1933–1945 Nazi Germany (the Third Reich).

1945 Unconditional surrender of Nazi Germany and the end of World War II.

Germany – and independently, its capital Berlin – was divided into four occupation zones until 1949 (Potsdam Agreement).

1948 The currency reform comes into force. The Deutsche Mark (DM) replaces the Reichsmark (RM).

1949 The Soviet zone declares itself an independent state with East Berlin as its capital. From this point on, there are two Germanies, each with their own political system.

1955 Rearmament of the FRG and accession to NATO. In return, the GDR joins the Warsaw Pact.

Establishment … European Economic Community (Treaty … predecessor of today's EU.

… closes its western external borders to … ight of its population. A wall is built … three western zones of Berlin:
= 155 km
… is in the city zone = 43 km
… now only accessible via three … nd by air.

OCCUPATION ZONES 1945–1949

BRITISH ZONE

SOVIET ZONE

AMERICAN ZONE

FRENCH ZONE

POLAND

Start of the Cold War (Cuba crisis).

1966 The Extra-Parliamentary Opposition (APO) takes shape in response to the formation of the grand coalition between Christian and Social Democrats.

1967 Student, Benno Ohnesorg, is killed by a police bullet during a demonstration.

1968 Assassination attempt is made on the student leader, Rudi Dutschke; this is a major trigger for student radicalism.

POPULATION TREND (ROUNDED)

1950 … Mill.

1961 … Mill.

1970 … Mill.

1990 FRG (62 Mill.) … Mill.; GDR (16 Mill.) … 8 Mill.

1972 Palestinian terrorist organization, Black September, attacks the Israeli team at the Olympic Games in Munich.

1977 The German Autumn ("der deutsche Herbst"): A series of terrorist attacks by the RAF (Red Army Faction) keeps the country on edge.

1985 Through his reform policy (perestroika), the new Russian Secretary General Mikhail Gorbachev initiates the turnaround that heralds the end of the Cold War.

1989 Due to growing pressure from the GDR population's demand for more freedom, the Berlin Wall falls on November 9th.

1990 Reunification of West and East Germany ("Deutsche Einheit").

ABOUT THE AUTHOR

Jan Reetze was born in Hamburg, Germany, in 1956. He completed a Sound Engineering internship, later studied Sociology, Political Science and Systematic Musicology at the University of Hamburg. He is the author of several books, documentaries, and radio features about music, media history, media research, and art topics. He was the managing partner of a music publishing company, in 2008 he relocated to Pittsburgh, Pennsylvania, where he lives with his wife.

TIMES & SOUNDS

Germany's Journey from Jazz and Pop
to Krautrock and Beyond

halvmall

First published in 2020 by

Halvmall
Buntentorsteinweg 172
28201 Bremen
Germany

publish@halvmall.com
www.halvmall.com

Design, illustration, maps/statistics, and typesetting: Thorsten Breyer
Editing and proofreading: Sapana Gupta
Print: BALTO print, Lithuania

Halvmall would like to thank all supporters for their help during this project: Christian Bordeaux, Melanie and Ida Gruhl, Hester Heilemann, Jan Portius, Manfred Rinderspacher, Benjamin Spils, Günter Stöppel

Bibliographic information of the German National Library:
The Deutsche Nationalbibliothek lists this publication in the German National Bibliography; detailed bibliographic data is available on the Internet at http://dnb.d-nb.de

This title is also available as an e-book (ISBN 978-3-9822100-1-8)

First edition, 2020

Printed in the EU
ISBN 978-3-9822100-0-1

For De

CONTENTS

FOREWORD

BY HANS-JOACHIM ROEDELIUS

Gladly, I comply with the request of music writer and sociologist Jan Reetze, who – for reasons of love – emigrated to the U.S. and has worked there for several years now, to contribute a foreword to his book about the specific internal matters within the historic evolution of contemporary German popular music.

As the co-founder of Kluster, Cluster and Harmonia, coincided with my solo career, I think I have contributed some important essentials to the story of this music. The main reputation usually was, and is, assigned to a couple of very special other individuals who have been mentioned over and over again within hundreds of publications (and will surely be mentioned again here), but now, in this book, some of them will be cut out for size while others will be added, which seemed to be bound for eking out an existence as a Sleeping Beauty up to this day.

It is not envy that makes me point this out so distinctly. It is, on the contrary, a delayed gratification about the fact that, in Jan's book, several protagonists will finally receive the appreciation they've long deserved. Several facts that had long been disregarded and never thought about are mentioned here, and the endless story that has been told in countless books is now, finally, conveyed by someone with profound knowledge on the topic.

For experts, as well as newbies, in the Krautrock field, this book does not only open up several new views for the first time, it presents a general overview of the big picture of rock music in Germany. It tells its history and illustrates the roots of the singular and successful musical movement called Krautrock – a movement that would not have been possible without its connections to Germany's then political situation, and "the little help from a good friend": the influence of the flower power movement that spilled from America over into Germany.

Having said this, Joachim Roedelius wishes you a good read – may this book get the attention it deserves.

WHAT'S IT ALL ABOUT?

When you happen to watch 40-year old TV commercials, they are not only something to smile about, but they will also give you a lot of background information about the time when they were originally shown. If you can read the signs, they will give you an idea about how people were thinking; you can see their wishes and their hopes, sometimes even their sorrows and problems. It's 40 years later now and you realize that in reality most things didn't happen the way they thought it would. In retrospect, we can see how and why.

What goes for TV commercials, goes similarly for music. Germany's daily life and culture mirrors itself in the music Germans listen to. When you read about it, you will learn a lot about Germany's cultural, political, and everyday background as well. These topics are interwoven; they are connected and influence each other. As music everywhere in the world, most German music came about not just "under the circumstances" Germans lived in, it came about *because* of the circumstances of certain times, and sometimes it had an influence *on* those circumstances.

You know the term "Krautrock". There is no clear definition, but it refers to German rock music from the late 1960s to the late 1970s. The title of FRUMPY's first album, *All Will Be Changed* (1970), clearly shows the atmosphere of departure this rising Krautrock scene had. Krautrockers, as one of today's several folktales about German rock music goes, followed their ideas in radical consequence. They defied all of the world and its brother, along with their audience and the A&R departments of their record companies (given they were signed), and did what the Lord or his chemical brothers planted into their heads. They were supposed to have done it this way because they were Germans, and Germans, as you know, always stand with one leg in the past and with one leg in the future, but you will never find them in the present.

But on their second album, FRUMPY already signaled a note of caution: "Take Care of Illusion". In reality, many bands had to walk several twists and turns before they finally found their niche, style and (if they were lucky) audience. Most of them failed or gave up. But to not exactly know one's path is not only something negative, it can also be seen as a chance. Bands fought with their record labels, they were in permanent financial trouble, ripped off by obscure managers. They had to solve technical problems. Band members had to deal with their families, friends, girlfriends, and boyfriends. They had to learn how to cope with sleepy radio hosts and the musical desert on German TV screens. They had to learn how to stand the often discouraging coverage done by the German music press. They had to deal with bizarre tour schedules, clueless concert promoters, agencies, and the employment office. There were also unruly and sometimes aggressive audiences, untrained to listen to new sounds and often unwilling to even pay entrance fees. (Several English and American bands touring Germany had to learn this the hard way, too.) Rock music in Germany was a product of permanent trial and error. To show this, this book will follow artists on their journey through decisions and learning processes.

This book rectifies several things that seem to be "common knowledge" especially in fan circles; it blows up some cherished illusions. It will give you some background about German music and some of its makers, many of which you've probably never heard of. You will hear about people like Siggi Loch, Peter Meisel, Manfred Weissleder, Mike Leckebusch. There are also names like Conny Plank, Dieter Dierks, Rolf-Ulrich Kaiser, along with some others whose names you've probably heard a thousand times, but not in the way they are portrayed here. You will hear about Bert Kaempfert or James Last, names you probably would never connect to German rock, but the connections exist. You will hear about the working conditions of professional musicians and the jobs they had to do to survive. You will have the chance to go behind the scenes of the studio and record industry. Last but not least, you will hear about the reception of German music in foreign countries and how it sometimes backfired for musicians, producers, and record labels.

This book is not a part of the current pile of "retro" books, and terms like "genius", "legend", or "icon", et cetera, will rarely be used here. This is a journalistic book, not a scholarly one. It's made for you to read, not for earning me a degree. It's about the stuff I grew up with and the way we (young people in Germany) saw things at a given era. Krautrock is only a part of it, but an important one. My intention is to give you a clue about the circumstances under which different German music styles came into existence, how they influenced each other, and what became of them after their downfall.

Could it be that Krautrock, especially, was a backlash on modernism? Could it be that the chaotic way of developing and making music had its roots deeply in the era of German Romanticism? Could it be that the way Krautrock musicians were thinking was not far from the artists' and "life movement" groups of the Weimar Republic – keywords being Worpswede, Hellerau, Monte Verità, et cetera? At least many Krautrock groups, as well as parts of the students' movement, had a similar attitude of "all or nothing" to their predecessors in the 1920s. And it was a similar radicalism that led to phenomena like the "2 June Movement" or the "Baader Meinhof Group" in the 1970s. There are connections, sometimes unpleasant ones, and you will read about them.

Imagine a hot air balloon: You'll get a wide view over the landscape, and from time to time you'll fly down to have a closer look at interesting details. When you listen to music from Germany, this book might be a sort of "making of". But, to plagiarize Stewart Brand: "If you're reading this book just to reinforce your present opinions, you've hired the wrong consultant."[1]

Here's a list showing all of the German 45s (singles) that reached the U.S. *Billboard* charts between 1955 and 2015:[2]

YEAR	ARTIST	TITLE	POSITION
1955	Caterina Valente	The Breeze And I	#8
1962	Bert Kaempfert Orchestra	Wonderland by Night	#1
1975	Kraftwerk	Autobahn	#25
1975	Silver Convention	Fly Robin Fly	#1
1976	Silver Convention	Get Up and Boogie	#2
1978	Boney M	Rivers of Babylon	#30
1982	Peter Schilling	Major Tom (Coming Home)	#14
1983	Nena	99 Luftballons	#2
1984	Scorpions	Rock You Like a Hurricane	#25
1988	Milli Vanilli	Girl You Know It's True	#2
1989	Milli Vanilli	Baby Don't Forget My Number	#1
1989	Milli Vanilli	Girl I'm Gonna Miss You	#1
1989	Milli Vanilli	Blame It on the Rain	#1
1990	Snap	The Power	#2
1991	Scorpions	Winds of Change	#4
1992	Snap	Rhythm is a Dancer	#5
1993	Real McCoy	Another Night	#3
1995	La Bouche	Be My Lover	#6
1996	Mr. President	Coco Jamboo	#22
1999	Lou Bega	Mambo No. 5	#3
2015	Omi/Felix Jaehn	Cheerleader	#1

In a way, the list shows what "the world" tends to expect from Germany: discopop, Eurodance, also sometimes techno. A little bit of innovation is always expected (as the Audi slogan says: "Vorsprung durch Technik" – advancement through technology), and if it's rock music that is taken note of in the U.S. or U.K., then it must be something very special. Kraftwerk was one group special enough to be noticed. Or the stage act consists of martial noise and fire magic, produced by sweating, bare-chested young men – that's the business model of Rammstein. Hard-rockers Scorpions are an exception to the rule: They are a German band, but nevertheless fit perfectly into the standards of a scene that is completely dominated by bands from Anglo-American territories.

Around 1970, some British music journalists glued the label "Krautrock" onto rock music from Germany. The V-2 had failed, and these krazy krauts dared to try it again, but this time with amplifiers and synthesizers? It couldn't be true.

But it was. Even in 1973 it was obviously not possible to imagine Germans without steel helmets, as this detail from a Virgin advertisement in the *Melody Maker* demonstrates:

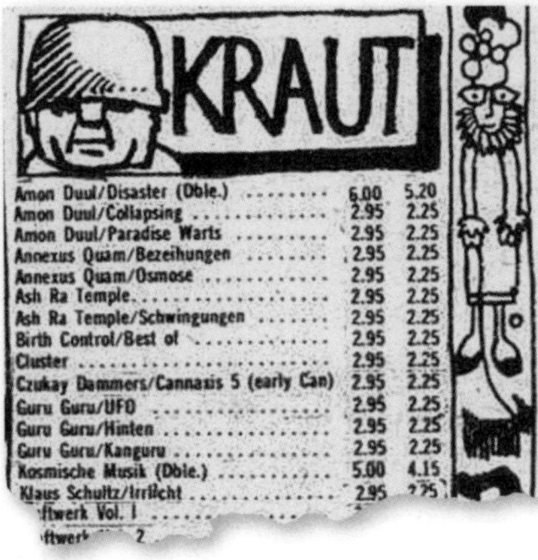

KRAUT

Amon Duul/Disaster (Dble.)	6.00	5.20
Amon Duul/Collapsing	2.95	2.25
Amon Duul/Paradise Warts	2.95	2.25
Annexus Quam/Bezeihungen	2.95	2.25
Annexus Quam/Osmose	2.95	2.25
Ash Ra Temple	2.95	2.25
Ash Ra Temple/Schwingungen	2.95	2.25
Birth Control/Best of	2.95	2.25
Cluster	2.95	2.25
Czukay Dammers/Cannaxis 5 (early Can)	2.95	2.25
Guru Guru/UFO	2.95	2.25
Guru Guru/Hinten	2.95	2.25
Guru Guru/Kanguru	2.95	2.25
Kosmische Musik (Dble.)	5.00	4.15
Klaus Schultz/Irrlicht	2.95	[illegible]
ftwerk Vol. I		
ftwer[illegible] 2		

If it wasn't a steel helmet, then you can bet they would use a Gothic-styled font for the headline. When David Bowie entitled a track on his "*Heroes*" album "V-2 Schneider", it was of course aimed at KRAFTWERK's Florian Schneider, but the "V-2" makes it a very ambivalent dedication – probably the reason why Schneider never commented on it. Some journalists, as here in the *New Musical Express*, were very amused about the German accent, and, as you would expect, let Germans call the shots:

Ve give ze orders here!

NICK KENT slinks unobtrusively into the bac[illegible]ething a little stronger

The British tabloids arrange similar nonsense in tiring conformity whenever a soccer game with England versus Germany takes place. It sounds a bit senile by now.

But in the 1960s and 1970s, some other countries also served with the big dipper, as this review of Kraftwerk's *Trans Europe Express* in Swedish tabloid *Expressen* might show: "First I didn't know if I dared to laugh. A German pop group with this name: Kraftwerk – is it a parody of the Fritz culture, or what ...? With excitement I put the record with songs like 'Europe Endless' and 'Franz Schubert' on the turntable and my laugh got stuck in my throat. Fascism is what it is, pure and simple. If there would be a work ban in West Germany it should be issued on Kraftwerk. Throughout the sound is synthetic into metallic monotony. Triads and march rhythm with lyrics like 'Europe Endless with elegance and decadence.' ... Here it just becomes a rhythmic tramp of boots in the latest synthetic packaging."[3]

If you think it would be hard to top this nonsense, then get ready for one that takes the all-time cake:[4]

If you ever need proof that British music press had a niche for brain-dead editors, this example should suffice.

But let's be fair: All these reviews didn't target the records, it was *Germany* they focussed on. Just think about when these critics and record industry guys were born. What did they hear from their parents and grandparents about Germany, what did they learn about it in school? Then add the fact that the first bands from Germany came off as really wacky, sometimes even arrogant. This was, of course, not much more than a way to deal with their own insecurities, but you can imagine the sort of vibes the critics received from this. For critics, Germany and these musicians were a heavy-loaded subject. And then, along with all of this, add the strange music! What did the critics do? They opened hate outlets and came out with a plethora of stereotypes they had heard of. The chief editors, usually the same age as their writers, maybe a bit older, supported this.

From the U.S. or the U.K. perspective, Germany was, and sometimes still is, an exotic place. WWII had still not been digested, and in many cases it was connected to personal or family experiences. Information about what was really going on in this mysterious country was hard to find. Sometimes facts were not even wanted – preconceptions were, and are, much easier to deal with. Most British or American music journalists, even the good-willed ones, had never been in Germany, usually did not speak the language, and didn't know much (if anything) about Germany's musical and cultural landscape. When journalists of this kind got into contact with the likes of Can, Amon Düül, Amon Düül II, Kraftwerk, Faust or Tangerine Dream, they were either shocked or amused, but in any case, they had no idea how to deal with this stuff. Still today, when I read articles about Germany in the *New York Times* or the *New Yorker*, I have the feeling they are written about a country that is small and puzzling, with people with overbearing or pushy characteristics living, mentally as if still in the 19th century, yet simultaneously perceived as quite cute sometimes.

Krautrock is what is most well-known about German music (except classical music) in foreign countries. In reality, there was a much wider spectrum of German rock and pop music than this, and it goes further back than you may think. German Krautrock musicians often love to tell the story of how they had no tradition to connect with - there was nothing but Beethoven and horrible German schlagers, and so they were forced to develop something completely new. In fact, there *were* traditions, and as you will see, they made use of them. There were jazz influences, as well as traces of cabaret songs. There were British, American and homegrown folk roots. There was skiffle, there was merseybeat, there were connections between schlagers and rock, there were composers like Stockhausen and Ligeti, there was "Sixty-Eight" (but nobody knew it then), and there was a sort of zeitgeist that simultaneously admired and bashed American culture.

While German schlagers had nearly no chance to be heard across the Channel or in the New World, Krautrock did. And while in the beginning, the term wasn't meant to be very friendly, after some time, something happened that nobody had predicted: Krautrock bands found an audience in the U.K. It was a small circle of listeners at first, but it grew. After a while, the Krautrock label turned into a sort of quality brand, first in the U.K., then in the U.S. and Japan, even making its way to Australia. Krautrock became a synonym for things to be found rarely in the mother countries of rock: strange sounds, sometimes endless ramblings and musical anarchy, ignoring the rules of the music industry, but also innovation of many kinds, radicalness, and intransigence. That was the point: The material coming from Germany had to be different from what Brits and Americans had in their own countries. The Anglo-American audiences – other than from their music press – had no prejudice, German musicians just had to learn some international rules.

To be presentable in the media, music needs distinctive personalities — great singers, extraordinary guitarists, people who are able to deliver crisp statements. But personalities of this kind didn't exist in Germany. Ralf Hütter of KRAFTWERK: "We're not too good at talking, that's why we make music"[5], and he was not the only one thinking this way. That's why a lot of guessing started among British and American music journalists. They were not able to categorize the sounds they heard from Germany (except schlagers – they had to be ridiculous by nature), they didn't know how to explain them in their magazines or radio shows. There was no internet and no Wikipedia, so only little background information was available, and even large parts of the information that *was* available were based on guessing – sometimes by intention, sometimes simply because the journalists didn't understand the meaning of German phrases some musicians used in interviews. The music fans in the States and the U.K. hardly had a chance to verify the press coverage about Germany, German music, and German musicians.

It was no miracle that it didn't take very long for some "fake news" to develop. Misunderstandings and false conclusions began to circulate – around the music itself, as well as around its makers and their abilities and intentions. Once these conclusions made their way into the public, they stabilized themselves and were perceived more and more as the truth.

Up until present day, this still hasn't really changed. Not all the information you find in the English language is wrong, but oftentimes, important context is missing. Once put into context, many things suddenly look different.

This book will provide you with context. It will show you how the music scene in Germany was embedded into everyday life – a search for the traces, done by someone who was present when the bulk of it took place. Krautrock is neither an isolated event, nor something that fell from the sky. It has lots of backstory, history, a sort of tradition, and at times, has led to the creation of something new.

This book is about the biotope in which German music generally came into being. It delivers background information on the artistic, cultural, sociological, infrastructural, political, and economic circumstances that were formative for the German music scene (and beyond the music scene) between the 1950s and the late 1980s. This book explains why musicians found ways of expressing that were different from the ways commonly used in the U.S. or the U.K. In this way, it also acts as a story about Germany, its everyday life, and its walk through the ups and downs during some strongly varied decades. You will smell the atmosphere we had lived in. You will see that musicians sometimes overvalued occurrences because they participated in them.

The "plot lines" of this book are organized chronologically, but I found that sometimes, it's more effective to follow a topic instead of keeping a strict timeline. The real changes in culture, arts, and music have always been a process anyway; they happen independently from the beginning of years or decades.

However, this book's content ends around 1990. The media landscape changed drastically, new technologies changed the music production, its distribution, and of course the music itself, and the German Reunification occurred in 1989. To bring all this together would require the creation of a whole other book in itself.

One more important point to bring up: This book is about West Germany and West Berlin. I'm well aware of the fact that there was an active jazz and rock scene in the GDR (German Democratic Republic; East Germany) with many excellent musicians, but this scene was relatively isolated and, because of the often strict ruling of the socialist GDR government, these musicians could hardly connect to the trends going on in the western world. It's not that I didn't know about East German bands, especially the ones prominent during the 1970s, but I think that their story should be told by somebody who lived in East Germany and can talk about the frame conditions they had to work under.

So then: Bon voyage!

Jan Reetze, April 2020

The ruins of the Reichstag, destroyed in World War II, are removed (March 18th, 1948)

THE BEGINNING

"We had to rebuild our culture because most of the interesting people were either killed or emigrated."

MANUEL GÖTTSCHING (ASH RA TEMPEL)

THE BEGINNING

RUBBLE YEARS

Werner Herzog, born in 1942 and one of the few German filmmakers known in the U.S. and the U.K., says: "As a German filmmaker, after the war, we grew up as - not only me, but all my peers - we grew up as a fatherless generation, as a generation of orphans. Our fathers either had fled the country, were chased out, or they had sided with the barbarism of the Nazi regime. So we had no one to learn from, and we started to look out for our grandfathers. And that was Murnau, Fritz Lang, and others. So I just needed to connect myself with a culture, with a legitimate, great culture of Germany. And that was the culture of the grandfathers or even earlier than that."[1]

Similar statements can be heard from rock musicians. In regard to KRAFTWERK's beginnings, Ralf Hütter says: "We realized back then: The Federal Republic of Germany has no contemporary sound. For us, this was a shock. But then we thought: Let's develop it. There was a giant space that was empty. Look at the late Sixties – there was nothing but schlager, and rock from Anglo-American sources … So, first we had to find the cultural identity."[2] "Schlager" is the German word for commercial pop songs. And, as is usually the case for statements like this, it remains unclear what that's supposed to be: "cultural identity".

Manuel Göttsching (ASH RA TEMPEL) states something similar, but he's more precise: "It was a period when many really interesting types of music were arising, especially in Germany, because of its situation. We had a cultural disaster after the Second World War. We had to rebuild our culture because most of the interesting people were either killed or emigrated. If they could. In the Sixties, the demand from young people to create something new was very strong."[3]

There we have it: Fatherless generation, no cultural identity, empty space, nothing but schlagers. It's tempting to see it this way. It would make a lot of things easy to explain. But in the late 1950s and 1960s, no musician seriously "felt the need" to create something new because he or she didn't see a tradition to connect with. In reality, the musicians copied Anglo-American music that came to Germany because it was attractive, or they had ideas of their own and tried to put them into effect. There was no thinking about tradition in the game. The only exception was the folk scene: Folkies had a unique problem, which, as we will later find out, *was* connected to traditions.

But how about taking a look at this situation through more of a general view? Did this "tabula rasa" really exist? Had there really been a so-called "Stunde Null" after the end of the war? ("Zero hour" was a frequently used phrase referring to the time immediately after the war, when all Germans were faced, equally, with ruin. But this has never been true. Most Germans did face ruin, but there were a few individuals who still owned a steel mill or a coal mine, or were professors or judges, and simply continued their careers as if nothing had happened.)

For filmmakers or painters, the situation was worse than for novelists or musicians. During the Weimar Republic, in the "Golden Twenties", Germany had been one of the leading film-producing nations. With directors like Fritz Lang, F.W. Murnau, G.W. Pabst, Robert Wiene, and others, German cinematography had become innovative, influential, daring, artful — but most of all, successful. German filmmaking became a role model for screenwriters, directors, and camera operators in Hollywood. But when the Nazis took over the film industry (one of the first things they did), German cinema lost most of its quality and all of its credibility. Although nearly 1200 films were shot during the Third Reich, there are, at best, only a handful worth mentioning. The most famous is probably *Münchhausen* from 1943, directed by Joseph von Báky, taken after a screenplay written by a certain "Berthold Bürger". In fact, this Mr. Bürger was none other than author Erich Kästner, who had been officially banned from publishing. For people who knew how to listen, he was able to put some discreetly subversive phrases into the dialogue.

When the Third Reich was over, Germany never managed to resurrect the golden era of film that emerged in the Twenties. It's not too exaggerated to say that it still, up to the present day, remains lost. In the 1950s and 1960s, the German movie production fell flat mainly due to sentimental films with regional backgrounds (so-called "heimatfilms") and harmless (and mostly unfunny) comedies.

And the music production? This was a bit different. The aforementioned statement by Herzog is not completely wrong, but in regards to music, it comes up a bit too short.

It might well be that many German rock musicians didn't know about the traditions of music in Germany, but that doesn't mean there had been no tradition at all. Germany had rich music traditions from earlier times: schlager, operetta, folk, classical music, cabaret, and jazz. There's the music from the 1920s and early 1930s, when Germany had its own highly original, cultural voice – COMEDIAN HARMONISTS (some consider them to be the first boy band) or WEINTRAUB'S SYNCOPATORS, composers, and lyricists Friedrich (Fredric) Hollaender, Werner Richard Heymann, Robert Gilbert, to name just a few. Some musicians later made use of this tradition without being aware of it.

During the Nazi era, a lot of this music was classified as "entartet" (degenerate), especially classical music by Jewish composers (like Erich Wolfgang Korngold or Berthold Goldschmidt), but also compositions that were somehow "difficult", or not compelling to the ear, like the ones of Paul Hindemith. There was also swing and jazz. Of course these were "copied" music styles, but both had a tradition in Germany; they had been an important part of the music of the "Golden Twenties" and early Thirties. Many people think that jazz in Germany was forbidden by law during the Third Reich, but this was not the case. The Nazi rulers did declare it "Jewish nigger jazz" (that's what they called it) and state that this "Hottentot noise" would not benefit the German national spirit, but this didn't lead to a full-out ban. This was, of course, not the kind of music the Nazis needed. What the Nazis wanted young people to do was to march lock-step[4], and you can't do this to jazz or swing rhythms. In 1935, it was declared and put into effect that Reich radio should no longer play jazz or swing. But jazz records, especially those imported, were still available. You just had to know where to get them. It was also optional for the regional gauleiters (leaders of the Nazi party districts) to declare local bans. Some did it, while others didn't. In 1937, in some areas, they created a ban forbidding swing dance in dance cafés, cabaret clubs, and bars. The waiters got the official order to stop bands from playing swing or jazz and to stop dancers from dancing to this music. Reich propaganda minister Joseph Goebbels declared this on the occasion of the opening of the annual "Reichsmusiktage" (Reich music days), saying that these pesky weeds had to be eliminated, and the state had to act as the gardener. What this meant became obvious with the exhibition "Entartete Musik" (Degenerated Music) in May 1938 in Düsseldorf.

For the "Swingjugend" ("Swing Kids") this led to hard times. Swing Kids were small fan groups, listening to British and American swing jazz. They consisted of teenagers and early twentysomethings, male as well as female. They listened to imported records or foreign radio stations like the BBC, and, of course, through this they received something beyond just music. They wore their hair relatively long, had a specifically casual fashion style, and communicated with their own slang, encompassed with lots of Anglicism. They greeted each other with "Swing Heil" or made fun of the Hitler Youth by calling themselves the "Hotler Youth". Some of them even dared to celebrate Churchill's birthday on November 30 by wearing a bowler, a rolled-up umbrella, and an old copy of *The Times* peeking out of their coat pocket.[5] If they were lucky, they were only pestered by waiters, teachers, overactive members of the Hitler-Jugend (HJ), and others (the HJ was the youth organization of the NSDAP (the Nazi party). All youngsters had to be members, and so the HJ organized 98 percent of all male Germans between 10 and 18. The girls were organized in the BDM (Bund deutscher Mädel), the female part of the HJ. Usually they had two meetings a week and several extra activities. Parents had to expect unpleasant repercussions if they didn't want to let their children go to these meetings). Later, Swing Kids who were seen as "ringleaders" were arrested or imprisoned in a concentration camp. This was more due to their assumed listening to foreign radio stations, which was strictly forbidden (since September 1939 it was under the threat of death penalty), and their generally rebellious behavior. In 1941, the Gestapo of Hamburg even founded a department aimed against Swing Kids; cafés and other meeting points were raided and teenagers had to run the gauntlet. They were brutally beaten up and had to stand at a wall in the Gestapo headquarters for hours, where, if they moved, the punishment started from the beginning.[6] Some dedicated swing and jazz musicians like guitarist Coco Schumann (1924–2018) went to prison.

In contrast, hundreds of dance bands continued playing in bars, pubs, cafés, and cabaret clubs all over Germany, and many managed to find ways to play swing or jazz, as large parts of their audiences demanded it. They camouflaged the "Tiger Rag" by announcing it as "Katzen-Foxtrott" (Cat's Foxtrot), or they invented completely new lyrics in German language, knowing the fans would accept this. They knew the musicians had no other choice; one could never know whether there was a spy in the house. The Nazis randomly sent out spies to check whether everything was "in order". But these spies were often too stupid to get the catch on to what was going on, while others deliberately played dumb because they loved this music themselves. If a singer used English lyrics, he had to be aware that somebody might protest and insist on songs with German lyrics. Sometimes the band fulfilled this wish by playing and singing "Bei mir bist du scheen", usually for the jamboree of the ones in the audience who knew the background of this song. But since at least after the so-called "Kristallnacht" (Night of Broken Glass), the pogrom against synagogues and Jewish shops in November 1938, jokes of this kind became too dangerous, and through time, the production of swing and jazz came to an end in Germany. It was, however, still possible to obtain imported swing or jazz records.

It's hard to believe, but even the Nazis themselves produced jazz and swing recordings. They needed them for the propaganda radio broadcasts they provided for foreign countries. These radio shows could be heard in several languages on shortwave frequencies all over the world, and it was clear to the Nazis that if they wanted people to listen, they needed music that would be attractive to an international audience. So, they brought big bands like TEDDY STAUFFER & HIS ORIGINAL TEDDYS (originally from Switzerland) or CHARLIE & HIS ORCHESTRA (a plain propaganda project) to secret studios and had them record first-class swing music, specifically for these radio shows. For Germans, of course, it was forbidden under death penalty to listen to these radio stations, but it goes without saying that all German swing and jazz fans knew the exact frequencies and schedules of these broadcasts (for safety reasons, usually by heart).

Later, during war time, when it became more and more clear that this war couldn't be won, the Nazis also used these recordings in the radio broadcasts for German soldiers to prevent them from listening to the German services of BBC or Voice Of America. The soldiers were not interested in folksy tearjerkers, marches, or polkas from home, they wanted real music.

You see, there was a tradition of music in Germany that continued even during the Third Reich. It is true that during the Nazi era, Germany misused and crushed most of its cultural assets that had come up in the Weimar Republic, but a handful of Nazi rulers, especially Reich Minister of Propaganda Joseph Goebbels, were intelligent. They didn't simply forbid unwanted left-wing phenomena (like the Wandervogel movement, which I will elaborate on later), they knew it would be more effective to get them on board. Today, when we think of the Nazis as traditionalists who acted as a reactionary force, we have to differentiate. The Nazis, during their founding days in the 1920s, gave themselves a very progressive image. Most workers and ordinary people at that time were fed up with the economic and political crisis of the Weimar era, and the Nazis responded to this by presenting what, at the time, seemed to be a positive direction of change. Similar to the Italian fascist movement, the Nazis included many progressive cultural streams in their program. They managed to recruit some of the best creative heads of their time – names like Leni Riefenstahl, Thea von Harbou, or the artistically great but politically naïve, Walter Ruttmann, among several others. Actors were especially easy to catch because, for their work, they depended on the German language. They couldn't offhandedly migrate to England or America.

The Nazi party promoted and supported the then modern media film and radio, massively. Simultaneously, they presented themselves as emphatically folksy. Their progressiveness always came with a sort of common sense that took away the menacing strangeness from modern arts. And finally, the Nazis didn't hesitate to create precedents if something didn't fit into their plans. In this case, oppressive actions – like the book burnings in May 1933 – were organized within moments. The music of Jewish composers, for instance, could be banned from being performed immediately.

Strange behavior? Yes. The result of all these actions was that, although people could feel on top of their time, these modern aesthetics seemed to be "grounded". It was backed up with lots of kitsch and bathos. If there was any real radicalism in works of art, the Nazi rulers cushioned it immediately, making it no longer look dangerous. People were taken by the hand and comforted by resoluteness. And last, but not least, the Nazis used newly-developed film and radio media to pick up and fuel moods and feelings that were hidden underneath a sort of common unconsciousness, like the latent anti-Semitism which had been there for centuries and was easy to activate, or common sentiments about intellectuals, artists, and other capricious elements. All this gave people a feeling of being sheltered, being "on the safe side" with the Nazis - the Nazis presented themselves as competent, their decisions were made quickly and resolutely. Things they supported couldn't be dangerous, and if something seemed out of the ordinary, one could be sure they would fix it very soon. This led to a feeling of overall safety that Germans had missed for a long time.

In the early 1930s, only few Germans had the clear-sightedness to realize where this might lead to. It's safe to say that in 1936 or 1937, had there still been free elections, a majority would have voted for the NSDAP[7], the Nazi Party (which was officially founded in 1920 at the Munich Hofbräuhaus, emanating from the DAP, Deutsche Arbeiterpartei). The Nazi ideology had a touch of religion tied to it, and as a believer you could lead a well-organized life without much trouble if you simply didn't break the rules. If something strange, irritating, or unwelcome happened, the Nazi propaganda knew how to explain it, and if you had a problem, the local Nazi organizations certainly had a solution.

It was the old game: The Nazis divided the world into "us" and "them". As long as you played along and didn't question anything, you were part of "us"; you were safe. Unless, of course, you were Jewish. Jews were "them" and acted as a necessary scapegoat for the Nazis. The feeling of "being part of a community" was something many had missed during the Weimar Republic. When the Nazis made clear that "we" were superior to "them", many people liked this idea. They wanted it to be true.

There were not many people who saw through this propagandistic fog, only some intellectuals — journalists, authors, artists, composers, filmmakers. It became more and more clear to them what this all meant. First for themselves, later for workers, employees, and everybody else. When an artist dared to walk a little bit outside the norm,, he was immediately ordered back inside. The same went for journalists. There was no free press anymore. Cinema newsreels, newspapers, and the airwaves became important parts of the Nazi's manipulation machinery, and they perfected it day by day. After 1938, latest, the followers of even apolitical and, more or less insignificant, small movements like the previously mentioned "Swing Kids", had to hide (and sometimes became, as a result, politicized).

In 1945, the whole story ended in rubble. The Reich that was meant for a millennium broke down after just twelve years. For the Germans, it was not only a party or a political system, it was their whole world that imploded. Everything they had believed in turned out to be wrong. And music was probably the last thing they were worried about.

Germany, country-wide, was destroyed. Nearly every survivor had lost somebody. Hundreds of thousands of German soldiers had either gone into war captivity or were missing. Slowly, very slowly, people developed an idea of the dimension of what had happened during the last twelve years, and it took even more time and energy to mentally *grasp* that it had happened. The last two or three years it had been – as philosopher Peter Sloterdijk calls it – an entire society's attempt to commit suicide[8], but many were simply unable to see this.

In the countryside, the situation was a little bit better than in the cities. There hadn't been so many bombings. In the cities, nearly no infrastructure was left. People had no other clothing than the broken material they wore on their body. They had no money and no food. They had their life, and that was all there was left. To make matters worse, the winter of 1945/46 turned out to be extremely hard. The temperature fell under negative 22 °F (negative 30 °C) and killed thousands in their destroyed homes. People had to deal with food ration cards they couldn't actually use because most stores had little or no goods left. People were busy with "hamstern gehen" (going hamstering), which meant taking a trip to the countryside to beg for food at farms or steal it from the fields. They walked dozens of kilometers along the railways to check for food or pieces of coal that might have fallen off of a wagon, and when they didn't find anything, some of them even stopped trains to steal coal or firewood. Shoplifting became a common thing. In the Ruhr area, they called it "fringsen", after Catholic Cardinal Josef Frings of Cologne had given his blessings to those who stole food to keep their families alive. People who, before the war, could never have imagined themselves doing such acts, broke into apartments, attics, or basements (even during the daytime) to steal metal objects, copper wire, and anything else that a scrap metal dealer (hopefully) would give some pennies for. There were also black markets for nearly everything, where people had the opportunity to barter things. Cigarettes quickly became the main currency because the Reichsmark wasn't worth anything anymore. Sometimes, these cigarettes were gifts from allied soldiers, and if they were not gifts — well, there's no need to get into the details of what else was done to obtain a couple of them. The 1946/47 birth statistics with the title "father unknown" is enough explanation. (I'm not talking about cases of rape here, which of course also happened. No army in this world will ever officially admit that rape is part of its business, but it is.)

But aside from all this trouble, there were also a few positive aspects. With the Allied Forces, winds changed in Germany. And they changed for the better – at least in West Germany. There's one thing that came with the end of the Nazi era that is important for this book's topic: The Allied Forces completely reorganized the radio networks. Among several other things, this meant that most households still had their "Volksempfänger", the cheap but durable radios the Nazis had developed to deliver their propaganda to the people. That's why, in the vernacular, these radios were called "Goebbelsschnauze" (snout of Goebbels). But now these devices started delivering fresh food for hungry ears — jazz, swing, popular music from England, America or France could be heard on the broadcasts, and this time no longer by home-made Glenn Miller copies, but rather the originals. For us, children of today's media, it is probably hard to understand what a prominent liberation of the mind this meant.

THE BEGINNING

TEENAGER MELODY

People sat in the middle of piles of rubble and asked themselves: How do we cope with this damned time between 1933 and 1945?

Had anything actually happened? If so, better forget about it. And so, they did. Twelve years went into oblivion. Nobody wanted to talk about it anymore. The nation buried their heads in the sand. Later, in the 1960s, this caused problems. At this time, however, the desire to forget the past proved to be one of the reasons why, after the currency reform in 1948, the *schlager* genre reached booming conditions.

HIT PARADES

The 1930s, 1940s, and early 1950s were prominent decades for music publishing houses, whose main job was printing and distributing songs. This sheet music, usually on a double page, contained the vocal melody, lyrics, and piano part of the song, sometimes also guitar chords. These scores were much more important than records at that time; still, in the Fifties, British pop charts were not based on records, but rather sheet music sales. It was the *song* that was successful, not the singer.

In the U.K. in the 1950s, the following procedure was common: Once a week, British music publishers visited record companies and the BBC to present demo versions of their new songs to them. If a record company considered a song to be promising, they licensed it from the publisher and recorded it with one of the singers who were signed to this record company. Because any song was open to be licensed by all record companies, it was not unusual that a song came out in four versions; any of the big four record labels (Decca, EMI, Pye, and

Philips) released their own one. In addition, the BBC presented songs by their own singers, accompanied live by the BBC orchestra. Only Radio Luxembourg, on its English program, (plus a couple of pirate stations) used to play music from records. It was not before 1955 that the BBC started one (!) weekly show where records were played: "Pick Of The Pops".

This program was not a hit parade as we know it today, but with its creation, the importance of sheet music diminished. The golden era of the 45 had begun. The music publishing houses immediately shifted their main areas of responsibility from printing and distributing sheet music to the administration of music and lyrics' copyrights. (That's what they are still doing today.) Now it was the *singer*, no longer the song. It didn't take long for the cover design of the sheet music to refer to the recording of the song, usually it was identical to the record sleeve.

SCHLAGER

In Germany, this was handled mainly the same way. Jazz (especially light jazz, like Glenn Miller) was popular, but it was not the music of the masses. Schlagers as such were nothing new, in earlier times they just weren't called this. Schlagers, in the beginning, were a crossbreed between folk songs and operetta melodies. The term goes back to 1881 when Vienna's *National-Zeitung* used it first; it probably comes from "Blitzschlag" (flash of lightning). The meaning of the term "schlager" is the same as "hit" – something that has an impact. But it was not before the 1920s, when this mix of folk and operetta was enriched with jazzy elements, that it became clear that this style was neither operetta nor folklore.

The rise of the schlager genre wouldn't have been possible without the mass production and distribution of gramophone records, later boosted by sound movies that used schlagers as film music or were completely built around them. Many schlagers of the 1920s and 1930s were nearly anonymous. The labels on the records noted the composers and sometimes the orchestra, but the mentioning of vocalists by name was rare. Most listeners were not interested in knowing the singers – their heroes at that time were mainly film actors and cabaret stars. One of the few exceptions was the Comedian Harmonists. They were already a marketing phenomenon: The record company knew the name would be a magnet. The schlager genre survived the Weimar Republic, the Third Reich, and WWII, and after Germany's collapse in 1945, it simply continued on.

Usually, schlagers are accentuated, apolitical songs. Sometimes, they deal with social or political topics, but that's an exception. If they do, it is mostly in a conservative, sentimental, sometimes humorous, but never aggressive way. Schlagers are not made to put anything into question. Their main themes are (failing) love relationships or messages to a (wanted) partner. It's important that a schlager has *one* singer (male or female); sometimes there are duos, choirs are very rare. The singer has to be able to *represent* the content with the sound of his/her voice and personality, otherwise the schlager will not work.

It is often said that listening to schlagers is bad because it may distract one from confronting reality for a certain time. This is true, but, isn't this the way most entertainment media work? Schlagers do indeed have the characteristic of picking people up where they are and putting their situation into words and melodies. When your lover has just left you and you are completely heartbroken, a schlager can mirror your situation and give you the impression that you are not alone. There's somebody out there who understands how you feel. This idea became a bit far-fetched in the 1960s when critics, journalists, and social scientists claimed that schlagers were products of what they called the "culture industry", and were intentionally made for distracting individuals from reality to keep people quiet and obedient to "the system". I will come back to this.

Several documentaries on German rock music claim that schlagers were exceedingly horrible songs. Usually the blond, sunglasses-wearing singer Heino is singled out as a typical example for the German post-war schlager scene – even good ol' auntie BBC couldn't resist bringing him up in a Krautrock documentary.[1] Aside from the fact that Heino didn't start his career before 1965, is this statement really true, compared to English or American hits?

Take the test. Go to *halvmall.com/times-sounds/schlager* and listen, with open ears, to a handful of typical German schlagers of the 1950s and early 1960s. Then compare them to British and American chart toppers of the same era. Listen to Bruce Low's "Es hängt ein Pferdehalfter an der Wand" (A Headstall's Hanging on the Wall; 1952), Margot Eskens's "Tiritomba" (1955), Fred Bertelmann's "Der lachende Vagabund" (The Laughing Vagabond; 1957), the HAZY OSTERWALD SEXTETT's "Kriminal-Tango" (Crime Tango; 1957), or Caterina Valente's "Spiel noch einmal für mich, Habanero" (Play It Once Again for Me, Habanero; 1958). Then compare these tunes to Patti Page's (or Lita Roza's in the U.K.) "(How Much Is) That Doggie in the Window?" (1953), Anne Shelton's "Lay Down Your Arms" (1956, a cover version of Swedish song "Ann-Carolina"), Gary Miller's "Aqua Marina" (1964), Mike Preston's "A House, a Car and a Wedding Ring" (1958), or Perry Como's "Magic Moments" (1958).

Even if you don't understand the lyrics, you will have to admit that all these tunes sound rather similar. They are all pure schlagers. Some might be better, some might be worse, but the difference between the German and the English ones is mainly the language, not their musical or lyrical substance. Giorgio Moroder is right: "Song structures are universal. It doesn't matter whether it was a British beat song or a German schlager."[2]

One audible difference between American and German recordings was a specific way to do the mix. American recordings had loads of reverb. Soon, German producers also learned how to make use of it, but as they didn't want their records to sound too "American", they usually mixed the instrumental backings more into the background. With that said, German vocalists were more in the foreground, and the lyrics were easier to understand.

Let's not forget that many popular German schlagers were, in fact, cover versions of British and American pop songs. Usually, German record buyers didn't know this because in the 1950s and 1960s, the cover versions were renamed with German titles. Most Germans, Austrians, and Swiss at that time didn't speak English too well (if at all), so in a record shop, they wouldn't have had a clue about how to pronounce the original title. My late great-aunt, who throughout her lifetime worked at the box office of a movie theater (or, as she always used to put it: "I'm in the film industry"), used to pronounce English film titles and actors names strictly as if they were German, and she was not the only one doing that. Many people had no real school training during wartime since schools had to be closed every so often. Record companies even preferred (sometimes absurd) German titles for the German release of foreign instrumentals because they sounded more familiar to the audience. As this record store's ad in a newspaper from September 1966 shows, this went both ways: "Back in stock! 'Mandy-Mandy'"[3] – which of course meant "Monday, Monday".

Cover versions, by the way, were not necessarily a one way street: Early in 1960, "Be Mine", with singer Lance Fortune, became a #4 hit in the U.K. This tune was a cover version of the German schlager "Alle Mädchen wollen küssen" (All Girls Want to Kiss), written and recorded by Leo Leandros in 1958. In the same year, U.S. listeners fell in love with the main theme of a German film named *Unser Wunderland bei Nacht* by Bert Kaempfert & his Orchestra. Polydor rejected the recording. Kaempfert, furious about this decision, sold it to U.S. label Decca. In the U.S., the tune was immediately covered by the Billy Vaughn Orchestra, but Kaempfert won: In January 1961, his original version, renamed "Wonderland by Night", became the first German recording ever to reach #1 on the *Billboard* charts and sold more than two million copies. (After this, Polydor woke up and organized the distribution for Australia, New Zealand, Canada and South Africa. The record reached top positions in these countries too.)

Several American and British stars came out with German versions of their own hits, among them Johnny Cash, Willie Nelson, Everly Brothers, Connie Francis, Elvis Presley, Cliff Richard, Dionne Warwick, Manfred Mann, Helen Shapiro, and many more. Even David Bowie gave it a try in 1967, but in his case, the result was locked up and the key thrown away. (Ten years later he tried his luck again with a German version of "Heroes" – that worked better). All these German versions were a phenomenon during, primarily, the 1950s and 1960s, and the singers' fights with German umlauts ä, ö and ü[4] or the pronunciation of "ch" were sometimes touching.[5] But musically, it was possible, even if the songs sometimes seemed to get more saccharine when translated into German.

You see: The schlager is an international phenomenon, not specifically a German one. Schlagers are three-minute-songs, structured simply, sometimes maudlin, sometimes cheerful, mostly apolitical, but sometimes well able to picture some zeitgeist phenomena. To become a hit, a melody has to be catchy, and even if one may think the lyrics are not too important because nobody seems to listen to them, they have to fit, and writing good schlager lyrics is far from easy. A well-crafted hit recording reflects the zeitgeist of its era in a similar way as illustrated magazines, TV ads, or movies. Usually, you won't notice this when the schlager is new, but 30 years later you will.

SCHLAGER AND ADVERTISING

If you watch German advertisements in print magazines or from that era's TV, you will see that most of them were somehow delicate, sentimental, kitschy, and spotlessly clean. After the currency reform in 1948, advertisements were dominated by "Es gibt wieder …" ("back in stores") slogans, bringing back familiar brands that had been unavailable during the Nazi era. In the 1950s, when this phase ended and life became more and more normalized, TV ads, especially, developed their own style. Now, everything from milk bottles to nicely polished furniture, cars at the gas station to coffee refills, was dancing and singing songs. Ads had smiling faces and a Disney-esque gleaming to it. Jingles were melodious, soft, and harmonic. Most of the spoken information came in rhymes, lyrics were long, the voices were soft, friendly, and persuading. Most Germans still had the barking voices of the Nazi newsreels, propaganda films, and radio broadcasts in their ears, and now this was the backlash.

One of the busiest advertising movie makers was animation filmmaker Hans Fischerkoesen (1896–1973; his real name was Hans Fischer, Kösen in Saxony-Anhalt was the city he came from). He developed this style to perfection. In 1919, he had made the first German (maybe full-length) animation movie, *Das Loch im Westen* (The Hole In the West). (No copy or screenplay survived, so even experts are not sure whether this was really a full-length movie.)[6]

As the Führer loved Walt Disney, the Nazis had planned for Fischerkoesen to become the German equivalent. Fischerkoesen was not a Nazi — actually, according to his son, he was completely apolitical — but he took the job anyway because it saved him from being sent to the front. This resulted in three animation shorts: *Die verwitterte Melodie* (The Weathered Melody, 1942), *Der Schneemann* (The Snowman, 1943), *Das dumme Gänslein* (The Foolish Gosling, 1944) – extremely sugar-coated, but somehow charming. In 1945, Fischerkoesen was captured as a prisoner of war by the Russians. After being discharged in 1948, he started his own production company. He kept his former style, and it immediately caressed tortured German souls. The 1950s and 1960s became his prime time. His commercials for cinema and TV were filled with dancing and blissfully smiling objects, singing cows or cars, stop-motion animated coffee cups or even abstract patterns in the expressionist tradition of Oskar Fischinger or Viking Eggeling, covered with syrupy music. If you want to see German zeitgeist of the 1950s and early 1960s in pics, the advertising art of Hans Fischerkoesen was a major part of it.

ELEVATOR TO THE TOP

The German schlagers had the exact same spirit as these commercials. In the early 1960s, they were sometimes arranged with little shots of exoticism, with latin or soft-jazzy dance rhythms, the upcoming bossa nova wave left its mark. The lyrics followed the time's main trends: First there was the "Fresswelle", the period of overeating in the mid-1950s after the hungry post-war years. The "Reisewelle" (period of traveling) followed when, in the late 1950s, Germans carefully began to discover the joys of tourism – this time without tanks. They especially fell in love with Italy, followed by Spain, and "Der weiße Strand von Surabaya" (The White Beach of Surabaya; HULA-HAWAIIAN-QUARTETT, 1954), which became a dream destination. With great pleasure, the schlager lyricists also sent their listeners to non-existing fantasy paradises somewhere in the South Seas. Finally, in the early 1960s, the "Wirtschaftswunder" (economic miracle) became a topic of schlager lyrics, sometimes with a dash of pride, sometimes even with a touch of irony – as in "Es geht besser, besser, besser" (Things Go Better, Better, Better) by Peter Alexander and Caterina Valente, 1956. This song even contained a sort of "hidden warning" already that, soon, things might go a bit too well. To prevent people from going boisterous, already in 1952, Peter Alexander and Leila Negra reminded Germans of the natural order of society: "Die süßesten Früchte fressen nur die großen Tiere" (The Sweetest Fruits Are Only for the Big Animals) – and because we are both small, we will never reach them. A ludicrous, sweetish and highly ideological song that still causes toothache today, but that's how the zeitgeist was: conservative to the max. Germans, after the chaos of war, didn't want to take any risks. What was more humorous was the Swiss HAZY OSTERWALD SEXTETT: "Der Fahrstuhl nach oben ist besetzt, Sie müssen warten" (The Elevator to the Top Is Taken, You Have to Wait; 1966). These guys already knew about the way things work: "The right elevator for you might possibly never go".[7] German cabaret stars, Wolfgang Neuss and Wolfgang Müller, placed a nicely ironic song in the 1958 satirical comedy film *Wir Wunderkinder* (We Miracle Children; in the English-spoken countries also known under the misleading title *Aren't we Wonderful?*): "Jetzt kommt das Wirtschaftswunder" (Now the Economic Miracle Comes). Even if you don't understand the lyrics, the pictures do all the talking. What is especially acid-tongued in this song are some lines about many old Nazis crawling back out of their holes and re-establishing themselves into politics and the economy. It was a fact nobody wanted to hear.

Around 1960, when the horror of the Third Reich seemed to look more and more like a scare that, luckily, was over, the slogan "Wir sind wieder wer!" slowly came into the collective consciousness. It translates to something like "We're someone again!" Schlagers reflected all these new German dreams and discoveries, as did "Heimatfilms" (homeland films) — sentimental, folksy movies, usually set in small Alps villages or in the wild woods of the Black Forest. A parallel development of that time were music comedies ("Schlagerfilme") that integrated schlagers into their plot or were completely knit around them. Germans also got

TV series about more or less happy families and their tiny little problems. Not really sitcoms like, say, *Father Knows Best* (1954–1960) – they were a bit more serious, but every episode always ended with the whole family having an "all's well that ends well" laughter. No problem was allowed to remain unsolved and the family was the most important thing in the world.

Schlagers were the soundtrack of this unreal world. They reflected the average German's wish for a little piece of an idyllic world. The real world wasn't idyllic, so it was the world of schlagers that allowed the listener to be carried away to beautiful, faraway places, even if only for three minutes. Schlagers transferred the listener under the white moon of Maratonga ("Der weiße Mond von Maratonga", Lolita, 1957), one of these non-existing fantasy paradises, or — a bit more specific — they sung of white roses from Athens: "White roses from Athen / say to you: Come back quite soon" ("Weiße Rosen aus Athen" by Greek singer Nana Mouskouri, 1961)[8]. Keeping in the back of one's head how German soldiers had ravaged in Greece, these lyrics might cause goosebumps. However, if someone wasn't able to travel that far, Paul Kuhn offered a good reason to stay at home: "There's no beer in Hawaii" ("Es gibt kein Bier auf Hawaii", 1963).

Sehnsucht und Ferne – yearning and distance: This combination has worked in German souls since the time of Romanticism, and, as we will see, German rock bands made good use of the same concept later on.

LONELY COWBOYS, WAITING GIRLS

You want a look into Germany's mental state of that time? Listen to typical schlager lyrics of the late 1950s and early 1960s! You will learn that most German men were named Jim, Johnny, or Bill, and they worked as sailors or cowboys. They always had to leave, their ship was always waiting at the pier, and their true bride was, forever, the ocean: "Seemann, deine Heimat ist das Meer" (Sailor, Your Home Is the Sea; Lolita, 1960). Men had to go out for dangerous adventures somewhere far away under the burning sun, their horse and/or their guitar being their only friends, sometimes not even these: "Restless I trek around the Earth / into the wide world / without a friend and without love / because I don't have a home" ("Rastlos", Jimmy Barber, 1961)[9]. It was a given that these guys never reached success – sometimes pecuniary: "Kein Gold im Blue River" (No Gold in the Blue River; Ronny, 1964), sometimes personally: "Jimmy wanted to love a girl / but another guy came along / and the only consolation left for him: / his guitar and the sea" ("Die Gitarre und das Meer", Freddy Quinn, 1959)[10].

In the worst case, both came together. Jim, a successful gold digger, makes the mistake to count his nuggets while riding home to his bride, not noticing that he was followed by a hidden rider with greedy eyes: "He heard the shot / but nevermore its echo / and never again / he saw Jenny Lee's golden hair" ("Gold in der Sierra", Donald Wolf, 1965)[11].

Sometimes, all these mountains of destiny and exoticism mixed together into one single tune, as done in "Heißer Sand" (Hot Sand) by Italian singer Mina from 1962: The black Tino, who once had to leave the lost land, wants to return home from his unrevealed, but apparently dangerous, mission in Arabia (as the music suggests) or Greece or Italy (as the lyrics suggest), while somewhere in an unknown port, his bride, the white Lina, dances for the boys. Why she has to do this and who these boys are remains a secret, but, regardless, Tino can't return to her, and so all that's left for him is "hot sand and a lost land / and a life in danger / Hot sand and the memory / That once it was nicer".[12] – This song's lyricist, by the way, Kurt Feltz (1910–1982), was a very active schlager lyricist and composer. In his day job, he was a music editor at NDR radio. They gave him the boot when it became too obvious that he mainly played songs he had written himself.

But even in the worst situations, when nothing else could help, there was always one person left to think of: Mom! Usually she had nothing better to do than worry about her son's fate and writing desperate letters to him: "Junge, komm bald wieder" (Boy, Come Back Soon; Freddy Quinn, a massive hit in 1962 and still well-known today): "I'm up in sorrows, sorrows about you / Think of tomorrow, think of me too!"[13] Freddy Quinn, originally from Vienna, was the prototype of this lonely sailor cliché of the 1950s and 1960s; to keep this image alive, Polydor bound him to secrecy about his being married, he was not allowed to wear a wedding ring and had to stay away from women in public (of course the unuttered suspicion that he was gay followed immediately). He sold more than 60 million records, making him one of Germany's most successful schlager stars ever.

And the ladies? According to the schlager lyrics, they were mainly busy with waiting. They had to wait for their cowboy, gold digger, or sailor to return, and if they had no sailor or cowboy, they hoped for a yet-to-be-discovered lover to come out of the rain. They were standing every night at the lantern on the pier: "Ein Schiff wird kommen" (A Ship Will Come"; Lale Andersen, 1960), always knowing that if this guy would show up, he wouldn't be faithful anyways – because, as we know already, his real and only bride was the sea, and maybe his guitar. This Lale Andersen, by the way, was a textbook example of a singer who had managed to get through the Nazi time by "muddling through". She was the original singer of the world-famous song "Lili Marleen" (1939) which was later covered by Marlene Dietrich. Willi Schaeffers, boss of the Berlin vaudeville stage "Kabarett der Komiker" (KaDeKo) had always protected her from the Nazis, but she was too dim and/or too opportunistic to appreciate this. As told in a KaDeKo chronicle: "The Secretary-General of the Reichskulturkammer, Hans Hinkel, admired and promoted this artist; she, in turn, used this connection ruthlessly and thoughtlessly to full capacity, until finally she was completely on his mercy. With sadistic joy he kept [her] on tenterhooks in his cobweb, but always protected her from worse."[14] After 1945, Lale Andersen remained a star. In the 1960s she was still the "voice of the sea" and a regular on maritime TV music shows. She passed away in 1972. On the North Sea island Langeoog, where she used to live, you can see a statue, in remembrance of her, as well as of "Lili Marleen". Rainer Werner Fassbinder's film *Lili Marleen* (1980, with Hanna Schygulla) is based on her autobiography.

Apparently it couldn't be helped; being lonely and always participating in dangerous missions under the Southern Cross was the way the Joes, Jims, and Bills ticked at that time. There was no way to change it, so the girls simply kept on waiting — maybe one day, while in a faraway country, the weather would bring the lover they waited for: "The day when the rain came / long desired, craved for / on the glowing fields / on the thirsty woods / Just then *you* appeared" ("Am Tag, als der Regen kam"; Dalida, 1959)[15], served with cathedral-like reverberation and strings that make your hair stand up.

The icing on the cake of this cowboys and sailors wave was the then 17-year old Gitte (at that time still without last name, Haenning) in 1963, covered in a sort of country cliché and hyped-up: Her clamoring mother wants her to marry a railroad man because of the social safeness it would bring, while her impatient father wants her to marry a film producer because of the possible career. But she has her own ideas: "I shouted no, no, no, no, no / these guys will fret my life away / I want a cowboy to be my husband!" And she knows why: "I don't care about the shooting / because I know that such a cowboy knows how to kiss!"[16] There you go. It was a giant success. The song jumped up to the #1 spot, stayed in the charts for 20 weeks, and launched Gitte's career in Germany. Even today, "Ich will 'nen Cowboy als Mann" is still well known, and in a certain way, it's a remarkable song: The girl (daughter) dares to make demands. This is really not something to be found often at that time.

It's easy to smile – today. After all the horror that had happened during the Nazi era and the years that followed, Germans had the feeling they earned this kind of escapism. One may criticize it, while another may understand it. And to honor the truth: Some of these schlagers, like the previously mentioned Dalida one, were simply well-crafted songs with larger-than-life drama and a touch of melancholy that made them irresistible, arranged often by first-class musicians, like James Last, Bert Kaempfert, or Ladi Geisler.

Another recipe that worked well was happiness. This kind of star was Caterina Valente. She was an exceptionally gifted singer from Italy; in German recording studios she went under the nickname "Lady First Take" because she was always prepared enough to lay down her vocals perfectly in only one take. In Germany, she gave the eternally good-tempered, but she was accent-free in several languages and did not only do schlagers, she also did Italian canzone, French chansons, as well as excellent jazz recordings in England, among others with trumpeter Chet Baker or the JOHNNY KEATON ORCHESTRA. Besides this, she was a brilliant guitarist. In sports you would say: She had all it takes. If you need to be convinced, listen to "Fiesta Cubana" (1955) – she sings all vocals and plays all the instruments herself.

The earlier mentioned Heino, by the way, didn't start his career before 1965, and he is a special beast. He was never a typical schlager singer, he was much more a starter of a musical crossbreed that, later in the 1970s, became extremely successful in Germany and was widely known as "Volksmusik" or "volkstümliche Musik" — music that is folksy, but it's not "folk music" and not "schlager", it's something between.

HALBSTARK

But all of this was only a segment of the German music scene. Do you have an idea what "halbstark" means? Literally, it would translate to "half-strong". In England they were mainly "Teddy Boys", in France they were called "blousons noirs", in Spain they were "Gamberros", sometimes they were also called "beatniks", but there is no real fitting translation. The term came up in the 1950s and meant teenagers – or better: adolescents – who were in opposition of the wonderful idyllic and conservative perspectives of life that adults tried to live. Most of them were male and had working class parents. Their behavior was rebellious and they looked at movie characters like Marlon Brando in *The Wild One* (1953) or James Dean in *Rebel Without A Cause* (1955) as role models. They used to meet in street gangs and they loved motorbikes (but in most cases this love remained unanswered for financial reasons; a moped had to do). Most of the time, they wore a quiff, jeans, red or checked shirts, boots, and leather jackets. Their musical heroes were the likes of Elvis Presley, Bill Haley, Tommy Steele, Buddy Holly and British skiffle star Lonnie Donegan.

Yes, this brand-new stuff, rockabilly and later rock'n'roll, the sound of electric guitars, had arrived in Germany; not so much on the German radio, but it could, of course, be heard on AFN or BFBS, in dance bars, the bumper car or the music express at the amusement park or in the jukeboxes of ice cream parlors. The 45s were available in record stores, and if you think these records had to be imported from England or the U.S., you don't know the German record industry: Even if it had taken a long time, the majors were finally on board. Rock'n'roll records were now available as German pressings; some record companies had even set up special labels: Telefunken used the sublabels London for music from the U.S. and Decca for music from U.K., for example. Fans especially saw London as a sort of credibility label. So the music was available in Germany, and it left its mark.

The halbstark movement (if you want to call it that) reached its climax in the succession of the film *Rock Around The Clock* (1956; the German title was *Außer Rand und Band* which means something like "cut loose"). The main title track by Bill Haley & His Comets hit #1 on German charts. In several movie theaters, the furniture didn't survive the first screening, and when Bill Haley toured Germany, the fans smashed the Grugahalle in Essen, as well as the Sportpalast in Berlin. When Haley sang "Let's Rip It Up", it was not just a song, it was a message, a signal. After a screening of *Außer Rand und Band*, 4000 Halbstarke met in downtown Dortmund, affronted passers-by, and smashed shop windows. The police reacted with bats and water cannons. This had never happened before. For a while after this, a group of a hundred policemen at concert venues became a common view; for a Bill Haley concert in Hamburg, the venue floor got prepared with potassium soap to force the audience to move slowly. Obviously the energy of this music was overwhelming, sometimes more than these juveniles could handle. They had never heard anything this powerful before.

It's hard to say whether these rencounters can be seen as serious riots. Probably not, but the participants certainly saw them as that. It was their response to the adults' world which – from the Halbstarken's view – was boring and dishonest. In a certain way, they got what they wanted: Press and media were full of disgusted coverage, and even in the parliaments, these "riots" led to discussions.

It's interesting that the Halbstarken of Germany accepted Bill Haley. Most British Teds had already given him the boot when they saw him face to face. They had adopted his music as their own, but, as music producer Simon Napier-Bell remembers, "the odd thing was, Bill Haley, the person responsible for bringing [rock'n'roll] to the world, was plump, in his mid-thirties, and with a kiss-curl more absurd than Hitler's moustache. When Haley toured England and arrived by boat at Southampton docks, [some Teds] were waiting to greet him, dressed in their best Teddy-Boy gear. 'He came off the boat and the minute we saw him, someone shouted, 'Fucking hell, he's old – he looks like my granddad.' So we left and went home. And we never played his records again – ever.'"[17] However, Bill Haley still had Germany. It could have been worse for him. Some Viennese fans even took a recording by the Ray Conniff Orchestra seriously ("Cross Over", 1956).[18]

But was being halbstark the reality of German juveniles in their entirety? Hardly so. In fact, no more than 5 percent of them were halbstark and saw themselves as part of this movement.[19] But even the kids who were not interested in being part of a movement listened to Presley, Haley, Holly & Co, and noticed: We have a voice. We can make ourselves heard. There's music our parents don't like and don't understand, and that's the important thing.

SCHLAGERS, COMING ALONG AS ROCK'N'ROLL

One of the main characteristics of the schlager has always been its ability to absorb any kind of influence as long as the result sounds interesting, without being too threatening or too far-out. So it was only a matter of time until the schlager genre developed its own rock'n'roll department.

It hadn't taken long for the four big record companies – Deutsche Grammophon Gesellschaft (DGG) in Hamburg, EMI/Electrola in Cologne, Ariola/Eurodisc (Bertelsmann) in Gütersloh and Munich, Teldec (Telefunken-Decca) in Hamburg – to become aware of the fact that there was a market, a target group that could be defined. As a doctoral thesis from 1958 showed, the mechanisms of the recording industry already worked fine. Nobody within these companies really liked this music, but they saw enough potential in it to jump on the train.[20]

To make one thing clear: Germany was hardly able to come up with a rock'n'roller who could rival the likes of Chuck Berry, Elvis Presley, Buddy Holly, Little Richard, Jerry Lee Lewis, Bill Haley. In Germany, guys like Peter Kraus, Ted

Herold, and some other singers, started their careers in the late 1950s, usually with German cover versions of hits from the popular U.S. teen stars, like Peter Kraus who first appeared on the budget label Tempo. Under the name Twist Boys he sang duets with himself there. These recordings were mostly a cross-breed between rock'n'roll, twist, or skiffle, and German schlager. But Bill Haley's tunes were attractive enough to release dozens of German cover versions; budget labels were especially active in this. Bear Family Records in 2015 released a collection of 25 of these cover versions on CD, entitled *...und dann kam Bill Haley* (...and then Bill Haley came).

To catch more attention, there was a sort of "good guy – bad guy" rivalry going on between Peter Kraus and Ted Herold. The glossy magazines, especially the weekly magazine *Bravo* (subtitled in the beginning: "The Magazine With the Young Heart", published since 1956 and in the beginning mainly a film magazine, later it became the leading music magazine for teenagers), were filled with stories about their latest love affairs, their parts in films, or other escapades. But this rivalry was systematically made up – actually, the two of them had the same management, and so the "fights" were well coordinated. Finally, "bad guy" Herold, who, in fact, was the better singer and performer, lost out. Kraus, a dream for all mother-in-laws, became the star, fully integrated into the schlager business and teen movies of the 1960s. This was the end even for the slightest trace of rock'n'roll. What remained was purely fake. The movie industry put teenage star, Connie Froboess, at Kraus's side and marketed them as the "ideal young couple"; in 1958, they appeared in a movie entitled, slightly suggestively, *Wenn die Connie mit dem Peter* (When Connie with Peter), followed by *Connie und Peter machen Musik* (Conny and Peter Make Music) in 1960 – stupid love comedies with even worse music, following the same pattern as beach party movies in the U.S. (But to be fair: Connie Froboess is a pretty good actress, still active today.) Gitte Haenning, who later became a schlager (and sometimes well acceptable jazz) singer, teamed up with schlager singer Rex Gildo (1936–1999), to build up another "dream couple" for schlager movies, puts it this way: "In these movies we had to fulfill all the unfulfilled dreams of the housewives."[21] Parents didn't need to fear them, the message these movies sent was clear: Your teenage kids might be a bit strange at times, but have them let off some steam, don't be worried, and in the end you will see: They are good kids, one day they will be on the same track as you.

All this stuff hit the top of the charts. In 1959, *Bravo* started the "*Bravo*-Starschnitt" with French superstar Brigitte Bardot, but the second and third were already Peter Kraus and Connie Froboess: Every *Bravo* copy included one page with a part of a photo. If after 15 or more weeks you had all the parts, you could glue them together to have a life-sized poster of your star to put on your wall. In the matter of reaching a high reader loyalty, the Starschnitt was a stroke of genius; we've got to hand it to the *Bravo* makers.

Ted Herold, meanwhile, switched to another record label and had to lower his sights. Of course, he never became a *Bravo*-Starschnitt. However, Herold finished his career just a couple of years ago. Kraus is still active today. He looks well preserved, and his latently blaring voice still jangles my nerves.

Another early rock'n'roller was Paul Würges (1932–2017) of Munich, who was seen as "the German Bill Haley". He was definitely a better singer than the aforementioned guys, and as a guitarist, he was talented enough to work as a session musician on recordings by Paul Anka, Tony Sheridan, and even Chubby Checker. But he was never able to score a real hit under his name; during his entire career he remained an insider tip, and most of the time, he had to work under several pseudonyms for budget labels. (I will come back to these labels in a later chapter; they were more important than you might think.)

As mentioned earlier, there were now also sounds coming to Germany that had been unheard of for a long time: jazz. Swing and pop from Great Britain and the U.S. was brought to the young generation's hungry ears by the Allied Forces and their radio stations BFBS and AFN. The listeners in the French zones weren't that lucky; their stations were more oriented to French-style chansons. If, in the 1970s, you asked adults about their all-time favorite songs, you could easily guess from their answers which zone they had lived in as teenagers. But this was not the only consequence of these zones' existence.

EARLY JAZZ

In the shipping channel of mainly AFN and BFBS, a tiny little jazz scene developed in Germany. In Düsseldorf, a certain Klaus Doldinger founded a Dixieland band named The Feetwarmers, another musician who started in the late Fifties was Peter Brötzmann, who later became a sort of "free radical" in the jazz scene. One of the consequences of their work was the re-opening of small music clubs in several cities, and these clubs were ideal breeding stations for new sounds beyond schlager and teenage rock'n'roll – they also served as meeting points for a new audience willing to listen to them.

Jazz musicians were the first to absorb these sounds from beyond the German borders. Multi-instrumentalist Klaus Doldinger already started his Feetwarmers in 1953 while studying clarinet and piano at Düsseldorf's Robert-Schumann-Conservatory. He didn't leave it at that. He added the saxophone to his roster of instruments (from the clarinet this is not a big step because the manner of playing is similar). In 1955, he founded Oscar's Trio, named in honor of Oscar Peterson, and won the "Coup Sidney Bechet". He also became a skilled sound engineer, which later turned out to be very useful for him. He then finished his first advertising jingle – a side job he would later become famous for. All this opened the door for him to write, play, and record film music professionally. In 1960, Klaus Doldinger toured the U.S., got in touch with George Lewis and some other jazz greats, played the Birdland, and became an honorary citizen of New Orleans. Back home, he worked with American musicians living in Germany: Don Ellis, Johnny Griffin, Kenny Clarke, Donald Byrd, and Benny Bailey. In 1962, he founded the Klaus Doldinger Quartet with Ingfried Hoffmann (organ), Helmut Kandlberger (bass), and Klaus Weiss (drums). This quartet recorded *Jazz Made in Germany* (1963) for the Philips label, followed by *Live at The Blue Note Berlin* (1964). Both albums were critically acclaimed.

What was also visible, was the beginning of what would later become the German free jazz scene. The term "free jazz", in all likelihood, came from Ornette Coleman's album, *Free Jazz: A Collective Improvisation* (1961). Free jazz was basically an expansion of bebop: It broke up harmonic tonality and the differences between sound and noise, and there was no dividing line between sidemen and soloists anymore – these were some of the main characteristics of early free jazz. Later, clear definitions of rhythm and metrics also fell apart. Somehow, this way of thinking landed on fertile soil. It didn't take long for musicians like Peter Brötzmann, Hans Koller, Gunter Hampel, Peter Kowald, Irène Schweizer, and others, to fall in love with this completely free, improvised music. And, as bassist Eberhard Weber says, soon the free jazz scene split up into two factions: the "hardcore" faction and the "happening" faction. Both couldn't stand each other.[22] For an audience used to the likes of Oscar Peterson or Stan Getz, the hardcore stuff was extremely hard to cope with, and the anarchic humor behind the happening faction was not accessible to everybody. But that was part of the game.

Within this bunch of free jazz musicians, we find two names that later became important for the German rock scene: Manfred "Mani" Neumeier and Uli Trepte (1941–2009). An excellent recording of this era is *Early Tapes* by Irène Schweizer Trio (recorded 1967, released in 1978 on the FMP label, with Neumeier and Trepte). It's clearly still a jazz album, but it shows that they had already absorbed some basic rock impulses. Neumeier: "Besides Jaki Liebezeit of Can, I was the biggest free jazz drummer in the whole Europe. … Then there came Jimi Hendrix who stunned me completely. From then on it was clear to me that I needed to integrate something electronic into my music. In Switzerland, I started Guru Guru with Uli Trepte. But to do something really revolutionary, Switzerland was simply too small. In 1968, there were just three venues for us to play our kind of music. Consequently, we became vagabonds, traveled to Germany to proclaim our mission. Thanks to some nice ladies and befriended bands like Amon Düül we always had a shelter there. And we could make a name for ourselves as Guru Guru. … First, we were outlaws. Merely because of our long hair. I would say we were anarchists, radical libertines. With our work and being different we wanted to blow away the dust of ol' Adolf H. from this country."[23]

Drummer Jaki (Hans) Liebezeit (1938–2017), after playing in Spain with Chet Baker, became a member of the Manfred Schoof Quintett and the Globe Unity Orchestra; he can be heard on *Voices* by Manfred Schoof Quintett and *Globe Unity* with pianist Alexander von Schlippenbach (both 1966). It was a relatively small scene; all of these musicians knew each other and jammed with each other, so it's no wonder that Peter Brötzmann and Mani Neumeier can also be heard on the latter one.

An important point about free jazz that many listeners didn't get was that these guys were virtuosi on their instruments. Of course, there was no longer any excuse for incompetent playing in jazz since Louis Armstrong had taken up his cornet. The musicians knew this, but in the audience it was not always common knowledge. These musicians now played free jazz not because – as many people suspected – they weren't able to play "real melodies", but because they felt it was time to break down some borders after the restrictions, jazz musicians, especially, had to suffer during the Nazi era. The Americans showed them how this could work.

This might be comparable to the shock that large populations of the art community experienced when abstract painting came into existence. Their first reaction was: These guys can't paint. But the more they got into this style, they realized: They can paint. They know all the rules, and if you know where to check, you can even see how they use them. As usual, artists were faster than their audience. But that's the way art works – just like music.

With the help of editors at German radio stations, it didn't take long for the European free jazz scene to become more radical than the American. It took a while until the listeners were able to appreciate what they were being served. And let's be honest: Seeing and hearing someone like saxophonist Peter Brötzmann snuffling, sweating, and permanently overblowing his instrument *was* a challenge. Often enough, these concerts ended up with a shocked and booing audience.

It was this virtuosity that made a big difference between these free jazz musicians and some later rock bands pretending to do a sort of "free rock".

SOME QUESTIONS OF INFRASTRUCTURE

The following paragraphs might fall a bit off track, especially timewise. Before we talk about music, it will be useful for you to have a basic overview about the post-war situation in Germany that musicians had to deal with.

FOUR ZONES

If you are a musician, artist, author, or filmmaker in the U.K., and want to make it, you don't go to Manchester or Bristol, you go to London. In the U.S., you go to New York City (because, as you know: If you can make it there, you'll make it anywhere), or, if your business is acting or screenwriting, Los Angeles. These are the places where important record companies, radio and TV stations, concert promoters, film production companies, agents, book publishers, and distributors are concentrated.

This isn't the case in Germany. After the war, there was no longer a capital where everything came together. Berlin had been the cultural center during the Weimar Republic, as well as during the Third Reich, but now it was an isolated island in the middle of the Soviet Zone (the German Democratic Republic, GDR). Even in theory, it had lost its function as a capital, if not in the early 1950s, then at latest in 1961 when East Germany erected the Wall. From then on, it became a nerve-racking act to even travel to West Berlin from West Germany because you always had to pass two (often harassing) GDR border controls, stay on a compulsory transit road full of police, and there were pettifogging traffic controls that only had one purpose: to cash in some of your West German money. The GDR bitterly needed this. When you traveled home, the same drama started all over again.

But why did no other city, like Hamburg, Frankfurt, or Munich, take the opportunity to become the capital?

There were two main reasons.

First: After the war, the Allied Forces divided Germany into American, British, French and Soviet occupied zones, and of course, every zone wanted to have its own center. To make things more complicated, Berlin, as the former capital, was now divided into four zones corresponding to the rest of Germany: There was an American, a British, and a French zone which made West Berlin. East Berlin, occupied by the Soviets, became the capital of the GDR.

As shown on the inside of the book cover, Berlin is in the middle of the Soviet Zone and is, itself, parted into four zones. This construction made it impossible to keep Berlin as Germany's capital, even for West Germany. So, the three Western Allied Forces decided that for the time being, Bonn, located on the Rhine River near Cologne, should be the political capital of West Germany.

Politically this worked quite well, but the sleepy, small town of Bonn could never become a cultural center. There's a colloquial saying that went: In Bonn, it either rains or the railway crossing gates are closed. If both happen at the same time, it's Sunday.

RADIO

The second reason for the lack of a real cultural capital was the reorganization of the German broadcasting system. During the Nazi era, all radio stations in Germany had been combined in one big radio network for all of Germany. It was directly controlled by Reich Propaganda Minister, Joseph Goebbels, and he knew exactly how to use it for purposes of communication of the Nazi party.

To prevent this kind of misuse of media power in the future, the three Western Allies decided that there should no longer be a centralized broadcasting system in Germany. It had to be organized regionally: one station for every federal state. The Allies decided to put this system under public law to prevent governmental radio; they also didn't allow any kind of privately run commercial broadcasting.

Following this decision, the Allied Forces started radio networks in their respective zones, each of them basically following the principles of the British BBC. (Eastern Germany did it differently; anything that is said here refers to West Germany, including West Berlin.)

In 1950, the ARD was founded. This acronym stands for "Arbeitsgemeinschaft der Rundfunkanstalten Deutschlands" (working group of the broadcasting corporations of Germany). The stations essentially followed the idea that each federal state should run its own radio network under public law.[1] Each station offered two radio programs, a more classic and informational one, and another geared more toward entertainment. These program structures changed a bit over the years, but the basic idea remained. In addition to the ARD stations, there was AFN (American Forces Network), mainly broadcasting in Bavaria, Hessen, and parts of Baden-Württemberg, and Rhineland-Palatinate; there was BFBS (British Forces Broadcasting Service), audible mainly in the Northern half of Germany. AFN and BFBS were service stations for American and British soldiers, the French Forces did not establish their own station. Finally there was RIAS (Rundfunk im amerikanischen Sektor), a radio station under American management in West Berlin, broadcasting in the German language, for the German public. One of the main points behind this was to have an American station that could reach East Berlin and the Soviet Zone. Obviously it was successful: It didn't take long for the GDR to start jamming RIAS broadcasts.

The only commercial station audible in Germany was Radio Luxembourg, which blew schlager, pop, small talk, and commercials over the border; its FM frequencies covered both the Ruhr area and Saarland. A shortwave frequency could be heard all over Europe, but the sound quality was weak. In the evening, from 7 pm on, Radio Luxembourg aired an English program over a medium wave frequency. These shows were produced in London and held value in the U.K., but turned out to also be something special for us young folks in the northern half of Germany; it was something we learned to love. I wouldn't even dare to imagine how we, the AFN-less lowland of North Germany, could have survived the late 1960s and 1970s without this English program of "208 Radio Luxembourg", named after its frequency (1440 kilohertz = 208 meters). For me, a thirteen-year-old with average school English, this was an eternal mystery because I always misheard the "Two-O-Eight" of their jingles as "two or late"; it never occurred to me what that could mean. It was simple Top 40 radio. No German schlagers – they had the latest hits from England and the U.S., and there was the easy-going way that the DJs did their job: They made it clear just how powerful and entertaining radio could be, contrasting to the always slightly stiff and "state carrying" radio stations we had in Germany.

There were also a couple of offshore radio stations we could pick up on AM or shortwave frequencies, mainly Radio North Sea International, Radio

Caroline, and Radio Veronica. They aired their programs from ships outside the three-mile territory limits or from abandoned military buildings in the Thames mouth. Their airwaves were hard to catch, mainly for technical reasons, but we were willing to put up with it because of their clandestine "pirate" image – apparently they outsmarted the stupid authorities that were always hunting them, and this made them lovable. From time to time, some illustrated magazines reported about these pirate stations; usually under fanciful headlines, like: "At Storm Force 10 the Turntable Skips" or "The DJs Have to Have Good Sea Legs" – as if the DJs were really working on board these ships. But we didn't know any better, so we believed it. Actually, all of the pirate stations' shows were pre-recorded on tape, somewhere in studios in London or Hilversum. Only the transmitters were installed on the ships. For the two or three technicians and tape operators on board of these barges, this must have been a pretty lonely and boring job.

"The Station of Your Stars", the English program of Radio Luxembourg, was no pirate radio, but even they pretended to be a live broadcast. The shows were pre-recorded in a tiny little studio on London's Hertford Street; day by day, the tapes were flown to Luxembourg by a private sporting aircraft. It was not until 1963 that the DJs physically moved to Luxembourg City (or, as they nicknamed it, to "Luxy"). From then on, they presented their shows live from the Villa Louvigny, where Radio Luxembourg was situated.[2]

Radio Luxembourg, as well as the pirate stations, made what the German radio stations lacked painfully clear. At this time, they were deadly serious in the way they presented their stuff; often, instead of playing the original hit versions, they preferred orchestral cover versions of hits, performed by their own orchestras.

In 1966, a unique problem arose. In Germany, there are two copyright societies: the GEMA (Gesellschaft für musikalische Aufführungs- und mechanische Vervielfältigungsrechte) that takes in the royalties for composers, arrangers and lyricists, and the GVL (Gesellschaft zur Verwertung von Leistungsschutzrechten) that takes in the royalties for musicians playing on records. Every radio and TV station in Germany has to pay a certain fee to these corporations for every composition and record they play. In 1966, the GVL had the idea to increase the fee they demanded from the radio stations by ten. Of course, the radio stations were not willing to accept this increase. Their response was a boycott toward records. They reduced their record-playing to only ten percent, and filled the rest of their time with music played by their own orchestras. This led to lots of protest from the audience, especially from young listeners. Whoever was able to catch

Radio Luxembourg, BFBS or AFN, went there. The conflict went on for several months until they came to an agreement. But a part of the audience, especially those from the Ruhr area and Saarland, where Radio Luxembourg was available on FM, never returned to the German radio stations under public law.

But even in "normal" times, the only way to get in touch with fresh, original music was mainly through the weekly hit parade that every station had, but these shows usually mixed English and American pop music with German schlagers, and it was only the latter that tended to reach top positions. Aside from this, most presenters (they weren't called DJs, they were called "moderators" or simply "announcers") were skilled actors who used to talk with sepulchral voices that gave us the feeling that, with the next time signal tone, the River Elbe would flood downtown. Talking into a microphone under public law was very serious business in the 1950s and 1960s. The first presenter to brighten this at least a little bit up was a guy from England: Chris Howland (1928-2013), starting in 1952 at NWDR radio in Cologne. No wonder "Heinrich Pumpernickel", as he used to introduce himself, became a somewhat radio legend, along with his enjoyable British accent, which he painstakingly cultivated. Besides Chris Howland, there was Jimmy Jungermann (1914–1987) at BR radio Munich.

It was not until the Seventies that the presentation style of most radio stations, in general, lightened up. Pioneering was, again, the BR Munich with Thomas Gottschalk who started his own radio show in 1971. Still, most presenters were not "DJs", they were journalists and primarily saw themselves as intellectuals, not as entertainers. This was exactly how they looked down on schlagers and pop music.

The German broadcasting system didn't change much until 1985, when a wide-ranging media reform took place. It allowed the start of privately run commercial radio stations. Most of them copied Radio Luxembourg or tried to present their program in what they thought might be the style of American radio stations. It didn't take long until public radio stations had to react and change their program styles.

TELEVISION

In 1954, the ARD started a nationwide television network. Because it was the first TV program we had, it's still, to this day, called "Das Erste" (the first). Every ARD station produces and delivers contributions to it.

In 1963, Chancellor Konrad Adenauer wanted to start another nationwide TV network – the difference being that this one be managed directly by the government, because Adenauer and his Christian Democratic Party (CDU)[3] had the feeling that the ARD was too critical and too left-wing. The Federal Constitutional Court overthrew the decision and ruled that every broadcasting network, no matter what, had to work under public law. So, finally, the Zweites Deutsches Fernsehen (ZDF) started, nationwide and under public law, and is still, to this day, called "Das Zweite" (the second). But other than the ARD network, it is one station, centralized in Mainz.

In 1964 and 1965, the ARD stations started developing regional TV programs for their respective federal states. These programs – you guessed it – were called "die Dritten" (the thirds); their job consisted mainly of local coverage, with a secondary focus on educational programs.

As with the radio stations, there were no commercial TV competitors allowed until 1984. All stations under public law were restrictive of commercial advertising: ARD, as well as ZDF, were only allowed to air TV commercials between 6 and 8 pm, no longer than 20 minutes per day. The "thirds" had no commercials.

These radio and TV stations became the docking places for record companies, sound recording studios, concert promoters, film production companies, and distributors. This is the reason why, in Germany, musicians and other artists had no "London" or "New York" to go to. The media structure of Germany was decentralized, which was fine, but, as you will see later, German musicians had to fight with this structure.

Similar to the BBC, ARD and ZDF were able to develop and produce shows, series, and events that no commercial station would even consider. They established one of the best networks of foreign news correspondents in the world. They ran symphony orchestras, choirs, big bands, and specialized ensembles. They commissioned and produced compositions and radio plays. They produced ambitious and informative radio features that sometimes became a prominent part of public discussion. They were extremely important for two music genres:

JAZZ AND ELECTRONIC MUSIC

One of the most famous radio institutions was the "Studio für Elektronische Musik des WDR" (Studio for Electronic Music at WDR) in Cologne, founded in 1953 by Werner Meyer-Eppler and Herbert Eimert. Both were well-known pioneers of electronic music. Since 1963, under the leadership of composer Karlheinz Stockhausen, this studio has been one of the most important impulse generators for electronic music of the mid-1960s and 1970s, world-wide. Still, today, it is seen as highly important and legendary. It had to move locations a couple of times and was closed down in 1999. It was planned to be re-opened at gallery Haus Mödrath near Kerpen, a former maternity home where Stockhausen was born, but WDR refused the offer. The studio's future is open.[4]

The SWF in Baden-Baden ran a similar institution named Experimentalstudio, founded by Heinrich Strobel. The SWF also founded a symphony orchestra that specialized in contemporary music. Without these institutions, the worldwide known "Donaueschinger Musiktage" for experimental music wouldn't be possible.

Another example for the importance of public radio is a series entitled "das neue werk" (the new opus, following the then zeitgeist, was decidedly written in lowercase letters). Through this series, since 1951, the NDR in Hamburg had commissioned, produced, and broadcasted many kinds of new and experimental music, including electronic and orchestral works, usually under direct participation of the composers. Karlheinz Stockhausen's *Gruppen für drei Orchester* is one of these commissioned pieces; today it is seen as one of the key works of the second half of the 20th century. The series is still in existence.

Some ARD editors had a special liking for contemporary jazz. One of them was Joachim-Ernst Berendt (1922–2000) whose "Jazzbuch", a book about the story of jazz, is still seen today as a benchmark. He built up the jazz department of SWF, and produced a lot of records in cooperation with the (later famous, now legendary) MPS label. In the Seventies, Berendt became more and more dogmatic about free jazz, which he saw as a highly political genre. Later, he drifted off into the nebula of New Age esoterics. But that takes nothing away from his importance for the development of jazz in Germany.

In 1958, NDR radio started the "NDR Jazzworkshop" series. First, under the keeping of Austrian saxophonist (and painter) Hans Koller, then later in the 1970s, under the aegis of jazz pianist, sociologist, and owner of an unforgettable voice, Michael Naura (1934–2017). The "Jazzworkshop" organized, commissioned, and recorded studio concerts with musicians from Lee Konitz to Keith Jarrett, Gary Burton to Miles Davis, and Albert Mangelsdorff to Pat Metheny. There has hardly been a better serial program for jazz fans in Germany since, and the Jazzworkshop archive is a pure treasure. (Today, we've reached the time to digitize these tapes before they deteriorate. The jazz editors at NDR have started doing this, but as always, it's a question of time and budget.)

These are just a few examples, but they might give you an idea about how important the radio and TV stations were, regardless of how stiff they initially came off as. Somebody, please show me a commercial radio station that would do all this! Only rock musicians, especially German rock musicians, tended to have a tough position with these stations.

If there was no real center in Germany, what happened to the music scene? Instead of one central location, there were four main cultural centers developing in the early 1960s: West Berlin, Hamburg, Munich and Frankfurt, plus a couple of sub-centers (Cologne, Stuttgart and some more), and later, Düsseldorf also appeared. Each of these music scenes had their own characteristics, mentalities, and ways of working, and as a musician, you had to know its specifics to be able to have any success. This way, a real "capital of music" couldn't come into existence. An important consequence of this is that, after WWII, Germany never had hit factories like Tin Pan Alley or the Brill Building.

RECORDS AND MARKETS

In 1929, 30 million records had already been sold in Germany. Due to the economic crisis, the number dropped down to just 10 million in 1933. There are no statistics from during the Third Reich, but in 1949, only 4 million records were sold – understandably; people had more important things to worry about than buying records. But, whether this would change again was a question of time and economic upswing. Only three years later, the record sales had more than tripled: 12.5 million copies were sold. In 1955, the industry caught up with the late 1920s: 31 million records were sold over counters; in 1956, 40 million.[5] For a while this didn't change. THE BEATLES, and other bands, were needed to increase records' sales again: 47.6 million records were sold in Germany in 1964.[6] The Golden Era of the record industry began and, for many years, the sales numbers rose, uninterrupted. In 1973, the industry sold 148 million records in Germany.[7]

A lot of 45s went into jukeboxes – you know, these wonderful Seeburgers, Rock-Olas, and Wurlitzers. Every bar and corner pub had one. These devices were an important economic factor for the inn-keepers and pub owners. When the jukebox was well-used, it could bring in nearly enough to pay monthly rent for the watering hole. In 1955, around 12,000 jukeboxes were found in Germany's pubs and bars, while in 1970 there were already 80,000, filled with records by around 5000 (usually self-employed) service operators. Every jukebox had around 100 singles in its belly – overall, that's 8 million. I remember that in the late 1960s, playing one song cost 20 Pfennigs, playing three songs cost 50 Pfennigs, and six songs cost 1 D-Mark. In 1970, the total turnover made by jukeboxes was 240 million D-Marks.[8]

In the mid-1960s, the yearly turnover with record sales was around 300 million D-Marks[9], and in 1973, it was around 1 billion D-Marks[10]. This might sound like big money, but everything is relative: The yearly turnover with Christmas tree sales in Germany had more or less the same volume.[11] In a macroeconomic view, music has never been a big market in Germany.

Usually Germany is classified as the third-biggest record market in the world, placing after the U.S. and the U.K., followed by France and Japan; sometimes Germany, France, and Japan trade places for a while. The record sales in the U.K. were around 33 percent higher than in Germany or Japan.[12] Germans are not a community of die-hard record buyers. In fact, around 60 percent of all German consumers never spent any money on music – not in the 1960s, not today, and most of the remaining 40 percent don't buy more than 15 or 20 records during their entire lifetime.[13] You just need to look at a typical German wall unit from the 1960s and 1970s (they are called "Schrankwand" and were a fad then) to see how little space was allocated for books and records, compared to the schnapps cabinet. Furniture designers always knew best what their target group really wanted.

Let's grab a magnifying glass and have a closer look at the record buyers. The record industry knew: 80 percent of the turnover is made by only 20 percent of the buyers. Record stores had a similar rule: When you have ten customers in your shop, eight of them have no idea what they are looking for. They feel lost, like the fathers, mothers, or uncles who look around for a while, unsure, before finally asking for "a record for a fourteen-year old". Or they sing a melody that they heard on the radio to the shopkeeper. These customers sometimes need long, intense guidance and will leave with one record (if any) in the end. The ninth customer is easy: He knows what he's looking for and buys it when he finds it. And then there's the tenth customer. He's the most interesting target group, but he's not always easy to handle. These guys are specialists. They don't leave the store without having bought five or more records. Sometimes they are the shopkeeper's best friends and like to talk shop. They know exactly what they want, and usually, it's not the Top Ten stuff – they look for more unique things.

They can also become sour when they don't find what they want, or, even worse, when the shopkeeper has never heard of it.

In the 1950s and 1960s, there were only a few big record stores which carried the full range of music in Germany. They were found in big cities, usually downtown, and some of them were connected to musical instrument stores like Steinway. Chains like Tower Records or HMV didn't exist and record companies didn't have their own stores. Then there were the department stores. Usually, they had a record department, but most of the time, they only carried hit records and some standard classical repertoire. There were some record shops specializing in unique genres (mainly jazz and classical). Records were also sold in small and medium-sized owner-operated radio and TV stores. Their main job was selling and repairing radios, TV sets, and record players; for them, selling records was only a side-job. The owners worked primarily as radio and TV technicians, not necessarily in music. If you (and they) were lucky, they had a 16-year old apprentice who could tell his boss which records he should keep in stock.

Germany had a couple of record clubs, like the Deutsche Schallplattenclub, the Bertelsmann Club, or the Büchergilde Gutenberg, the latter was connected to the trade unions. You know this concept: They send a catalogue to you, you have to order three records quarterly, and if you don't order, they send you three records of their choice. Usually the records were called "club edition" or something like this, had a different cover but were identical to the ones you could buy in stores, but a little bit cheaper. The clubs also had some special offers you could only take advantage of there. The prime time of these record clubs were the 1960s and 1870s; in the 1980s their relevance went downhill.

Records were subject to fixed prices until 1966, when the Bundesgerichtshof (Federal Court of Justice), much to the annoyance of the industry, declared the fixed prices void. But the industry didn't give in. They now installed a "recommended retail price", and all the retailers knew exactly how to read this "recommendation". So the price for records in Germany remained very high: 18 D-Marks for an album and 4.50 D-Marks for a single in 1965, which around 1969, went up to 20 and 4.75 D-Marks, and, shortly after, increased again to 22 and 4.95 D-Marks. If you see that the German average income in 1965 was just 400 D-Marks gross per month (in 1970 it was around 580 D-Marks)[14], you can easily understand how expensive it was to buy a record. These were the golden times for the record industry, and this did not change before 1972. We will have to come back to this because German rock music had an important role in this process.

CLUBS AND LIVE MUSIC

Musicians don't only need electronic media, they also need places to meet their audience face to face. Most cities had music clubs and, sometimes, record stores and fashion boutiques also had a little stage. Even some head shops already existed, but they weren't called this. They were all important in building up a local scene. These were the places where musicians learned about the latest trends from London. Here, musicians and fans met one another.

In Frankfurt, there was the Sinkkasten, a famous jazz club. There was also a basement bar named Heidi Loves You, which was a cross between a pub, club, and head shop, run by Paul-Gerhard "Hadayatullah" Hübsch and Bernd Brummbär, authors and, at that time, well-known dudes. It was a sort of meeting point for the early (still small) Frankfurt psychedelic scene. Because this establishment offered alcohol without holding a concession, the police paid it a visit, and, in September 1968, when they found some grams of hashish and hookahs, Heidi Loves You was shut down.[15]

Munich had the PN Hit-House on Leopoldstraße in the posh Schwabing neighborhood, where cover bands played during the week and international top acts on the weekends. Later, Amon Düül became their in-house band. There was the Blow Up, the P1, the Domicile, the Big Apple, and a well-stocked record store named Pudding Explosion. This shop always carried the latest albums from England and America. One album they had in heavy rotation was by Hapshash & The Coloured Coat, entitled *Feat. The Human Host and the Heavy Metal Kids* from 1967. This band was originally a London-based underground advertising, poster design, and music crew, and their wild music had an audible influence on what would later become Amon Düül II.

In West Berlin, the Riverboat called itself an "action center". It had big interlaced rooms, up to four bands, and a DJ, all of which were simultaneously performing. There were several more clubs, three different ones called Eden, and the Badewanne, which was mainly a jazz club. In 1969, the Tangerine Dream "Bathtub Session" was recorded and filmed there. But the most important club was the Zodiac Free Arts Lab in the Kreuzberg neighborhood, which consisted of two rooms (one painted in black, one in white) in a building that was used by the Schaubühne theater, founded in 1967. One of the founders was Conrad Schnitzler. He, with Hans-Joachim Roedelius, Boris Schaak, Elke Lixfeld, Christoph Sievernich, Beatrix Rief, Verena Schirz, Broderick Price, and Norbert Eisbrenner, started a project named Human Being and used the Zodiac to perform fully improvised noise events that left audiences disoriented; later bands like FAUST, AGITATION FREE, PLUS/MINUS, ASH RA TEMPEL, or Edgar Froese's TANGERINE DREAM predecessor, THE ONES, also played at this club and left stunned listeners (and sometimes destroyed equipment). The Zodiac closed its doors after only two years, but its impact on the West Berlin rock scene cannot be underestimated.

In Düsseldorf, there was the world-famous Kunstakademie (Academy of Arts). Sigmar Polke, Gerhard Richter, Blinky Palermo, Jörg Immendorf, Bernd and Hilla Becher, and other important artists held chairs there – and of course Joseph Beuys, who probably had the biggest community of followers (which was not too big of a feat because, as a matter of principle, he never rejected any applicants). One of his students was Conrad Schnitzler. In the neighborhood of the Kunstakademie, several clubs and galleries were situated. One of them became especially important for Düsseldorf's music scene later on: the Creamcheese, a pub and gallery. KRAFTWERK, as well as CAN, started there. Later, there was the Ratinger Hof, but that's a thing for the Eighties chapter.

But it was not only the big cities – things also happened in the backwater. Like most cities with American or British soldiers, the Hessian garrison town, Hanau, had a very vivid and relatively big red light district, and there were, of course, music clubs. The most important one was the Jolly Bar – THE MONKS played here regularly and became influential on the just-forming German rock scene.[16] German and American musicians mingled and played together here. A (kraut-)band from Hanau that later appeared was ORANGE PEEL. An important painter and record cover designer also lived here, Helmut Wenske.

Session musician and later AMON DÜÜL II saxophonist, Olaf Kübler, has many anecdotes about the start of his career in Gießen (another Hessian garrison town) – Café Baumann, the Casanova Club, which was again a mixed scene, something between jazz clubs and red light districts.[17] Later, there were better opportunities to play in Germany, but in these early years there was nothing more for young bands other than jazz clubs, bars, and cafés. Without question, all these clubs, galleries, et cetera, were important. Regardless of their importance, their impact remained mainly local.

But there was one music club that topped them all. Its influence was nationwide and its opening in 1961 had, once and for all, finished "the time of oompah music". We will visit this club after the following chapter.

But before any music, the wirtschaftswunder (Germany's economic miracle) had to come.

Franz-Josef Degenhardt at the “German Song Night” (opening of the “Internationale Essener Songtage” – September 25th, 1968)

THE SIXTIES

"No Experiments!"

KONRAD ADENAUER
(CHANCELLOR OF GERMANY, 1949–1963)

CHOO-CHOO TRAINS AND TELSTAR

In 1960, I was four years old – not an age at which rock music gives you goosebumps. In 1961, the Beatles were already around (don't forget I lived in Hamburg), but they were not much of a topic under our roof, and the Rolling Stones were still widely unknown in Germany at that time. The most important topic that came up with these bands was their "long hair". These haircuts were seen as criminal and caused a lot of head-shaking whenever family and friends gathered together for coffee klatch at granny's birthday party. You could bet there was one uncle proclaiming what he'd do with these "monkeys" if he'd get the chance. Until about 1965, the Beatles' music had rarely been played on the radio, the music of the Rolling Stones was played even less, but you could buy "Beatle wigs" or giant "Beatle combs" at joke article shops or department stores for the carnival season.

When I listened to music, it came mainly from the radio, and what they played there was a lot of big band music or orchestral, easy-listening stuff – what was unforgettable for me, just for its name, was the Tanzorchester ohne Namen (Dance Orchestra without a Name) conducted under Franz Thon, a radio orchestra mainly playing cover versions of the current schlagers.

My parents had a pile of records, mainly 45s, maybe two or three dozens of schlager records, usually stuff they had heard in the jukebox at their favorite watering hole. Everybody had one at that time, and Eimsbüttel, the Hamburg neighborhood where I grew up, had four at every intersection. Besides this, my parents were motorcycle riders, and one or two times a year they took their motorcycle with a sidecar and visited some friends at a small village in the Rhön area near Würzburg. One of their friends worked at the local gas station there, while another was a sales representative for an herbal schnapps distillery. Another pair of siblings they knew owned a pension with a roadhouse named "Gasthaus zur Krone" (a common name back then – we will hear it again later), and this was a place where in the back room typical 1960s weekend parties took place every Saturday night. My parents, when they were back in Hamburg, used to buy some of the records they had heard there in the jukebox as a sort of souvenir. The jukebox at the "Krone" was their main source to get information about the latest hits. Whenever they celebrated one of their three-month house parties, alternating with three befriended couples, these 45s rotated over and over on their Telefunken record player (of which you could put a pile of ten records on).

When they were alone at home, they preferred popular classical music, like Edvard Grieg's "Peer Gynt Suite" or Beethoven's "Moonshine Sonata". My father would have liked to be a marine engineer, but he was an accounting clerk at a home loan bank and my mother had been an assembly-line worker, but quit her job when I popped into their lives, so we could hardly be called "middle class". We didn't have much money, which is why they used to buy classical records from budget labels, especially from Opera, the label with the sewn sleeves. Some recordings of this label weren't even bad. My parents are both long deceased and many records got lost. Nobody knows where they are. The ones we've managed to keep lay in shoe boxes in my book shelves today.

I wasn't interested in classical music during my childhood, especially since the interpretations of Beethoven's music from that time were extremely heroic, buried under pathos and grim; destiny kept knocking at the door – this was the way the conductors had perceived Beethoven's scores in the 1950s and 1960s, and that was the way my parents tried to explain this music to me. Apparently, they expected me to shiver with awe, but I simply felt screamed at by these recordings. The only classical exception for me was Leopold Mozart's "Toy Symphony". I loved that one. The rest of the classical world was something I discovered much later.

My favorite records were "Witch Doctor" by David Seville (1958) with the double-speed voices that later became the CHIPMUNKS, and a 45 named "Die kleine Bimmelbahn" (The Little Choo Choo Train) from 1958 by the HARZER MEISTERJODELPAAR (which probably translates to something like "Harz Mountains Master Yodel Couple") – and they did that at the top of their lungs. I still have the record today. Another one I loved was "Swinging Sweethearts" by RON GOODWIN & HIS ORCHESTRA (1958); I'm still carrying this melody with me, its bouncy rhythm and arrangement running through my head. I loved to listen to the BERT KAEMPFERT ORCHESTRA which was played on the radio relatively often; I especially loved "A Swingin' Safari", "Happy Trumpeter", "Mexican Road" and, of course, "Afrikaan Beat" (all 1962); these were all cheerful, optimistic-sounding earworms. I didn't know who played these tunes, but I always recognized their sound immediately.

BERT KAEMPFERT

Bert Kaempfert (1923–1980) of Hamburg was an arranger, composer, and orchestra director. He worked as an in-house producer for Polydor, wrote some international hits like the ones mentioned above, plus Al Martino's "Spanish Eyes" (1965, originally an instrumental entitled "Moon Over Naples") and two of Frank Sinatra's biggest hits, "Strangers in the Night" (1966) and "The World We Knew (Over and Over)" (1967). Sinatra *hated* the fact that these two songs had been written by a German. Usually, at his concerts, he gave recognition to the composers and lyricists of every song he performed, but he *never* mentioned the name Kaempfert.

Kaempfert built his own orchestra and developed a specific sound. It was mainly based on Rolf Ahrens' drumming with pedaled hi-hat, wire brushes, and (seemingly) randomly played bass drum accents, combined with Ladi Geisler's characteristic "knackbass" (or "click bass"); some back-up strings, flutes, and female chorus were added, plus a good portion of Ray Conniff inspired brass. It took me a while to get behind the secret of this bass sound, but one day I cracked the mystery: It's not one bass, it's a combination of *two* basses. One was a soft-plugged deep bass (in the beginning it was an upright bass, but later they used an electric bass guitar), and the other was a tuned-down acoustic guitar that was plucked very quickly with a pick. Together, these two sounds created the "knackbass". Kaempfert had a way to arrange melody lines and instrument groups that gave me the impression that the main melodic phrases were commented on, answered with, or echoed by other phrases. For me, the instruments talked to each other, they were chasing each other like young cats. Kaempfert never used multitrack recording for his orchestra, he worked with one single stereo microphone for the entire orchestra. Instead of balancing the sound on the mixing desk, musicians were placed here and there, a bit more in the foreground or in the background, a bit more to the left or the right, until the overall balance was what Kaempfert wanted to hear. The sound quality and plasticity of his recordings is awesome, still today. (These stereo mics are still available today. Their price starts around 10,000 Euros; Holger Czukay used one of those for his live album *Radio Wave Surfer* (1991). Also Max Raabe uses one of those for the recordings of his PALAST ORCHESTER.) I'm always cautious to use the term "genius", but I'm confident to say: Bert Kaempfert was very, very good in what he was doing (some people used to call him "the thinking man's James Last"), and his sound was probably one of the biggest influences on my young ears.

By listening to the difference between his sound and the contrasting sound produced by Tanzorchester ohne Namen or other orchestras, I somehow recognized that, independent from the melody, a piece of music sounds different whenever different orchestras play it, even when they use the same instruments. The way the instruments combine could be organized in one way or another, and this makes an overall different sound, even when the same melody is played. Of course, as a five-year old, I didn't know that we call this an "arrangement".

In case you miss Germany's most famous orchestra leader here: James Last, at this time, was still referred to by his real name, Hans Last, and for ten years he had played the upright bass in the NDR Big Band. Later, however, he had a significant role in the Krautrock scene, so we will come back to him.

There were more musical adventures waiting for me. When I was six years old, I heard "Telstar" by the Tornados on the radio. Of course I didn't know what caused these strange sounds at the intro and the fade-out, and nobody could explain to me how they might have done it. But this tune brought the open universe into my bedroom (which I had to share with my parents at that time, our apartment was small and constricted), and it became clear to me that these sounds could not have been made by trumpets, flutes, or guitars. I realized that there were more possibilities to create music beyond using orchestras or bands.

Something I will never forget is my first experience with a sort of real rock music – if you want to call it that. It hit me on New Year's Eve 1963/64. My parents woke me up shortly before midnight and we went outside to shoot fireworks. After that, my parents and several of our neighbors somehow spontaneously gathered together in the apartment above us. The children were allowed to join. This neighbor had a Grundig reel-to-reel tape recorder – something I had never seen before! Record players were relatively common already, but tape recorders were rare devices in private households; most people didn't find them important enough to purchase. But he was a music freak. Suddenly, with a sly grin, he cranked up the volume and started his tape machine: What exploded in my ears was "Jack the Ripper" by Screaming Lord Sutch. I swear I will never forget the running steps, the breathing, and the terrible female scream this song begins with. It was a shock. Could it be that *this* was the mysterious *beat music* my parents, my aunt, or my cousin sometimes spoke of? It was at least different from anything I've heard before. It really got me. I wanted to know more about it.

Another song I fell in love with a bit later, although it was played not often on the radio, was "Have I The Right" by the Honeycombs (1964) – the extremely noisy drums and trampling sounds floored me, and I always hammered along with it on the table whenever it played on the radio.

By the way, it was not before the mid-1970s that I discovered that all three of these songs – "Telstar", "Jack The Ripper" and "Have I The Right" – had something in common: They all had the same producer, Joe Meek. It wasn't completely clear to me *what* exactly it was this guy did, but it was obviously something that already resonated with me when I was little.[1]

In 1966, German television came up with a series entitled *Raumpatrouille* (Space Patrol). It consisted of seven episodes in black and white, each of them one hour long, showing the adventures of the crew of the "fast space cruiser Orion" in the year 3000. (Still, today, many people think *Raumpatrouille* was a reaction to the U.S. series *Star Trek*, but this is wrong; actually, *Raumpatrouille* is the slightly older production.) I was stunned. Even seen from today, the special effects are not as bad as they are sometimes described. Of course the silly way people danced at the "Starlight Casino", the water taps the crew used as microphones, or the flat iron and pencil sharpeners they used to navigate their space cruiser are funny today, but at that time, we simply didn't notice. There were lots of subtle special effects that are still impressive because you have to take a second look to see them. Of course as a 10-year old you are not able to notice all the subtle references hidden in the plot about society in 1966, so I took it very seriously. Interestingly, most adults also took it this way. They were not used to hidden irony or humor beyond plain jokes in the media. The music of *Raumpatrouille* came from composer Peter Thomas (with his PETER THOMAS SOUND ORCHESTRA), and the noisy mix of trumpets, trombones, high-pitched women's voices, electronic organ, the sounds of a Thowiphon (an early synthesizer with twelve sound generators; Peter Thomas himself developed this device with Viennese engineer Hansjörg Wicha), lots of tubular bells and cymbals hit on the bell, and all that was drenched in cathedral-like reverb. It was probably the most futuristic music I'd heard after "Telstar". Peter Thomas (1925–2020) had the crème of jazz and session musicians in his ensemble; sometimes Klaus Doldinger, Charlie Tabor, Lothar Meid, Olaf Kübler, Jan Hammer, Ingfried Hoffmann, Albert Mangelsdorff were among them. Some of you readers will already recognize the Munich studio circle we will meet again later. Big parts of the music were improvised in the studio and cut down for the final mix. And there was a sort of robot voice used for countdowns and machine messages – an unbelievable sound. It sounded a bit like a deep-voiced man speaking into a watering can with a clothespin on his nose, but as much as we children tried this, it didn't quite match this specific sound. Back then, we had no idea what it really was. What we heard was the first functioning model of a *vocoder*, modulating ("voice-coding", that's where the name comes from) the sound of a bowed cello. This device belonged to the Siemens Studio for Electronic Music in Munich, founded in 1956 and led by composer Josef Anton Riedl (1929–2016). Famous composers like Pierre Boulez, Henri Pousseur, Mauricio Kagel, Dieter Schnebel, John Cage, and David Tudor worked there. The studio closed in 1968 and, since 1993, the equipment can be seen at the Deutsche Museum in Munich. Director Edgar Reitz used it as the setting for his fictional composer Hermann Simon (who is a combination of Riedl and Reitz himself) in the second part of his monumental *Heimat* trilogy (1984 to 2004)[2], which is probably one of the best productions that German TV has ever made.

THEY WILL NEVER BE FREE AGAIN THEIR WHOLE LIFETIME

All this happened in the 1960s. This was a weird decade, even children could feel it. During the 1950s, people had been mainly happy that the war was over. They had enjoyed that things were becoming better and more stable. But now it got more complicated. The war and the postwar period seemed to sink more and more into subconsciousness, but nevertheless it stayed present in a strange way. It was like a nightmare you had last night: It's still present when you wake up, but it fades away very soon and, somehow, overshadows your day. You know there has been something horrible, you don't really remember what or why, but the feeling stays and there's not much you can do about it. That was the way Germany felt.

When life had slowly normalized during the 1950s, Germany began to pick up steam. But it was still visible that something had happened. There were still bomb-damaged locations, ruins, neighborhoods that nearly erased, and construction sites wherever you looked. One-armed or one-legged men out in the streets were normal to see. There were signs in the trams, saying: Please give your seat to pregnant women and war invalids. All of us born in the 1950s have our memories of debris in the cities, streets that led to nowhere, ruins, and houses which were visibly damaged by shots or burned by phosphor bombs. Many of these places were great playgrounds, but we children were not allowed to play there. Our parents found it much too dangerous. Of course they were right, but we played there anyway. I saw more than one accident and experienced more than one myself. Fortunately, children have rubber bones.

When listening in on adult conversations, you could hear dark, strange things. “The war”, on the one hand, was something everybody refused to name directly, but, on the other hand “the war” was also ever-present, especially when men were talking to each other. When our mothers had a chit-chat in the stairwell or the laundry room and thought we weren’t listening, they talked about the war as if it had been a natural phenomenon. We had no clear idea about this “war”, except that it must have been something scary. When we asked about it, we usually got the answer: “It’s been a different time. You can’t understand.”

Through time, this “war” transformed. It morphed into an abstract, ghostly thing, like a dragon attack or something unreal. But somehow, we knew this dragon attack had been real, and the consequences could still be felt and seen everywhere, from all the ruins around us, to the fact that there were only very few male school teachers. For us, this was nothing special, we didn’t know it any other way, but our mothers apparently found it abnormal. And there must have been something with “Jews”. Most of us school children (Yours Truly started school in 1963) had no idea what Jews were. There were Protestants and there were Catholics, and that was it. Nobody told us there were more religions than these, and during my whole school time (which ended in 1974), none of my classmates ever identified themselves as being Jewish. It was an unspoken topic, except for when the school custodian blurted out: “You behave like in the Jewish school!”

What had happened to the Jews – there was not even a word for it, and even if there had been a word, we probably wouldn’t have been able to comprehend it. Terms like Holocaust or Shoah didn’t exist yet. It was not before 1978 that the (in Germany, highly controversial) broadcast of the U.S. TV series *Holocaust* gave us a word. Most people pronounced it as an English word, and also the news magazine *Der Spiegel* introduced it as an English term. But children have a sixth sense for things that are wrong. We could feel that there must have been something so monstrous that even our teachers or parents were unable (or unwilling?) to explain it to us – perhaps unable to fully realize it themselves. It was never mentioned *what* exactly had happened, but I remember that one day in the stairwell, I heard two of our neighbors gossiping: “Not everything was bad, but with the Jews, that was a mistake.” The other neighbor answered: “I’m not sure he knew about that at all.”

“He” was Adolf Hitler, of course. Even while sitting in the midst of the rubble, it was impossible for many adults to admit that “he” had been the driving force behind all this horror, that they had been taken in by him or, at least, that they had followed him. To avoid these uncomfortable feelings, flimsy excuses, and shiftless attempts to defend each other, Germans settled on putting all their energy into work. This was the power that ignited the wirtschaftswunder years – dig yourself into work and strictly look forward.

The German government, led by the conservative CDU[3] with Chancellor Konrad Adenauer (1876–1967) and Minister of Economic Affairs Ludwig Erhard (1897–1977), had the maxim "Keine Experimente!" (No experiments!) and managed to grow the plant that became known as "das deutsche Wirtschaftswunder" (the German economic miracle). It wasn't a big feat to start this miracle: The German economy was lying flat on the ground, so politicians could have done more or less whatever they wanted. Setting up political plans or dancing around a hollow oak tree at full moon: The economic situation would have improved no matter what.

However, Ludwig Erhard, as a minister, not only had the right idea, but he managed to execute that right idea. He was a professor of economics and, in 1935, he had co-founded Germany's first market research institute[4]. He had never been a Nazi (actually, he had carefully supported some forms of resistance), and his concept of "soziale Marktwirtschaft" (social market economy) was an intelligent system that tried to establish a relatively fair balance between entrepreneurs, as well as employees and consumers. Erhard pushed this concept into power, against the will of the Allied Forces. The Allies did, however, end up accepting it when it started to work like crazy.

Erhard's appearance – well rounded, always with a cigar in his mouth – became not only his personal trademark, but an ideal symbol for the years of economic progression. There was even a folksy schlager about him in 1963: "Lasst doch mal den Dicken ran" (Put Out For the Fat Man) with the lines: "As long as still the cigar glows, things will go well".[5] Erhard's social market economy became a giant success. Germans worked obsessively, leading the economy to fly up to the sky in the late 1950s and early 1960s. The wirtschaftswunder era is still legendary today.

Erhard's fame fell apart in 1963 when he became the successor to Chancellor Adenauer. As a minister, he had made the right decisions, but now as Chancellor, it became obvious that he was not the gripping "maker" with shirt-sleeve approaches the people wanted to see. He was a thin-skinned thinker with a fondness for Bauhaus furniture and modern arts, and so, for the Chancellorship at that time, he was the wrong person. After a couple of bad mistakes and verbal faux pas, he resigned in 1966. His successor for the next three years was Kurt-Georg Kiesinger, who soon got into hot water: He had been rated as a hang-er-on, but in reality, he was much more than that. He hadn't been a civil servant during the Nazi era, but as assistant manager of the radio department at the Ministry of Foreign Affairs, he had been responsible for propaganda broadcasts to foreign countries.[6] Strangely (or maybe not strangely), nobody cared about the fact that eight (!) SPD members of Kiesinger's cabinet had also been involved in Nazi organizations. (SPD = Social Democratic Party of Germany, slightly left-wing and forbidden during the Nazi era.)

Around 1966, Germany's unemployment was nearly nonexistent. On the contrary, German entrepreneurs were more and more desperate about finding qualified employees. Applicants were able to request salaries and working conditions that, just five years earlier, would have been unthinkable. In 1963, the trade unions had already pushed through a five-day working week with a free Saturday; their campaign posters had shown a happy blond girl, maybe eight or nine years old, under the headline: "Samstags gehört Vati mir!" (On Saturday, Dad belongs to me!). Not only was a five-day work week on schedule, but the unions also came up with wage demands of ten, twelve, or even more percent extra, vacation and Christmas bonuses, and more – and they got what they asked for.

When we children grew a bit older and heard about Germany's recent past, we had to deal with two speechless generations: parents and grandparents. No answers to our questions were to be had. We learned that our parents and grandparents had apparently generated a human, political, and cultural disaster beyond all imagination, but they didn't want to take any responsibility for it. Many of them were not even willing to listen to questions: "Shut up. You weren't there, you can't understand." We had to deal with school teachers, sports club coaches, and apprentice instructors who *must* have somehow been involved in these twelve years of Thousand Year Reich – some of them actively, some of them passively, some of them against their will, but most of them out of indifference. Many benefitted from the social systems and the labor market policy the Nazis set into power. We learned that they all reacted passive-aggressively when – even without criticisms or accusations – we asked: "Where have *you* been? What did *you* see, what did *you* know? And what did *you* do?" Maybe this was just me, but there was always one question that came up to me when I saw pictures or films of Adolf Hitler: It's possible to fall for a charismatic or powerful political leader – but for *this guy*, of all people? (As Hitler never gave any interviews or press conferences, he was only known from his public speeches.) We were scolded in such a way, as if, during dinner, we had asked about grandpa's hemorrhoids.

My father was 14 when the Nazi rulers came into power and 26 when the spook ended – the prime years of his youth and adolescence. He had experienced the Hitler Youth. He had an office job in the low rank of the administration of justice. As this was a job in a public authority, his boss gave him the "recommendation" to join a Nazi organization. As a motorcycle fan, and to avoid further requests of this kind, he joined the NSKK (Nationalsozialistisches Kraftfahrkorps, National Socialist Motor Division). He always told me that this was a sort of automobile club, like the AAA. Maybe he really thought this, and maybe it was indeed the lowest level available, but, as I hadn't found out before conducting research for this book, the NSKK was, in fact, the motorized section of the SA. (SA = Sturmabteilung, Storm Detachment, was an early paramilitary wing of the Nazi party, mainly installed to beat up politically-opposing individuals,like the Red Front Fighters League, terrorizing their meetings and protecting the meetings of Nazi organizations.) Later, he got drafted for the Wehrmacht. He sometimes talked about how he had been in France as a radio operator. But that was all he said. When I asked him what kind of jobs they had to do in France, or what kind of messages he had to send, he usually told me about the Morse code, radio waves and how hard it was at times to find the right place to set up the antenna without being discovered by the enemy, and he always mentioned the heavy boozing that was part of the deal. No more specific answers were to be had from him.

For all of his later lifetime, my father never got rid of his alcohol problems. And there was a wall of glass around him. It was unbreakable. In a way, it became true what Adolf Hitler had predicted in a speech about his plans for youth education under the swastika: *They will never be free again their whole lifetime.*[7]

My grandfather on my mother's side was a Social Democrat and trade union man his entire life. He and his wife had met in the "Wandervogel", a part of the German youth movement of the 1920s. The roots of the Wandervogel movement can be traced back to German Romanticism. Usually, the Wandervogel (an old expression for bird of passage) was seen as part of the progressive, some say socialistic, life reform movement of the early 20th century, with vegetarianism and anti-alcoholism, nature protection, singing, hiking, and free love, and I'm sure my grandparents lived it this way. This sounds positive in a sense, but from its start, this movement had (maybe unwanted) parallels in its ideology and worldview with the later upcoming Nazi movement. It was relatively easy for the Nazis to corrupt it and incorporate parts of them. There's a lot of literature about this overlapping of ideologies.[8] I'm sure my grandparents stayed mainly on the social democratic side of this movement, but they had some thoughts that could work well for both sides – like Hugo Höppener's (a.k.a. "Fidus") kitsch postcard *Lichtgebet* (Light prayer)[9] which, for their whole lifetime, was framed next to their hallway mirror. This painting was an icon of the youth movement, and still today, it's easy to find a copy at flea markets.

My grandpa had survived WWI, but all he ever said about it was that it had been a horribly long time. In WWII as a soldier, he was sent to Russia. When I was around 14, he told me a couple of times that his SPD membership book saved his life when he and some comrades fell into the hands of Russian communist partisans who were busy damaging railroad tracks. It was something he was a bit proud of, but when I asked questions, my grandma usually cut him off: "Stop playing this old record again, nobody wants to hear that anymore." Much later, after he passed away, I had the opportunity to read a notebook, a sort of keyword diary he had written during his time in Russia. Obviously, he had been honest in what he said, but it was my impression that he had never really looked into the system of injustice he had been involved in. He had been drafted, he got orders, he hated it, but he did what he was expected to do. In a certain way, and as a somewhat left-wing person, he knew that what he was doing was against his own conviction, but he was no resistance fighter. His wife's (my grandma's) main concern was that he might have had an affair with a Russian woman. Even in the last days of war, when Germany was long reduced to rubble, she had been convinced that the Führer had a sort of "silver bullet" up his sleeve.

Luckily, he didn't.

Most of my contemporaries (if they asked at all) had similar experiences with their parents and relatives, especially with fathers, uncles, and grandfathers who had been soldiers or members of the Nazi party, the SS, or the SA. If we got answers, they were one-sided, often confused and didn't make much sense, or they opened out into one of the three big folktales about the Third Reich: (1) "We didn't know anything," (2) "Nobody asked us whether we wanted or not," and (3) "The Wehrmacht soldier as such dealt fairly."

Parents, grandparents, and teachers were not willing to speak out about what they had done during this ghastly war time, either staying at home, or living as a soldier somewhere in one of the many invaded countries. Apparently, they had been present, but hadn't heard anything. They had been under gun fire, but hadn't seen anything. At home, everybody must have seen the half-dead concentration camp inmates who, every morning, were openly chased by SS guards through the streets to a factory where they had to do forced work. But apparently nobody had ever seen them. Everybody knew somebody who, for little money, had bought furniture, winter coats or household articles from apartments of communist or Jewish neighbors who "were gone". The local Nazi organizations sold their belongings on the street, at farmer's markets, or at auctions. Nobody had asked them why the owners "were gone" or where they went. People were proud and happy to have made a bargain. They didn't want to know anything about it, and in case they couldn't avoid knowing, they couldn't help it.

Sometimes there were people claiming to have "helped" Jews (yes, some people had really done this, sometimes risking their lives). But this was another one of these contradictions that were impossible to solve for us: Why had there been a need to "help" when, at the same time, it had been impossible to know anything? Children and young people have a keen sense for illogicalities like this.

Nearly no one had admitted to being a follower or a member of one of the several Nazi organizations, and if somebody couldn't avoid claiming that he had been in one, it meant that he had been forced against his will or "to prevent something worse from happening". Hitler must have hit Germany like a plague epidemic, coming out of the blue sky.

If today you see feature films set in Germany during the Nazi time (there are many of them, especially from the U.S.), you can easily get the impression that Germans during this era lived in permanent uproar, with shouting and singing SA uniforms patrolling through every street, HJ boys beating up people, Gestapo leather coats constantly shadowing everyone, the blockwart (block warden) knocking three times a day at your door, neighbors getting visibly deported at any time by "Schweinhund!"-shouting SS men, and a constant atmosphere of terror and fear, created by newspapers, cinema newsreels, and the radio, hovered in the air.

But this was not the way the Nazi regime really worked. Most people simply lived their lives. They didn't ask anything, they ignored what they saw, and they did their jobs to pay their rent. They laughed, they cried, they fell in love, they married, they had children. They didn't think much about the political system they were involved in. As long as it gave them food and social security, they kept the system alive by not questioning it. When they finally became aware that husbands or children were just food for the cannons, it was too late. Other than in 1914, when WWI started, most people didn't want a war, but when it started, they had no choice but to go through it.

In exactly the same way, Germans simply moved forward when the Nazi era was over.

Of course, there were people who had supported the Nazi system actively. Many of them didn't seem to feel even the slightest responsibility for anything, not to speak of guilt. Many of them were proud of what they had done and couldn't see any mistakes.

When, in February 1943, the death sentences on members of resistance, Sophie and Hans Scholl and Christoph Propst, were announced, 3000 students in the Auditorium Maximum of the University of Munich applauded. Still today, we remember the three who got executed, but nobody ever lost a word about these 3000, later becoming part of Germany's "elite", who gave their consent. Nobody ever asked them what they were thinking when they clapped their hands.

These people were the problem. These people are the problem in any system. They are, as Kurt Tucholsky wrote, the ones who never broke the vase they broke.

Worse: Most police officers, public servants, professors, judges, and federal prosecutors could carry on working in their profession after 1945 without any career slump, even when they *had* been glowing followers of the Nazi regime. This was because, as Chancellor Adenauer used to say: We don't have any others.

The so-called "denazification" – researching every German about his life during the Third Reich and calling those responsible to hold accountability – as the Allied Forces tried to do, is seen by today's historians as, mainly, a failure. Too many people were classified and cleared as "blind followers" and too many of the relatively few who were put on trial were found "not guilty", probably because many judges had skeletons in their own closet. Novelist and essayist Ralph Giordano (1923-2014) later called this "die zweite Schuld" (the second guilt): The murderers, with few exceptions, got away scot-free.[10]

Call it pragmatism, call it coldness, call it repression: This is what psychoanalyst, Margarete Mitscherlich (1917–2012), called "the inability to mourn"[11]in 1967. You see the double meaning of this phrase. Some people simply didn't see any reason to mourn, while others weren't able to mourn when they realized the extent of what had happened. It went beyond anyone's imagination. Mitscherlich received a lot of trouble and outrage for her remark.

If someone tried to call the murderers to account, as federal prosecutor Fritz Bauer did in Frankfurt, politicians and his colleagues put so many spokes in his wheel that no result could be made. When somebody told Bauer where Nazi mass murderer Adolf Eichmann could be found (in Argentina), Bauer didn't trust the German government and found it better to give the information directly to the Israeli Intelligence Service instead. They caught Eichmann and put him on trial. This trial is documented on film, and when you see how Eichmann tried to portray himself as a victim in court, all you can do is cringe. His emotionless, droned reading says a lot about the Nazi mentality – and you'll get an idea about what author Hannah Arendt meant when she spoke of "the banality of evil".[12]

Whether it was a teacher, a policeman, your grandparents, or your own parents: You saw a friendly face, but couldn't be sure whether there was somebody respectable, a victim, a sheep trudging with the flock, or a monster behind it. This uncertainty became formative for the generation of children who were born in the postwar period – many of them never developed a real loving or respectful connection to their parents, relatives, or teachers because they couldn't know for sure what to think about them.

But let me make one thing completely clear: All our problems with our parents, teachers, and so on are just hot air compared to the psychic deformations Jewish, communist, gay, lesbian, mentally handicapped, Christian, or other inmates had to carry when they survived Auschwitz, Treblinka, Buchenwald, Dachau, Neuengamme, or any of the many other concentration camps there were. One might think they were freed by the Allied Forces and could happily go back to their former lives. But this was impossible. One may not see it, and oftentimes, they tried to hide it, but they remained branded, had the mark of death with them, and many of them never found a way back into this world. They were permanently aware their life could fall apart again. They hoarded food in secret places in their apartments. They sat on packed suitcases and never let their passports expire. I wouldn't even dare to think about the people who survived the concentration camps and stayed in Germany. What did they see when they looked into people's faces?

If there's one song that catches this feeling, it must be Austrian Jewish singer-songwriter Georg Kreisler's song "Weg zur Arbeit". It still gives me goosebumps.

If you ever saw the film *Cabaret* (1972)[13], surely you remember the scene in a crowded countryside beer garden, where Brian and Maximilian are having a beer (Max is one of the many people who thought this Nazi spook would be a short episode and it would be easy to get them under control once they are in power). Then, suddenly a blond youngling starts crooning a pathetic song: "Tomorrow Belongs to Me". It takes a few seconds until the camera zooms out a bit and we can see that he's wearing a Hitler Youth uniform. First, only a few people care, but then, one by one, they start listening to him, smiling at him, and some even start singing along with him – in the end, all the beer garden guests, young and old ones (with the exception of one elderly man whose face shows that he doesn't like what's happening here), sing full-heartedly and with Nazi salute along with this HJ boy about the glorious future that's going to come. Brian and Max leave, and while getting into Max's car, Brian dryly asks Max: "Still think you can control them?"

Of course, we can be sure that something like this scene has never happened in reality, but what's better than many scientific analyses is that it shows, in a nutshell, one of the mechanisms that brought Nazis into power. The point is this: When *Cabaret* premiered in German movie theaters in 1972, this scene was cut out by the German distribution company. Still, in 1972, it was found to be inappropriate to confront Germans with a scene that symbolically showed that the Nazis had not fallen from the sky.

FLUXUS & CO.

Although (or probably just because) the economy was on a high flight, the social atmosphere in Germany was extremely conservative. People still had the hard days in mind after 1945. They were full of fear, thinking they could lose the material prosperity they had just gained, and had no sympathy for abnormal ideas, strange music, and art projects that didn't make themselves immediately clear without explanation.

The art scene was actually already quite active at this time. Since the mid-1950s, a group of artists worked under the label ZERO – Otto Piene, Günther Uecker, Heinz Mack, and some others tried to redefine and expand the concept of sculpture.

In Cologne, there was the artist Mary Bauermeister who lived with Karlheinz Stockhausen and his wife at that time. On the top floor she had her studio, and she used it for meetings between artists: Joseph Beuys (I will have to come back to him), Wolf Vostell, Nam June Paik, John Cage, George Maciunas, Christo, David Tudor, and Hans G. Helms were some of the frequent visitors. These meetings with happenings, actions, readings, and the newest music performances prepared what was to become the Fluxus movement. In June 1965, at the art gallery Parnass in Wuppertal, a cracking twenty-four hour happening opened a Fluxus group exhibition with works of Beuys, Vostell, and several others. It was here that, inspired by Beuys, Nam June Paik developed his concept of video sculptures made from old TV sets, and with cellist Charlotte Moorman, he performed something that would later be called "performance art" – because there was no better label for it. This exhibition caused quite a stir in the media.

And that's the point: The stir happened in the media and *remained* in the media. Average people got angry about all this, but most of them reacted by shaking their heads or didn't even take note of it. It didn't make any sense to them why it should be considered art to knock over a piano or deform a TV picture with a magnet. It had no connection to their lives.

There was not much time in the 1960s for cultural questions. First, the Germans had to catch up on all the commodities they missed out on in the 1950s and – here we are again – during the war; no time for breathing until this goal had been reached. Culture was a sort of luxury article that nobody really needed or was interested in.

Besides this, the Germans became sensitive. If somebody asked about the past, they reacted huffish, especially when somebody came along and brought up memories nobody really wanted – like the schlager "Hundert Mann und ein Befehl" (1966, a cover version of "The Ballad of the Green Berets"): "Hundred men and one command / and a way nobody wants to go / Day in, day out, who knows where to / Burnt land, and what's the sense about?"[14], on TV presented by Heidi Brühl with burning eyes, accompanied by a military drum rhythm. Even though this song didn't name any concrete culprits or ask for accountability, it could lead to heated discussions between co-workers or ruin the mood at family gatherings.

BIG WHITEWASHING

More and more, things turned into their opposites. Suddenly the Soviet Union became "the enemy". I still remember our geography teacher in 1967, warning us that "the Red Army sits only 40 tank minutes away from Hamburg", so we should be prepared. In a history lesson, one of my classmates stated: "Since there is no treaty of peace yet, the war didn't end, it's only cease-fire" – he probably just repeated what he had heard from his parents or some relatives, but our teacher didn't straighten this nonsense out. Chancellor Adenauer also resurrected the army with the argument: Soviet Russia has to realize that attacking Germany is a big risk for Soviet Russia itself.[15] No mention of the fact that, a couple of years ago, it had been *Germany* that attacked the Soviet Union.

More and more people from East Germany (the Soviet Zone) took flight and went to West Berlin or West Germany. To stop this, in August 1961, the GDR immured itself and left West Berlin as a sort of island. The Cold War started.

Later in the 1960s, the NPD (National Democratic Party of Germany, a sort of NSDAP replacement party), was able to increase their membership and won a couple of mandates at some regional elections (1966: 7.4% in Bavaria, 7.9% in Hessen; 1967: 8.8% in Bremen, 7.0% in Lower Saxonia; 1968: 9.8% in Baden-Württemberg). Obviously, there were still a number of incorrigible morons who either never learned anything or had never gotten anything anyway. The NPD never had big successes, but young people and university students especially noticed these trends and found them dangerous, or at least irritating and worrying. Under the surface, some things began to boil in Germany, which later led to certain consequences.

A MUSIC SCENE DEVELOPS

I'm sure you get the picture. Blind economic upswing and the will to forget the past, this was the 1960's atmosphere rock musicians and singer-songwriters meant when they later referred to Germany in the Sixties as a cultural desert. You can see where they came from, but they were not completely accurate. Germany was not a desert – in arts and music, a lot of things were going on, but whatever it was, it had nearly no resonance with the average audience. So the musicians were right in the sense that they were not interested in an "avant-garde" audience, they were interested in reaching everyday people and everyday radio programs. But reaching this audience with rock music was not the easiest thing.

Of course, this book is not the right place to clear up the entire Nazi history and the way the Federal Republic of Germany dealt with it. But all this was going on in Germany in the 1960s. It led to several political and sociological disturbances, especially between the generations. It makes some things that happened in the music scene clear, especially why the Germans loved their schlager scene so much: Schlagers were the soundtrack of these years – the Sixties never came back, but the schlager genre persisted.

But was it really the described situation in Germany that became the inspiration for musicians to invent new musical styles? That's what they often say in interviews, but there is no easy answer to this. Behind the curtains, there was a very vivid arts and music scene, but it was a sort of parallel world, and only a handful of musicians had a background as artists and knew about this scene.

Most of the later rock musicians didn't know much about it. They ignored it, or it was not their tradition, and so they misunderstood what had happened there.

Only a handful of jazz musicians left the safe grounds of traditional Dixieland jazz or swing and went on to more challenging horizons. But that was jazz. This was not a tradition rock musicians could use for themselves (at least not now; later this changed a bit). Most German rock musicians who started their career in the 1960s were too young to have their own memories of the war or Nazi era. What had happened *before* the Nazi era, they knew only by hearsay, if they were interested at all. Even if they were interested, there was no internet, no archives that were available immediately and without problems. Most libraries only had a small stock of records, and these were mostly classical ones. Aside from modern jazz in some special niches, the radio programs were not a good place to retrieve information about music tradition – most radio stations played classical music, schlager-oriented music, or had news, radio essays, radio plays, and stuff like that. Very often, these radio shows were high quality and very informative, but not really something young folks like us wanted to listen to.

You might imagine the impact of Elvis Presley, Bill Haley, and Buddy Holly in the atmosphere described above. Newspapers, and especially tabloids, were angered about Bill Haley's German tour in 1958; the cinema newsreels, in an unbelievably disgusting tone, tried to ridicule this "monkey-like" rock'n'roll dancing, as a fever that had infected Germany's youth. They didn't even notice (or didn't want to notice) that the Nazis had used the exact same method to ridicule jazz from America. Parents didn't know what to do to keep their teenagers away from this oh-so-disgusting stuff.

Following these role models, first rockabilly and later rock'n'roll bands came up. But they had no real big impact. The rock music evolution became more interesting in the early 1960s, when bands and musicians like JOHNNY & THE HURRICANES, THE BEATLES, THE ROLLING STONES, Lonnie Donegan, Cliff Richard, Ray Charles, Emile Ford, and Screaming Lord Sutch came to Germany – first over the airwaves and then in person. Now Germany's teenage musicians had role models they could adapt to.

FIRST GERMAN ROCK BANDS

It's impossible to say which was "the first" German rock band. Somehow it was in the air, the success of The Beatles pushed guitar sales forward, and a lot of folks in basements and garages all over Germany started "Beatgruppen" (beat groups), as they were called then. Most of them were named after the scheme "X & his Ys", others were simply "The Xs". In any case, it had to be in English. It's impossible to say how many "X & his Rhythm Rockers", how many Starlighters, Fireballs, Four Aces, Roulettes, or how many bands named "The Beathovens" there were. I knew at least three of the latter in Hamburg alone (in a Düsseldorf one a certain Wolfgang Flür played the drums – we will meet him again).

One of the first bands that made it to a record contract was The Lords of West Berlin. "Hey Baby, lass den Anderen" (Hey Baby, Drop the Other Guy; 1964) was their first 45, with German language written by a professional schlager lyricist named Carl Ulrich Blecher. The music was written by a band member, Peter Lietz. The flipside was a cover version of the famous "Tobacco Road". It was not successful.

The other important band was The Rattles. But before they could reach nationwide success, both bands, The Lords as well as The Rattles, had to win a competition in Hamburg's Star-Club.

THE SIXTIES

THE STAR-CLUB: WHERE IT ALL STARTED

This is the story of Germany's most famous music club. Without this institute, the story of German rock music wouldn't have been the same. No, I won't tell the story of The Beatles in Hamburg for the umpteenth time, there are other excellent books on that topic. It was, indeed, the place their career really took off, and this might in itself already say a lot about the importance of this club. Citizens of other towns may see it a bit differently, but I don't hesitate to say: German rock started here, in the heart of Hamburg's world-famous red light district St. Pauli.

The man who pushed the start button was Manfred Weissleder (1928–1980) of Dortmund (not to be confused with cyclist Manfred Weißleder of Weimar).

Weissleder came to Hamburg in 1955 as an employee for the electric company AEG. It didn't take long for him to quit that job and become an electrician and house technician in the striptease club, Tabu. He was a tight-lipped lone wolf and seemed to work around the clock. But he did this very effectively. He even used his hobby, diving, to take a few prostitutes and strippers traveling with him to the South Seas to produce a couple of underwater porn movies. As it turned out, he ran into money with these films.

He was a mountain of a man which alone gave him a lot of respect in the scene, but also his short fuse soon became notorious. He once threw photographer Günter Zint down the stairs. Immediately after, Weissleder felt very sorry about this, but, you always had to be aware that he might act this way.[1] Zint later became the club's in-house photographer, his wife sat behind the pay window

– however, when Weissleder noticed that Zint used one of the display cabinets in the entrance area to put his photos out for sale, he pinched 60 D-Marks per month from Zint. In short, Weissleder knew where the money was and how to deal with business partners in the kiez, and so he quickly climbed up the St. Pauli hierarchy. – "Kiez", by the way, has locally different meanings in Germany. In some cities, like Berlin, "my Kiez" refers to the immediate vicinity you live in, while in Hamburg "Kiez" always means the red light district. This kiez is only a part of the entire St. Pauli neighborhood, it includes (just in case you want to visit it) the famous Reeperbahn and its even-more-famous side street Große Freiheit, and a couple of small streets and squares in the area, like Hein-Hoyer-Straße, Silbersackstraße, Talstraße, Hans-Albers-Platz, or the infamous Herbertstraße. At daytime it's a sad-looking area.

Back to Manfred Weissleder: After only five years, in 1960, when he was just 32, they called him the "King of St. Pauli." He had twelve establishments at this point ("mainly the left side of Große Freiheit," as he used to say): a bordello named Rote Katze (red cat), strip bars, pubs, a porn movie theater, and some bars in the Paradieshof (Paradise Yard), a backyard behind Große Freiheit you could only reach through a gateway. One of these bars was the Erotic Night Club in the upper floor, a place where, early in the morning, non-stop porn movies were shown – his self-made underwater ones among others. After an inspection, the fire authority told Weissleder that he needed to open up a second emergency exit. The only way he could do that was to break through the wall to the building next door. This was the Stern-Kino, a movie theater. Its licensees, however, were not very fond of this idea. Weissleder, without further ado, bought the Stern-Kino. Now he had the emergency exit he needed and a movie theater which he did not really need.

One morning in February 1962, a guy named Horst Fascher entered the café where Weissleder used to have breakfast. Fascher had been a featherweight boxer in the 1950s but had to give up his career – he had had a quarrel with a sailor over a girl and had finished the dispute with some punches. The next morning, the sailor was found dead in his berth with a cerebral hemorrhage (even today, it might happen that Fascher bursts into tears when somebody asks him about this incident – boxers, as we all know, are sentimental guys). This caused a great stir in the press. The local boxer's federation saw Fascher's name as "contaminated" and refused to book him for further fights.

Now, he worked as a waiter and bouncer at several St. Pauli clubs, among them Indra and Kaiserkeller. These were two of the places where, in 1961, THE BEATLES had played, so he had become friends with them; today, Paul McCartney still calls him "Horsti". After some bad blood with Kaiserkeller's boss Bruno Koschmider, a former trapeze artist, he became manager of the Top Ten club at the Reeperbahn. During his Kaiserkeller time he had made some excellent connections to English bands and agents, and now, he wanted to make use of them.

Fascher had introduced himself to Manfred Weissleder who cut him short: "I know who you are." (Of course he did. To know who's who was a precondition of becoming king of St Pauli.) However, Fascher was able to plant his idea in Weissleder's head: to open up a music club – a *real, grand* club, not just another simple juke joint with a band playing somewhere in the corner. Weissleder's answer: "Give me three days." To Fascher's surprise, after three days, Weissleder really came back to him: "We could use the Stern-Kino, if you think that would work." Fascher was happy with that. Weissleder had already decided that he would call it *Star-Club* then – typical for his economic way of thinking, because in doing so he could continue to use the old neon star on the front of the building. He also hired Fascher as the club's "manager and booker" as they called it.

The Star-Club opened on Friday, April 13, 1962, at Große Freiheit 39. By now, "the misery had an end" and "the time of oompah music was over", as countless flyers and posters in blaring orange all over Hamburg had promised.

The basic idea that was supposed to differentiate Indra, Kaiserkeller, Top Ten, or Blockhütte, was to not only have one band playing per night again and again for several hours, alternating with the jukebox. The Star-Club offered three, four, or sometimes even more bands, playing one-hour slots. This way, known names could be used as magnets to introduce newcomers.

The first thing Fascher had managed to do was to set up a stage with a yellow curtain. The stage was big enough to offer space even for a 20-piece big band. He installed a sound system that was excellent for that time (and hellishly expensive, but Weissleder was willing to pay for it because he saw the need), and he hired Erwin Ross to paint the Manhattan skyline as the stage scenery. Ross did nearly all the wall paintings and pin-ups within the kiez; he was called "the Rubens of St. Pauli." Several of his paintings can still be seen there.

Of course, the bands knew they were competitors, and sometimes this led to brawls and backstage fights, but usually they were friendly with each other. This allowed them to learn from each other – special chords, tricks on how to play, new words, meaningful lyrics. German bands especially learned from the English ones. This way, several gifted bands got the last kick to become professionals, and professionalism was something the German rock scene needed badly. But it also worked the other way round: Most Liverpool or London bands were originally cover bands with the classic line-up of "three guitars + drums". Most of them specialized in a certain style to build up and keep their own circle of fans – rockabilly, rhythm & blues, skiffle, rock'n'roll, dancehall, Cliff Richard songs, Top 40 hits. These bands tried to copy the originals as closely as possible. This worked quite well at home, but when they came to Hamburg, they had realized they were expected to be more well-rounded. Even for the best of them this meant that they had to work hard on their style and repertoire. They received a special kind of finishing in Hamburg this way, and this showed up in their sound.

Entrance of the Star-Club, Hamburg

This is what musician Kingsize Taylor of Liverpool called "the Hamburg Sound". When these bands finally returned to Liverpool, they took this sound home with them, where it became what is known today as "Mersey Sound". So it is not completely overstated to say that the Mersey Sound was, in fact, a Hamburg Sound, but it's important to note that it was a result of exchange from both sides.

Horst Fascher booked nearly every band that had a name or wanted to get a name; bands and artists from Germany as well as from England and the U.S., later also from the Netherlands, Belgium, France, or even Indonesia: The Searchers, The Liverbirds (the first all-female beat band), Johnny Kidd & The Pirates, Bill Haley & The Comets, Chuck Berry, Chubby Checker, Little Richard, Gene Vincent, Tony Sheridan, Screaming Lord Sutch, The Tornados, The German Bonds, The Blue Flames, The Rivets, The Rattles, and many, many more – and of course The Beatles three times. "We had nearly all the stars that were available at that time, with the exception of Elvis Presley. But he didn't appear on stage anyways, he only made movies," Weissleder said retrospectively. "We also had a way of doing business that was very different from today's places, where comparable groups perform. For example, we only had a minimal entrance fee – at maximum it was 5 D-Marks, but those were acts like Fats Domino and Bill Haley and things like that, which cost 60,000 D-Marks per night. I always lost money with these star appearances. I was able to do this because I had my other places. Maybe that's something the guys today can't do, and that's the reason that something like the Star-Club cannot exist anymore. I made money on normal days, and when the stars performed, I frequently lost money."[2]

More than once, a star had to learn what "St. Pauli" meant. Chuck Berry, to name one example, sat backstage in his cloakroom, and when Fascher told him they were completely sold out, he said, "Okay, then pay me 10,000 dollars more, otherwise I won't play." Obviously, he knew little about where he was. Weissleder immediately gave an order to his waiters to block the stage door and all emergency exits. Then he paid a visit to Chuck Berry in the cloakroom: "Well, Chuck, it's up to you whether you want to play or not. But if you decide not to play, you'll have to leave through the front door, and Horst will let the people know why you won't play. I can't guarantee your health then." Chuck Berry played.[3]

The name "Star-Club" became a seal of quality very soon. The club's logo became famous, and Weissleder and Fascher developed completely new ways to market this brand. They had a stencil of their logo, and many bands who played the Star-Club wanted to have it spray-painted on their flightcases or bass drums – sometimes even before they got their fee. The Star-Club sold merchandise articles like tees, pullovers, scarves, cigarette lighters, pins, umbrellas, posters, stickers, postcards, and key rings. But this wasn't everything. Weissleder licensed the name and the logo to music clubs in several cities for 1000 D-Marks a month; finally, there were around 20 Star-Club clones all over Germany – and of course, they all had to book their bands via Weissleder's and Fascher's booking agency.

All these clubs hosted band competitions, and since the Star-Club was known for fair conditions, lots of bands made use of them. A winner of one of these competitions was Wolfgang Flür's band THE BEATHOVENS, as the Star-Club logo on their bass drum shows[4]. The winners were usually sent to tour several Star-Club clones, and as strange as it may sound, this way, high quality, stage-tested rock music was distributed all over Germany.

To get the house filled, there were also competitions for the audience, like a Twist competition in 1962 between Star-Club guests from Hamburg and French marines whose ship was moored in the port – the first prize was 500 D-Marks, the second was 250 D-Marks, and the third was 125 D-Marks. This was a lot of money: 500 D-Marks at that time was approximately a month's salary for an office employee or a shop assistant.

The Star-Club team sent talent scouts to England and even to America to discover new bands and bring them to Hamburg. It became a question of prestige for English or American bands to have played the Star-Club – having done that meant a much easier career start, not even in Germany, but also at home. The image benefits of having played the Star-Club worked as a plus factor internationally.

Interestingly, having had success at the Star-Club could also turn out to be a trap. Successfully playing at the Star-Club opened important doors, but the band or artist still needed to actively cross the threshold into wider fame. If they forgot to do this or waited too long, basking in their Hamburg success, they could easily miss the train to a nationwide or international career. One of the most prominent guys who had what it takes to become an international act was Tony Sheridan, but he ended up as a sort of local hero. There were some more bands like this – THE GERMAN BONDS, THE RIVETS – the list is long.

In 1964, Weissleder started a monthly magazine named *Star-Club News* which, in the beginning, was not more than just that, but it didn't take long for it to morph into a serious music magazine; even political topics became part of its content at times. It had some excellent writers, and included photos taken by in-house photographer Günter Zint. Every edition had a list of all the bands that had ever played the Star-Club, so there was no way for any band to pretend that they had played at the club; it was easy to check out whether this was true or not.

The magazine became a serious competitor to the then glossy teenager gazettes like *Bravo* or *Musikparade*. Eventually, it was distributed by Heinrich Bauer Verlag, one of Germany's big publishing houses for illustrated magazines.

Even a pirate radio station in the North Sea outside the territorial limit was planned and announced, but unfortunately, around the same time, Germany signed a convention against radio piracy, so this did not happen.

STAR-CLUB RECORDS

Another leg of the Star-Club empire became very successful: the record label. Siegfried E. "Siggi" Loch, record producer and A&R man at Philips Records in Hamburg, had discovered Klaus Doldinger and several other musicians, mainly in the jazz area, and produced their records. During The Beatles's second guest performance at the Star-Club, he got in touch with Manfred Weissleder. Loch talked to him about the idea of starting a Star-Club label as a sub-label of Philips. He mainly had live recordings in mind, and was especially interested in acts like the Everly Brothers, Ray Charles, Fats Domino, and Little Richard. It was a risk; Loch's boss at Philips, Hans Schrade, had not been too happy about this idea, and an even worse reaction to this idea had come from the sales representatives whose job would be to pitch these records to dealers. But, finally, Schrade said: "If it doesn't cost more than the technical equipment, then let's give it a try."

Weissleder, however, immediately realized what a giant advertising platform a record label with the Star-Club logo could be. He was clever enough to add some conditions: Philips wouldn't have to pay extra fees for the musicians, he (Weissleder) would take care of that, and he provided an empty room behind the stage for the recording equipment. But he insisted that before the name "Star-Club" would appear on a record label, a test album had to be released which should present the main Star-Club stars, and if this record would sell more than 10,000 copies, he wanted 5 percent of the sales of this recording and all future ones. Loch was fine with this, but as a precaution, Weissleder gave him a little taste of St. Pauli: When they both went upstairs to the office to set up the contract, Weissleder suddenly grabbed Loch's upper arms, lifted him up into the air and said, "Keep one thing in mind: Never play tricks on Manfred Weissleder."

The test LP appeared on the Philips label: the sampler *Twist im Star-Club*. It became a bestseller, Weissleder was happy, and suddenly everyone at Philips had always been ecstatic about the new Star-Club Records idea. So the new label was launched.

Several albums and, all in all more than 200 singles, were released under the Star-Club label, selling millions of copies – a real gold mine. Even Edgar Froese's TANGERINE DREAM predecessor THE ONES was among these 45s: "Lady Greengrass" (1967).

But then, one day, Loch did "play a trick" on Weissleder: He thwarted a 10,000 D-Mark deal between THE SEARCHERS and Decca Records that Weissleder had triggered. Loch was simply faster and released the album *Sweets For My Sweet – The Searchers Live At The Star-Club Hamburg* (1963) on his home label Philips. You can call that chutzpah. Weissleder, of course, foamed at the mouth when this happened, and it would take a very special event to make him forget this brazenness.

Such an event, luckily, did take place just one year later, when Weissleder got into trouble and Loch became a sort of knight in shining armor. The Jamaican singer Millie had a world-wide smash hit in 1964 with "My Boy Lollipop". Because her producer, Charles Blackwell, had had a big success in Germany with the SPENCER DAVIS GROUP, he now wanted Millie to enter the Star-Club stage at any cost. The problem was that she appeared without a band to back her up. In this situation, Siggi Loch was the one who had the right idea and the right connections. He talked one of his label acts, Paul Nero and his band, into jumping in. But on the day of the concert, another problem came up: Blackwell had forgotten to send the sheet music, so the band couldn't rehearse and had no idea what to play. It was unclear whether the concert had to be called off. Then, in the afternoon, Loch gave Millie's records to the band and the musicians practiced by listening to them. In the end, they were able to play live with Millie for around half an hour. Of course this was not enough for a concert – but once they were on stage, Paul Nero and his musicians proved what real musicianship means: They managed to pump up "My Boy Lollipop" to a red-hot, improvised 25-minute jam. The audience went bananas, the evening was secured, and Weissleder and Blackwell became best business friends, which was important for future concerts. Paul Nero, the boss of the band, was no other than Klaus Doldinger, wearing a blonde, curly wig that looked rather strange, but he didn't want to get recognized in case the concert went downhill. Not many musicians would have been able to rescue a concert under these circumstances, but it worked out. On this night,

Weissleder definitely figured that some things in the music business needed more than just money to be solved, and his trouble with Siggi Loch was settled.[5]

Manfred Weissleder had to withdraw from the Star-Club in 1964 when police and fiscal offices decided that they wanted to see him go. Of course – remember, we walk under red light here – the police often had to stop brawls in the club, more than 90 times in 1963 alone. There were prostitutes in and around the club, and since most of these ladies – as well as the musicians and the waiters – used to be on speed, there were drug dealers found inside and outside the building.

Another problem was that guests under the age of 18 had to leave the club at 10pm – it was the law. Every evening at 10 to 10pm, this had to be announced, and the waiters, if in doubt, had to check IDs. Of course, they always missed some folks, intentionally or not. So when the police decided to raid the club (something they did from time to time), they always picked up some under-aged boys or girls.

A third problem was that there was constant trouble between waiters and the guests who either drank too much or didn't want to drink enough. With the former, the waiters didn't discuss, they solved the problem physically. In the case of the latter, they expected to be given some "tip", and if you followed this "recommendation", they left you alone with your Cola or whatever you had. If you didn't, the same solution took effect as with the drunk guests. It has to be said that this was not a problem special to the Star-Club, it was a common thing at most kiez places. I remember a friend of my parents visited a strip bar with some out-of-town business friends. He made the mistake of complaining a bit too loudly about the overpriced drinks. He was then "asked" by two bouncers to follow them. In the backyard he was given the short shrift – and they knew how to do this without leaving visible traces. This was also the usual procedure at the Star-Club.

That made a nice list of sins. But, the authorities were not willing to make Weissleder a martyr in the eyes of the public – the Star-Club was popular and Weissleder had his *Star-Club News*. So they constructed a slightly adventurous theory to checkmate him: They claimed that all the bands that had played at the Star-Club for three or more days in a row had to be seen as employees – and this meant that for all of them, Weissleder had to pay supplementary social contributions. Suddenly, he was deep in the red – In reference to the under-18 problem and the brawls the authorities imputed "breach of the duty of supervision". All in all, that was enough to confiscate Weissleder's license. Horst Fascher even went behind bars. For a couple of days, the Star-Club remained closed. This led to public protests in the streets of St. Pauli. In order to keep the club alive, Weissleder had no choice but to lease it to somebody else.

It took him more than two years to get his license back, when he finally won his lawsuit against the City of Hamburg, but he was never able to really get back into business. In 1965, he had to give up the *Star-Club News* because the Heinrich Bauer Verlag planned to start a glossy youth magazine named *OK* and wanted to get rid of their critical, cheeky in-house competitor.

Of course, Weissleder didn't fall into poverty immediately. He still had his other places and made a living from the leases. But his prime time was over – the same goes for kiez kings as for boxers: They never come back.

THE POST-WEISSLEDER ERA

The Star-Club management changed a couple of times during the following years. The new leaseholders tried to keep up with the evolution of the music scene. More and more of the "classic" Star-Club bands gave up. When, around 1967, stars like Jimi Hendrix, The Nice, Colosseum, East Of Eden, Cream, Vanilla Fudge, Spooky Tooth, or The Earth (who later became Black Sabbath) hit the Star-Club stage, it was a bit like trying to use a local airport to launch rockets to the moon.

In February 1969, musicians Kuno Dreysse (The Rivets), Achim Reichel, and Frank Dostal (The Rattles, Wonderland) became the last renters of the Star-Club, but even they weren't able to stop the downfall. Not only was their incompetence a problem, it was more and more the Star-Club tradition itself that made the venue look outdated. In the eye of the public, the Star-Club stood for rock'n'roll and beat, not for prog rock. Other clubs, like the Top Ten which had become a disco, were more attractive now, even more the Grünspan, an abandoned public pool, just 300 meters away from the Star-Club. The Grünspan was the first club in Germany that was equipped with strobe lights, and it became a Mecca for the fans of the growing psychedelic scene.

The Star-Club tried to catch up; The Nice were announced in the press with the pointer: "The first time in 16,500 watt lighting!"[6] But all this didn't help, and Reichel and his friends were too inexperienced to even deal with simple management duties. Frank Dostal: "When the janitor told us we were getting low on toilet paper, we had no idea where to order it."[7]

HOT FINALE

On New Year's Eve 1969, HARDIN & YORK played the final concert, with a special one-hour long homage to the venue. They had to stop at 10pm – then the yellow Star-Club curtain fell forever. At midnight the building was cleared and the Star-Club became history.

A sex theater named Salambo, run by René Durand, took its place. It made good business for over a decade. But in the 1980s, these sex revues attracted less and less people, and Durand heaped up a loss of nearly one million D-Marks. In 1983, the building finally went up into flames. Still today, there are rumors about arson for insurance reasons (in Hamburg we use to call this a "warm debt relief"); other sources say some competitors had set the building on fire to get rid of an unwanted competitor[8], but this doesn't make much sense because the Salambo was a bust anyways. However, the destroyed building remained untouched for three years. Then, Lee Curtis, who over the years had played the Star-Club dozens of times, played a final concert in its ruins, accompanied by a sort of ballet by Durand's girls and boys. Immediately after, a wrecking ball did its job and the building was torn down.[9] You could see grown-up couples in tears, watching from across the street. A part of their youth fell into rubble.

Today, there's a faceless red-painted transient hotel with a bar on the ground floor at this site, along with the Paradieshof, which is now a beer garden with karaoke bar. Among what's left of the original Star-Club memorabilia is Erwin Ross' Manhattan Skyline stage painting and the old neon star from the building's front, now exhibition pieces at the Museum for Hamburg History.

On a wall at the end of the former Paradieshof gateway, not visible from the street, you'll find a memorial tablet in the form of the former billboard over the entrance, initiated by photographer Günter Zint – first with a "Jimmy Hendrix" engraving, but in a second version the flaw was corrected. That's all that's left.

Manfred Weissleder passed away in 1980 at the age of only 52, and it was not the happy kind of a story. He became addicted to alcohol and pills. He grew more and more lonely, his last remaining friend being Erwin Ross, the Rubens of St. Pauli. He didn't starve, but the only income source left was the rent he got from the Salambo, his other places weren't his anymore, and the money he had saved for retirement got lost when his last wife eloped with it.

The end of a St. Pauli king. Oh well.

RED LIGHT MEANS: GO!

From today's perspective, and especially when you keep the atmosphere in Germany during the first half of the 1960s in mind, it's not a miracle that, all over Europe, innovative impulses didn't come from serious concert halls and venerable music clubs, but sparked in the neighborhood of striptease bars, porn cinemas, peep shows, and pubs in red light districts. All over the world, in New Orleans as well as in Chicago, London, Vienna, or Paris, these are the places where people can go overboard without being judged as crazy. It's always been just these places, where owners and innkeepers accept even the strangest ideas and quirks as long as they fill up the cashbox.

Bruno Koschmider, the Indra's manager, had always shouted to the Beatles and his other bands, "Macht Schau!" ("Make show!") – and they did. The more they did, the more the audience loved it. The bands had to play at least three slots every night (which could add up to six or more hours, all in all!), which was nearly impossible without speed and alcohol, so their stage performances became wilder every night. Since this was something the young people had never seen before, it became the talk of the town, and as a result, these shows had increasing repercussions. In some middle-class residential areas, this wouldn't have been possible.

THE SIXTIES

BEAT OF THE WIRTSCHAFTSWUNDER

So far, I've mentioned two important Star-Club bands: The Lords and The Rattles. Both started their careers by winning a Star-Club competition.

The Lords probably can be seen as Germany's first original rock band that went professional, even when, at that time, they were called a "beat group". They had started in 1959 as The Skiffle Lords in Berlin. In 1964, they won a competition, connected to the German premiere of the Beatles' movie *Yeah Yeah Yeah*: "Who are the Berlin Beatles?" The Lords, as they had shortened their name now, were not really "Berlin Beatles", but they were good enough to qualify for the finals at the Star-Club in Hamburg.

This became the start of their recording career. EMI in-house producer and schlager specialist, Heinz Gietz, took them under his wing. After "Hey Baby, lass den Anderen", their first 45 in the German language, had flopped, Gietz accepted their wish to sing in English. They were right: "Shakin' All Over", a relatively well-done cover version of Johnny Kidd & The Pirates' hit, went up to #11 on German charts in August 1965. Their first self-written composition, "Poor Boy", soon followed and peaked at #12.

It's better not to pay too much attention to The Lords' lyrics. None of these guys were really competent in the English language, they often translated their grammatically shaky Berlin working class lingo into English, word by word: "When I was born, you know / I couldn't speak and go / My mother worked each day / And she learned me to say ..." But this didn't matter. Not many Germans at that time were fit enough to become aware of these flaws, and the song itself worked well. If you see the band's live video from the TV show "Beat-Club", it is impossible not to smile at their operetta uniforms, mop-top haircuts, and inept dance steps.

Although The Lords never had a #1 hit, they were able to place at least twelve songs in Top 10 positions and sold around 7 million singles; their cover versions of Huddie Ledbetter's and Lonnie Donegan's "Have a Drink on Me" (1965) and "Glory Land" (1967) can still be heard today on oldies radio stations. In the early 1970s, they split up, but reunited a couple of times until the death of their singer Ulli Günther ("Lord Ulli") in 1999. They even recorded an image song for the North Rhine Dental Association: "Die Zähne von dem Zahn" (The Teeth of the Tooth, 1978; a pun based on the youth slang of these years: "Zahn" [tooth] also could mean a girl; an especially sexy girl was called a "steiler Zahn" [steep tooth]; a steady was called "Stammzahn" [regular tooth]).

Of course, one never knows what happened in the cellars or garages deep in the backwater of nowhere, but it's relatively safe to say that The Lords were the first German beat group that got signed by a major record label. The Rattles of Hamburg started later than The Lords, but they were the first German rock band that became commercially successful. While The Lords were still doing skiffle, someone else was preparing the scenery for the beat of The Rattles: a young schlager singer named Drafi Deutscher (1946-2006).

Peter Meisel (1935-2010) was a music producer and publisher in Berlin. In 1962, he had founded Hansa Music Production, which, two years later, became a record label of the same name. His main demesne was the schlager genre with singers like Conny Froboess, Manuela, Giorgio Moroder, and others. Drafi Deutscher, under the aegis of composer/producer Christian Bruhn, had already had a decent amount of success with "Shake Hands" in 1964, but it was never a hit. Now, Meisel took him under his wings. In 1965, Meisel and Bruhn produced Drafi Deutscher & His Magics's 45 "Marmor, Stein und Eisen bricht" (Marble, Stone and Iron Breaks), a textbook example of a catchy tune. The song contained the unforgettable lines: "Weine nicht, wenn der Regen fällt / *dam dam, dam dam* / Es gibt einen, der zu dir hält / *dam dam, dam dam* / Marmor, Stein und Eisen bricht / aber unsere Liebe nicht ..."[1] ("Don't cry when the rain falls / *dam dam, dam dam* / There's one who sticks with you / *dam dam, dam dam* / Marble, stone and iron breaks / but not our love"). Still today, every German first-grader knows these lines, and whether you admit it or not, this song was not simply a schlager, it had *beat* in it. "Marmor, Stein und Eisen bricht" flew up to the #1 spot of German and Austrian charts and stayed there for five weeks; in the Netherlands it climbed up to #3. An English version soon followed ("Marble Breaks and Iron Bends"; #80 in U.S. charts). Not to say that this song was "hard rock" or something like that, but it was the first real fusion of beat and schlager; it combined the sound of a beat group (The Magics were a real band) with the German language and became accepted on a broad front. The only station that banned the song was BR radio Munich: "The title is grammatically incorrect." Through a strict perspective, they were right; three elements are mentioned, so it has to be plural, making it "Marmor, Stein und Eisen *brechen*" – but my sprachgefühl, at least, has no problem with "*bricht*". The whole affair was ridiculous anyways, and when the song topped the charts, BR radio finally gave in.

The major labels, by the way, never had any problems mixing genres if they thought it might sell. The schlager sampler *Die großen 16, 1967/68* on the German EMI/Columbia label combined tunes in intimate togetherness by, among others, Graham Bonney (an ex-member of British band Riot Squad from Joe Meek's roster), The Lords, Ralf Bendix, Gitte, Adamo, a female singing duo named Die Peanuts, Gilbert Bécaud, Heino, Howard Carpendale – and Pink Floyd ("See Emily Play"). Seriously.

For the growing beat music genre, this was probably a good thing. Albums like this and schlagers like "Marmor, Stein und Eisen bricht" brought rock music to untrained listeners, opened doors in the media, and paved the way for the future. We shouldn't underestimate this, because in fall of 1965, when the Rolling Stones started their first German tour, the press coverage was still mainly pejorative – a strange mix of fear and hate. The Stones' first performance took place in Münster (Westphalia), and it was short. The band that was marketed as "hardest band in the world" and antithesis to The Beatles, had a live repertoire of just eight songs, so the duration of the show was only 22 minutes. This was enough for the very serious nationwide paper, *Frankfurter Allgemeine Zeitung (FAZ)*, to complain about this "wretched uninspired primitive music"[2]. Nothing spectacular happened – the precautionary police marched up, but their water cannons didn't come into operation. This changed four days later when the Stones played the Waldbühne, an open-air venue in West Berlin: Some fans jumped on the wooden bench-seating and seesawed, and of course some benches broke. Other fans tried to climb up on stage. The concert ended very suddenly, with no encores given, but some fans simply went on seesawing on the benches. This was the signal for police to start beating the audience. Most people left immediately, but on their way home, many angry fans destroyed street lights and urban railway cars. 87 people were injured – the physical damage cost around 400,000 D-Marks, and the press wrote about a "battue of deadbeats."[3]

This might give you an impression of what it, at that time, meant in the public eye to play "beat music" – as The Rattles did.

The Rattles were founded in 1960 in Hamburg by Achim Reichel and Herbert Hildebrandt. Both were St. Pauli natives and knew each other from school. They covered English and American songs, from records and the radio. They didn't understand much of the lyrics, so they shouted out what they acoustically heard – which sometimes ended in strange results, but it worked since the listeners didn't understand the lyrics either. As the instruments had eaten up most of their money, they had no amps. Instead, they used old tube radios, with the guitar plugged into the record player jack. This set-up must have produced adventurous distortions, but that was what they wanted.

This was the way many bands at that time started in basements and garages. While in default of talent, most bands actually had to remain in their garages and basements forever. Not The Rattles. In February 1963, they won a Star-Club competition. This became their launching pad. It made them a sort of in-house band there, which led to their album *Twist im Star-Club Hamburg* (1963, released by Philips). It mainly had cover versions of English tracks; only one tune was composed by the band ("Mashed Potatoes", which became a 45 later). The album was also released in the U.K., and Philips marketed them as "the German Beatles". In 1964, a second album followed, released now by Ariola Records, but again under the title *Twist im Star-Club Hamburg* and again, mainly with cover versions.

The Rattles recorded their first studio single in 1965, entitled "La La La", a song with lyrics that didn't need much translation. It was released under the Star-Club label and reached #19 in German charts. "Stoppin' in Las Vegas" became their second 45, another being "Come on and Sing" (both again with loads of "na na na" lyrics), and several more followed.

The Rattles were the first German band to be part of a package tour through Great Britain; five weeks with Bo Diddley, Little Richard, and the (then still relatively unknown) Rolling Stones. Hans Joachim Kreutzfeldt, singer and guitarist, left The Rattles to become a schlager singer; as one half of the duo Kim & Hajo, he released "Junge Liebe"/"Wenn du weißt" on the Ariola label, later making a German cover version of "Mademoiselle Ninette", a catchy little pop song out of Herbert Hildebrandt's kitchen.

In 1966 in Munich, The Rattles were the best of the three supporting acts to play at the so-called "*Bravo*-Blitztournee" which headlined The Beatles. They were so successful that for the remaining tour stations (Essen and Hamburg), the Beatles manager, Brian Epstein, had them playing the first slot, far away from the Beatles.

In the same year, The Rattles appeared in a full-length feature film: *Hurra, die Rattles kommen!*, which was promoted as "Germany's first beat movie". It was a variation of the typical teenage schlager films, and Achim Reichel later called it "a complete washout"[4] – even their dialogues were lip-synched by professional actors. The Rattles were also used as the band for a German tune by French singer Johnny Hallyday ("Lass die Leute doch reden").

The success of The Rattles story had a setback in 1966 when Achim Reichel got drafted. He tried to file a lawsuit against the Bundeswehr (Germany's army), but of course he failed. The judge could see no sign that beat music might go out of style within the next couple of years. So Achim's long blonde hair had to fall and teenager magazine *Bravo* published his new military autograph address ("Panzergrenadier Achim Reichel" at Hamburg's Boehn-Kaserne). But the Bundeswehr was clever enough to use his popularity. They provided him a press officer who reported whatever Reichel said, did, or planned to do, to the media.

Producer Siggi Loch also talked Reichel into recording a 45 in German: "Trag es wie ein Mann" (Take It Like a Man). It was an embarrassing attempt to grind some money from Reichel's military service. Relatively soon, both Reichel as well as Loch saw this record as highly forgettable, but it took them a long time to be able to laugh about it. On Youtube you can find more than 100 videos of Achim Reichel – but not this one. Still today, somebody seems to take care of that. I can understand why.

For The Rattles, there was no other choice than to replace Reichel during his service. The replacement was singer, guitarist, and organist, Frank Dostal (1945-2017) of Flensburg. Not a bad choice, as can be heard on "Cauliflower" (1967).

WONDERLAND, JAMES LAST

After his service, Achim Reichel did not return to The Rattles. He saw that the music had clearly changed and The Rattles were no longer a fit for him. In 1968, he founded Wonderland with Frank Dostal, Reinhard "Dicky" Tarrach, Helmuth Franke, and Les Humphries, following an idea from teen glossy *Bravo*. The name was chosen by the readers of the tabloid *Bild*.[5] This band delivered music somewhere between beat, pop, and a sort of blues rock. A poll taken by music journalists nominated Wonderland as the third-best German rock band of 1969. Their output was of varying quality, but several tracks are worth a second listen. The producer of this project was none other than party king and "happy music" producer, James Last. How did this happen?

Around 1963, Hans Last (1929-2015) of Bremen became more and more terrified by the idea of ending up as a life-long bass player in the last row of the NDR Big Band, although it would have been a secure job for life. Besides this, he was not able to have his compositions played by this orchestra – it was frowned upon there. So he decided to jump into cold water, wave goodbye to the NDR Big Band, start working as a schlager arranger for Polydor, and finally found his own orchestra. Several members were his former colleagues from NDR who were allowed to do some side jobs – many of them were also playing in the Bert Kaempfert Orchestra and later also in the very jazzy Peter Herbolzheimer Rhythm Combination & Brass. James Last mainly recorded dance music. Since he was not the only one doing that, not even on the Polydor label (there were also Bert Kaempfert's and Max Greger's orchestras), he wanted to add something "special", but he had no idea what this could be.

It was more or less by chance that he found what he was looking for when, after a recording session, the musicians and several other people had a drink in the studio and listened (at a relatively high volume) to the potpourris of the current hits they had just recorded. Beer, schnapps and cocktails did their job; some people started singing along with the music, dancing, clapping, whistling, humming, clinking glasses, talking, and making noise. Last's flash of genius in this moment was to tell the technician to press the "record" button to make a recording of this atmosphere. Later, they mixed these party sounds under the prerecorded music. This turned out to be the "special" he had looked for: Suddenly Hans Last's party sound was born. When the final mix was done and played for the A&R guys of Polydor, they found it quite nice but asked why this background noise was present – but Last closed the discussion with a bone-dry: "Das bleibt so" (This remains as it is). The result was Last's first album, *Non Stop Dancing '65* in 1965, and because Polydor suddenly saw potential for international success with this sound, they thought it would be better (without asking him) to change "Hans" to "James".[6]

They were right: During his lifetime, James Last sold around 100 million records all over the world and received 17 platinum and more than 200 golden records – except in the U.S., where he was never able to get his feet on the ground, for what reason ever. He recorded one of his finest albums, *Well Kept Secret* (1975), with the crème of studio musicians from Los Angeles (Larry Carlton, Ernie Watts, Tom Scott, Jim Gordon and many more), but it flopped. In 2008, the album was re-released, now entitled *James Last In Los Angeles*, but again it sank like a stone. Obviously, this "American" sound was something the Americans didn't need, and the Germans didn't want.

He could live with this flop. In the 1970s, the James Last Orchestra produced up to twelve albums per year. Last is also a record holder in selling out London's Royal Albert Hall: He managed to do this 90 times. Most of his recordings were cover versions of nearly everything – schlagers, pop, rock, soul, folk songs, classical, polka, waltzes, usually two or three tunes combined into potpourris. He had top-notch musicians and singers in his orchestra who could play every kind of style – including guitarists Peter Hesslein, Erlend Krauser, and "Big Jim" Sullivan, trumpeters Manfred Moch and Derek Watkins, singers Simon Bell, Katie Kissoon, P.P. Arnold, and the Weather Girls. But Last was also a composer, some of his compositions became world-wide smash hits: "Happy Hearts" (1970), "Games That Lovers Play" (1970), "The Lonely Shepherd" (1980, with pan flutist Gheorghe Zamfir playing lead), "Biscaya" (1981). Dozens of film and TV soundtracks may be mentioned; in Germany, "Morgens um sieben ist die Welt noch in Ordnung" (1968) is the most famous one.

After giving up his day job as an orchestra musician, it didn't take long for James Last to start working as a producer. Which brings us back to WONDERLAND. While critics saw him as the maker of "elevator music", musicians knew better. For WONDERLAND, he created powerful brass arrangements, surprisingly psychedelic treats, and special sound effects. "They were great guys, really willing to work hard for their success," Last said in regard to the band.[7] In a short spoof on the tearjerker "Mama" (which in 1969 was a megahit by Heintje, a 12-year old import from the Netherlands), WONDERLAND even used an original recording of the JAMES LAST ORCHESTRA as a backing track.

James Last used his skills as an arranger and producer in the same year for his version of the musical *Hair*, which, still today, is one of his best recordings ever. It's not possible to say whether he used his experiences from recording *Hair* for the WONDERLAND sessions or if it was the other way round, anyway, it worked. This guy could have easily been Germany's Quincy Jones, but he decided to go on with his highly successful "happy sound". In the 1970s, the JAMES LAST ORCHESTRA produced a third of Polydor's entire turnover. In these years, it was impossible to escape, his music was omnipresent. But who could hold it against him? He simply knew his audience. James Last passed away in June 2015 in his adopted home of Palm Beach, Florida, after a severe illness.

WONDERLAND's first single was "Poochy" b/w "Moscow" (1968). As sometimes happens, the flip side became the hit: Nobody cared about "Poochy" (which could have also been a second-rate DAVE DEE, DOZY, BEAKY, MICK, & TICH number), but "Moscow" reached #15 of the German charts. The band had several TV appearances with the song, and they performed as the supporting act for none other than the BEE GEES. "Moscow" or the follow-up "Boomerang" (1968) even had what it takes to become an international hit. But, somehow, it didn't happen, and nobody can tell why. Even in Germany, "Moscow" remained their only hit, so Reichel finally went his own way.

Helmuth Franke became a guitarist in the JAMES LAST ORCHESTRA. Frank Dostal later became a producer, music publisher, and schlager lyricist. As such, he was involved in inexcusable garbage like "Das Lied der Schlümpfe" (The Smurf Song) by Vader Abraham or "Yes Sir, I Can Boogie" by the female vocal duo BACCARA. Later, Dostal also became a member of the supervisory board of the German copyright society GEMA. He passed away in 2017.

And The Rattles? Their biggest hit had yet to come. It happened in 1970 after a couple of line-up changes. The members now were Edna Béjarano, Frank Mille, Herbert "Borny" Bornhold, und Kurt "Zappo" Lüngen; Herbert Hildebrandt was still in the wings as their songwriter and producer. Musically, they were now very different from the former "beat" Rattles; their sound tended towards psychedelic hardrock, and singer Edna Béjarano brought a good load of soul feeling into the band. (Edna's mother, by the way, is Esther Béjarano, one of the last survivors of the Woman's Orchestra of Auschwitz. In the 1980s, with daughter Edna and son Joram she started Coincidence, a vocal group presenting Jewish and anti-fascist songs. She's co-founder and chairwoman of the International Auschwitz Committee.)

"The Witch" had originally been the flip side of "Geraldine", a single from 1969 with Henner Hoier on vocals (a former member of The Rivets, another Star-Club in-house band), but in 1970, the new Rattles line-up re-recorded the song. This new version of "The Witch", powerful and dramatic, made it to #4 in Germany, #8 in Great Britain, #10 in the Netherlands, #15 in Ireland, #20 in Austria, and it even reached #79 in the U.S. *Billboard* charts. (Interestingly, NDR radio in Hamburg always played the old flip side version in its weekly "International Hit Parade". They did not even notice that this was not the hit version. This says something about how much German radio and TV editors cared about the world outside their office doors at that time.)

Two other 45s became minor hits in Germany, "You Can't Have Sunshine Every Day" and "Devil's on the Loose", both 1971, but after these, they were not able to come up with adequate follow-ups anymore. The Rattles split up in 1977. Later, they had a couple of reunions, but these happened outside of this book's timeframe. From time to time they get together on stage at some oldies nights, and besides this, they are active studio musicians, like on recordings of schlager singer Juliane Werding.

Other follow-up projects, side projects, or solo careers of the Rattles, aside from Wonderland, that made it to record releases were the Hamburger Blues-Gesangsverein von 1970 (not to be taken too seriously), Birgit Sommer, Birgit & Iris, Herbert & Birgit, Pegasus, Moti Special, Kuno & The Marihuana Brass, Randy Pie, Hajo, The Gorillas, Edna, Propeller, Toni Pepperoni, The "In" Kraut, The Fixx, Our Gang, Sunshine Band – probably this is not even the complete list.

Henner Hoier became involved with the Les Humphries Singers, and later he worked as a schlager singer for a while. His biggest successes were probably a German cover version of Daniel Boone's hit "Beautiful Sunday" (1972) and a tune called "Ich hör' Musik" (1973). He wrote and produced songs for several other schlager singers like Jürgen Drews (who came from *Hair* and was also a member of the Les Humphries Singers), Hans Hartz (1943-2002), Wencke Myhre, and also for The Lords; later, he toured as a musical singer. Sometimes, for strange reasons, his name is connected to Can as having been their roadie, but this is nonsense; nobody knows where this rumor comes from.

John Leslie "Les" Humphries (1940-2007), originally a skilled military musician, alongside his Singers and Wonderland, had a sort of afro-hardrock project named Megaton with singer and songwriter Jimmy Bilsbury. Their self-titled album from 1971, which was probably made with musicians from the circle around Rattles, Lucifer's Friend and the James Last Orchestra, is inspired by Wonderland as well as bands like Osibisa, but it didn't go anywhere. Bilsbury, who also had been one of the lead singers of the Les Humphries Singers, passed away in 2003 somewhere on the street as an impoverished alcoholic. The Les Humphries Singers sold, overall, nearly 50 million records, but their time drew to an end with the end of the decade. In 1992, they tried a comeback as the supporting act for schlager star Howard Carpendale. Later, in 1998, Les Humphries, who had grown lonely, faked his own death to get his name into the media again. Jürgen Drews, without knowing the actual situation, delivered an obituary on BR radio.

Herbert Hildebrandt went on working successfully as songwriter, producer, and session bassist. Under the headline "The Rattles present" he released a duo recording by Herbert & Birgit (= Herbert Hildebrandt and Birgit Sommer, real name Birgit Schmidt), a German cover version of "Hey Jean, Hey Dean" (1967; originally sung by U.S. duo Dean & Jean, 1964) on the Star-Club label. It became a minor hit. In 1971, he included Herbert & Birgit in a project called Pegasus and released the recording a second time. Pegasus ended with the death of Birgit Schmidt in 1973; she fell asleep while smoking in bed. One of Hildebrandt's biggest hit productions was probably "Mademoiselle Ninette" by The Soulful Dynamics of Liberia which went gold in 1971; it's still well-known in Germany and often played on oldies radio stations. At least once, Herbert Hildebrandt was also working anonymously for the budget label Europa, which you will learn more about in the following chapter.

MUSICIAN'S DAILY ROUTINES

What a wonderful life this must be: being a star, loved by everyone, from time to time singing some songs for a new album, everybody will hear you on the radio or see you on TV! Sounds good, doesn't it? Well, here's the truth about the various jobs many professional musicians had to do to survive in the 1960s and 1970s.

In the Choo-Choo chapter, I mentioned so-called *budget labels*. These labels are nearly as old as the record industry itself. In German, they are called "Kaufhauslabels" (department store labels) or simply "Billiglabels" (low-price labels); in the U.S. we know them as "drugstore labels". They are record companies that usually work outside the "big" market, but make their profit from it. Most of them have two lines of business: The first is the production and distribution of cover versions of popular hits. Often, they prefer the EP format for this because, this way, they can put four hits on one record. The second line consists of recordings of folklore, popular classical music, operettas, military marches, comedy, et cetera.

Interestingly, just these budget labels – Baccarola, Bella Musica, Fass, Hallo, Opera, Starlet, Tempo, Tip, Die Volksplatte, to name a couple of them – had a part in German rock'n'roll that shouldn't be underestimated. Their releases were mainly cover versions of popular English pop songs or bestselling German schlagers (which in fact means they were often cover versions of cover versions). The productions had to be made as fast and cheap as possible, the session musicians who recorded them usually didn't have more than three hours to lay down the two recordings for a 45, including the time they needed to set up instruments and equipment, and have a coffee break.

One of the few real existing bands able to do this was The Rocking Stars, an amateur band of Rastatt. They made some recordings for Hallo, but later they switched over to CBS and went professional. In most cases, the musicians for budget label recordings came from professional big bands, show orchestras, and beer tent bands, or they worked as music teachers. They had to be able to read music, as well as play everything without any assistance, from schlager to waltz, country to Dixieland, and polkas to rock'n'roll. Usually, they were not really familiar with the latter, but in their simplicity and rough-and-readiness, some of their "rock'n'roll" recordings were more authentic than the high-gloss tunes coming from major labels like Polydor, Telefunken, Ariola, et cetera. The major labels often worked with the same session musicians as the budget labels, but they had more time to polish the productions. In a way, it's a pity that many of these budget label recordings are lost forever. Today, the best places to find some of them are flea markets. In the mid-1960s, the importance of budget labels even grew.

It's rare that budget labels produce unknown new compositions, but it happens sometimes. When it does, it usually means music that fits into a rampant fad. In the late 1950s and early 1960s, as mentioned earlier, some of these labels produced rock'n'roll recordings with the likes of Paul Würges, Benny Quick, Flip Gering, The Rocking Stars, and others. Their rawness sometimes made these recordings more interesting than the polished productions of major labels. Budget label recordings were apparently made by unknown artists. Sometimes they are not even named. But as you will see, they were not always as unknown as one might think.

Budget label records were not sold at normal record stores, they were to be found at supermarkets (usually in a stand-up display near the cash registers), low-priced department stores like Woolworth (which even ran its own budget label named Embassy) or Kepa, a long-gone cheap subsidiary of Karstadt. The department store chains Karstadt, Kaufhof, Horten, Hertie (the big four in Germany then), carried them in their record departments, but on a special shelf, away from the "real" records. Sometimes you could also find them unsorted in special bargain bins near the entrance doors, often mixed with major label cutouts. After the invention of cassettes, and later CDs, gas stations became another important outlet for budget labels. A budget label 45 had usually cost 1.75 D-Mark, an EP 3.95, and for an LP you had to pay 5 or 6 D-Marks.

A special sideline of the budget record business were one- or two-sided flexidiscs or "sound postcards" that had a foil with playable grooves laminated on them; this kind of stuff was usually made by magazine publishing houses and came as a gimmick with teenager magazines and dime novels, or was sold at tourist souvenir stands – but explaining this further would require another book in itself, so I'll leave it at that.

The prime time of budget labels were the years from the 1950s to the late 1960s. Not all, but many of these labels went broke and gave up in the 1970s and 1980s; a handful survived and are still active today. Some of them worked independently, some were subdivisions of major record companies, some belonged to mail order outlets, like Neckermann Records, run by Germany's then largest mail order store of the same name. Quelle, Neckermann's toughest competitor, did the same with its label Quellux, later renamed Universum which also became Quelle's house brand for radios, TV sets, and record players.

One of these labels, Europa, switched its focus over to records and cassettes with audio plays for children and teenagers in the 1970s and became phenomenally successful (we will come back to these). Europa was initially part of Miller International and recorded German bands and orchestras for the U.S. market at very cheap prices. This ended up working very well, so they expanded into the German market. Aside from Europa, Miller International ran the labels Parade and Somerset. Later, Europa was sold to the U.S. corporation MCA and is now part of Sony Music, but it's still a budget label.

Budget label records were especially attractive to people who were interested in "some nice music", but were not willing or able to pay much money for it. They didn't get the original singers or bands this way, but they accepted this for the low price. Others simply didn't know or care about the difference, and there were many of these people. It's hard to get exact sales figures, but in Germany during the 1960s, hundreds of thousands of budget label records must have rotated at allotment garden parties, monthly ninepins evenings (the German version of bowling, a fad in the 1960s and 1970s, up until the mid-1970s, when bowling became established), and of course in many, many private party rooms. If you owned a house at that time, the "Partykeller" was a must-have: a typically carpeted and heated, often maritime-styled, basement room with a lounge, usually a fishnet under the ceiling with plastic sea stars in it, a little bar with stools, starboard and portside lanterns on the bottles' storage shelves, a cheap blaring stereo, and a little dance floor equipped with red, blue, and green lights. In the 1970s, the stereo equipment improved and the light bulbs became connected to the dernier cri: a light organ ("Lichtorgel"), rhythmically triggered by the frequencies of music. Almost no male teenager's room was without one.

To show you that budget label records had sometimes played a role, here's an example: In 1968, Europa Records released an LP entitled *Supreme Psychedelic Underground*, by a band named Hell Preachers Inc. It circulated in my school, was highly admired, and even our music teacher – a jazz buff – played and attempted to "analyze" it. Nobody was interested in his opinion, but it was a nice opportunity to listen to music during class. We were around 12 years old then and had no idea about budget labels. We never realized that this LP was somehow too cheap to be a regular one. There was this "psychedelic" cover picture with a melting day-glo font. The band's name had an evil sound to it, there were church bells, gunshots, sirens, and other sound effects in its tunes, stuff you could associate with protests or riots, and all of this was enough to make us school kids believe that Hell Preachers Inc. was a rebellious, hardcore underground band from England or America, and we handled this LP with awe-stricken respect. The fact that neither musicians nor composers were named on the album's sleeve made it even more mysterious.

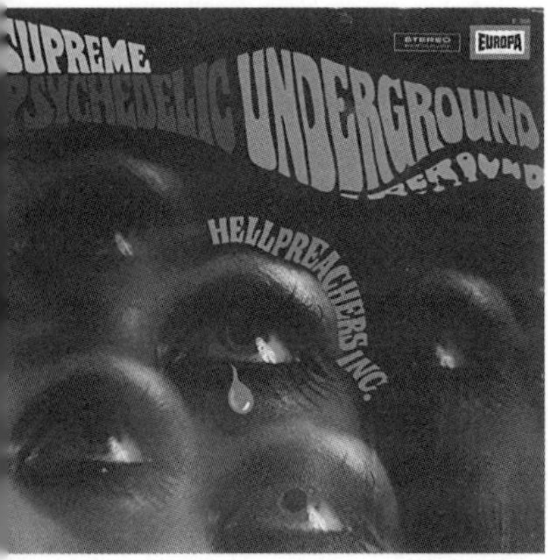

There is a reason why I mention just this album. Still today, *Supreme Psychedelic Underground* is seen in some Krautrock or hard rock communities as a sort of insider tip or well-kept secret; some internet sources even claim that Ritchie Blackmore, and maybe some more Deep Purple members, might have been involved in this record – probably because there are some, well, let's call them "similarities" that connect its sound to some Deep Purple tunes.

But no. Here's the simple truth: Hell Preachers Inc. were not from England or America, they were not even a real band. Like most budget label acts, they consisted of various musicians from several bands. In this case, it was the bass guitarist, Herbert Hildebrandt (former Rattles) with The Tonics of Hamburg – who were guitarist Helmuth Franke, guitarist Hermann "Rugy" Rugenstein (later The Rattles), bass guitarist Benny Bendorff (who was a schlager singer, member of The Rattles, later of Lucifer's Friend, and the James Last Orchestra), guitarist Hajo Teschner (who later joined Krautrock band Silberbart), and drummer Herbert Bornhold (later Lucifer's Friend); not all of them appear in every track. The Tonics were formerly known as The Four Renders and had won a Star-Club band contest in 1963, through which they went on to become professionals. In the 1970s, The Tonics were the backing group of schlager singer Manfred Oberdörffer, who went by the stage name "Tony"; Hildebrandt had worked with him for a while. Tony's biggest hit in Germany was "Mädchen mit roten Haaren" (Girls With Red Hair; 1971); the backing band you hear on this schlager (without the brass section) is, for the most part, the same that went under the fantasy name Hell Preachers Inc. If only we 12-year olds would've known where this band would end up ... but well, we didn't.

Just for fun: The Tonics, with or without Tony Oberdörffer or Herbert Hildebrandt, recorded music for major labels (Polydor, Philips, Fontana), as well as for budget labels (Tip, Elite-Special, Joker). They appeared under the names Herb Allen, The James Anderson Band, James Anderson Brothers, Automatic Blues Inc., The Black Kids, Memphis Brown's Band, Buster Churchill & The Beat Tigers, The Ginger-Rockets, John Hamilton Band, The Happy Beat Boys, Holt & McIntosh Inc., Humpty Dumpty, The Increasing Hot Patters, The Lightning Soul Players, Phil Morris & His Tigers, The Pick-Ups, The Pop Spots, The Ravers, Rémon-Biermann-Band, The Rock Ravers, Little Joe Rover & His Party Riders, The Seven Souldiers, The Shotguns, The Soho Gamblers, The Spots, Ten O'Clock Bubble Gum Train, Toni Tornado, and probably a dozen more. Besides schlagers and hellish preaches, they did a couple of relatively well-made cover versions of hits by The Sir Douglas Quintet. The Tonics split up in 1970; afterwards, Franke, Bendorff, Bornhold, and Teschner joined the James Last Orchestra.

In the mid-1960s the Munich budget label Tempo released more than 100 cover versions of hits by The Beatles, The Rolling Stones, The Spencer Davis Group, Dusty Springfield, and many more. Just a hair away from the original names, the "bands" were called Blue Cats, Venture Five, Gamblers, The Lovers, The Dynamits, High Tops, The Stars, Beat Kings; singers like Johnny Smash, Ben Cash, Teddy Todd, Jimmy Fields, Rusty Greenfield, and several more appeared. Usually, their accents alone made it immediately clear that the vocalists were Germans. One of the masterminds behind all of these names was Christian Bruhn. He was connected to Peter Meisel of Berlin (Hansa Production) and later became a schlager composer and producer, and another individual whom we will meet again in the context of Krautrock. The only exception on Tempo seemed to be the Beat Kings who were a real, existing band from Liverpool – not to be mixed up with another band named Beat Kings, whose singer was Rio Reiser, the later co-founder of Ton Steine Scherben.

Another first-class musician was drummer and composer Carsten Bohn (a.k.a. "CeBee") of Hamburg. He had been a founding member of the folk rock project, City Preachers, and later of the well-known blues-rock band, Frumpy. He was one of a couple of musicians behind the pseudonym "Bert Brac". He wrote the music for nearly 200 episodes of budget label Europa's audio play series *Fünf Freunde*, *TKKG*, *Die drei ???* and some more. This stuff sold like hot cakes. *Die drei ???* series alone sold 45 million copies, mainly cassettes. If budget label records would have been included in German charts, they would have permanently taken the top five spots for several years leading up to the 1980s.

After producer Heikedine Körting had started these series, she did not even notice their success – not until she suddenly received 64 golden records in one fell swoop. Up to the present, she's produced more than 2000 audio plays.[1] These were sales numbers German rock bands or even schlager stars could only dream of.

As usual goes with recordings for budget labels, the musicians just had one studio day to lay down the whole album. This explains the many flaws and timing problems you may notice on *Supreme Psychedelic Underground*, but it also explains why the budget labels needed professionals to make these records: It would take too long otherwise, and that would be more expensive. *Supreme Psychedelic Underground* has been rereleased a couple of times by several labels, also on CD, and is still available today. With a dash of humor, you can see it as a sort of scrap icon.

Bassist Dieter Horns explains how these kinds of budget productions had worked: "Per track [the budget label] paid 60 D-Marks. In the morning I worked at Studio Maschen [a schlager studio not far from Hamburg], in the afternoon I was at Polydor Studio, and in the evening sometimes at, say, Drafi Deutscher's private studio. You had to make ends meet." His colleague, guitarist Peter Hesslein: "This gave us the idea we could work as a group this way." The result was hard rock band Lucifer's Friend who got signed to Philips. Dieter Horns: "Sometimes, when we had a sort of creative episode, it got us more tunes than would fit on one LP. In one fell swoop we had material for three LPs. Then we filtered out: The best material we took for Lucifer's Friend, the second-best was for Asterix [a side project of Lucifer's Friend, they released one album on the Decca label in 1971], and the garbage of our 40 tracks ended up on Europa."[2]

The Lucifer's Friend musicians were active as or with The Air Mail, Asterix, Bokaj Retsiem (which, read backwards, is "Meister Jakob", a popular children's round), Brother T. & Family, Children Of Quechua, Electric

Food, The Fantastic Pikes, The Foundations, The Four Renders, The Giants, Hell Preachers Inc., Lake, The Pink Mice, Rebel, Rudolf Rock & die Schocker (a play on the name of the well-known opera singer Rudolf Schock), Spinning Wheel, Stonewall, Tone Band, Tony & The Kingtones, and they also gigged for childrens records by Rolf Zuckowski – and several more which they probably don't even remember themselves.

Peter Hesslein talks about the routine of these session jobs: "They said to us: 'Today we want to record an LP which will be entitled *Easy Rider*. You know, Woodstock-like stuff with power guitars, really good rock tunes. Twelve tracks. Do you have something in store that would fit into such a concept?' And we were sitting in their studio and said: 'Well yeah, we have some stuff like that …' And they said: 'Okay, go ahead then.'"

ADVERTISING

Another source of income for many musicians was music for advertising – composing as well as playing. In a way, this seems to be strange when you think about the way "beat" or rock musicians were seen by wide parts of the public; society tended to view them as unwashed long-haired monkeys mistreating their instruments. But the advertising agencies knew better. When they wanted modern sounding jingles and short music tracks for commercials, they knew whom to ask.

In the U.S. this was nothing new; musicians always did these kinds of jobs. The money was always welcome; even top songwriters from the Brill Building, like Doc Pomus, didn't miss out on an opportunity. The Rolling Stones delivered music for Kellogg's Rice Krispies in 1964, Iron Butterfly made music for Ban Roll-On deodorant in 1968, the Pontiac GTO was decorated with music by Paul Revere & The Raiders, Jefferson Airplane made a (gruesome) jingle for Levi's jeans in 1971, and the examples go on.

In Germany, Klaus Doldinger was one of the earliest and most productive guys in this business. Since the early 1960s, he wrote and recorded an unbelievable number of jingles. Most of them were "one off" productions, but some, like the one for a soap named "Fa", continued to exist through the decades with consistent changes in its arrangements, but the melody remained.

One big Star-Club band was The German Bonds. Under this name, they released a couple of albums, first on the Fontana label (a sub-label of Philips), then later on Star-Club. They also, however, had a connection to session jobs like recording jingles for commercials et cetera; in 1966, they released a 45 with a

Coca-Cola song. They also gigged for the Europa label. In 1970, the band broke up. Some of the musicians joined the LES HUMPHRIES SINGERS, while others were hired by the JAMES LAST ORCHESTRA. Parallel to this, they founded LUCIFER'S FRIEND, but didn't stop doing session jobs.

Another band that did ad jobs were the JAY FIVE of Würzburg. Their "official" stuff was released on Polydor, and later on Cornet, but they also did film music and advertising music. Their Coca-Cola song "Frischwärts", made up of three different arrangements, even appeared on a 45 released in 1971 as the B-side of an advertising song by THE NEW SEEKERS: "I'd Like to Buy the World A Coke", which became a world-wide hit under the title "I'd Like to Teach the World To Sing".

In 1988, even EINSTÜRZENDE NEUBAUTEN joined the advertising community: They provided a jingle for Jordache jeans.

Around the late 1980s, the high time of producing jingles for advertising ended. The ad agencies came up with a new fad: More and more, they used original hits, usually oldies, for their commercials. But the musicians found a new market: When in 1984, a new law in Germany allowed commercial radio stations, hundreds of call signs were needed. Usually these consisted just of name and frequency of the station, but these couple of syllables had to be set to music and needed to be recorded.

THE LIFE OF TELEPHONE MUSICIANS

What all of this shows is that instrumentalists and singers who appear on budget labels or do commercials may not necessarily equate to second-rate musicians. Some instrumentalists who worked for the Munich-based budget label, Tempo, were known for being members of the MAX GREGER ORCHESTRA, while others were active in schlager productions or worked as music teachers.

Session musicians didn't participate in the record sales, they were paid per recording session. That's why the vocalists, especially, had to work under several names for several labels: It was pure necessity; they couldn't have survived otherwise. These guys and girls could really be called pros. Without any fuss, they deliver what they are asked for, and do it fast, without significant flaws or too much personal style. There are specialists among them who are able to imitate voices or styles. They are hired when the real star becomes hoarse or is not available for some overdubs. In the morning, these guys or girls will sing a cover version of a #1 schlager, in the afternoon, they'll play a rock'n'roll song in another studio, and on the next day, they'll record an entire LP with folk songs in a third studio. Many of them, sometimes as a hobby, played in a rock band. Some of them, like LUCIFER'S FRIEND, made the jump. Professional musicians in Germany never had big problems with switching between roles and genres, otherwise they wouldn't have been able to survive.

For the budget labels, it made sense to use these kind of professional musicians. They needed to place their cover versions of hits as soon as possible because they had to surf the wave of the original's success. To produce an EP fast and cheaply, they needed musicians who sight-read, were capable to deliver four top hits within a tight three-hour studio schedule, and able to lay down any track in no more than two or three takes.

The pseudonyms used by singers and musicians who appeared on budget labels are nearly impossible to decipher, particularly since, sometimes, these record companies released a recording under pseudonym A themselves, and licensed the same recording to another budget label (or even more than one) where it appeared under pseudonyms B, C, and D. The opposite was also common practice: Budget labels pooled recordings of several different singers on one LP under one collective pseudonym. The voices are recorded and equalized in a way that makes it nearly impossible to recognize that "the singer" of the album is, in reality, five different people.

This worked because radio and TV never played budget records, so the real people behind the pseudonyms always remained unknown. GEMA and GVL, where of course all pseudonyms are registered, never give out any information, even if the name holders became deceased long ago.

Many musicians tried to use budget labels as a launch pad, but the success was hit or miss. Holde Fee of Braunschweig, founded in 1971, shortened their name to Fee after two self-released albums, and then released the album *Notaufnahme* (produced by ex-Rattles guitarist Frank Mille) on budget label Marifon. Their idea was that, this way, their album would be available where people had to do their shopping anyway, and it would be cheaper than the records from major labels. This has a certain logic to it, but the target group apparently did not buy records at supermarkets. Fee went on to indie label Risiko and was finally signed by Teldec.

When, in 1970, the exiled Czech saxophonist Hanus Berka was stranded in Munich, he founded Emergency; their album *Get Out to The Country* (1973) is a jazz-rock gem. Among several others, drummer Udo Lindenberg played with them, as well as guitarist Frank Diez, who later joined Frumpy's follow-up Atlantis. But Berka also worked for many schlager productions, usually connected to producer and arranger Rainer Pietsch (who had a soft rock band named Tanned Leather himself; album: *Child Of Never Ending Love*, 1973, which remained an insider tip). In this connection, Berka appears on the album *Wir sind die Meiers* (1973) by Austrian schlager singer/lyricist Wolfgang (full name Wolfgang Hofer). In 1970, Wolfgang had a smash hit in Austria and Germany with the song "Abraham (Das Lied vom Trödler)" (Abraham (The Junk Dealer's Song)), and he was one of the few pieces of proof that "schlager" does not necessarily mean "stupid". In the line-up of the session musicians on his records, you find the Tanned Leather band, Lothar Meid (later Amon Düül II), Wolfgang Schmid, Curt Cress and Keith Forsey (later Doldinger's Passport), as well as guitar virtuoso Wolfgang Schwab. But he was not mass-compatible, after ten 45s and three albums, he left his singing career in 1975 and switched to writing lyrics for various singers; more than 100 songs for Udo Jürgens alone.

In general, working for schlager productions was nothing special for German rock or jazz musicians. Somehow, it's always about money. Inga Rumpf (Frumpy, Atlantis) had started as schlager singer; her first 45 was "Bonnie And Clyde" (Decca, 1968), recorded with John O'Brien-Docker under the name Inga & John. In 1976, Inga was part of a package tour through the USSR: 28 concerts through Moscow, Kasan, Tashkent, and Alma Ata with schlager singers

Mona & Michael, Herbert Reiner, and the Jochen Brauer Sextett, the latter mainly known in Germany as the in-house band of the successful TV game show "Dalli-Dalli". Inga's band Frumpy gigged as a backing band for schlager singer Stephan Remmler before he founded NDW project Trio. The Rattles of Star-Club fame worked as a backing band for schlager singer Juliane Werding. Amon Düül II's offspring 18 Karat Gold became the backing band of schlager star Peter Maffay. Karl-Heinz "Carlo" Blumenberg (1948-2016), singer of Thrice Mice, comedic rock'n'roll band Leinemann, and jazz rock band Altona, was active as a schlager singer and made horrible horror songs under the name "Harry Horror". Werner Stephan, singer of Kin Ping Meh, made several schlager recordings under the names Stephan or Marc Stephan, mainly on the BASF label; as part of the duo Steve & Lee he was also active in electro dance pop. The later singer of Jane, Bernd Pulst, made a 45 for Metronome in 1972: "Ein Mensch ohne Namen" b/w "Du bist genauso gut". The A-side was a cover version of America's "A Horse With No Name" with lyrics by Karlheinz Freynik, while the B-side was written by Klaus Hess, also a later member of Jane. The song flopped, but it was a start – you see the rope teams, and they worked.

Gitta Walther was a singer from the 1960s up to the 1980s. For producer Erich Storz (remember: "Die kleine Bimmelbahn" by the Harzer Meisterjodelpaar – this was Marianne Vasel and him), she recorded back-up vocals for folksy oompah and yodel music, sang with the orchestras led by Werner Müller, Ambros Seelos, and Addy Flor, recorded an album named *Liverpool Bluebeat* with The Thunderbeats for Eurocord (the club label of Intercord), and did solo schlager recordings under the pseudonyms Simone and Jackie Robinson, under the latter of which she, in the 1970s, reached #5 of U.S. *Billboard* disco charts with "Moving Like A Superstar". She sang with the Cornely Singers who, in 1969, changed to Love Generation; under the new name, they had a minor hit with "Hör' wieder Radio" (Listen to the Radio Again) in 1975. Then, again as Jackie Robinson, she became one of the voices of producer Michael Kunze's "Munich Sound" trio Silver Convention, a sort of spin-off of the circle around Moroder/Bellotte. "Fly Robin Fly" was a world-wide hit in 1975 – Gitta Walther's salary was just 1200 D-Marks for the session (not too shabby for one day's work, but compared to the sales numbers this record reached …). She also provided the high-pitched screams in Penny McLean's hit "Lady Bump" (1975), another international hit produced by Michael Kunze. After this, Gitta Walther worked as a back-up singer for Marius Müller-Westernhagen, a German superstar in the 1970s and 1980s. In the 1980s, she founded the vocal quartet THE HORNETTES; they had two minor hits. After the German reunification in 1989, Gitta Walther moved back to her hometown in the former GDR and started recording for budget labels again, this time under her real name – Christmas and folk songs in the dialect of the Erzgebirge area for the budget labels, Laserlight and Phonica. Gitta Walther passed away in 2014.

This kind of career, with its unbelievable ups and downs, jumps between genres and labels, successes, flops, and simple routine gigs, was typical for many musicians in Germany in the 1960s, 1970s, and even the 1980s. Working under pseudonyms for budget labels could be a lucrative source for an extra income, especially for instrumentalists. Sometimes, this was actually their bread-and-butter job, allowing them to play music they really liked under their real names. Sometimes, they did these jobs in the hope of amounting to some "big" career one day. But only a few musicians were lucky enough to achieve this; schlager singer Mary Roos would be an example for this. Most ended up as session players, back-up singers for schlager productions, or recorded cover versions of hits for budget labels, and this remained their main job. Usually they called themselves "telephone musicians": A record company or a studio called them in for a job tomorrow afternoon, and they did it, got their check, and that was about it. They had no influence on what the record companies did with these recordings or under which name they were released.

What all this might show you is that the borders between schlager, pop and rock, advertising jingles and utility music, budget and major labels, and band A and band B were always permeable (and still are). Behind all these pseudonyms, non-existing bands, and pure studio projects, you see a music scene that was (and still is) quite easy to grasp. All these musicians, composers, lyricists, arrangers, and producers knew each other. They did all kinds of musical jobs, from budget label recordings to advertising jingles to funeral gigs, they performed with each other, created bands and broke them up, were orchestra members, or had a day job somewhere. This was and still is the reality for most musicians in Germany. They might not be interested in the kind of music they have to play, but they are the ones who at least *make* a living from being a musician. In this sense, one could say they are privileged; most musicians are not that lucky. Being well-known at one point in time has never been a guarantee that, in the future, you could turn down session jobs for budget labels. But now you see why there are so many pseudonyms on record sleeves.

When, for a schlager production, strings are needed and the sampler presets won't do, then the string section from the local opera house gets called in – the highest-qualified classical musicians. Usually, they grumble for a while about the "primitive stuff" they are expected to play, but in the end they take the job. Today's universities and conservatories qualify a lot of musicians, many more than the existing orchestras can absorb. Most of these classically trained musicians are not aware that these kinds of studio gigs will be the main part of their future. It's even more unintelligible that situations like playing in a studio with headphones on still is not something taught during their studies.

Many musicians, especially jazz musicians, can make ends meet as employees of one of the four big bands of WDR, HR, NDR, or SWR radio. From the 1960s to 1980s, there were also the Bert Kaempfert Orchestra, the James Last Orchestra, Peter Herbolzheimer's Rhythm Combination & Brass, the Max Greger Orchestra, and some more independent orchestras (which means they were not funded by state or a radio station) that were hubs for musicians. In the 1960s and 1970s, many musicians even worked in more than one.

In the 1980s, after the big success of *Cats*, musicals became a new source of income for musicians who were able to sight-read. Even a top-notch drummer like Pierre Moerlen (1952-2005; he was a former member of Gong and his own project Pierre Moerlen's Gong, and later played with Mike Oldfield and Swedish band Tribute), had to waste his talent on the Stuttgart version of *Miss Saigon* for a while. But as the situation is, even the best virtuosos can (or have to) be very pragmatic sometimes.

Or, during the summer months, musicians simply traveled through the pedestrian zones, busking. That's where Holger Czukay and Jaki Liebezeit spotted Damo Suzuki.

Musicians without jobs like these usually had day jobs as copyists at music publishing houses, private teachers like Bröselmaschine's guitarist Peter Bursch, the author of Germany's probably most successful guitar hornbook (even Yours Truly learned the usual five guitar chords with it), or saxophonist Helmut Hachmann from Ardo Dombec, school teachers, or, if they are very lucky, they hold a chair at a conservatory or a university. But many were simply working at some office or garage. This can turn out to be problematic, as the later the example Novalis will show.

Of course, all of this is background information. But if you really want to know how the German music scene worked, you have to know the scenery in which it happened, and this jumping between genres, bands, labels, and day jobs was and still is an important part of the scenery.

It might give you an idea about what a monstrous decision it was for a hobby rock musician in the 1960s or 1970s to say: "I want to make a living from music. I can't develop my potential while having this damned day job. I have to give it up. I want my band to be professional." The jazz and rock musicians who were really able to make a living from their music was a very small circle.

But some of them never gave up and made the jump.

BEAT-CLUB & CO.: MUSIC ON GERMAN TV

During the 1960s, TV had platforms for traditional music. What was missed, was a forum for new developments. This changed with the founding of a TV show called "Beat-Club". Of course, there had previously been a couple of so-called "talent shows" on TV, mainly meant for up-and-coming schlager singers and singer-songwriters (who in Germany are called "Liedermacher", which translates to song makers).

TALENTSCHUPPEN

The SWF (Südwestfunk) in Baden-Baden (Baden-Württemberg) presented "Talentschuppen" (Talent Showcase) once a week and, yes, they made some interesting discoveries there. Besides a couple of schlager singers, The Petards of Willingshausen in Hesse appeared there in July 1967; they released their first album, *A Deeper Blue*, on the Europa budget label, then switched to Liberty. When Klaus Ebert, one of their members, left the band to play with Amon Düül II and later became label manager at Metronome Records, The Petards replaced him with Bernd Wippich. This guy later played with Randy Pie and worked as a schlager duo with his wife Freya. The Petards also released Creedence Clearwater Revival cover songs under the names Zonk and Flitter Mouse. Joy & The Hit Kids with their remarkable singer, Joy Fleming of Mannheim, appeared in March 1967. Joy Unlimited were there in December 1970; they were more or less the same band as Joy & The Hit Kids; one of their members was guitarist Hans Lingenfelder who later became known for his schmaltzy guitar playing under the pseudonym Ricky King. Hard rockers KIN PING MEH of Mannheim performed in the same show, and again, Joy Fleming appeared in November 1974, this time as a soloist. Other discoveries of the overall 67 episodes of "Talentschuppen", were Ute Lemper, Juliane Werding, Reinhard Mey, INGA & WOLF, and Penny McLean.

BEAT-CLUB

Jazz musicians also had some forums on TV. But there had never been a real music program for young people – not until the smallest of all German ARD-TV stations, Radio Bremen (RB), which had always been one of the more creative ones, changed this. Michael "Mike" Leckebusch (1937-2000), a theater specialist and fan of traditional jazz, worked as an editor at Radio Bremen and was responsible for classical TV shows. The task to develop a concept for a new show, targeted for young people, was handed to him. Because this was not really something he felt competent in, he teamed up with Gerhard "Gerd" Augustin who was a DJ at the discotheque Twen Club in Bremen, where Leckebusch used to hang out from time to time. Augustin had lived in the U.S. for two years and was competent in the field of music, especially when it came to soul and British pop. Leckebusch became his star student.

As a role model for their upcoming show, they used the U.S. show "American Bandstand", the British "Ready Steady Go", and some other similar foreign shows. They mixed and adapted them to German TV needs. They decided the show should be aired live, but the bands and singers should lip-sync because the sound engineering would be too complicated for their mere two-and-a-half minute appearances.

They hired Ursula "Uschi" Nerke to co-host the show. At that time, Uschi Nerke was a 21-year old woman who had just won a dance competition when schlager producer Hans Hee took her under his wing. Under the name Karina she tried her luck as a schlager singer for a while ("Ein kleiner Traum" b/w "Hier ist mein Platz", 1964 released on the Telefunken label), but without noteworthy success. Hee also sent her to some TV test shootings. Later, she studied architecture and became a structural engineer; in 1968 she started her own architect's office. Her only flaw was that her English sounded rather German, and she didn't have much knowledge about the music she had to present. But since she didn't have to write her scripts herself, nobody noticed. For her entire TV career, her presentations sounded recited (which they probably were).

The show was called "Beat-Club". On Saturday afternoon, September 25, 1965, it aired for the first time, 45 minutes nationwide, with 150 young people from Augustin's disco and some friends dancing in the studio, hosted by Uschi Nerke and Gerd Augustin, and introduced with a warning: "This is the first show made especially for you, young people. But those of you who you don't like beat music, we ask for your understanding." THE YANKEES of Bremen acted as opener with "Halbstark", another guest in this first episode were THE LIVERBIRDS of Liverpool, the first full-female beat band and a former Star-Club regular (one of its members was married to RATTLE Frank Dostal). There were also three go-go-girls who became a sort of cult after a while. Besides this, there were also shown film snippets with well-known artists. This was a new thing on German TV screens; singers were usually expected to appear in person on the show. And the "Beat-Club" was the first show on German TV that made use of jingles. The theme music was initially "Rinky Dink" by SOUNDS INCORPORATED, later it changed to "A Touch Of Velvet, A Sting Of Brass" by MOOD MOSAIC FEAT. THE LADYBIRDS; this latter tune somehow became legendary – everybody knew it, but nobody knew the title or band. (These LADYBIRDS, among many other gigs, also did backup vocals on Jimi Hendrix' "Hey Joe" and were a Joe Meek act under the names LEA & CHESS, THE SHARADES and FLIP & THE DATELINERS.)

In the beginning, Radio Bremen had problems with getting bigger acts for the show, especially from the U.S. and Great Britain, because nobody there could imagine that such a show could exist in Germany. But after a while, this changed. The reason behind the change was none other than our friend Manfred Weissleder. He now used his former Star-Club connections to book acts from England and the U.S., and as he was well known there, this worked quite well. In December 1965, the "Beat-Club" was even able to present SONNY & CHER. The German record market became more and more interesting for foreign artists, and the "Beat-Club" was the main forum for pop music, from the SMALL FACES to Chris Andrews. Some of the bigger German acts like THE LORDS, THE GERMAN BONDS, THE REMO FOUR, or THE RATTLES also became regulars. German schlagers were a no-no, and Leckebusch made clear one point: Every song presented in "Beat-Club" had to be a German TV première. As far as I know, there has never been an exception.

Gerd Augustin left the "Beat-Club" after only eight episodes; he later became one head of the Munich-based Liberty label. Still today, he claims that Leckebusch elbowed him out for flimsy reasons.[1] He was followed by Dave Lee Travis, a DJ from pirate station Radio Caroline, and after him came a nice line-up of male hosts. The most prominent of them was Dave Dee (real name David John Harman, 1941-2009) of DAVE DEE, DOZY, BEAKY, MICK & TICH. After a while, the "Beat-Club" left the small Radio Bremen studio and moved into a storehouse in the suburbs of Bremen. This location was owned by Leckebusch himself. He now produced the show independently and licensed it to his former employer, a practice which is standard now, but uncommon at that time.

The viewer's reaction to the "Beat-Club" was extreme in both directions – positive as well as negative. Many adult viewers, my parents among them, were appalled – I can still see my father sitting on the sofa, shaking his head, complaining about these "long-haired cavemen" and the way they treated their instruments. This was a common reaction. The, at times, highly aggressive reviews and letters Radio Bremen received from critics and viewers are legendary. Mike Leckebusch went on leaving the TV audience feeling unsettled; he started using more and more new devices for electronic picture manipulation, and there was nearly no psychedelic effect he left out: melting faces, optical echoes and feedbacks, alternating between negative and positive, hard contrasts, permanent zooms and variation in camera angles, and strange picture-in-picture crossfadings – and all of this became even more extreme with the added fact that, in 1969, Germany finally developed colored TV.

It should be mentioned here that there was a Dutch director named Bob Rooyens who also launched visual effects in his shows on German TV; not as heavy as Leckebusch did, but he introduced them into "normal" schlager music shows, especially at ZDF – and of course, he too harvested head-shaking audiences and furious letters. But there was no way back. TV aesthetics, especially of TV advertising, followed these new technical possibilities. It's what normally happens: Give the makers a new toy and they will soon play with it to death until the next new toy is created.

In the same year, 1969, the "Beat-Club" changed its concept radically. The audience and go-go-girls were sent home, double-hosting stopped, and Uschi Nerke hosted the show on her own, sometimes underpinned by written inserts. The duration was extended to 60 minutes, with no more than two or three bands featured in one episode, sometimes only one, and most of them now actually played live. Sometimes the psychedelic effects went overboard to the extent that you couldn't recognize anything anymore, and a couple of times the camera operators went on strike because a band was extremely loud. Part of the studio decoration was a backline built from Orange amps and speakers. This was of course product placement and, as such, forbidden on German TV – officially.

But Leckebusch was not "official" TV, he was his own company, meaning that he was able to squeeze product placement into public TV. It usually worked quite well, and regardless of whatever there was to complain about, the "Beat-Club" became the most important platform for bands referred to as "progressive", like Atomic Rooster, Black Sabbath, Caravan, Curved Air, Deep Purple, Jethro Tull, Santana, Soft Machine, and many others. German bands like Can, Frumpy, or Kraftwerk also had a platform here now, and much of the stuff you can buy on DVD today that has to do with these bands comes from "Beat-Club" episodes.

The "Beat-Club" era ended in December 1972 after 84 episodes, when it became obvious that this concept wasn't widely compatible enough for Saturday afternoons anymore.

MUSIKLADEN

The follow-up became "Musikladen" (Music Shop). It was produced by the same team in the same studio "Beat-Club" had been and had the same theme music. Uschi Nerke had a co-host again (Manfred Sexauer, a radio host from Saarbrücken), go-go-girls and an audience were brought back, and the whole show now traded under the subtitle "TV Discotheque International", now primarily presenting what was popular in the charts at that time. Nonetheless, the "Musikladen" is worth mentioning for three reasons:

First: it was the first show to present promotional videos from the U.S. or England on German TV. This was something really new; the screening of the "Fade To Grey" video (which was directed by 10cc's Godley & Creme) pushed Midge Ure's then band, Visage, up to #1 on German charts.

Second: As a result, "Musikladen" became the TV show that established New Wave and New Romantics on German TV screens; acts like Blondie, the New York Dolls or Spandau Ballet appeared here first.

Third: From time to time there were "Musikladen Specials" with 45 minutes featuring only one act. All in all, 59 of these specials were made, and the important episodes had The Police, Roxy Music and Abba; the latter received numberless re-runs and was licensed worldwide. "Musikladen" changed its hosts a couple of times, Uschi Nerke left in 1979 (but today she's still radio-active, and runs a restaurant), the show was finally closed down in 1982 after 90 episodes.

4-3-2-1 HOT & SWEET

Other music shows on German TV were "4-3-2-1 Hot & Sweet" on ZDF TV, hosted mainly by schlager singer Suzanne Doucet and actor Ilja Richter. The basic idea was to introduce international pop stars, but this show never made a real breakthrough. Musically, it wasn't very interesting or important – the most unusual aspect was probably Suzanne's short haircut; something that was not really common on TV at that time. ZDF gave her the boot when it leaked that she did a similar show on Swiss TV; the TV top dogs were thin-skinned in things like that. "4-3-2-1 Hot & Sweet" aired from 1966 to 1970, ended after 23 episodes, and is widely forgotten about today. Suzanne lives in California as New Age music producer today. For Ilja Richter, the show became the start of "Disco".

DISCO

This one became more famous. Richter always appeared properly dressed in a suit and tie, and acted like an actor who had to take on the role of a music show host. For 45 minutes, "Disco" presented a cheesy collection of nearly anything available: schlager, pop, oompah folk, country, Liedermacher, and (later) Neue Deutsche Welle songs. There could be Mud with "Tiger Feet", followed by Tina York and the "Liechtensteiner Polka", followed by Gilbert O'Sullivan with "Clair", followed by Middle Of The Road with "Chirpy Chirpy Cheep Cheep", followed by Gloria Gaynor with "Never Can Say Goodbye", followed by Phil & John with a German cover version of "Hello, Mary Lou" – it was completely topsy-turvy. In contrast to other music shows, there was no real stage in the studio. The audience was placed on the floor or on low pedestals, and the singers and bands mimed to playbacks in the midst of their fans.

At one point during the show, there was a quiz: The viewers at home had to recognize a singer and send in a postcard with the name. Third place's prize was a transistor radio, second place's prize was a record player, and first place's prize was an invitation to the next taping of the show in Hamburg. The winner got to appear on TV. This was something very special at that time, so it was celebrated. Ilja used to shout: "And now, the absolute top winner of the first prize! Today live with us at 'Disco'! Lights down!" (Audience: "Woom!" – lights blacked out). "Spotlight on!" (Audience: "Yeah!" – spotlight on the winner). "Karla Knietschmann of Bielefeld!" Then, in the spotlight, usually a girl or boy between 12 and 14 with a sheepish grin appeared, sweating, shaking, not knowing where to look or what to do with their hands. Ilja went over to him or her for a handshake, asked two or three smalltalk questions, and handed a (usually humorous) gift to him or her. Fifteen seconds of fame, and on went the show. There was also a second running gag in every episode: Two or three times, pre-produced sketches were shown between the music pieces. They were a mix of 1950s comedy movies and 1920s piano chansons and were presented by Ilja Richter himself, sometimes with guests like his sister Janina or a celebrity from various categories. These sketches were written by Richter and his mother, and with all due respect, *never* have I *ever* met a single person who found them funny or wanted to see them. All of this happened in front of a teenage audience clapping along – they seemed to love simply everything.

All in all, *Disco* had 133 episodes and continued to air until November 1982. It was hard to tolerate, but we weren't too spoiled with the three TV programs we had at that time. We had to deal with what we got. I remember, however, that when a schoolmate managed to get ahold of two tickets for the show, they showed them proudly to everybody on the schoolyard – and to be fair, Ilja Richter is a friendly guy with a unique voice. He later became a light comedy actor and recorded several audio books.

ROCKPALAST

From 1974 to 1986, there was "Rockpalast", invented by Peter Rüchel (1937-2019), editor at WDR TV. These now legendary rock nights happened two times a year and usually consisted of three full live concerts from 11 pm until birds started to sing in the morning. The "Rockpalast" nights were broadcasted live by Eurovision all over Europe in mono on TV and – this was the real clue – simultaneously in stereo on most FM radio stations in Germany, Austria, and Switzerland. "Rockpalast" brought us acts like Willy DeVille, Rory Gallagher, Grateful Dead, Van Morrison, Mother's Finest, Joe Jackson, Little Steven, The Police, Patti Smith, Spirit, Roger McGuinn's Thunderbyrd, The Who, Johnny Winter, ZZ Top, and many more; even a Prince concert was shown via satellite. Youth centers organized "Rockpalast" parties, and tens of thousands of cassette decks were probably running in homes all over Europe.

In the mid-1970s, the "Rockpalast" concept was a sensation so completely new that it took a couple of episodes until the British and American artists' managements finally believed that this show really existed. On British TV networks, and even more on American, showing several hours of live rock concerts would have been unthinkable.

In addition to these live rock nights, "Rockpalast" had smaller shows, recorded live at different locations and usually cut down to 45 minutes. I remember the Steve Hillage Band or Graham Parker & The Rumour, but these smaller shows also were a podium for several German bands like Grobschnitt or Guru Guru – which was a sensation in itself at that time.

"Rockpalast" stopped in 1986 when it became obvious that the concept had jumped the shark. The last act, if memory serves correctly, was Kid Creole & The Coconuts. They had a pretty good show, but the audience didn't know what to do with them – usually, people had bought their tickets long before the acts could be announced, trusting it would be something good. But the "Rockpalast" team couldn't guarantee this anymore because they had to live more and more with so-called "package deals" – artists' managements said: You get act X only when you also take act Y. This didn't always end well.

In 1995, "Rockpalast" was reanimated, but as the music scene had changed, this time the show was connected to existing rock festivals like the Burg-Herzberg, Bizarre, or Loreley open airs with acts like PJ Harvey, Portishead, or David Bowie.

FURTHER SHOWS

Of course, there were more music shows on TV, but the ones mentioned here were particularly important for the music focussed on in this book.

There was "Musik aus Studio B". There was "Hits à gogo" with the Les Humphries Singers as the in-house band. There was "RockPop" on ZDF TV, where Kraftwerk's "Die Roboter" premièred (the excellently produced studio presentation can still be seen on Youtube). "RockPop" also had a sister show called "RockPop in Concert" which was a sort of response to the "Rockpalast" nights' full-length concerts, but they were pre-recorded.

There was "Bios Bahnhof", hosted (and produced) by Alfred "Bio" Biolek, broadcasted live from an old streetcar depot near Cologne. The in-house band was Peter Herbolzheimer Rhythm Combination & Brass. The show had an innovative concept: *Anything* was possible, from folk music to Stockhausen, Nam June Paik's video art to Mauricio Kagel's multimedia compositions, Reinhild Hoffmann's strange dance performance "Couch" to Folies Parisiennes. Sometimes, Biolek teamed two artists up who otherwise never had anything to do with each other, like Angelo Branduardi and Esther Ofarim, or Udo Lindenberg and Nana Mouskouri. Since this former depot had a railroad track and a platform, the stars sometimes entered the venue in historic wagons, like the legendary Trans-Europ-Express "Rheingold". Everything in this show had to be live, Biolek never made any exceptions. "Bios Bahnhof" facilitated the first appearances of Kate Bush, Laurie Anderson, Klaus Nomi or Sting on German TV screens, and a performance in this show often became a hot topic in German offices and schoolyards the next morning.

There was "Na sowas", hosted by Thomas Gottschalk; KRAFTWERK's "Das Model" had its German TV premiere there. "Szene" from BR TV Munich was a short-lived music show that was aired nationwide in the late 1970s; I remember a strange playback presentation of LA DÜSSELDORF's "Rheinita" there, as well as – in the same episode – the YELLOW MAGIC ORCHESTRA, which, as far as I know, never appeared anywhere else on German TV. They presented a song from their first album and had me immediately hooked.

WDR TV had two comedic music shows, "Plattenküche" and "Bananas". The first one was hosted by comedian/singer Frank Zander and actress Helga Feddersen, and mimicked a TV show where everything that could go wrong, went wrong. However, they had some top-notch acts in their show, CAN with "I Want More" was one of them, also LA DÜSSELDORF. "Bananas" had a similar concept; popular hits mixed with sketches presented by a group of comedians. The difference between both shows was that in "Plattenküche", the musical acts were part of the sketches and had to tolerate some nonsense done to them, like storm-producing wind machines, tipping sceneries, or stuff like this.

Then there was the very popular "ZDF-Hitparade". This was, as the name states, a classic hit parade, shown once a month and hosted by former car salesman and Radio Luxembourg DJ, Dieter Thomas Heck (1937-2018). The music was selected through an audience poll via postcard. In this show, only schlagers in German were allowed. A small exception was made when songs in English were also allowed to be voted for. Sometimes, this led to a red-letter episode when – for example – a schlager of schmaltz king Roland Kaiser was followed by a bluesy rock ballad by Joe Cocker, a combination that always left one part of the studio audience distressed, and after a couple of months this concept was stopped. For the schlager scene, this show was important. A rule of thumb stated: One appearance in the "ZDF-Hitparade" means around 30,000 sold records during the following week. For rock musicians, the "ZDF-Hitparade" was not of interest, except in the 1980s when the Neue Deutsche Welle came up – these acts usually led to unsettledness in the classic schlager-affine audience.

There were also several regional shows that had appearances from singers and bands. One of them was "Die aktuelle Schaubude" (which translates to something like "The up-to-date show booth") on NDR TV, broadcasted from 1957 to 2009, Saturdays between 7 and 8 pm, live from a car dealer's showroom in downtown Hamburg, usually with a small in-house audience and hundreds of spectators in the street, pressing their noses against the big store windows. With the start of color TV, the show moved into a real TV studio. The "Schaubude" was an adaptation of the American "Today's Show", a sort of magazine with regional policy, interviews with local politicians, fashion tips, gossip about movies, stars, and starlets – and the appearance of singers and bands, making it a must-see for us children in the 1960s. Usually, these performances contained a spectrum from schlager singer Ronny to British chart toppers like Barry Ryan, and without exception, they were lip-synced presentations in cheap-looking scenery sets. I remember when John Mayall & His Bluesbreakers appeared on this show, probably around 1968 or 1969. These guys had very long-hair at that time, and were consequently put into a scenery set that made them look like Neanderthals cowering somewhere in the woods. When the song was over, the host (a former fashion model) asked some people in the audience about the haircuts. It was embarrassing, and I don't dare to imagine what kind of impression John Mayall and his band mates took home with them after the show. But this was exactly the main understanding of popular entertainment at that time on German TV. This show was already outdated when it was new.

I will stop here. There will be more on music TV starting in the 1980s.

THE MISLEADING MAGIC OF SIXTY-EIGHT

1968, a magical number! Looking back, 1968 must have been a year that simply changed everything. But *in* 1968, the year was a year just like any other year. On New Year's Day of 1968, nobody knew how this year would be perceived in the future.

In his book "Der Wendepunkt" ("The Turning Point"), author Klaus Mann (1906–1949), son of Thomas Mann, had some very perceptive things to say about the German youth movement of the early 1920s:

> "The youth movement, like the dance art of Mary Wigman or poetry of Stefan George, can be understood only in the country of its origin. This boastful self-glorification of youth as an idealistic-revolutionary agenda, the establishing of a certain biological phase as an autonomic way of life: Only in Germany, something like this was possible. How unmistakably, how *dangerously* German is this mix of systematics and nebulousness, of revolutionary panache and malicious obscurantism that we find to be characteristic of the youth movement! Without question, the romantic rebellion against our mechanized epoch has seminal, truly progressive elements, but at the same time, it also holds the seed of disaster. Who could object to the heartfelt-enthusiastic penchant for old German songs and dances, against the pathos of *retour à la nature* with guitar, backpack, and alcohol-free drinks? But alas, these harmless games did not stay free from pretensions of a quite fatal kind. The 'Wander-

vogel' movement was not satisfied with just shocking a fossilized and prissy older generation by wearing fancy costumes or haircuts; instead, it aggrandized itself with a 'weltanschauung' in which the most manifold moods and confused tendencies are jumbled. Anti-progressive, nationalist-racist tendencies that were visible already on the ideological founders of the youth movement ... soon went out of hand. Finally the 'revolution of the youth' fell apart into a variety of certain groups, of which the most influential turned out to be the trailblazer of National Socialism."[1]

Leave out "National" and exchange Wandervogel with the upcoming European backpack tourism movement of the 1970s[2], and you will see: There is a parallel between the youth movement of the 1920s and the student movement of the 1960s and – later – the "alternative movement" of the 1970s. There is a certain radicalism that goes through the decades and centuries, starting in the era of romanticism. The "alternative movement" of the 1970s stood in the cycle of a tradition without being aware of it.

1967 had somehow been a relatively happy year in Germany. But for those who were willing to see, there were dark clouds approaching in the horizon. Economically, Germany had just survived a phase of an overheated boom. Things were going a bit downhill now – quite naturally, but some people used this as a signal to *think*; during the wirtschaftswunder years, Germany had gone nearly berserk with consumption – but could this go on forever? "Konsumterror" (consume terror) became a common phrase among students and some intellectuals. First, subtle ideas came up about how the pendulum might swing back. Consumer protection became a topic, especially in the media.

This year brought Flower Power, Mary Quant, Twiggy, and *Magical Mystery Tour*. Frank Zappa and his Mothers Of Invention were in talks in the upper grades of our school. Nobody really understood what Zappa and his gang did, but the magazines sold them as "progressive", and that was all you needed to know to share this vision.

The power suppliers placed TV commercials propagating the wonderfully endless new source of energy, nuclear power, and they used electronic music for these commercials, which had a great impact on me. The then popular and trusted TV science presenter, Professor Heinz Haber, was enthusiastic about it, especially about the fast breeder technology which, as he said, would "result in nuclear waste that gives us even more energy than the primary fuel rods." At that time, only few people realized that this concept strongly resembled a perpetual motion machine. Only few people recognized (and Haber didn't tell us) that nuclear waste would live extremely long, be extremely dangerous, and would have to be secured in safe places for thousands of years to keep clear of radiation exposure. Haber had learned his job at Disney's, and he had been a good scholar.[3] Critical minds, somebody like, say: Carl Sagan, were rare in Germany, and so for me, at least, nuclear energy sounded like the future itself. 1968 gave us Terry Riley's *A Rainbow in Curved Air*, a real milestone album, and Riley fantasized a future vision on the album's back sleeve: "... The energy from dismantled nuclear weapons provided free heat and light." Obviously I was not the only one whose ears found "nuclear energy" to sound fantastic (but well, I was 12 then).

Marshall McLuhan's book "Understanding Media" was published in German as "Die magischen Kanäle" and infused certain ideas into our brains about "the global village", something that sounded like both home and the entire Earth at the same time – a little touch of Stewart Brand, but Germany had nobody like him focusing on such ideas. The future and electronic media were main topics at that time. Everybody, even we school students, were discussing "The Hidden Persuaders" (originally released in 1957, but the German version, "Die geheimen Verführer", was not released before 1968), in which the writer, Vance Packard, told stories about "invisible advertising" that could manipulate consumers into buying anything the Mad Men and their accomplices from the psychology faculty wanted us to. In school, our German teacher recommended this book to us. With a little bit of logic, he (as well as everybody else) could have already seen, even then, that "invisible advertising" cannot work. Actually, what Packard hoaxed us into was a textbook example of selling "the emperor's new clothes": The whole "invisible advertising" thing was made up by (of course) an adman who wanted to sell "invisible ads". It was fraud, but it sounded so utopian, so true, and so American, it couldn't be wrong.[4] We *wanted* it to be true, just to have something we could object to. Why? In those days, advertising was one of the most hated things (because of the "Konsumterror" it was made for), nobody wanted to "fall for it". But at the same time it was one of the most fascinating things available. Ads were the place where the latest and newest graphic designs could be seen, especially the ones with the multi-colored melting fonts and the TV commercials with the strangest music. All this stuff was druggy without blatantly referring to drugs. Something we hadn't seen yet. "Druggy" – that was also one of the enthrallments of the time. It was not about cocaine or heroin yet (both came later), but we didn't know what was really behind this drug thing. Pot had been a topic for a while already. In the U.S., the main substance was "pot", "grass", or "weed", meaning marijuana. In Germany, if memory serves correctly, grass was not widely used – or I, at least didn't see it often. Hashish was en vogue (again, it should be said that it had already been en vogue in the 1920s[5]); the most popular cultivars were "Black Afghan" and "Red Lebanese". It was mostly called "dope"; I don't want to trot out the dozens of slang names it had locally. Most of them I've never heard of anyway. Now there were horror articles about LSD – sometimes *relatively* serious, as on TV or in the news magazine *Der Spiegel*, in political magazines like *Konkret*, and a bit too sensationally in magazines like *Stern* or *Quick*. In progressive pop magazines like *Sounds* it was a bit up tight, and in the German edition of *Reader's Digest* or the usual glossies, it took the form of pure horror stories. So it was clear to us that this must be something interesting.

The sounds coming over to Germany from England and the U.S. were also different now. The song structures were different, the musicians' appearances were different, and their approaches to music were different. Instead of the noisy and rather simplistic rock'n'roll or raw skiffle, bands now played much longer tunes with more sophistication and complex structures – a *Sounds* reviewer went skywards about GRATEFUL DEAD: "The music you can hear on *Anthem Of The Sun* is the most progressive pop music up to date: Use of electronics, modern forms, and rhythmic as well as harmonic complexity did not go – as usual in pop music so far – into symbiosis because of modernity, but here, for the first time in the history of pop music, with all these stylistic devices a masterpiece has been made."[6] This was the overall sound many reviews at that time had. Nobody knew exactly what was going on, but it sounded very concrete.

Sounds, by the way, was one of the most important voices for fans of all this new stuff. The magazine had been founded in 1966 as a jazz magazine, but then, one year later, starting with a review of Frank Zappa's *Freak Out*, it began to change more and more into a rock magazine and eventually became the most influential German rock music journal. When, in the late 1970s, *Sounds* started reporting more and more about Neue Deutsche Welle, it turned out that many readers were not interested in NDW, so *Sounds* went bust in 1983. The name was sold to Swiss publisher Jürg Marquard who already owned *Pop* and the Munich *Musik Express*. He combined them into *ME/Sounds*, but most of the better writers left and went to *Spex* (which was founded in Cologne in 1980).

Back to 1968: Many guitarists who thought they were talented had to learn that someone named Jimi Hendrix outdid anything ever played on their instrument. There were singers like Julie Driscoll or Janis Joplin who simply blew away most (white) vocalists in expressivity and skills. There were virtuosos on drums, like Ginger Baker or Keith Moon, who no longer saw themselves as rhythm slaves but as soloists in their own right. There was a bass guitarist named Jack Bruce who was able to take over the melodies on his bass that were typically played on the guitar – something that simply didn't exist before. There were bands like the previously mentioned GRATEFUL DEAD or JEFFERSON AIRPLANE, who didn't exactly know what they would play when they entered a stage, and their studio recordings were based on structures that were new, complex, and virtuosic. They had lyrics that were far from the simplicity of the early 1960's teenage broken hearts dramas. They came with elements of serious poetry like Bob Dylan, but also with witty, ironic nonsense like in JEFFERSON AIRPLANE's "White Rabbit": "Feed your head", as they invited us, and we did. Maybe not in the way it was meant, but at least acoustically.

One heard about psychologist Timothy Leary and his drug experiments at Harvard, and, although that had been in the early 1960s and was nearly forgotten about, his name continued circulating around. When Richard Nixon called him the "most dangerous man in America"[7], we found it a bit exaggerated (Nixon had problems of his own making and needed to deflect attention away from it). When Leary asked his audience to "turn on – tune in – drop out", he was not just calling for drug consumption to change one's mind, it was the other way round: A change of mind is required in order to detach from conventions and social rules. This claim is clearly different from what later drug generations had in mind when drugs became more and more a thing of party entertainment. Interestingly, the phrase came to Leary's mind while in the shower, after Marshall McLuhan had advised him to come up with "something snappy" to advertise his ideas. Leary himself hated to be called a "guru" or "priest"; he saw himself as "coach".[8]

THE TIMES, THEY ARE A-CHANGING

The record industry soon noticed that the 45 sales were on a downfall and the album was climbing up – not such a big deal in the beginning, but still big enough for the A&R people at major labels to see that something was going on that needed their attention.

These were all consequences of the fact that a couple of general changes had happened within the mid-1960s pop scene in England and the States. The most important one was that the prominent task sharing between songwriters and singers had ended. Since The Beatles, The Beach Boys, and singer-songwriters like Bob Dylan or Joni Mitchell became part of the scene and grew more and more successful, an increasing number of bands and solo artists followed them not only in writing their own song material, but in taking over the helm completely.

This had, of course, put the role of music producers into question, and the record labels lost a big part of their power over artists. The traditional producer who decided "his artists" by fiat and dictated songs, sound, image, styling, and pseudonyms to them, was no longer helpful for these new musicians. What artists needed now were producers who were able to recognize individual talent and willing to build the right working conditions to convey the musician's ideas in the best way. Without a doubt, the Brill Building people initially had no clue what to do with these new kinds of artists. But they figured it out.

German record companies and producers ignored most of these developments. Around 1966/67 in the U.S. and U.K., the album became more and more a medium of interest. This had not only to do with the musicians, but also with the fact that in the U.S., FM radio stations had discovered rock music, and with FM, terms like "hi-fi" and "stereo" came up. German record companies went on producing, primarily, two-minute-thirty-second tracks for the well-established 45, and whenever a producer or A&R man listened to the demo tape of a German band, the first thing he complained about was: "I don't see the single." The developing German rock scene, however, wasn't interested in this format anymore. They got along well with longer tracks that had a much wider dramaturgy.

There had always been a time gap of two or three years before trends from the U.S. spilled over to Germany. The album trend reached Germany around 1968/69, and at that point, some record companies reacted. This acted as a sort of starting line. The music that was on its way to becoming "Krautrock" couldn't have happened without this trend.

But it was not only the album trend that was vital. There were more things that left their mark on music itself. Much more beyond just music had changed during the time between circa 1964 and 1968. Slowly over time, the atmosphere in Germany had developed a latently bad smell. You could try to ignore it, but it disturbed the recently redeemed coziness. The economy was still up in the clouds, but this turned out to be precisely the problem; the overheated economy meant that crisis was in the air.

All the while, another danger was growing: the Cold War between the East and West, between the "free world" and "communism". The generation who had experienced WWII (or both wars) was in real fear that one of the many little conflicts in the world could explode and turn into another big war.

German society as a whole was re-established now, and now it experienced a mix between optimism, especially among young people, and uncertainty among older people who saw that some things were changing and did not know how to deal with it (but this might be the way life goes and every generation has to learn this).

In 1962, a group of 26 filmmakers had met at a festival for short films in Oberhausen in the Ruhr area and wrote the "Oberhausener Manifest": "Papas Kino ist tot!" (Dad's cinema is dead!). They developed new aesthetics in film; the "Neue Deutsche Film" movement lifted off and freed the silver screens from traditional conventions and taboos. Names like Rainer Werner Fassbinder, Werner Herzog, Edgar Reitz, Volker Schlöndorff, Alexander Kluge, Helma Sanders, and others, came up and made themselves known with a new concept they called "Autorenfilm" (author's film), which meant they held roles as screenwriters, directors, and (often) producers, all as one person. This didn't always work; sometimes it's quite useful to put these three jobs on three pairs of shoulders, but this was an experience they still had to make. However, to document the new concept, they called themselves "Filmemacher" (filmmakers) from now on. "Making" was en vogue anyway. The filmmakers' constant fight against old-fashioned institutions had finally led to the "Filmförderungsgesetz" (film funding act) in 1967, a law that started public film funding. The idea behind this was to take film production away from pure commercialism, making it possible to produce films independently with a main focus on art and quality, instead of the primacy of the box office. (What sounded positive in 1967 has become more and more problematic today. The public film funding system in Germany now has grown into an entanglement of local boards, panels and connections between funding institutions and the TV stations that practically nobody can see through anymore, all the more, as now also the EU is involved. No film producer today is willing anymore to take the risk of making a movie without being funded by one of these boards and a TV station. That means that in fact today it's no longer the producer, in the end it's the boards who decide which movie is made and which movie isn't. Anything but an ideal situation.)

When, in the mid-1960s, the pill came in use, Germans discovered sex. Okay, even before they must have known that something like that existed, but at this time, in movie theaters, a sex documentary film had become a big sensation: *Das Wunder der Liebe* (The Miracle of Love) by a Dutch-German journalist named Oswalt Kolle (1928-2010). On one hand, this movie was seen as scandalous, there was even a (mainly catholic) initiative named "Aktion saubere Leinwand" (something like "initiative for clean silver screens"). They had already targeted Ingmar Bergman's "scandalous" film, *Das Schweigen* (The Silence) from 1963, and then its members began to stand in front of movie theaters that showed Kolle's film and handed out flyers to the moviegoers about the increasing decay of morality: "Wir wollen saubere Filme" (We want clean movies) – that was the goal.

On the other hand, filmmakers had opened a new door, and it began to dawn on many people that it was long overdue to talk about love and sexuality more openly. Young people especially did it, although it sounded a bit contrived sometimes. One of the strangest outcomes of this new freedom was a series of cheap sexploitation movies under the main title *Schulmädchen-Report* (Schoolgirls Report). They were soft porn movies somewhere between ridiculous and sleazy, too harmless to be porn, pretending to be scientific reports about the love life of "today's schoolgirls". The *Report* series didn't stop before there were no less than 13 episodes, plus an offspring of several further "report" movies, from a *Hausfrauen-Report* (housewives) up to a *Blitzmädchen-Report* ("Flash Girls", during the Third Reich a common moniker for young women who were detailed to assist soldiers at the anti-aircraft gun; they were called this because of their collar patches: a stylized flash). All this stuff was lousy, yet successful, and the movie theaters around train stations had especially good business. One of the leading soundtrack composers of these "report" movies was Gert Wilden (1917-2015), schlager producer, arranger, and former leader of the TANZORCHESTER DES BAYERISCHEN RUNDFUNKS. Alongside this, he wrote a lot of advertising music. Today, he has a sort of "cult" status among fans of "German Sixties Easy Listening"; soundtrack records under his name can be easily found. Some of them are interesting to listen to because he was able to pick up and imitate the "vocabulary" of beat and soul without having much of a clue for what that really meant.

HIPPIES

In 1967, the media had given us lots of rumors and reports about a "Summer of Love" in San Francisco. There was a real leftist scene in the U.S., and there was a sort of "alternative scene" for people who tried new forms of community life and solidly united ways of acting. Hippies didn't need to be left-wing – some were, some were not. There were Korea and Vietnam veterans, many with psychological baggage, there were grassroots activists, lovers of macrobiotic food, communists, communist haters, acid heads, music lovers, free thinkers, gun freaks, whatever you want. Writers like Tom Wolfe, or later T.C. Boyle, transferred this amalgam into (sometimes brutally honest) novels.

But in Germany the real social background of the flower power movement was hardly reported on, so we heard about the hippie movement without knowing who and what it really was. The general opinion Germany had of the U.S was inconsistent. On one hand, America was the imperialist, half-fascist, capitalist, war pig, who occupied Germany, and owned the nuclear bomb. But on the other hand, America was also connected to all the good things we loved – freedom, democracy, progression, Donald Duck, Ginsberg, Dylan, Burroughs, great music, Hollywood – and the hippie movement. In the late 1960s, German media coverage focused mainly on the colorful surface: Hippies, pot, and free concerts in Golden Gate Park. It sounded like pure sunshine, and it came from the U.S., so it was perceived as fun and couldn't be bad.

Usually, and still today, the lore circulates in Germany that 1967 was the "happy" summer of love, while in 1968, problems started. In the summer of 1967, everything seemed to go well – but only from outside. San Franciscans were able to deal with incoming crowds peacefully (as long as the kids had money on them), music was great, radio DJs weren't venal, acid was clean, trips were full of rainbows, thanks to the Diggers the food was free, Hell's Angels were nice guys, nobody had a hump and nobody was cross-eyed, and the Mafia was somewhere far away in Italy. The future looked sunny to everyone.

But then, to everybody's surprise, in the summer of 1968, paradise fell apart when masses of clueless people flooded San Francisco because they had heard about 1967 and thought this could be repeated. Many of these kids came from the countryside and had never seen a city before. A growing number of psychos populated the streets and needed to be cared for. The trips got mixed with methamphetamine, and suddenly, heroin entered the game. Kids either puked their magic mushrooms all over the Golden Gate Park flower beds or were simply left alone to endure bad trips. The free kitchens realized it's true that there is no such thing as a free meal. Behind the scenes, Hell's Angels and Mafia took over the helm.

The chaos of 1968 had already laid out in 1967 – people simply enjoyed themselves too much to notice the infrastructure that was needed to keep this hippie paradise going. There had been an unbelievable naiveté among the now helpless helpers, and in 1968, their inexperience became dangerously obvious. Hippies had no idea how much the disdained civil society had already done in 1967 to avoid a disaster. The aggressive panhandling in the streets had been ignored and the organized crime that was part of the system had been overlooked. Few people wanted to see this in 1967. The few media that reported unadorned about the situation were seen as "poisoning" and, wherever possible, got blocked out. If you want to have a look at the dark sides of the glorious summer of love, Joan Didion's essay "Slouching Towards Bethlehem", written in 1967 (!), is a disillusioning eye-opener.[9]

The American music industry, of course, immediately saw the money that was in this movement. All major labels began to open branches in San Francisco. Between summer 1967 and summer 1968 no less than eight large, professional sound recording studios were founded in the city. In 1968, these new businesses increased the economic value of San Francisco by 6 million dollars. The city was the new center of American rock and pop music.

Successful rock groups didn't see any problem. They lived in their own bubble and had enough money to not be reliant on looking under the golden surface. They had their footboys. As much as I love the Airplanes, listening to armchair-anarchistic songs like "Volunteers" or "We Can Be Together" makes you shake your head. At the latest, when "San Francisco" by Scott McKenzie became a giant hit, everybody could have seen that something was wrong in paradise. Woodstock already was a sort of open-air fancy-dress ball of the hippie movement – Altamont sealed it in 1969.

GAMMLER

Germany, as described earlier, had no such center where an ignition like the San Franciscan could happen. What we heard was double-edged. Everything that came from America was fascinating, yet, simultaneously, so far away, nobody in Germany had seen the commercial and social aspects of the San Francisco scene – in a good way as well as in a bad way: There was a fearfulness, but also a certain naiveté in view of the hippie movement. Papers and news magazines, especially the tabloids, wrote about it more or less as a sex & drug story, but nobody (particularly in the German music industry) had the idea to make use of this trend yet. German parents at this time were afraid this movement could spill over to Germany with all of its uncontrollable anti-authoritarianism. They were shocked when the first so-called "Gammlers" (deadbeats) appeared in parks and streets, sitting around, drinking beer, smoking, playing guitar, smooching ... When, in a TV report, some passers-by were asked about them, things like "concentration camp", "they should be gassed", or "into the labor camp with them" were stated openly into the camera. We can be sure the reporters had to search a while for these extreme statements, but it was possible to find them. The extremely hateful reactions that these men and women harvested from the so-called "average people" for just sitting on public lawns and doing nothing were unbelievable. Apparently, it was impossible for adults to imagine (and even more to accept!) that someone could have focused on life other than work, marriage, children, a car, and a garden with a trellis-work fence. Germans always have the tendency to go overboard when they fear that someone could live off them.

Sometimes in TV reports about Germany, and also on some Sixties samplers (like *Hippies, Hasch und Flower Power – 68er Pop aus Deutschland* [various artists, 2008]), you can hear a recording by Freddy Quinn from November 1966, entitled "Wir" (We); a harsh protest song against gammlers, hippies, and other troublemakers.

In a malignant way, this song puts "them" against "us" – "us", of course, refers to the society of respectable citizens. It's a bit reminiscent of Merle Haggard's "Okie from Muskogee", but it is more acidic. The song was on the B side of "Eine Handvoll Reis" (A Handful of Rice), a hardly bearable hommage to military missions somewhere in exotic foreign countries which, in 1967, went to #6 of German and #7 of Austrian charts. I never heard one of the songs at that time, both sides of the 45 obviously had little airplay. Freddy himself, I heard in a recent interview, is not very proud of "Wir", but in the 1960s, schlager singers were simply expected to sing what their producers had chosen for them. Had he not done it, Polydor would probably have made no bones about firing him, even more so since he was not the label's top act anymore, like he had been ten years before.

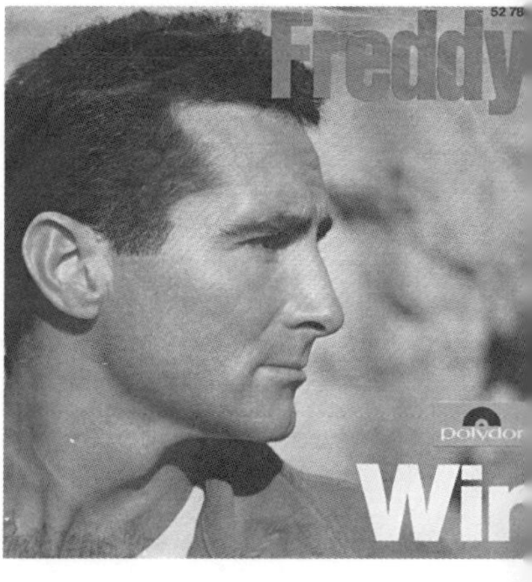

However, it wasn't rock music, it was the schlager industry that was first to finally jump on the hippie bandwagon. How else could it have been? Schlagers were always quick to join trends. Suddenly, schlager singers appeared with long hair on TV – as semi-tolerant adults tended to say: "I don't have anything against long hair, but it has to be well-groomed." When the news about "Swinging London" reached Germany, it only took a few weeks until schlagers talked highly about it, usually in a slightly humorous way, and in view of only the colorful surface – like Peggy March: "In der Carnaby Street" (which was originally a flip side, but later became a major hit).

RIOTS

There was not only fun and good moods at this time – there was also a war in Vietnam, and that angered students: Although they, as mentioned, felt deeply connected to the music and culture of the U.S., it was the same U.S. that was fighting and feeding into this obviously dirty war. On TV and in the papers, German students saw protests led by their fellow American and French students, and something unpredictable was accumulating across universities. All of this was in the air, but the trigger for the following riots was a trinity of events that stirred up students and other young people.

First was Shah Mohammad Reza Pahlavi of Persia and his wife Farah Diba, visiting West Berlin on June 2, 1967. This visit led to a protest against him, his politics, and his visit. It was during the daytime and the protesters were not a crazy large group – something between 400 and 1000 people. They created a lot of noise but weren't violent. There was also a group of well-dressed, probably planted, Persian students who rallied *for* Shah. They went into the vernacular as "Jubelperser" (cheering Persians), meaning "claqueurs" or "wrong applauders". They had banners on wooden slats with them, and suddenly, as if on cue, they took these slats, steel pipes, and nightsticks, and started brutally beating up the protesters. Several dozens of protesters were badly hurt. Hundreds of policemen, many of them on horseback, watched the scene and did absolutely nothing. Finally, after several minutes, also as if on cue, they reacted. But don't think they stopped the Jubelpersers – no, they helped them beat up the protesters. Baton-wielding, with unbelievable brutality and aggression, they chased the protesters through the streets. This led to counter riots and the power exercised by police officials went completely out of control. Water cannons and tear gas followed – scenes you wouldn't forget if you had seen them on TV. Even more, if you got the message directly hammered onto your skin.

Part two of the trinity followed only a few hours later: RIAS radio had reported on the incidents of that day and, because of these reports, more people decided to protest in the evening against the Shah and his wife who had planned to visit a performance of Mozart's *Zauberflöte* at the Deutsche Oper Berlin. Most of the protesters had the intention to go home when the Shah and his entourage entered the opera house, but then the Jubelpersers struck a second time. During the chaos that followed, police officer Karl-Heinz Kurras felt "threatened" by a non-armed, 26-year old student named Benno Ohnesorg. From a short distance he fired a shot into the back of Ohnesorg's head. Ohnesorg died immediately. Kurras fit the image of an "old Nazi". (As we know today, Kurras was a so-called "IM", an informal cooperator of the "Stasi", the State Security Service of the GDR. But that doesn't make anything better.)

Now, the student movement had its first victim of excessive police violence. Many protesters were convinced that on this day, the "fascistic government" had shown its true colors, and they radicalized themselves.

Students grew more and more critical about their own situation, as well as politics in general, and protests became more radical and better organized. In West Berlin, the "Kommune 1" became a focal point of resistance. It had been founded by, among others, Dieter Kunzelmann (1939-2018), Fritz Teufel (1943-2010), and Rainer Langhans; at the beginning, this was not much more than a politically motivated idea for a room-sharing community, but after a while it was not only rooms that were shared. It became an attempt to develop new forms of living together, privately as well as politically – and everything private was now seen as political.

The communards prepared the so-called "pudding assassination" on U.S. Vice President Hubert H. Humphrey when he visited West Berlin. This was meant to be a satirical action, but of course, the police didn't find any satire in it. Eleven students, among them Kunzelmann, Langhans, and Teufel, were remanded in custody, and even the *New York Times* described their actions as dangerous.

When parts of the "Kommune 1" relocated to Munich, the more radicalized "Kommune 2" (or in short: K2) was created in West Berlin. It was a sort of second generation. One of its members was Jan Carl Raspe who later connected with the "Baader Meinhof Group". Hans-Joachim Roedelius was in touch with the communards: "I knew some guys like Andreas Baader and Ulrike Meinhof who were later infamous because of their 'Red Army Faction' (RAF). I frequented the political K2 commune. But it was just out of curiosity, just to watch how they behaved. I couldn't agree to their extreme programs because they only cared about themselves, they were always freaked out on chemicals. I ended up looking after their children who'd been left alone while their parents were in eternal discussions. I decided it was better for me to protest in my own way, with my own 'art of noise.'"[10]

Rudi Dutschke (1940–1979) was a student of sociology, ethnology, philosophy, and historical science at the Free University Berlin. He was the publisher of a magazine called *Anschlag* (which in German could mean "attack" as well as "placard"), and he worked actively with the SDS (Sozialistischer deutscher Studentenbund, translated to Socialist German Students' League) on organizing protest marches and other actions against the emergency legislation, the grand coalition, and the war in Vietnam, so he had become a sort of spokesman of the student movement. At a rally, speaking in front of around 12,000 students, he had requested all American soldiers in Vietnam to desert from the army. This led to a reaction: On February 21, 1968, West Berlin saw a pro-America rally. Some people carried banners, spelling "Public Enemy No. 1: Rudi Dutschke". A passer-by who happened to look like Dutschke had to thank his stars that the crowd didn't strike him dead when they spotted him.

On April 3, 1968, later RAF members Andreas Baader and Gudrun Ensslin set two department stores in Frankfurt on fire. "In consent with Andreas Baader I want to declare: He and I did it at the 'Kaufhaus Schneider' … We did it in protest against the people's indifference about the genocide in Vietnam"[11] is what Gudrun Ensslin later stated to the judge.

All of this was accompanied by more and more instigative media coverage, especially by the tabloid *Bild*. On April 7, 1968, *Bild* commented: "We are not allowed to go back to normal from what is currently happening. And we are also not allowed to leave all the dirty work to the police and their water cannons. Are our judges sleeping? Are our politicians sleeping? How long will they continue to accept that our young people get incited by red agitators, that our laws get questioned, undercut and violated?"[12] A few days later, *Bild* called on their readers to "capture" the "ringleaders".[13] Implicitly, this was not far from being a call for vigilante justice, and every reader knew exactly who it was meant for.

This finally led to the catastrophe that became the third major trigger event: In West Berlin on April 11, 1968, an instigated right-wing scatterbrain shot Rudi Dutschke three times, then took flight into a basement nearby and tried to commit suicide with 20 sleeping pills, but he was found and rescued. Dutschke survived after several hours of surgery. His brain was damaged, he had to relearn how to speak from scratch, and suffered from epilepsy for the rest of his life.

An epileptic seizure led to his death: Rudi Dutschke drowned in his bathtub on Christmas Eve 1979. Whether you like him or not: It was Dutschke and his companions who cracked the encrusted way of thinking that was a basic part of the German society during the 1950s and 1960s.

TERROR

These three events, that's my conviction at least, were the original triggers for the start of a terror movement in Germany. The first terror group that came up was connected to the shooting of Benno Ohnesorg: the "Bewegung 2. Juni" (2 June Movement), founded in 1971. Two of its founders, Ralf Reinders and Ronald Fritzsch, later said: "The real politicizing didn't come before the shooting of Benno Ohnesorg on June 2, 1967. After all the poundings and floggings, we had the feeling that the cops had shot all of us. Partly, you could resist against being beaten up. But when someone simply gets bumped off, that goes a bit further."[14]

This "movement" was accountable for several bomb attacks, bank robberies, and the murder of the President of the Berlin Superior Court of Justice, Günter von Drenkmann, in a kidnapping attempt. In 1975, they took the CDU frontrunner for mayor, Peter Lorenz, hostage and obtained the release of several imprisoned terrorists who were then brought to South Yemen. While the later "Red Army Faction" was more on the Marxist side, the "2 June Movement" was an anarchist sect – in some parts, there were the same people involved.

Then, partly in personal union with this movement, there was the "Baader Meinhof Group"; later, they called themselves "RAF" ("Rote Armee Fraktion", translated to "Red Army Faction"). First, they had no real impact. But the situation became more and more heated. In May 1968, the Bundestag, Germany's parliament, had the unfortunate idea to establish a new law called the "emergency act". Its purpose was mainly to make it so that some basic constitutional rights could be declared out of power in case of crisis situations. Conservative politicians saw this as inevitable in order to react in an appropriate way to such situations. The flaw was that they didn't define what "crisis situation" meant. Of course, the student movement and its leaders saw this law as a reaction to protests and other acts of civil disobedience. So, they reacted. In all main cities, further fueled by the students' riots that happened in Paris at the same time, this led to some of the most aggressive protests ever seen in Germany, something that is still known as "Easter riots" and "hot May". All of this marked the beginning of the time of terrorism which finally ended in the "Deutsche Herbst" (German autumn of terror) later in the 1970s.

SIGNIFICANT CHANGES

Reading the above paragraphs about riots, student protests, and terror, can easily give you the impression that Germany must have been in permanent uproar at that time, and that's exactly what many "kraut" musicians state in interviews. But is this true? What did the Sixty-Eight student movement do to German society?

Naturally, the student riots made a lot of wind in the media, but let's face it: No, Germany was not in uproar. Germany was not even in danger of getting in any kind of serious trouble. The more documentaries you watch about these riots, the more you will realize that it's always the same three or four clippings of street protests that are shown. To be able to classify what these "student protests" meant, it's quite useful to know these numbers: In 1960, only 6 percent of all 18 to 20-year-olds were enrolled at a university. Doing academic studies was a privilege of few. In 1970, this already increased to 12 percent. In 1980, it continued to 19.5 percent, in 1990 to 30.4 percent, and in 2010 to 45.2 percent. If you prefer absolute numbers: In 1965, Germany had a total of 245,000 students at universities, in 1975 there were 836,000, in 1989 1.5 million, and in 2013 2.6 million.

These significant changes in the mid-1970s came when, after the elections in 1969, the conservative CDU lost to a coalition of the social democratic SPD and the liberal FDP (Freie Demokratische Partei, Free Democratic Party) for the first time after the war. ("Liberal" is meant here in the way the term is used in Europe. Americans usually see it as "left-wing", but in European countries the term is connoted with liberty, civil rights and a government that acts reservedly.) Germany's new Chancellor became Willy Brandt. If you didn't experience it yourself, you probably can't imagine what this meant after 25 years of a conservative government. One of the first things the new government started was the "education offensive" with the goal of bringing more people to universities, especially working-class children.

The latter was something not everybody liked. Many of Germany's established academics were not happy – they would have preferred to remain a closed elitist circle. A lot of professors were, let's say, irritated. At that time, their academic culture was still very traditional, they even wore black gowns during their lectures. It was all the more refreshing when, in 1967 at the University of Hamburg, some students crashed a university director ceremony by entering the Auditorium Maximum with a banner spelling "Unter den Talaren – Muff von 1000 Jahren!" (Under the gowns – bad smell of 1000 years!). The resulting photo circulated and made this one of the central slogans of the student movement.

The number "1000", by the way, was not chosen randomly; it was meant as a reminder to the "Thousand Year Reich" in which many of the professors had already been professors or were at least climbing up the academic ladder. Now, suddenly, this venerable magnificence was open to attack and became a joke. This was a shock for many professors.

At this time, it was still a real privilege to be able to visit a university. Most young people never saw a university from the inside. They finished school, decided what profession would be right for them (or what parents, uncles and friends decided would be best for them), and then they went into an apprenticeship for three years. After finishing this, they were certified in their profession, and at that time a profession was seen as something you would learn once and execute for the rest of your life, until retirement.

Sometimes, when talking about these years, one might think there were only students and adults living in Germany. When you watch documentaries, especially, it's easy to get this impression. But the real changes that resulted from 1968 were much more subtle.

MUNICH RIOTS AND THE START OF KRAUTROCK

From 1966 to 1969, Germany had been ruled by a grand coalition of both its major parties, CDU and SPD. Together, they had a two-thirds majority in the Bundestag. Only one small party was left as their opposition: the liberal FDP. This led to the formation of the APO (Außerparlamentarische Opposition, translated to extra-parliamentary opposition), formed mainly by students and trade unions.

In Munich, one of the most active towns in the context of student and APO protests, composer, conductor, and musician Eberhard Schoener fired off a cultural multimedia spectacle with readings, music, and acting entitled *(A)lter (A)ction* at the Haus der Kunst. It started on Easter Monday 1968, three days after the assassination attempt on Rudi Dutschke. Schoener was not only conducting, but had also organized the entire presentation. *(A)lter (A)ction* was a sort of opera, written by Egisto Macchi, about poet and actor Antonin Artaud's last days in the madhouse. (Artaud, 1896–1948, was a French playwright, director, actor, poet of ecstasy and morphine addict, had been declared a public danger and was sent again and again to a psychiatric ward where he was diagnosed with schizophrenia. He was treated with electric shocks, mercury, bismuth and several other unhealthy things. He died of cancer, two years after being discharged.) In Rome, this work's premiere had been prohibited by order of police. In Munich, the opera was now scheduled to be shown for 14 days. It was set on four stages with simultaneous actions. It used ballet dancers, the Munich Chamber Opera Orchestra (a festival orchestra Schoener had founded in 1965), a rock band, some singers with extreme voices, and professionals as well as laypersons. Toys were used as musical instruments, there were slide and film projections, strobe lights (the latest sensation then), and dancer Heino Hallhuber, performing as Artaud, was hanging topsy-turvy from the ceiling for nearly 20 minutes.[1] In a way, with the Haus der Kunst, Schoener had found a fitting place for the show: In 1937, the Nazis had presented their infamous exhibition about "degenerate art" at this location. Now, used as the set for this piece, the high room had an atmosphere of emptiness and looked strangely absurd, nearly frightening.[2] Florian Fricke, future head of POPOL VUH, working as a critic for the influential newspaper *Süddeutsche Zeitung*, wrote a review for the evening: "Aside from the result, as well as from the fact that the 'new' is not always really new outside of Munich, the attempt deserved to be welcomed and is interesting, even in its failure."[3] Other critics, however, spoke of the "360-degree-event"[4] as "mammoth dilettantism"[5]. Boulevard paper *Abendzeitung* even ranked the event as "stammering of a morphine addict"[6]. News magazine *Der Spiegel* complained that "outside, in the streets of Munich, there was much more provocation going on at the same time, that is for sure."[7]

It was exactly this that turned out to be the problem. The students, who Schoener and his team had counted on as being the main audience, didn't show up. They were busy blocking off the delivery of the tabloid *Bild* to retailers. *Bild* was seen as being accessory in the assassination attempt on Rudi Dutschke, and the APO protesters were furious. Of course, this led to loads of trouble – to put it mildly. It led to what is known as the "Easter riots" in Munich: 60,000 people (most but not all were students) in several street battles all over the town collided with 21,000 policemen. Around 1000 people, many of them not involved in any fights, were arrested. A press photographer was fatally injured by a stone, more than 4000 people overall were injured, and one died.

Schoener, who in actuality sympathized with the students, was in hot water. Sponsors pulled out when they saw that only a handful of spectators came to the show. Schoener, however, quickly tried to turn things around by showing paid advertisements on the silver screens during intermissions. This was a completely new idea; no one had done this during an opera performance before. Nevertheless, he was finally left with a deficit of 40,000 D-Marks; for him at that time, this was an unaffordable amount. A TV production of *(A)lter (A)ction* for BR TV Munich followed, but even this didn't bring him out of the red. Schoener: "This meant going on, to see to it that money came in. I felt very committed to Fassbinder who used the budget for a new film to pay off his debts for the old one."[8]

The situation in Munich remained high-voltage. Protests went on, now (as described before) against the "emergency act", and they were more furious than before.

It was on one of these days in the heat of May 1968 – nobody remembers the exact date – that somewhere in one of the squatted rooms of Munich University, the first public performance of Amon Düül took place.

THE DNA OF KRAUTROCK

This event, I believe, marks the birth of the first generation of bands playing what later became known as "Krautrock". Amon Düül wasn't the only one; there were several bands playing rock music of different variations, but the true early "kraut" projects you can count, were: Amon Düül, Amon Düül II, Can, and Guru Guru Groove – that was more or less it in the beginning. These four projects can be seen as the pioneers that started the metamorphosis of German bands from being carbon copies of British or American bands into forming something completely new. They formed into something that turned out to be an adventure, but nobody knew it at the time. In Düsseldorf, Kraftwerk's predecessor, Organisation, hadn't really started yet, and in West Berlin, Tangerine Dream (former The Ones) was already active, but in this early state it was not much more than an unknown guitar band with a psychedelic touch. Conrad Schnitzler's and Hans-Joachim Roedelius' Human Being had been a more or less spontaneous project, not quite a band. Later, Dieter Moebius joined them and the three of them founded Kluster, but this was not before 1969. In Munich, connections between Christian Burchard, Lothar Meid, and Dieter Serfas already existed, but Embryo had not been founded yet. The only thing that seemed to be clear to everyone was that the beat era was dead – nobody was interested in playing "beat music" anymore.

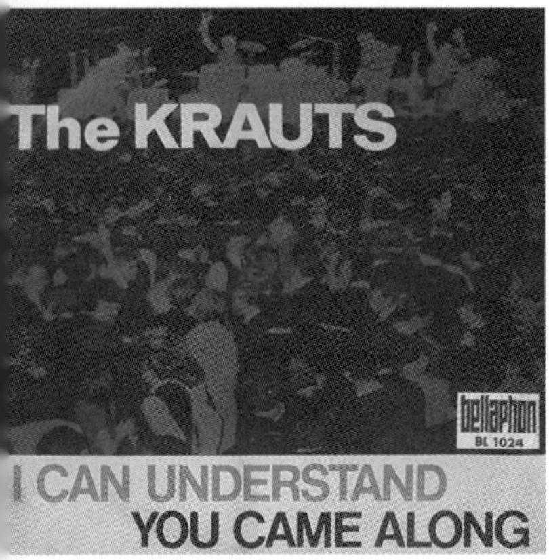

There are several explanations for who invented the "Krautrock" label. Jean-Herve Peron of Faust ascribes it to the co-head of Virgin Records: "The term was created by Simon Draper of Virgin when he scouted for new German acts. The English press was thankful for that tongue-in-cheek term. We wanted to show that Germans also have humor, and decided: 'You call it Krautrock – so we gonna krautrock you.'"[9]

But no. The term's initial use was much earlier, by a long forgotten band from Frankfurt: THE KRAUTS – "I Can Understand"/"You Came Along" (1965). And when AMON DÜÜL, on their first album *Psychedelic Underground,* had a track entitled "Mama Düül und ihre Sauerkrautband spielt auf", British journalists just needed to pick it up, and there was the boilerplate.

There has never been a clear definition of what that "Krautrock" really is. The term has never been (and was never meant to be) a seal of quality. It is a sort of stopgap definition for a small sub-category of rock music, produced by German bands between 1968 and circa 1977. The term was especially connected to music that was (or seemed to be) drug-fueled, psychedelic, included long improvised passages, was often played using strange electronic instruments and smashed classic song structures and pop music's three-minute scheme.

On the production side, there were just a handful of producers recognizing that something new was growing in the garden of music, but none of them had a clear idea about what these bands needed. Some lonely folks prepared ground, but to really ignite German rock, producers and sound engineers like Conny Plank, Dieter Dierks, and Rolf-Ulrich Kaiser were needed. They, however, were not part of the game yet. Siggi Loch and Gerhard Augustin were now in Munich at work, managing the German branch of U.S. label Liberty Records. They mainly worked in the schlager, folk, and Liedermacher (singer-songwriter) area, with acts like Vic Dana, Suzanne Doucet, Katja Ebstein, and others, but at least they were willing to sail out to new territories.

The first producer who actually jumped on the German rockwagon was Peter Meisel (1935–2010), schlager producer and music publisher from West Berlin. In 1962, with his brother Thomas and composer Christian Bruhn, he founded Hansa Music Production, which two years later became a record label of the same name. At the Essen festival he had signed AMON DÜÜL, TANGERINE DREAM, XHOL CARAVAN, and BIRTH CONTROL.

AMON DÜÜL was a chaotic bunch, mainly consisting of non-musicians, viewing themselves as a collective of artists. Some of them could play two or three chords on a guitar, while others were able to tap on the bongos. At that time, this sort of cheap percussion instrument and wandervogel guitars were found in every flat sharing community. In the beginning there were no "real" musicians; but regardless, making music was one of several projects of this artists' community that had named itself after the Egyptian divinity "Amon" (or "Amun"). Nobody knows where the (meaningless) word "Düül" came from. Sometimes it's said to be Turkish for "moon", but that's not true. I remember, darkly, that for a short time we kids used the phrase: "Willst du mich düülen?", which meant something like "Are you kidding me?". So there might be a connection, but even if there were, nobody could tell whether the phrase followed the band or the band followed the phrase. The main thing, however, was that the name sounded mysterious.

Peter Meisel had no idea how he could seriously produce a record with this bunch of weirdos, so he simply put them into a studio and recorded what happened. This way, after endless hours of editing and tape splicing, AMON DÜÜL's first album, *Psychedelic Underground,* became an adventure of a very special sort: uncoordinated, spontaneous, chaotic, and psychedelic. Not only "Mama Düül's Sauerkrautband" was striking up here, the band also took a walk "Im Garten Sandosa" (In Sandosa's Garden) – the latter of course was a bow to Albert Hofmann, the "father of LSD", who worked as a pharmacologist at the Sandoz corporation in Switzerland. The recording session was a spontaneous trip in its truest sense. There was no finished composition and no concept; nobody had a clear idea about what should happen next. So, a guitarist beat one and a half chords out of his guitar, a percussionist showed that he hardly had any idea about rhythm, a singer screamed incomprehensible syllables at the top of his lungs, fashion model Uschi Obermeier and some other c-list celebs rattled with maracas and tambourines, and somewhere in the background, a child was crying. The sound engineer, whoever he was, gave up any kind of control, and the entire LP became heavily distorted from beginning to the end. But maybe that was intentional – I have no idea.

Meisel didn't know what to do with this stuff, so he shut the tapes away. He unblocked them not before *Phallus Dei* (the first album released by AMON DÜÜL's split-off project AMON DÜÜL II) was out; he thought he might append to it.

Psychedelic Underground was released in 1969 on Metronome, which was not just a major label, but the well-established German branch of a Swedish parent company specializing in mainly jazz (Stan Getz, Sonny Rollins, Zoot Sims and others), sixties pop, and schlager (THE EDSELS, Jørgen Ingmann, Siw Malmkvist et cetera). At that time, the Hamburg-based Metronome was the German distributor of Meisel's Hansa label; in the 1970s, it became important for the German rock scene as the home of Brain Records.

I know: Some hardcore Krautrock connoisseurs consider *Psychedelic Underground* to be a special gem. I, for my part, consider it to be one of the lousiest albums ever produced. A nameless reviewer in the German *Sounds* claimed to hear "numerous reminiscences to American archetypes": "From the Mothers to Grateful Dead to Velvet Underground every new idea is present"[10]. It's hard to believe that this critic ever even listened to the record. How can anybody with functioning ears and a functioning brain between them not realize that there's a *world* of difference between the Velvets and Amon Düül, and what do you have to smoke to compare this record to the Dead – even if you set their experimental early works like *Anthem Of The Sun* as a benchmark? It's a mystery. Maybe the reviewer simply had no idea what to make of this album and didn't want to say anything wrong. Commercially, *Psychedelic Underground* was not successful. Admittedly, it is a unique document of the beginning of a trip into the unknown. But whatever one might call this album, there's no way to take it seriously in the context of music.

The follow-up, *Collapsing Singvögel Rückwärts & Co.* (Collapsing Songbirds Backwards & Co.; 1969), probably used material from the same sessions. Some sources say the material was recorded during a second session, shortly after the first one, but there's no way to confirm this. The same players shot again and the album was not much different from the first one, except maybe a bit more advanced in editing techniques. Obviously the post-production process had been handled a bit more thoughtfully. Another album with material from these session(s) was *Disaster/Lüüd Noma*, a double LP that was released in 1972 when the band had already been buried. This release was obviously an attempt from the BASF label to use up the remains, while their press info proclaimed that all mistakes and glitches were intended. (Nice try.)

Amon Düül's *ParaDieswärts Düül*, which was chronologically the third album, was a different kind of beast. It was recorded in 1970 at Cineton Studios in Munich and released on Rolf-Ulrich Kaiser's Ohr label. The producer was Julius Schittenhelm who had also produced the first Guru Guru album, *UFO* (later he became a political singer-songwriter, creating his material himself). The sound quality is much better here, and the tunes have a recognizable structure. This is no wonder: Aside from some of the usual non-musician suspects, John Weinzierl, Ulrich Leopold, and Christian Thiele (a.k.a. Shrat) are involved here, the guys who later switched over to AMON DÜÜL II. So there's a little bit more talent and professionalism available to the ear. It doesn't make this an interesting album, but at least a noticeable stride in progress and learning had happened.

In 1977, Peter Leopold, who was involved in the first AMON DÜÜL album and later became AMON DÜÜL II's drummer, in an interview with NDR radio host Klaus Wellershaus commented on this chaotic phase: "The ideologists came and said, 'Everybody has to make music now. Music has to be made by all people. Everyone who somehow is able to do so is allowed now.' First of all, this was mainly a social need, like watching TV together, having conversations, or going to the movies. Then we tried to transpose this concept onto the stage. But the stage somehow produces distance. Only things that stand out from the norm should be put on a stage. If you get into a situation where twenty people in the audience are better guitarists than the guitarist on stage, it turns down the whole audience. But at that time, we thought, 'That's a good model, we should stay the course.' And with that attitude, we were able to do this for a while."[11]

Not only AMON DÜÜL thought this way. Several bands, especially a bit later in the early 1970s, developed this attitude as well. They heard the first VELVET UNDERGROUND album and thought: "Oh, that should be easy. We can do that." But no, they couldn't. Somehow, this was the same error in reasoning that many people had made about free jazz: They took being incompetent as a qualification to make noise. Several bands didn't see this difference, or didn't want to see it. They called "improvisation", what was in fact just blind chaos and an unwillingness to practice and rehearse, and when they got booed off the stage, they put the blame for their failure on the audience, claiming the audience was "not yet ready" for them.

The opposite was also possible. This idea that "everybody has to make music now" made portions of the audiences feel invited to "participate" in performances, even in different genres. Karlheinz Stockhausen wrote about a performance of *Stimmung* (which could mean "Mood" as well as "Tuning"), a meditative vocal composition for six vocalists that uses overtone singing and requires a lot of concentration to be performed: "In 1969, at the Holland Festival in Amsterdam, in the sold-out Concertgebouw a performance of *Stimmung* which started especially well, after around 20 minutes got disturbed by circa a dozen 'Provos', so-called 'left radical students', with cats' meowing to the point that we had to stop the performance. Among the many disrupters, as the papers wrote, were 'modern' Dutch composers; and in a following panel discussion, which was more a manifesto, some declared they wanted to 'participate', and if the music wouldn't make this possible, it would be 'authoritarian'. The journalism screwed this up and distended this incident so much that in German radio broadcasts finally got divulged, the work 'lacked social necessity.'"[12]

IS EVERYBODY AN ARTIST?

Behind the concept of Amon Düül, Peter Leopold's statement, behind this whole way of thinking about "participating", you can always hear a famous Joseph Beuys quote: *Everybody is an artist.* It is spun off of a quote by poet Novalis (1772–1801): "Everybody can be an artist." Many referred to Beuys' quote, but it had been misunderstood then and has been misunderstood up to the present day.

Joseph Beuys (1921–1986) held the chair for "monumental sculpting" at the Kunstakademie Düsseldorf; large parts of his work dealt with social philosophy, humanism, and anthroposophy. He saw himself as a sort of modern shaman: "With great intent, by using this picture of the shaman, I tried to say something like this: We have a materialistic concept of science claiming that everything the shaman claims does not exist. Now, a person appears who definitely knows the methodology of materialism and, again, demonstrates that there are completely different forces in the world, from which man is currently being systematically cut off by the political systems."[13] We are allowed to assume that the "person" Beuys mentions is himself. Beuys knew that, of course, not everybody has the talent to be an artist, when it comes to the meaning of "painter", "sculptor", "musician", or "composer": "With this, I don't say anything about quality. I only speak about the general possibility that lies in everybody."[14] What he meant, in his own words, was this: "There is an invisible and a visible world. The invisible world includes an imperceptible balance of power and energy processes; it also includes what is usually called the inside of man. The human being is the ground control for something much bigger, and works of art are the stations on Earth releasing something that has a metaphysical, spiritual character."[15] Beuys' somewhat deeply religious concept was something he called "soziale Plastik" (social sculpture). Through his eyes, all of society had to be seen as a living work of art. To keep society going, work had to be done. For Beuys, anybody who did any kind of work existed as a creative part of society and therefore held equal importance, regardless of whether they worked as a janitor, manager, painter, bookkeeper, or children's caretaker. Art for Beuys meant working on a personal resurrection. Beuys: "This is the real meaning of the word 'creativity'. Any other interpretation of the word would just have the meaning of fashion."[16] Now, when you define society in its entirety as a piece of art and the work done within it as creativity, as Beuys did, then *everybody* who does any kind of work, for better or for worse, *is an artist*.

This is the real meaning of Beuys' statement "Everybody is an artist". This was also the reason why, consequently, Beuys never rejected any applicants for his class at the Kunstakademie Düsseldorf, although he knew that most of his students would never be successful sculptors or painters.

45S VS. ALBUMS

One more thing needed to happen in order to clear the way for Krautrock. Before it came about, the record business was mainly defined by 45s. The seven-inch single format with two three-minute songs was what counted. The 45 was what people bought and what radio stations played. U.S. radio stations saw the three-minute limit as downright mandatory. When Phil Spector promoted the 45 "You've Lost that Loving Feeling" (1964) by the Righteous Brothers, with its duration of 3'45", he printed 3'05" on the label to get the record played – when the DJs noticed the "mistake", it was too late (with more than 15 million plays, the song still holds the record for most airplays ever today). The album format was used for classical music. For pop music and schlagers, it was not much more than a way to assemble a handful of 45s on one record. It hadn't yet occurred to anyone that a longplayer could be more than that.

This changed around 1966 in the U.S. and U.K., when a handful of rock bands started leaving the 45 format behind. Groups like The Beatles, Grateful Dead, Iron Butterfly, It's A Beautiful Day, Jefferson Airplane, Quicksilver Messenger Service, and several more, either came out with longer tracks that would go beyond the available running time of a 45, or they composed song cycles that had to be listened to in their entity. For most of these bands, this was not an easy fight. The first thing their record companies asked them when they came up with the material for a new album, was: "Where's the single?" It was hard for the musicians to get through with the idea that there was no single and explain that they were not interested in writing two-and-a-half minute songs.

After a while, however, record managers noticed that this album format, with its new content, seemed to sell fairly well. So, they accepted this new concept – not enthusiastically, but they did accept it. Which, in the U.S., was possible because they experienced another change: Before this point in time, Top 40 radio stations mainly used AM frequencies, while several others also used FM frequencies to broadcast the same programming in parallel. FM had a much better sound quality and, since the late 1950s, it offered stereo reception. Unfortunately, the operating range of transmitters was much smaller, so FM was useful primarily within cities. But in July 1964, the Federal Communications Commission decided that radio stations were no longer allowed to broadcast the same programming over both their AM and FM outlets. Now radio stations had to change something. Most of them now started using FM for classical music and a little bit of jazz. This influenced the way in which DJs used their voices. The AM station DJs usually fired off a speech staccato of high volume and speed. The FM DJs discovered that they could talk unagitated, almost as if being "in your living room", with lower voices, often bringing more content, and this more natural sound quality made the audience listen to them longer, with more concentration.

Around 1966/67, some FM station DJs started playing parts of, or even full, stereo LP sides. It was not a big deal in the beginning – it didn't take off before the early 1970s, but it was a start. Longer tracks and, because of the better sound quality, more complex rock music now had a chance to be played on the airwaves.

It took a while until even the few open-minded German record producers and companies took note of this U.S. trend. They saw that the new homegrown rock bands were not interested in recording 45s, too. But the record companies were not interested in only selling LPs. They knew there was only a slim chance to get airplay on German radio stations without a 45. Producers, as well as label managers, first had to thoroughly watch the U.S. market to reassure themselves that the album-only concept might also work in Germany.

It's relatively clear that producers and A&R guys, like Siggi Loch and Gerhard Augustin, who had both worked in the U.S. and had strong connections to the American record industry, were the earliest birds to see this. Peter Meisel apparently also saw it.

German radio stations were still not willing to play the game yet. Although they were broadcasting most of their programs on FM frequencies, they were not interested in playing long tracks – except classical ones, but classical music had its own stations anyway. This was a huge problem for German bands, and remained one for several years.

In 1969, Yours Truly was 12 years old. On my 13th birthday that year, something changed: One of my schoolmates gifted me a record, a sampler. *Electric Rock.*

I still have it today. It was a double LP and my first ever album (I only had a couple of 45s at that time). The record was a release on the S*R International label, which I knew was a label that the Bertelsmann Schallplattenclub used for license deals with other labels; I described this "record club" concept earlier. For reasons unknown, I was already interested in record companies and labels at the age of 12. Another school mates' parents had subscribed to the *Musikmarkt*, a trade magazine of Germany's record industry which I devoured whenever I had the opportunity. Besides this, my parents had a motorcycle friend who was the CEO's chauffeur of record company Teldec; their head office was two minutes away from our home. He must be long deceased by now, but this gives you at least a bit of background on where I got a lot of this information from during my early years. My schoolmate's parents were members of this Bertelsmann Schallplattenclub, and I'm certain that *Electric Rock* was a record this club had sent to them when they missed out on ordering three records of their own choice. When their son told them that he needed a birthday gift for one of his classmates, they gave it to him to give it to me.

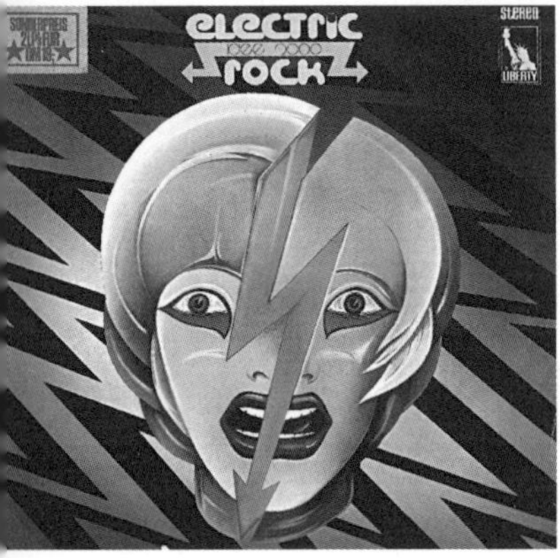

This album only carried Liberty/United Artists acts, and it turned out to be anything but scrap. There were British, American, French, and German acts I knew by name at that time: Amon Düül II, The Can, Canned Heat, Jean-Luc Ponty, Johnny Winter, as well as bands I had never heard of: The Aynsley Dunbar Retaliation, Klaus Doldinger's Motherhood, Floating Bridge, The Groundhogs, Krokodil, The Petards, Pookah, and Valhalla. All this came with surreal liner notes created by Karlheinz Freynik: "When the grass did not get greener, although the paint was waterproof. The recovery remained the same. Amon Düül II: 'She Came Through The Chimney'." This instrumental caught me head-on; still today, it's one of my Amon Düül II favorites. "When the genius got rid of the pen and disappeared in the big park. He wanted to be first when trees would grow only downwards, rivers would flow back to the spring and moles would crawl on hands out of their holes. Life was the biggest disappointment for him. The Can: 'Thief'." The pure emotion of this track left me breathless. "When the hippies noticed that sand wouldn't get more sandy, flowers wouldn't get more colorful and dirt wouldn't get dirtier. Motherhood: 'Sahara'." I felt hypnotized by the clockwork-like four-

Klaus Doldinger, live at Heidelberg City Hall (1971)

to-the-floor monotony of this one, it could have gone on forever and ever. It was the first time I heard of Klaus Doldinger. The version of "Sahara" presented on this album was played by Klaus Doldinger, Olaf Kübler, Joe Quick, Lothar Meid, and Swiss drummer Kurt "Düde" Dürst (from KROKODIL), and never appeared anywhere else on a record. This is a pity and even more astonishing, since Doldinger still plays this tune today on stage with PASSPORT. CAN's "Thief", by the way, is also around 30 seconds longer on this record than on the later release of CAN's album *Delay 1968*, where Holger Czukay deleted some of Malcolm Mooney's most excessive vocals.

There was more stuff to like on this sampler. But I noticed that these three – my favorites – came from German bands. I noticed they had a special sound that the British and American bands didn't have. I had probably discovered what Freynik wrote when concluding his liner notes: "The electric revolution has a hymn." Freynik, by the way (though I didn't know this at that time), was a screenwriter and schlager lyricist in the circle of producer and composer Ralf Arnie. Both will turn up again later in this book.

This was my first contact with what would eventually become Krautrock. Most of it came from Munich. West Berlin was not yet on my map at that point. It's not that there was nothing going on, but it was different and remained mainly within city borders. We will come back to it, but for now, let's stay a bit longer in Munich.

ANGELS OF CHAOS

Rolf-Ulrich Kaiser, who was a music journalist in 1968, had organized the "Essener Songtage", Germany's first real rock festival. This was the event where producer Peter Meisel heard and signed, AMON DÜÜL and TANGERINE DREAM. Shortly after this, a few of the chaotic AMON DÜÜL musicians left the band and started AMON DÜÜL II.

In the beginning, this new band consisted of Chris Karrer (guitar), Dieter Serfas (drums), Falk Rogner (organ), John Weinzierl (guitar), and Renate Knaup (vocals). Like AMON DÜÜL, they were also a chaotic combo, but the musicians had a little bit more of a professional approach and were able to handle their instruments to create something beyond just random noise. Because AMON DÜÜL II played gig after gig in Munich and the surrounding area, it didn't take long for them to get noticed.

Music journalist, Ingeborg Schober, knew AMON DÜÜL II's singer Renate Knaup, they had been schoolmates. Ingeborg and her boyfriend, the to-be filmmaker Rüdiger Nüchtern, attended an AMON DÜÜL II performance at the Jazzkeller in Munich's famous Schwabing neighborhood: "I can hardly remember any of the details of this performance, it was, overall, an overwhelming impression. This might explain what this music did. I was so completely paralyzed by the noise, the visual spectacle of the lightshow, the intense mood in this smoky and run-down basement, I left after a couple of hours with a blackout. Apparently I talked to the group, but in contrast to them, I can't remember."[1] AMON DÜÜL II's shows blew audiences away with hypnotic music, extreme volume, and psychedelic lights.

Soon, the name AMON DÜÜL II circulated among the media and record companies. Ingeborg Schober tried to spark some interest in them by sending a couple of live recordings to the well-established Munich label, Ariola, but the label "didn't see any possibilities for cooperation at the moment", as their reply letter to "Liebes Fräulein Schober" states. It was also difficult for her to set up a usable Amon Düül II press kit because the members were camera-shy – it was almost impossible to get them all together for a photo session in the garden. When one of them came home, another one had just left – but they also didn't trust record labels anyway.

Someone like Olaf Kübler was needed to get the job done. He was ten years older than the Düüls and a well-known studio saxophonist and flutist with connections to Klaus Doldinger, Eberhard Schoener, and others. The record company's officials weren't able to have a reasonable conversation with the Düüls. "They didn't even survive the second joint", Kübler once said. "I was an approved madcap and local hero at the Domicile, I knew Dieter Serfas and Chris Karrer, and I arranged that Mr. Wewerka, a publisher, threw in some money for a demo tape."[2]

Now think back to the connection between Klaus Doldinger and Siggi Loch: As someone who had worked with Doldinger, Kübler's voice carried weight with Loch. When he played the demo tape for Loch at Liberty Records and invited him to see the band on stage, Loch reacted positively: "In May 1969, jazzer Olaf Kübler took me to a Amon Düül II performance, who, in sharp contrast to the spherical music of Tangerine Dream, sounded nearly like an early heavy metal band. I signed them immediately ..."[3]

In reality, it was a bit more complicated. Loch was clever enough to have Kübler finance the production in advance. Kübler accepted. With the help of a lawyer he drafted contracts. With these contracts, he went to a bank. The bank approved them. Now Kübler was able to overdraw his account. With this money, he first went to Herrsching (a municipality at Lake Ammersee, 20 miles southwest of Munich, where the Düüls resided in an old villa) and first made an arrangement with each band member. Later, he made a contract with all of them.[4] When he returned to Liberty with the signed contracts, the company put money for three days of recording time on the table in spring 1969 at Trixi Studio.

Kübler: "These three studio days turned out to be a never-ending session."[5] Dave Anderson on bass, Holger Trülzsch on Turkish drums, and Christian Burchard on vibraphone were added as core musicians. As a professional studio musician, Kübler was able to guide this inexperienced band through the recording process, but it must have been strenuous work for everyone involved. The sound engineer at Trixi's, Willy Schmidt, had recorded acts like Doldinger, Hans Koller, and lots of schlagers, folk and film soundtracks, but was not familiar with rock bands. The DÜÜLS were not able to overdub or start at a point in the middle of a tune. With every mistake, the whole recording had to start back from the beginning – and they made lots of mistakes because the tracks were mainly improvised along some basic ideas. Kübler: "Everything was recorded. Later we cherry-picked what to use for the record."[6] The resulting record was a work of artful tape editing.

Phallus Dei became the title of the album. Olaf Kübler: "This was not a commissioned production. Loch had said: Just do it, and then we will see. If this thing had turned out like shit, I would have had to pay for everything and Liberty probably would have said: No, thanks."[7] Siggi Loch describes the affair a little bit less prosaic: "We released the already produced *Phallus Dei*, even though we had the – unfounded – concern that the album could get banned because of its title."[8] From today's perspective, you can call it faith in God that Liberty released the album anyway.

The record hit the stores in 1969. Still today, it's not quite clear whether the long title track was meant to be side 1 or side 2, but whatever: Something like *Phallus Dei* had never been heard before from a German band, and more importantly, there was also no English or American band that had done something like this.

Phallus Dei is a typical "first album": It lacks a clear concept, nothing is polished, but you can already sense the direction this band would take on future recordings. The music is destructive, while sometimes beautiful; hypnotic moments rise out of chaos, but fall back in after a few seconds. Many ideas come up, but none of them get worked out. The album jolts from moment to moment without any flow. Parts of the lyrics are written in a made-up ancient German slang, setting up a strange atmospheric mix of the Middle Ages, biblical phrases, and fantasies about things connected to BDSM and pedophilia – Loch's concerns were not completely unjustified; if someone would come up with these lyrics today, he would probably face heavy critique.

When composer Karlheinz Stockhausen was asked by weekly paper *Die Zeit* what he finds interesting and not interesting on the title track, he answered in short terms: "Not interesting: The three-part form (A: bubbling, reed-organ sound; B: D major with icing, lunatic singing, amusement park ghost train; C: bass part F minor with clarinets / harmonically tonal with Christmas crackers / periodic knocking in constant tempo). For phallus Dei ('God's penis') it's much too short and remarkably thin. Interesting: The five-layer concept with increasing complexity that starts at part C / irregular variations of the bass theme / gradual establishing of tempo 152. Extra-musical basic mood: Film music for the inexperienced."[9]

Olaf Kübler: "When the record reached stores, it sold like hotcakes. The record companies were stunned by this success. Nobody had put such lunacy past a German rock group. The pop magazines wrote very benevolent reviews, and one headline read: 'Germany awakens with AMON DÜÜL II!'"[10] Well, "hotcakes" might be slightly exaggerated. Of course, *Phallus Dei* got no airplay, except the track "Kanaan" sometimes, and it never appeared in any chart. A couple of pop magazines did, however, present the band and review the album, but not always positively. But, as the old saying goes: Any publicity is good publicity. It was a première, and many people were curious. *Phallus Dei* was good enough to be a door-opener, that's for sure.

AMON DÜÜL II PLAY PHALLUS DEI – THE MOVIE

It was no planned promotion coup that Ingeborg Schober's boyfriend, film student Rüdiger Nüchtern, had the idea to make a film about AMON DÜÜL II's *Phallus Dei*. In fact, it was the other way round: The film came first, then the album was recorded. But the film turned out to be very helpful in spreading the name of the band.

The basic idea came up during another concert night. On New Year's Eve 1968/69, Ingeborg and Rüdiger stayed in Frankfurt, visiting friends – an act of despair because there was lots of trouble and chaos going on in their flat sharing community in Munich, and they needed to escape from it for a couple of days. On a wall in Frankfurt, they saw a wildly hand-painted poster: A new club named Underground would open that night with AMON DÜÜL II, leading Ingeborg and Rüdiger to spend their evening there. The Underground was situated in a basement, it was bedraggled, smokey, and unpleasantly hot. The DÜÜLS, angels of chaos as always, didn't show up on time because, on the way to Frankfurt, their bus got stuck somewhere in the snow. Schober: "After waiting a long time and enduring several debates, AMON DÜÜL II finally lifted off. Never again I heard them so hard-lined, aggressive, and belligerent. The whole basement seemed to melt into nothing. Rüdiger and I were completely hypnotized by the light show. This was when he said for the first time: 'Imagine this as a movie!' And at that moment, for us, the film was a done deal. But we knew how distrustful the DÜÜLS were of the media, considering all the world and his brother were after them. First, I talked to Renate because she seemed to be the most approachable one. We then scheduled a meeting in Munich, but it was very vague. The night ended in a wild happening – and like that, we staggered into 1969."[11]

The band was not really interested in being part of a movie. Gerd Stein, then photographer at the court of Amon Düül II, remembers: "During a session, the Düüls talked about this movie. Renate said: 'There's this guy, a filmmaker, he's pretty crazy and spaced-out. He's now selling his car and wants to make a movie with us, so we just have to go there.'"[12]

Nüchtern started several more activities to get his film funded. He wrote a three-page proposal (in Germany we call this an "Exposé"), entitled *Amon Düül II spielt Phallus Dei – eine elektronische Oper* (Amon Düül II Play Phallus Dei – an Electronic Opera) with lots of notorious buzzwords and some hip Marshall McLuhan quotations. It ended with "[This] will be an attempt to let the movie, or rather its presentation on TV, find a new form which has its equivalent in the union of theater and music: the opera. An attempt to tune the sequence of pictures in such a way that, parallel to the music, a new continuity will be established, and under no circumstances will the optic-acoustical balance be destroyed. The duration of the movie will be as long as the music piece, which will be edited especially for this movie, to roughly 30 minutes. We will see long tracking shots of landscapes, the group onstage in front of a rear projection screen showing a lightshow. The musicians will look like beautiful pictures, signs of their music, not real persons anymore. We will see the face of a gorgeous girl. The girl will cry out, yelling, at the same time we will hear loud drumming – and nobody saw or heard such a scream ever before. We will treasure it like people before our time used to treasure a Titian painting. The movie will be shot in color. Instead of a screenplay there will be a tape and color slides."[13]

What a wonderful mix of naivety, nonsense, and a smooth megalomania! But this was the way stuff like this was done at that time, and it was probably exactly this cheekiness that impressed Clemens Münster (an old stager and head of the TV department at BR Munich since 1954) when Nüchtern knocked at his door. Today, it would be hard to push through such a project this way, but at that time, some people at broadcasting stations were open enough to recognize interesting ideas (remember the TV version of Eberhard Schoener's *(A)lter (A)ction* project – it had also been produced by BR TV with Münster's backing). Nüchtern left Münster's office with an option contract and an option fee of 1000 D-Marks – not an amount he could get rich with, but it was a start.

Since the band members were not willing to enter a studio without being paid in advance, Nüchtern gave them 800 D-Marks. If the movie got sold, the Düüls would receive an additional 25 percent of the profit. The remaining 200 D-Marks went to Kineticlights, a lightshow collective founded by Vincent Schaab; if the

Amon Düül II at the second British Rock Meeting (Germersheim, May 22nd, 1972)

film got sold, they would be paid another 400 D-Marks. Ingeborg gave up her temp job to prepare the shooting, and Rüdiger did indeed sell his "Ente" (duck), as this car model was nicknamed in Germany – a Citroën 2CV, the typical student's vehicle. The proceeds were just enough to buy some film footage, but it meant they had to borrow a car if needed for shooting or transportation. As camera operators, Nüchtern hired Matthias "Ufo" Weiß and, none other than Wim Wenders; at that time, both were still film students like Rüdiger, but had collected some shooting experience. Mr. Münster made something nearly impossible, possible: For one day, they got ahold of three professional 16-mm cameras from Bavaria Studio, and they were able to use a professional TV studio (the ZDF Studio III at Unterföhring near Munich) – and the Munich Film Academy would pick up the bill for all of this.

The first shooting took place on March 28, 1969, and it turned out to be a day nobody can forget. When the whole bunch of people – the film crew, the Düüls, the lightshow team, roadies, boyfriends, girlfriends, family, entourage, pets – entered the studio area with the psychedelic-colored lightshow bus and several adventurously painted cars, and the studio staff caught sight of all these extremely long-haired guys in their full-length leather coats, hippie clothing, sunglasses, and mothy fur coats, they probably weren't sure of whether this was a fancy-dress ball or if the revolution was about to start.

It soon turned out that the studio lighting outshined the lightshow, so a 1000 watt back projection pistol had to be organized somewhere. Then somebody noticed that drummer, Peter Leopold, was missing. Nobody knew where he was, so a few people had to search for him. It took two hours to get hold of him, somewhere in downtown Munich, he was tripping on acid. When he was finally brought to the set and started playing, he hit his drums so hard that he slid through the whole studio with his kit, although it was placed on a carpet. Both the drums and the carpet had to be nailed to the floor. Falk Rogner, playing organ, was more or less still practicing. Because of the incense sticks the Düüls had placed all over the studio, they got into a bit of a hassle with the firefighter on duty. Nüchtern installed the three cameras, but the shortage of footage made it necessary that only one of them could be used at a time. Because of this, he had to operate one camera himself and signal to Wim Wenders and Matthias Weiß when to start and stop theirs by nodding or waving. As the Düüls consistently ignored all stop signals when they or someone else made a mistake, the whole 25-minutes tune had to be played again and again. The band, as always, also pushed the volume up to a level that in all surrounding studios the work had to be stopped. Their staff came over, and half-angry, half-amused, they stood in the open door and watched what was going on – which in turn led to problems with stray light. As if all of this wasn't enough, in the end, the cameras gave up their ghost, one after another. The team had to work with two cameras while Wenders, somewhere backstage, tried to fix the broken ones. At 7 pm the studio time was over and not a single meter of usable film had been shot.

Mr. Münster was the rescuing angel, making a second session possible. Three days later, on March 31, the whole spook started again: Same place, same people, but this time, the mood and atmosphere were frustrated and aggressive straight from the start. Inevitably, the cameras failed again – this time the angles of view couldn't be varied. What this failure led to is the annoying phenomenon that the whole band is never pictured or shown together, and the wrong image detail always appears: We see the singer exactly when she's *not* singing, and when the organ plays a solo, guitar player is shown. At least the light show was well presented.

In the end, not all the music that had been taped could be covered with visuals. Cutting down the music was not an option for Rüdiger Nüchtern. Amon Düül II's music was holy to him, so he developed the plan to shoot a sunrise and sunset somewhere in the countryside. This, in fine synchronicity with the music, should fill the gaps.

Of course this turned out to be another adventure: Sometimes there were too many clouds or it started raining, sometimes the team slept too long and the sun was already out. One time, their borrowed car ran out of gas and Nüchtern had to walk several kilometers to the next gas station (which of course was still closed because it didn't open before 11 am). Another time, everything seemed to be alright, but then they ran into a group of cyclists. There was always *something*.

In between these adventures, the landscape tracking shots were made. Since it was early in April, they only found boring, bald trees somewhere in the Bavarian uplands. The camera was fixed to a luggage rack, and Ingeborg operated the stopwatch, while Rüdiger tried to push the gas pedal in sync with the music that came from a tape recorder. Later, they synchronized the film to the music.

As if all this had not been enough trouble: Later, when they had a first look at the developed film strips, they realized they had footage made for artificial light, so the film had a blue tint. It made things look a bit surreal, which was fine but not intentional. Parts of the film were damaged and showed wrong and changing colors. There were still three gaps left, which they filled with pieces of black film. Since they had used all of their film , including the ends of the reels, there was a sort of washing out effect in the picture, an effect Wim Wenders had already used for his student short film *Silver City* from 1967, but of course, intendedly.

Somehow, it was a miracle that *Amon Düül II Play Phallus Dei – An Electronic Opera* finally finished. It premiered at the Munich Film Academy. Most DÜÜL members missed it, some of them have still never seen the film. Rüdiger Nüchtern and Ingeborg Schober were completely out of money, but it was Rüdiger's first TV production. It started his career as a professional filmmaker. The film was shown at a film festival in Edinburgh (of course it started with a film tear) and went through a couple of other festivals. BR TV used its option and bought the movie, which meant 8000 D-Marks for Nüchtern: "A small fortune – it sorted me out for half my time at university."[14] The film was shown on BR TV and even had some reruns during the daytime (!) program. Critics especially loved the wrong and washed-out colors and black segments; they felt reminded of the colors seen while hallucinating during LSD trips. The American director Samuel Fuller saw the film and critiqued it with: "It's rough, it's vicious, it's a drama."[15]
After the previously mentioned showings, *Amon Düül II Play Phallus Dei* more or less disappeared from the face of the Earth. It was not before 2003 that Repertoire Records released the film on DVD. Unfortunately, the visuals and audio are horribly out of sync in this edition. Today, you can find the film (taken from the DVD with these flaws) on Youtube easily.

With the movie and their first album on board, AMON DÜÜL II was now able to follow up with a double album. Kübler still was their producer: "Because I had carried out the whole transaction [the production of *Phallus Dei*], I had a certain power at United Artists [Liberty's mother company] now. But the band tried to con me. … Some of them, I think Renate, Falk and Peter were involved, tried to get me out of the next production. At Liberty they blackened me as the evil King Kong. But Siggi Loch was straight. He gave me a call and said: 'Listen, your freak show is sitting here in my office, and I'll show them the door now. Try to check out what's going on with them.' It was an effective try, but I don't give a hang, things like that always repeated themselves. AMON DÜÜL II always tried to eliminate some authoritarian things that belong to life."[16] Friendly words. But even within their innermost circle, the DÜÜLS were able to surprise each other. In the band's early days, for example, they simply credited "AMON DÜÜL II" as the composer, and when their royalties from the GEMA rolled in, the money, a five-digit amount, was paid to only one contact person. But this guy – who he was isn't important here – didn't share the money with the other members. He just looked at the money in his hands and bought a new car. Of course, it didn't take long for the band to notice that the money was gone. But now there was a sort of group solidarity developing. Instead of firing him or taking him to court, the other members said: Well, this was not okay – of course he has to pay the money back, one day, when he's able to do so. While this was said, everybody already knew that this guy would never be able to pay the money back. But as a precaution, on their future records, all composers were credited individually, so the GEMA would pay all shares directly to every respective co-composer.

In April 1969, AMON DÜÜL II took part in a sort of happening at the Circus Krone Building in Munich, with GURU GURU GROOVE, Paul and Limpe Fuchs, action artists Peter Weibel and Valie Export, and a theater group called WATH THOLL. The whole thing was announced as "music, theater, film, light, action". It turned out to be not so inspiring; AMON DÜÜL II opened the evening, and as usual, they conquered time and space. But after half an hour, the performance fizzled out into nothing. GURU GURU GROOVE apparently had the most impressive performance of the evening with a talked-about drumming portion – Mani Neumeier was already a great drummer then; his free jazz training with IRÈNE SCHWEIZER TRIO paid off. Paul and Limpe Fuchs delivered their usual performance of piano, flute, self-made instruments, and screaming that didn't surprise anyone anymore. Peter Weibel and Valie Export finally jangled the audience's nerves by splattering water over the spectators and terrorizing them with a whip. But the evening was not sufficient enough to become the calculated scandal it was supposed to be. The press reactions were at best lukewarm – "bang without impact", as *Süddeutsche Zeitung* wrote.[17]

AMON DÜÜL II's second album, *Yeti* (1970), was produced by Kübler and Loch, still slightly reminiscent of a recorded live performance, but it delivered a better impression of the band's potential. They didn't play to their full potential, but the album was audibly better organized than its predecessor.
Immediately, it was obvious that the DÜÜLS had learned a lot of things in terms of music. They had absorbed some JEFFERSON AIRPLANE records, however, it was also obvious that there were no Grace Slick or Marty Balin on vocals. The vocals always remained a problem for the group. But Renate surely was more of a rock singer than most other female singers in German bands or schlagers, especially because, in the upper regions, she avoided falsetto singing, she sang powerfully, right from the stomach.

The concept of *Yeti* was not very different from their first album, but this time the musicians knew better about what they were looking for. The tracks were obviously structured, the improvisations were target-oriented, they had discovered some effects the studio electronics offered (like the frightening ring-modulated vocals in "Eye-Shaking King"), and the overall sound of AMON DÜÜL II had become more recognizable. That does not mean that *Yeti* wasn't wild stuff – it was, and we can be sure that, for this album tape, editing was also a big part of the deal, especially in regard to the improvised parts.

The "Grim Reaper" on the cover is Wolfgang Krischke; the photo was one from a series taken by Falk Rogner. Krischke was one of several people who belonged, in some way, to the band's entourage. He was involved in the lightshow, a sensible guy who saw AMON DÜÜL II as a sort of ersatz family for his depressing home – maybe not the best choice, since the DÜÜLS always had lots of trouble with themselves and were hardly able to even solve that. Shortly after the photo session, Wolfgang froze to death in the ice-cold winter woods during an LSD trip. It never became clear whether this happened intentionally or by accident.

Even a 45 was extracted from *Yeti*: "Archangel's Thunderbird", b/w excerpts from "Soap Shop Rock". "Archangel" should have been a hit. It has this "special something" – you listen to it once and you find it's coherent and won't get it out of your head for a while. But there was no chance to push it into the media. The acid-fueled lyrics and Renate's otherworldly singing made it impossible.

Liberty U.K. released this 45 backed with "Fortunate Son" by Creedence Clearwater Revival – what an unbelievable combination! As no sleeve is known to exist, and they have two different catalogue numbers, nobody could tell whether the idea was to interconnect the unknown Amon Düül II with a successful hit band, and through this, make them known, or if the 45 was simply a misprint. My guess would be the latter. Today it is a sought-after rarity.

I remember that a music magazine (it might have been *Pop*) compared the band to "nuclear waste": Once you've heard their music, you'll be contaminated for the rest of your life, but in a positive way.

A second Amon Düül II 45 was released in 1970: "Rattlesnakeplumcake" b/w "Between The Eyes". If I can trust my ears, these tracks must have been recordings from the *Yeti* sessions, but they were never released on an official album. Amon Düül II's overall four 45s, plus some album excerpts, were released in 1974 on the compiler *Lemmingmania*.

KRONWINKL 12

In the meantime, the band had left their housing at Herrsching where rats played billiards on the kitchen table and the garbage men refused to pick up the trash that piled up in front of the door. As in many flat sharing communities, all occupants always were very enlightened, but none of them felt the need to take on household work – doing the dishes, taking out the garbage, dusting, vacuuming, and so on. Nobody was responsible for paying the electricity bill, so the power was cut off and the oven had to be started with a blow torch. Somehow, the Düüls were not able to get a grip on this chaos. Furthermore, it was apparently impossible to live in peace with the citizens of Herrsching. It's like buying a new car just because the old one's ashtray is full – but the band looked for a patron, found one, and moved to Schloss Kronwinkl near Munich. It was a manor house from the 12th century, located in Kronwinkl, a one-horse town so small that it only had house numbers, no street names. Today it is part of the township Eching.

It took them a while to notice, but living in a place like this meant the end of any budding hopes of "alternative living". The band described this place musically on their 1972 album *Carnival In Babylon* with the track "Kronwinkl 12", and it didn't sound very cozy. I don't remember which pop magazine, but one wrote something along the lines of, "Imagine a competition – first prize: one day with AMON DÜÜL II, second prize: two days with AMON DÜÜL II."

However, the film *Amon Düül II play Phallus Dei* made the band known to filmmakers, and so in 1970, AMON DÜÜL II contributed a song to Rainer Werner Fassbinder's first TV production *Die Niklashauser Fart* (The Niklashausen Journey; "Fart" in this case is an old way of spelling "Fahrt") and later delivered the soundtrack for Hans-Jürgen Syberberg's film *Chamsin* (after a story by Heinrich von Kleist). The film opened in cinemas in 1970 under the title *San Domingo*.

It was not successful, but for the score, the band received the prestigious "Deutsche Filmpreis" (the "German Oscar", so to speak; today its name is "Lola"). The soundtrack makes up the entire second LP of AMON DÜÜL II's album *Tanz der Lemminge*. They could have made good use of the Filmpreis, but as always: Nobody in the band cared about things like this, and nobody was interested in learning how to care.

Although there was a sort of "core membership" – Renate Knaup, Chris Karrer, Christian "Shrat" Thiele, John Weinzierl, Daniel Fichelscher, Peter Leopold (1945-2006), Falk Rogner – the line-up started changing now, from album to album and from live gig to live gig.

TANZ DER LEMMINGE

Tanz der Lemminge (1971) became AMON DÜÜL II's third album, another 2-LP set, and probably their most versatile work; this time is was also released in the U.S. as *Dance Of The Lemmings* and in Italy as *Vaggio in un sogno* (Journey Into a Dream) on the United Artists label. Bass player Dave Anderson, left for HAWKWIND and session musician Lothar Meid (1942-2015) had taken over. He was a soul-loving professional, jazz musician, co-founder of EMBRYO, and you can hear all of this in his excellent bass playing. The overall sound of this record is even more compact and organized than the previous ones, but nevertheless, still heavy, distorted, psychedelic, and distinctive. The improvised parts on sides 3 and 4 are especially remarkable. Falk Rogner did an excellent job on the electronics in "The Marilyn Monroe Memorial Church". Renate Knaup only appeared in "Riding on A Cloud", and interestingly, she's credited as a "guest". Another guest (a real one) was actor Rolf Zacher (1941-2018) who appeared on the track "H.G. Wells' Take-Off". One can clearly hear that every side of the record carries a signature style of one "directing" musician.

Another 45 was released in late 1971, right at the start of a planned tour: "Light" b/w "Lemmingmania", for unknown reasons with the robot face from Fritz Lang's *Metropolis* on the cover. The A side sounded astonishingly song-like, and with German lyrics it could have even been a schlager. But the single didn't amount to much.

ENGLAND

In January and February 1972, Amon Düül II had their first successful tour in England. They played five concerts, one of which was at the University College of London. As always, the chaos never left them. Their tour bus broke down, they missed a city, or showed up to a concert too late. A second tour in June was better organized; they even played at London Roundhouse. Music journalist Winfried Trenkler wrote: "The eagerly awaited tour debut in England took place on June 13 in the city hall of Orford Ness. A 'Hitler fan' added a special smack to this performance. During every break, he jumped up, lifted his arm for a 'Führer salute' and shouted 'Heil Hitler!' On his shoulder dangled a machine pistol, a real one. Bobbies took care of him. ... Uxbridge near London, for the time being, was the climax. The whole audience at the university gave an interminable standing ovation ... Comparisons to English groups brought up two names over and over again: Hawkwind and Pink Floyd."[18]

CARNIVAL IN BABYLON

Carnival In Babylon, the 1972 follow-up album, included the previously mentioned "Kronwinkl 12" and "All The Years 'Round". If you were able to decipher the lyrics, these two tracks told a lot about the band's behind-the-scenes situation. Aside from this, it wasn't a remarkable album. They now had a backup singer named Joy Alaska; her head-voiced singing voice was enervating and didn't match with Renate's voice. With that said, it makes sense that this was her first and last appearance.

During the recording sessions, all hell must have been let loose. Olaf Kübler: "*Carnival* really was the big argy-bargy."[19] Chris Karrer: "With revolvers circulating in the studio, it was mainly a pure Karrer-Weinzierl mafia. On *Lemmings* we had written one side each, and now we mimed the composing giants: now play, you folks! Looking back, this was the wrong method to get closer to, for example, Leo [Peter Leopold]. We thought he would go beyond himself when we put him under pressure, but basically, this was a bit of a perverse method."[20]

This record was followed by another England trip. One of these gigs (December 16 at the Greyhound in Croydon) was recorded and, in parts, released as *Live In London* (1973). It was recorded by the professional Pye Mobile Studio, but the sound quality of the original LP is gruesome. Later CD releases have been denoised and remastered, so they are better but still far from being considered *good*. An improvised part that starts off very promising, suddenly stops. However, there is no better alternative. The album *BBC Radio 1 Live*, recorded in 1973, has better sound quality, but only *Live In London* shows the degree of power Amon Düül II could deliver at that time when they were in a good mood – which was not always the case.

WOLF CITY/UTOPIA

The follow-up album was *Wolf City*, released later in 1972. This was probably their most developed album. But, remember how I said that Amon Düül II was a chaos combo? Well, this album definitely reconfirms this notion.

Lothar Meid (who had taken over the bass again) and Olaf Kübler grew exhausted of the chaos and constant quarrels, so they rented Bavaria Studio when the Düüls were not using it, and, with the idea to make a deal with the BASF label, they hired additional session musicians, Kristian Schultze (1945-2011) from Passport, Jimmy Jackson (a Pittsburgh-born pianist who also played with Embryo and Passport), Keith Forsey, and jazz drummer Joe Nay (1934–1990). With this line-up, they recorded their own project; it was initially untitled, but later they named it Utopia. Of course the other Düüls got wind of that and wanted to be part of the project. Long story short, the whole thing grew into a fight about who played what and where, who got his composition recorded first for which album (because it was clear that if member X got his composition recorded, there would be no space left on the album for member Y's composition). Lothar Meid: "The famous pistols' war began. Pistols, poison, LSD, and I don't know what else was, again, passed under the table."[21] This statement, I must make clear, is not to be taken at face value. There were lots of troubles and quarrels, and the band members put themselves under permanent psychological stress. In fact, they were all sensitive folks, and they knew each other well enough to know exactly how to hurt one another most effectively. But, as far as I have been told, there was never any *real* violence between them. This has to be stressed because, during my research, I came across a couple of blog entries about Amon Düül II's history, written by people who have obviously taken these statements seriously without knowing their source and context.

In the end, Olaf Kübler had managed to get the most striking track, "Deutsch-Nepal", recorded for *both* albums and in parts with the same musicians. This couldn't be more "düül".

Kübler then flew to their American record label, United Artists, played them both albums and told them he would like to have the Utopia one released under the band's name 'Olaf & His Electric Nazis'. Kübler: "Most of the record company bosses sitting there at the conference table were Jews. Of course they went bananas – they didn't fancy that in the slightest. Although, they actually liked me. I did something – I don't remember what – to calm them down, and they bought the record and put 40,000 D-Marks on the table, which covered the production costs. So, in general, the whole thing did sort of clear things out between Lothar and me, but the jive it got was a totally different thing."[22] It was one of their strangest releases ever. In 1982, the self-titled Utopia album got rereleased under Amon Düül II's name, with *Utopia* now as the album title.

FIRE

In 1971, during a tour through Germany, Amon Düül II lost all of their equipment in a fire that destroyed the discotheque Keks in Cologne. Four people in the audience died that evening. The band's equipment, what a surprise, was not insured. To avoid bank debt, the Düüls accepted an offer from Liberty Records to advance the money for new equipment. This went quickly, so the band was able to continue touring – which they had to; their record sales were not high enough to make a reasonable living for all of them.

Of course, Liberty wanted to get this money back. Due to the on-going personnel changes in the band and Liberty's transition into United Artists, contracts between the band and the record company became more and more complicated until finally, nobody knew what was going on with them. When, in 1974, Siggi Loch left the company to become head of WEA Music, it was finally decided to set up a cancellation agreement that ended all further contracts between Amon Düül II and United Artists Germany. The band was clear of debt, but until the equipment was paid off, they wouldn't receive any money for the records they had produced. This meant that after five years as an active professional band, AMON DÜÜL II had to start from scratch.

Olaf Kübler remained AMON DÜÜL II's producer until *Vive la Trance* in 1973. After this, he was still with the band, but the band itself acted, "officially", as its own producer.

Lothar Meid, with Jörg Evers and Keith Forsey, founded 18 KARAT GOLD as a side project; they released one album titled *All-Bumm* in 1973. Jörg Evers originally came from EMBRYO. In 1978/79 he wrote the soundtracks for the TV mini series *Schluchtenflitzer* (English title *Whizzer*), in 1985 for the TV movie *Bolero*, both directed by Rüdiger Nüchtern (see how nicely the Munich network worked!), and under the pseudonym Manni Ickx, he composed the music for *Manta Manta* and some other God-awful 1980s comedy movies. Evers was a board member of Germany's royalties collecting society GEMA until 2012. Keith Forsey worked in the circle around Klaus Doldinger, Giorgio Moroder, and Harold Faltermeyer, and did lots of disco and schlager jobs.

Other members of AMON DÜÜL II, especially Renate Knaup and Danny Fichelscher, started working with Florian Fricke's POPOL VUH. But AMON DÜÜL II continued to exist.

MADE IN GERMANY

In 1975, on *Made In Germany*, for the first time, Jürgen S. Korduletsch appeared as co-producer and backup singer. He was a very active producer, his bandwidth ranged from disco soul to pop, schlager, and later, Neue Deutsche Welle (NDW), and with him, AMON DÜÜL II's music changed dramatically. The band now signed with Teldec in Germany and Atlantic Records in the U.S. – which turned out to not be the best idea. The 1974 album *Hijack* (as it appears on the sleeve, on the label it says *Hi Jack*) appeared on Teldec's sublabel Nova, later records went down to Nova's sub-sublabel Strand (both infamous for suboptimal press quality). With Atlantic, trouble began to brew.

The basic idea of *Made In Germany* sounded big: It should be a musical. Yes, somehow, the DÜÜLS would have been the ideal cast to stem such a project. They had the fitting image and the required quantum of madness. But it didn't work. Maybe it was already too late for them, or maybe there were other reasons. However, they gave the game away. Korduletsch ironed the psychedelic sound and the original heaviness of Amon Düül II down to pleasing, mostly boneless pop music with orchestral parts. He added unimaginative electronic vignettes and, under the title "La Krautoma", a cover version of evergreen "La Paloma". There was also an "interview" with Adolf Hitler, edited from several of his speeches – of course one could do that, but it has to be satirical or at least contain a bit of humor. Unfortunately, it was neither.

In Germany, *Made In Germany* was released as a 2-LP-set. Liner notes came from Ingeborg Schober, the cover showed the band in historic uniforms and dresses, but the more you look at the photo, the more you will see how mothy and broken the clothes and the costumes were – this might give you an idea about what the original intention of this project had been. Although they had a nice, nationwide TV appearance, at the music show "Phonzeit", where they celebrated a wild version of the mentioned "La Krautoma", the album flopped. It sold around 10,000 copies, and that was it.

In the U.S., Atlantic was not willing to accept the double album, and the label also didn't accept the Hitler interview (which is understandable because everyone would have recognized the voice, but only a few would have been able to understand it). So Korduletsch had to cut the album down to one LP, and, unfortunately, he made the mistake of removing the "strange" parts, leaving only the "standard pop" tracks. On the cover, they put Renate Knaup in a rather silly Marlene Dietrich pose.

The album sank like a stone. In this version it was, as Siggi Loch used to say, like trying to sell German Coca-Cola to Americans. If there is one thing a German band has to keep in mind when they try to enter the U.S. or England, it's this: You have to do something spectacular, something people see as "German", something English or American bands would never do (we will touch on this phenomenon again).

This, more or less, ends the story of Amon Düül II. Of course, they created more albums. Pop albums. They weren't as bad as some critics portrayed them, but their typical Amon Düül II flavor was gone – that rough, slightly self-destroying, lemming-like charm. Somewhere along the way, they had lost their touch.

The band fell apart. For a while, Amon Düül II existed mainly as a sort of studio construct with alternating musicians. Lothar Meid's project 18 Karat Gold became schlager singer Peter Maffay's live band. The Düüls, now under the guidance of Stefan Zauner and Klaus Ebert (who came from the Hessian Petards and had been a Liberty labelmate) with singer Tommi Piper, started touring again, but in 1981, with the album *Vortex*, Amon Düül II, came to an end for the time being.

Zauner, consequently, founded the schlager pop group Münchener Freiheit. They had a couple of major hits in the 1980s, especially "Ohne dich (schlaf ich heut' nacht nicht ein)" (1985) and "Solang man Träume noch leben kann" (1987, recorded pompously with the London Symphony Orchestra).

It was not before 1995 that Amon Düül II returned with a new album entitled *Nada Moonshine #*, this time on the Schneeball label. This one went back to their old roots with the old team.

By the way: From the start, the band members played with ear protection, while the audience always got the full dose.[23] I can confirm this at least in parts. I saw Amon Düül II two times on stage. The first time was in Easter 1974 – I think they had just released *Hijack*. It was at a German rock festival and they played on Easter Sunday in the late afternoon. Lothar Meid, who stood in for (probably) Robby Heibl on bass, remembers this appearance as "catastrophic"[24]; I remember it as somehow neutral – I can still see the band on stage, I especially remember Renate, looking a bit clueless. They had no lightshow (it was in the afternoon and the Ernst-Merck-Halle was not dark) and they were loud, but in no way over the top. Although I knew their records quite well, I couldn't identify most of what they were playing.

In a certain way, I was lucky to have seen them at all that day: The next day, they had to play a festival at Lake Constance, but only Lothar Meid arrived. After a while it became obvious that the other members wouldn't show up, so he drove back home to Munich. This says a lot about the condition the band was in, at that time.

The second time I saw Amon Düül II on stage was probably in 1977 at the Winterhuder Fährhaus, an old ballroom in Hamburg. It was the line-up with Klaus Ebert and Stefan Zauner – *Almost Alive* had just been released. It was relatively crowded, and I think this is the only concert I've ever attended where the audience escaped in rows. I don't even remember what the band played because of their unbearably high volume. Finally, the venue was about half empty and we gathered on the lawn in front of the building. Neither the band nor the guy at the mixing desk cared about anything. Apparently *Almost Alive* could be synonymous with "half-dead".

CONFOUNDING THE GHOSTS

In connection to rock music, Cologne has never been too important of a city, with few exceptions like Turk rock gem Alex, ZELTINGER, BAP, and some others. But here, we will meet another first generation Krautrock band: CAN, or, at their start, THE CAN. They never saw themselves as a Krautrock band, maybe not even as a rock band. But they became a rock band.

"Confounding the ghosts is always dangerous", Irmin Schmidt once said to a reporter. "It's not good to talk about these things if you cannot control them."[1] Ghosts or not ghosts – it's easier to deal with CAN than with AMON DÜÜL II. The reason is quite simple: When CAN started, all core members (except Michael Karoli) were already over 30 years old, were professionals, and more or less out of the woods. Sometimes there are some rumors on the web or in other sources that make people think CAN was living at the Schloss Nörvenich as a flat sharing community with their own vegetable garden,[2] but they never were. The members of CAN were very close as musicians and as a band, but they never tried to live together. I'm sure this was important to keep the band project alive.

Irmin Schmidt had studied piano and French horn, was an aspiring conductor and composer, studied music theory with Karlheinz Stockhausen, Luciano Berio, and György Ligeti, and had been employed at an opera house as choir director. He had also written film soundtracks and stage music, been awarded the German Radio Award as "best prospective conductor", and had been commissioned with a composition for orchestra and rock band by NDR radio in Hamburg. But more and more, Schmidt realized "that there was nothing I had in common with the classical audience."[3] In New York, he had drum sessions with Steve Reich and La Monte Young. These experiences left their mark, and he got in touch with rock music there.

Jaki (Hans) Liebezeit (1938-2017), as mentioned earlier, had been a jazz drummer at Manfred Schoof's for two years, but felt that free jazz had come to an end: "Anything followed the rule: All notes are on an equal footing. This also means that any kind of doubling or repeating is forbidden. There were ideas like playing as a mountain stream, running down into the valley, sometimes faster, sometimes slower, barrage, down the waterfall. For drummers, this is a big frustration. A *big* frustration. … I had never been a hundred percent convinced when I played this way."[4] So, when Irmin Schmidt asked him whether he knew a drummer who would be willing to start a new band, he answered: "Yes, I think I know somebody" – and to Irmin's surprise, he showed up himself at the founding meeting.

Holger Czukay (1938-2017) studied upright bass and composition, worked as a music teacher at a Swiss boarding school, had had classes about Early Music, and had been a participant of the "Kölner Kurse für Neue Musik" (Cologne Courses for Contemporary Music) from October 1965 to April 1966. One of his lecturers there was Karlheinz Stockhausen; another participant of this class was Irmin Schmidt. (Stockhausen has a list of all 38 participants and 13 teachers. Czukay is listed under his civil name Holger Schüring. Also in this class, were Jon Hassell, Bruno Spoerri and David Johnson. The latter became an early member of CAN but left to become sound assistant for Stockhausen. His voice can be heard in Stockhausen's *Hymnen*, *Region 2*.)[5] In general, Stockhausen was not a big fan of rock music, but he followed CAN's career for many years. Holger Czukay had, especially, always stayed in touch: "Stockhausen was the church in the village", he said.[6] In a certain way, Stockhausen adopted the band. Schmidt: "During the CAN years there were moments when we were in touch with each other, and one time he helped us very much. He accepted the music of CAN with open arms and liked it. I have to tell you a story: In the Seventies, he made a blindfold test for a newspaper about new rock music.[7] He found most of it rather crackbrained and spoke out about most of this stuff in an unfriendly manner. And then they played 'Aumgn' from *Tago Mago* to him. He found it super-duper. Then they told him that this was CAN. He said: 'No wonder, they were once my students!'"[8]

Michael Karoli (1948-2001) was a guitar student of Czukay and introduced him to the music of Jimi Hendrix and other rock guitarists. After his abitur (graduation), he studied law for a while, but he gave it up to join CAN in 1968.

CAN wouldn't have been what it was without Hildegard Schmidt, Irmin's wife. When, during a train ride to Berlin, she met Irmin for the first time, she was 17 and had a job in real estate management. She didn't know much about the rock music scene, but she knew what a contract was and how it had to be set up correctly. "I also had a great deal of luck at the start: I met two people who loved CAN and supported me in every respect. They were Martin Davis, managing director of United Artists, from whom I learned a great deal, and upon whose advice I still rely today; and David Platz, a music publisher of the old school, who took me under his wing. ... I founded my first English publishing company, Messer Music, with him."[9] The rest was learning by doing.

How did Malcolm Mooney join the band? Hildegard Schmidt: "I met Malcolm in Paris. There, I visited Serge Tcherepnin, who, along with Irmin, had been a student of Stockhausen's. This was in June 1968, directly after the May riots. Malcolm, a friend of Serge's from the U.S.A., had just returned from India, and, because of the Vietnam War, he didn't want to go back under any circumstances. He looked for connections to galleries and hoped he would find a studio somewhere, so that he could work as a painter and sculptor. My first impression of him was that he was very nice and absolutely charming. I thought I could perhaps use Irmin's and my connections to the art world to help him find something in Germany. So I invited him to visit us in Cologne. It happened rather quickly after that. I was visiting my family in Witten [in the Ruhr area], and when I returned, Malcolm, or Dessie, as we called him then, was in Cologne and had become the singer in CAN."[10] Malcolm Mooney had a special liking for slightly erratic, improvised lyrics and monomaniac repetitions; to listen to his desperate screaming in "Thief" or "Soul Desert", or his repeated, shouted phrases like "Are You Waiting for the Streetcar" over and over and over can be an unforgettable experience, especially on high volume (and CAN was rarely a quiet band). In concert, Malcolm sometimes lost his self-control to the point that he would leave the stage or attack the audience. Aside from that, after being part of the band for a while, he started showing a mix of psychological problems and homesickness; he was afraid of getting into trouble with the army, and he became more and more unreliable. Finally, in 1970, he left CAN and returned to Harlem, New York City, to work as an arts teacher.[11] Later, he released three records with the Bay Area band TENTH PLANET and three or four collaborations with other musicians, but none of these ever came close to his work with CAN.

Kenji "Damo" Suzuki crossed paths with CAN by chance. He was busking in front of a Munich café when Jaki and Holger, going for a stroll, saw him there. They listened to him for a while and then asked him to join the band at the Blow Up, and he did: Damo entered the stage with the band that night – and stuck with them. The *Melody Maker* described his vocal style as "not so much singing as breathing words into the microphone."[12] He also had the ability to improvise lyrical phrases. I, for my part, like most of his vocals on the studio recordings; on stage he had an unpleasant tendency to screech. He left the band in 1973 when he fell in love with a woman who turned out to be a Jehovah's Witness. Later, he made some records worth listening to; his best one might be *In The Night* with Cologne band, DUNKELZIFFER (1984). He's still an active musician today.

Many of you readers will probably shake your head when I claim this: Both singers, Mooney as well as Suzuki, had strong personalities, are part of CAN's history, and left massive marks. Nevertheless, I'm convinced that they were not too important for the musical impact this band had and still has up to the present day. Of course, it was Mooney who drove this primarily experimental group of German intellectuals into becoming a rock band, and so his influence shouldn't be underestimated. After these two vocalists had left, the group tried to find another singer, but, as Irmin stated, "the flaw with them was always that they could really sing."[13] Finally, Michael and Irmin shared the vocals. CAN continued without a new singer, and this worked quite well. But imagine what would happen if only one of the core members – Schmidt, Czukay, Karoli or Liebezeit – were to go missing: Then CAN obviously wouldn't work anymore. CAN needed all four of them.

The band was mainly a closed circle; guest musicians were only used on "Red Hot Indians" from the album *Landed* (our friend Olaf Kübler on saxophone); later on *Saw Delight* (1977), there was percussionist Reebop Kwaku Baah (1944–1983) and bassist Rosko Gee, both from TRAFFIC. But at that time, CAN was already out of balance. The project still continued on, exerted, more or less because all core members were still present. But I remember watching a live concert on TV in 1977 with Klaus Schulze and CAN. After the concert, there was an interview session, and when you watch Czukay and Schmidt in this interview, you can almost physically feel the tension between both of them.[14] When, on stage, Reebop pulled the plug of Holger's amp, Holger said: "If you do this again, I'll leave."[15] Reebop did do it again, and Holger left CAN after *Saw Delight*. The follow-up *Out Of Reach* (1978), still with Rosko and Reebop, turned out to be a characterless collection of meaningless songs. A core part of the band was missing and the circuit wasn't closed anymore. CAN was a different band now and the original concept started floundering. The remaining members, Irmin, Michael, and Jaki, felt this change and tried to get rid of what they recognized as the disruptive factor. Their next album, the self-titled *Can* from 1978, was more compact and somewhat better than its predecessor – nevertheless, it was pale and turned out to be their last one. The original group spirit was gone and could not be restored.

Hildegard Schmidt: "The conflict with Holger was very painful. Apart from musical reasons, there were private reasons that I don't want to talk about. I simply wished that Holger would be able to build a career for himself, and I did everything I could to help. I'm very happy that Holger trusts me with my work. I believe he never would have taken the decisive step to leave the band – which was very important to his career – without talking to me about it."[16]

It has to say a lot about the social construction of the band that members of Can appear on most of Holger's later solo recordings. Even during serious conflicts, they were able to find a way to deal with it. No one was ever kicked out; the living organism of Can was never destroyed.

Along with managing themselves, the band followed a couple of self-created, basic rules. They never credited their music other than with "Can" (or the names of all members), independently from who was actually composing or playing, and they put all incoming money into a shared can. Legend has it that this is where the band got its name from. There are various stories about its origin, but this one seems to be the most plausible.[17] Each member, no matter the circumstances, got the same share. In contrast to Amon Düül II, they never had any trouble with royalties this way – well, let's say, *almost* never: The only exception was the album *Out Of Reach,* when Rosko Gee insisted on having individual composing credits. In the end, this was one of the reasons why the band said goodbye to him. Again, there was (and is) Hildegard, who even in times of crisis, when the can was empty, somehow managed to never leave anyone high and dry.

She denies it, but from the beginning Hildegard was also involved in artistic decisions: "I didn't have and never wanted to have influence over artistic decisions. I was attentive and I gave my opinion. I did find the material on *Tago Mago* so wonderful that I managed to persuade both Can and United Artists to make a double LP."[18] In 1988, it was also Hildegard Schmidt's idea to bring the band together again – including Malcolm Mooney (Damo Suzuki was asked to join, but he declined) – to lay down the straggler *Rite Time.*

Irmin Schmidt had always had connections to theaters and filmmakers. In 1969, Can had played in *Prometheus* by Max-Peter Ammann at the Stadttheater Zürich for three months. Another job during that same year was the music for a soft porn movie named *Kamasutra – Vollendung der Liebe* (directed by Kobi Jaeger, long forgotten, just like the movie). Not just a "glorious chapter", as Schmidt says: "We weren't even Can, we were still Innerspace, when a film producer came and hired us. At least we made some money with that. But not immediately. Malcolm Mooney, our singer, first had to beat up the producer in a bar in Munich before we got our money."[19] However, film music jobs soon became an important part of CAN's work as well as their way to make ends meet.

CAN's *Kamasutra* experience shows what rock musicians in Germany always had to be aware of. They weren't taken seriously. Record companies, bookers, and concert promoters tended to see them as – TANGERINE DREAM's Edgar Froese once nailed it – "carnival idiots"[20]. Even if it was not that extreme, working with rock musicians was usually seen as an opportunity to make a fast buck or get a soundtrack for little money.

OFARIM

Setting up a management was a similar sort of trouble that rock bands had to prepare for. CAN had experienced this annoyance – keyword: Abi Ofarim (1937-2018). It was, again, Hildegard Schmidt who piloted the band out of the trouble they had gotten into with him. What had happened? This guy had been well-known (duo ESTHER & ABI OFARIM), and now he was a solo singer, songwriter, choreographer, and dancer. He had founded a music promotion company named Prom. (Of course Prom was meant to be a management company, but it was better to keep plans like this behind closed doors; I will come back to this later.)

In a near-live situation at Schloss Nörvenich, CAN had privately recorded their first album, *Monster Movie*, but no record company was interested in it. So, in 1969, they made a private pressing with the soon-to-be Music Factory label, founded by Karlheinz Freynik. For some reason, on the back sleeve of the LP, it said "Scheisshouse Records Production presents" ("Scheißhaus" is a vulgar German slang expression for a toilet stall), but it was never intended to start the record company under this name. The print ran 600 copies.

I already mentioned Freynik in connection with the *Electric Rock* sampler for which he had written surreal liner notes. He had released an unsuccessful album named *Ich bin ein Deutscher* (I am a German) in 1966 on Star-Club Records, had been a member of Hamburg's CITY PREACHERS, had gotten into drug problems, and had later written a libretto for one of the two or three different German versions of the musical *Hair*. As some singers from the Munich *Hair* ensemble – Donna Summer, later schlager singers Jürgen Marcus, Jürgen Drews, and Su Kramer – were signed to Liberty, Freynik became known to Siggi Loch. So one day, Freynik gave him a test copy of *Monster Movie*. Loch: "I was immediately fascinated by CAN, just like I had been by AMON DÜÜL II. Their music was original but also included many elements from all kinds of styles, even from jazz. I made Kalle Freynik an offer for a license deal with Liberty, and we made an agreement soon after. He wanted to pick up the advance license payment of 10,000 D-Mark the next morning after signing the contract. He was in a hurry and on his way to vacation."[21]

But Loch waited in vain for Freynik the next morning. Instead, he received a call from Abi Ofarim, who informed him that Freynik was already on his way to Greece, and that he (Ofarim) now owned CAN's recordings. Loch: "So I drove down to Abi's place, where he lived with the very young, unbelievably beautiful, Iris Berben. [She later became an actress, known mainly for appearances in TV series.] Abi Ofarim was a clever wheeler-dealer. It took hours, and, in between, the captivating Iris served cake. I was too busy with the negotiations to help myself to it, but my assistant helped himself nicely – and he returned to his office not before two days later. The sweet seduction was a hashish cake and it had given him a total blackout. After driving a hard bargain with Abi, I finally made an agreement with him and bought *Monster Movie* a second time, but now for twice the amount."[22]

The problem that resulted from this successful deal was that Ofarim now saw himself as CAN's manager and demanded a share of their incoming money. Hildegard Schmidt: "At the beginning, Abi Ofarim had given the band the idea that, with him as manager, they would go straight to the top. At that time I never dreamed of becoming CAN's manager. That absolutely did not come under discussion. But afterwards the first euphoria wore off, and, despite Abi, we were left standing there with no money. However, the CAN virus had taken hold of me, I couldn't resist my fighting spirit anymore and simply got going."[23] Of course, Abi Ofarim was not willing to accept this and gave the band an unpleasant time. He even sued out a temporary restraining order against the release of their album *Tago Mago*,[24] but Hildegard Schmidt was able to sort it out and officially took over the band's management.

As rational as all this may sound, CAN was not an easy project to manage or deal with. The core members, as well as the singers Malcolm and Damo, were strong and very different personalities. There was constant tension between the members, things were discussed endlessly, sparks flew, especially between Holger and Jaki – Jaki always found that Holger played too many notes. Many other bands would have probably given up. But, luckily, the CAN members found a much better outlet: They transformed all these tensions into an operating power which pushed the band forward. Hildegard Schmidt: "They hung around with each other so much that, for instance, for a couple of years I had to go on holiday alone with our little daughter. CAN never had time for such things."[25] Probably it was exactly this sort of intensity of working, as well as the diversity of their characters, that is the main secret behind CAN's artistic success.

STUDIO

CAN was the first band that could clearly see that they couldn't execute their ideas without having their own studio. Holger Czukay: "Before we came together as CAN, Irmin already had a film music commission. … The movie was *Agilok & Blubbo*, really a 1968 underground movie, with a shaky camera and all that. Topic: How to go your own way. We delivered rather acceptable, intelligent music for it. … We assembled our equipment at [David Johnson's] apartment. We did not go into a studio. Irmin, quite rightly, said: If we want to make it as a band, we need our own studio from the beginning to do our recordings without restraints from outside. Compared to the way it was usually done, this was the opposite. … We got a room at Schloss Nörvenich because we had played there at a Picasso exhibit. We got it offhandedly."[26] The "Schloss" was a manor house, first erected around 1400 in the Düren area of North Rhine Westphalia, not far from Cologne. From 1963 to 1971, sculptor Ulrich Rückriem lived there with his family and provided several rooms to artists who used them as workshops.

CAN needed their own studio because the band was improvising, experimenting, editing, overdubbing, and rerecording, and all of this took up a great deal of time. They had no other choice because CAN – unlike most other bands – didn't compose a track, developed it, rehearsed it until they had it perfectly down, and then would go into a studio to record it. With CAN, every moment could be part of the final tune or become the backing track for an overdub. Irmin Schmidt: "It was our concept that nobody composes but we all invent. You have to concentrate very hard on listening, it's nearly a 'monkish exercise', because it's not so much about what you are playing yourself, in the first place it's about opening your ears and listening to what the others do! And maybe then you can do something yourself, when it fits in. That's a rather ascetic exercise! It's not improvising in the sense of 'jamming'. We never did that. We always worked highly focused, with a lot of discipline."[27]

A rock band doesn't usually operate on low volume, so Schloss Nörvenich couldn't be a solution for eternity. But they were lucky; it didn't take long until CAN found an unused movie theater in Weilerswist township, near Cologne. This building became the Inner Space Studio (named after the band's first name). The band acoustically insulated it with a load of old Bundeswehr mattresses, while the original curtain, made from flags of several countries, remained where it was. The old box office and much of the decor were left untouched.

CAN was also lucky in another respect: They never got into serious trouble with the neighbors. At first, they were observed with a bit of skepticism – the band members looked dangerous at that time. But after a while, the townsfolk realized that they were friendly people, not planning to destroy park benches, chase their daughters, or beat up shopkeepers, so they got used to them. The town of Weilerswist completely accepted the band in 1971, after CAN had written the soundtrack for the three-part TV crime movie *Das Messer*[28] that nearly everybody watched. In Germany, we call this kind of a TV event a "Straßenfeger" ("street sweeper"); all the streets were empty during its transmission because everybody was watching it. "Spoon", its theme song, became a veritable radio hit and entered the charts in December 1971 and stayed until April 1972, peaking at #6. The 45 sold around 350,000 copies in Germany, gave a nice push to the album *Ege Bamyasi,* and brought them more TV and movie soundtrack jobs: *Das Millionenspiel*, *Ein großer graublauer Vogel*, *Alice in den Städten*, *Tote Taube in der Beethovenstraße*, and *Die letzten Tage von Gomorrha* followed.

On February 4, 1972, CAN played a free concert in front of around 10,000 people at Cologne Stadthalle with an illusionist, acrobats, and fire-breathers. The show was filmed on behalf of the band by Peter Przygodda (who was the editor of most Wim Wenders films; the band knew him through their soundtrack for Wenders' *Alice in den Städten*). The film was edited by Przygodda into a 50-minute documentary and was shown on WDR TV, which gave another push to CAN's popularity. After this, they started their first U.K. tour.

The *Sounds* poll 1972 listed CAN as "band of the year", and the band was awarded the "Goldene Europa" by SR radio Saarbrücken.

STUDIO ROUTINE

CAN's usual work routine in the studio (Nörvenich as well as Inner Space) went like this: They showed up around 10 am, the time they would leave the studio varied. Somebody – it could be a single musician or the whole band – started improvising something. The improv could consist of playing instruments as well as drumming on blue trash bags that they had filled with paper and used as sound insulation at Nörvenich, it could be listening to music, it could be listening to Irmin telling the plot of a film. Whatever the improv was, it could go on for hours. Both Malcolm and later Damo were able to spontaneously improvise lyrics or at least some singable lines. Most of what the band played was taped. Holger used only five Sennheiser microphones (three of those for the drums and some room atmosphere). These, along with two Revox tape recorders and a modest mixing desk, were all of the equipment.

The second step was usually that Holger edited the tape that came out of this first session. He cut away the stuff the band considered not worth keeping and spliced the remaining material into one piece. Often, these cuts are not even camouflaged; you can clearly hear them on several CAN recordings. Holger had designed the studio in a way that there was no separation between the recording room, mixing desk, and control room. Via a studio PA system, this tape was then played back to the band as a sort of backing track, and they added a second layer of (again improvised or now already structured) music to it – then, the result was edited and cut down once more. This is the reason why, sometimes, there exist segments that can't possibly be played in one go; some drumming parts (like in "Vitamin C" or "Mother Sky") would be physically impossible to do, even for a drummer like Jaki.

I'm not sure whether they knew it back then, but the method of using a studio PA system instead of headphones was very similar to the recording procedure producer Phil Spector had developed to create his "wall of sound". This way, parts of the sound coming from the PA speakers bled into the microphones during the second go. This is also the reason why all CAN recordings up to *Soon Over Babaluma* have such a "roomy" sound.

This method worked quite well, but it used up enormous amounts of expensive recording tape – which is why, as Irmin said, they needed to be rather disciplined and focused. Of course, the tape material that had been edited out was erased and reused, sometimes hundreds of times, including audible splices and magnetic drop-outs. This was the only way for them to cope with costs.

In 1974, CAN acquired a 16-track tape recorder. This machine changed the working process dramatically, because now, individual members could work independently from the other musicians. The first album this new mode of recording was used for was *Landed* (1975), and you can hear the difference immediately. With this 16-track machine, it was possible for any of the musicians to add new parts to a track themselves, without the others. They still could work improvising as they did before, but technically, there was no need to anymore. A not unimportant part of CAN's charm became lost because of this.

Both recording systems meant that all studio productions of CAN were heavily edited, post-processed, and thus always different from CAN on stage. There are strong parallels with the production methods of producer Teo Macero: Masterworks like Miles Davis's *In A Silent Way* (1969) or *Bitches Brew* (1970), have never been played in the studio as we hear them on record. These records are the result of significant tape editing. Still today some purists are outraged that something like this was possible in jazz – they see it as comparable to cheating. I, for my part, see it as using the studio as an instrument.

As already said, CAN was not originally intended to be a "rock band", it was meant to be an ensemble to transform into music whatever the musicians had in mind. The important part of this was the ability and willingness of all CAN members to listen to what the others did or didn't do. Regardless of whatever one of them did, they could all be certain that no one would respond with: "Hey, what is this nonsense supposed to be?" Each member could be sure that at least one of the others would pick up the idea and *do* something with it. Anything could be an inspiration: "With CAN, we were often sitting together for a long time without talking to each other," says Irmin Schmidt. "Maybe we smoked a joint and listened to the room, as if it were a sound installation to harvest sounds from. A lot of CAN music came out of this feeling, but it's also present in my solo works."[29] Listening to each other also meant that not everybody had to constantly play. Usually, when a rock band improvises, they act as a collective: Sometimes all musicians play together, sometimes one instrumentalist is featured and the others back him or her up. However, they are all with their instruments and play. This wasn't the case with CAN. A musician's contribution could also be *not* to play. But even then, by facial expression or gesture, they could feed something into the tune. That's another reason why they were different from other bands.

GHOSTLY IMAGE

CAN might not have seen their project as a rock band, but they were interested in furnishing the band with an image. In their early years, they especially tried to get the band connected to the occult. CAN made good use of the media to spread anecdotes about unexplainable things that had allegedly happened to them, and parts of the press willingly followed. Music journalist, Pierre Granini, mysteriously whispered: "Inexplicable things happen again and again in the surroundings of CAN, about which the musicians are willing to speak only reluctantly and with all due caution. For example, there was the thing with the studio clock at the recording of the British TV show 'Old Grey Whistle Test'. After the start sign and the beginning of the tune, Jaki noticed that something with his drum kit was wrong. He stopped the recording, and, at the same moment, the second hand of the clock stopped running. Minutes later, the drummer signaled 'Ready!', and the hand started running again. None of the musicians had noticed it, but the whole scene had been recorded by four video cameras and was verifiable. A camera operator, chalky: 'Really, there's something odd with you guys.'"[30]

Four cameras – wow, it must be true then. This story wasn't put in *Bravo* or other trash magazines, it appeared in "Rock Session", a relatively serious annual book series on rock music from the renowned publishing house Rowohlt.

There are more stories like these about CAN. We shouldn't take them too seriously. Their purpose was to construct an image. But in a way, there might be a grain of truth in them: Since CAN's musicians were sometimes very well-tuned, mentally, with one another, they might have reacted a bit over-sensitively to coincidences that were *seemingly* connected to what they were just doing. Granini: "Michael was able to stop and restart the penetrant hissing of the old, seldom-used Selmer organ by only mental effort and verbal order – this cannot be explained physically."[31] Of course it can't, simply because there is nothing to explain. I guarantee that. It's an old and well-known phenomenon: Everybody has probably made the experience once or a couple of times in their life, where you think of your mother or another close person, and in this very moment, you receive a phone call or text message from them. If something like this happens, it sticks in your mind. But have you ever counted the times you've thought of this person and nothing happened? No other secret is hidden in case of CAN's old Selmer organ. But it is this kind of story the press (and let's be honest: also the fans!) loves.

I-CHING

Another "esoteric" thing about CAN is the I-Ching hexagrams they placed on some of their record covers. On *Future Days* it's *dĭng*, the number 50, meaning "crucible" as well as "succeeding" or "holding":

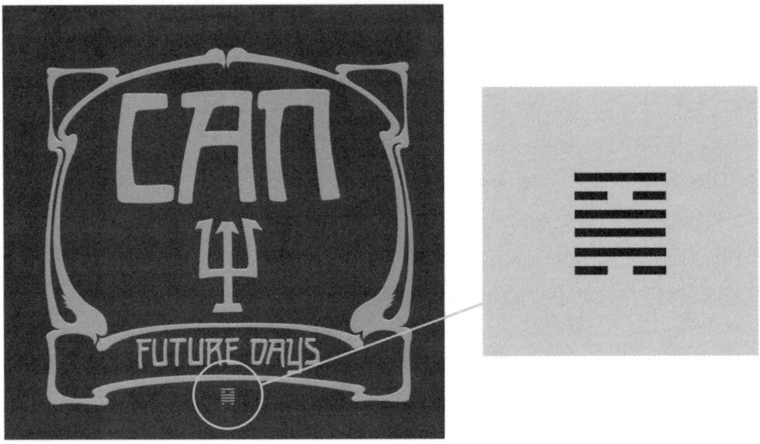

On *Flow Motion* we find two hexagrams, *kăn* (number 29), meaning "the abysmal" and "water", leading to *huàn* (number 59), meaning "decay" or "dissolution":

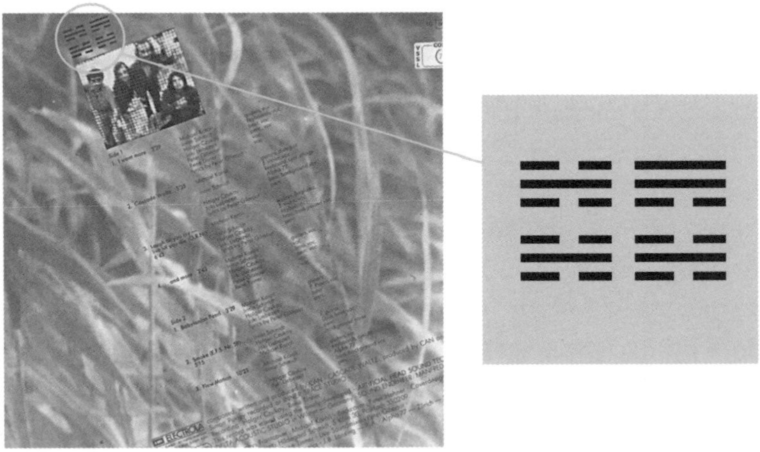

The I-Ching is the Chinese "Book of Changes". This is not, as many people used to think, a sort of horoscope or prophecy, it's more an empiric vade mecum, based on hundreds of years of life experience. Its basic idea is: Nothing will remain as it is now. In Buddhism, you'll find the same basic idea. The I-Ching is a sort of modular construction kit made to answer a carefully worded question. The latter is important because formulating a question means that you have to think about, and define, what you want to know as precisely as possible. Precisely defining the initial situation does, however, usually already lead you halfway to the solution. The I-Ching demands that you need *two* hexagrams, because the answer you get is always the description of a *process*. Which of the hexagrams you get is usually decided by flipping coins. The first hexagram you get marks the current situation, the second one marks the result to which the change will lead to. This process of changing is what the I-Ching is about. It transforms experiences we all know into universally valid comments: If you are successful, there will come a tipping point where it ends and your situation may go downhill; if you are unhappy, there will be a change for the better; if it rains for a long time, know that sunshine will come – you get the picture. (I'm tempted to say: It's the same kind of wisdom that schlager lyrics are made of.) This sort of thinking can be applied to nearly every possible problem or question. If interpreted well, the I-Ching can be a helpful tool to sort out the chaos in your brain, making it potentially easier to come to a decision. That's the whole secret.

In regard to the hexagrams on CAN's records, we don't know what question the band had asked, so for us, the hexagrams are meaningless. In regard to *Future Days,* there's not even a second hexagram, so no process can be described. But, the hexagrams looked nice and a bit mysterious, and I'm quite convinced that this was the main point behind their use.

However, one thing about CAN is safe to say: The band's secret was this way of thinking and working in closed circuits. I think we can even use the term "autopoietic"[32] to refer to the way CAN worked, and it made the band, musically, nearly invulnerable. The musicians picked up and absorbed the strangest influences and made them their own, be it French musette, street noise, the radio, Pierre Schaeffer's *musique concrète*, an urban legend in a newspaper, reggae, disco or waltz. Sometimes influences were made into numbered experimental tracks that are known as "E.F.S." ("Ethnological Forgery Series"). Some of these tracks should be taken with a pinch of salt – CAN's music isn't "funny", but there's often humor in it, if you are willing and able to recognize it.

The result of all this is that no two CAN albums sound similar, yet they all still sound like CAN. Each CAN album is its own universe; they are all full of surprises and hidden things, and even when you've heard one thirty times and think you know it like the back of your hand, there might still come a day when you discover something you never noticed before.

ELECTRONICS

For some reason, CAN is often seen as a pioneering "synthesizer" or "electronic" band. This is misleading. Of course, CAN experimented with several sources of sound and/or inspiration. If there's one sentence that makes this completely clear, it's Irmin Schmidt's description of *Tago Mago*: "Sides 1 and 2 offer a certain idea about what we wanted to do, while sides 3 and 4 resulted from the mood in which we made sides 1 and 2 – a sort of history of origins of that record."[33] CAN had unusual ways of playing instruments and used heavy tape editing (but rarely worked with tape loops); they integrated the sound of short wave radios, like the signature tune in "Unfinished" on *Landed* which is audible at 6'15". I remember that Holger once assigned it to Radio Moscow, but in fact it was the then signature of the Deutsche Welle ("Es sucht der Bruder seine Brüder" from Beethoven's *Fidelio*). They manipulated voices, like Damo's vocals on "Come sta, la luna", or the seemingly vocoded voices on "Full Moon on the Highway", which are actually just ring modulated, and if you ever saw Michael Karoli standing with both feet on several guitar control pedals, you know the musicians were willing to use whatever was in reach. They were also one of the few bands experimenting with "dummy head stereo" (on the albums *Flow Motion* and *Saw Delight*, but the result is not too impressive), and even Assi, Irmin's schnauzer, made an appearance – you can hear him bark in "Aumgn" on the *Tago Mago* album.

CAN, to my knowledge, was also the first German rock band to use a rhythm machine, first in 1971 on "Peking O" from *Tago Mago*. This track was recorded on the first day the band owned this machine; what you hear is the band members' immediate reaction to the new device[34], and it's interesting that they use it more as a sound source than as a rhythm generator. Later, they used it on the previously mentioned TV theme track "Spoon", but even there the machine is only used as a sort of additional sound source; it adds an artificial color to the band's natural overall sound. In both cases, the machine is not replacing Jaki's drums, it's an additional instrument in its own right. (Let's not fight about who was "first". Robin Gibb had already used a rhythm machine on his 45s "Saved By The Bell" in 1969 and "August October" in 1970, simply replacing the drums. SLY & THE FAMILY STONE's use of a rhythm machine (a Maestro Rhythm King) in "There's A Riot Goin' On" (1971) was a bit more innovative, but there it's also only used as an interesting sounding replacement of drums.)

How about synthesizers? Well, Can has never used a synthesizer in the usual sense. There was only Irmin Schmidt's "Alpha 77", but this device was mainly an extended filter bank, combined with a ring modulation unit: "It was not a synthesizer with a keyboard, but it has three inputs where you can plug in the organ or the electric piano, and there's an oscillator. You can re-modulate, filter, and shift around all three lines with different electronic possibilities. So that's what I needed. I could ring modulate for instance, which is one of the basic early electronic features. I designed it, not technically, but the idea, and then an electronic engineer built it for me."[35]

LIVE

Compared to their studio recordings, Can's live performances were a different beast. They had their circle of fans, and their overall number of concerts shows an increasing popularity: In 1971, Can played 15 concerts, in 1972 it was around 20, and in 1973 it was already 40.

I have only seen Can live once, at a point late in their career. It took place at the Fabrik in Hamburg, probably in April 1976. As mentioned, they experimented with different singers; on this tour they had Michael Cousins (a.k.a. "Magic Michael") with them. This didn't work, and he left the band only a few weeks later. Luckily, he wasn't on stage for the whole show, he only appeared for a couple of tunes. But what the four core members played was remarkable.

As a supporting act, they had a jazz rock band; the only thing I remember from them is the singer who suffered, visibly, from stage fright. Then, after this band had finished their set, nothing happened. The air became more and more blue with smoke (yes, at that time most young people smoked, cigarettes and whatever else, and nobody felt the need to stop this in concert venues – even the musicians sometimes smoked on stage). We expected that some roadies might appear to set up some more equipment, but the longer we waited, the more we realized that everything the band would need was already there – Jaki's blue-transparent acrylic drum kit with two bass drums (heavily en vogue at that time), Holger and Michael's amps, Irmin's keyboards, his Alpha 77, the PA left and right, a wall of speakers at the back of the stage. There were strange rumors circulating in the audience about these speakers: Some people spread word that they "knew for sure" that Can would use "dangerous ultrasonic sounds". Which, of course, they did not. It was crowded and had become more and more overheated. The audience sat mainly on the floor in front of the stage, and after nearly an hour of waiting, people became impatient.

Then, suddenly, without warning or announcement, the musicians stormed the stage, plugged in their instruments, and kicked off without hesitation. For some reason, I had the impression that backstage, they must have had a quarrel (maybe about the singer), and maybe that was the reason why we had to wait this long. They performed without any break or intermission for, I think, around two hours. Michael Cousins entered and left the stage a couple of times, dancing wildly and jumping around, but without leaving much impression. Finally the band ended their set and disappeared without any form of goodbye, leaving a stunned and ecstatic audience. There was no encore. Something special I remember about this concert was that Holger Czukay constantly watched me. You've probably heard of this old musician's trick of picking one person in the audience and playing "for him (or her)". That night, apparently I was the guy Holger had chosen, and Holger noticed that I had noticed – a strange but intense sort of communication; we both had to smile a couple of times.

As impressive as this concert was, all live recordings I know by CAN are a double-edged sword. There are several live recordings out now, official and unofficial ones. They show that CAN, on stage, did more or less the same they did in the first go of their early studio recordings: They would improvise until something interesting emerged, and then they would work off of that. In the studio, this searching process got edited out, only the essential parts were kept (they once made a nice collage track from these edited out snippets: "Cutaway", released on the album *Unlimited Edition* from 1976), while in concert, what you got was the entire searching process. At the concert that I attended, they seemed to have a sort of set list, but the known tracks were usually only touched on and immediately transformed into something different, something that goes for most of CAN's live recordings. Again, this is a bit reminiscent of Miles Davis: He can start with whatever he wants, it might even be a schmaltzy Disney ballad like "Someday My Prince Will Come", but no more than two minutes later, the tune has morphed into something completely new.

On the other hand, once they really found their shtick, they could get absolutely hypnotic on stage – it could last two, maybe three hours; their longest performance lasted, allegedly, for seven hours, somewhere in West Berlin. It's fascinating and exciting to watch this searching process, inching forward and growing, but you really have to be in the audience. On record, without seeing the band and their communication with each other, and not being part of the crowd, this process tends to circle around itself. I prefer CAN's studio albums for that reason. In addition, many CAN live recordings were not made to be released, so the sound quality leaves a lot to be desired.

CAN is respected more today than during their active time. They were one of a handful of German groups who really developed a musical style that nobody else had. One reason for this is surely the fact that (except Michael Karoli) they were all already over 30 when they started the band. The other reason is that they were all highly skilled on their instruments and had a highly qualified musical background they could fall back on. This is why they were able to improvise. Many other "improvising" bands, in truth, simply reproduce the same structures again and again – today in this order, tomorrow in another order – but it's always the same stuff. Or, they develop a tiny little chord chain or melody, but never work out any details or variations, because they don't know how to really execute their ideas. The results are usually long tunes that go round the houses forever, but never arrive anywhere. Not with CAN. They were able to bring the term "improvisation" back to its original meaning: *instant composing*. That's why CAN's music still works.

SOLO

In 1960, Holger Czukay, with three unknown friends, had already recorded three jazz tunes at WDR radio. One of these tunes appeared as "Mellow Out" on the CD version of *Canaxis 5*; the same piece exists under the title "Konfigurationen" as part of the *Cinema* box set (2018).

One night in 1965, he had the chance to sneak in the Studio for Electronic Music, in the basement of WDR. There, with Rolf Dammers, he recorded two tracks that ended up as *Canaxis 5* (1969): "Boat Woman Song" and "Canaxis"; early experiments with tape loops and sampled vocals.

After leaving CAN, Holger went to Thailand into a Buddhist monastery for one year to rebuild his confidence. When he returned to Germany in 1978, he took on a job as a production assistant at Conny's Studio for a while where he helped record DAF, KILLING JOKE, BLÄCK FÖÖSS, ULTRAVOX, and some other bands. One of them, BLÄCK FÖÖSS of Cologne, on the cover of their 20-year jubilee album *Et es 20 Johr jenau jetz her* (1990) "rebuilt" the BEATLES' *Sgt. Pepper* album cover and put Holger at exactly the place where the original collage showed Karlheinz Stockhausen – isn't that a compliment?

At Conny's Studio, Holger began recording solo albums that became masterpieces: *Movies* (1979), *On the Way to the Peak of Normal* (1981), *Der Osten ist rot* (1984), *Rome Remains Rome* (1987), and some more. He also made two amazing ambient collaborations with David Sylvian (*Plight & Premonition*,

1988; *Flux + Mutability*, 1989). All these albums are outstanding, especially the tracks on which Holger does not try to be funny. He loved to play the "mad professor"; journalist Karl Lippegaus, who had the opportunity to follow Holger for several months while Holger worked on *Der Osten ist rot*, even compared him to a sort of "holy madman" who used to talk to his equipment – but after a while he learned more and more that Holger was neither mad nor holy.[36] In all the bizarreness he loved to celebrate in interviews or in front of cameras, Holger Czukay was a very sensitive musician and serious composer. His ears were open to different sound sources that might go together, and, after several years of tape editing and splicing with CAN, he had gained the ability to create soundscapes that were much more than just collages. They were his way to organize the world into something he could live in. You can call this a sort of acoustical philosophy. In interviews, Czukay loved to downplay this aspect of his music, but don't be fooled by his humor. He was a pretty good guitar and bass player and had an excellent feel for musical structures. Tracks like "Träum mal wieder" (Just Dream Again) or "Music in the Air" can catapult you into other worlds.

During his last years, Holger lived with his wife, Ursula (a.k.a. U-She), in the old cinema at Weilerswist. In the end, he was hardly able to climb the stairs anymore, and in his last radio interview it was audible that he had trouble breathing. On September 5, 2017, when Holger passed away at the age of 79, only five weeks after U-She, the world lost a truly original artist. I think he would smile at the fact that he died in his studio, of all places.

In 2019, the City of Cologne installed an annual pop music prize and named it "Holger-Czukay-Preis für Popmusik".

Irmin Schmidt is now the last survivor of the classic core of CAN. He went on composing film music after the end of the band, and he belongs to the best composers in Germany doing that, although his last film music compilation *Filmmusik Anthology Volume* 6, 2015) might produce a sort of "same as ever" feeling. CAN had already been active in film composing; their second album *Soundtracks* (1970) is a compilation of some of these tracks. More film music tracks appeared on the latecomer *The Lost Tapes*. CAN also contributed the theme music for the weekly ZDF cultural magazine "Aspekte". It was in use for several years; a longer stereo mix of the track appeared on CAN's self-titled album from 1978 as "Aspectacle". When you listen to Schmidt's several film music anthologies, it becomes obvious that he has developed a style of writing that is unique and recognizable, but it never destroys the film it was made for. He avoids what German film composers call "mickey mousing" and what has become a plague since Disney developed it – Schmidt hates it: "Playing one track after another onto a tape, following the pictures precisely, is, first of all, a boring work, and second, the boredom is carried in its sound. There are these monotonic synchronicities that are constantly used in films that make a sort of 'Punch and Judy effect', when someone falls on his head and the music makes a 'boom'. … I don't play live alongside a video. I watch the movie a hundred times, if necessary, but in the studio I work without a picture."[37]

Aside from this, Schmidt has released a couple of solo albums. *Musk At Dusk* (1987) and *Impossible Holidays* (1991) are, in particular, just exquisite pop music. You have to get used to Irmin's strange singing style, but after a while you can't even imagine these records with a "real" singer (interestingly, schlager singer Gitte Haenning sings backup on the latter one – you can immediately recognize her voice). Another gem is Schmidt's collaboration with Swiss saxophonist Bruno Spoerri, an instrumental album entitled *Toy Planet* (1981). Spoerri plays a lyricon here, which is a synthesizer played not with a keyboard, but with a saxophone-like breath controller. Irmin Schmidt's fantasy opera *Gormenghast* (2000) after Mervyn Peakes's trilogy, recorded with the BRANDENBURG SYMPHONY, several classical singers, and the usual CAN suspects, is not my cup of tea. But maybe that's just me. Another more "classical" record is *5 Klavierstücke* (2018) for solo piano, sometimes a prepared one. The title obviously refers to Stockhausen's cycle of *Klavierstücke* (1952-56), but it's different from these. Schmidt's piano pieces are mainly improvised – but in a special way: "I don't like the word 'improvisation' in this connection. These are spontaneous compositions. It's what Stockhausen called 'playing intuitive music'. You don't play simply along, the tunes originate from listening to yourself. It's like Japanese calligraphy, where the ink drawings also originate from the first go – they stem from the first movement. One brave brushstroke – that is it. Nothing will be changed or revised, and there are no sketches or drawings. The calligraphy originates in this single moment. In this way, I recorded the piano album."[38]

CAN, as well as the solo works of Holger Czukay and Irmin Schmidt, will remain an important part of the music of the second half of the 20th century – much too good to be counted simply as "Krautrock". One day, this will be common knowledge.

Mani Neumeier of Guru Guru, live at Heidelberg Thingstätte (1970)

THE SEVENTIES

"We are working on the production of cultural soup cubes."

RALF HÜTTER
(KRAFTWERK)

THE SEVENTIES

FUTURE'S CALLING

The future was calling, but sometimes people were not too enthusiastic to answer the call. We're in the early 1970s now. The 1960s had left its traces, and more and more, 1968 became a magic number. Germans still enjoyed economic growth. But something had changed – let's say, the overall climate.

In large numbers, university professors went into retirement, and those reaching out for their empty chairs were former student movement activists from 1968. They started their careers as scientific assistants, finished their habilitation (something we don't have in America), and got a professorship, somewhere, not least because every small-town now opened its own university.

Another popular way to continue on after graduation was to pursue a civil service career, working as a "Beamter", which is non-redeemable and provides people the security of receiving a pension after retirement. As a student you may have disliked the oh-so-bourgeois society, but becoming part of it has its advantages.

A career in the media was also frequently chosen, especially as a radio or TV editor. The early Seventies were a good time to land a job there. A lot of young freelance journalists were able to reach a permanent position at one of the radio and TV stations under public law (remember, there were no commercial stations in Germany yet) by doing this: As soon as their fees for freelance work exceeded a certain amount in the given year, they filed a lawsuit against the broadcasting corporation with the goal to reach a takeover into employment. The courts usually saw this as a justifiable claim. (This trick had an unwanted flip side: After a while, the radio and TV stations fired back and stopped using a freelance journalist when he had reached a certain (not very high) amount of fees in the given year. This became a problem for many freelance journalists of my generation.) Most of these journalists, once they got hold of a position, kept it until retirement. It was a well-paid job, and nearly as safe as being a "Beamter". Many of them had been part of the student protest movement, saw themselves as "somehow left-wing", and had the idea that it was impossible to keep a certain degree of objectivity or to differentiate between report and opinion, so they didn't waste much time on this. They saw themselves as a sort of people's educators.

Some of these journalists switched to a job in politics after a while, became spin doctors, spokespersons of politicians, or speechwriters. Others, especially the ones from the arts and entertainment departments, left journalism and switched over to the record or film industry.

The "Generation Sixty-Eight" called this "the march through the institutions". They became quite successful with this strategy. There were some irreversible traces 1968 had left. In ethics, politics, fashion, and art, things that would have been unthinkable just five years earlier, became possible, and that was not at all bad. This generation articulated some unpleasant truths about the German society and especially the way the society handled the German past, and they showed directions for a different future. But it's also true that this sometimes resulted in a new compulsion of conformity, and this is historically more and more romanticized today by some of the pioneers. They forgot about the dubious idols *they* had rendered homage to at many protests. The year 1968 and its concomitants slightly evanesced. The atmosphere of departure that 1968 had created had already become self-evident.

Among students, the concept of flat-sharing communities became a common thing. But now, living in such a community was no longer meant to be an experimental social experience, in the first place it was something practical – sharing apartments reduced individual rent. Having your own apartment as a student was nearly impossible. For many courses of study you had to change your place of residence, and staying at your childhood home was not possible anymore (and in contrast to today's German university students, staying at "Hotel Mama", your parents place, was not a popular choice). By this point in time, many young men around 17 or 18 thought about relocating to West Berlin: The city had the reputation of being a place of eternal youth. There were two attractive universities, the cost of living was cheap, you could easily find an apartment, a room, or a community, and – the main point – because of the special political status of West Berlin, you couldn't get drafted into the military if you stayed in town for at least five years. There was a lot of space for experimentation in music, art, love, and life. The point when you saw yourself as an adult was negotiable, and this created a special atmosphere no other city had.

Following the zeitgeist, most flat-sharing communities, but also "normal" apartments, changed their color schemes to brown, beige, and orange. For several months, Pril, a common dish detergent, came with flower stickers on the bottles, and soon there was nearly no kitchen tile, no refrigerator, no apartment door, and no bathroom mirror without Prilblumen (Pril flowers) on them. The standard, black telephone was now also available in screaming orange or woodman's green, and for the sake of convenience (and when you paid extra) its cable now was a sensational six meters long instead of two. Some very early avant-gardists even had an answering machine now; these were clumsy devices that had to be connected to a tape or cassette recorder and gave the usually completely untrained caller 30 seconds to leave a message: "Please start talking at the sound of the tone – beep!" Most people had no idea what to say after the beep.

DARK CLOUDS COMING UP

The time of prosperity slowly petered out, but Germany was not in an economic crisis mode yet. Far in the horizon, some dark clouds, like the shortage on apprenticeship openings, became visible; those who wanted to, saw a slightly growing joblessness, and voices could be heard in the media, saying: Now it's only a problem for few, but just wait – unemployment will grow, and when it exceeds one million, people will rise in protest. Actually, joblessness in the following years climbed up to more than five million people, but only one thing happened: The Federal Government changed the way the unemployed were statistically counted, so the numbers appeared to go down. Trade unions started protests, but besides this, not much else happened.

In 1973, some Arabic countries shut off oil supply. This crisis led to three Sundays when, in car-crazy Germany, it became forbidden to use your car. Every street was free of traffic, people walked or cycled on the autobahn, or climbed bridges that were usually blocked for pedestrians.

Then, first environmental problems became a topic. The suspicion came up that the gas used in spray cans might damage the ozone layer. But it was still easy to ignore the writings on the wall.

WINDS OF CHANGE

Since 1969, the conservative CDU hadn't been the reigning party anymore, and social democrat Willy Brandt had become Chancellor of a social-liberal coalition. His party, the SPD, brought some "winds of change" to Germany. One change in particular was the reforms they made in the school system: They believed more children from working class families should be able to receive a higher education and ideally be able to achieve a university degree. This worked; Yours Truly is one of these people. Another important thing was that Brandt steered a course of openness concerning socialist East Germany, which finally led to the formal acceptance of its existence, which was unthinkable a few years earlier, and many conservative people didn't hesitate to call Brandt a traitor (or worse). But they had to admit that the GDR authorities now reduced their enervating chicaneries on the transit ways between West Berlin and West Germany – the GDR police didn't stop it completely; they still tried to cash in D-Marks from the drivers, but all in all, it was a little bit less uncomfortable now to visit West Berlin. In 1971, Brandt received the Nobel Peace Prize for his New Eastern Policy.

In 1972, the parliamentary group of the CDU in the German Bundestag finally tried to get back into power: A man named Rainer Barzel, who had the appearance of an overzealous head-clerk, wanted to become Chancellor by trying to overthrow the SPD/FDP coalition with a "constructive vote of no confidence" against Brandt. The parliamentary debate and vote was broadcast live on all radio and TV channels. The streets of Germany were deserted; whoever was able to, planted themselves in front of their TV. People on buses and streetcars carried transistor radios with them. Crowds of people stood in front of TV stores' shop windows or went to the TV department of the nearest department store to watch the broadcast. When the President of the Bundestag finally announced the results and it became clear that the CDU with Mr. Barzel had failed, many people, strangers to one another, sank into each other's arms, applauding and cheering. It was unbelievable, and it says a great deal about Brandt's popularity after two conservative decades. Shortly after this, re-elections were called. The election battle that started then is probably the most vivid I can remember. Even among us teenagers, feelings ran high and sometimes went overboard. It was officially not allowed in school buildings, but I still remember that I wore the orange-colored "Willy wählen" (vote Willy) badge on my jacket, and teachers didn't care. Out in the streets, you saw people across all generations wearing this badge. The SPD won, again with the help of the liberal FDP as coalition partner.

Sounds good? Well, relatively. It was like a cold shower when the seemingly progressive SPD installed the "Radikalenerlass" (decree against radicals), meaning that people who didn't fully accept the German Constitution were not allowed to work in public service anymore. In theory, this was meant for Nazis and neo-Nazis as well as for communists, but, since there were not too many openly organized active Nazis left, the whole thing leveled mainly against members of the DKP (German Communist Party, oriented at the ideas of the Soviet Union and the GDR and mainly funded from there) and its subdivisions, MSB Spartakus (Marxistischer Studentenbund Spartakus, active at universities) and SDAJ (Sozialistische Deutsche Arbeiterjugend, organizing apprentices and young workers).

Outside these organizations, in the shipping channel of the 1968 student movement, several left-wing extremist splinter groups were founded. There were especially the so-called "K-Gruppen" ("K" groups):

KB (Kommunistischer Bund), a primarily undogmatic left-wing party, had a monthly paper with the ludicrous name *Arbeiterkampf* (Worker's Fight) that, at least sometimes, had articles substantial enough to be worth a discussion;

KBW (Kommunistischer Bund Westdeutschland) was a strictly Maoist party with members who, at protest marches, acted as disciplined as soldiers, and when you talked to one of them, you felt like you were talking to someone who had been brainwashed;

KPD/ML (Kommunistische Partei Deutschlands/Marxisten-Leninisten), was oriented towards Albanian socialism.

I remember some even more obscure left-radical groupings – like the MRI (Marxistisch-Reichistische Initiative), which tried to combine the analyses of Karl Marx with the sexual theories of Wilhelm Reich. All of these groups, to put it nicely, were sects mainly made up of muddleheads, and not always in a funny way. None of them ever had the slightest chance of getting anywhere, but they existed, their members were drilled to talk your ears off if you gave them the slightest chance, and they usually destroyed any discussions outside their line with a sort of ad hominem filibuster technique.

What the main intent of the Radikalenerlass was, was to prevent the members of one of these groups from becoming school teachers, police officers, judges, or other public officials, but in reality, it also hit locomotive drivers or mailmen. This practice sparked a lot of headshaking, especially in France, but also in other neighboring countries. They saw it as disproportionate; in their view, German democracy was stable enough to deal with splinter parties without getting hysterical. In the end, the whole idea turned out to be unsuccessful. Around 1975, the Radikalenerlass was handed down to the federal states where it more or less faded out.

But the Radikalenerlass left atmospheric traces – sometimes strange ones. Due to the fact that, at a certain age, it's always nice to see yourself as highly dangerous, it became a fad especially among high school and university students to see themselves as radical enough to be surveilled by the Verfassungsschutz (Federal Office for the Protection of the Constitution). I remember completely harmless people seriously thinking that their telephone lines were bugged because they had, seven years earlier, signed a protest resolution against the raise of streetcar fees or something like that: "We always have this strange crackling noise in our telephone. This can only be them, monitoring us." "Them", of course, was the Secret Service, if not the 'secret Secret Service'. Or, they were convinced that somebody had opened and read their mail, or some spooks were following them on the street to check out their "contact persons".

Today, you can smile about this. But in some circles, this was a deeply serious topic. It was serious enough that some folks from the former protest movement became real radicals and went underground. Around 1971, with a little help from ideologies supporting the liberation of the working class, this turned out to be the beginning of the era of the "Baader Meinhof Group" (or "Baader Meinhof Gang", as they were called later).

BAADER-MEINHOF & CO.

This is not the place to delve deeply into the story of this self-proclaimed "Red Army Faction" ("RAF"), but a few lines might be of interest because their activities shaped the atmosphere in Germany in a way nobody could ignore. From the beginning, the RAF had been a media phenomenon – which was intentional and well taken into account by its members.

Political scientist Wolfgang Kraushaar, explains in an interview: "In the Federal Republic of Germany, the chapter of 'armed fight' significantly started with a bomb attack at the Jewish Community Center, on November 9, 1969, at a commemoration for the victims of the so-called Reichskristallnacht. [The "Kristallnacht" or "Night of Broken Glass" on November 9–10, 1938, was a pogrom against Jews, Jewish institutions, stores and synagogues, carried out by paramilitary Nazi forces, especially the SA.] The culprits came from a precursor organization [of the RAF], the Tupamaros West Berlin. Like the RAF, they had been trained on weapons and explosives by Palestinians. Without this anti-Israeli cooperation – first with the Fatah, later then with the PFLP [Popular Front for the Liberation of Palestine] – none of these local underground groupings would have been able to start any actions at all."[1]

Between 1970 and the late 1980s, the core of the first and second terrorist generation consisted of no more than around 60 people. Based on scatterbrained political ideas, they conducted bomb attacks, bank robberies and hostage-takings, seeing themselves as the avant-garde of revolution, who were going to blast the mask off the fascist face of the German State. Of course, this was ridiculous. Although the German State had been conservative and sometimes authoritarian, it was far from being fascist. Many people on the left side saw this clearly, but words couldn't stop this train anymore.

The RAF members had persuaded themselves to be in a situation of self-defense, and they used this as justification for their actions. With these actions, the RAF members maneuvered themselves into a more and more hopeless status that left them with no way to return. The resulting bunker mentality blinded the Baader-Meinhof members and their entourage even more. In the end, they were accountable for 33 homicides, at least 200 injuries, dozens of bank robberies, and around 250 million D-Marks of property damage.

To give you an idea of what was going on in their heads, here's Ulrike Meinhof in her own words:

> "This is a problem, and of course we say the cops are pigs. We say the guy in uniform is a pig, he is no human being, and this is the way we have to deal with him. This means we don't have to talk to him and it is wrong to talk to these people at all, and of course there might be a shooting. Because we don't have the problem that they are humans, as it is their function, or rather their job, to protect the crimes of the system, to defend and to represent the crimes of the system. And when we have to deal with them, they are just criminals, then they are just pigs, and that is a completely clear front."[2]

In view of this inhuman drivel it's hard to imagine that Ulrike Meinhof had been a well-respected journalist in the 1960s.

The German government nearly went bananas about this small group of extremists that – as aggressive and dangerous as it was – never would have been able to kick society or government into instability. In the end, their actions were not even political anymore; they consisted mainly of procurement crime and the need to get their own people out of prison.

But there were heavy overreactions by the authorities, and some politicians tried to use the fight against terrorism for things they had always wanted to push (more rigorous laws, more monitoring, more control). Sometimes, there were denunciations of long-haired and/or pot-smoking students by their neighbors; left-wing intellectuals especially came under observation, along with artists.

Hamburg-based singer-songwriter Hannes Wader, to name a relatively early example, was going to start a concert tour in 1971, when he was asked by an acquaintance whether it would be possible for a reporter from NDR radio to stay at his apartment during his absence. Wader saw no reason to deny the favor. When he returned home after his tour, he found his apartment desolate and got arrested by the police. It emerged that the "reporter" had been – under a fake name, of course – terrorist Gudrun Ensslin, and she had experimented with explosives in the apartment. The police didn't buy that Wader had had no idea of his "guest's" identity, and the press took the same line, especially (but not only) the tabloid *Bild*. A smear campaign against Wader started. The singer, surely left-wing and socially critical, but far from having any sympathy towards terrorism, was villainized as "Baader Meinhof sympathizer" and "helper of terrorists". It took him years to get rid of this label, and without the help and solidarity of fellow singers, especially of Reinhard Mey, this could have easily ended his career. At the beginning of terror hysteria, it was easy for the media to stir up some paranoia to sell more newspapers.

Real, massive police actions that could affect everybody did not start before the mid-1970s, and they increased in 1977, in the 44 days known as "Deutscher Herbst" (Germany's fall of terror). In that year, the Baader Meinhof terror reached its climax.

In September 1977, RAF terrorists kidnapped Hanns Martin Schleyer, head of the Confederation of German Employers' Association and of the Federation of German Industries; he was called "boss of the bosses". His Nazi past was just as well-known as his callousness. The terrorists shot his chauffeur and three of his security guards. They kept him hostage and demanded 15 million U.S. dollars, along with the release of eleven imprisoned RAF members. With their brutal videos of holding Schleyer captive, they used the media to emphasize their demands.

After nearly five weeks of negotiating, the Federal Government under Chancellor Helmut Schmidt rejected all of these demands. (Willy Brandt had stepped back in 1974 when it came out that his personal aide Günter Guillaume was a spy from the GDR. Helmut Schmidt of Hamburg became Brandt's successor.) Because it had been a big mistake to give in to the demands of the 2 June Movement when they had kidnapped Peter Lorenz, the crisis squad had already decided on day one of Schleyer's kidnapping that the German State would not give in and would keep absolute silence about this decision – knowing that this decision might turn out to be a death sentence for Schleyer.[3] The reaction was immediate: Two female and two male PFLP terrorists, confederated with the RAF, at Palma de Mallorca hijacked a Lufthansa tourist plane with 86 people, including the crew. After an odyssey through several Arabic countries and the shooting of one of the pilots, the plane finally ended up empty on fuel at the Mogadishu airport in Somalia. For a nerve-wracking week, the plane stood there in the heat without air conditioning or freshwater. Several ultimatums expired. The terrorists finally drenched their hostages in alcohol and set up several explosives.

Then, in only one night, all of the terrorists' pipe dreams collapsed. The plane got stormed by the GSG-9, a specially-trained group of the German border police. Three hijackers were shot and all hostages were freed. When the plane's rescue was reported in the German radio news early in the morning, Andreas Baader and Jan-Carl Raspe shot themselves in their prison cells, Gudrun Ensslin hung herself with a cable (at the same crossbar Ulrike Meinhof had hanged herself one year earlier), and Irmgard Möller tried to stab herself, but survived.

Yours Truly was doing his civilian service at that time, in German called "Zivildienst". (All young men were drafted at age 18 for military service, except they lived in West Berlin, but if, for reasons of conscience, you refused to do this service, your conscience was then tested by an examination board. If they accepted your motivation, you had to do an alternative service. Usually, this was some unskilled labor in a house for handicapped, a hospital or psychiatric clinic, or something like this. You had to serve 18 months, while the military service took only 15 months.) I still remember some co-workers of my age at the place where I did my civilian service, who didn't believe in the RAF suicides; they were convinced the government had actively conducted, or at least knew about, what was happening, and didn't try to prevent these suicides. They constructed absurd theories for why it would have been impossible for Baader to shoot himself in the back of his head as he had done (indeed it must have taken him some contorted maneuvers to make it look suspicious). Still today, there are some ludicrous myths about these suicides.

Hanns Martin Schleyer was shot the same night and his kidnappers left his body in the trunk of a car somewhere near the French border.

It was a nerve-wracking time for everybody. The actions taken by police in response were drastic: During the crisis, a total press embargo took place (the media accepted it without exception) and a communication ban ("Kontaktsperregesetz") prevented the RAF prisoners from getting in touch with their lawyers. This meant that the German Bundestag had been put out of power; for 44 days, Germany had been governed by a crisis squad.[4] Some further laws, like the "Rasterfahndung" (dragnet investigation) or the passage of several "anti-terror laws" in the Bundestag were, to say the least, questionable in terms of constitutional law.

BLURRED ATMOSPHERE

A long-lasting, vague anxiety was in the air all over the country. In 1974, even world-famous novelist Heinrich Böll, who argued with the RAF and especially with Ulrike Meinhof a number of times[5], got under press treatment. His reaction: He took the campaigns against him, the atmosphere, and the governmental overreactions, and transformed them into a novel called "Die verlorene Ehre der Katharina Blum, oder: Wie Gewalt entstehen und wohin sie führen kann" (The Lost Honor of Katharina Blum, Or: How Violence Develops and Where It Can Lead). The novel was made into a film by Volker Schlöndorff one year later.[6] The prefix of the novel, as well as of the film, especially triggered angry reactions from the tabloid press and some politicians: "The characters and storyline of this novel are imaginary. Should the narration of certain journalistic practices show similarities with the practices of newspaper 'Bild', then these similarities are neither intended nor accidental, but inevitable."[7]

When you read articles or literature about Germany, or interviews with some rock musicians of that time, you get the impression that the police were constantly terrorizing the streets all over the country, and that everyday, people lost themselves in the shuffle. Let me assure you: This is not how it was. The more or less most unpleasant thing that could happen to the average person was a traffic check like this one: I think it was in late 1977, while I was serving my time doing civilian service, when one night I was driving home. It was around 1 am and somewhere on an inbound street to Hamburg I was stopped in a stop-and-search operation. A police officer wanted to see my vehicle license and driver's license. The scene was lit by some bright headlamps, but out of the corner of my eye I noticed that, in the darkness, outside the circle of light, four uniformed police officers with machine pistols were standing around my car. Had you seen my car, you would understand what a surreal scene this was: I had an old, white, rusty Renault 4, which would probably have fallen into pieces without the half a dozen bumper stickers against nuclear power, and it was a bit noisy because of a damaged alternator. My hair was at shoulder-length and I wore big round glasses (my Janis Joplin Memorial Glasses, as my then girlfriend used to call them). It is safe to say that the real RAF terrorists at that time never would have touched an unreliable old clunker like mine; they preferred BMWs, wore business suits, all of which were financed by bank robberies. They had short conventional haircuts, and looked like IBM salespeople. I thought it might be better to do what the officer wanted, so I put my hands on the wheel and told him in which pocket he would find my wallet with the driver's license. Surrounded by these four firearms I feared it might be risky to put a hand into the pocket myself – one of these guys might have a nervous index finger. But they checked my name and license plate, returned the licenses to me, wished me a good trip, and told me to do something about the noise. This is the only experience I've ever had with the police in this context. If some of these police actions look a bit disproportionate today, let's not forget: There were reasons for them.

There are some movies, especially *Deutschland im Herbst* (1978)[8] and *The Baader Meinhof Complex* (2008)[9], that try to find artistic ways to deal with the connections between society and terrorism. Both are worth watching, but still today, my toenails curl up when, in *Deutschland im Herbst,* Baader, Ensslin, and Raspe's funeral is shown, overdubbed with the song "Here's To You" by Joan Baez from the movie *Sacco e Vanzetti* (1971) with the diligently repeated lines: "Here's to you [Nicola and Bart] / Rest forever here in our hearts / The last and final moment is yours / That agony is your triumph." You won't hardly find a song more out of place than this one.

The Baader Meinhof Complex is a well-crafted feature film with several of Germany's then movie darlings. It portrays some of the involved persons quite accurately, but attaches an inapt sort of "buccaneer romanticism" to the whole affair – as if these terrorists had been nothing more than some well-meaning but naïve sheep going a bit astray. This way of looking at it couldn't be more wrong. Wolfgang Kraushaar on this film: "Apparently it was mainly the delight of adventure and the admiration of the existential – the life-or-death struggle – that is attractive here. These are the same mechanisms that work in action movies. When in the film adaptation of Aust's [book] 'Der Baader Meinhof Komplex' we see how Andreas Baader wildly fires all over the place at night out of a driving car, then this is the scene where the exceedingly hollow fascination is put in a nutshell. However, what I don't understand: What could be 'cool' about spreading fear and terror, hitting banks, kidnapping people, or even killing them?"[10]

For a while, we had the same phenomenon about this Baader Meinhof spook as we did earlier, about the fancied telephone bugging – some people thought purporting things like that would make them look more interesting at cocktail parties. I already mentioned my civilian service colleagues whose speculations about the RAF suicides had a clear undertone of admiration. At nearly every party in the outgoing 1970s, you could bet there was at least one person who claimed to know not Holger Meins, but at least Holger's sister, personally. Nobody knew whether Meins even had a sister, but this wasn't the point. There was a connection insinuated that made this person "close" to a terrorist. (A similar phenomenon happened after 9/11 – it was perplexing to see how many people suddenly claimed to know somebody who had known Mohammed Atta.)

UNWANTED PARALLELS

It's an interesting parallel that, like our parents and grandparents, most of the surviving RAF terrorists, as well as their sympathizers and helpers, were and are not willing to talk about the details of what they were doing or thinking during their "active" time. They remain silent. When asked, they trail off into meaningless gibberish, or take flight into cynical anecdotes. Of course, no one can look into their heads and know anything about their real feelings today, but it seems to me that even the few who talk didn't learn very much. One of the rare exceptions is Peter-Jürgen Boock who now thinks: "It is a big fuck-up to be a killer"[11] – a very delayed insight and a bucketful of self-pity, but maybe a first step.

THE MUSIC SCENE AND THE RAF

Sometimes, when you read interviews with some pioneering Krautrock musicians (especially the ones with a clear political standpoint), you might find they don't get tired of talking about how often during their concert tours they got stopped and frisked by the police, or their apartments got searched because of terrorists, and what a drag it was then to outsmart the officers about the pot or whatever else they had hidden in the refrigerator or elsewhere. Interestingly, I've noticed more than once that, for some reason, their memory sometimes sets these incidents back to a time when the RAF was not even active yet. But musicians often live on the road, and they had to drive thousands of kilometers, so logically, their chance to get into a stop-and search operation was greater than for the average Joe – and as we all know, memories are not a static thing.

You still find this phenomenon today. One member of the Neue Deutsche Welle band Östro 430 of Düsseldorf, to single out one example, still talks about the stop-and-search-operations of September and October 1977 as if they had been a daily cops and robbers game that she had been a part of.[12] She's not the only one. Older, as well as younger folks, use the RAF era to fantasize a sort of private myth centered around themselves. But the RAF was no adventure playground.

Actually, in the music scene, there was not much reaction. Some agitprop bands (more about them later) felt validated in their distrust against "the state", but this was part of their logic. Some singer-songwriters made the RAF a topic without directly mentioning it, like Franz-Josef Degenhardt ("Bumser Paco", 1980). The schlager scene, of course, remained completely silent. Only the avant-garde showed some reactions, but it took long.

The most important work that directly dealt with the Baader-Meinhof topic was probably *Das Mädchen mit den Schwefelhölzern* by composer Helmut Lachenmann.

This opera (or "music in pictures", as he calls it) premiered in 1997 at Hamburgische Staatsoper, a recording did not appear until four years later. This extremely complex composition uses Hans Christian Andersen's fairytale "The Little Match Girl" as a sort of interlayer to mix in the story of terrorist Gudrun Ensslin. Lachenmann and Ensslin had been childhood neighbors; the composer's father was Ensslin's father's boss. In an interview, Lachenmann said: "Gudrun Ensslin wrote a letter in her Stammheim prison cell using some ugly, violent language, but in the end her words are of touching beauty – beautiful because she calls a spade a spade – so that I do not only simply see the unleashed preparedness to use violence and her broken spirit, but also the love for the individual who breaks under the strictures of society."[13] Lachenmann uses parts of this letter in his libretto.

The equation of Gudrun Ensslin and Andersen's Match Girl (who hallucinates a sort of paradise while in reality she's freezing to death) might look far-fetched. It is a tough go indeed, but it is an attempt to find access to a worldview that made a sensitive, intelligent woman a terrorist, arsonist, and murderer, and in combination with the music, it might come closer to an answer than the mentioned films. And Lachenmann is not a dreamer: "The mutually exacerbating brutalities in the struggle with the not too gentle forces of order disfigured her being. There is no excuse for her criminal deeds. But with her conviction in court, the question of our responsibility is not yet answered."[14]

NUCLEAR POWER PLANTS AND PERSHING II

Two other phenomena of the 1970s shouldn't be left out here because both added their part to the political and sociological climate:

First, people's initiatives started organizing resistance against the nuclear power plants that mushroomed everywhere – later you will hear about Hans-Joachim Roedelius and his fears about the two nuclear power plants near his home, and he was by far not the only one.

Second, in 1979 the NATO Double-Track Decision took place and brought Pershing II middle-range missiles and other new weapons to Germany to rebuild the state of Mutual Assured Destruction. This led to a substantial willingness to offer resistance. This arms race between East and West defined, in large parts, the mood the Germans were in when they entered into the 1980s.

Nuclear power plants and missiles: These were the two points where all the aforementioned radical splinter groups could meet. They were joined by some grass roots organizations like "Strobo" (Stromzahlungsboykott), a short-lived initiative of people who refused to pay the percentage of their electricity bills that utility companies would invest in building nuclear power plants. This and other groupings made it into the political day-to-day business. They entered the citizen's initiatives – the earlier mentioned KB (Kommunistischer Bund) became especially active. None of these groups were able to dominate the anti-nuclear or anti-Pershing movement, but because of their already well-organized infrastructure, they became helpful in printing flyers, putting up information campaigns, protest marches and so on. It has to be mentioned that there were also some right-wing groups and persons joining; many in Germany will remember Baldur Springmann (1912-2003), an extreme right-wing organic farmer with a long Nazi past who, for a while, was a permanent apparition on German TV screens. Somehow, with his white beard and his blue or green smock overalls, he attracted every TV camera; you couldn't escape him. After a while, you could recognize these right-wing folks and their way of thinking by their vocabulary. The initiatives sometimes had a lot of trouble getting rid of them. But fights between different ideologically gridlocked leftist splinter groups also led to permanent quarrels, hostilities, and foundations of splinter groups of splinter groups.

However, the fight against nuclear power plants and new missiles became two of the "big points" of Germany's 1970s and early 1980s. They politicized many citizens and brought people together – many of them had been completely apolitical until then. They even became the trigger for some rock festivals, like the series of "Rock gegen Rechts" concerts, inspired by the British "Rock against Racism" initiative.

Finally, these movements and initiatives resulted in the founding of the Green Party in 1980.

AND WHAT DID YOURS TRULY DO IN THE 1970S?

Besides having a lot of trouble at school and home, for me, the Seventies were a time when I discovered films, sometimes excessively. Usually with one or two friends, I became a sort of fixture at Hamburg's art house cinemas. Sometimes, we were there every evening. After a while, the employees knew us by name, and we knew theirs. We watched all the 1970s stuff that went under "Neuer Deutscher Film" (New German Film) – Kluge, Wenders, Fassbinder, Reitz, Herzog, but also the big ones from France and Italy. Nobody at that time dared to say openly that Wenders' or Herzog's films were appallingly boring and far-fetched, which in fact several of them were. But their camera work was often stunning, and sometimes they had great music; there were the great Popol Vuh soundtracks for Herzog's films or the music Improved Sound Limited made for Wim Wenders' *Im Lauf der Zeit* or Erwin Keusch's *Das Brot des Bäckers*. Wenders also used to integrate some original American rock music into his movies, like Creedence Clearwater Revival. But sometimes also cheap comedies like *Car Wash* (1976) or action movies like *Vanishing Point* (1971) were on our watch list.

With two friends, I started a lightshow group. The motivation for this probably came from our love for the Jefferson Airplane and other San Franciscan bands, but also from a Nektar concert (of several) we saw that had left its traces. First, if memory serves, we called ourselves X-Lights, then later we became Waves. The basic idea was to build a lightshow set-up small and compact enough to be suitable for small and medium-sized venues like clubs, youth centers, or school auditoriums. We worked with spotlights, strobes, rotating lights, slides, oil projections, liquid wheels, and a couple of inventions we made ourselves (like foam projections, to name one).

Waves Lightshow in 1978, at a youth center somewhere. Standing on the right is Uwe, projectionist (today an organ builder), left (outside the picture) is Ralph, projectionist (today a car dealer), and Yours Truly is at the lights mixing desk. © Frank Thiele

We made a projection screen from white bed sheets sewn together and used tent poles to set it up (and I will never forget the moment when this construction broke down one evening; luckily it happened before the audience had arrived). At one Nektar concert, we asked their lights operator Mick Brockett what they used to dye glass plates. We needed them to be put in our projectors to have colored light, but our attempts with varnish or tinted water didn't work satisfactorily. Mick told us to use stamp-pad ink (it worked fine, thank you for this, Mick!). Waves existed for five or six years, and after a while, we had a handful of bands in and around Hamburg that we worked regularly with (or they with us). One of them was an interesting electronic improvisation duo whose name I forgot; they were a bit like Seesselberg, but better. During our active time we already knew that lightshows were a bit nostalgic, but the way we did it was unique, no "professional" show ever would have done it our way, and for the audience it was a glimpse into a psychedelic show era that most of them had never seen live on a stage before. We were around 20 years old, and it was a lot of fun.

In the following chapters you will see how music both formed and blended into this zeitgeist, simultaneously.

THE SEVENTIES

AMATEURS AND PROFESSIONALS

In the early 1970s, the beat era was definitely over and "German rock" became more visible, but one thing still remained the same: No matter what record companies and musicians tried in the early 1970s, German rock music remained a special market for special people.

When a band started, the members were usually amateurs who knew each other from school. The first thing they had to find was a rehearsal room. In the countryside, this could be dad's garage, a barn, or the local youth center. In a city it could be more complicated; sometimes schools or parish halls offered their rooms, sometimes there were (and still are) air-raid shelters from WWII that hadn't been torn down. Their walls are massive, it was nearly impossible to demolish them at reasonable costs or without damaging the neighboring buildings, so the local authorities often made a virtue out of necessity and rented the rooms cheaply to rock bands. This was not a bad solution because, inside, you could crank up the volume to 11 without disturbing any neighbors. I, however, always felt uncomfortable inside such a building. I could never stop imagining what might have been going on in this place during air strikes, and I could feel these people's fear crawling down the walls. But maybe that's just me.

One of the first things the band now had to decide was: Should we play cover versions or should we try to write our own compositions? If you do cover versions, you will be compared to the original; in addition, playing covers was a thing of the beat era. Most bands tried to play their own compositions, usually in a style between melodic and hard rock without many individual tricks. Self-written songs followed the song scheme of intro, verse, refrain, verse, refrain, instrumental bridge, refrain, outro. The irony with the latter was that, sometimes, nobody wanted to do it like schlagers did, and so the self-written songs were usually longer but still followed the basic schlager structure. Lyrics were usually written in the English language. Sometimes it was more a sort of fantasy English, but it didn't hurt because not many people in the audience paid much attention to the lyrics. Later, in the 1970s, it became more and more unthinkable to simply "copy" foreign bands, but then, simultaneously, many bands bent over backwards to avoid "sounding German". This contradiction remained unsolved for several years – in most cases, bands *did* have a German sound, but it took a while until they realized that this must not necessarily be seen as negative. It could also be a way to differ from British or American rock.

The next step was to build up a local fan community. In cities, bands had to compete with several other music events, if bands lived in the countryside, they knew their competitor would be the Saturday night disco at the local youth center or inn. A certain sense of togetherness could arise, especially in small towns, where everyone knew each other, and a band could well be part of it – after a while, they became a sort of fixture in the youth center or the local clubs and were seen as the town's "very own". In addition, the young folks in small-towns and villages had a much more emotional tie to their local youth center or club than their contemporaries in big towns. In these youth centers, they had painted the walls, built the photographic laboratory, played tabletop soccer or table tennis. They had donated posters, installed the obligatory lighting effects or other technical things, took on counter duties, brought their records or made cassette tapes, and sometimes had to fight against local authorities. All this counted in making the youth center a second home. Usually, there were four categories of folks hanging out: the beer and alcohol faction, the pot faction, the sports faction, and the political faction. They were not too close with each other, but they all knew that this was *their house*. If a concert was scheduled, it was easy to understand that the audience reacted to it in a completely different way than the folks in a big town club with at least three other bands competing in other clubs the same evening.

Of course, all this had to work without getting in the way of day jobs, school, friends and family life. If you asked musicians, they would say: "We just do it for fun, we have no professional intentions." Most bands were all-male; the tone within bands was often latently misogynic, and when band members had girlfriends, they were allowed to attend the concerts, but they weren't welcome in the band's rehearsal room. The only exception was a female singer, but female instrumentalists were rare.

The music had to be straightforward, harmonic, and not too complicated – "honest", as they used to call it. Instrumental virtuosity, on the one hand, was well appreciated and every guitarist had his hero, but when a musician was *too* much of a virtuoso, he was not seen as "honest" anymore. This was a strange, yet common way of thinking – as if a musician who really mastered his instrument was somehow disingenuous. Even if a band was able to integrate some psychedelic effects they had lifted from records or concerts into their tunes, most of the musicians never had any of their own serious experiences with psycho-active drugs, except maybe a joint from time to time. They mainly left it at beer; chumminess and good mood was the important point of the whole band project, not ecstasy.

There were definitely hundreds of bands like this in Germany. If they were not completely talentless, they could become well-known in their region; this led their pay for performances to increase from maybe 50 D-Marks plus free beer to something in the 500 D-Marks range, when they became "locally world-famous". This was the maximum you could get as an amateur band. In most cases, fiscal authorities showed some consideration, classified the band as a hobby project and didn't cash in any taxes from them. This was indeed discretionary, given that bands cashed in 500 D-Marks per evening and played every Saturday, leading them to make roughly 2000 D-Marks per month or 400 D-Marks per person (for a five-piece band). 400 D-Marks in the 1970s could cover both the monthly rent for your apartment and the fuel for your car, so it was not an absurd idea to classify the fee as "income". If the tax office didn't play ball with the band, the members were advised to become a "GbR" (Gesellschaft bürgerlichen Rechts), a partnership organized under the Civil Code – which meant that somebody had to be the band's treasurer and bookkeeper; a job that was usually left to one of the girlfriends.

If the band had managed to become known in their area, it was common to, after about three or four years, privately make a vinyl record with live, rehearsal room, or cheap studio recordings at a print run of, say, 300 copies. 200 of them were sold at the concerts, 50 were given away to friends, the local press, and sent to some record companies as demos, the remaining copies were piled up on one member's attic, collecting dust, and when the band was finally shut down, they were thrown away because space was needed for other things. In some cases, the pile of LPs may have remained, and been discovered by a British record dealer in 2015 who took it with him and sold the records for a lot of money on eBay as a "hidden gem" and "extremely influential part of the German Krautrock era".

These bands usually played clubs, youth centers, and small multi-purpose halls within a 50 kilometer radius around their home. Sometimes, they were part of nearby festivals. If they were very lucky, they got hired as local supporting acts for a touring, professional Krautrock band. This was certainly the highlight of their career, and later, with the photo album on his knees, dad would tell his grandchildren: "Look, this is Guru Guru on stage, we were their supporting act, and I still remember how their drummer Mani Neumeier, after we had done our set, turned to us behind stage and said: 'Wow, you seem to be well-known here!'" To receive such a comment from them had felt like a sort of honour.

The lifetime of these bands was around six, sometimes seven years. They fell apart because family, other hobbies, or day jobs became more important. Somebody may have relocated, or the members got into a more and more intractable row about their repertoire. But in some cases, the one big question finally came up: Shall we turn professional?

This could be a hard question, and you could damage or even destroy a potential career if you waited too long. The Hamburg band Novalis, for example, got a record deal with Brain in 1973, but they kept their day jobs (logistics manager, record dealer, advertising clerk, telecommunications technician). This seems reasonable, but the consequence was that they were hardly able to promote their albums in a proper way. They couldn't go on tour; they could only play single concerts on weekends and during their vacation time. Their first concert tour with 35 dates to promote their already fifth album *Brandung* didn't happen before 1978 – five years after their record deal. When they finally made the decision to give up their jobs, the band's career had already turned into stagnation. All in all, Novalis sold around 400,000 albums (a fifth of them in Japan), which wasn't bad, so we can't say they missed the bus, but I'm sure they could have done a lot better if they had decided to give up their jobs earlier. But this is easy to say in hindsight. At that time, the risk was real, and they surely didn't make this decision lightly.

At least Novalis *did* the jump. Most bands turned down the idea of getting professional – the talent scout they waited for never showed up, turned out to be all talk and no connections, or wanted to be paid in advance (which is an absolute no-no!). The demo tapes were rejected, girlfriends and wives didn't like the risk, there was a house or a car that had to be paid off (not to talk of having children!). Being a professional musician would have been too big of a step into an unsafe area. There was always a dad or an uncle who pointed out that there was no money in music – as the German saying goes, it's "brotlose Kunst" ("breadless feat") – so they insisted that you at least had to get a "real" job first. Often enough, fights with parents broke out just to be allowed to even *play* in an amateur band – there were so many horror stories about rock music in the tabloids that parents feared their children would miss school or their apprenticeships, fall into bad company, or get on the syringe. In most families (as in mine), it was not even *considered* that the junior might become a musician. It was simply too far out. I don't know a valid statistic about this, but when you read professional musicians' biographies, you will find that many of them had parents who were musicians themselves, worked as music teachers, church organists et cetera, or were at least connected to "artful" jobs, like architecture, acting, or something like this. Or – the not so funny alternative – parents didn't care much about what their offspring was up to.

THE STONY WAY TO PROFESSIONALISM

What if a band was artistically fit enough and willing to jump into cold water?

One basic difference between musicians in Germany and the U.S. is that most German bands saw themselves as an inseparable unit (in parts, this goes for British bands too). If, for whatever reason, one member left, the whole project was in danger. Musicians in the U.S. usually viewed their jobs through a business lens. When they wanted to be professionals, they knew New York or Los Angeles were the places to go. Musicians were hired for a band and changed as needed. The Byrds, for example, were a project of Roger McGuinn and a couple of employees, and this was the norm. Unthinkable in Germany! When, in the 1990s, Wolfgang Flür and Karl Bartos left Kraftwerk and it became known to fans that they had just been "employees" for the core members, Ralf Hütter and Florian Schneider, many fans were deeply shocked.

MANAGEMENT

In the 1960s and early 1970s, privately managing a rock band was risky business. In fact, it was forbidden by law. Artists' management was officially seen as an employment service, and the monopoly for providing this service was with the local job offices. These centers had a special department called "Künstlerdienst" (service department for artists). The problem was that the job placement officers were usually fit to find local gigs for emcees, stand-up comedians, allround-DJs, conjurers, magicians, children's hospital clowns, and all-purpose dance bands for weddings and old-age homes. But most of them, even the younger ones, didn't have much knowledge about rock music, not to mention the necessities of band management. They were of no use for rock bands, and that's why there was no other reasonable way for a band than to set up its own management.

These private managers had to be very careful about revealing what they were doing – especially when they had to negotiate with municipal youth centers or the heads of multi-purpose halls run by local authorities. Some bands tried to avoid the legal pitfalls by declaring their manager a member of the band, but there was still risk. Even the relatively well-established label head, Rolf-Ulrich Kaiser, was once fined 10,000 D-Marks for managing bands from his roster.

Another problem resulted from the fact that many of these self-made "band managers" saw themselves more as artists or wild rockers than serious managers. They had no clue about business and came up with abstruse ideas about musicians' fees, catering at concerts, advertising, et cetera. Even for good-willed, negotiating partners, dealing with these guys sometimes meant riding the razor's edge.

It was not before the mid-Seventies that this law became suspended and bands were allowed to run their own management officially and legally.

ON TOUR

In Germany, there were no professionally organized concert tours for German rock bands before 1973. MaMa Concerts (run by *Ma*rcel Avram and *Ma*rek Lieberberg) and Lippmann + Rau, both in Frankfurt, probably Germany's best-known big concert promoters (in Germany they are called "Konzertagentur", concert agency), only organized tour productions for big fish, like The Rolling Stones, foreign show stars, popular schlager acts, and classical concerts. Horst Lippmann (1927–1997) and Fritz Rau (1930-2013) had a special love for German jazz, blues acts, and singer-songwriters; Fritz Rau, originally a jurist, organized his first concert with Albert Mangelsdorff in 1955[1] and made concerts and festivals after that. But even he was not interested in organizing concerts for German rock bands before 1973. In 1975, when Fritz Rau was asked why he didn't support more German bands, he downright exploded: "I'm not a nationalist, for me there are no German rock groups, for me there are only rock groups! I don't have to fulfill any duties for the German nation, I don't have to push up German rock in terms of a Reichskulturkammer!"[2]

Rau has always been a poltergeist, but of the likeable sort. Born in 1930, he had spent his childhood and early teenage years under the Nazis, and he was fed up with any kind of nationalism for the rest of his life. Later, he became one of the most important concert promoters, which included German acts. Through a business perspective however, his fierce reaction was somewhat understandable: The number of tickets you could expect to be sold when German acts toured was small – too small to cover the costs of a professionally organized tour. Concert promoters knew that dealing with these bands was extremely risky, and even if it worked out, they couldn't make much money with their target group. In addition, club owners, innkeepers, or runners of youth centers were neither interested nor trained in dealing with professional concert promoters; they were used to hiring bands on their own account. Even after 1973, when some promoters (usually start-ups) finally began organizing concerts and tours with German acts, it took long until they learned what was needed for such concerts. Small local concert organizers especially had no idea about rock bands, their needs, and what or when to pay them. Most of them acted in good faith but simply didn't have the know-how yet to do it right.

This is the reason why most bands had to organize everything on their own. To make a living, they needed to accept every gig they could land, and this made it nearly impossible to flesh out reasonable tour schedules. The band members had to ride highly absurd roadway arrangements and distances with their typically packed Ford Transit, Volkswagen Bus, or Variant (or, like FRANZ K., an old hearse). – One day they would have a gig in Gummersbach near Cologne, the next in Augsburg (Bavaria), and the day after they played Amsterdam. You get the picture. In Germany we call this "tingeln" – doing small time. A gig in West Berlin was attractive, but meant dealing with border controls to pass the transit way through the GDR, and if the band was unlucky, all their equipment would be weighed and sometimes disassembled by the border guards on the way to Berlin and again on the way back to West Germany. Not every band had the nerve touring like CLUSTER: Roedelius and Moebius drove from museum to museum and gallery to gallery, knocked on doors and asked: "Are you willing to let us perform here tonight?" Some did, and some didn't. Being a rock musician meant hitting the road with decrepit vehicles, "fahr'n, fahr'n, fahr'n auf der Autobahn", thousands of kilometers – you see where KRAFTWERK probably dredged up the idea for their tune.

CONCERTS AND FESTIVALS

If you ask them what they think was the most important thing for youth culture in general at that time and the number one place for collective life and shared experiences, many people would answer: rock concerts. Anecdotes about the Sixties are full of quotes like that. But political scientist Wolfgang Kraushaar sees it a bit differently: "At least in the second half of the Sixties in this country, concerts did not play a decisive role. This didn't change before 1970 when the impact of the *Woodstock* movie and the triple album that was spread by mass media and present everywhere, was tried to adopt and to imitate. … Before this, without any doubt, the central way of collectivization for all those who saw themselves as somehow oppositional or rebellious had been protests and manifestations."[3]

You couldn't get rich from playing concerts, but it was the main source of income for most bands. In the mid-1970s, a well-established band like KRAAN could usually make between 3000 and 5000 D-Marks per concert,[4] but this was already "all inclusive". The "average band" was far from such amounts.

GURU GURU sold about 4000 copies of each of their first two albums (1970 and 1971). The third one, *Känguru* (1972), sold 12,000 copies, but then the figures went back down again. Mani Neumeier: "We made our living from live performances. We said to ourselves that window washing in between or screwing something together, or sawing, or office jobs, was something we did for years, and we won't do it anymore – verboten! Better save money and make ends meet with music only. Nothing came from the records, and the advanced money, sometimes 5000 D-Marks or so, that went into our equipment. It was a modest life, but after a while, you get used to it. What's important is the time you have for yourself, and the dough enough to live."[5]

To get booked for clubs and youth centers, bands had to deal with negotiating partners who also were not professional. Youth centers in the countryside were oftentimes run by local school teachers, pastors, deacons, or social workers, more or less in their free time. Usually, these guys were fair to deal with, but sometimes they had their own ideas about what the exact meaning of "fair" was, or how to organize a concert. Besides this, they had their day job, so it was a common incident that the band stood in front of the closed door and had to wait for hours until somebody came to let them in (there were no cell phones and no twitter at that time). You could bet that on stage (if there was one at all!), they only had one wall outlet, and when you plugged in more than one amp, somewhere in the basement, the fuse melted. So you had to knit adventurous cable chains from the stage to another circuit, which could be in the middle of the tearoom or somewhere in the photo darkroom, and of course, during the concert, somebody would pull the plug, just out of curiosity.

You always had to be prepared that only seven people would show up because the club owner "forgot" to hang out the band's posters they had sent to him two weeks in advance. There were several backstairs methods to cheat bands, and this didn't change until there were serious concert promoters involved.

AUDIENCES

To appreciate German rock at that time, you needed the willingness to be open to experimentation, sounds you weren't used to, and you needed a good amount of tolerance for mistakes, failures, flaws, incompetent singers, or guitarists who had good ideas in their head but not in their fingers. Actually, in the early 1970s, fans of German rock were a sort of community. At concerts in Hamburg and the surrounding area, I always saw the same faces in the audience – after a while we began to recognize each other, and this happened over Germany.

For the musicians, it was not always fun to deal with these audiences. The German audiences in the late 1960s and early 1970s could be a special beast, but not only for German bands. Several British and American bands also had to learn this the hard way. Many young folks had no understanding that bands asked for entrance fees and didn't play for free. The entrance fee could be as small as imaginable, yet was still always too high. Every so often, groups of fans smashed doors or windows of venues, entered violently, barged into already (over-)crowded auditoriums, and sometimes provoked perilous situations, or they physically threatened or simply ignored the cashbox guy or girl. By doing so, in their worldview, they occupied the moral high ground. This was a sort of Sixty-Eight leftover: "What, a band wants money? Obviously they try to sell out now, we can't accept that!" Bands with a political approach, like the EDGAR BROUGHTON BAND, VOLKS-MUSIK or TON STEINE SCHERBEN, had to be especially aware of this phenomenon. More than once, the police had to be called to calm down ticklish situations, often against the resistance even of the bands themselves – they didn't want to be associated with the "bulls", as police officers were called at that time, but sometimes there was no other way. When, in 1970, CREEDENCE CLEARWATER REVIVAL played the West Berlin Sportpalast, they were shocked to see armed police in front of the venue.[6] I don't dare to imagine the impression of Germany they took home with them. On the other hand, the GRATEFUL DEAD had had the experience of fans breaking doors to get into a venue already at home in the U.S., so this might have been an international phenomenon.[7] However, it took a couple of years until German audiences finally learned that you can't expect professional music from hobby musicians.

For some reason, Germany, especially West Berlin, had the most aggressive autograph hunters in the world. As GRATEFUL DEAD bassist Phil Lesh describes, they lay in wait for the musicians in hotel lobbies or in front of the stage entrance, hunted them even to the airport and drove them into a corner there. They seemed to believe they had a right to get autographs, insisted on it with commanding voices, and they didn't ask for *one* autograph, they came up with piles of 20 or more records to get them signed. You could be sure that within a short time the autographed records would show up for sale in the classifieds of respective music magazines (today they would be on eBay within three hours).[8] Ringo Starr stopped signing things for this reason.

LODGING

Even musicians on tour need to sleep sometimes. How about in hotels? Not an option, as long as we talk about German bands. Even when hotel rooms were booked and pre-confirmed, the usually long-haired and often wild-looking musicians had to be prepared to meet a desk clerk who sent them packing – usually with words like "We are very sorry, but one of our apprentices had made a terrible mistake, we don't have any vacancies tonight." Most musicians were used to that, even more since they had probably already gotten thrown out of the Autobahn-Raststätte (highway restaurant) around noon. Most of these places are still as horrible as their food. In small villages, sometimes one had to be cautious about getting provoked and beaten up by groups of "respectable citizens". Many long-haired American musicians had the same problem in (but not limited to) southern areas of the United States.

But in many cases, hotels were much too expensive for poor German bands anyway, so it was common that local flat-sharing communities hosted them. Sometimes the bands, after they finished their gig, asked directly from the stage whether someone in the audience would be able to host them for the night. Sometimes there was a friendly teacher who let them sleep in his school building. Sometimes, especially in villages and small towns where a couple of hippie communities existed, there were downright competitions between them – the communards already waited at the door after the concert, and the game was:

Who will be able to catch the band tonight? To host a rock band at home was seen as a sort of attraction, and if it couldn't be the STONES, the better-known German bands were a decent alternative. The musicians could then sleep on air mattresses, sofas, or in sleeping bags – if mattresses weren't already spread out on the floor anyway instead of having sofas and seats. Of course, they were then expected to yarn cock-and-bull stories about their minstrelsy till four in the morning, trash talk the horrible hotels, youth centers, or clubs in other villages, play a private acoustic session for the residents, write crazy things into the guest book, autograph the resident's guitars or bongo drums (every flat-sharing community had at least one pair of those), and share their pot with them (the smallest problem, usually). At least this way there was nothing the bands had to pay for; they got free wine, free beer, and free breakfast, and sometimes also free sex.

FESTIVALS

When, after the Woodstock festival in 1969, an open-air festival fever broke out in Germany, most local governments rarely had an idea about how to deal with the arriving rock fans. Soon, access roads were blocked by illegally parked cars, neither roadies nor ambulances could pass, sometimes the fans had to walk two miles through mud to reach the festival area. Sanitary arrangements were overflowing, poor, or completely missing. Nobody felt in charge of profanities like these. There was no garbage management, soon the lawn was laced with broken bottles and the first-aid wards were completely overstrained.

Often, sound systems were underdesigned, gave up the ghost when it rained, or the wind carried the sound away into nowhere. It was rare that somebody had ever heard of delay lines, and when they existed, they were often balanced incorrectly because there was not enough time for a real soundcheck. So from many standpoints, you heard the music once and, with a short delay, a second time. Usually, the organizers heavily miscalculated the time the bands needed to set up their equipment, so between sets nothing happened for an hour or longer.

The most annoying thing, when festivals were a new development in Germany, was the habit of organizers to print out posters, flyers, and press releases with all the bands and musicians they would like to have – without asking them. These hobby organizers simply thought that if they invite a band, the musicians would be happy to play for them. How could they not come! This, of course, led to disappointment at festivals when promised acts didn't play because they had never confirmed to appear, and the audiences sometimes reacted aggressively

Audience at the second British Rock Meeting on the island Grün near Germersheim (1972)
© Manfred Rinderspacher

with riots and destroying stages or equipment when poor emcees had to break the news to them.

In summer 1972, the Bavarian federal state government sent the "recommendation" to all communities to not permit open air rock festivals for the time being. The main reasons were the problems with garbage, traffic, alcohol, drugs, and noise. This edict was hardly attackable because it was only a "recommendation", but the communities got it completely right. So for a while, Bavaria was not the best place for rock festivals anymore.

For several bands and artists who played Woodstock – like Joe Cocker or Santana – this festival marked the start of their world career, and they referred to Woodstock throughout their lives. Nothing like this can be said about a German rock festival. No German band became famous for having played Fehmarn or Scheeßel. Ton Steine Scherben might be the exception: The riots after their Fehmarn performance were mentioned in Germany's main news broadcast "Tagesschau" and gave them 15 minutes of fame.

Besides this, there was often a sort of unexpressed separation between German and foreign bands. Only every so often they shared the same festival stages; otherwise, we had lots of "German Rock Festivals" with exclusively German acts, except the appearance of Nektar, who were originally from England but were definitely part of the Krautrock scene, as well as Sweet Smoke, and maybe singer-songwriter Jack Grunsky from Canada. It was a bit as if German bands didn't have the heart to contend directly with British or American bands. Or maybe it was the festival organizers who had the feeling that these were two different worlds?

Some of these German festivals had (sub-)titles that made puns of Nazi vocabulary or slogans, like already the Essener Songtage: “Deutschland erwacht – Popmusik aus deutschen Landen”. “Deutschland, erwache!” (Germany, wake up!) had been an anti-Semitic slogan of the Nazis, and it was known for having been this.[9] Didn't the organizers know this? I think they did, and they either found it funny or wanted to “provoke”. Most of the audience didn't care either. But some Jewish singers or bands from the U.S. knew this connection quite well from their parents or grandparents, and even if they didn't say it, they felt appalled. And they were right, this was more than a question of taste. Anti-Semitism has always been a latent problem in Germany. It was not something the Nazis invented, they just made use of it, and it did not go away after the Nazi empire had fallen (and if we Germans get upset about some British ads like the examples shown in the introducing chapter, we should keep in mind that when you point a finger at something or somebody, then three fingers on the same hand point back at you).

EQUIPMENT

A big problem for German bands that played live was the sound. While in U.S. sound equipment, PA systems and stage monitors could already be rented, there was nothing like this in Germany. Most clubs or youth centers in the 1960s had no or inadequate in-house sound equipment; the Star-Club and a handful of others were rare exceptions. In smaller venues, the bands simply used their guitar and keyboard amps, the drums didn't need any amplification, only the singer needed some speakers to get his microphone amplified. There was no monitor system on stage and no mixing desk in front of the stage. For many bands, parts of the required equipment, like speakers or amps, were do-it-yourself constructions; many bands had or knew somebody who was able to solder and work with the electronic stuff they needed.

If bands had the opportunity to play bigger halls like the multipurpose halls that existed in most towns, the problem came up. These venues usually had their own sound system, but in the first place it was installed to bring announcements to the audience, and it was operated by a technician or a caretaker who didn't belong to the band. These systems were not made for music and sounded horrible. In the 1970s, the stage setups changed anyway, so the bands started bringing their own sound systems and technicians. Even in the more professional U.S., this could sometimes be a shock for venue managers, as concert promoter Pat DiCesare remembers when in 1969 he brought Big Brother & The Holding Company with Janis Joplin to Pittsburgh's Civic Arena: "When they backed a 40-foot truck up to the stage door, I said, 'You have that big of a truck with just sound equipment?' Sure enough, they did. I had never seen so many speakers for a concert, and we had to move seats to accommodate a soundboard. ... The head usher was bent out of shape. 'What's all this fuss about the sound? They're blocking the view of people behind the stage and on the ends of the stage,' he said. 'And what will I do about the people who bought seats where that soundboard is located? Those were good seats. Where do I put those people?' Roy Clair, who was by my side at the mixing board, said, 'Sir, you better get used to this, because this is the way it is going to be for all the bands.'"[10]

In Germany, interestingly, it was not a rock band who first came up with their own PA system. It was Manuela, a schlager singer who'd come to fame in 1963 with "Schuld war nur der Bossa Nova", a cover version of Eydie Gormé's "Blame It on the Bossa Nova". She brought her own professional live band (named The Five Dops) and three back-up singers, and around 1966 she was fed up with the poor sound systems that clubs and venues provided and decided to not be dependent on in-house sound systems any longer.

The big drawback: A usable PA system, consisting of power amps, several microphones, a mixing desk, and of course several speaker cabinets, had to be bought, and inevitably this put most bands in deep financial troubles. Amounts between 50,000 and 70,000 D-Marks for the equipment soon accumulated. If the band also used special electronic instruments like a synthesizer or mellotron, it could be 100,000 or more. Some lucky musicians had rich parents or patrons, but it was usually the record company throwing money in. A record company, even a big one, has nothing to give away for free, so the company deducted the advanced amount from the band's record royalties. If the records didn't sell well, the band was under monetary pressure from then on. Think back to when Amon Düül II lost their equipment in a fire in Cologne – later in this book, you will read about Rolf-Ulrich Kaiser's "sunshine contracts", as he used to call them.

Having their own PA system brought two further problems for bands: First, all this stuff had to be moved, and that meant that the Volkswagen Bus wouldn't do anymore. Second: Some stages were too small for such a system. The bands now had to figure out how much space they needed on stage and make this part of the contract they negotiated. Club owners often had no idea about stage equipment, or they didn't take this part of the contract seriously and guaranteed specifications that weren't actually available.

At that time, most PA systems were not as good as we know them today. They were loud, but the sound quality often left a lot to be desired, and distortions made your ears ring for hours after the concert, sometimes even for days. Today, the industry is able to build stronger magnets, so the speaker membranes can be made from other material combinations rather than pure cardboard – PVC, carbon, sometimes light metal. Today's PA systems usually consist of hanging midrange speakers and tweeters, combined with subwoofers. These systems are smaller, but even on very high volumes, the sound is clear, undistorted, and tortures your eardrums much less than the old PAs. You also don't need to buy them anymore, you can rent them as needed.

LIFE

If you're in good health (and maybe have some chemical assistance), you can live this way as a musician for a couple of years. At the age of 25, we all are immortal. But nobody can live on the road this way forever. The day will come when, after your concert, you want a decent hotel room for yourself.

Like it or not, that's the time when it becomes clear to you that you need to make money with your music, and this includes setting up a functioning tour management. Not to mention tiny little things, like keeping a romantic relationship alive or family life going. There's an old musician's rule, saying: "What happens on the road stays on the road", but that doesn't mean the partner at home has no intuition about what "happens on the road", and this can be extremely harmful for a relationship. Of course, it was possible to have your partner come along with you on tour, but they usually didn't do this more than once – a concert tour is boring and frustrating when you have nothing to do, so most girlfriends, wives or lovers simply preferred to stay at home. And a musician's life on the road doesn't end back home. After a tour, you still remain in a mental state of emergency for several days, maybe longer. The job continues on with writing new songs, rehearsing, and recording, and the next tour might come soon.

For many musicians, these circumstances meant the end of their career after a couple of years because they had to come to a final decision. As a single person, you can do a lot of things you cannot do when you're in a relationship. This sounds like truism, but for a touring professional musician it can simply be bitter reality.

THE SEVENTIES

BEING PROFESSIONAL

When a musician made the decision to go professional, a lot of follow-up decisions came up. I'm not talking about classical musicians – Germany had around 150 professional symphony orchestras back then, so most musicians who had finished a conservatory found a job, and most were well-paid. For rock musicians, there were no show schools or degree courses like today. You had to learn your instrument and find your way.

Diedrich Diederichsen, Germany's leading rock theorist (if something like this exists), writes that a rock career doesn't start with guitar or piano lessons, it starts with a look in the mirror, and then the question: How do I want them to see me?[1] But most German rock musicians in the Seventies acted just the opposite way. They were not interested in building up a visual image, a special look, or remarkable habits. They wanted to be seen solely through their work. Their stage appearance was, let's say, reserved. Krautrock bands usually didn't go for show; they didn't dance, they didn't wear special stage clothes like glitter jackets, or adventurous coiffed hair (if so, it was meant ironically, but irony was never their strongest point). They were the hippies next door. They looked more or less like we all looked at that time (except for if you had an office job or something where business attire and neat hairdos were mandatory): long-hair, patched or colorful embroidered bell-bottom jeans, the obligatory parka, which in winter became the obligatory Afghan fur coat (Yours Truly had a white one – it looked cool, but was scratchy), and self-rolled cigarettes in hand (Van Nelle and Samson were the tobacco brands of choice). KRAFTWERK was probably the first band that worked intendedly *against* this kind of image, but even they didn't do this until 1975, when *Autobahn* had entered the charts and they started touring the U.S.; on the album's back cover photo they were still shown as long-haired hippies.

There's a lore by psychologist Paul Watzlawick (1921-2007) that states one cannot *not* communicate. Because of this, after a while, the seemingly "unintentional" habit of most German musicians to have no image outside the stereotypical "hippie" turned out to grow into a sort of "anti-image". Wanted or not, an anti-image is still an image. This allowed fans to recognize each other.

Kraftwerk: Autobahn, German back cover, 1974

But this anti-image was not the way the "mainstream rock audience" (for lack of a better term) wanted to see their favorite bands and musicians. The term was not yet commonly known in Germany, but let's not forget that it was the rise of Glam rock, coming over from the U.K., acts like The Sweet, T. Rex, Slade, Mud or Gary Glitter, that dominated the charts. But even the more prog-oriented audience usually was not willing to take risks. People mainly wanted to hear slight variations of what they already knew, they were not interested in being confronted with big surprises. When these fans appeared at a concert with German rock, or when at a festival, a German band suddenly appeared between two British acts, the situation could easily get uncomfortable. If this band was Karthago, Jane, or maybe Nektar, it could work out, but woe betide a band like Kraftwerk, Cluster, or Faust if they entered the stage. The spectators were neither able to make head or tail of what they saw, nor were they willing. Even the artfully ironic Roxy Music, although from Britain, failed miserably on their first German tour, and somehow this had to happen – most of the German audience simply did not understand what these guys were up to. The band was taken deeply seriously. On top of this, Brian Eno played a synthesizer on stage, and so, Roxy Music was immediately seen as an "electronic" band. "Geeeeze, no, go away with this plastic crap, this is not even music, nobody needs that," was the standard reaction. Consequently, "Virginia Plain", their first 45, was rejected upon its introduction by "Hit oder Niete", the German radio version of "Juke Box Jury". Finally, Roxy Music caught the German audience with their third album, *Stranded*, when Eno and his synthesizer had left, but even today, this band is still latently misunderstood.

MAKING A LIVING

Arno Steffen, singer of Cologne band TRIUMVIRAT, opened up a calculation in the early 1970s: "As a German band, if you sell 100,000 copies of your LP, and the band has five members, then, depending on the deal you have with your record company, let's say you might get 100,000 D-Marks on royalties." (In 1972, this was equivalent to just under 30,000 dollars.) This is already an amount on the upper end; as long as you were not a star, a record company usually paid the band an amount between 50 Pfennigs and 1 D-Mark for every album copy sold. Steffen: "If you do a lot of touring and write your own songs, you can add another 100,000 D-Marks, coming from the GEMA [the German copyright society]. All in all, that is 200,000 D-Marks. Now we have to divide this by five, so that is 40,000 D-Marks gross. No taxes are paid yet, no health insurance, nothing. And now think about how long it might take to sell 100,000 LPs – this might come up to a year and a half. That means: You've made 40,000 D-Marks gross in a year and a half. So now divide this by 18 and you end up with a monthly gross of roughly 2000 D-Marks. If I'd work as a streetcar conductor, I'd have a salary of 2800 gross, maybe 2900 including bonus for doing night shifts."[2]

For most German bands, selling 100,000 copies of an album remained a dream. At home, even a top act like KRAAN sold just 30,000 copies of their *Live* double album (1975). Some thousand copies of this album were sold in Denmark, but neighboring countries were not a factor a band could rely on – KRAFTWERK, at that time, had already entered the U.S. charts, but that doesn't mean they were successful everywhere. In Denmark, for example, *Autobahn* had only sold 800 copies. The KRAAN musicians numbered their monthly income as "the salary of a clerk at a record company: under 2000 D-Marks gross".[3]

The musicians of LA DÜSSELDORF had to work on a building site during the production of their album *Viva*. In his early years, Edgar Froese worked as a graphic artist for the BVG, the local public transportation company of West Berlin.

GERMAN ROCK RECORDS IN NUMBERS

An average production of an average German rock band in the early 1970s usually didn't sell more than somewhere between 1000 and 3000 copies. The market had an extremely small volume: Only a half percent of all rock albums sold in Germany originated from German bands, 99.5 percent allotted to British and

American records. In 1973, 148 million records were sold in Germany.[4] Now do the math: The German rock records share was about 750,000 copies with a turnover of circa 5 million D-Marks (turnover, not profit!). Kraftwerk's first album, released in fall 1970 on the Philips label, sold around 60,000 copies within one year; Frumpy's debut *All Will Be Changed* from the same year sold around 15,000 copies. The then Phonogram board members "were and are very satisfied with the sales figures of our progressive German groups Kraftwerk and Frumpy"[5], but it's pretty certain that, internally, they were not happy with these numbers, especially not the Frumpy ones. Numbers like these also marked the dimension that top sellers of Ohr and Pilz (Tangerine Dream, Guru Guru, Ash Ra Tempel) had reached. An album by Les Humphries Singers or James Last Orchestra selling 15,000 copies would have been seen downright as a flop. A schlager 45 broadcast at the monthly TV chart show "ZDF-Hitparade" was expected to sell around 30,000 copies during the following week.

Even after German rock music ignited (or let's say, after it became accepted by a couple of record companies and small parts of the public), the sales numbers remained bleak. In 1977, likely the peak level year of Krautrock, German rock albums ended up selling circa 2 million copies. Here are the twelve best-selling German rock records in 1977 (the number of copies sold in 1977 are in parentheses)[6]:

- Udo Lindenberg: *Panische Nächte* (120,000)
- Jane: *Live At Home* (71,000)
- Kraftwerk: *Trans Europa Express* (67,000)
- Eloy: *Dawn* (65,000)
- Jane: *Between Heaven And Hell* (54,000)
- Scorpions: *Virgin Killer* (46,000)
- Lake: *Lake* (45,000)
- Novalis: *Sommerabend* (40,000)
- Michael Rother: *Flammende Herzen* (40,000)
- La Düsseldorf: *Düsseldorf* (35,000)
- Kraan: *Wiederhören* (33,000)
- New Triumvirat: *Pompeii* (32,000)

Again, do the math: That's 608,000 records on this list. Because the sales number of German rock records was around 2 million, the remaining circa 1.4 million sold copies spread over the approximately 250 acts that were signed by a record label.[7] Mathematically, this results in a medium of just under 5600 sold copies per act – and as mentioned, this was the top year of Krautrock.

None of the albums listed above, not even Udo Lindenberg, reached a position in Germany's general 1977 Top 100 album charts, and there were no 45s by a German rock act that made it into the 1977 Top 100 single chart.[8] Worldwide, TANGERINE DREAM sold 250,000 copies of *Phaedra*, 300,000 of *Rubycon* and 350,000 of *Ricochet*; in Germany these albums sold 10,000, 12,000 and 15,000 copies, in France it was 40,000, 45,000 and 50,000 (France had always been a bigger market for German electronic rock then Germany itself). Klaus Schulze's records mainly sold in the same range.[9] AMON DÜÜL II, BIRTH CONTROL, CAN, KIN PING MEH, and RANDY PIE, who all released albums in 1977, didn't make it into the Top 100. They shared their fate with several dozens of acts who hadn't sold more than the aforementioned numbers between 1000 and 3000 copies – maybe even less.

Heinz-Gerd Lütticke, in the 1970s A&R man at EMI: "I was furious about how bad these musicians were treated. If someone came from a Scottish village, then the people fell down on their knees in awe. When Frank Bornemann of ELOY came into the office, having sold 20,000 to 30,000 LPs then, he felt more or less like being the interoffice messenger."[10]

Around 1971, all major labels slowly discovered that there was a sort of creative potential available at home. They had started sublabels for German rock, and they tried to inject some German acts into the orbit. CAN and AMON DÜÜL II appeared on Liberty/UA in Munich, which, under the direction of producer Siggi Loch, became one of the first labels to risk releasing German rock bands. As written before, he had already been involved in German music with Klaus Doldinger earlier when he worked at Philips and managed its sublabel Star-Club. Later, Philips signed not only KRAFTWERK and FRUMPY, but also CLUSTER, JADE WARRIOR, SILBERBART, SIXTY-NINE, ZWEISTEIN, and several more, some of them were released on Philips's sublabel Fontana. Another one was EILIFF, the name taken from Bertolt Brecht's *Mother Courage and Her Children* (but spelled wrong). They were an interesting jazz rock project somewhere near SOFT MACHINE, founded by guitarist Houschäng Nejadepour and top tier pianist Rainer Brüninghaus who later worked with Volker Kriegel, became a permanent member of the JAN GARBAREK GROUP, and released two remarkable albums under his own name on the ECM label: *Freigeweht* (1981) and *Continuum* (1984), the latter with trumpet virtuoso Markus Stockhausen – which might once more show the deep interconnections between the jazz and rock scene.

Other record companies also started special labels for German rock:

- Intercord of Stuttgart started Spiegelei (Brainstorm, Eulenspygel, Hoelderlin, Kraan, Tomorrow's Gift).
- EMI in Cologne added some German acts to its Harvest label (Janus, Nine Days Wonder, Tanned Leather, Triumvirat, later also Can and Holger Czukay).
- In Munich, producer and musician Eckart Rahn, with schlager singer and radio DJ Mal Sondock in partnership with an advertising agency and distributor Polydor, started the Kuckuck label (Armaggedon, Deuter, Peter Michael Hamel, Ihre Kinder, Eberhard Schoener). In the 1980s, Rahn became the founder of the U.S. New Age label Celestial Harmonies.
- Polydor established a sub-label named Zebra (Abacus, Epitaph, Joy Fleming, Franz K., Randy Pie, Achim Reichel, Kin Ping Meh, Night Sun, Ougenweide), but it didn't take off. The artists were re-integrated into the mother label, the name was sold to Metronome.
- Hamburg-based Polydor itself, the pop label of Deutsche Grammophon Gesellschaft and a textbook example of a crisscross label with acts from Caterina Valente to Cream and Mikis Theodorakis to Jimi Hendrix, signed Abacus, Drosselbart, Faust, Frumpy, Joy Unlimited, Niagara, Ougenweide, Sunbirds, later Michael Rother, and several more. (The name "Polydor", by the way, is a sort of "dog Greek", meaning something like "much gold").
- Teldec (Telefunken-Decca) in Hamburg signed Amon Düül II, Les Humphries Singers, Udo Lindenberg & Das Panikorchester, Message, Satin Whale, and many more, then started sublabel Nova and its sub-sub-label Strand (Amon Düül II, Duesenberg, Gift, Kin Ping Meh, La Düsseldorf, Missus Beastly, Parzival, Achim Reichel, Satin Whale, Scorpions, Jutta Weinhold).
- Bellaphon in Frankfurt, a label specializing in schlager and some rock and jazz, was also the German distributor of Chess, Fantasy, Sun, and other important U.S. labels. This way it had Creedence Clearwater Revival, Chuck Berry and even Johnny Cash, Archie Shepp, John Scofield or early Miles Davis recordings in their roster. Bellaphon bought Bacillus Records, an independent label that had gone broke in 1970, and turned it into a sublabel. It became one of Germany's most important labels for the hard & heavy side of Krautrock. Bacillus was the child of arranger, producer, and drummer (The Rollicks) Peter Hauke. Acts were Dzyan, Epsilon, Jeronimo, Ka-

Lacakra, Karthago, Nine Days Wonder, Pell Mell, Tiger B. Smith, Wyoming; Hauke successfully integrated Krokodil from Switzerland and Omega from Hungary. Viennese singer-songwriter Wolfgang Ambros also found his place in the roster, but Bacillus' main act was definitely Nektar. The Bacillus record covers, in addition to the label's orientation to hard rock, had a characteristic look by graphic artist Helmut Wenske.

- Bertelsmann's Ariola in Munich, mainly an important schlager label, was the German distributor of Island, MCA, and other labels, and had several international acts this way, like Desmond Dekker, Neil Diamond, King Crimson, Renaissance, Cat Stevens, T. Rex, Traffic, or Uriah Heep. An especially important label distributed by Ariola was Virgin from London. Virgin had given the starting shot for German rock in England by signing Can, Faust, and Tangerine Dream. Virgin's co-founder, Simon Draper, explains why Virgin was better in selling German acts than other labels: "All the Soft Machine and Canterbury sort of acts, the German acts, Tangerine Dream, the instrumental music, it was all incredibly sellable throughout Europe. So right from day one we sold records throughout Europe while all of the other record labels were focused too much on the U.K. and America. And of course America was a hard nut to crack. It's much easier, actually, to sell records to Europe."[11] Virgin's distributor Ariola itself was not involved in German rock except with early Eberhard Schoener.
- Deutsche Metronome (the German branch of a Swedish company) distributed Ohr and later established Brain.
- BASF in the first place was founded to produce German schlagers; they focussed on collecting schlager singers who had jumped the shark. Every established schlager singer who ended up under the BASF label knew that he or she had now reached the bread of charity. But BASF also distributed the MPS label with its highly-ranked jazz records. The label had chaotic marketing and was somehow indirectly connected to Polydor. Some Polydor productions with low selling expectations, like singer-songwriter Knut Kiesewetter, were "parked" at BASF. This way, Polydor fulfilled its contract without putting the act on the "more valuable" Polydor label.[12] BASF stopped its journey through the music industry in 1976. BASF became important for German rock as a distributor of Pilz Records (more about this connection later).
- There were also several small independent labels – Sky Records was one of them.

The main starting location for most artists was Hamburg. Liberty and Ariola were located in Munich, Intercord domiciled in Stuttgart, Bellaphon in Frankfurt, EMI in Cologne, but almost all other important labels at that time were located in Hamburg (including Sky, Brain, and the distributors of Ohr and Pilz), so this was the address to send demo tapes to.

Once the Krautrock avalanche was triggered, every label tried their luck. In 1973, the market was downright flooded with German rock; even samplers with several acts were released. Some journalists already saw this as the beginning of a sell-out. Actually, it was far from being "big business", but at this time German rock was definitely released and distributed.

KRAUTROCK & MEDIA

Released and distributed? Yes. But not necessarily promoted to the media. This was a long-time problem all record companies had with German rock. At that time, there was no radio station in Germany that specialized in rock music. In the early 1970s, there was nobody like BBC's John Peel on German airwaves. Later, that changed a little bit when Winfried Trenkler hosted "Radiothek" and "Rock In" (on WDR Cologne since 1973). In addition, there was Klaus Wellershaus (1938-2016) at NDR Hamburg (very "dry", but always perfectly informed). Walter Bachauer (1943–1989, you may know him musically under his pseudonyms Clara Mondshine and Anatol Arkus) could be heard on RIAS Berlin. Alan Bangs, who had worked at BFBS since 1975, probably came closest to Peel, but you could only catch this station in the former British zones of Germany. And there was Ingeborg Schober hosting "Club 16" and later "Zündfunk" at BR radio Munich. But they all were rare exceptions.

Some ARD radio stations had just started so-called "Autofahrerwellen", le dernier cri, car driver's service programs with constant music (inoffensive rock, schlager, instrumentals), little talk, but hourly news and lots of traffic jam alerts. These programs offered music non-stop, but they were not the environment for rock of any origin. And most of the existing rock music shows centered on British or American music anyway. Many editors acted in a highly arrogant way against homegrown bands and were not willing to play any of them in their shows.

In the U.S., there existed around 5000 radio stations. Several of them were part of a chain and offered identical shows, but in contrast to the U.K., nearly no station could reach the entire country. For this reason, record companies could hark back to several hundred well organized, independent, professional "record pluggers" travelling from station to station. These guys were paid on a commission basis – they promoted records to the DJs, and the more often the DJs played these records, the better the pluggers were paid. What a miracle then that payola was always the little devil in this business: While in the 1940s and 1950s, you usually had to slip 50 dollars to the (mostly underpaid) DJ to get your new record aired, in the 1980s, the top DJs in the key areas (New York, Los Angeles, Bay Area) expected 10,000 dollars or more.[13] Sometimes they expected other means of exchange, such as trips to exotic places, goodies, drugs, or sex (there were female pluggers especially for country music stations). All of these costs far exceeded the amount a U.S. label could earn with a German band's record. That's why German bands had almost no airplay in the States.

In Germany, such an organization of record pluggers did not exist. There were promoters, of course. Every record company had its own ones. Sometimes these were the A&R persons themselves, but usually they were young, predominantly good-looking and females, but not limited to this description. "Senderbetreuung" (support of broadcasting stations), as it was called, was not a job in its own right, it was a sort of stepping stone for people who wanted to start a career in a record company's A&R department. Nobody liked this job, but it had to be done. These people then had to hit the road with 20 or 30 new records in their suitcase, know the radio station's music shows, and get in touch with the appropriate editors and (sometimes) hosts, which meant they had to be well informed about *all* music genres the company was active in – schlager and pop as well as classical, rock and spoken word. Payola has never been a big deal in Germany. The promoters were advised to know which brand of whiskey or arts calendar had to be put on whose desk for Christmas – that, mainly, was the dimension. Sometimes they offered a weekend trip to some "trade meeting", they had giveaways, like the little pocket calculator with Kraftwerk imprint that was made to promote their *Computerwelt* album. I once got an LP that was made completely out of chocolate (I don't remember which album it was – I ate it). Sometimes the promoters gave tickets to the editors for concerts that had already been officially sold out. The promoters could make connections between artists and editors, and usually the artists were sent on a "Sendertournee", a trip through the radio stations where they got interviewed live on air about their current release. Bigger acts – like Udo Jürgens – recorded special LPs with lots of answers to frequently asked interview questions, so the radio hosts could fake a live interview. The bigger companies, like Teldec, pressed so-called "information records", which were albums made for and sent to music journalists, radio editors, and important dealers, previewing the highlights of the upcoming quarter. All of this is highly sought after by today's collectors.

Some artists frequently attack A&R people for "not doing enough PR", as well as the record companies and concert promoters for "not doing enough advertising". This, for the most part, is not really justified. It's a common belief that advertising can make people buy things they don't want or need. This might work once, but when the record isn't convincing and the buyers are disappointed, they will never buy a second one from this artist, no matter how great the advertising is. A record company trying to sell an album by, say, Asmus Tietchens, could come up with whatever marketing you can imagine: The record will sell around 2000 copies world-wide, and that's it.

The record companies, of course, knew which record stores were in the sample the weekly charts were determined from. Sometimes, the bands or the A&R people then tried the old trick of sending paid customers (usually friends or apprentices) to these stores "to buy a record into the charts". In the U.K., this could work because a record went automatically on air through the BBC when it entered the Top 40. In Germany, this didn't make much sense because there was no Top 40 radio, so this was not a usable method to get records aired. It was more effective to activate fan clubs that could bomb radio stations' hit parades with postcards, thus carrying a schlager singer into the Top 10.

These poor A&R people, even when they bent over backwards, usually ran against a wall of disinterest at the radio stations with their German rock records. Because they knew it would be like trying to get blood from a stone, the promoters didn't put much energy into this specific area.

One big problem was caused by the artists themselves: Many of them refused to do 45s that could have been used as an appetizer for an album or as a door opener to be aired. They saw themselves as "album acts", and were proud of their long, sometimes wildly foamed tracks with durations of ten, fifteen, or even more minutes. They were not willing or able to accept that these monster tracks didn't fit into the existing radio formats. Of course, the exception proves the rule, but to get tracks like CAN's "Halleluwah", KRAFTWERK's "Kling Klang", or NEU!'s "Hallogallo" into a radio show was hard to do. This didn't go for German bands only. Long tracks like "Tarkus" by EMERSON, LAKE & PALMER, "Valentyne Suite" by COLOSSEUM or "Nine Feet Underground" by CARAVAN were a little bit easier to get into radio shows, because they were prog, successful and British, but even those were rare events on German airwaves. NDR radio in Hamburg, for example, had a show called "Nach der Schule – Musik für junge Leute" (After school – music for young people) which was 25 minutes in the afternoon, so you can imagine that they rarely used their airtime to play only one track. When – miraculously anyway – on one fine day, they decided to play TANGERINE DREAM's "Phaedra", they ran it on 45 RPM instead of 33 because obviously neither the host nor the sound engineer were listening. And when KRAFTWERK came out with the *Electric Cafe* album, the track "Musique Non Stop" was used as background music for some event notes. This was the usual treatment German rock had to expect on German airwaves.

BOOM

Let's honor the truth: There was a lot of scrap on the market. Around 1972/73, with an acceptable demo tape even second- and third-rate German rock bands were able to land a record deal. The A&R people were often not familiar with the demos the postman delivered daily, but they signed the acts anyway because they saw a "trend" and "one never knows". So a flood of half-baked records hit stores during the following two or three years. The production and sound quality of even third-rate records was often quite good because the record companies at that time still used to cover the expenses for the studio. Of course, most of these bands and artists failed in the end, but this is nothing special: A failure rate of 80 percent or more is standard in the record industry. There is no formula to bake a hit, so music has always been a business of throwing spaghetti at the wall. One or two successful records have to cover not only their own production costs but also the costs of the eight or nine records that fail.

A&R man Heinz-Gerd Lütticke of EMI sums up the production costs in the 1970s: "You can estimate 100,000 D-Marks for marketing and direct promotion. I have to hit the road, all over Germany, to place the group in the media. That means 20,000 D-Marks for flights, telephone and entertaining business friends in restaurants. Then there's the effort for marketing: Ads, decor for record stores, and so on. 100,000 D-Marks is an average amount. Some international artists cost easily two or three times that much. A standard LP production on a technically international level means another 100,000 D-Marks. A day at the studio is around 2000 D-Marks. And that's not a 'first-class' studio, it's an average one. If you do your job painstakingly, maybe you get bogged down once during the mixing process and have a second attempt a week later, you will end up with 60,000 D-Marks in production fees for only the studio. Depending on where the production is done, you have to add the costs for hotel, food, arrival and departure, the daily transport to and from the studio. For four musicians that is 250 D-Marks per day. The tape material is expensive: A master tape costs around 500 D-Marks, and you'll need five or six of them, because these tapes don't run 90 minutes like cassettes. And yet we don't have the expenses for the cover design or a special remix of the record for discotheques. 100,000 D-Marks is quite a normal amount, all in all."[14]

You see, once the decision to sign an act was made, the record company dealt relatively professionally with it. Even though musicians complained (and still complain today), German rock acts usually received the same treatment as most schlager acts. This professionalism is the reason why we still find many original Krautrock albums in second hand stores today, but it's also the reason why we shouldn't hope for lots of "forgotten treasures" in record labels' drawers. It is really an exception when a failed record later emerges as a masterpiece.

MUSIC PUBLISHING HOUSES

As mentioned, several musicians from German bands still don't get tired of complaining about how their record label palmed an especially bad record contract off on them and how they got shortchanged by the "record bosses".

There is no easy answer to this complaint because, sometimes, it was true. But it was the exception. You have to keep in mind that a rock musician's income has more than one source: There are, as mentioned above, record fees. But there's also live performances, being aired on radio or TV, and royalties for composing and writing lyrics.

For lyrics and composition, the creators receive royalties from the GEMA (the German copyright society) whenever the tune is played live or on radio or TV; but as seen in the AMON DÜÜL II chapter, this can sometimes be tricky if a band is disorganized (which was the standard situation in most of them). Usually, there is a little catch. If you are a composer or lyricist, it makes sense to leave the copyrights administration to a music publishing house (which is not the same thing as a record label!) because it takes care of collecting the money internationally, cash in the royalties for cover versions of your tune, and do a lot of administrative work that a musician usually can't or doesn't want to do him- or herself. Of course, they don't do this for free. That's why the GEMA has an (always highly controversial) allocation formula that says: 60 percent of all incoming royalties go to the artist(s), 40 percent go to the music publishing house. When you sign a contract with a record label, the label usually demands that you choose a music publishing house that is owned by the label or its mother company. For small independent labels, the money they receive this way can be especially substantial; most of them couldn't survive from record sales alone. The band can, of course, start their own music publishing house, but you had to simultaneously already be well-known and a good record seller in order to push this through. CAN did it (Messer Music), KRAAN were able to do this (they founded their Wintrup Verlag in 1974), and KRAFTWERK had started their own publishing company (Kling Klang Verlag) in 1973. As a newcomer in search for a record deal, you had nearly no chance of becoming your own publishing company. The label's answer was almost always: We decide on the publishing house, otherwise there will be no record deal – take it or leave it.

As you see, a music publishing house can be a useful thing. But it can be misused. Some bands or musicians, like Wolfgang Dauner, CAN, or IMPROVED SOUND LIMITED, made a good portion of their income by writing and playing music for film and TV, and they were put under real pressure. Wolfgang Dauner: "The tendency of TV stations having their films produced by private production companies led to the consequence that more and more pressure piles on the composer! Private film production companies immediately start their own music publishing house, and in the contract they secure the rights for record productions to themselves. ... The tendency is obvious: to use the composer's royalties from the GEMA, to reduce the production costs, and to produce cheaply!"[15]

However, for most other musicians who were not involved in film composing, most record deals in the 1970s were more or less fair. Many people won't believe or won't like to hear this, but we should honor the truth: They were fair in the sense that there were no special conditions for German rock musicians. The record deals that German rock musicians and bands received were the same as most of the other acts under the same label, schlager singers as well as bands.

ALTERNATIVES

In the 1960s, there were a couple of jazz musicians in the U.S. – Bill Dixon, Archie Shepp, Cecil Taylor, Ornette Coleman, Sun Ra, Albert Ayler, Milford Graves and some more – who wanted to produce, record, and publish their works independently. With Paul and Carla Bley, Michael Mantler, Pharoah Sanders, Don Cherry, and the JAZZ COMPOSERS ORCHESTRA, this led to the founding of the New Music Distribution Service that would break the dictates of usual labels. This founding went down in history as the "October Revolution of Jazz".

A bit of this spirit was behind the start of the jazz labels ECM (Edition of Contemporary Music) in Munich and FMP (Free Music Production) in West Berlin. It's not a coincidence that both labels prepared their start in 1968, and in both cases, the idea was to find an independent way of producing and publishing jazz. ECM's founder was Manfred Eicher, a musician himself; the first ECM production was a record by Mel Waldron, and not without reason, entitled *Free At Last*. ECM still works independently today.[16] FMP was powered by musicians Peter Brötzmann, Peter Kowald, Alexander von Schlippenbach, and producer Jost Gebers; the company had to be shut down in 2011.

In 1976, four bands, Ton Steine Scherben, Embryo, Missus Beastly and Sparifankal, started their own label and distribution called April, which later, at the instigation of CBS Records, had to be renamed and became Schneeball. After a while, the Schneeball network grew; finally, a dozen bands were involved. With a little help from left-wing book publishing house Trikont of Munich, named after the Italian magazine *Trikontinentale*, they self-organized the pressing, packaging, and distributing of their records. Schneeball records were hardly available in record stores, they could be ordered directly from the bands, were sold at concerts, and, based on the Trikont model, were delivered by local Schneeball members directly to local left-wing bookstores. There were approximately 200 of these stores in Germany, many of them situated near universities or in collegiate neighborhoods. Schneeball, as well as Trikont, were clearly children of Sixty-Eight. Many of the book stores made a part of their turnover with pirate editions of books that were officially out of print but seen as important for the discussion in student circles.[17]

For a while, this worked. But all participants involved had to spend a lot of effort and time on this process, and they couldn't reach a wide market this way. Ton Steine Scherben, for example, sold around 10,000 copies of their album *Keine Macht für Niemand* using this distribution, and this was already one of the bestsellers. To use bookstores as sales points was surely a "second-best" idea, but it was not really an alternative to well-stocked record stores. When a Schneeball band was finally able to sign a record deal with one of the usual record labels, most of them jumped on the chance (as did the jazz musicians of the New Music Distribution Service when a major label came with a lucrative offer), and suddenly there was a gap in the distribution network. Nobody in their region could sell records at concerts and nobody was available to deliver them to local bookstores anymore. So, after a couple of years, the Schneeball project fell flat.

But the idea left its mark, not as a label, but in its shipping channel. Alternative distribution companies followed: Efa (Energie für alle) and later Indigo made good use of the know-how from Schneeball's project. Only Trikont still exists as an independent record label with a hand-selected repertoire (the book publishing department sadly had to be closed a couple of years ago).

LICENSE DEALS

In 1973 and 1974, some of the previously mentioned German labels were able to place license deals with labels in the United States. KRAAN and NEKTAR, for example, appeared on the Passport label of South Plainfield, New Jersey, and Billingsgate Records of Chicago released LUCIFER'S FRIEND, FRUMPY, EPITAPH, NEU!, and SCORPIONS.

Inga Rumpf (FRUMPY) and Peter Hesslein (LUCIFER'S FRIEND) were particularly unhappy with their deals. Although both bands successfully toured the U.S., the responsible A&R department of the record company didn't see anything interesting in them, so the records were promoted badly, received no airplay, and were hardly available in stores. In the end, the artists never received any money.[18] KRAFTWERK was a bit luckier in this regard; their *Autobahn* album in the U.S. appeared on the much more professional Vertigo label, a sublabel of Mercury (which itself was the U.S. dependence of Philips), so for them it was a sort of in-house deal. It's an eternal mystery and must have been very frustrating for musicians to understand why KRAFTWERK's label mates, FRUMPY and LUCIFER'S FRIEND, didn't get the same deal – even more so when you know that KRAFTWERK actually had no record deal anymore: Their contract with Philips had ended after the four stipulated albums, and EMI wasn't in the game yet.

What was even more aggravating for some German bands, was that unsold copies of U.S. records were exported to Germany only to end up there as cut-outs in bargain bins – much to the annoyance of the artists and their German labels. In cut-outs lie no profit; their only function is to keep the loss to a minimum.

THE END OF THE FIXED RETAIL PRICE

In Germany, records were seen by law as objects of cultural value, similar to literature. Like books, they had a reduced sales tax rate of 7 percent, while the standard sales tax rate was 11 percent. (Interestingly, the reduced rate has never changed. While today's sales tax went up to 19 percent, the reduced sales tax is still 7 percent.) And records – unthinkable in the U.S. – had a fixed retail price. Of course, dealers and the record industry were happy with the fixed price and not willing to even discuss alternatives. Everybody who knew the business knew that records were overpriced. In 1966, the Federal Court of Justice had already ruled that fixed retail prices of records were illegal, but the industry as well as retailers simply continued this practice. Retailers played ball because they, too, profited well from the fixed price. Usually, a third of the retail price stayed in the retailer's cashbox – easy money for them.

This changed in 1971. In that year, Frank-Michael Wiegand of Hamburg founded a company named Govi Schallplatten, first as a mail order store, but soon the company established a couple of shops. After a while, Govi had 23 stores all over Germany and published a nice little monthly mail order catalogue named "Govi Collector" (a collectible today, they are sold on eBay now).

Govi was the first retailer to break the rules. They offered albums for prices between 13.90 and – at its highest – 18.90 D-Marks, and special offers sometimes went down to 9.90 D-Marks. At that time, this was simply sensational, compared to the usual price of 22 D-Marks. Of course, the record industry wasn't thrilled and reacted by setting up a boycott, but it didn't last long. Govi found ways to import records, so the industry finally had the choice of delivering or leaving the profit to foreign record companies. With gritted teeth, they decided to do the former.

In Hamburg, there were three Govi shops. The one in the neighborhood of Eimsbüttel was just around the corner from my apartment, in a former bread shop where I had often bought our breakfast rolls. Later on, I had to walk past the store daily on my way to work. It didn't take long until I knew the salespersons by name, and they knew me; after a while, they even knew my taste well enough to give me useful recommendations.

Another important reason why Govi could be relatively cheap was that they didn't offer all genres. This way, they reduced the risk of carrying too many shelf warmers. Govi specialized in progressive rock and pop music, and had a small share in jazz. No schlager, no classical, no 45s. But, from the beginning, Govi had a special love for homegrown rock. If there was a new record by CAN, CLUSTER, or KRAFTWERK, Govi had it first – something that did not go without saying at that time. Even more: Most record stores had a special shelf for "German Rock", as if the records needed to be put under quarantine. Govi was one of the very few stores that saw German rock records on an equal footing with the international ones, and sorted them into the standard A-Z shelves. In a way, this was a statement.

I remember in 1974, Govi released an album entitled *Ameurope* by Wolfgang Michels' folk-rock band Percewood's Onagram. The record came with a swastika – as known from Hitler's party's flag, just inverted.

Somebody probably had had the idea to try the good old "marketing by calculated scandal" method to push the album into the media by triggering an agitated controversial debate, hoping a swastika would do the trick. So one morning, Govi's shop window was entirely decorated with dozens of these covers. I was perplexed, to say the least. When I went past the shop again later that afternoon, I couldn't help entering and asking the shopkeepers whether they had lost their marbles. I told them they wouldn't see me in their store again as long as this crap would be in the window. Apparently, I wasn't the only one who didn't appreciate this decor, and it took less than two days for the window to change.

I'm telling this because the *Ameurope* cover was not just a simple faux pas (which could have happened at any time, anywhere) – it was a bad omen for what was planned: *Ameurope* was the first album to be released on the brand-new Govi label. The Govi owner had decided to reach for the stars; he wanted to follow Richard Branson's example and intended to make Govi into a sort of German Virgin. But he soon had to learn that Wolfgang Michels was not Mike Oldfield who had been the first act of Virgin Records, sold millions of *Tubular Bells* copies (in the U.S. not least because it was part of the *Exorcist* soundtrack), and took Virgin with him up to the sky. *Ameurope* failed miserably (I'm sure the cover had its part in this) and remained Govi's only original record release. A couple of German Rock samplers in cooperation with Brain Records followed, but this was all there was.

In addition, it became more and more obvious that Govi had too many shops. Finally, in 1979, the company was sold to WEA Records, and it didn't take long until it went bankrupt.

The era of the fixed record price was irretrievably over. Other stores took up the idea of breaking the price regime. Zweitausendeins, a book and record mail order store from Frankfurt, continued the idea, mainly by selling remainders and imported records. This chain also opened 14 stores, little by little, mostly around universities (the last one had to be closed in 2017, the mail order still exists). But the most important step came from Friedrich Wilhelm "Fritz" Waffenschmidt, who had founded a photo store named Hansa-Foto in Cologne. Finally, in 1972, this became Saturn-Hansa which had a well-stocked record department with low prices, and this store developed into a chain. There was no chance for the industry to get back to fixed record prices anymore. Today, Saturn, with its sister company Media-Markt, is the biggest European store chain for records, DVDs, computers, electronics of all kinds, and white goods. In fact, Saturn and Media-Markt are two brands of the same company today; Saturn is found in downtown areas, while Media-Markt mainly exists in shopping malls outside cities.

What was even more important for German rock was that Günter Körber (1946-2013) and Bruno Wendel had left Rolf-Ulrich Kaiser's Ohr label (more about this later) and were co-founders and A&R men at Brain Records. When Körber had the idea of starting his own label, it was ex-Govi owner Frank-Michael Wiegand who supported him with the necessary funds. This was the start of Sky Records in 1975. Wiegand later became a real estate agent and, for two legislative periods, he was a member of the Bürgerschaft, the parliament of the City of Hamburg.

STUDIOS AND PRODUCERS

There are two main kinds of producers: the *executive* producer and the *record* producer. Then there's also the *independent* producer who is a mix of both. There is no exact job description, but as a rule of thumb: The *executive producer* is usually an employee at a record company. They govern the budget, arrange and control timetables, and keep deadlines in mind. They hire and pay the record producer, pay for the studio (if it's not a company-owned one), the needed session musicians, and back-up singers. The executive producer is not directly involved in the recording process.

The *record producer* (or, in short: *producer*) is comparable to a movie director. They might be an employee of the record company (a so-called *in-house producer*), or work independently and the executive producer hires them to produce a record the label wants to release. In any case, the record producer has to know the music field the artist is active in, and must have an idea about how a record with this artist should sound. They know which studio and which sound engineer would be right to do the recording. They sit at the mixing desk next to the sound engineer; sometimes, they are both the producer and sound engineer, simultaneously.

In the 1960s, most producers in Germany were in-house producers; they were employees at a major label and worked for the acts the A&R department had signed. They were mostly busy doing schlagers, and they used the "all-purpose studios" the record company owned. One of these producers was Bert Kaempfert who worked as an arranger and producer for Polydor. In 1961, one of the Polydor schlager singers called his attention to The Beatles. They gigged at the Top Ten Club at the Reeperbahn as the backing band for Polydor act, Tony Sheridan. Kaempfert liked them: "Polydor wasn't very interested in their sound. I talked to the company until I was blue in the face. I said: This is something new! Something different! Refreshing! Let's try it!"[1] Against the heads of Polydor's resistance, he was finally allowed to produce some recordings with the musicians at the Friedrich-Ebert-Halle, a concert hall in the Harburg neighborhood of Hamburg. Polydor sometimes used it because of its beautiful natural reverb. Tony Sheridan already had a name, so Polydor marketed the results of these sessions under TONY SHERIDAN & THE BEAT BROTHERS, as several of Sheridan's backing groups were called. Kaempfert: "It was obvious that they were enormously talented, but nobody, not even they themselves, knew what to do with this talent and where they were possibly heading."[2] Therefore, when Brian Epstein asked Polydor to release THE BEATLES from their contract, the label simply let them walk. And that was that.

This shows in effigy how the situation was. For German artists, however, it was even worse. There were just a handful of producers recognizing that new plants were growing in the garden, but most of them had no clear idea about what these bands needed or what to do with them. "Who will buy this stuff?" was probably the question they asked themselves most often.

The earlier mentioned Siggi Loch and Gerhard Augustin were already at work, as well as Peter Meisel. You heard about Günter Körber and Bruno Wendel; they were both A&R employees at Rolf-Ulrich Kaiser's Ohr label. When they were finally fed up with his management style (let's call it this), they went to Ohr's distributor, Metronome Records, and founded the sublabel Brain Records there. Günter Körber later found a financial backer in the former Govi owner, left Brain, and started Sky Records. Both were important labels for German rock. But Körber, as well as Wendel, were not really producers. Wendel was still an A&R man, and Körber something between an executive producer and A&R man of his own company.

INDEPENDENT PRODUCERS

One link in the chain didn't exist yet: the *independent producer*. These guys are not employed by record companies; they find artists and produce music with them at their own risk. They license these recordings to major labels, and sometimes they also run their own label (which is then usually distributed by one of the major companies). They are often sound engineers and have their own studio. They are the talent scouts who leaf through shoe boxes full of unsolicited demos, walk through youth centers and venues to listen to new acts, are responsive to hints from musicians they know, and are the ones who try to walk unknown roads. They are (usually) children of the musical scene they keep under surveillance, so they not only have an idea about what the audience might want, they also know what these musicians want and need, as well as which studios and sound engineers would be the best to record them.

Usually, they are paid with a fixed fee, an hourly or daily rate, or by a percentage of participation in the royalties the record might bring in. It is hard to name amounts here, but it is something between 300 and 10,000 D-Marks per track, or 20 to 25 percent of the artist's royalties, or 3 to 5 percent of the sales price of the 45 or the album. There are no written rules. The year when the producer makes the master recordings official and gives it to a pressing plant is usually marked on the label or the sleeve with "℗". Women, by the way, are rare in this business. In Germany, Gille "Sternenmädchen" Lettmann, Hildegard Schmidt, Annette Humpe, Hanne Haller (1950-2005), Kristina Bach, Gudrun Gut, Barbara Morgenstern, Ulrike Haage come to mind, but with the exception of Lettmann and Schmidt, they all didn't start until the 1980s, and again, were a mix of schlager, pop, and rock.

Often, it is said that British sound engineer, Joe Meek, ("Telstar" by The Tornados) was the first independent record producer in Europe. But he wasn't. Joe Meek, for his part, learned his trade from working with jazz producer Denis Preston (1916–1979). Preston was not an employee of a record company, he worked with jazz bands and some early skiffle acts (Chris Barber, Acker Bilk, Humphrey Lyttelton, Lonnie Donegan, and others), produced music with them at his own risk and licensed the recordings to major labels. Preston was also the first independent producer in Europe who founded his own recording studio (Lansdowne Studio in London), and later, he established his own record label under the same name. Preston didn't invent this method, it had been common practice in the U.S. for many years before, and he knew it from there. Joe Meek learned about independent production during his time as Preston's sound engineer at Lansdowne Studio, and around 1960 he adopted the concept for himself. He failed with his own label, Triumph Records, but his production company RGM Sound became a pioneer of independent pop music production in Europe (RGM are the initials of his real name, Robert George Meek).

The idea of producing recordings independently to license them to an established record company for exploitation looks quite convincing. But there were two catches: Once the license deal was done, the producer had to let go of control over the tune. He had no impact on what the label did with the tune or how the record was marketed. Second, in the 1960s, independent producers were anything but welcome at major labels. The majors had their in-house producers, as well as A&R departments, and they saw no reason to accept help from outside. Independent producing deals mainly worked through networking, and these personal contacts were the first things that needed to be established. Gay networks were especially effective in this business.[3]

When, around 1966, the music scene became more complex and developed new and more sophisticated music styles, the established major A&R departments noticed they had no real connection to this new stuff. This was the moment that help from independent producers became more and more welcomed, and this was also the moment when independent producers could set conditions on how major companies had to deal with licensed tunes. It was none other than Phil Spector who established the "Number One Independent Producer's Rule" for himself and others: "If you ever find a group to record, never let the group sign directly to a major, nor use the record company's own studios. By using your own studios and licensing the masters to a record company, you'll keep control and earn much more money."[4]

INDIES IN JAZZ

People had to first start preparing German ground. To really ignite German rock, it needed not only studios, but also producers and sound engineers like Conny Plank, Dieter Dierks, Rolf-Ulrich Kaiser. But they were not part of the game yet.

One of the most famous addresses for excellent independent jazz productions in Germany is MPS. The name stands for "Musikproduktion Schwarzwald" (Music Production Black Forest), located in Villingen-Schwenningen, a small town somewhere between Freiburg and Lake Constance. Since 1958, Hans Georg Brunner-Schwer (1927-2014), the moneyed inheritor of electronics company Saba (then well-known for TV sets and radios, they also invented Germany's first TV remote control), had had a sound recording studio and recorded jazz and schlager productions for his Saba label. As a sound freak and tinkerer, one of his ideas was to place microphones inside a grand piano, which gave the listener a similar sound impression to what a pianist had while playing. In 1964, Brunner-Schwer invited jazz pianist Oscar Peterson to have a recording session in his (Brunner's) living room. This recording turned out extremely well, and Peterson was absolutely thrilled. The recording was released as *My Favorite Instrument* (1968).

Brunner-Schwer now decided to move his studio into the attic of a building in the back, equipped it with some top-of-the-line tape recorders, mixing desks, and microphones, and changed the name to MPS. In collaboration with Joachim-Ernst Berendt (the jazz editor of SWF radio Baden-Baden) as producer, the label as well as studio became a sort of legend. The studio saw artists like Charly Antolini, Kenny Clarke, John Coltrane, Miles Davis, Duke Ellington, Bill Evans, Ella Fitzgerald, Stephane Grappelli, Freddie Hubbard, Jean-Luc Ponty, Baden Powell, George Shearing, and many others. Top German artists also recorded here, like Eugen Cicero, Wolfgang Dauner, Hans Koller, Friedrich Gulda, Peter Herbolzheimer, Volker Kriegel, Joachim Kühn, Rolf Kühn, Albert Mangelsdorff, the DAVE PIKE SET – the list is endless.

Overall, MPS released more than 500 albums. The records were first pressed and distributed by Deutsche Grammophon; the quality was excellent. Later, in the early 1970s, when BASF took over distribution, the label also reached the U.S. market. The MPS record covers were known for their distinctive graphic design; it's still easy to recognize today.

The MPS studio was closed down in 1982. In 1983, Hans Georg Brunner-Schwer sold the MPS label to Philips. He never made much money with his studio – he just loved jazz and wanted it to be presented as best as possible. In 2004, Brunner-Schwer was tragically killed in a car accident. The MPS label changed its owners several times and, in 2014, the Edel Company bought the entire MPS catalogue.

In 2011, the original studio in Villingen was declared a "cultural monument of music history". It re-opened in 2015 under the name HGBS-Studio (after Brunner-Schwer's initials), and is still one of the finest analogue recording studios in the world.

Another early independent producer in Germany also came from the jazz field. The previously mentioned Manfred Eicher, a former double-bass player with the BERLIN PHILHARMONICS, had a little bit of experience as an assistant for Deutsche Grammophon, so with the help of local businessman Karl Egger he founded his "Edition of Contemporary Music", in short ECM, in Munich in 1969.[5] With a loan of 16,000 D-Marks, without a clear plan, but with an idea of the sound he wanted to hear, he produced four albums (MEL WALDRON TRIO, ALFRED HARTH'S JUST MUSIC, PAUL BLEY TRIO, Marion Brown) and sold them by mail order, which, to everybody's surprise, led to a success in Japan. This was the start of what would become one of Germany's most prestigious record labels. Among later top acts are Gary Burton, Chick Corea, Wolfgang Dauner, Jack DeJohnette, Jan Garbarek, Jon Hassell, Keith Jarrett, Pat Metheny, Terje Rypdal, and many others – a kind of jazz you wouldn't find on "classic" jazz labels like Impulse, Blue Note, or Verve. It was jazz with a clear European, sometimes "Nordic", touch, and some people described it as "chamber music with improvisation". The timelessness of ECM's recordings is stunning. Critic Joachim-Ernst Berendt had his problems with this. Manfred Eicher: "In jazz criticism of the Seventies, it became a fad for a while to vehemently mock any hint of beauty. Joachim-Ernst Berendt, for example, didn't mince matters on this aspect, which didn't make much sense"[6] – as if there hadn't also been recordings like Circle's *Paris Concert* (1972) or Wolfgang Dauner's *Output* (1970). For being the "jazz pope", Berendt was simply ideologically blinkered, but this was a "thing" at that time. Eicher: "As a basic principle of our productions, clarity was always more important than beauty."[7]

In 1984, Eicher started a sublabel called ECM New Series that specialized in contemporary classical music by John Adams, György Kurtág, Meredith Monk, Arvo Pärt, Steve Reich, and others, but also released new recordings of Early Music.

To this day, ECM has issued around 1600 records between classic and modern jazz and contemporary classical, most of them produced by Eicher himself who always followed his own curiosity. The recording quality of ECM productions is excellent and known world-wide for crystal-clear, compression-free, and spacious sound. Eicher always says that there is no special ECM sound, but I say there is. Maybe "sound" is the wrong word, maybe it's more of a sort of synesthetic quality which originally may not have been intended, but the time formed a sound that makes ECM records recognizable.

At the time of vinyl, Eicher produced all ECM LPs under the quality rules that were otherwise used for classical records. Among other things, this meant that every copy had to be pressed for 30 seconds to avoid warps, and the pressing matrix had to be replaced after 800 to 1000 pressed copies.

ECM also developed a recognizable cover design style very early on, starting with the talents of Barbara Wojirsch and Dieter Rehm. Their layouts, typography, photos, and graphics were later good enough to fill gallery exhibitions and art books – ECM records "know that ears have eyes"[8], as the *New York Times* wrote in reference to their design. Manfred Eicher also knows quite well how to present himself to the press, and as the saying goes: When you forget your coat or jacket at ECM's office overnight, it will be black or dark blue the next morning.

Eicher never had his own studio, but he used to work in a few handpicked studios, with a small number of sound engineers. First he worked at Tonstudio

Bauer in Ludwigsburg with engineer Martin Wieland, and later at Talent Studio and Rainbow Studios in Oslo with engineer Jan Erik Kongshaug (1944-2019). Eicher knew the characteristics of the studios, and the engineers knew the characteristics of the producer. ECM is distributed by Universal today, but it's still an independent label; Eicher always refused to sell the company. And his double bass still has its place in his office.

INDEPENDENT STUDIOS

In the 1960s, there were few independent labels in Germany (most of them were budget labels, as shown earlier), and the existing studios were not made for rock recordings. Even around 1967, there were only a small handful of studios that could be used by rock groups, but most of them did their main business with schlager productions. Usually, these were run by one of the major companies Deutsche Grammophon, Polydor, EMI Electrola, Teldec, and their sound engineers had little (if any) experience in recording rock music. When a band was setting up their stuff in one of these studios, the musicians had to expect that the engineer would say: "Okay, you are four people, so I need four microphones." Then, when the band answered that this isn't the way a rock recording works, he might reply: "Listen, I've learned my trade and I know how to do my job. It's up to you now to adapt." The result then sounded like this.

But there were also some private studios, not connected to record companies, like *Bavaria Studios* in Munich (Amon Düül II, Doldinger's Passport or Eberhard Schoener recorded there) or Studio Tonndorf in Hamburg (where The Monks recorded their album *Black Monk Time* from 1966 as one of the earliest rock recordings at that place). Both were connected to film studios and a little bit more flexible, but they usually specialized in dubbing commercials or lip-syncing foreign movies or TV series.

Windrose-Dumont-Time, a studio in Hamburg's not really attractive Dulsberg neighborhood, fifteen minutes away from the airport and not far from the Brain Records headquarters, was also part of a film and TV production company, founded in 1967 by TV reporter and U.S. correspondent Peter von Zahn. He and his black-and-white TV reports of the 1960s had an enormous influence on what we Germans knew about America and its unbelievable "way of life". I can still hear his voice, and I will always connect it to futuristic kitchens in suburban houses, parents with children looking like dollhouse figures, and wonderful giant cars in the driveway. In the 1970s, Windrose-Dumont-Time became one of the leading recording studios for German rock; nearly 150 German rock albums were recorded there, including those by NOVALIS, NEU!, GURU GURU, GROBSCHNITT, YATHA SIDHRA, and many more, especially acts from the Brain roster. Since around 1980, the place has been called Chameleon Recording. The original building was torn down and the studio was completely rebuilt. It still has the same address as Windrose-Dumont-Time, but has nothing to do with it anymore. Today, it specializes in schlager and pop.

There were some more independent recording studios where rock groups were welcome. Several of these studios mainly recorded advertising jingles, film music, (of course) schlager, and sometimes jazz. Here, in alphabetical order, are some names you can find on German rock record covers:

- *Alster Studios* were situated in Hamburg's suburban Ohlstedt neighborhood. Achim Reichel, Marius Müller-Westernhagen, OUGENWEIDE, BLONKER, TON STEINE SCHERBEN, WOLFSMOND, PERCEWOOD'S ONAGRAM, and several others recorded there; usually, the sound engineer was Richard Borowski. (And Yours Truly enjoyed his sound recording internship at this place.) The last big project this studio was involved in was the mix of the German lipsynced version of the film *Das Boot*. Shortly after finishing this job, the studio was closed and, in parts, torn down. Today there's a meadow where Yours Truly once had the honor of having lunch with James Last in the cafeteria.
- West Berlin had the *Audio Studio*, usually with sound engineer Ottmar "Otto" Bergler. The studio in the Lichterfelde neighborhood recorded several TANGERINE DREAM albums, solo works of Edgar Froese, and Peter Baumann, but also acts like AGITATION FREE, Georg Danzer, KARTHAGO, LOKOMOTIVE KREUZBERG, Ulla Meinecke, Reinhard Mey, NENA, RAINBIRDS, Rio Reiser, SPLIFF, Stefan Waggershausen, and many more. The studio was shut down in 2006.
- More interesting for early German rock was the *Beatstudio*, located in the basement of a school building in Berlin-Wilmersdorf, run by the City of Berlin and headed by Swiss composer Thomas Kessler. The Beatstudio was originally the rehearsal room for Lutz "Lüül" Ulbrich's (then) school student band AGITATION FREE, and in 1968 it was equipped as a simple but nevertheless professional studio, open for everybody, subsidized widely by the Berlin senate. It became an important part of what would become the "Berlin School"; TANGERINE DREAM, ASH RA TEMPEL, Klaus Schulze, and Manuel Göttsching worked here. GURU GURU's first album *UFO* (1970)

was recorded here. The sound engineer of this album was Julius Schittenhelm (1926-2012) who became known as a producer in Rolf-Ulrich Kaiser's Ohr circle. Later, he worked for April Records, but was also known as a singer-songwriter himself. After the studio relocated to a school building in Berlin-Halensee, Klaus Lage, Morgenrot, Rammstein, as well as Ideal, recorded at Beatstudio.

- You are probably already waiting for the very famous *Hansa Studio "at the Wall"*. But, astonishingly, this place in West Berlin's Kreuzberg neighborhood was not one of the big players for recording German rock music of the early 1970s and before. The most important role this studio had in German rock was the Big Moog synthesizer Peter Meisel had bought from Mick Jagger. They didn't really know what to do with it, so they hired Christopher Franke to tell them (but more about this story later). Hansa was essentially a schlager studio, opened in 1964 by Will Meisel and his sons, Peter and Thomas, in Berlin-Halensee. In 1974, the studio relocated to the "Meistersaal", a former ballroom in Berlin-Kreuzberg, in visual range of the Berlin Wall that gave it its name; the Meisel brothers had used it earlier as a recording space sometimes because of its excellent acoustics. The engineer was usually Eduard Meyer. You know all the international acts who recorded here – David Bowie, Iggy Pop, U2, Marillion, Diamanda Galás, David Byrne, Mark Knopfler, Nick Cave, Pet Shop Boys and many more. But from Germany, there's not much more than Einstürzende Neubauten, Eloy, Tame & Maffay, UKW, Camouflage, Nina Hagen, Tangerine Dream, and a couple of others which would bring us far into the 1980s and 1990s. Since 1998, the studio has been headed by Thomas Meisel's son, Sven (1966-2016). The studio still exists, but of course, is no longer "at the Wall". This wall fell in 1989, but the name sticks.
- After Can's breakup, their sound engineer, René Tinner, took over their *Inner Space Studio* they had established in an old cinema in Weilerswist near Cologne and started using it commercially. In 1978, he renamed it *Can Studio.* In 2007, parts of the studio, including instruments, floor, some decor, and furniture, were transferred to the Rock'n'Pop Museum at Gronau (the birthplace of Udo Lindenberg) near the border of the Netherlands. Joachim Witt, Marius Müller-Westernhagen, the Bläck Fööss, as well as Julian Dawson, and many others, produced records there. The Can Studio still exists today. Holger Czukay later used the old place at Weilerswist for himself as both a studio and apartment; finally he died there. His ghost, hopefully, keeps the place in good shape.

- Kraftwerk's *Kling Klang Studio*? Nobody except the masters themselves ever used this backyard loft at Mintropstraße near Düsseldorf's main station. Since Ralf Hütter in 2009 relocated the studio to a business park in Meerbusch near Düsseldorf, Florian Schneider used it for a while but eventually gave it up. The old rooms with the faded "Elektro-Müller" sign over the entrance gateway are now home to a multimedia production company and sometimes used as a (very small) concert venue.
- *Musicland Studio* was located two floors below ground in the multi-story Arabella House in the Bogenhausen neighborhood of Munich. The studio was founded in 1974 by Giorgio Moroder who also used to have his apartment somewhere in the upper floors of this building. With its sound engineer, Reinhold Mack (who simply calls himself "Mack", like the American trucks) it became famous enough to attract acts like Elton John, Led Zeppelin, Meat Loaf, Rory Gallagher, Queen, Deep Purple, or the Rolling Stones. To get different acoustic conditions, Mack sometimes incorporated rooms and spaces outside the studio for recording. To get the resounding drum sound of Led Zeppelin's "When the Levee Breaks", for example, Mack placed John Bonham and his kit on a landing of the concrete stairwell. Among the relatively few German acts who recorded at Musicland were Neu!, BAP, Edo Zanki, the Scorpions, Sahara, Tame & Maffay, and of course Moroder himself. Because of the latter, many people think Musicland had a Big Moog synthesizer, but it didn't. Moroder's Moog recordings were mostly made at Bavaria Studios (which were connected to a Munich film studio) and then further processed at Musicland (more about this will follow in the chapter about Eberhard Schoener). In the mid-1980s, after Moroder relocated to Los Angeles, the studio was headed by Mack, but the fun didn't last very long: When the City of Munich built a new subway line through Bogenhausen, the tunnel turned out to be so close to the studio that the vibrations made it impossible to do further recordings there. Today, the building is a hotel.
- *Rhenus Studio* in Godorf near Cologne was located in a black building that was part of an abandoned oil refinery, which gave the whole area a bit of a bizarre air. It was founded by Karl-Heinz Münchow, husband of Fifties and Sixties schlager star Margot Eskens. Rhenus recorded jazz, big bands, classical, and contemporary stuff (Isang Yun, Karlheinz Stockhausen, Bernd Alois Zimmermann, Mauricio Kagel), but mainly schlagers, and many of them for budget labels. The studio would have probably been rather meaningless for

German rock, had Conny Plank not worked there as an assistant to sound engineer Wolfgang Hirschmann; the latter ended up teaching sound engineering at Robert Schumann Hochschule Düsseldorf. Since Plank was able to get good conditions for using the studio at night (apparently he specialized in this), Rhenus became a pioneering recording place for KLUSTER, ORGANISATION, KRAFTWERK, SATIN WHALE, SWEET SMOKE, Peter Brötzmann, PETER HERBOLZHEIMER RHYTHM COMBINATION & BRASS, NOSFERATU, and ANDROMEDA – but that's about it. One of the sound assistants was Klaus Löhmer who recorded parts of KRAFTWERK's first album. The studio is gone today, in its place, you'll find an Ikea branch.

- The *Rüssl Studio* in Hamburg-Eidelstedt was founded in 1976 by comedian Otto Waalkes and his manager Hans-Otto Mertens. "Rüssel" means "elephant's trunk". It became the name of the studio because of the elephant cartoons Waalkes used to draw for a newspaper ("Ottifanten"). With sound engineer Thomas Kukuck, KRAFTWERK recorded parts of *Trans Europa Express* here. Ralf Hütter hated to have "Rüssl" on the record cover, but as this was Germany's best-equipped studio at that time, he had to grudgingly accept it. Other bands that recorded there were NOVALIS, LUCIFER'S FRIEND, Udo Lindenberg, KRAAN, SCORPIONS spin-off ELECTRIC SUN, Randy California, Roger Chapman, and several more. Its name today is *Gaga Studio.*
- *Star Studio* in Hamburg was located in a bourgeois city villa in the Hoheluft neighborhood. It was owned by schlager composer, lyricist, producer, and music publisher, Ralf Arnie (= *Ar*tur *Nie*derbremer, 1924-2003), who wrote more than 800 songs; the most famous one was probably "Tulpen aus Amsterdam" (Tulips From Amsterdam, 1958). He was still active in Germany's schlager scene of the 1970s and was willing to support new talent. He allowed Conny Plank to use the studio for free at night. The deal then was that Arnie got the publishing rights of the recorded works. The special thing about this studio was its architecture: As it had been an inhabited villa, it consisted of two floors without a window between the recording room and the control room. KRAFTWERK, NEU!, CLUSTER, JANE, TOMORROW'S GIFT, ASH RA TEMPEL, and lots of Brain acts recorded here. There are also many recordings from Windrose-Dumont-Time that were mixed at Star Studio. The house still exists but is not used as a studio anymore.
- *Studio Maschen* at Maschen in Hamburg's commuter belt, visible from the autobahn, run by schlager and country producer and composer Joe Menke, is itself a little monument because Hamburg's country band, TRUCK STOP, made a

hit record that mentions the studio ("Der wilde, wilde Westen", 1980). Alongside them, the studio had visits from the Scorpions, Thirsty Moon, Novalis, To Be, Lake, Eulenspygel, Randy Pie, Achim Reichel, and others.

- *Studio Nord-Bremen (SNB)* in Bremen-Oberneuland was founded in 1966 by songwriter, schlager and volksmusik singer, and skilled sound engineer, Wolfgang Roloff (1930-2011). As a singer, he was known by his stage name, "Ronny", and several other pseudonyms. SNB is Germany's oldest private studio. It is still active today and remains one of the very few studios big enough to record an entire orchestra. It was originally a ballroom; later it became a country inn for day trippers. Eloy recorded there, as well as Thirsty Moon (Ronny himself sings backup on their album *Starchaser* from 1981), Munju, Alphaville, Dissidenten, Heinz Rudolf Kunze, and many others.
- *Trixi Studio* in Munich mainly specialized in soundtracks for film and TV. Popol Vuh's *In den Gärten Pharaos* was recorded there. Joy Fleming, Ralf Nowy (Drosselbart), Wolfgang Dauner, Hans Koller, Klaus Doldinger, and others also worked at this place. The engineer was usually Willy Schmidt.

Of course, there were other studios. *Amber Studio* in Berlin could be mentioned (Tangerine Dream, Edgar Froese), *Tonstudio Bauer* in Ludwigsburg with engineer Martin Wieland (Einstürzende Neubauten, Curly Curve, United Jazz & Rock Ensemble, Erlend Krauser, Tritonus, Joy Unlimited, Floh de Cologne, and lots of Pläne and early ECM productions), *Cornet* in Cologne-Junkersdorf (Udo Lindenberg, Kraftwerk, Peter Herbolzheimer Rhythm Combination & Brass, Bläck Fööss, Gomorrha, and others), *Panne-Paulsen* in Frankfurt with sound engineer Eberhard Panne (where Klaus Schulze recorded some of his most important records – *Mirage*, *Moondawn*, *Body Love*, and *X.*; even parts of Harald Großkopf's *Synthesist* or Ashra's masterpiece *Correlations* were laid down there), *Zuckerfabrik* in Stuttgart (Missus Beastly, Volker Kriegel's Mild Maniac Orchestra, Exil, United Jazz & Rock Ensemble, Wolfgang Dauner, Anne Haigis, Anyone's Daughter, Lok Kreuzberg, Steinwolke, Eulenspygel, and more).

It's no coincidence that many of the studios are/were located in or around Hamburg – as long as the GDR existed and West Berlin was an island, Hamburg was Germany's place for media companies, record labels, and advertising agencies.

But Germany's two most famous and important studios were situated around Cologne and require their own chapter.

CONNY PLANK, DIETER DIERKS

Two of the most important German studios, however, were not located in Hamburg: *Conny's Studio* in Wolperath, southeast of Cologne, and *Dierks Studio* in Stommeln, northwest of Cologne – both small villages. Both cannot be seen without their founders, Konrad "Conny" Plank (1940–1987) and Dieter Dierks. These two shook up the German record industry in a way nobody had before. Without Plank and Dierks, German rock would have taken a different direction. Their working attitudes were different.

Interestingly, both set up their studios in the countryside, in operating distance to a big city. Dierks did it because he could use the attic at his parents' as a small studio. Plank did it because he wanted a place where undisturbed and relaxed working would be possible. It wasn't only cheaper to live outside the cities; Plank made the ambiance, the beautiful Bergische Land with its hills, woods and meadows, part of the working atmosphere he offered musicians. When you run a sound recording studio in a small village, you'll be looked at a bit skeptically for a while, but when it starts to thrive, it will become an important economic factor, and the township, with its officials, will give you any support you need.

Dierks, as well as Plank, probably unintendedly, anticipated a trend that would kick in around 1973: Go to the countryside – and many hippie communities followed the calling, making the countryside a hip place for studios.

CONNY PLANK

Conny Plank started as a high voltage engineer and later worked as a broadcasting technician at SR Radio in Saarbrücken. He resigned because he didn't like the atmosphere of a radio and TV station under public law and worked as a sound assistant at the private Rhenus Studio. There, he mainly recorded things like cover versions of popular schlagers for budget labels. "I had a good technical teacher who showed me how it's done. This was Wolfgang Hirschmann, a real old-fashioned ace of sound engineering. He was really good at making sound. He had already worked with Marlene Dietrich. I've learned a lot from him."[1]

Wikipedia and other sources say that Plank "began his career as a soundman for Marlene Dietrich"[2]. This is a bit exaggerated; he was actually an assistant to Wolfgang Hirschmann who balanced the radio transmission of a Dietrich show. It's also sometimes said that Plank had been a sound recording assistant to Karlheinz Stockhausen at the Electronic Music Studio of WDR Radio in Cologne. The truth is that when, on the occasion of the "Beethoven Bicentennial 1970" in Bonn, WDR Radio commissioned Rhenus Studio with the production of *Kurzwellen mit Beethoven* (which is a special variation of Stockhausen's classic *Kurzwellen* from 1968), the sound engineer was Hirschmann; Plank was *present* at this production, but not involved in it. According to Stockhausen's long-time partner and assistant Kathinka Pasveer, Plank was never involved in any Stockhausen productions.[3]

Plank was a hobby jazz musician ("When I heard boogie woogie as a child, I completely freaked out"[4]), he didn't want to go professional as a musician, but he was musically curious and open to nearly anything. It was frustrating for him to not be able to work independently. To change this, around 1969, he started working as an independent music producer and sound engineer.

DIETER DIERKS

Dieter Dierks is the son of a conductor and originally wanted to become a stage director. He studied acting and dramatics, played bass guitar in a more-schlager-than-rock band named Hush ("Oh Darling" b/w "Schau mir in die Augen", 1969, with later Bläck Fööss singer Tommy Engel) for fun, and had his first recording experiences with two Revox reel-to-reel tape machines. In 1969, Dierks and producer/songwriter Michael Schepior also rearranged and worded a Greek song and recorded it with a raspy-voiced singer named J. Bastós: "Loop di Love". In 1971, this record became a disco hit, especially in the Netherlands and Belgium, and eventually found its way back to Germany. It reached #30 in summer 1971.

In 1971, Dierks moved from the attic at his parents' house to a newly built studio in their yard – the first original Dierks Studio. His second step was converting the dwelling into a sort of hotel, equipped with a kitchen run by his mother. What he had now was a place where musicians could record, mix, and live at during the time of their work – which, in some cases, could take several weeks.

It didn't take long until this Dierks Studio became a topic in the media, which finally brought it to producer Rolf-Ulrich Kaiser's attention (who will be the topic of the next chapter). Most of Kaiser's Ohr, Pilz, and Cosmic Couriers releases were recorded or mixed here: Ash Ra Tempel, Jerry Berkers, Birth Control, Bröselmaschine, Embryo, Emtidi, Floh de Cologne, Sergius Golowin, Guru Guru, Hoelderlin, Klaus Schulze, Tangerine Dream, Wallenstein, Walter Wegmüller, Witthüser & Westrupp, and more.

Bands that were no Kaiser acts also recorded here, like Annexus Quam, Gila, Grobschnitt, Ihre Kinder, Jeronimo, or Peter Meisel's protégés Amon Düül. Klaus Doldinger recorded at least four Passport albums here; his legendary album *Doldinger Jubilee Concert* (1974), recorded live at Rheinhalle Düsseldorf, was mixed at Dierks Studio. Can came to mix their *Landed* album; it was the first one they had recorded on their new 16-track machine, but the Inner Space Studio was not yet equipped for mixing.

Dierks also started his own record label named Venus Records, signed Atlantis of Hamburg, the successor of Frumpy with Inga Rumpf, and tried to establish them in the United States. Although Atlantis did a relatively successful tour there, the record sales remained unsatisfying – a rarity in Dierks's career. Other temporary acts on Venus were Galaxy, Mythos, and Pell Mell; the label was closed down in the early 1990s. To be in a better position when dealing with record companies, Dierks founded a management and production company named Breeze Music.

What was more successful than the Atlantis collaboration was Dierks's work with producer Peter Hauke and the hard rock acts he released on his Bacillus label, especially Nektar. This collaboration, along with his former work with Birth Control and Jeronimo, gave Dierks a reputation for being a specialist in the matter of hard & heavy productions. RCA hired him to produce *In Trance* (1975) by the Scorpions, and later he could sign the band for his Breeze company. This was the beginning of a successful, long-time collaboration; between 1975 and 1988, Dierks produced and recorded eight Scorpions albums. Gold and platinum records came with them, and the name Dieter Dierks became prominent, even in the U.K. and across the Atlantic.

The main reason behind this success was that Dierks not only had a hot hand in his business decisions, but was also, simply, very good at sound engineering.

Walter Westrupp: "When you listen to what we actually recorded and then listen to the final result, it was not for nothing when we used to say: 'He has a magical hand.' You could say to him: 'Let this sound pad just walk from right to left, and then send it up vertically', and he did it. It was simply fantastic. I could play a 'bling' on my ukulele, and with him it sounded as if a whole orchestra made a 'bling'."[5]

Edgar Froese: "I have very fond memories of Dieter Dierks. He was among the first sound engineers who put all of their professionality into these alternative music styles. He never said: 'Okay, here we have some stoned idiots, fine, that's an easy job, let's just get it over with and cash the check.' He was really dedicated, he wanted to *understand.* I still give him credit for making full use of the potential his innovative recording technologies had to offer for our work."[6]

By 1973, Dierks had already enlarged the studio with three smaller recording rooms and a control room, all in the basement under the hotel section, so that more than only one act could work in parallel. Dierks always kept his studio state of the art. He invented some reverb and room simulation systems and was able to offer quadro recording when this became a fad. This especially resonated with Rolf-Ulrich Kaiser, who was always interested in getting the latest tech results. When, in the mid-1980s, the classic rock band concept went a bit into descent, Dierks opened two new studios with hard disc recording systems – ideal for the upcoming techno and hip-hop artists' use of sound samples.

In 1974, Dierks started a 16-track mobile recording unit – the Dierks Mobile – which was used for live recordings. WDR radio and TV hired this mobile for the "Rockpalast" nights at the Grugahalle in Essen. The "Rockpalast" sound was mixed in three versions: Mono for the TV broadcast, stereo for the radio transmission, and in addition, all concerts were recorded on a 16-track tape. These mixes and recordings were done by the Dierks Mobile. Through this, Dierks built up connections to TV stations that he could use later on in the 1980s, when he started an outside broadcast vehicle for TV transmissions.

Today, the entire studio complex can be compared to the best, big studios in New York or Los Angeles. Besides this, Dierks invented and patented the *dual disc*, a double-sided disc that is a DVD on one side and a CD on the other.

While Dieter Dierks already ran his own studio, Conny Plank still worked as sound engineer for various producers in various studios all over the country. He had produced some demo recordings by ORGANISATION (KRAFTWERK's predecessor) which, in 1969, finally became their album *Tone Float*. In addition, he produced the first KRAFTWERK album in 1970, along with GOMORRHA, PARZIVAL, VIRUS, the two KLUSTER albums, and was familiar with Michael Rother and Klaus Dinger. This put his name on the map.

He relocated to Hamburg where he lived in a flat-sharing community with comedian Otto Waalkes and his manager Hans-Otto Mertens (who also was a concert promoter), Udo Lindenberg, Marius Müller-Westernhagen, pianist Gottfried Böttger (1949-2017), violinist Lorenz "Lonzo" Westphal (1952-2001), and radio host and humorous schlager singer "Willem" Wilken F. Dincklage (1942–1994, real name Wilken F. Müller). Temporarily, there lived up to 14 people in this house, and they were all somehow connected to music or show business. The community was situated in Winterhude, one of Hamburg's finer neighborhoods, in the former villa of the Canadian ambassador. Nicknamed "Villa Kunterbunt" after the chaotic house that Astrid Lindgren's anarchic creation Pippi Langstrumpf (Pippi Longstocking) used to live in, this community became the initial nucleus of the "Top Scene Hamburg" – I will have to come back to this later.

Plank, in collaboration with the skilled merchant Dincklage, started a music publishing company called Kraut Musikverlag. This company published anything between volksmusik (KASTELRUTHER SPATZEN), pop, and music comedy. The reason for this was the same as what Dieter Dierks had in mind when he founded Breeze Music: It gave him business background, connections, and a better position when negotiating with the record industry. Plank also worked as a freelance sound engineer, mainly at Windrose-Dumont-Time and Star Studio. At these studios, he recorded ASH RA TEMPEL, CLUSTER, GURU GURU, KRAFTWERK, NEU!, and the SCORPIONS' debut album. These jobs furthered reputation as a sound engineer, but also grew his connections within the record industry. Later he knew how to use them.

Plank was not completely happy with his situation, so in 1973, he found himself an old farmhouse near Cologne and remodeled it to his needs. The former pigsty became a studio.

The main difference between Plank and Dierks is that Dierks knew how to get the sound a musician or producer wanted, and he delivered what they asked for. Plank, on the other hand, found it more important to keep full control of the whole process. It's not that Plank didn't know how to use his equipment; he even equipped his mixing console with joysticks to be able to change two sound parameters with one fingertip. His real strong point was something different: He was able to spot skills (sometimes skills the artists themselves had no idea they had) and then set up an atmosphere that made it possible for the musicians to develop and work with said skills. In his own words: "Basically, I do nothing more than try to establish situations for good music. I don't care whether it's electronic music or folk music. I don't see the power of music in its style, I see it in its expression. I would even produce a ländler band – actually, I do so with ZUPFGEIGENHANSEL."[7]

While working with bands, he did much more than just recording what they played. He got involved in the entire production process and shaped its result – he told the guitarist not to use the Gibson and try the Telecaster instead, he developed synthesizer sounds, he changed atmospheres, he sat down with musicians and edited recordings. When they got stuck on something, he strolled around in the woods with them, and kept view of the big picture in a way most musicians were not able to. The studio didn't have its own hotel, but it was possible to stay overnight in one of the buildings.

Unlike Dieter Dierks, Conny Plank never strove for an empire. He had his studio, and that was all he wanted and needed, besides a mobile recording unit he started. He could be an edgy companion. If he felt he couldn't work with an artist, he sent them packing, as he did with David Bowie and U2. His prices were moderate; a day at Conny's Studio cost something between 600 and 1000 D-Marks (other studios sometimes charged 200 D-Marks or more per hour). He used to help bands when they were negotiating with a label to stop them from falling into contractual pitfalls, and set up label deals for them.

KRAFTWERK, especially *Autobahn*, made the name Conny Plank internationally known. Plank produced DEVO as well as the EURYTHMICS, CLUSTER as well as Holger Czukay, DAF as well as ULTRAVOX, RHEINGOLD as well as Gianna Nannini, Brian Eno as well as IDEAL. But the majors could never be sure about him: "My market value within these systems is higher now, but for all intents and purposes, I'm still presumed to be an unreliable personality. I think that's very good. This way they can't have any influence on me. That is a good situation. I think this is the principle of getting out of this dilemma: building up a field around you that is healthy. Maybe this impregnates the landscape. ... The industry is just a monster that made too much money to keep the balance. And that's why they paddle like crazy and don't feel obliged to the music anymore, but rather to its profitability, and then such a process perverts."[8]

While Dierks' empire got bigger and bigger, Plank intendedly tried to work within self-imposed limits: "Chris Blackwell once said: We have to shrink to stay healthy. Island Records [Blackwell's label] became insanely successful and an excessive bureaucracy, and Blackwell was one of few in the business who realized that we need to become smaller in order to function. I see it the same way. I'm for sure not going to enlarge my studio to get more capacity – I'm not interested in that. I want to make the place more interesting for the people living here. Keep it colorful, not persist in what we are now, but keep it in balance with the size of the structure. That will give me further freedom to go on with my lunacy."[9]

As a copy of a golden record is traditionally given to the studio that did the recording, Plank received lots of golden records. Conny used to hang his golden records in the bathroom – a bit childish, with all due respect.

There's no need to repeat all the hymns many important artists use to sing about Conny Plank. Hans-Joachim Roedelius can speak in their regard: "Conny was a friend, and beyond that, through his very own way of sound engineering, he was a musician himself who, in respective productions, ideally played a part by contributing several things, and he acted as a third member of CLUSTER this way. But this was never mentioned publicly. Being an ideal producer, visionary in sound quality, and artistic contents, he always felt strictly obliged to the requirements of true art. With his productions, he never aimed ostensibly at their possible salability, he always stayed true to his idea as the most innovative sound engineer and co-musician that he was all his lifetime. Conny and his companion in life, Christa Fast [1942-2006], an ideal team at this place Wolperath at an old pilgrimage road, a side way of the Jakobsweg [Way of Saint James], which, seen from just this spiritual meaning, was the best possible place of activity for such an exceptionally gifted 'producer' that Conny was, and his wife as helper. An oasis of creativity which could be used by all those who ever had the chance to work with him there."[10]

A part of Conny Plank's idea of living, I'm convinced, was burning himself in the work he was doing – as Joseph Beuys once put it: "It is completely meaningless what profession you abrade yourself, but you have to abrade. You have to burn yourself down to the ashes. Otherwise it's all useless."[11]

Conny Plank passed away in December 1987 at the age of only 47. Christa Fast and their son Stephan Plank kept the studio going until Christa's death. The studio was torn down in 2009 – truly the end of an era.

THE SEVENTIES

KAISER'S REICH

"Currently, I make 6000 D-Marks a month. This shows how much an idea of mine is worth."[1] Rolf-Ulrich Kaiser said this in 1968. He should have listened to his girlfriend, Gille Lettmann: "Everybody creates his own reality."[2] This chapter will show you why.

The story of the German record labels Ohr, Pilz, and Kosmische Kuriere – and of course of Rolf-Ulrich Kaiser and Gille Lettmann who ran them – is an especially interesting chapter of German media, music, and contemporary history. These names still come up pretty regularly on discussion forums today.

Rolf-Ulrich Kaiser and Gille Lettmann were important figures for the German rock landscape. When nearly no one else dared to, they bet on German rock music without reservation. Few people have been thrown down to the pit as mercilessly as them. Even their former followers in the music press doused them with buckets of malice. Some still do it today. It's easy. There is nearly no risk that Kaiser could suddenly reappear and hit back.

Kaiser and Lettmann were not the only ones who rendered outstanding service to the beginnings of German rock music. But when it comes down to when German "beat groups" transformed into rock bands, leaving behind their imitation phase and starting to develop their own musical style, we can't ignore them. Kaiser and Lettmann's importance becomes obvious when we look at the endless questions about their whereabouts. Speculations have become more and more abstruse over the years. Some claim to have seen Kaiser at the Frankfurt Book Fair. Others say he lives on the street, supposedly walking around the central market in Cologne in the early mornings, begging for food. He's said to live in the U.S., working as Erich von Däniken's promoter. He's also been declared dead at least two times.

All of this is nonsense.

Rolf-Ulrich Kaiser, sometimes nicknamed "RUK", was born June 18, 1943, in Buckow (in Brandenburg, near Berlin). He was raised in Osnabrück (Lower Saxony) and Berlin. Later he studied German language and literature, philosophy, sociology, and dramatic theory in Cologne.

ESSEN

His first enduring contact with German music, aside from the radio, was the first of today's legendary folk festivals at the Waldeck Castle in the Hunsrück area (Rhineland-Palatinate) in 1964. Kaiser became an active part of the rock scene in 1968 when he managed to get a guarantee of 300,000 D-Marks from the City of Essen to start the "Internationale Essener Songtage" (International Song Festival Essen). To give you a clue about what this was worth, today, this would equate to around 550,000 euros or 625,000 U.S. dollars. Kaiser praised the event, in all modesty, as "the biggest thing that ever happened in Europe". It was at least Germany's first real rock festival. Bernd Witthüser was the managing director, press work was done by Henryk M. Broder, and the program was designed by graphic artist Reinhard Hippen – these names will re-appear. The performing artists from Germany were kabarett artist Hanns Dieter Hüsch (Kabarett is not the same as cabaret; more about the difference in the "agitprop" chapter), political bard Franz-Josef Degenhardt, singer-songwriter Hannes Wader, jazz musician Peter Brötzmann, the bands TANGERINE DREAM, AMON DÜÜL, GURU GURU, THE CITY PREACHERS, FLOH DE COLOGNE; from the U.K. and U.S. there were JULIE DRISCOLL WITH BRIAN AUGER & THE TRINITY, FAMILY, Alexis Korner, THE FUGS and THE MOTHERS OF INVENTION with their boss Frank Zappa. The latter turned out to be irritated: "Apparently the audience can't decide whether they want to *discuss* music or *listen* to music." The AMON DÜÜL members were stoned enough to play the same riff over and over again like a loop; some festival visitors still remember the repeated announcements: "AMON DÜÜL, stop playing please, we need to set up the stage for the next band!" At least the DÜÜLS (and some other bands) were interesting enough to be signed by producer Peter Meisel of Berlin, who was a festival visitor. In the thick of all this chaos, Rolf-Ulrich Kaiser ran around. To him, this whole event was a giant, adventurous playground: "A music happening that, mind-expanding and mind-expanded, psychedelically, opens up new ways of experience and, in an emotional way, puts the vested and accepted habits into question", as he stated somewhat foggy-minded. He tried to minimize the organizational confusion he had caused with his inexperience and unconsciousness with "irrefutable orders" and a walkie-talkie: "We will crack down on this."

Not everybody was happy with the festival. Newspaper *Kölnische Rundschau* wrote: "The revolution did not happen. This, more or less, is the conclusion of the eagerly anticipated Internationale Essener Songtage that attracted nearly 40,000 spectators to come to the Ruhr area during four days and around 40 events. Songs and sex, rock and shock, in parts excellent music, in parts incomprehensible stammering. But the performers' protest shouting didn't catch up with the audience. The audience wanted to watch, not take action. People also were not willing to get involved in big discussions. The U.S. band Fugs played proper rock, but besides this, they came across as vulgar. So did the kabarett group Floh de Cologne of Cologne. The many psychedelic shows tired the fans. … Luckily there were no riots coming up."[3]

The festival ended with a loss of 80,000 D-Marks – real money; today this would be circa 145,000 euros or 165,000 U.S. dollars. Kaiser tried to get money by selling broadcasting rights, but ended up playing the stations off against each other in such a clumsy way that no more than 4000 D-Marks came in. Editor Hendrik Wuermeling from BR TV Munich: "Had Mr. Kaiser negotiated early and seriously enough, he could have proceeded a much higher amount."[4]

PANOPTIKUM

Around the same time, Kaiser, under the pseudonym "Fritz Baas", used the Protestant news service *Kirche und Rundfunk* to slam all German radio shows targeted at young people as "boring" and "a real pest". Parallel to this, he praised a new radio show by WDR radio Cologne that had not even aired yet as "up to date" and "ambitious", and called in advance for more airtime.

The show was called "Panoptikum", describing itself as a "radio collage", and miraculously, Kaiser himself was a freelancer in its editorial staff. One of his co-collaborators was, again, Henryk M. Broder (who later became a columnist for news magazine *Der Spiegel*, now works for newspaper *Die Welt* and is still an excellent writer and highly gifted polemicist).

We'll have to come back to "Panoptikum" later because for Kaiser, this radio show became important for a completely different reason.

Several books followed. Kaiser was a good and efficient writer, busy as a bee, and in contrast to other people who simply discussed their ideas, he put his ideas into practice. His never-tiring typewriting was legendary; as an early bird, he could already be found at his desk at 5 am. Sometimes, he worked under several pseudonyms for around 60 newspapers, magazines, and radio stations.

Some of his books were regarded as more serious than others, and were released by respected publishing house. Others were obviously shots from the hip, released by "kinder der geburtstagspresse" ("children of birthday press", decidedly in lower case letters) – which essentially meant they were self-published. Kaiser had founded this business in 1968. As his shrill house advertising said, it was the "super publishing house of German underground" and remained in existence for a couple of years. Kaiser published not only his own books, but also two or three books written by others.

He also published a magazine (he called it a "counter newspaper") named *popopo – Zeitung für Pop & Politik & Pornographie* (paper for pop, politics, and pornography), edited by Henryk M. Broder, Reinhard Hippen, Rolf-Ulrich Kaiser, and Fred Viebahn. In one of his later books, Kaiser praised this magazine for its "especially psychedelic layout". Via mail order, he offered a couple of U.S. music magazines that were hardly available elsewhere in Germany. But his cash cows were some American porn magazines – he imported them for 25 cents and sold them for 5.50 D-Marks.

"Das Buch der neuen Popmusik" (The Book of New Pop Music) from 1969 and "Rock-Zeit – Stars, Geschäft und Geschichte der neuen Popmusik" (Rock Time – Stars, Business and History of the New Pop Music) from 1972 are still worth reading. The former was translated into Dutch, Portuguese, Spanish, and Italian (strangely there was never an English translation), while the second one only exists in German. Both are out of print for a long time.

When read consecutively, these books show Kaiser's development in a stunningly precise way. His talent of putting facts and circumstances into short, crisp sentences and labelling them with catchy buzzwords is obvious. In "Rock-Zeit", Kaiser delivers lots of hot air, slips (he continuously misspells Bob Dylan's famous album as *John Wesley Hardings*, to name just one), and arbitrarily constructed arguments, but there are also bright, sometimes razor-sharp analyses. But his conclusions are oftentimes over the top and set their sights on simplistic blow-offs instead of serious insight.

Interestingly, Kaiser seemed to be well aware of the fact that he was in danger as a journalist writing from the perspective of a fan. He tried to make a virtue out of necessity by admitting this openly: "This book carries a contradiction in itself. Apparently. In it, I strictly criticize the rock music that ended up being purely for-profit music, and I identify myself exposedly with a part of this rock music. … This is different from the non-fiction books we are used to, and I'm well aware of this. I didn't write an abstractly so-called objective paper, I compiled the musical aspects that are currently most important to me and have been part of my life for several years. And I think it is a good thing when the reader can recognize the author."[5]

A comparison of the first "Pop Music" edition with the extended second edition had already shown the author's increasing affinity to drugs, hashish, and especially LSD. But now, in "Rock-Zeit", he openly mentions "the trip" as an important part of his perception of music: "It is – read this way – an intimate and dedicated book."[6] This is true. Besides this, Kaiser didn't leave out any chance to promote his own artists.

These two books offer a key to his way of thinking. Here, in rough outline, the developing imaginary world in which he was going to lose his way during the following years already becomes visible.

Kaiser wrote more books, like "Underground? Pop? Nein! Gegenkultur!" (Underground? Pop? No! Counterculture!; 1969) or "Fabrikbewohner – Protokoll einer Kommune und 23 Trips" (Factory Residents – Journal of a Commune and 23 Trips; 1970). These are less important, but also revealing. Both books are printed multi-colored and are collages from short essays, transcripts of talks, interviews, photos, and drawings, made in collaboration with Reinhard Hippen, and they show a couple of Kaiser's special quirks. One of those is the persistent urge for a hierarchic numeration of text paragraphs to suggest the existence of essentials where, in reality, no essentials exist. His constant use of the term "trips" for each chapter is also notable.

The constant mentioning of addresses in both books is even more interesting. The idea of "Gegenöffentlichkeit" (counter public) fascinated Kaiser. It's obvious that when he studied sociology, he had delved deeply into "Strukturwandel der Öffentlichkeit" (The Structural Transformation of the Public Sphere) by German sociologist Jürgen Habermas, published in 1962, a "must-read" at that time, and Kaiser now puts these perceptions into use for the scene he writes about. This is why he profiles domestic and foreign flat-sharing communities, projects for the arts or alternative manufacturing, musicians, theater people, and other artists – he calls them "neue Leute" (new people). Following his idea of a counter public sphere, he tries to let the reader be able to cross-link with all these people. For this reason, he filled pages by listing their addresses and telephone numbers. It might be understandable that names like Allen Ginsberg, Andy Warhol's Factory, or FUGS boss Tuli Kupferberg (Kaiser deeply admired this band) are listed, as well as "Rechtsanwalt Schilli" (he means Otto Schily, a lawyer who then acted as defense counsel for several Baader-Meinhof terrorists; the tabloids described Schily as terror sympathizer for that reason, which he never was). But Kaiser also lists several dozen completely unknown persons without letting us know who and what they are. Even the private New York address and telephone number of singer Nico (1938–1988) is listed (if somebody is interested: 134 E 16th St, but she doesn't live there anymore). She surely never had the slightest interest in any sort of "counter public sphere". Collecting addresses must have been a personal quirk of Kaiser's; he kept a file with thousands of them.[7]

Kaiser saw society's future in building up alternative networks everywhere. There were lots of them. One may bemoan it or not, but most of these alternative projects fell apart after, at the latest, one or two years. Kaiser was far from being the only one running after an illusion, but most participants woke up after a while. It is hard to say whether Kaiser eventually woke up too, but while he continued his publicist course without any changes, he started his following career as a music producer under the roof of a fully commercial group of companies. And – in spite of his existing analytical perspicacity – he became a barker in the matter of mind-altering drugs, ruining his own credibility and that of his artists. Eventually, he ruined his own existence.

OHR

1970. Peter Meisel enters, then 35 years old, working as a music producer and publisher in Berlin; you've read about him already. He was producer of schlager singers Conny Froboess, Manuela, Drafi Deutscher, Giorgio Moroder and others, but he also had signed Tangerine Dream and Amon Düül, Xhol Caravan and Birth Control. At this point in time, he was a bit clueless about what to do with these groups. So when Kaiser entered Meisel's sphere of activity, he was exactly what Meisel needed. This resulted in the founding of Ohr Music Production.

The company had its place in Berlin-Wilmersdorf, in the same building where Meisel's other companies and branches were based. Its catch phrase "Macht das Ohr auf" ("open the ears") came from graphic artist Reinhard Hippen (now Ohr's design head), and it was not without subtle humor: It was a pun on the slogan "Macht das Tor auf!" (Open the gate!) which West Berlin's edition of the tabloid *Bild* had on page 1, framed with barbed wire. Of course, what *Bild* was referring to was the closed Brandenburg Gate as a widely visible symbol for the inaccessible border crossing between East and West Berlin. Hippen hit the zeitgeist with this pun because, at that time, rock music was usually expected to be politically left-wing, and *Bild* was one of the most aggressive identity-forming enemy images of the student protest scene. Kaiser and Hippen knew exactly how to adjust Ohr ads to this scene. (Reinhard Hippen later published several books and anthologies on German kabarett history and founded the Deutsche Kabarett Archiv in Mainz, which he ran until 1989. He passed away in 2010.)

After Kaiser's entry, Ohr Records hit the market in March 1970 with three LPs: *Fließbandbabys Beat-Show* by Cologne-based agitprop band Floh de Cologne (more about them in a later chapter), which was already their sixth stage show, but only their first based on music, a song cycle in a contrived cool language, straying between sexual revolution and class struggle; *Mandalas* by Limbus 4 from Heidelberg; and *Lieder von Vampiren, Nonnen und Toten* (Songs of Vampires, Nuns and Dead People) by singer-songwriter Bernd Witthüser of Essen; Walter Westrupp was involved, but the record hadn't yet gone under both of their names. In April, *Opal* by Embryo from Munich followed, in June *Electronic Meditation* by Tangerine Dream from Berlin, and then *UFO* by Guru Guru from the Heidelberg area. The three latter albums are widely seen as classics today – rough, unpolished diamonds, but it was obvious that there was potential.

A couple of 45s were also released. The first, "St Pauli, du mein Loch zur Welt" by Floh de Cologne, went to nowhere; the first one that might have had chances to sell commercially was the fourth, "Hope" by Birth Control.

While some of the first recordings, among them *UFO* and *Electronic Meditation*, had been recorded at Thomas Kessler's Beatstudio in Berlin and sounded a bit raw, Kaiser was soon able to acquire Dieter Dierks, later also Conny Plank, as sound engineers for his productions. The recording quality and production creativity of many of Kaiser's productions are still remarkable today. Kaiser was also an early adopter of new trends. Several of his records were mixed in SQ quadro, a four-channel system that could be pressed into standard vinyl records and was compatible with stereo equipment, but it wasn't successful.

The Ohr LPs had a lavish design, usually gate-fold sleeves, good graphics, and often came with posters or gimmicks, like a balloon clipped to the cover or gadgetry like the extricable giblets on the cover of FLOH DE COLOGNE's second album *Profitgeier* (something like "Vulture Capitalist"). The record itself came in day-glo red vinyl.

Soon it became Kaiser's strategy to present an increasing number of new discoveries. The problem with this was that the pool was not exactly overflowing with qualitative acceptable German bands. In nearly no time, Kaiser had signed around 30 acts to his label, among them were bands like TANGERINE DREAM, GURU GURU, POPOL VUH, and ASH RA TEMPEL who probably would have made their way even without Kaiser. But there were several "second-tier" bands – ANIMA, EMTIDI, HÖLDERLIN, MYTHOS, WALLENSTEIN, WITTHÜSER & WESTRUPP and others – of which we probably would have never heard without Kaiser. Soon, he claimed to have signed "the best German rock groups"[8], but this, actually, was a matter of taste. He did not have AMON DÜÜL II, CAN, CLUSTER, KRAFTWERK, and later NEU!, so it could be rightfully stated that some of the most important bands were missing from his roster.

Ohr probably would have been a good place for AMON DÜÜL II, but it's hard to imagine that the likes of CAN, KRAFTWERK or NEU! would have participated in the marketing circus Kaiser now ignited. His record output grew in such a way that Deutsche Metronome (the company that distributed the Ohr records) had to finally put the brakes on.

PILZ

Kaiser's and Meisel's response to this was founding the Pilz label, which required a second distribution channel. In 1971, they finally found the chemical giant BASF that had stepped into the record industry in 1969. BASF's product manager, Jürgen Schmeißer, had developed a sublabel named Mouse and had already prepared a couple of productions. But when the inquiry from Kaiser and Meisel came in, BASF decided to turn down the Mouse project and took over the distribution of Pilz instead. The finished Mouse recordings were transferred to the new label; the distribution was managed by Ulrich Rützel (who in 1979 became co-founder of Ars Electronica, which is probably the most important European festival for electronic arts; in 1981 he founded his own label, Erdenklang). In principle, Pilz was meant to release more folk-oriented productions, while Ohr was dedicated to (psychedelic) rock. But this got mixed up very soon.

Kaiser never had any problems with the fact that music had to make money. But in his main target group, this was frowned upon. Many rock fans at that time defined themselves as "somewhat left-wing"; critics from music magazines, the "art & entertainment" sections in the papers, or cultural programs on TV did so even more. When watching today, an early-1970s issue of a TV magazine like "aspekte" can give you chills. The pseudo-left wing complacency these journalists showed is breathtaking. But this was good form back then – everybody wanted to be seen as critical. Music critic, Bernd Gockel, for instance, closed his review of Amon Düül II's album *Wolf City* in *Sounds* with the conclusion: "It would be a great pity if we would find Amon Düül II in the hit parade one day."[9] At that time, charts had a maximum disgust factor. If a band really managed to place a record in the charts, then this immediately made them inauthentic in the eyes of their fans and, even more so, in the eyes of "progressive" journalists: For them, the band was now "on the commercial trip", as the saying went, meaning that the band sold out and couldn't be taken serious anymore. Nobody realized that the charts only show which records are currently selling well, and critics (especially salaried ones like Gockel) didn't seem to understand that with conclusions like the one just mentioned, they expected the bands to prove their credibility by making no money. How should they make ends meet? Who cares!

The same spirit could be seen when, in 1971, WDR TV live aired a round-table discussion, titled "Pop & Co. – Die 'andere' Musik zwischen Protest und Markt" (Pop & Co. – The 'other' Music Between Protest and Market): Panel member Nikel Pallat, manager of West Berlin-based agit-prop band Ton Steine Scherben, berated Kaiser as a vassal of high finance, acting in cahoots with capitalists. Kaiser stated his point of view: His record label would never tell its bands what to do or not to do, but of course, Ohr couldn't be a benevolent society. Pallat, who called TV an "instrument of repression in this mass society", finally closed down the (as he called it) "fucking liberal" discussion by pulling an axe out from under his jacket and trying to smash the studio table. But the table was very stable, only a couple of ashtrays broke. Pallat then stole some microphones ("I need them for people in youth prison!") and disappeared with the words: "Now we can discuss further". Probably still today he has no clue what he wanted to let us know with this action.

By the way, it was just Ton Steine Scherben who had to learn the hard way where this attitude could lead to. A concert excerpt from 1976 shows their singer Rio Reiser, highly on edge, trying to explain to the audience that even a political band cannot only play solidarity gigs without being paid. Even left-wing musicians need a minimum income to make ends meet. The audience stared at him like: "What the heck is this guy talking about?"[10]

As shown earlier, it was better to be careful with messages about economic success – they could backfire. However, according to their own statement, capitalist Meisel and his vassal Kaiser had sold around 250,000 albums in their first two business years. Not overwhelming, but not too bad – but only at first glance. Why? Assuming this number is correct (nobody can verify it anymore), we have to see that it refers to no less than 18 productions. In addition to this, at that time, the costs for production and studio were usually covered by record companies; license deals were still the exception. The problem was that the two or three best-selling Ohr albums might have been successful and profitable, but the revenues they generated were not high enough to cover the costs of all the other albums that had been produced and didn't sell. Ohr had sold a quarter of a million records, but yielded only a small profit (if any) at that time, although the company was able to land some license deals with foreign labels.

One year later, in early 1973, Hansa stated that of all the now circa 50 albums that had been released under Kaiser's reign, especially the seven records with the new electronic "cosmic music", were selling well. But this time, as a precaution, no figures were given.

Kaiser now included more and more obscure and half-baked products in his roster and obviously mixed up turnover and profit. He planned on boosting the market share of German bands from 0.5 percent to more than 90 percent – just within a few months! To succeed in this, he compensated missing artistic quality with increasingly strange promotions and massive ad campaigns.

We've got to hand it to him: It seemed to work for a while. There was this psychedelic and politicized scene, and Kaiser knew how to sell them their own pipe dreams: records plus image. He didn't sell records, he sold a lifestyle. He probably didn't even have any qualms about it; we can be sure that Kaiser believed in his own writings – don't forget that at that time, many still saw him as a serious journalist. He knew the slang of his target group because it was his own. It worked so well that the music press didn't hesitate to adopt his catchphrases – just read album reviews from that time in *Sounds*, *Musik Express,* or the Swiss *Pop*. Kaiser started a bi-weekly PR magazine called *deutsche popszene* with background stories about his artists and the zeitgeist in general. It was sent to various editing staffs, journalists, and media people. For every new album, Ohr and Pilz designed voluminous press kits and sent them to any magazine, radio, and TV station within reach.

Kaiser also knew how to make use of the well-tried "calculated scandal" concept. The best-known example for this strategy was the BIRTH CONTROL album *Operation* from 1971.

Its tasteless cover, which had not even a connection to the songs, was a "precisely and deliberately" developed part of the band's "career plan"[11]. The cover shows a giant insect eating babies under the blessing hand of Pope Paul VI, who in 1968 had released the much-disputed encyclical "Humanae vitae – On the Regulation of Birth". Today, this provocation may look harmless, but in 1971 it was enough for catholic priests in Germany to mount barricades against "this porn group". In Switzerland, concert posters of the band were banned, and in England the workers of a record distribution center refused to dispatch this record.

Ulrich Rützel: "Kaiser was enormously talented in PR and marketing, and we thought it was absolutely amazing to see how he systematically started dusting off this completely boring German music industry." Kaiser remained busy as a bee. Rützel: "You know, we had no answering machines at that time, and often enough, Kaiser called me up at night because he had a new idea. In the beginning, I said to myself: 'Okay, that's rock'n'roll.' But after a while one would like to go back to sleeping without interruptions …"

Finally, Kaiser got to a point of overdoing his activities in such a way that Hansa's marketing head, Hans Blume, got the feeling it would be time to talk to his boss: "As someone with his feet on the ground, I soon had the suspicion that this thing was going to go wrong. And I said to Meisel: 'Peter, you have to slow this guy down!' But we were in the record industry, so we always wanted to try something new. And well, it could have been ..."[12]

GILLE

Meanwhile, Meisel would have needed to slow down not only Kaiser, but also his companion Gerlinde Lettmann, nicknamed Gille, a textile designer from Cologne.

It was in spring 1968, when Düsseldorf-based journalist Hubert Maessen took a train to go to WDR in Cologne. He had a suitcase full of LPs with him, flipping through them during his train ride. Vis-à-vis in his compartment sat an 18-year-old: That was Gille, asking him about the records. For a short time, a little love affair resulted from this chance encounter. During the following weeks, Maessen took Gille, who still lived with her parents at the time, along with him a couple times to editorial conferences for the radio show "Panoptikum". The relationship between Gille Lettmann and Hubert Maessen ended soon, but it didn't take long for Gille to find herself a new boyfriend: Rolf-Ulrich Kaiser, the "monk", as he was called, the berserk writer, who, as depicted before, worked as a freelancer for this editorial team. It must have been the love of their lives; they always came as a package from then on.

Hubert Maessen describes Gille Lettmann as "wide awake, self-confident, resolute, inquisitive".[13] In the beginning, she was mainly Kaiser's girlfriend, but in 1971 she began to take on an increasingly decisive role in the company. To slow her down was nearly impossible; she and Kaiser drove each other from idea to idea.

LEARY

Another thing happened in 1972 – from today's perspective, we can call it the beginning of Kaiser's and Lettmann's downswing: The American psychologist, LSD trickster and fired Harvard lecturer, Timothy Leary (1920–1996), after his escape from U.S. prison via Algiers, finally ended up with his wife in a luxurious flat in Villars-sur-Ollon, Switzerland, near Lake Geneva, hosted by arms dealer Michel Hauchard whom Leary's part-time companion Brian Barritt (1934-2011) used to call "Goldfinger".[14] Barritt had gotten in touch with Leary in Algiers when he asked Leary to write a foreword for his unpublished book "Whispers". Later, in the 1980s, their relationship ended on bad terms: Leary "named Barritt as the instigator of his [Leary's] heroin use" and called him a "lying junkie".[15]

It was Ash Ra Tempel's bass player, Hartmut Enke, who first got directly in touch with Leary. This was a strange story in itself: When Ash Ra Tempel, at that time Manuel Göttsching, Klaus Schulze and Hartmut Enke, had produced their second album *Schwingungen* (1972), they quoted lines from Allen Ginsberg's poem "Howl" on the cover. Because of this, they had the idea it would be nice to meet him in person. They asked Kaiser to bring them in touch with Ginsberg. Although he had Ginsberg's address in his files, Kaiser had no idea how to do this. But he had heard somewhere that Timothy Leary was a friend of Ginsberg and stayed in Switzerland. So they sent Hartmut Enke to Leary to bring him a copy of *Schwingungen* – with compliments from Ohr.

Leary and Barritt, of course, had never heard of Ash Ra Tempel, but as Barritt later recalled: "We liked it. They weren't trying to be pop stars or anything like that, they didn't really have any pop star traditions. They were more like a crowd of people who liked playing music … It sounded great to us because we'd got tired of Pink Floyd, and the stuff we were getting from the States and England was pretty sort of low-key compared to the lifestyle we were living."[16] *Schwingungen* gave Leary the idea to make a record with them, a record that would be based on a theory he had worked out: a "mindmap model … which classifies what the mind is capable of in both normal and expanded states of consciousness. It was always a theory that was going to sound baffling when explained to the general public, but might it become easier to comprehend if it was represented musically?"[17]

Hartmut Enke at least understood the idea immediately. So, Ash Ra Tempel and the whole Ohr clan, including Kaiser and Lettmann, came to Switzerland, and what had to happen, happened: In Leary, Gille found her personal guru, and in the drug he propagated, she saw the way to go. Or, as Barritt put it: Kaiser, who didn't need to be convinced about LSD anymore, tried, from now on, to be for Gille what she saw in Leary. This constellation seems to mark their entry into a personal labyrinth.

Still in Switzerland, they schlepped the Ash Ra Tempel musicians to Sinus Studio, a professional but strange basement place in the historic center of Bern, and had them record what would become *Seven Up*.

Lyrics were written by Leary and Barritt, the musicians were Hartmut Enke on bass and synthesizer, Dieter Burmeister and Tommy Engel on drums, Manuel Göttsching on guitar and synthesizer, Micky Duwe on flute, Steve Schroyder on synthesizer, and his Highness Timothy Leary himself on vocals. As a fan of German bands, one was used to incompetent singers, so Leary's vocals didn't stand out very much. It was – as often is – owed to the class of the musicians and not least to sound engineer Dieter Dierks, that the resulting album, with lots of sound effects and atmospheric noise, was tolerable. But overall, *Seven Up* is not an interesting album. Without the name "Leary" on it, it would be one more album in the pile of mediocre Krautrock leftovers.

SOME GOODBYES

Watched closely, the forthcoming decay was already visible. In 1972, two of Kaiser's most important collaborators quit: Bruno Wendel and Günter Körber, who both felt that things were going downhill. They talked to Deutsche Metronome, the distributor of Ohr, and developed the sublabel Brain Records with Metronome. It didn't take long until Brain became the top address for German rock music – and Kaiser's biggest competitor, especially because Wendel and Körber had taken a couple of important Ohr acts with them. In 1975, Körber finally founded Sky Records, which became meritorious in its own right.

In May 1973, Peter Meisel quit his collaboration with Kaiser. It had become obvious to him that this ship was now heading for the iceberg. Kaiser and Lettmann paid him off with a loan from Gille's mother.

Meisel, in 1984, migrated to the U.S. where he became a joint partner of the fast food chain Wendy's. After the Fall of the Wall, he returned to Hansa to be a producer again. Among others, he discovered DIE PRINZEN, a vocal group from Leipzig, and later Lou Bega. Peter Meisel passed away in his adopted home in Pinehurst, North Carolina, in 2010.

The Ohr & Pilz Musikproduktion, now solely under the direction of Kaiser & Lettmann, moved to the Europa-Center, a shopping mall with an office tower in the Charlottenburg neighborhood of West Berlin. Kaiser's old home address in Cologne's Dellbrück neighborhood became a second headquarters.

COSMIC COURIERS

"We are the Cosmic Couriers. First, we send our music, later we will expand into a more beautiful world", stated the press release. Under Leary's lasting influence, Kaiser and Lettmann now became irrevocably struck by cosmic lightning. They started a third label and called it Kosmische Kuriere (Cosmic Couriers) because this was what they felt they were. Only three albums later, they renamed it to Kosmische Musik (Cosmic Music) and changed the visual appearance. The name "Cosmic Music" had been stolen anyway. It was the title of an album by Alice & John Coltrane in 1968, but it's likely that neither Kaiser nor Gille (or anybody else in their circle) was seriously interested in their music.

Not that there hadn't been any drug connections on the Ohr or Pilz releases. This was not only Kaiser's private quirk, it was part of the zeitgeist, evident not only in music but also, and especially, in advertising – find an "Afri-Cola" TV or cinema commercial created by Charles Wilp on Youtube and you'll have an example. Psychedelic graphic elements or typography could be found nearly everywhere, Ohr and Pilz were no exception.

First, the psychedelic messages came as graphics, were musically encrypted, or – as in case of Witthüser & Westrupp – borrowed from Tolkien's "Lord of the Rings", often mixed with friendly-absurd humor.

With the establishment of Cosmic Couriers, Kaiser and Lettmann now saw hallucinogenic drugs as a sort of savior for themselves and the rest of mankind. The playful atmosphere, to a large extent, was turned into plain propaganda. Leary's trip-advising instructions were incorporated in songs without much modification; one example is "Interplay Of Forces" by Ash Ra Tempel from their album *Starring Rosi*.

LSD SESSIONS?

It is said that sometimes in the studio, Kaiser and/or Lettmann dosed the musicians with LSD in their drinks, without telling them beforehand. Klaus Schulze states in an interview: "Partially, we've been forced to take drugs to be allowed to take part in those monster sessions."[18] As often is the case, what actually happened cannot be verified anymore, but we can be sure it did not happen at gunpoint. Doubts about "being forced" come up (at latest) in Walter Westrupp's online autobiography, when he fiddles around with the term "Kaiser's Kaffee" ("Kaiser's Kaffee-Geschäft" was the name of a supermarket chain rich in tradition at that time). It is clear that most musicians knew quite well what this coffee was about.[19] But apparently not all of them. Bettina Müller-Hohls, who participated in the *Seven Up* sessions as a backup singer, did not know about the content of the soft drink she was offered. Gille later asked her whether she had "come through well". The same happened to drummer Burmeister.[20] Klaus Schulze: "Rolf-Ulrich would like to always have us high in the studio, but I can't improvise while tripping."[21] Let's hope that this remained their biggest problem, and in most cases, luckily, nothing further happened. But "from the inner Kaiser circle … at least five ended up in a psychiatric ward."[22]

PROMOTION OVERDOSE

All of Ohr and Pilz's activities were now bundled into the new project, Kosmische Musik. Had the promotion of Ohr and Pilz already been quite something, then what the Cosmic Couriers now started turned out to be a promotion overkill that had rarely been seen in Germany before and would not be seen again until the Neue Deutsche Welle in the 1980s. The space pilots denoted their albums as "sonic LSD", nothing went without cosmic connections. Lavish ad campaigns were placed in the press, and the press kits now turned out to be something between linguistically spaced-out and infantile. Finally, even good-willed fans and journalists couldn't help but smile or shake their heads: "You are invited to a flight through your childhood, into the fields of joy, to the centers of your nerves, into the white light of the elemental force of your life" – this came with the release of the previously mentioned Leary album. A "guided trip through the seven levels of consciousness" was promised, the sapience of "magicians and alchemists, philosophers and psychologists" were announced, and the blurb of *Lord Krishna von Goloka* by Sergius Golowin stated that "Krishna is not a legend from India! Krishna is you! … Let's go to the White Alp where Radha and Krishna dance their love." Golowin (1930-2006), a librarian, politician and writer, was another one of Timothy Leary's hosts in Switzerland. (He had been a member of the Swiss Federal Council, and on his initiative, the canton Bern accepted special minority rights of the Didicoy, a topic of several books he published. Golowin was friends with playwright Friedrich Dürrenmatt and artist H.C. Artmann.)

Facsimile of an Ohr/Pilz ad

Most of this promotion kibosh was no longer written by Kaiser, it came from Gille Lettmann. She took over the helm more and more now. It was her idea to put the musicians in fantasy costumes that she had designed herself. These clothes would have been okay for acts like THE SWEET, SLADE, Gary Glitter, or other Glam acts from Ilja Richter's "Disco"; news magazine *Der Spiegel* stated, Kaiser and Gille now wore "beautiful new clothes, velvet and latex with silver sequins and several sorts of bling-bling"[23], but none of their musicians were ever seen in these costumes. Kaiser and Lettmann were apparently the only ones wearing her creations.

Kaiser rented a railway car, had it colorfully painted, put his artists in it, and visited local newspapers all over Germany. He gave journalists a bus ride to press conferences somewhere in the woods where he had installed a sound system and assembled inflatable, white, plastic seats. For the release of Walter Wegmüller's (1937-2020) album *Tarot*, they even designed and printed a complete Tarot Deck.

In the U.S., Kaiser was able to score an especially big whopper when he managed to place a double-page advertisement in the U.S. *Rolling Stone* – an ad that looked like an editorial report on German rock music. Advertising pros call this method "native advertising". If that was a kicker, then the icing on the cake was this: In one of his German press releases, under the headline "*Rolling Stone* presents the German Rock Musicians", Kaiser said the following in reference to the ad: "The bible of rock critics has discovered 'German Rock'. The American rock journal *Rolling Stone,* with editions in San Francisco and London and a print run of 500,000, presents in its latest issue the new German rock scene. Under the title 'German Rock Musicians', in a lavish two-page photo story, *Rolling Stone* portrays six German groups: EMTIDI, FLOH DE COLOGNE, HÖLDERLIN, MYTHOS, POPOL VUH, and WALLENSTEIN. With this, the world's most influential rock magazine has made 'Deutsch Rock' (*Melody Maker*) irrevocably and internationally respectable."[24] Call that chutzpah.

Parts of these PR activities were handled by a specially founded company, Sternenmädchens Media Service GmbH in Cologne.

It was at this time that Gille Lettmann transformed herself into a new personality she named "Sternenmädchen": "Hello, galactic people. I am the Sternenmädchen. I've been blown to Earth to bring you joy. Now you have one of the records I produced for you. Close your eyes and dig it. From a cloud, with regards – Gille, Sternenmädchen."[25]

Gille still signs this press release with her handwritten real name, and introduces herself as *the* Sternenmädchen. Later she changed this.

Today, many of the company's musicians claim that they were always "against it". But this seems to be more or less a sort of "protective statement". Of course, from time to time there were quarrels about the royalties and conditions of contracts, but it rarely ended as it did with XHOL: In March 1971, they released their new album under the title *Hau-RUK*. This pun is hard to translate. In German, "Hau-ruck!" means something like "Heave ho!", but "hauen" also means "to hit". So, "Hau-RUK" can be read as a call to beat RUK up. It speaks in Kaiser's favor that he didn't stop this title.

Kaiser's "sunshine contracts" (after the street name of his preferred LSD compound) were a controversial topic of discussion among musicians. These were a way to pin bands to the label long-term. To understand these contracts, you need to recall that at that time, every band had to purchase their own PA system. There were no PA rentals like today. The consequence was that most bands had to go through a lot of trouble to buy this equipment, otherwise there would have been no way for them to play on stage. Kaiser's sunny offer was providing equipment that amounted to 40,000 D-Marks plus a monthly advance payment of 1000 D-Marks. In return, he demanded 25 percent of all earnings the band made from creative activities. (For ordinary people, 40,000 D-Marks were an unreal amount at that time. To give a comparison: An office clerk, working somewhere for an industry company, made circa 1200 to 1500 D-Marks gross per month.)

Kaiser did not invent this kind of contract – several other record labels offered similar conditions. In general, there is nothing unfair about them; it's a clear deal the band could accept or refuse, and usually, the record contract did not depend on it. But once the band accepted it, they were deep in debt to their record label, and that meant they were nearly unable to leave. If they wanted to leave, they had to pay back the money. Most bands couldn't afford this, not even TANGERINE DREAM at that time. So it was understandable when Edgar Froese wrote to Kaiser: "What you do is simply to utilize a situation at the expense of others. If this is your principle of joy, I decline politely."[26]

However, when *Der Spiegel* wrote that Kaiser drugged the musicians of a group named HIMMELFAHRT with five joints to make them sign the contract,[27] it is safe to say that something didn't smell quite right (and it wasn't the joints). Even if the boys really smoked five joints: They were underage[28], so in any case it would have been their parents who had to sign the contract.

Many stories about Kaiser and Lettmann are of this half-true quality. Musicians tried to show off by telling this kind of drivel, while others wanted to camouflage their own inability to do business.

It might be interesting to know that, apparently, when you had to deal face to face with Kaiser and Lettmann, the two of them were not always as spaced-out as one might think. In an article, music journalist Archie Patterson of Portland, Oregon, describes an interview a friend of his conducted at their (rather middle-class furnished) apartment in Cologne: "He spent the afternoon with them, and he told me when he returned they were nice, rather reserved, and not at all the spacy cosmic type of their public image. In fact, he said they were very business-like and their reality did not seem to match at all the mythos their promotion suggested."[29]

However, most of Kaiser's musicians believed in the hype, at least for a while. They took part in it, and probably not even unwillingly. If you're skeptical, it's useful to take Kaiser's "Rock-Zeit" and read their own statements. Even many years later, WALLENSTEIN's keyboardist, Jürgen Dollase, said: "Kaiser had the idea to include magicians and spiritual teachers in the productions as an energy source – and he had a point in that."[30] (Today, by the way, Dollase is the well-known restaurant critic of the *Frankfurter Allgemeine Zeitung*.) The whole Kaiser-Reich was sort of one big family: "I had rats in my apartment, but in the studio I felt safe and secure", says WALLENSTEIN's drummer Harald Großkopf. "Mother Dierks cooked for us, Rolf-Ulrich and Gille, who were a couple of years older than us musicians, were eloquent and literate. As the generation of our parents, seen from our Sixty-Eight perspective, was still part of the Nazi generation, I absorbed anything there that otherwise only a family could have conveyed to me. I was all the more distraught in my tiny little love-and-peace hippie world later, when all these lawsuits started."[31]

LAWSUITS

It all was a pipe dream. For the business year 1973, Kaiser and Gille had set up a finance plan that is reminiscent of the proverbial "wondrous increase of currency": They envisaged a turnover increase of more than 600 percent, which meant revenues of nearly 3.5 million D-Marks; they intended to re-invest 1.8 million in new productions.[32]

Besides this, they had the idea of handing the management of several bands over to Liz Elliot and Brian Barritt, Leary's remaining European followers

(Leary meanwhile had been taken into custody again). Edgar Froese, to put it mildly, was not too happy with this plan: "We know from definitive experience to what extent they are addicted to the syringe," he wrote in a letter to Kaiser. That wasn't all: "It's coming along that I cannot comprehend your interpretations of necessary drug use."[33]

Froese, as well as his label mate Klaus Schulze, had become fed up with all of this excessive hype, and they felt peeved by being constantly pushed to use drugs. Tangerine Dream as well as Klaus Schulze wanted to cancel their contracts with Kaiser, but of course, Kaiser was not willing to let his top sellers walk away. He feared that other artists might follow suit. He insisted on keeping the contracts.

In June 1973, Froese and Schulze went to court. In May 1974, the Berlin District Court announced: "There is no need to further explain that the magniloquent style [of the record company] is exceedingly liable that the musicians affiliated with him [Kaiser] are seen as ludicrous by a not insubstantial part of the expert circles."[34]

Froese then filed another lawsuit, this time for outstanding royalties. He had a long way to go. Four years later, after going through all levels of jurisdiction, the Federal Court of Justice finally proved him right. But Froese never saw any money – no wonder, all the money had existed only in Kaiser's and Lettmann's feverish fantasies and business plans. Nothing was real. In fact, Kaiser and Lettmann were not even able to pay their lawyer.

It is safe to say that it was not even intentional fraud. Kaiser, as Jürgen Dollase puts it, in the end "was taken by his own delusions."[35]

COSMIC JOKERS

In 1974, Kaiser and Lettmann struck out on a new coup – their last, as it turned out. They took several tracks from their label repertoire, slightly remixed them, added some unreleased session stuff by Klaus Schulze, Wallenstein, Tangerine Dream, Jerry Berkers, Ash Ra Tempel, Witthüser & Westrupp, and some others, and dubbed some echo-laden, reverberated comments and break-ins by Gille, Kaiser, and Rosi Müller into the mix.

They made five albums from this material and released them under the project name Cosmic Jokers – *Cosmic Jokers, Galactic Supermarket, Planeten Sit-In, Sci-Fi Party, Gilles Zeitschiff* (all 1974): "The time ship Sternenmädchen floats through the galaxy of joy. In the sounds of electronics. In the flashes of light.

Here you will discover Science Fiction, the planet of Cosmic Jokers, the *Galactic Supermarket* and the *Sci-Fi Party*. That is the new sound. Space. Telepathy. Melodies. Joy."[36]

Rolf-Ulrich Kaiser and Gille Lettmann, with (from left) Timothy Leary, Klaus Schulze, Manuel Göttsching, Rosi Müller, Harald Großkopf & Jürgen Dollase, and Dieter Dierks

They even managed to get *Planeten Sit-In* sponsored by *Hobby*, a German magazine for techies (shut down in 1991).

But from the beginning, the offered joy was flawed. The fifth of these records, *Gilles Zeitschiff – Sternenmädchen zu Besuch bei den Magiern, Vol. 1 (Gille's Time Ship – Sternenmädchen Visiting the Magicians, Vol. 1)*, reflected a conflict between Kaiser and Lettmann and the pop magazine *Sounds*. In its edition from April 1973, the magazine had reported in plain language on Timothy Leary's layover in Switzerland, and this report was not what Kaiser and Lettmann wanted to read about their hero. So Gille published a press release (she called it an "open letter"): "Timothy Leary is being hunted by the CIA. The magazine with a supposedly 'progressive' image has, so far, printed three photos of Timothy Leary that come from the CIA archives. The CIA doesn't need *Sounds*. But the *Sounds* editors don't understand how the CIA works … They publish hate instead of joy … By doing this, *Sounds* has turned against Leary and the principals of joy. In favor of fear, horror, and the CIA. We predict: This *Sounds* is dead."[37]

Under the headline "My Spaceship" (not "Time Ship", for some reason), the sleeve of *Gilles Zeitschiff* in German and English had the following liner notes, as confused as it is choppy:

> "Come in. We are flying to America. We've met Tim, the Sci Fi Courier. And with him, more than 30 millions young people. Then, the C.I.A. steps in. Tim is arrested. He flies to Algier. To Switzerland. Ar-

rested again. Friends showed up. Lord Krishna from Switzerland. He's also a Cosmic Courier. Hartmut, Rolf and I went to see Tim at home on the lake. Tim is Joy. Tim is busy making the LP. Seven Up. His first SciFi Rock LP. I Am The Changer. This is the second one. The four big adventures of our life. Here. On Earth. And when we are flying, we meet the Cosmic Courier 'Bon Chance' Brian Barritt. He explains us, why he and Tim and a lot of other Cosmic Couriers are with us. We are flying to Basel. Walter Wegmüller. The Cosmic Painter. We played Tarot together. Is Tim a wizzard? Mr. Tarot gives us the answer. And we have already stepped into TIME. TIME is the new dimension. In it grows the Cosmic Music. TIME contains three big experiences. They make you fly to the Queen of Sunshine. Love is in TIME. Flight in Joy. –Gille."

This drivel on the record sleeve was the last time that the names "Gille" and "Sternenmädchen" appeared in parallel.

The Cosmic Couriers stopped all advertising orders for *Sounds*. As they learned a bit later, with this boycott, they punished not only the magazine, they also shot themselves in the foot: Without *Sounds* they couldn't address a big part of their target group anymore.

Allegedly, as some of the musicians later complained, Kaiser and Lettmann had not informed them about the Cosmic Jokers albums and didn't ask for permission to release any of the session material. There's a story that Ash Ra Tempel guitarist, Manuel Göttsching, to his surprise, heard one of the Cosmic Jokers recordings play in a record store without having been told by Kaiser that he was part of it. This is another case that cannot be verified anymore, but at least Göttsching disagrees: "Of course I knew about the releases, of course I had contracts before, and of course I received royalties, even in advance. This was all very little money, but that shouldn't be any reason to spread rumors like this. You can say many things about the producer Rolf-Ulrich Kaiser, but I have no reason to accuse him of acting incorrectly so far."[38]

It may lead you to your own conclusions to learn that, in his autobiography "Flashbacks", Timothy Leary doesn't mention any of all these episodes. There's not a single word, not even in a footnote. This might show how important he perceived the Cosmic Couriers. The Leary biography by Robert Greenfield also doesn't mention any of these episodes, only Sergius Golowin is briefly mentioned. The only biography that allocates a couple of pages for the *Seven Up* sessions is the one written by John Higgs.

TAKE YOUR HEADPHONES

One of Kaiser and Lettmann's last activities was a promotional LP titled *The Cosmic Couriers present: Take Your Headphones* that opened and closed with the final movement of Beethoven's Ninth Symphony (the "Ode to Joy" choir) and presented samples of several of their label acts.

Kaiser and Lettmann announced and commented on these samples, but their confused talk is drenched in echo and reverb effects and covered with electronic noises. This is done very unprofessionally, so large parts of the commentary are hardly understandable. The album had a print run of 500 copies, was numbered on sleeve and label, packed in a white cardboard sleeve with a red wax seal, and came with a letter signed by hand. These LPs were sent to U.S. radio stations where they were probably kept as curiosities or were made into Frisbees.

CRASH LANDING

However, it is obvious that Rolf-Ulrich Kaiser and Gille Lettmann had made a mockery of themselves and their music production company. In the music press they were called "komische Kuriere" now ("funny couriers" or "strange couriers"). It was not only their own reputation they had damaged; as music journalist Barry Graves wrote, Kaiser had even ruined "the reputation of his bands by publicity that used dubiosity nearly as a sort of stylistic feature."[39]

In 1975 it was quitting time. The space ship went into bankruptcy. The remaining LPs were sold off in piles in the bargain bin at Karstadt (a big German department store chain) at a ridiculous price; if memory serves, it was around 5 D-Marks – not even the price you had to pay for a cut-out. Many of the original Ohr, Pilz, or Kosmische Musik vinyl albums circulating today come from this bargain-sale.

The crash of Kaiser and Lettmann was short and hard. First, the Cosmic Couriers had to leave their West Berlin headquarters at the Europa-Center because they couldn't afford the rent anymore. They retreated to their Cologne apartment, but shortly after, they also got evicted from there because they didn't pay the rent. As writer and publisher Werner Pieper states, "Finally, an execution sale of their belongings has taken place. In the Nineties, [journalist] Uwe Husslein found a couple of books from Kaiser's library at a Cologne flea market, some of them with very personal dedications by Tim Leary."[40] Soon, the whereabouts of Kaiser and Lettmann became the subject of a wide variety of wild and sometimes colorful speculations.

The truth is less colorful. When they had to leave their apartment in Cologne, they relocated to Gille's mother's house in Frechen-Königsdorf near Cologne, where they lived until 1990. For several years, when you phoned in, you heard the same echo-laden, spacey sounding message from their answering machine. You couldn't leave a message, Gille's voice sent you down to a telex number that was long disconnected.

They abandoned the world completely. Kaiser appeared for the last time in the late 1980s, when the Hessian record company Zyx Records re-released the Ohr, Pilz, and Kosmische Musik catalogue. Kaiser contacted the company to get his producer's share of the royalties, but Zyx head, Bernhard Mikulski, (1929–1997) had to point out to him that he (Kaiser) had no rights over the recordings anymore. The rights are mainly with Dieter Dierks' company Breeze Music now.[41]

FINALE

Since then, Rolf-Ulrich Kaiser has remained silent. He has not been seen in public and doesn't accept mail. When WDR radio re-ran an old radio show by Kaiser, they sent him a royalty check, but he never cashed it.

Gille Lettmann does not accept her former name anymore. She is only addressed as "Sternenmädchen". She's no longer *the* Sternenmädchen, her name is without the article now. If you are not a friend, you have to address her as "Frau Sternenmädchen". In a blog post, I once translated her name into "Star Maiden", and she reacted allergic. As she stressed in one of her letters to Yours Truly, "Sternenmädchen" is her name and therefore cannot be translated. She refers to Gille Lettmann, her former identity, as "this person."

"Over the decades [she] seems to have adopted nearly all of the quirks, ideology, manner of writing, even the identity of her companion whom she calls 'Meson Cristallis'."[42] Her only sign of life is that, for over 30 years, Sternenmädchen – philosopher now, according to her letterhead – publishes an esoteric photocopied magazine named *Sternenmädchens Planetenschau.* It's mainly about "Intelligenz" (often written in uppercase letters) and problems that result from too much greed. You cannot order the magazine; it's Frau Sternenmädchen's own decision to whom she mails it – mainly to old friends, politicians, CEOs of big companies.

After mother Lettmann's death in 1990, the two of them moved to "a rented apartment not far from a German brewery at the Möhnesee" in the Sauerland area.[43] This had gone well until 2003 when they stopped paying the rent. The landlady first got in touch with Walter Westrupp (which shows that she was well aware of who her tenants were) and asked him whether he could try to reason with them. He tried, but without any success, so she finally had to call in the appropriate authorities. Westrupp says he lost contact with them in 2006.[44]

In the same year, for a book project, publisher Werner Pieper tried to track down Rolf-Ulrich Kaiser. His report[45] confirms what journalist Andreas Hub had already found ten years earlier: "As it looks, all written contacts to the world … come from Sternenmädchen, without exception."[46] Pieper tried to get in touch with Kaiser using Sternenmädchen's correspondence address, but according to her reply letter, Cristallis cannot be reached under her address.

Cristallis and Sternenmädchen, who, in a former life, a thousand moons and a thousand trips ago, were once Rolf-Ulrich Kaiser and Gille Lettmann, live in a small town on the edge of the Sauerland area today in a facility of the Catholic Church. Sternenmädchen's letters are still written with a classic golf-ball typewriter. Sometimes, once or twice a year, they use the public wifi at a wellness therapy center in a neighboring town to check the web.

Cristallis is invisible. Sternenmädchen can only be reached via general delivery; if you want to write to her, there are a couple of rules you have to follow, otherwise you won't get an answer. Cristallis and Sternenmädchen are private persons. They are not interested in their former life anymore, they don't want to be traced, they don't wish to see any visitors. This has to be accepted.

Our world is not theirs anymore. Or maybe vice versa.

STOCKHAUSEN, CARLOS, SALA & CO.: ELECTRONIC REVOLUTION

It was a revolution. But in the Sixties and early Seventies, there were many who didn't want to believe it. Edgar Froese (Tangerine Dream) remembers: "In those days, people were not very polite about what we did. In a *Melody Maker* interview in 1973 or 1974, I said, 'In about ten years' time, everybody will play synthesizers.' The guy stopped his tape recorder, said, 'You're an idiot', and walked out. They thought we were aliens, just fooling them."[1]

Kraftwerk had similar experiences: In the States they were seen as a sort of novelty act; a poll from the U.S. magazine *Cash Box* had no fitting category and listed them as "New Vocal Group".[2]

However, if there is one thing German rock is internationally known for, it's the use of electronic instruments and devices, especially synthesizers. This leads to two questions: What made the synthesizer more usable than other electronic instruments already existed? And why was it just in Germany that electronic rock became a whole new genre?

When you talk about "Electronic Music" to people who are born after 1990, they usually assume you are talking about electronic dance music. But they should know that electronic music existed already since the 1920s. And they should know there's a difference between "electronic music" and "electro-acoustic music". The difference lies in how the sound is generated. Only when the sound itself is electronically generated, music scientists speak of "electronic music". An instrument like the (original) Hammond organ is not an electronic instrument; it generates its sounds with rotating rack-wheels. Under "electro-acoustic" goes any kind of music that uses natural sounds manipulated by effect units or tape.

But let's not get too scholarly here. Early electronic or electro-acoustic instruments were the *Telharmonium*, *Dynamophon*, *Sphärophon*, *Mixturtrautonium* (a sort of sister instrument, the *Subharchord*, was invented in the GDR in the late 1950s and early 1960s, but its further development was blocked by officials for "musically political reasons"), *Hammond organ*, *Theremin*, *Clavioline*, *Ondioline*, *Ondes Martenot*, and several more. Starting in the 1950s, there were several electronic studios, most of them connected to universities or radio stations: the Electronic Studio of WDR in Cologne, STEIM in the Netherlands, Radiophonic Workshop at the BBC, Siemens Studio in Munich, Heinrich Strobel Studio at SWF in Baden-Baden, Centre de Recherches et Formation Musicales de Wallonie (today "Centre Henri Pousseur") at Liège, Belgium, Center for Computer Research in Music and Acoustics at Stanford University, IRCAM (Institut de Recherche et Coordination Acoustique/Musique, a sort of gift of the French government to composer Pierre Boulez) in the basement of the Centre Pompidou in Paris, and several more. Usually, these institutions started with devices from measuring and control technology and "misused" them in a creative way as sound generators or sound manipulators.

STOCKHAUSEN

When it comes to electronic music, one of the most famous names is Karlheinz Stockhausen (1928-2007).

Many musicians call him an important influence, but I'm sure this is not always based on actual knowledge of his works. Miles Davis at least knew him: "While recovering from my car accident, I studied a lot more of Stockhausen's concepts of music. I got further and further into the idea of performance as a process. I had always written in a circular way and through Stockhausen I could see that I didn't want to ever play again from eight bars to eight bars, because I never end songs; they just keep going on. ... Through Stockhausen I understood music as a process of elimination and addition."[3]

In the Krautrock scene it was always en vogue to drop Stockhausen's name, even more in Germany, but his direct influence on German rock music is actually not as big as one might think. This mainly has to do with the fact that he started composing far back at a time when synthesizers didn't exist yet. When he discovered electronic music, he had already written lots of works for conventional instruments. Then, he transferred his compositional ideas to electronic sound sources and technologies. This happened at a time when most electronic music was produced with several devices that were often not even made for musical usage. Later, Stockhausen also had very specific ideas about rock music, and some of them are well worth thinking about.

What made him important? Stockhausen was probably one of the most famous composers of the second half of the 20th century; his ideas were outstanding, his records in the 1950s and 1960s were released on the prestigious Deutsche Grammophon label and usually turned out to be bestsellers. His reputation has gone from "wacky" to "brilliant" and everything between. His pioneering has affected three main points:

- the use of electro-acoustics, electronics, and tape editing
- the spatial positioning and moving of sounds, including problems with sound projection
- the integration of non-musical occurrences (like projections, theatrical elements, costumes, gestures, landscapes, starry sky, shortwave radio sounds, et cetera) into musical works.

Gruppen (Groups, 1955–1957) is a work for three orchestras placed around the audience. It has no electronics, but it makes the spatial position of sounds part of the compositional process. This was not completely new; think of Thomas Tallis (1505-1585) and his motet *Spem in Alium* for eight choir groups of five voices each, arranged in a circle around the audience; space is part of the work this way. Also known are offstage instruments or choirs (Fernorchester/Fernchor); Gustav Mahler used these effects in five of his symphonies. But Stockhausen was the first to split a symphony orchestra into three groups and place them around the audience like a horseshoe: one group in front, one on the left, and one on the right side. The result is still adventurous today – if you ever get a chance, listen to it in concert; today, the piece is usually performed twice so that the audience has a chance to change seats. No record can reproduce the spatial impression of such a performance.

Stockhausen's name is inseparably connected to the Studio für Elektronische Musik at WDR radio Cologne, founded in 1951 under the aegis of WDR editor Herbert Eimert (1897–1972), and has become the center of what is known as "Cologne School". It was not, as the name might suggest, a big, futuristic studio with all the latest devices; it was a lousy room without air conditioning on the third or fourth floor below ground level of the broadcasting center. When more than three people were in there, there was no place left for chairs and they had to sit on tone generators. When they all smoked (as nearly everybody did then), you could cut the air with a knife. But it was an incredibly creative place.

The studio was equipped with lots of devices that were originally made for control engineering. First, mainly technicians were working at the studio to find out and show "what's possible" with these devices. Later, composers and music scientists like Karel Goeyvaerts, Gottfried Michael König, Giselher Klebe, Henri Pousseur, György Ligeti, and others worked there. But as much as these composers tried, it was probably Stockhausen's *Studie I* (1953) that was the first pure electronic piece not only composed of melodies, but that also consisted of tone colors resulting from a compositional process. Consequently, it didn't have its première in an auditorium, but late at night on the radio.

In 1962, after Eimert retired, Stockhausen became head of the studio.

Stockhausen's most famous composition (and usually the only one people have ever heard from him because it's relatively short and easy to find on the web) was created at the studio in 1955/56: *Gesang der Jünglinge im Feuerofen*, (Song of the Youths in the Furnace), commonly known simply as *Gesang der Jünglinge*. It is a tape composition of electronic sounds and a boy soprano; the singer was 12-year old Josef Protschka who later he became an opera tenor. The lyrics are based on a Biblical story from The Book of Daniel. The composition was planned to have five channels; as the legend goes, four speakers were supposed to have been placed around the audience, one speaker fixed on the ceiling. But since there was only a four-channel tape recorder available and it was not possible to synchronize the four-channel tape with one extra channel from a mono tape recorder, Stockhausen mixed the fourth and fifth channel into one track, and a four-channel version became the definitive one. Electronic sounds and voices are mixed and cross-modulated with and by each other – something nobody had ever heard before. Today, it is probably impossible for us to imagine the bafflement the audience has experienced at the première in view of the empty stage and the four big Altec speaker towers in the corners of the auditorium (Stockhausen has never been known for low volume; the equipment he used, without exception, had to be the best available, and somehow he was always able to get his way). The lyrics are cut down into words, syllables, and phonemes, it's hard to understand anything beyond single words. But this is not the important part. The main point is the mixture of a natural voice with electronic sounds, on an equal footing: This had never been done before.

Kontakte (1958-60) followed, another electronic four-channel tape composition. As in *Gesang der Jünglinge* there are no synthesizers involved yet, but the piece only uses electronic sounds. (For live performances there is also a version of *Kontakte* with tape and some acoustic instruments which is also available on record, but it's not as interesting as the pure tape version.) Stockhausen used tape and electro-acoustic devices in a way that was unheard of before and could not have been done with any conventional instrument. The short moment (at the beginning of Structure 10) when the sound slides down the frequency scale and becomes deeper and deeper until it decays into click impulses – which then define the rhythm – is legendary. *Kontakte* is still one of the most important works in electronic music, and for the unprepared listener, it remains a challenge.

Stockhausen's, in my opinion, most impressive work is *Hymnen* (Anthems, 1966/67), another four-channel composition using all the ideas he had developed before, but now in one go: concrete sounds, radio sounds, vocals, sounds from the tape archives of WDR radio, national anthems, and electronic sounds – "Region III" and "Region IV" belong to the strongest works Stockhausen has ever made.

I'm sure Stockhausen's hippie-esque appearance in the 1970s and later – long-haired, dressed in white, typically wearing embroidered Mexican shirts and living with two women – had its part in his reputation among rock musicians, so it's no surprise that he became a sort of role model for many, especially musicians who dealt with electronic music.

It can certainly be said that Stockhausen himself was not very interested in most rock music. In one of his rare interviews about this topic he said: "[Pop music] never brings me into a higher sphere. It confirms my vital sphere; but even this only when the intellect is in consent with the language of such a piece – the rhythmic as well as the melodic language – so that I don't think: 'Oh dear, that's all cliché, that's crap.' The intellect is permanently active and filters out the banalities, because I don't want to have things like that around me. I don't accept any old kind of furniture around me, and in the same way I don't accept any kind of musical event. You're not going to put any kind of rubbish around yourself."[4]

But Stockhausen knew quite well to differentiate: "Within pop music there are many grades – depending on who does it. Of course it is an important difference whether you compose only all these sweetish chords, or you write harmonic combinations that include *all* chords."[5]

One exception he accepted was Can because Irmin Schmidt and Holger Czukay had been his students, and he had always stayed in touch with them. He knew KRAFTWERK who always indicated the importance of modern electronic instruments – Ralf Hütter: "In our opinion, in 20 years there will be hardly any bands still performing with guitars and drums. For us, these instruments are already a thing of the past."[6] Stockhausen criticized them for not making real creative use of their equipment – to have an excellent vocoder and simply use it for producing nothing more than some robot-like vocal lines was just too simple of an idea of modernity for his taste. (If you want to know what Stockhausen himself did with a vocoder, listen to "Tonszene 4" and "Tonszene 5" from *Freitag aus LICHT* (1996).) In California, he met JEFFERSON AIRPLANE and the GRATEFUL DEAD; he knew that the DEAD's Phil Lesh had studied composing and electronic music with Luciano Berio[7]: "There are some rather gifted composers among them who try this music because it correlates with their age."[8]

The *Zeit* article[9] I have cited a couple of times about Stockhausen's opinion on a handful of German rock records shows the criteria Stockhausen applies to music quite well, and they don't have much to do with the dimensions rock musicians use to think in. He had no problems with rock music as an idea, but he could get angry when it was too predictable or worked with too many clichés and standard formulas: "When you listen to American Dixieland music or other jazz music from the Twenties with a bit of historic distance, it appears more elaborate, more like chamber music, and more transparent than what pop music has produced in the last ten years. … [Pop music] is crammed with sound effects from the 'new music', but it's so dirty and structurally primitive that all the Dixieland music, every boogie-woogie, is melodically, harmonically, and rhythmically more interesting. Just think about how primitive melodies are today; they never leave diatonic three-note or four-note motives and are simply repeated numberless times."[10] But don't think Stockhausen's only scale was the ivory tower of classical avant-garde; he knew what he was talking about: "For five years of my life, I played schlager music and jazz nearly every night myself."[11]

Never in his entire life did Stockhausen stop checking the limits or try to leave them behind – he went farther than most rock music ever did. It is quite clear that this didn't always work, sometimes he re-used old ideas to highlight new ones, but obviously, he never accepted that something was "not possible". This had a side effect: He was often asked why his music couldn't be more approachable. For him, no listener had the given right to get into his music easily. But, at the same time, he never saw his compositions as "elitist" or written only for a special audience. When you want to learn something about quantum physics, you have to get deep into it, and that means mental receptivity and a lot of work; this was the way Stockhausen saw his music. Indeed, it often means that, to listen to Stockhausen's music, one has to *work*, but when you take the chance and get into it, your musical sensitivity will never be the same.

I hope this makes it clear that I consider most comparisons between Stockhausen's work and rock music meaningless. Although some of his records were available in rock music stores (Polydor, in 1973, even compiled a double album entitled *Greatest Hits*), Stockhausen played in a completely different league.

Most pop and rock music fans are not willing to take on the work of listening. Which is fine, nobody is forced to. Stockhausen's music may be seen as meaningless or simply "noise" by the fans of standard rock or pop music, but even they should be able to recognize that his compositions are more elaborate than most rock compositions. To use Stockhausen's own words: "Pop music touches its fans in the same way as people who always spend their vacation in the same area. It shouldn't be exactly the same as last time, but not too different and, moreover, not too unfamiliar: that would be much too stressful … and what would it be good for …"[12]

SALA

It's an interesting question why it took so long for the "Cologne School" composers to work with "real" electronic instruments, although a couple of them had already existed for a while. It might be that these instruments didn't deliver the (sometimes mathematical) precision that Stockhausen and his colleagues wanted for their compositions, but he never mentioned this specifically.

Let's have a look at one of the most interesting of these instruments: the *trautonium*. This instrument is inseparably connected to the name Oskar Sala. The trautonium virtuoso, composer, and electronic music pioneer was born in 1910 in Greiz (Thuringia). He had intended to become a pianist, but this didn't happen. He studied composition with Paul Hindemith's who introduced him to engineer Friedrich Trautwein (1888–1956). In 1922, the physicist had developed an electronic musical instrument which he called trautonium. The special feature of this instrument was not only its sound diversity, but also the way it was played: In contrast to the Ondes Martenot or the Hammond Organ it had no keyboard. Instead, it had a steel string that had to be pressed down onto a horizontal steel rail like a violin string.

Sala was immediately thrilled by this instrument. He asked Hindemith to write a piece for the trautonium. Hindemith (1895–1963), an excellent violinist himself, was also fascinated by the fact that the manner of playing was so similar to the violin, so he composed *Seven Trio Pieces for Three Trautoniums*. They premiered in Berlin in 1930; a three-movement *Concert Piece for Trautonium with String Orchestra Accompaniment* followed in 1931.

Commercially, the trautonium was not a big success, although there were several variations of the instrument: the *radio trautonium*, several *concert trautoniums*, and Telefunken even made a *volkstrautonium* (popular trautonium) for music making in the home.

Sala remained the only musician who dedicated his life to this instrument. He even developed it further until, finally in the 1950s, the *mixturtrautonium* was ready to be used in his studio in Berlin's Charlottenburg neighborhood. It had two string manuals, making it two-voiced, and was equipped with touch-sensitive liquid resistors under the manuals.

Sala placed a film editing table beneath the instrument to compose and play mainly film music from then on, directly mostly to the pictures. He specialized in soundtracks for animation movies and several award-winning industry image movies (best-known probably *Stahl: Thema mit Variationen* from 1960 for Mannesmann Steel Company) and documentaries up until the 1990s; the last film composition he finished was the main theme for *Das war die DDR* (This was the GDR), a seven-part documentary (1993) made by MDR TV Leipzig. But Sala also wrote music for a few feature films, like the Edgar Wallace movie *Der Würger von Schloss Blackmoor* (1963); his soundtrack was probably the best thing about the whole movie. But his most famous work was undoubtedly his beautifully eerie sound backdrop for Alfred Hitchcock's *The Birds* (1963) – Sala's electronic bird screams were scarier than any natural bird calls could have been. Besides this, Sala did numerous pieces for theater and radio plays. All in all, he wrote and recorded around 300 compositions – not only film soundtracks but also free compositions that are documented on records, which he also used to perform on stage from time to time.

Sala never warmed up to electronic music as it came up in the second half of the 1950s from Cologne. It was too dogmatic for his taste. His tunes were usually developed from improvisation, and this didn't correspond to the mathematically determined minds of these "gentlemen from Cologne", as he used to call them with slightly lifted eyebrows. The animosity was reciprocal. Sala, if he is even mentioned in music handbooks, is just seen as an instrumentalist and someone on the fringes. His work as a composer and pathfinder of electronic music is rarely noted.

During the 1960s, Sala had lived quite comfortably with this kind of public disdain. He was busy with film music jobs throughout the decade. This changed when the Moog synthesizer came up. The trautonium fell more and more into oblivion, and so did Sala himself. For him and his wife, the 1970s must have been a hard time; he became rather tight-lipped when I asked him about it. But he never gave up; the walk from his apartment to the studio remained a part of his daily routine.

Then, in the 1980s, the trautonium and Sala's remarkable life's work were rediscovered – this time mainly by pop musicians. There lies a little bit of logic in this because, unlike other composers of "serious" music, Sala never had any problems with playing entertaining music; on Youtube you can even find some dance music recordings he had participated in. Florian Schneider, founding member of KRAFTWERK and now owner of one of Sala's original instruments, described him as the one who transferred electronic music from avant-garde to popular music.

In 1987, Sala was awarded the "Filmband in Gold" of the German Film Awards (one could call it the "German Oscar"; since 1999 it's been known as "Lola") for his film music. In the following years, Ulrich Rützel's Erdenklang label had released three Sala CDs, among them the Hindemith compositions, and this way the "serious" critics also finally discovered him. A couple of new trautoniums were built, first by a team of professors from the Hochschule der Deutschen Bundespost in Berlin, then later by a company named Trautoniks. It's now based on modern microelectronics, and there seem to be some young musicians working with these instruments; the most active one of them is Peter Pichler.

Having a chat with Oskar Sala meant experiencing a highly vivid and very eloquent man, who up to a ripe-old age, had been able to speak enthrallingly and with astute humor about his pioneering years, yet never lost sight of the present. Oskar Sala passed away in 2002 in his apartment in Berlin-Charlottenburg, three years after his wife. I am grateful for having had the pleasure to meet him in person.

MOOG

Electronic music made a giant jump when the American engineer Dr. Robert Arthur "Bob" Moog (1934-2005) invented an instrument that became known as the *synthesizer*. This was more than just introducing a new musical instrument. Actually, I would go so far as to say that Moog invented a new social context for existing technologies. He didn't do this intentionally, but as always, once a new idea enters the world and the moment is right, it paves its own path. This is what happened to Moog's invention.

What does "new social context for existing technologies" mean? There were a couple of attempts to build synthesizers before Moog; the RCA synthesizer comes to mind, as well as the Russian ANS and the Buchla synthesizers (used by Morton Subotnik in *Silver Apples on the Moon*, 1967, by Douglas Leedy in his triple album *Entropical Paradise* from 1968, by Laurie Spiegel in *The Expanding Universe*, 1974–1976, and by Suzanne Ciani in her music for commercials between 1969 and 1985 as documented on *Lixiviation*, 2012). The Durrett synthesizer can be heard on the self-titled album by THE UNITED STATES OF AMERICA, 1967, still a milestone record. But they all worked differently and were somehow more of a "technician's toy", rather than what musicians wanted.

Wendy Carlos worked as a sound engineer at Gotham Records Studio and had studied electronic music at the Columbia-Princeton Computer Music Center in New York City. Bob Moog met her around this time at one of the annual Audio Engineering Shows (AES). Carlos was able to oversee the musical aspects Moog didn't have much knowledge about, and with her help, Moog took all of these technologies and devices, modified and converted them, and built them following the three elements of sound: pitch, tone color, and volume path. Each of these elements got their own independent generator: oscillator, filter, and amplifier. To shape all of them, an envelope generator was added. These generators (and this, actually, was Moog's stroke of genius) were based on the same regulation system: voltage control. So we have four basic modules: the voltage controlled oscillator (VCO), usually including a noise generator, the voltage controlled filter (VCF), the voltage controlled amplifier (VCA), and the envelope generator (EG) that delivered control voltage in a shape the user wanted ("amount of contour", as Moog called it). Of course, you need a device to play the whole thing. Moog decided that this should be done using a keyboard – which, in a way, is self-evident, but technically it would be possible to use different devices, like strings (there were guitar as well as violin units), a theremin, or a breath-driven controller (like the lyricon).

There you have a synthesizer. It's *very* basic and simple; but that's all you need to be able to play. It's a sort of "compact electronic studio", and once you understand this system and the idea of voltage control, you will be able to successfully use a synthesizer. You can also add several other voltage controlled units, like a sequencer, a pitch bending wheel, a low frequency oscillator (LFO) to add tremolo and vibrato, you can split the filter unit into low pass and high pass filters – the possibilities are endless, and Moog came up with many ideas very fast.

Wendy Carlos, by the way, was paid in kind for her help: with Moog equipment – and she used it for her record *Switched-on Bach*, released in 1968.

The early Moogs had each of the four units in its own chassis. That's why they were called "modular synthesizers". They were as big as refrigerators and had to be connected to each other with patch cords. Later, with further development of microelectronics, these units could be built smaller, were hardwired, put into a smaller chassis, and had a stationary mounted three-and-a-half octaves keyboard – in this form, around 1971, the *Minimoog* came into existence. It was not cheap (it was about 1500 U.S. dollars, which was around 5000 D-Marks at the time – for comparison, a new Volkswagen Beetle in 1971 cost roughly 6000 D-Marks), but it was an amount one could somehow afford, and so this great-sounding instrument became a hit. It didn't have the flexibility of a modular Moog, but it was relatively easy to handle, even on stage. Around 1973, it became a sort of standard for most keyboardists, parallel with the classic Hammond B-3 and a Solina String Ensemble.

You see why I said: what Moog did was invent a new social context for existing technologies. Instead of musical scientists in their experimental electronic studios, now rock musicians were the recipients. Their approach to the instrument was different and rock listeners became the consumers of the sounds the musicians produced with this new device. To see it this way means to construe technological progress as a social construction. It might be interesting to know that similar formulae were used in U.S. advertising campaigns for the Volkswagen Bus in 1970 or for the first Macintosh computer in 1984.[13] The products themselves were not the message; the products answered to a social trend, and *that* was the message.

The biggest practical problem synthesizers had was probably that they used to go out of tune after a while, especially under the warmth of stage lighting, but sometimes the audience's entrance produced enough heat to impact its tune. Another big problem was that if you had found a sound you liked, you couldn't store it. If you needed this sound a second time, you always had to reconstruct it, and because the slightest changes in settings could lead to big differences in sound, this could really be a drag. (This was not only a Moog problem; the synthesizers of other manufacturers, when they came up a short time after the Minimoog's big success, had the same problems. It was an issue having to do with the electronic components available at that time.)

Admittedly, this explanation is extremely simplified, but I don't want to torture you with more technical details. There's only one thing I would like to point out very clearly about synthesizers in general: A synthesizer doesn't play automatically and is not "artificial" – at least not more artificial than a violin or a guitar. No musical instrument grows "naturally" on trees. They all are products of technology. An analogue synthesizer, as described here, is a musical instrument that offers a wide spectrum of sound creating possibilities that no other instrument has. But – and this is the point – it doesn't do anything on its own. You have to *learn* how to play it. You have to learn it the same way you have to learn how to play guitar or trumpet or drums. You cannot learn this in just a couple of hours. Many rock musicians thought: Great, it has a keyboard, so it must be a sort of "super organ" with a built-in multi effect rack. These musicians, without exception, had to learn that this is not how a synthesizer works. If this is what you have in mind when you touch a synthesizer, you will experience that the instrument plays with you, not the other way round. There's no need to explicate here how many rivers of acoustic slurry flooded thousands of record productions because of this misconception.

It's hard to say who had the privilege of being "the first" rock musician to use a modular Moog. The honor probably goes to The Monkees and their album *Pisces, Aquarius, Capricorn and Jones Ltd.* (1967). Another early rock record making a not spectacular but relatively effective use of a modular Moog was *The Notorious Byrd Brothers* (1968) by The Byrds. Roger McGuinn had discovered the instrument at the Monterey Festival where Bob Moog had a demonstration booth. As McGuinn found it too complicated, it was played by Paul Beaver, an electronic music pioneer who had played the Moog already before on The Monkees' album, The Zodiac's *Cosmic Sounds* and some more recordings. But on all of these records, the synthesizer is more or less a kind of side effect. The album Beaver made in 1968 with partner Bernie Krause, *The Nonesuch Guide to Electronic Music*, was more playful. But this was not rock music, it was experimental stuff. *Moog – The Electric Eclectics of Dick Hyman* (1969) or Christopher Scott's *Switched-on Bacharach* (1972) were more entertaining – Hyman's recordings use the Moog as a source of funny sounds, and Scott's record does to the hits of Burt Bacharach what Wendy Carlos did to the hits of Johann Sebastian Bach. It works, but in both cases I prefer the originals.

ELECTRONIC SOUNDS IN GERMANY

Who was the first one to use a synthesizer on a German record? This is also a hard question. If you follow Wikipedia[14], it happened in a schlager: "Arizona Man" (1970), sung by Mary Roos. (Her real name is Rosemarie Schwab, she had worked for budget labels under dozens of pseudonyms since the early 1960s.) "Arizona Man" was her first and, up to today, biggest hit and started her long-time schlager career; the record entered German charts in July 1970, reached #9, and stayed in the charts for 18 weeks. The song had been written and arranged by Giorgio Moroder. But I think Wikipedia has it wrong here. "Arizona Man" in Mary Roos' hit version had an electrifying sound with a swirling hookline, which, if I can trust my ears, was played using a Stylophone, with probably two or three overdubs. Besides this, the song is drenched in wah-wah and fuzz guitar, dramatic drums, piano, some winds, and it has a nicely built-in radio DJ trap – it didn't end where you thought it would. But I don't hear a synthesizer at any point. In 1970, Moroder simply had no Moog.

The fame for bringing the first synthesizer sounds to German pop music has to go to somebody else. You won't be surprised to learn that in all probability it was our old friend James Last who did it. His keyboardist Günter Platzek played an EMS Synthi 100 during a concert at the IFA (Internationale Funkausstellung) in Berlin 1971.

Moogs were not easy to obtain in Germany. For a couple of years, the only authorized Moog dealer was a recording studio in Hamburg, owned by sound engineer and film composer Heinz Funk (1915-2013). He had a demonstration device, and I have a special relationship to this synthesizer because Mr. Funk gave me the opportunity to put my fingers on it. I was looking for an internship at a sound recording studio and had applied to Studio Funk. They invited me for an interview and showed me around the studio which was situated in the souterrain of a big old apartment building. There was one special room with big windows – and there it was: a modular Moog with a sequencer unit, but this one had all its modules combined into one big chassis, usually known as "Moog III".

There was also a mixing desk, an eight-track tape recorder, and two big speakers in the room. Funk was just fiddling around with the synthesizer. Through the window, he must have seen my big eyes and waved at me to come in. He was a bit surprised that I even knew what this thing was; most people who saw it apparently mistook it for a telephone switchboard. I asked something about it, he started explaining it to me, and when he noticed that I understood what he was saying, he was hardly stoppable. He demonstrated several things and let me try it myself. It was late in the evening when Mr. Funk finally threw me out.

Some years later, the studio (which mainly specialized in lip-synching movies and recording sound for commercials) relocated to bigger rooms. Musician Okko Bekker took over the place, including the Moog, and renamed it Audiplex Studios. In the 1980s, most records of electronic artist Asmus Tietchens were recorded there (but he never used the Big Moog). The instrument eventually ended up in a museum.

EMS

How about the Studio for Electronic Music of WDR? Shouldn't they have had a modular Moog? Nope. They thought about it – financially it wouldn't have been a problem. But they decided against a Moog. This was advised by Karlheinz Stockhausen who preferred getting an EMS Synthi 100. It was ordered in 1973 and delivered the following year. The Synthi 100 was a combination of three VCS-3 synthesizers with a couple of additional features like sequencer and vocoder; all in all, only 40 units were built. The reason why Stockhausen preferred this device was not that the Moog might have been too complicated. It was because, unlike the monophonic Moog, it could be played with two keyboards, four-voice polyphonic, and also offered the possibility to use alternative tunings. Stockhausen's *Sirius* (1977) uses the Synthi 100 extensively. But in the end, he was not really happy with the instrument: "The Synthi 100 has never performed completely satisfactorily; it is terribly unstable and the filters are very bad."[15] There is always something.

Other users of a Synthi 100 were Wolfgang Dauner (1935-2020), as can be heard on his album *Changes* (1978). The BBC Radiophonic Workshop also had one of these devices; Delia Derbyshire used its sounds for the title theme of the TV series *Doctor Who* (1973).

The small version, the VCS-3, could also be used to manipulate external sounds; something the Minimoog didn't offer. Brian Eno did a lot of treatments with this device, and Sonja Kristina's voice on Curved Air's *Phantasmagoria* (1972) was distorted with it.

Now let's go to Munich – that's where synthesizer music in Germany first started.

SCHOENER, FRICKE, MORODER: THE MUNICH MOOG PIONEERS

It wasn't in Berlin or Düsseldorf where electronic rock started. It was in Munich. Amon Düül II had already made use of electronic effects, but without being an "electronic" band. The first musician in Germany who owned a Moog modular synthesizer was Eberhard Schoener.

SCHOENER

It's an interesting story, how this instrument came to him.[1] Schoener was not a big fan of the kind of electronic music that came from Cologne. As a classically trained composer, conductor, and violinist he could see its potential, but he considered these compositions to be "pure head music, without phenomenology, without arcs of suspense, without sensuousness."[2] Like many later lovers of electronic music, he got his first kick in 1969 when he heard *Switched-on Bach* on the radio. But it was not the whole album that caught his attention, it was only one track: the second movement of Bach's *Brandenburg Concerto No. 3*. This movement only has a few written notes. Schoener: "I remember exactly when I heard [the Carlos version]. I was not interested in this imitation. I was only interested in the improvisation in the Third Brandenburg Concerto. Bach requests the musicians to improvise [on these few notes]. And Wendy Carlos gave it an electric shape that was mind-boggling to me, with an instrument I had never heard of, and I simply thought: This is unbelievable! Suddenly I realized that it was possible to have suspense in music again, and that this could be something I would be interested in."[3]

He found out this instrument would cost around 60,000 D-Marks, an amount that was completely out of reach for him. For comparison, in 1969, the average annual income in West Germany was 11,800 D-Marks gross. The price of a Moog synthesizer would have been more than five years' worth of the average employee's salary. Accidentally, a solution was found: Schoener had talked about his discovery to a friend of his, Ulf von Gienanth, the offspring of an old nobility family. Ulf, in turn, told his mother, Heidi von Gienanth, about Eberhard's enthusiasm, and she said: "Okay, Eberhard, why don't you go to this Mr. Moog and buy one? I will lend you the money." She told Schoener she would set up a foundation so there would be no need for him to pay the money back before having some commercial success.

With this unexpected money in hand, Schoener and his wife Stefanie (a journalist at *Süddeutsche Zeitung*) flew to New York without knowing where to find Mr. Moog. In a shop for rock'n'roll accessories, they found somebody who knew his whereabouts. The two of them then traveled to Trumansburg, a dreamy village of 1500 souls in the middle of the Finger Lakes area, in Upstate New York. What they found was not the expected factory, but rather Moog's family home including a workshop annex where two engineers assembled theremins – and synthesizers. There was no "store" you could enter to choose and buy a synthesizer. These early Moog modular synthesizers were custom-built units. They got type designations, "Moog Series I", "II" and so on, but the numbers were more or less meaningless because the devices were commissioned productions. You had to tell Mr. Moog what specifications you wanted, he did the price calculation, and you had to make a down payment of 50 percent. With this money, they purchased the parts they needed, and then it took around half a year until your synthesizer was finished and ready for pick-up. This was the way it was handled, and they were used to capacity with that.

Consequently, when Schoener knocked on Moog's door, Moog told him: "I'm sorry. I can only put you on the waiting list. Due to the success of *Switched-on Bach* everybody wants a synthesizer now. If we are lucky, we can help you in two years. Feel free to come back then."

But Schoener stayed. Maybe he had a feeling that something would happen. He and Stefanie got settled in a motel in the neighborhood, and somehow, he talked one of Moog's engineers into explaining to him how a synthesizer works. As Schoener's English was not the best, the main parts of this conversation went by drawings – waveforms, oscillators, filters, envelope generators, flow diagrams, and so on.

Then, one week later, indeed something happened: A truck delivered four black boxes and unloaded them in the yard in front of the workshop. Schoener espied them immediately. It turned out to be John Lennon's synthesizer, the

Eberhard Schoener and his Moog

second one ever built, including a sequencer unit. Lennon returned it because he found it too complicated and preferred to wait for further technical developments. Schoener immediately jumped at the chance: "Don't unpack it, I'll take it as it is." It was probably Schoener's curiosity, persistence, and patience that finally convinced Mr. Moog to sell him John Lennon's synthesizer.

That's how the first Moog modular synthesizer came to Germany. Then a technician named Robert "Robby" Wedel heard about it somehow, rang Schoener's doorbell in Miesbach (a small village in the alpine uplands, some kilometers south of Munich), and asked whether he could have a look at this miraculous machine. In the end, Wedel became Schoener's assistant and probably the only person who, technically, got the hang of this device. (Wedel later also worked at some Munich-based studios with Giorgio Moroder, Donna Summer, Siegfried Schwab, the Carla Bley Band, Popol Vuh, and others.)

A couple of months later, Schoener accepted an assignment to set up an electronic department at Bavaria Studios in Munich, and he moved his Moog from out of his house to the studio. It remained there for around ten years, and other musicians made use of it – Giorgio Moroder was one of them. In 1980, Schoener founded his own studio on the slope of Mount Wendelstein near his home (you always need half an hour to get used to the thin air up there). That's where his Moog has lived for many years, in good shape and sometimes still in use. Finally in fall 2019, Schoener donated the instrument to the Deutsche Museum in Munich, as well as big parts of his archives.

What about the 60,000 D-Marks Heidi von Gienanth had lent to him? She had inspected the Moog once, said "uh-huh", but never talked about it again. When she finally passed away, Schoener asked his friend Ulf about the foundation, and how they wanted him to pay back his debt now. Ulf was puzzled, he had never heard about this foundation. They discovered that there was no foundation, there had never been one. It sounds like a fairy tale, but it's true: Heidi von Gienanth had invested her private money into Eberhard's dream. She had "invented" this foundation to spare him from having to owe her this great deal of money.

Schoener had become a composer and conductor from his own strength. But his career as an electronic music pioneer is owed to this lady.

What a wonderful story.

The first record Schoener made using the synthesizer was *Destruction of Harmony – The Living Sound of Synthesizer based on Bach & Vivaldi* (1971), a sort of expanded and more experimental *Switched-on Bach.*

In June 1971, Schoener used an air-inflated marquee for a series of meditative Moog concerts. It belonged to art collector and photographer (and yes, playboy) Gunter Sachs (1932-2011) who used it for exhibitions. With his financial backing, the marquee was equipped with lots of water beds, so visitors could lie down and look at monitors showing videos of optical feedback by Brian Wood. The sound of street cars coming in from outside had to be ignored, as well as the noise from the generator that pumped air into the tent. First, six visitors came, then only one. But this one was a critic, and he was very impressed. His review brought more people in; they had to give several shows per day. After five days, the show had to end because in the morning the marquee and the water beds were found slashed and destroyed; all the water had flooded the street. Even in 1971, the world was already full of idiots.

Another Moog concert took place during the Berliner Festwochen 1971 at National Gallery Berlin. 200 people were expected. In the afternoon, already 500 stood in line, and in the evening around 1000 people thronged into the hall – which made the gallery director extremely nervous. There were paintings by Mark Rothko not only on the walls, but some were even hanging free from the ceiling, each one of them beyond price. But Schoener calmed him down, and he was right. His contemplative Moog improvisations and compositions in combination with these paintings made the audience completely relaxed and silent, and no damage happened.

You can get an idea of what this music was like from Schoener's first record made with nothing else but the Moog: *Meditation*, released on the Ariola label, produced in 1973 on a 16-track at Bavaria Studio, mixed in SQ quadro and delivered in a beautiful tri fold sleeve.

It has always been Schoener's strong point to combine things that nobody would have considered possible. His most important work in the 1970s was probably *Bali-Agúng* from 1975, recorded in a hotel lobby in Bali with the Big Moog, drummer Pete York, guitarist Siegfried Schwab and the Gamelan orchestra of Prince Agúng Raka of Saba and Pinda. When Schoener went to Bali, he didn't just listen to this orchestra for a few hours, he listened to it for several days to get fully into the music it played, and to see how the musicians interacted. This patience was apparently the reason why the prince finally gave his blessings to this experiment. *Bali-Agúng* is not a record to make gamelan music compatible with western tourists. In fact, it is still a tough go today. This record is the result of two completely different music cultures *listening* and *reacting* carefully to each other, and that's still an adventure. (A 2010 reissue of *Bali-Agúng* on the MiG label has been remastered and comes with a "making of" TV docu in German. This DVD is very useful to get an idea how this album came into existence.) I still remember how absolutely puzzled the audience was when the band and the Gamelan players appeared in a TV show.

One of Schoener's later, important records is *Trance-Formation* (1977), originally released under Eberhard Schoener & The Secret Society and partly recorded in a church. Moog, Mellotron, piano, and organ are played by the maestro himself who also conducts his Orchestra of the Munich Chamber Opera (a sort of festival orchestra he founded in 1965), vocals by Mary Gregoriy and members of the Tölzer Knabenchor, plus Gregorian chants by monks of the monastery of Sama (long before Michael Cretu for his project Enigma discovered the special charmingness of Gregorian singing mixed into electronic backgrounds). Further session musicians Andy Summers (guitar), Raimund Elleder (keyboards), Nippy Noya (percussion) and Hans Peter Ströer (bass; also known for interesting film soundtracks) play on it. Follow-ups were *Flashback* and *Video Magic* (both 1978). The latter one closed with a track entitled "Koan" which has Andy Summers on guitar and Olaf Kübler on saxophone; I consider these twelve minutes to be one of the most substantial and most important tracks German electronic rock of the 1970s has to offer. It's an eternal mystery to me why *Video Magic* never got rereleased on CD.

I have seen Schoener twice on stage at the CCH (Congress Centrum Hamburg); once in 1977 and once in 1978, playing with these musicians (the monks and the Tölzer Knabenchor came from tape, of course). I vividly remember the energy all these mixed elements in his shows brought to the audience and how well it worked. In the 1977 show, what was especially impressive was the combination of wafts of different scents – they used the venue's air conditioning system for this. It took the CCH weeks to get rid of the smell. In the 1978 show it was the combination of music, lights, slides and laser projection (by Laserium from Los Angeles) that made it attractive, and it was an opportunity to see a band that nobody had yet known at that time: The Police. Schoener was working with guitarist Andy Summers in preparation for this tour, when Summers said to him: "You need a good drummer. I know somebody …" Of course this somebody was Stewart Copeland, and he turned out to be extremely interested in the rhythms of Balinese gamelan music. Then it was Copeland who said to Schoener: "You need a good bass player …", and well, this was Sting, of course. So The Police became part of Schoener's circle of musicians. Their 45 "Roxanne" was out but didn't sell yet. They were a bit depressed about this, but on the other hand, they were also open-minded enough to be interested in Schoener's offer to integrate them into his tour project. Schoener also offered them to play as a supporting act, which they did.

It is still remarkable that Sting's and The Police's later cooperation with Schoener on three albums and their attendance at these albums' respective tours was never mentioned in The Police's official band biography. Their manager Miles Copeland (Stewart's brother) blocked any further contact between the band and Schoener. Not only did it not fit into the band's image that Miles Copeland tried to build up, it seemed to be downright inconceivable for him to reveal that a German classical musician and conductor had been the first to discover this band's talents. Apparently Miles Copeland feared that a breakthrough in the U.S. would be impossible if this Munich experience became a known part of the band's story.[4]

FRICKE

The second German musician to own a Moog modular synthesizer was Florian Fricke.

He had won a couple of piano competitions when he was a teenager, and had just started Popol Vuh, but he was mainly still involved in his freelance job as a music and film critic for *Süddeutsche Zeitung*, acting as a protégé of this paper's music critic doyen Joachim Kaiser. Fricke and Schoener were immediate neighbors in Miesbach. They were not friends, but they knew each other well enough to be informed about what the other was up to. When Fricke learned about this new, wonder of an instrument his neighbor had, he was stunned: "The music you can produce with the Moog incorporates essentially all possible human sensation."[5] Fricke's wife, photographer Bettina von Waldthausen, asked Schoener to use his connections with Bob Moog to make it possible for Fricke to get his own Moog synthesizer, and he did.

It was 1970, and Fricke now owned the second Moog modular synthesizer in Germany. Its serial number was 1068, including a sequencer unit. Edgar Froese: "Fricke was moneyed by birth, he could afford his own system."[6] So, the first two Moog modular synthesizers in Germany stood just 300 feet away from each other in this little Bavarian mountain village. Since no user's manuals came with the instrument, Schoener as well as Robby Wedel tried to explain to Fricke how this thing worked. This was not an easy job; Fricke's understanding of technology was limited. Schoener and Fricke never held any sessions or recorded any music together.

Shortly after this, as many of his generation did, Fricke, his wife, and the then members of Popol Vuh relocated into a picturesque former parsonage at Peterskirchen near Wasserburg in the Bavarian countryside east of Munich. The house was owned by Gräfin von Lehndorff, the mother of Popol Vuh's percussionist Holger Trülzsch's girlfriend, Veruschka von Lehndorff (a former fashion model and friend of Florian Fricke's wife Bettina von Waldthausen; she became well-known from acting in Michelangelo Antonioni's film *Blow Up*). The house was a meeting point for all kinds of artists and jet-set bohemians that were hip at that time – Rainer Langhans, Rainer Werner Fassbinder, Hanna Schygulla (who also lived there for a while), Warren Beatty, Jack Nicholson, Paul and Limpe Fuchs, and others. The house can be seen in a video entitled "Improvisation (1971)", easily found on Youtube.

During his stay in the U.S., Gerhard Augustin of Liberty Records had heard about the Moog, loved it, and wanted to produce an electronic album immediately upon returning to Germany. He learned there were only two Moogs that existed in Germany and got in touch with Fricke.

The result was *Affenstunde* (1970), a title connected to the "Codex Florentinus", a collection of Aztec legends. It was the first Popol Vuh album, recorded at Bavaria Studio. Holger Trülzsch: "The idea of *Affenstunde* was to imagine a marketplace where people meet, talk, and make music. … It was really a resounding success. Through Veruschka, we handed it to John Lennon who was enthusiastic about it. Bob Dylan liked it too, and Avedon, the great photographer, played it in his studio for half a year. In certain intellectual circles it was a big thing."[7]

When he was asked about *Affenstunde*, Karlheinz Stockhausen had mixed feelings. In regard to the track "Dream, Part 4", he noted: "Japanese-Indonesian atmosphere by repeating pentatonic rising melody in C. Emotional memories: Pulsations in a nightly express train, far-away boat in the night. Much space. Not interesting: partition of form A – B – C / sound colors too naturalistic / melodics – harmonics completely banal (predictable), single turn from major to minor. Interesting: sensitive organization of volume (several different grades of quietness) / rising melody movements with development to highest note B / driving nighttime sounds."[8] Critics saw *Affenstunde* as a "mystic trip" and a "strange flowing world of sound" (*Pop*)[9]. The *Sounds* critic picked the Moog out as the central theme: "What is most notable on the tracks of this LP … is for all that noise-related electronics, how simple and clear Popol Vuh's music is. … The Moog synthesizer may be ill-reputed as a cold, too much technical instrument, but on this record it becomes an expressive instrument. … [For me], *Affenstunde* by Popol Vuh is the best and most satisfying LP with German pop music up yet."[10]

Affenstunde sold 3000 copies, so commercially it was a flop. It is, without a doubt, an interesting and pioneering album, but my feeling was always (and still is) that, what we got through that album is not so much a well-thought-out composition as it is a search for something. The sounds Fricke produced with his Moog always seemed to be a bit arbitrary.

In April 1971, Popol Vuh appeared in the TV show "Beat-Club" with a confused improvisation called "Bettina". The three musicians are nearly invisible behind a wall of electronically generated colors and flickering effects that director Michael Leckebusch contributed, but nonetheless, it's easy to see that Fricke was more or less cluelessly twisting the knobs of his Moog.

Another TV appearance of Popol Vuh (with Fricke, Fiedler and Trülzsch) is the previously mentioned "Improvisation 1971". The improvised tune shows once more that Fricke had no coherent idea of what to do with his synthesizer.

Fricke's second record production using the Moog was *In den Gärten Pharaos* (In the Gardens of Pharaoh), recorded at the collegiate church Baumburg with the synthesizer, pipe organ, and several percussion instruments, released 1972 on Rolf-Ulrich Kaiser's Pilz label. The track "Vuh" (the whole side 2 of the LP) is a mighty and, still today, intense work of improvisation, but the main part of this intensity lies with the organ, not with the synthesizer. A "somehow sacred, deeply touching music"[11], produced by "a group of people who make music, but are not a music group"[12], as Fricke put it. In a certain way, this statement shows that Fricke saw himself not so much as the leader of a band but as an individual working with other musicians under a project name. He undoubtedly saw the project Popol Vuh as his own. Later, this perception led to problems.

Besides using it for the Popol Vuh recordings, Fricke shared his Moog with two other important record projects, *Bury My Heart at Wounded Knee* (1973) by Gila and *Zeit* (1972) by Tangerine Dream. Edgar Froese remembers the latter contribution: "He produced completely different music with it, not based on sequencers, but more layers, long melodies. Of course we were interested in this, and we became even more interested when we found out what else could be possible with this box."[13]

During the preparation for Popol Vuh's follow-up album *Hosianna Mantra* (1972), Fricke went back to his original instrument, the piano: "I don't want to use the synthesizer in connection with Christian-religious music."[14] This sounds plausible, but I doubt it's the real reason. Putting it this way made it easier for Fricke to get rid of the synthesizer without damaging his image as an "electronic pioneer". Fricke was a highly educated and always very soft and spiritual looking guy, and because he used to give his tunes titles with religious or at least spiritual associations, he was seen by many as a deeply religious man. This was well-accepted brain food for the growing "alternative" and "New Age" scenes in which Popol Vuh's music was popular. Fricke was, indeed, interested in various religions and sacred myths, but according to Bettina von Waldthausen, this was mainly a sociological kind of view. Fricke was very interested in learning about the functions and consequences that religions and rites had for the societies they were practiced in, but he was not a practicing follower of any religion. He knew that his fans saw him as religious, and he wanted to avoid destroying this successful image. He used exactly this spiritualism as an argument to say goodbye to the synthesizer.

The true reason was simple: Fricke had always been on the warpath with technical devices, and he never got what he wanted from the synthesizer. Percussionist Holger Trülzsch: "Of course Florian had no understanding of the synthesizer. Everything went by plugging or unplugging."[15]

As said earlier, the analogue synthesizer is an *instrument*, and you have to *learn* how to play it. This will take you several months, if not years. Otherwise, the results might be unpredictable, frustrating, and disappointing – at best, and if you are lucky, they might be "interesting". Of course, for a listener, it is often hard to decide whether a sound is "intended" or not, but think back to the Stockhausen chapter: Tone colors can be composed like melodies, and as a listener you can train your ears to get a feeling for whether a sound "fits" or "doesn't fit". It's a bit like developing an ability to judge whether wine is of quality or not, or whether a piece of art is really art or just craftwork.

Fricke's musical thinking and feeling was based on the piano which he played in a classical fashion and usually for more than five hours a day. He sold his synthesizer in 1975 to Klaus Schulze who was already an active musician in the electronic field (Ash Ra Tempel, Tangerine Dream). Schulze – I think it's not overstated to say this – owes his artistic breakthrough to this Moog.

Consequently, Popol Vuh's really interesting phase started when Fricke's Moog was gone. With Daniel "Danny" Fichelscher, a rock and jazz guitarist from Amon Düül II whom Fricke had met at Gila, as well as guitarist Conny Veit (who also worked with Guru Guru), percussionist Holger Trülzsch, singers Djong Yun (daughter of the renowned Korean composer Isang Yun), later Renate Knaup (from Amon Düül II) and guests Robert Eliscu (from Peter Michael Hamel's band Between), Olaf Kübler and some others, they developed a kind of music that was (and still is) unique. The mental connection between the musicians was intimate. Fichelscher: "I was in the recording room and he [Fricke] was in a cubicle with giant windows. We could only hear each other through headphones. Suddenly, while playing, we looked right at each other. We weaved each other together, into the music; it was a wonderful exchange. For me, that was the initial spark, and I think it was for him too: Come on, let's do more together."[16] This became a sort of love/hate relationship and seems to be the essence of Popol Vuh's music. Fichelscher on *Einsjäger & Siebenjäger* (1974, recorded by Dieter Dierks and named after two characters from the "Popol Vuh" book): "There is this mood, there is this wonderful floating, in the most beautiful way we were peacefully enjoying this together, that's what is in there. Wonderful piano playing, wonderful work by Conny, completely reduced, devoting himself to the work – this, for me, is *the* Popol Vuh record."[17] There might be a flaw in Fichelscher's memory: Conny (Veit) plays on *Hosianna Mantra* from 1972, *Seligpreisung* from 1973, and later probably on soundtrack album *Aguirre* from 1975 (uncredited), but not on *Einsjäger & Siebenjäger*. Nobody knows anymore, and it seems to be that sometimes, the album credits are incomplete – intentionally or not.

It is not a mystery that director Werner Herzog became attracted to their music: "Popol Vuh was a godsend for me because in the pictures there's always something hidden which sleeps deep in the darkness of our soul, and this is made visible by the music of Florian Fricke. The pictures suddenly got a new and unique and strange quality. The music has something cryptic. Especially in the cinema it can reveal qualities and characteristics and rhythms in the pictures that would have never been noticed without music: When, for example, I filmed the jungle in *Aguirre*, initially, the jungle is just a landscape. Then the music of Popol Vuh changes this landscape. Somehow the landscape turns into a quality of soul, a human quality."[18]

As soft and peaceful he may look in photos, Florian Fricke was anything but easy to handle. He was always in trouble with business matters and furious about it. He was able to entertain a party for hours, but he could also snub all the party guests with harsh and arrogant remarks. It was especially not his style to acknowledge the big creative share his co-musicians infused into the music of Popol Vuh. He was, as Fichelscher says, "dogmatic, [and had] horrible demands – 'I come first, and then the others may come'. He always saw himself in the center – 'You are nothing without me.' Never let the others live out their power … These incidents [Herzog] had with Kinski, these checks and balances of power: I had them the same way with Fricke, only the preconditions were different. It was the same crock, the same destruction. I could tell you stories which are anything but nice. There were people who witnessed that. It was catastrophic. And on the other hand there was this enormous love, and often we hugged each other, crying, when we saw that something beautiful was there, something first-class, a living thing. And luckily sometimes you can hear this."[19]

Fricke loved to travel. He had visited Tibet twice, where, with long-time fellow musician and friend Frank Fiedler, he shot the movie *Kailash – Throne of the Gods* (first released in 1995). His soundtrack for this movie is magical, although he mixed in some tracks from earlier records.

In Molfetta, Italy, Fiedler and Fricke presented *Messa di Orfeo* (1999), a multimedia performance and another great work, but the record flopped.

Fricke had always been a chain smoker; he used to be nearly constantly stoned, and if he wasn't stoned, he was drunk. It was his will to live this way, and he executed it with all consequence. In his last years, after he and Bettina got divorced, he lived an isolated life at his home back in Miesbach. Renate Knaup: "He harvested all warmth from his solitude and did this in a way that firmed him up. All this 'you have to deliver' from his time as a wunderkind, all this strange stuff he had to experience, that must have been the time when he started building his own spiritual house, and probably he said to himself: 'Okay, then I get my warmth from somewhere else.' Which is not completely bad, I think. However, he was very extreme, a real maniac."[20]

In his last years, Fricke's drinking increased in a way that can only be described as intentionally self-destructive. Even close friends now preferred to cross to the other side of the street when they spotted him. Danny Fichelscher: "Very often I saw him and really thought: It's now time for him to rise like a phoenix, otherwise nothing will remain. He looked exhausted, and not only exhausted, he was sad, deeply sad."[21] Renate Knaup: "In this later time, I was especially scared of meeting him in the street, because all this madness would come up again, this whole package of life, of sadness. He had given himself up. Don't ask me why, I don't know. Whether it was the drinking, whether it was something else he had dealt out with himself, something we don't know about – I have no idea. It was the eve of destruction, purely."[22]

Florian Fricke passed away in December 2001, at the age of just 57 years. Bettina von Waldthausen: "I think that this was just the right point in time for him. I'm not sure whether he would understand the world as it is today. I think it was the right thing for him."[23]

So, Fricke, a pioneer of electronic music? Yes and no. In fact, as the second owner of a Moog in Germany, he was a pioneer, and he is seen as such by many fans of German rock. But I think his true significance lies somewhere else. Not all of his music is really remarkable; his later productions in particular are sometimes a bit weak and probably food for Californian New Age communities. But several works of his "middle phase" without electronics – especially the ones for Werner Herzog's films – belong to the finest moments the German rock scene has produced, still unrivaled today. Those are the works he will be remembered for.

MORODER

Former schlager singer Giorgio Moroder from Peter Meisel's kitchen discovered his future trademark at the Bavaria Studio in Munich: "Composer Eberhard Schoener had this big Moog synthesizer. He played a bass figure to me that reminded me of musique concrète. I liked it, but of course I wanted to know what else could be done with this Moog. Synthesizers were as big as closets at that time and horribly complicated to handle. Patch cords everywhere. You really had to know a thing or two about it. When I wrote 'I Feel Love' with Donna Summer, I wanted to do something that could be the future. What could represent the future better than the synthesizer?"[24]

In 1972, Moroder used this Moog for a production named "Son of My Father", written by him, Pete Bellotte, and Michael Holm, with the British band Chicory Tip. The song landed in the charts. A second success, done by the same team and again with a striking use of the Moog, was "What's Your Name" in 1972.

From Schoener, Moroder learned one of his later signature sounds: a sequence doubled by stereo echo (Schoener calls it the "Black & Decker effect" after a TV commercial). Schoener's assistant Robert Wedel, brought this effect along when Moroder hired him. Schoener was slightly surprised when he heard the sequence produced this way on Donna Summer's recording "I Feel Love" one day in New York (this led to a lawsuit then).

Moroder developed a sort of formula that melted two things together: his schlager experience and modern electronics. From the beginning of his career, he had worked with professionals who knew their stuff – Peter Meisel, Pete Bellotte, Harold Faltermeyer, Keith Forsey, Kristian Schultze, and Michael Holm are a handful of names that show this. Michael Holm, real name Lothar Bernhard Walter, worked with Moroder as a duo under the project name Spinach and started a successful schlager career in his own right in 1969 with a cover version of "Mendocino", originally by the Sir Douglas Quintet. But Holm had already been active behind the scenes ten years earlier as a lyricist, composer, and arranger. With Kristian Schultze, he became extremely successful in the 1980s and 1990s with New Age music under the project name Cusco. Moroder himself added his sense for sounds, simple but catchy melodies, and some atmosphere he had probably picked up from some discotheques in New York. The result of all this became formative for electronic dance pop; the long version of "I Feel Love" with singer Donna Summer (1977) is a classic. Some of Moroder's film soundtracks are also still worth listening – "What A Feeling" with Irene Cara (1983, from movie *Flashdance*) is a powerful song, and some instrumentals from his cut-down version of Fritz Lang's film *Metropolis* are not as bad as some people had expressed when this version was released. Moroder defined a style of electronic pop that was international, yet always remained connected to Munich.

The works and styles of the three musicians this chapter focuses on are very different from each other. This is probably the reason why there's no "Munich School" of electronics as we know from Berlin and Düsseldorf.

THE SEVENTIES

BERLIN SCHOOL

When we talk about German electronic rock or pop music (I'm well aware that these are different kettle of fish, but let's not make a big deal about the difference in this connection), it's a question of time until the keywords *Berlin School* and *Düsseldorf School* come up. The difference seems to be quite clear – but in reality, this is a vastly artificial separation.

TANGERINE DREAM

A third Big Moog came to Germany in 1973. Production-wise, it was also a very early one. For a few seconds, the device appeared in Donald Cammell's and Nicolas Roeg's film *Performance* from 1970. One of the leading actors was ROLLING STONES boss Mick Jagger, the owner of this instrument. He used it to produce some music for Kenneth Anger's short film *Invocation of My Demon Brother* from 1969. But, similar to John Lennon, he found this instrument too complicated; at the MIDEM music festival 1972 in Cannes, he sold it to Peter Meisel, who transferred it to his Hansa Studio in Berlin. The team there had the intention to use it for pop and schlager productions, but it didn't take long for them to find out that this machine was complicated, and getting reasonable sounds from it was nothing you could do in a hurry. So they asked TANGERINE DREAM drummer Christopher Franke (former member of AGITATION FREE) for advice because they knew he owned a VCS-3 and had a little bit of experience from working with electronics at composer Thomas Kessler's Beatstudio in Berlin. Franke's first contact with a Moog modular synthesizer had taken place at Eberhard Schoener's studio in Munich; Schoener had shown him some basics.[1]

So Franke came to Hansa and checked the Moog out: "In doing so, I brought a virus into the band because now everybody wanted to use one. The first record to feature these abstract electronic sounds was *Alpha Centauri*. This was my first album with Tangerine Dream."[2] The group's first direct contact with a Moog had been Florian Fricke's guest appearance on *Zeit*, but they didn't have much electronic equipment of their own yet. Their first four albums, *Electronic Meditation*, *Alpha Centauri*, *Zeit*, and *Atem*, were mainly produced with rock instruments (guitar, Farfisa and Vox organs, drums, et cetera) and with the stuff that Kessler had in his studio – sound generators, filters, and so on – just the "classic" equipment electronic studios used to work with.

The band had left Rolf-Ulrich Kaiser's Ohr label and management and signed with Richard Branson's Virgin Records. With an advance payment from Virgin, Franke bought Jagger's Moog in 1973 at a price of $15,000. Later, he added a second Moog that was formerly owned by the Moody Blues.[3]

For Tangerine Dream, this was the start of a new era. Virgin had its own recording studio, The Manor in Shipton-on-Cherwell, Oxfordshire (shut down in 1995), where Tangerine Dream could work. None of the musicians – at that time this was the "classic" line-up, Edgar Froese, Peter Baumann, Chris Franke – had a clear plan for what to do with the Moog. They more or less fiddled around with it, and as a result, they eventually discovered what they could do with the sequencer. Tangerine Dream were not the first or only ones to use sequencers, but they did it in such a memorable way that sequencing formed the basis of their music and became a sort of trademark. Froese: "What was commercially available on the market at this time was mainly Walter Carlos with *Switched-on Bach*, some things by Tomita and the first beginnings of Keith Emerson playing along with it, but none of that was based on what we started to do, doing the pure sequencer work."[4]

The resulting album was *Phaedra*, released in 1974. It was an innovation in the truest sense. *Phaedra* was miles away from the music produced by all the electronic music studios in Cologne, Baden-Baden, or Paris; it had the smell of rock music without being rock music. Among prog fans, the Virgin label acted as a seal of quality at that time, so the album caught the attention of rock listeners, but was simultaneously experimental enough to irritate them. It also caught a new group of listeners who were willing to walk into the unknown. Nobody had heard such an album before. Some critics were not even sure whether this could still be called rock music. Chris Franke: "No one could predict or believe what happened next. When Virgin released *Phaedra*, it went into the Top 20 after three or four weeks. A year later, we were awarded a golden LP for this instrumental, twenty-minute-long, non-vocal music. All this happened with no promotion and little airplay. Musical popes like John Peel proclaimed that this would be the music of the future. All this started an avalanche. We had never expected such a big success. I found this incredible. We were at the right place at the right time."[5]

Yours Truly discovered TANGERINE DREAM in 1973 when – if memory serves – the cultural TV magazine "Aspekte" published a short report on German rock groups. It was enough to pique my curiosity, so I went to the nearby Govi record store the next day and found the album *Alpha Centauri* from 1971; it was not new anymore, but it was the only one they had in stock that day. I bought it blindly, listened to it at home, and liked it – especially side A. After a while, however, I lost my interest in both the album and the band.

One late night two years later, there was a radio documentary about David Bowie (a series by Heinz Rudolf Kunze), and following this broadcast, they had some 20 minutes left until the midnight news. They filled this time with the second part of TANGERINE DREAM's album *Ricochet* (1975). This was completely different from the TANGERINE DREAM music I had known up until that point, and I was floored. There is no other way to describe it. It hit right into my heart. I owned the album only a day later, and having this experience, I went through TANGERINE DREAM's back catalogue. It didn't take long until I had them all and, similar to Ingeborg Schober, became obsessed; for the next two or three years I was hardly able to listen to "normal" music anymore.

The first time I saw TANGERINE DREAM on stage was in February 1978 in the Auditorium Maximum at the University of Hamburg. This concert was not the most convincing experience. The band had just released *Cyclone*, which included a drummer and a singer for the first time. I'm well aware that some people consider this one of their best albums ever, but it didn't do much for me. The live performance included drums and vocals, the volume was so extremely loud that the PA system clipped miserably (after the show I was half-deaf), the mix was unbalanced and blurred. Finally, the laser show – performed by LASERIUM of Los Angeles with a 2000 kilogram, water-cooled laser projection machine – partly gave up the ghost and delivered only a pale idea of what it was supposed to be. (An audience recording of a part of this concert is officially available on TANGERINE DREAM's 7-CD box *The Bootleg Box Set, Vol. 2*.)

That strange thing, by the way, on top of Chris Franke's Big Moog that looks like a devil's trident – you may have seen it in some photos – was a metal

"E" profile from an old neon sign, laid on its side. It's only function was to look mysterious. This same synthesizer also survived a fall from the cargo area of an (of course not flying!) airplane.

There is a rumor that, around 1981, the band sold Jagger's synthesizer to East Berlin musician Reinhard Lakomy (1946-2013), but Edgar Froese rectifies: "What went to Lakomy had nothing to do with [Jagger's] device. In the 70s we had other modular Moogs, all in all we had four systems. But it was only parts of these four systems, Lakomy's Moog does not have the original sequencer anymore"; Jagger's original one was "cannibalized and scattered. I still have one system, but it's not usable anymore."[6] Tangerine Dream's four Moog modular systems had been partially modified by the companies PPG and Projekt Elektronik. Reinhard Lakomy: "I bought the Big Moog around 1981/82. ... Maybe some parts, like the sequencer, are the originals, but the oscillators may not be the ones it had when the Stones bought it."[7]

Lakomy paid with the help of credit granted to him by the (West German) copyright society GEMA. Nobody knows exactly how the Moog crossed the Berlin Wall – it happened with an East German Barkas lorry that wasn't checked by the East German border guards. This is one of these eternal German-German mysteries: It actually was not unusual that East German bands received instruments and equipment from West German colleagues, and this probably wouldn't have been possible without clandestine help from East German officials. The border guards at least knew exactly which cars or trucks they were *not* allowed to check. However, for the time being, the trace of Jagger's Moog ends at Lakomy's studio. Reinhard Lakomy passed away in 2013; maybe the instrument is still in his former studio, maybe it was sold on eBay. Lakomy's heirs remain silent.[8]

After the 1978 concert, I saw Tangerine Dream four more times; the last time was in 1982 during their "Logos" tour.

After *Stratosfear* (1976), when Peter Baumann had left the band (which obviously was "his" album, as a comparison with his first solo album *Romance '76* clearly shows), church organist and sound engineer Johannes Schmoelling took his place; he was one of the few able to one-handedly roll a cigarette in their pocket – a feat I never managed to do. This line-up had remained stable for around a decade and led to the production of more classics, like *White Eagle* (1982) and *Poland (The Warsaw Concert)* (1984). *Force Majeure* (1979) should be mentioned here, recorded by Froese and Franke with drummer Klaus Krüger. "Cloudburst Flight" on this album contains one of Froese's most inspired guitar performances ever; interestingly, it was recorded at half speed – you can hear this when you know it. After their, in my opinion, last interesting album, *Hyperborea* (1983), the band began touching the foothills of New Age Land a bit too closely. They also lost themselves in an increasingly confusing mass of film soundtracks, of which only a few are worth listening to. I'll mention *Sorcerer* (1977), *Thief* (1981), and *Wavelength* (1983), but that does not necessarily mean that the films are must-sees. The band did, however, make good money with these works.

After that, Tangerine Dream ran through a fast-turning merry-go-round of people. The only remaining stable factor was founder Edgar Froese – and if you listen to his solo albums, it becomes clear to what extent he had always been the band's heart and soul.

Because Tangerine Dream had always tried to stay on top of technological developments, their sound and musical style began to change in the 1980s as fast as new synthesizer models were pushed out into the market. For a band like this, it might be fine (you might end up being a museum piece otherwise), but somehow they lost sight of themselves and the technology prevailed over the music. Tangerine Dream eventually found themselves back to a more individualized style in the 2000s, but that takes us beyond this book's timeline.

SYNTHESIZER MUSIC – A "GERMAN" THING?

As fun as it is to follow the traces and stories of specific old synthesizers, I will stop here. In 1972, after moving to Williamsville, New York, Moog's workshop morphed into a real factory, and buying a Moog synthesizer was no longer a problem as long as you had the funds. In addition, because there was the Minimoog now, most rock bands didn't need to get the big modular system. The Minimoog offered all the features they needed.

Or should we put it the other way round? To what extent did the synthesizer and its size define the music you got out of it? Among some electronic fans, as well as the brighter part of music journalists, this soon became a point of discussion.[9] Using a modular Moog, the musician was forced to construct and find sounds, as well as a way to shape them, because there was no default way to do it. There were not even instruction manuals.

Klaus Schulze commented on this problem: "In the first stage, when you get to know your synthi, you can easily slide down into a state that will make you love anything the synthi does. It looks like this: You play a sequence, and what you hear is so beautiful, sound-wise, that you completely freak out. You have to get over this stage as soon as possible, otherwise you become permanently dependent on the synthi playing beautiful things to you; it's not you who controls the synthi, it's the synthi that controls you! But when you go on working and really try to discover the synthi rationally, then you finally get over the fascination of pure sound, although the danger of 'sinking into the sound' is still given."[10]

Klaus Schulze was – and still is – the one who defines the term "Berlin School" (although he left Berlin long ago) more than anybody else, besides TANGERINE DREAM. Without knowing where this would lead him, he took the trouble of walking down this sometimes stony way to find out what the electronics could do for him – not what he could do for the electronics. Starting out as a drummer, he had already had a strong rock feeling. When he switched over to keyboards and left Rolf-Ulrich Kaiser's circle, this feeling was what made the difference between his music and the electronic music that came from the academic field – Cologne, et cetera.

Inside the device, the sections of the Minimoog were pre-wired and the patching couldn't be changed. There were still a lot of ways to change and manipulate the sound, but it was much easier to operate. As a result, it didn't take long for the Minimoog to be used as a solo keyboard that every listener could immediately recognize. The price that had to be paid for the convenience: The sounds got more uniform. After a while, it became more and more evident that a couple of "standard sounds" were recognized as "*the* synthesizer sound". Most prog bands used them. They sounded well, but it was exactly the opposite of what a synthesizer was originally meant for: creating new and unheard sounds. It was possible, but it needed ideas and effort, and it was still not easy to do this on stage, so it remained undone in too many cases.

Several other manufacturers also came up with synthesizers. They all had their own specific sound qualities. The Moog, however, had a uniquc sound, cspecially in bass. Moog devices had a patented filter with a higher rate of attenuation than other synthesizers. This led to a "fat" sound, but it also created some distortion, or, let's say put some "dirt" on it, and it's just this dirt that we sense as "warmth". You can also turn the filter resonance up to a degree that starts self-resonance, which leads to interesting percussion sounds (well audible in KRAFTWERK's "Numbers" or Herbie Hancock's "Rockit").

But still: Why is it that just German bands and musicians developed a style of electronic rock that became "the musical German export hit"? Why did they have no real competitors from the classic rock countries, Great Britain and the United States?

Edgar Froese: "The inducement is plain easy. It's our inability to do what Americans and Brits did for decades: playing with the same intensity and, first of all, with the same musical feeling, to the point of groove, of playing technique. I think I can say with all arrogance that, still to this day, German musicians haven't learned how to do that. At least, this must be added, not when playing in an ensemble. I don't know a band here that grooves like it is completely normal in any New York rock venue. Because listening experiences, traditions, and also the hard work that is behind it, are not really common here. So to develop a sort of originality at all is why German musicians tried to get some orientation: What do we want to do musically, and which field offers possibilities to reach this goal? This was the basic idea."[11]

Froese is not wrong here, but he might have thought a bit too much on the intellectual side. It is reminiscent of video artist Nam June Paik's answer to the reporter's question of why, in the early Sixties, he had become the first artist to work with old TV sets: "The only way to win a race is to run alone."[12] As true as this is, most rock bands, when they started in the Sixties, didn't think this way. They simply tried to copy what they had heard from rock records or on the radio. They went to the Star-Club and similar venues, listened to British and American bands and tried to play like them. Only very few of them asked themselves: "Which untilled field offers us the opportunity to do something without competition?"

German bands playing at the Star-Club already had to fight with the phenomenon that they sounded a bit stiff. Don't get me wrong, bands from Liverpool or Manchester also didn't produce the kind of groove a band from, say, Louisiana did. Which is no wonder because Liverpool or Manchester are located just as far from the banks of the Mississippi River as Hamburg or Berlin. The answer to this question is probably tradition. "Groove", which – similar to "swing" – is a musical quality that can't exactly be defined. It is something you have to imbibe from your infancy. Groove is a feeling that is important for rock music, and you can only learn it by listening to it from early childhood on. American musicians who were exposed to black radio stations throughout their lives had developed this feeling much easier than European or Japanese musicians.

Groove has never been very common in German music, so the musicians couldn't get this feeling early enough to be able to play it themselves. Even German jazz bands playing swing often meant a sort of relaxed foxtrot, and hearing German bands grooving is a rare experience – ATLANTIS comes to mind, some Doldinger recordings, HIGHWAY, LAKE, maybe RANDY PIE (at least sometimes).

But you can go further back, to 1927: Germany's most famous boy group, the Comedian Harmonists, modeled themselves on The Revelers from New York, and it took them a whole year of daily rehearsals until they had found out how to reach this relaxed, laid-back singing style that nobody else in Germany had. They were all experienced professionals, but it soon became clear to them that they were bound to the traditions they came from – classical, "lied", opera, operetta. They had to work willfully against their knowledge and skills to become successful in this new style they were looking for. It was very hard work for them, but they never gave up.[13] It's exactly this kind of hard work that German "beat bands" of the 1960s also would have needed to put a "British" or "American" feeling to their music. Very few were able to actually reach this goal.

You can see how hard this was when you think of the German bands who actually tried to sound "American": They usually failed in the States. Seen in the light of day, this is not even a mystery. Why would you need Randy Pie or Highway when you have Steely Dan in your country? Why would you need a German soul band when you can hear an original American one at the club next door three times a week?

But there are some things in which American bands or musicians don't seem to be proficient. One of these things is the use of electronics in music. Some German musicians who initially had no real idea of what exactly they wanted to do with these new electronic instruments, suddenly hit a gap. They lived in Germany with no Mississippi far and wide, so without any intention, they hammered out something nobody else in the world had done. It brought them attention after a while, so they stuck to it.

Yes, there were non-German bands working with synthesizers. As mentioned, The Byrds played a Moog on their album *The Notorious Byrd Brothers*, and so did the Monkees on their album *Pisces, Aquarius, Capricorn & Jones Ltd.* Even Stevie Wonder, with the help of Malcolm Cecil and Robert Margouleff a.k.a. Tonto's Expanding Head Band, had a Moog and other synthesizers on his album *Talking Book* from 1972.

The difference between them and Tangerine Dream, Klaus Schulze, et cetera, is this: They tried to *integrate* the Moog and other electronic instruments into their existing music style and equipment; they wanted to use them as an expansion of available sounds, while Tangerine Dream and company *abandoned* most classic rock instruments and developed a music genre that was *tailored* to these new electronic instruments. This, exactly, is the meaning of *Berlin School.*

Why couldn't this happen in the United States? One reason is that synthesizers were antagonized by extremely conservative musicians' unions. Synthesizers, as the unions saw them, were devices that could imitate conventional instruments and replace the musicians who played them. They perceived synthesizers as crutches for people who couldn't play a real instrument and thus were not fully valid musicians – in short, synthesizers were the devil's work, made only to cut the jobs of real musicians.

Tangerine Dream said goodbye to a good part of their classic rock instruments and produced *Electronic Meditation* (1970) at Beatstudio Berlin under the wings of avant-garde composer Thomas Kessler (but still without synthesizers). Klaus Schulze put his drum sticks away and made *Irrlicht* (Will-o'-the-wisp; 1972) – instead of synthesizer, with electronic keyboards and lots of studio effects. Interestingly, *Electronic Meditation* was not even made to be published; the tapes just fell into the hands of Rolf-Ulrich Kaiser who heard them and said: "This stuff needs to be released." These records (and some others) became the foundation of what we know as Berlin School today, and what Tangerine Dream and Klaus Schulze, maybe even Mythos, Ash Ra Tempel, and Manuel Göttsching essentially mean. The main feature of this music style was probably its use of short tonal sequences, often pushed through several keys, and embedded into (usually) harmonic and melodic synth and mellotron sounds. But pads without rhythm, endlessly stretched-out chords (we would call them "drones" today), and moments of noise could also be part of the Berlin School concept.

EQUIPMENT AND PLAYING LIVE

Karlheinz Stockhausen never made any compromises about the equipment he used. He never had to. Rock musicians weren't usually in such a good situation. But after a while, some were, and they showed it. Tangerine Dream and Klaus Schulze had made electronic equipment a special part of their image and their stage show. The altar-like setup of modular Moogs, keyboards, and other technical equipment with its flashing control lights, played in semi-darkness at earthquake-like volume, sometimes the musicians with their backs turned to the audience, left an overwhelming impression on the (primarily male) spectators. This aesthetic was meant to be overwhelming.

The album sleeves continued this vibe with long lists of the allegedly used electronic instruments and effect devices – for some fans, this information seemed to be more important than the music itself. Many believed the quality of the music correlated with its use of devices: It must be great music because the band uses devices X, Y and Z.

Sometimes, parts of the equipment on stage were not even plugged into a mixing desk, they were just decoration. The bands also used backing tapes sometimes. They didn't like talking about it, but usually, this was no cheating, no incompetence, no amenities. There was simply no other way to keep the show going for two hours. You couldn't register an analogue sequencer during the show. As mentioned earlier, there was no way to store sounds or sequences, so the feeding of pre-produced parts has always been a topic in electronic music. In general, this was not a big problem; most people in the audience knew about and accepted it. In a way, Stockhausen's tape concerts with the empty stage were more "honest". Avant-garde musician, Asmus Tietchens, sometimes demonstratively pushed a button to start a tape or a CD player in his stage appearances, then took a seat in the front row, and let the music run. His audience usually accepted this, but of course, this is not what a rock audience expects. But today's laptop musicians do it the same way. Of course they don't use tapes anymore, they use a hard drive, but does this really make a big difference?

Klaus Schulze: "I have had experience with live concerts now. … What is so nice about playing synthi, and making music in general, is to go crazy with music, simply said. But the synthies don't accept that. When you work with these devices, you go crazy with one ear, and with the other ear, you need to listen very precisely, because all sound changes, effects, and timbres you want to retrieve have to be adjusted very rationally and strategically. Often it's only millimeters of governor settings of filter buttons, oscillators or faders that have to be changed, and when you're in such a freaky mood, it's impossible to grab the buttons and faders [by intuition], because then some sound might thunder around your ears that has no connection to the music you are just playing. … To reduce it to a common denominator, this means that you always have to be rational and emotional at the same time. This is why it's inevitable for live performances to have some things pre-programmed. These recordings run and then I can go crazy on the keyboards, based on this."[14]

One consequence of this insight was the idea to share a stage or studio with guest musicians. Schulze did this with drummer Harald Großkopf, guitarist Manuel Göttsching, keyboardist Rainer Bloss (1946-2015), percussionist Michael Shrieve (from SANTANA), cellist Wolfgang Tiepold, singers Arthur Brown, and Lisa Gerrard.

Later, Schulze had his modular Moog modified with MIDI technology. In 2005, he still used it in cooperation with Pete Namlook (= Peter Kuhlmann, 1960-2012) for the *Dark Side of the Moog* series, then it was sold via eBay to an anonymous buyer. According to reports, Schulze's Moog, pre-owned by Florian Fricke, was then re-modified to its original technical condition and is now located somewhere in Switzerland.

Klaus Schulze is the one who stuck closest to his basic ideas, which already go back to his appearance on Ash Ra Tempel, Cosmic Jokers, and several other recordings produced by Rolf-Ulrich Kaiser. He's the one who, today, still best represents what the meaning of Berlin School was. He developed his style and continued on, following his intuition without caring about what others did. His use of analogue sounds was exquisite. Later, with the upcoming digital synthesizers, his use of often boring preset sounds got out of hand, and over time, the number of albums he threw on the market became a bit questionable – it was simply too much, and this became apparent in the quality. However, his albums *Timewind* (1975), *Moondawn* (1976), and *X.* (1978) are classics; *Mirage* (1977) will save him an eternal seat on the Mount Olympus of electronic music, and with *Silhouettes* (2018) he landed a late highlight that, without any difficulties, ties in with his early masterpieces.

MUSIC FROM THE ROAD OF FAIRY TALES

Not everything that came from Berlin remained "Berlin School" forever. To be an "electronic group" or artist, or to even make electronic music, it was not necessary to use a synthesizer. The price made this impossible for most musicians; it was much easier to use cheaper instruments and replace technology with fantasy. Something like an electronic organ, an e-piano, a cello, a watering can, or a metal rod, picked up with a contact microphone, played through echo units, a wah-wah pedal, phasing, or flanging devices, could already be very impressive.

HUMAN BEING

Hans-Joachim Roedelius had founded Human Being in 1968, a project with artists Boris Schaak, Beatrix Rief, Christoph Sievernich, Elke Lixfeld, Broderick Price, Norbert Eisbrenner, and Verena Schirz. They made free improvised noise at Berlin's Zodiak club. Human Being used a Farfisa organ, some electric guitars (although none of them could really play them), saxophone, and lots of percussion instruments, as well as oil drums and other "found objects", sometimes mixed with pre-recorded tapes. Roedelius: "We just fiddled around with feedback, echo machines, prepared tapes and loops. None of us were academically trained ... We didn't care much about what reactions we got."[1] It was very loud and very long, but the audience's reactions were not too bad.

Roedelius' biographer Stephen Iliffe compared Human Being's improvised performances to Stockhausen's cycle *Aus den Sieben Tagen* (From the Seven Days), especially to "Prozession".[2] These pieces were performed in Berlin at the same time, and they were improvised. But comparing Human Being to those is a misinterpretation of the term "improvisation", the way Stockhausen used it. The improvisations he called for were not completely free; every piece of the cycle was based on a short instruction that defined the way the composition had to be played. Before entering the stage, the performers had to remain silent for a couple of days or had to stay by themselves for a week, had to do praying gestures or meditation exercises, or they had to complete a week-long fast. When they got on the stage, they were certainly in an unusual mental state. And different from the HUMAN BEING members, they were virtuosos on their instruments. It's easy to imagine that their performances had a spiritual level that HUMAN BEING was never able to reach.

It was a lot of fun for the HUMANS to fiddle along this way, and it was probably an interesting adventure for the (usually stoned) audience. But if you listen to a recording, you will have to admit that their music was objectless. HUMAN BEING's album *Live at the Zodiak – Berlin 1968*, released in 2009, attests to it. But well, it was the start of something new. Let's face it: The early works of TANGERINE DREAM et al were not much different from HUMAN BEING. The only, and important, difference is that, since the TANGERINE DREAM members had already been rock musicians before (Edgar Froese had played in THE ONES, Chris Franke had played in AGITATION FREE, Klaus Schulze came from PSY FREE and ASH RA TEMPEL), they had a more deliberate approach to their work. This does not mean that their firstling *Electronic Meditation* is easy listening, but the follow-up *Alpha Centauri* clearly already has a "rock feeling" to it, and the double album *Zeit* comes along with a sort of perseverance and thinking in long distances. They couldn't have done this without a great deal of patience and discipline. It's not "composed music", but the musicians, especially guest musicians Florian Fricke on synthesizer and cellist Joachim von Grumbkow, had a classical background, so they had an idea of what they wanted to bring in.

KLUSTER

After the end of HUMAN BEING (of course it was not a project made for eternity), Hans-Joachim Roedelius, with Beuys student Conrad Schnitzler (who also played on TANGERINE DREAM's first album) and Swiss graphic artist and part-time saloon keeper Dieter Moebius, started KLUSTER. They essentially continued what HUMAN BEING had started, but under the guiding hands of producer Conny Plank. This resulted in a new sort of harsh electro-acoustic music that had not been heard yet. In December 1970, Plank recorded a quasi-live album entitled *Klopfzeichen* (Knock Signals) with the three of them at Rhenus Studio and managed to sell it to Schwann, a record label focusing on pedagogy and contemporary church music. To get this company to release their album, they had to mix in short poems by Liselotte Rauner, Rudolf Otto Wiemer, Dorothee Sölle, Wilhelm Willms, and Uwe Seidel, recited by actress Christa Runge. Two months later, *Kluster zwei – Osterei* (Kluster Two – Easter Egg; a paraphrase of a children's counting-out rhyme) followed, using the same scheme: This time the reciter was actor Manfred Paethe, and the poems were written by Rudolf Bohren, Kurt Marti, Hilde Domin, and again by Dorothee Sölle, Rudolf Otto Wiemer, and Liselotte Rauner. The print run was 300 copies each. It wasn't a money-maker, and surely it was not an ideal solution, but at least now they had two longplayers in their backpack. The fact that KLUSTER was available on record now opened some doors to galleries, museums, youth centers, and other culture institutes, making it easier for them to obtain live gigs.

CLUSTER

After the relatively successful firstling of KRAFTWERK from 1970, the Philips label in Hamburg smelled a market and quickly signed on more German acts. One of them was CLUSTER (Roedelius and Moebius renamed KLUSTER after Schnitzler had left to find his own way). Conny Plank used his reputation and connections again by making it possible to record this album at Star Studio in Hamburg. They paid owner Ralf Arnie, as usual, with the publishing rights of the recorded compositions (which was probably just enough to cover a nice dinner out with his wife).

The basic idea of the self-titled first CLUSTER album (rereleased in 1980 as *Cluster '71* on the Sky label) was the same as before: harsh, improvised electro-acoustic soundscapes, but the absence of Schnitzler is noticeable. You can feel that two very different yet like-minded souls are trying to create a sort of music they could both find themselves in. The track "15:34" already anticipates a little bit of one of CLUSTER's later masterpieces, "Im Süden" from *Cluster II*. Music critic Rainer Blome wrote in *Sounds*: "Currently there are only two bands in the world using contemporary electronic material in terms of New Pop Music: POPOL VUH of Munich and CLUSTER of Berlin. … This record is one of few valid pieces of evidence that electronic music can be generated not only intellectually, but also emotionally. This is something that musicians working in pop have as an advantage over their colleagues from contemporary classical."[3] I remember that, on the schoolyard, I picked up how one of my older school mates said to some of his classmates: "If you think KRAFTWERK is too conventional, then CLUSTER is for you."

Cluster II (1972) was their first recording for the freshly founded Brain label and, for a while, the last relic of their early musical style. Recorded again at Star Studio and produced by Conny Plank, *Cluster II* became CLUSTER's most advanced recording of abstract, swirling electronics, without a synthesizer, but now, sometimes even with a touch of lightness and humor. For my taste, it is the summit of early CLUSTER; other people saw this album as emotionless and boring, like Roedelius' biographer Stephen Iliffe: "An inspiration-free zone for completists only."[4] Winfried Trenkler, who hosted some of the few important radio shows, like "Radiothek" or "Schwingungen" at WDR radio in Cologne, wrote in *Sounds*: "You don't want to believe that CLUSTER consists of only two people when you hear their music. It doesn't become understandable until you recognize the amount of electronic equipment they use."[5] This is an interesting perspective because Trenkler was another one who seemed to think that the quality of the music stood lineally to the quantity of equipment that was used for its production. Actually, the equipment CLUSTER used at that time was relatively cheap anyways – it had to be. They had two simple organs, a Hawaiian guitar, a cello, some tone generators, several Echolette and Schaller effect pedals, and a cheap Echolette rhythm machine. Later, they added a simple synthesizer named "Davolisint", brought out in 1972 by the now long forgotten Italian manufacturer Davoli. A little misunderstanding resulted from one of the track titles, "Live in der Fabrik", which apparently some listeners took as a live recording made at the Fabrik, a well-known venue in Hamburg's neighborhood of Altona. It's not. They had played the Fabrik a couple of days before the studio sessions started and simply liked it as a title.

SEESSELBERG

Eckhardt and Wolf-Jürgen Seesselberg of Hamburg made music comparable to *Cluster II*, but they already worked with real synthesizers. Their devices were home-made, built by Eckhardt, while Wolf-Jürgen had been involved in electronic theater music at Deutsches Schauspielhaus in Hamburg in the 1960s. Similar to CLUSTER, SEESSELBERG performed in galleries and art museums, and their music was mainly based on sound structures. We can call this "Berlin School", they just weren't from Berlin. On their only album *Synthetik 1* (1973, self-published with a print run of 1000 copies), this is relatively diverting, but I had the opportunity to see them live at the Fabrik and remember that on stage, the whole affair became more and more tiring after a while. There was no recognizable compositional concept; the two of them just sat there and fiddled around on their control dials, and after half an hour, it became obvious that they had no clear idea where to go with their machinery. FAUST sometimes ran into the same trap. They had an ARP synthesizer, it can be seen in some live-recorded videos.[6] Even worse: Their debut concert in Hamburg in 1971 turned out to be disastrous because they were not able to get the machinery under control.[7]

ALTER WESERHOF

Cluster II is early industrial (a genre that didn't exist at that time), but unlike its predecessors, it carries a sort of atmosphere with it. "Im Süden" already has traces of warmth and foreshadows things to come.

There is a reason for this change: When they recorded *Cluster II*, Roedelius and Moebius weren't living in Berlin anymore. Like CAN, FAUST, and KRAFTWERK, they noticed that what they had in mind couldn't be done without their own studio. CLUSTER had relocated to the countryside of Lower Saxony, to a little village in the Weserbergland area called Forst (forest; today it is a district of Holzminden-Bevern); the next bigger city you might have heard of is Göttingen. A friend, an antiques dealer, had pointed out a 16th-century farmstead called "Alter Weserhof" to them (which translates to something like "Old Farmyard at the River Weser"); a big house in midst of a group of smaller buildings, situated a little bit outside the village, surrounded by deep woods, a view of old castles, meadows with horses or typical black and white cows, situated within eyeshot of a River Weser's bend. Villages in this area have lovely names like Gottstreu ("devoted to God") or Gewissenruh ("calmness of conscience"), and that's how they look. This area is part of the so-called "German Road of Fairytales" – in fact, many of the fairytales we know from the Brothers Grimm are set and were originally collected somewhere here; the Sababurg, to name one example, is said to have been the castle of Dornröschen (Sleeping Beauty). Bodenwerder, home of Baron Münchhausen, is also only a couple of kilometers away. This must have been an adequate place for Roedelius and Moebius, the musical storytellers. "The building was a two-floor stone outhouse formerly used for storing corn and beer and at other times as a courthouse. It was where farmers who hadn't given up their tithe – ten percent of the harvest – were tried and gaoled", Roedelius recounts.[8] One of the buildings also included a bar and a tiny little neighborhood whorehouse; both are long gone.[9]

Roedelius and Moebius accepted an offer to rent the Weserhof for 99 years for very little money – but that meant they had to renovate it. The building had nothing. There was no heating and no running water. The rooms were empty, damaged, and as good as uninhabitable. They had to put lots of work into it, but in the end, it was worth it.

The only factor they didn't like was the two nuclear power plants nearby, Grohnde and Würgassen. Roedelius hated this and always had the feeling that radioactivity would harm them. But in the mid-1970s, Germany had around 30 active nuclear power plants. So, wherever you went, there was always at least one near you. For this reason, Roedelius, along with his wife and daughter, left Forst in 1978 and relocated to Austria. In a referendum that year, Austrian citizens had decided not to accept any nuclear power plants in their country (which didn't turn off the ones around Austria, but well, you can't have it all). Although he later centered his life back in Berlin again, Moebius still had a place at the Alter Weserhof until his death in 2015.

HARMONIA

The Alter Weserhof and the magical environment of the Weserbergland had changed Roedelius' and Moebius' way of thinking, which of course resulted in a change in their music. Here, at this Weserhof, Berlin and Düsseldorf, figuratively, kissed. In Easter 1973, the spirit of Düsseldorf came to Forst in the shape of guitarist Michael Rother. He was originally from Hamburg, but due to his father's job (a Lufthansa pilot) he had lived in several places, like Munich, Wilmslow (near Manchester, U.K.), and Karachi (Pakistan). He had played in SPIRIT OF SOUND with Wolfgang Riechmann and Wolfgang Flür, in KRAFTWERK and – most important – NEU! (more about this project later). His NEU! partner, Klaus Dinger, had had the idea of starting a "supergroup" named EUROPA, consisting of Rother and himself, his brother Thomas, and Hans Lampe, and he also wanted to hire the two CLUSTER guys with their keyboards. So, Dinger and Rother came to Forst to check out what might be possible. Dinger tried to push the idea through in a way that Moebius and Roedelius didn't find acceptable. EUROPA never saw the light of day, but Rother fell in love with the Weserhof, occupied a couple of empty rooms, and started renovating them. Just for fun, he also started jamming with Roedelius and Moebius. This turned out so well that in 1973, Harmonia resulted from it – which, in Germany, is a name that makes you think of a "Gesangverein" (choral society or glee club) singing choral pieces by Schubert. That's actually where the name came from: They took it from a gesangverein concert poster they had seen somewhere on a wall. Rother: "My Cluster colleagues had very little money, so we were happy that at least the advance payments for Harmonia came in. We also played concerts, but it was very hard to survive with that. I was lucky that the record sales of Neu! yielded enough money for me to be able to carry the loss-making project Harmonia."[10]

The hope for a bit more commercial success remained unfulfilled, but Harmonia at least became a highly interesting project that caught David Bowie, Brian Eno, and several other important artists' attention. The first Harmonia album, *Musik von Harmonia*, released in 1974 on the Brain label, was recorded partially at Alter Weserhof and partially live. Michael Rother: "We were so poor! Together, we had three Revox A-77, these nice stereo tape decks, and a very simple, not great sounding mixing desk by Echolette. The great thing was: We had time."[11] The result was remarkable: "Hypnotic rhythm, meditative sound streams, passages full of inner tension between them. Music to listen to, that lets you enter the musicians' world of imagination", as Hermann Haring wrote in *Sounds*. But this was only a ten-liner somewhere in the midst of a collective review of several records. Not to mention that Haring speaks of "Michael Roth" and "two Cluster people" without naming them, and he concludes: "Stylistically they didn't change".[12] One would like to know where this guy's ears were; he was probably sitting on them. But this kind of inadvertence – or should I say: ignorance? – was typical for the way many German rock records were treated by the German music press. Consequently, Haring later stuck to his judgment when he rated Rother's solo records as "saggy gloss rock"[13].

In the meantime, Moebius and Roedelius worked on another Cluster album, released by Brain in 1974: *Zuckerzeit* (Sugar Time) If they ever did a pop album, it's this one. The cheeky cover photo and sugary lettering underscored this impression. Although the LP carries the name Cluster on its sleeve, *Zuckerzeit* was not a duo recording. In actuality, it contains five solo tracks by Roedelius and five by Moebius. When compared, one clearly hears the different ideas the two of them had about music. But, somehow, they were a good match because of this. Moebius did more irritating tracks, preventing the Cluster music becoming too sweet, while Roedelius mainly focused on soft and substantial melodies which were sometimes in danger of becoming kitsch, if Moebius hadn't set counterparts. On their later solo recordings, Roedelius' and Moebius' respective parts in Cluster became much more audibly clear. "Rosa", the closing track of *Zuckerzeit*'s side 1, was Roedelius' welcome to his daughter – she had seen the light of day at Alter Weserhof, which, in fact, was the light of the fireplace.

It is sometimes said that Michael Rother was the producer of *Zuckerzeit*, but this is not the case. They used his Revox tape recorder, but that's it. The fact that the publishing rights were with Ralf Arnie again indicates that Conny Plank gave the recordings a bit of post-editing at Star Studio (Conny's own studio hadn't been opened yet).

Zuckerzeit stood with almost no reviews; only *Sounds* mentioned it in an article as "a little masterpiece of ironic synthesizer art".[14]

The second Harmonia album, entitled *DeLuxe* (1975), was also recorded at the Alter Weserhof, but this time Conny Plank brought a 16-track tape machine. Sound-wise, this was a jump ahead. Rother: "We were very happy to have Conny in our space. I'm not exactly sure how long he stayed. Maybe two weeks? … Then we met in Conny's studio a few weeks later to do the mixing and record the vocals. That was something we did spontaneously. Roedelius, Moebius and I were all rather shy on stage. We played with our backs to the audience because we couldn't look at people, not even speak to them. So this was worrying me. I thought: 'We have to overcome this shyness, this fear of the audience.' One step would be to open your mouth. So in the studio, 'DeLuxe (Immer wieder)', the title track, was originally conceived as an instrumental. We came to the decision: 'Let's open our mouths and stand around the microphone.' We sat down for five or ten minutes, scribbled down some lyrics and jumbled them together. That was very refreshing and liberating. Then we did the 'crazy' version, the track 'Monza', the very dynamic stuff, and that was pure fun!"[15] The lyrics are a little bit similar to the nonsensical lyrics of Kraftwerk's *Autobahn*, but this was probably unintentional.

On *DeLuxe*, Harmonia had a guest musician play with them: Mani Neumeier of Guru Guru played drums on three tracks, "Walky-Talky", "Gollum" and the crazy "Monza (Rauf und runter)". His drumming on the latter tune is similar to Klaus Dinger's style on the Neu! albums, and I wouldn't have recognized Neumeier. "Walky-Talky", to my mind, is one of their strongest tunes. *DeLuxe* is a wonderful and timeless album; for me, it was a companion through many nights.

The music press completely ignored it, as did radio stations, even though there was a 45 available (shortened edits of "DeLuxe (Immer wieder)" b/w "Monza").

They even recorded a special track for a radio station. Rother: "'Tiki-Taka' is an example of how we worked in the studio in 1975; it's this track we recorded for the only German radio journalist who played our music occasionally. We were really totally ignored by nearly everyone. But he offered us airtime. He said: 'If you record something for me, I will play it on my show.'"[16] This track appears on *Documents 1975*, which is the fourth album of Harmonia's *Complete Works* box set, released in 2015 by Grönland Records. The journalist Rother talks about can only be Winfried Trenkler of WDR Cologne. He remained more or less the only one; besides him, there was only Ingeborg Schober who, as far as I know, played a Harmonia track on her show on BR radio Munich. Of course the project turned out to be a washout: Both Harmonia albums didn't sell more than around 1500 copies each within one year.

When Harmonia played clubs or youth centers, sometimes 20 people appeared, sometimes 50, sometimes only three. I was lucky enough to see them twice, both times at the Fabrik in Hamburg. The first time happened to be the concert where Brian Eno spontaneously joined them. Today this sounds spectacular, but back on that evening, it wasn't. Eno didn't know Harmonia, Winfried Trenkler had taken him along to Hamburg to introduce him to the band. For what it's worth, Eno was in reach of me but I didn't recognize him – from what I knew, Eno was the long-haired, glitter-wearing, colorful bird of paradise of Roxy Music, but at that time, he was just dressed in black, had short hair, and nothing special about him except that he spoke English. After the intermission, he joined the band, but unfortunately I don't even remember what instrument Eno played – probably guitar. However, to give you an idea of how a Harmonia concert felt, here's a short report I wrote for a radio station about the second Harmonia concert, which I saw in 1976:

> Tonight, *They Came From Beyond Space* is shown on German TV. At the Fabrik, Harmonia is playing. This band does not come from beyond space, but from a tiny little village named Forst. For most citizens of Hamburg, there's no big difference between Forst and Outer Space. The name may remind you of a folksy choral society: The music of Harmonia is more utopian than the movie.
>
> Harmonia is one of those bands who doesn't know exactly what they will play before they take the stage. Sometimes, this can result in

endless rambling, but it can also lead to unforgettable moments that can only happen when something "clicks" between free, interacting musicians. On this evening, in 1976, it worked.

Because the shape of the old factory building suggests it, the band plays on two levels. On the left side in front of the stage, there's Michael Rother with his leopard-spotted Fender Mustang that was formerly owned by KRAFTWERK's Florian Schneider. On the right side, there's Hans-Joachim Roedelius at his tower of electronic devices. Onstage there's the band's trademark, the parasol with several blinking colored light bulbs. Under this parasol, Dieter Moebius reigns over his castle of electronics. A drum kit is also put up on the stage, but it won't be used before the second half of the evening starts. *DeLuxe*, HARMONIA's second album, has just been released, and guest musician Mani Neumeier plays the drums on it. Since he can't join the band this evening, Lutz Oldemeier takes his place. Actually, Oldemeier comes from a different musical field; he comes from jazz rockers AERA and MISSUS BEASTLY, but his style fits into HARMONIA's music well. For cushioning reasons, his kit is covered with white cloth. An old trick, even Ringo Starr already knew how to make use of it. It's done because HARMONIA plays on a low volume – so low that the sound of the uncovered drums would stand out too much. Only at the finale of their last regular track does the band pump up the volume for a couple of moments.

The encore is soft again: "Es war einmal" which appeared on the then brand-new CLUSTER album *Sowiesoso*. As always, when it gets later at the Fabrik, the sound of the music mingles more and more with the sound of smashing beer glasses, tipped over by spectators walking around.

The audience wants a second encore, but instead of playing another track, Roedelius, to the amused pleasure of the audience, shouts out: "Macht ihr doch mal was!" (It's your turn now!)

Over the in-house PA system, Lou Reed's *Transformer* starts, the record that every evening signals: We would like to clock off now.

There are not many spectators at the Fabrik tonight, maybe 50 or 60. That's at least a little bit more than the legendary 16 that were the audience on HARMONIA's *Live 1974* album[17]. Even if there are many details I can't remember anymore from this event that happened four decades ago, the concert as a whole still sticks in my mind. There are not too many concerts I can say that about.[18]

Commercially, as said, HARMONIA was a fiasco. This was one reason why the project couldn't be continued. The second reason was that Moebius and Roedelius hadn't given up on CLUSTER, and their plans to go on with it were not compatible with Rother's more commercial ideas about HARMONIA. Roedelius: "Moebius and I were unable to adapt ourselves to the conditions of the music business, to kowtow to what is called success, or to let producers meddle in our concept."[19] This turned HARMONIA into a dead horse, and they gave it up.

CLUSTER's album *Sowiesoso*, recorded again at Alter Weserhof and mixed at Conny's Studio, had been released in 1976 on Günter Körber's recently started Sky label, and it is CLUSTER's definitive masterpiece. No other album has the two of them closer together, or has a deeper overall atmosphere, than this one.

In 1976, during a trip from Berlin to Lausanne, Brian Eno stopped by the Alter Weserhof just to say hi and check out what the guys there were up to. They had invited him after his appearance in Hamburg. He ended up staying with them for eleven days. There were no plans on making an album, playing live or doing anything else, but of course, sessions took place. In an interview from 2005, Eno described his stay: "Working there was a very pleasant time. It was a sort of an air bubble in my history, partly because it was such an outlying area. We worked not far away from this mighty course of the river. The song 'By this River' from my album *Before And After Science* is bound to this place. We lived in this very quiet old farmhouse. There the Weser was a very fast, nearly raged river. For me it seemed to be like a picture of the immensely fast-running time. Compared to that, life in this old house seemed to be even calmer! The music that was created there had something magic. How can we make *something* from *nothing*? That was the main question. Like a legerdemain. We only had simple instruments, a simple studio. I don't even remember whether I had brought some equipment with me. We just used what was in this room, and that wasn't much."[20]

The meeting resulted in a couple of recordings; Eno took most of them with him. Two of these tracks later appeared on Roedelius's album *Theaterworks* from 1994. After Roedelius found some more tapes at Eno's home (Eno didn't even remember he had them), he gave the hissing recordings a Sonic Solution treatment out of his own pocket and released nine of them in 1997 as *Tracks And Traces* on Sony's S3 label. The project was marketed under the name HARMONIA 76. In 2009, Michael Rother added three recordings from his archives (cassette recordings that were preserved astonishingly well) for a rerelease of the album on Herbert Grönemeyer's Groenland label.

As the collaboration between Eno and CLUSTER had worked out fine, they met again at Conny Plank's studio. These meetings resulted in two records: *Cluster & Eno*, released in 1977, and *After The Heat*, credited for some reason not to CLUSTER but to ENO MOEBIUS ROEDELIUS (1978). Both albums had Holger Czukay as a guest musician, and both belong to the finest of their creations, beginning with the wonderful atmospheric cover photos and not ending with their smoothly melancholic overall mood. They turned out to be a blessing for the musicians, as well as for Sky Records: None of them entered the charts, they were slow burners, but the sales figures of both albums amounted to six-digit figures each.[21] Roedelius and Moebius lived off of the royalties they made with these two records for several years. If you need an example for what the name "Brian Eno" could do when it appeared on a record cover – here you have it.

A little anecdote about *Cluster & Eno*: When Roedelius, Moebius, and Eno had recorded 30 minutes of music, Eno ran out of time and had to leave. Thirty minutes were not enough to fill an album, but the date for cutting the master disc was already fixed. So, Hamburg-based musician Asmus Tietchens received an emergency call from Roedelius: Another track needed to be recorded to fill the gap, and it needed to happen very quickly.

Asmus Tietchens and Okko Bekker helped out. At Bekker's Audiplex Studio in Hamburg they recorded a six-and-a-half minute track, using guitar, prepared piano, and sitar, which became part of *Cluster & Eno* – but neither Roedelius, nor Moebius, nor Eno are in the track far and wide. They entitled it "One" – I wouldn't be surprised if this would be "Eno" spelled backwards; it would fit Tietchen's sense of humor. Interestingly, in his album review, music critic Manfred Gillig of *Sounds* wrote about just this track, with its "oriental-colored sitar and percussion sounds [it] takes much more a firm stand [than the rest of the album]" and reminded him of Eno's *Another Green World*.[22]

All these mentioned recordings belong to the most important works German rock musicians have produced. Who wants to decide whether this is "Berlin" or "Düsseldorf" School? We should call it "The School of the German Road of Fairy Tales".

SOLO

It's worth mentioning that there are a couple of albums Hans-Joachim Roedelius did solo or with a guest musician. Not all of these works are electronic albums. So far, Roedelius has recorded nearly 100 albums under his name, so it's hard to pick a handful of them, but I would like to highlight his first one, *Durch die Wüste*, recorded in 1976 and released 1978 on the Sky label (although it's a stereo recording, the CD release of *Durch die Wüste* on the Sky label is mono, probably by mistake. The Sky LP version as well as the later Bureau B rerelease is stereo). I'm convinced that the track "Regenmacher" influenced even Jasper van't Hof's success, *Pili Pili* from 1984.

Roedelius's *Selbstportraits I, II* and *III (Reise durch Arcadien)*, recorded during several years at Alter Weserhof at the open window, mainly with his organ, are still a nice listen; sometimes a cheap rhythm machine is ticking along. The albums were released in 1979 and 1980.

One of my personal solo Roedelius favorites is *Jardin au fou* (1979), produced and recorded by TANGERINE DREAM's Peter Baumann at his Paragon Studio in Berlin. Baumann had gotten the job and a good amount of money from the French label Barclay/Egg to produce three albums with electronic artists from Germany. One of them was Asmus Tietchens' adventurous first solo record *Nachtstücke* (Night Pieces), another one was Conrad Schnitzler's *Con*; both probably put the Barclay people in gray desperation. The third was Roedelius. Interestingly, he doesn't like this record. Paragon was a nearly perfect studio, with a first-class Steinway and all the modern recording possibilities you otherwise could only dream of, but Roedelius felt blocked by just that. He missed the sound of a river from outside, cows mooing, horses snuffling, and ducks quacking in front of the window. He filled track after track on the 16-track recording machine, but they, both Roedelius as well as Baumann, fell more and more into desperation about the results. Finally, Baumann gave up and left the recording work to his assistant Will Roper who mixed the final record from this material.[23] I can't help it, but for me this is a beautiful record.

Roedelius took the leftover recordings from these sessions home with him, and later finished and mixed them in Vienna. They became the album *Lustwandel* (1981) – another nice one. The CLUSTER album *Großes Wasser* (1979) is also a Paragon recording, which was recorded in parallel to the *Jardin au fou* sessions. It's not a bad album, but compared to its predecessors, you can feel it's a bit "undercooked". The studio's atmosphere comes through.

There are more. There's the mellotron-loaded *Geschenk des Augenblicks (Gift of the Moment)* from 1984, played on a mellotron that Roedelius discovered by chance in somebody's attic. The album exists thanks to Brian Eno's wife Anthea, who spontaneously decided to release it on their EG Records label. Another remarkable one is *Sinfonia Contempora No. 1 "From Time to Time"* (1994, a collage made from older recordings).

Beginning in the late 1980s, Roedelius turned more and more to the acoustic piano. He didn't trust electronically generated sounds anymore; after a woman had fainted during a CLUSTER concert, he feared the sounds could trigger health problems.[24] A Korean piano had been given to him by the Austrian Alban Berg Endowment (they also helped him with some home studio equipment, amounting to around 9000 dollars). The result was *Piano Piano*, first released on the Italian Materiali Sonori label in 1991. These were not his first solo piano recordings, there had been live recordings before, but they were not released before 2011 as *Roedelius Plays Piano (Bloomsbury Theater, London, July 28, 1985)*.

Roedelius, as I write these lines, is 86 and still active. Since around the year 2000 it's been obvious that – after a really adventurous life – he now finally receives the world-wide appreciation he had been entitled to for decades. It's only consequent that in 2017, he made it to Deutsche Grammophon's prestigious "Yellow Label" (*Einfluss*, with Arnold Kasar).

There are a couple of later albums by Dieter Moebius one should know; I would like to point out his solo work *Tonspuren* (1983), *Rastakraut Pasta* (1980) by MOEBIUS & PLANK, and *Moebius & Tietchens* (2012) by Dieter Moebius and Asmus Tietchens.

There is an unfortunately unfinished one from 2016: Moebius had been invited to write a score for Fritz Lang's silent masterpiece *Metropolis*. It should have been performed live with the film. Sadly, the Grim Reaper had his say before this could happen. Some finishing touches were added by Irene Moebius, Tim Story, Jon Leidecker, and Jonas Förster. What we have now are four pre-recorded backing tracks with a duration of about ten minutes each. The track titles are "Schicht", "Moloch", "Tiefenbahnen" und "Mittler"; if you ever watched the film, you will know which scenes they refer to. They were meant to serve as backing tracks that he would improvise live to. Several sorts of rhythmic statics melt together in a sort of collage, on this carpet colored noise, lots of metal sounds and ringing bells are dancing, and somewhere there's also a sample from the album *Cluster II*. The tracks provide an idea of what Moebius probably had in mind. I'm not sure whether this would have really been a good soundtrack for *Metropolis*; it's more my impression that the film was the inspirational source for this music. The movie doesn't only feature utopian architecture and technology, it also has a very strong romantic side. The original orchestral score by Gottfried Huppertz covered both aspects, and Moebius' music clearly misses out on the latter aspect. But this is not a flaw. Just take *Musik für Metropolis* as an album, and you will get Moebius "at his best". On this record, he does exactly what had always been his strong side: design irritating soundscapes you can live in after a time of orientation.

Here's one that's a bit out of line: *Liliental*, recorded in 1976, released 1978. It is not made by a "band", it's mainly a sort of spin-off product. Asmus Tietchens considers it "not really important"[25], but it's his first contribution as a musician that found its way on an album. Originally, *Liliental* should have been another solo record by Dieter Moebius, but he invited Tietchens and Okko Bekker to take part in it, and they couldn't say no to the opportunity to work for a whole week at Conny's Studio for free. By chance, because of a running Kraan recording, bass guitarist Hellmut Hattler and sax player Johannes "Alto" Pappert also appeared. Conny Plank himself played guitar, and in this way, the album came into existence, more or less out of session situations. Tietchens, Bekker, Moebius, and Plank can be heard on all six tracks; Hattler plays on the tracks on side 1, Pappert on side 2. The album swings between experiment and entertainment, is a convenient listen, and is seen today as a sort of insider's tip.

Cluster themselves also did several further albums. They are all worth listening to, but none of them tops *Sowiesoso*. The duo suffered at least two unpleasant breakups, followed by reunions, but in the end, the quarrel between the two of them couldn't be settled, so Cluster split up in 2010.

In 2017, Bureau B released two old live Cluster recordings on the album *Konzerte 1972/1977*, the first one is from the Fabrik in Hamburg, the 1977 recording is from the Festival International de la Science-Fiction in Metz (France). Listening to them makes it disconcertingly clear that the kind of unorganized noise from the *Cluster II* era was still part of their live act in 1977. You can barely hear any stylistic differences between the two recordings. For whatever reason, there hadn't been any development – what a strange rollback, happening at a point in time when *Zuckerzeit*, *Sowiesoso*, the Eno collaborations, and the Harmonia albums were long in stores. It becomes immediately clear why the Harmonia project couldn't be continued. What Michael Rother had in mind at that time was definitely already in a different league; it would have been impossible for him to go along with *this* stamping of Cluster. Roedelius puts it the other way around: "Michael strongly referred to himself or his own artistic ideas, with a stable opinion on how to tackle things and pull them through, and meanwhile we know how successful he was with this."[26]

"Isi" from *NEU! '75* already foreshadowed what was going to come. Rother now had his own studio at the Alter Weserhof, and because he was in a constant strife with Klaus Dinger (or Dinger with him), he asked CAN's Jaki Liebezeit to play the drums on his solo project – probably the best decision he could make.

After nine months of working at home and at Conny's Studio came out a fresh breeze of guitar and keyboard instrumentals that simply nobody had expected. When I walked by the neighborhood Govi record store, as I did every day, one of the salespersons was busy sorting new arrivals onto the shelves. When he spotted me through the shop window, he waved me in and handed me Michael Rother's first solo album: "Here, this is something for you!" And he was right. *Flammende Herzen* (Flaming Hearts) was melodic, excellent sounding, easygoing but not simple, well-thought-out. Rother's basic idea had been to develop a guitar style that worked without vibrato or pitch bending and had no connection to blues. The album was released on Sky Records in 1977. The Deutsche Austrophon, the company that distributed Sky's records, only ordered 150 copies – ridiculous, but somehow understandable after the experiences with CLUSTER and HARMONIA, and you had to know at least NEU! and the backstory of KRAFTWERK to have any clue about who Michael Rother was.

Most critics reacted enthusiastically. Manfred Gillig in *Sounds* wrote: "These 'Flaming Hearts' hit the bull's eye, a feast for the ears! Aloof from all Teutonic earnestness and uptightness and unconcerned of all archetypes or comparisons that may come to mind about this music category – see Eno, CLUSTER, KRAFTWERK – on his record, Michael Rother has figured out a kind of music that's not only clever, not only peaceful and relaxed, not only melodic and mellow, not only electronic, but also electrifying and animating to hum along with (even without lyrics), and it has this air of simple grandeur that has become rare today – the stuff hits are made of."[27] Even the *New Musical Express* stated "striking body of music of an unusual making."[28]

But Austrophon seemed to be right, the record was a shelf-warmer – until finally Winfried Trenkler played the record in his "Schwingungen" show at WDR radio. After it had gotten airplay, *Flammende Herzen* climbed up the hill: All in all, the album sold around 150,000 copies[29] – which was a sensation for both German rock conditions and Sky Records, and suddenly Michael Rother even became a household name in the wider rock circle.

Director Walter Bockmayer (1948-2014) used music and title for his low budget film *Flammende Herzen* (1977/78), a sort of romantic tragicomedy about a shy Bavarian bachelor who wins a trip to New York City, where in the subway he meets a dirndl-wearing blonde. Later at an Oktoberfest imitation festival, the two of them win a living cow which they walk through the streets of Manhattan with – finally to the abattoir.

Rother's next albums, *Sterntaler* ("Star Money", after a Grimm fairytale, 1978) and *Katzenmusik* ("cat music", but the word in German also means "caterwauling", 1979), both again with Jaki Liebezeit, followed on seamlessly. In the *Sounds* poll 1978, the readers voted Rother as "best German musician" and "best instrumentalist"; *Sterntaler* was voted third-best record of the year.[30]

The follow-up *Fernwärme* (literally "long-distance heating", but it could also be read as "warmth from far away") took three years, and the success of his first three albums made it possible to sign with the Polydor label. But this story already belongs in the 1980s, and we will come back to it later.

DÜSSELDORF SCHOOL

Going from Michael Rother to Düsseldorf and to KRAFTWERK is a small step. KRAFTWERK's story is well documented and can be found in several books, as well as on the web. But we have to see that, artistically, KRAFTWERK is one of Germany's most influential bands and an important article of cultural export; it's only in this connection that TANGERINE DREAM, Klaus Schulze, (later) EINSTÜRZENDE NEUBAUTEN, and (even later) RAMMSTEIN, could keep up with them. There are German pop projects like BONEY M or MILLI VANILLI who were commercially successful in certain foreign countries, but musically, they are not something that needs to be discussed here. But what is interesting is the *reception* of KRAFTWERK in Germany, compared to their reception in foreign countries.

It needed someone like Conny Plank to transform the many half-baked ideas that flew around in Düsseldorf's air into sellable albums.[1] Reading Rüdiger Esch's oral history "Electri_City" from 2014 makes two things apparent:

First, Düsseldorf was a relatively closed circuit, small, and good parts of it were organized around the Kunstakademie and affiliated places like the Creamcheese, a pub and gallery furnished by artists Günther Uecker, Ferdinand Kriwet, and filmmaker Lutz Mommartz. Since around 1975 there has also been the Ratinger Hof, seen today as the birthplace of German punk.

Second: Musically, KRAFTWERK was the center of it all. Today, bands and musicians from Düsseldorf still revolve around KRAFTWERK, try to work off of them, are at odds with them, try to sail in their shipping channel, try *not* to sail in their shipping channel, try to play them down, or try to ridicule them. Up to present day, KRAFTWERK has been seen as "our very own" in Düsseldorf and is still a benchmark, although the band has been playing in a completely different league since *Trans Europa Express*, and now, more or less, has turned into being its own memorial.

Kraftwerk started in 1968, at that time under the name of Organisation, after Ralf Hütter and Florian Schneider-Esleben (1947-2020) had met in a class at the Remscheid Academy. Schneider came from a band named Pissoff with Eberhard Kranemann, Hütter had played organ in several amateur bands, among them the Phantoms and the Rambo Zambo Bluesband. As Organisation, they had already come under the wings of Conny Plank. He found "some nice stuff" in the demos they played to him and considered it worth working with these guys. Organisation – the original full name was Organisation zur Verwirklichung gemeinsamer Musikkonzepte (Organization for the realization of collective music concepts) – was a quintet consisting of Hütter, Schneider, Basil Hammoudi, Butch Hauf, and Alfred Mönicks. Their music, as well as their stage appearance, was purest Krautrock, with all its bells and whistles. Plank produced the first album with them at Rhenus Studio and managed to sell it to RCA Records in England: *Tone Float* (1970); it was never officially released in Germany.

Ralf Hütter and Florian Schneider probably needed this quintet to realize that this was not what they wanted to do, although I'm sure at the time they had no clear idea about what they could be up to instead.

But they were part of the Düsseldorf art scene. There, they lived their lives, and being part of the art scene left traces and opened doors. Hütter: "We were lucky. We started performing at a time, since 1968, when there had still been great freedom. We could play for five hours just to try to explore our limits, without somebody telling us what to do. The director of Kunstmuseum Mönchengladbach, Johannes Cladders, like me, was from Krefeld. He hired us completely spontaneously: 'Just come to us and play next Saturday at the opening of the Joseph Beuys exhibition.' We really could do whatever we wanted to do there! I had an electronic rhythm machine, and the music was like running by itself, then slowly we left the stage, mingled with the audience on the dancefloor and danced. At that time this was possible! … When you're on the Ratinger Straße in the evening, playing the pinball machine or table soccer with Beuys and his team, you can't make schlager music the next day."[2]

The first Kraftwerk album was different from *Tone Float*. And not only this, it also was different from almost everything all other bands in Germany did at that time. Hütter: "We were looking for our way, and we stuck to this way."[3]

Like Can, Faust, Cluster, and some others, they came to the conclusion that they needed their own studio. Their initially nameless studio, a loft in a business house in the red light district near the Düsseldorf main station, became their headquarters for around forty years, although their early albums were not recorded there. They said goodbye to most classic rock instruments. Florian Schneider played several flutes, a violin, tone generators, a Framus eight-string lap steel guitar and an early ARP Odyssey synthesizer; he had even played as a session flutist alongside Olaf Kübler with Klaus Doldinger (on the album *El Condor Pasa – Paul Nero in South America* by Paul Nero Sounds, 1970). His father, architect Paul Schneider-Esleben, would have liked to see his son become an architect too, but Florian preferred going into professional music. At the Remscheid Academy, Florian met Ralf Hütter of Krefeld. Hütter, son of a textile entrepreneur, studied architecture and – at that time – was serious about it. He had a Hammond L-100 and a Farfisa organ and e-piano (the same one Can's Irmin Schmidt had). In 1972 he purchased a Minimoog: "My first synthesizer was monophonic and cost exactly as much as my grey Volkswagen Standard, the Beetle from our record cover." He bought it "at Studio Funk in Hamburg, which was the only dealer in Germany who carried it. I still have the receipt: 5500 D-Marks. I had to save up my money for a long time for it."[4] Kraftwerk (as all Düsseldorf bands, for some reason) never owned or used a modular Moog or a Synthi-100.

There are parallels between early Cluster albums and tracks like "Stratovarius" and "Megaherz" from Kraftwerk's debut album, the pre-industrial side 2 of *Kraftwerk 2*, "Tongebirge", and the intro section of "Ananas Symphonie" from *Ralf & Florian*. For some reason this is rarely recognized. There are even more remarkable parallels between "Sowiesoso" and "Es war einmal" from Cluster's album *Sowiesoso* and Kraftwerk's "Heimatklänge" and "Tanzmusik" from *Ralf & Florian* and "Mitternacht" and "Morgenspaziergang" from side 2 of *Autobahn* – it is not the melodies, but the ideas behind the tunes, which are similar. Waves were swinging between Düsseldorf and Forst. This is not really a mystery: The musicians knew each other; Roedelius had been friends with Florian Schneider's sister Claudia for a while; in 1971, Cluster and Kraftwerk had a joint concert at the Audimax in Hamburg. They watched each other, and through doing so, they influenced each other.

Now add the fact that Michael Rother played not only with Kraftwerk, but also with Spirit of Sound, where later Kraftwerk percussionist Wolfgang Flür started; another offspring of this band was Wolfgang Riechmann (more about him later).

Klaus Dinger, for a short time, had been KRAFTWERK's drummer. Rother played with him in NEU!. For around half a year, Michael Rother and Klaus Dinger were even part of the KRAFTWERK trio line-up without Ralf Hütter. KRAFTWERK, in their early years, sometimes even jammed with CAN from neighboring Cologne, and CAN's Jaki Liebezeit later played the drums on Rother's first four solo records.

You see, somehow all of these musicians were connected, or at least part of a biotope of creative people who all knew and influenced each other. This went on for several years.

When KRAFTWERK's first album came out in 1970, Yours Truly was 14 years old, and I remember that I heard it for the first time from the record I already owned. It was the second LP I bought myself. (The first one, if memory serves, had been IRON BUTTERFLY's *In-A-Gadda-Da-Vida*, just a couple of weeks before – yes, the one with what is likely the most tedious drum solo of all time, but back then, the album was a sort of "must have".) Since I was little, I have had a liking for typefaces and special graphic elements, so it was the sleeve in a shop window, this day-glo red drawing of a traffic cone on white ground, the lettering (probably from the big Stencil font family or something similar) that touched a nerve and gave me the impulse to buy this album without knowing it – which, for a fourteen-year old, meant putting a lot of money on the table. But I didn't regret it. In my room, I only had an old Telefunken mono record player that was more of a saw than a player. At least it was connected to a great-sounding Telefunken "Concertino" tube radio, but I wanted the stereo sound, so I gave this record its first spin on our Dual stereo turntable in the living room and immediately fell in love with "Ruckzuck", especially with the tone color of the organ and the phasing effect. "Stratovarius" was fine; I used the noise in the middle of the track for some adventurous sound collage stuff I did with a microphone, a radio, a metal ashtray, two cassette decks, and a borrowed Grundig reel-to-reel tape deck. "Vom Himmel hoch" was not my favorite – it was okay, at least I liked the drums (played by Klaus Dinger; on the other tracks we hear Andreas Hohmann). "Megaherz" was initially not my cup of tea, but interestingly, after a couple of spins, it became my favorite track on the album. The entire record had a sort of softly enigmatic dark humor and technological romanticism that hooked me. I was used to listening to "serious" electronic music on the radio, and I loved a lot of it, but that stuff was *really* serious. Now, for the first time, I heard something like this in combination with the feeling of rock music. I had been looking for it without knowing it.

The black and white photo taken by Bernd and Hilla Becher on the inner sleeve was also something I loved about this record. Of course I had no idea then who they were, but this picture of a transformer on rails looked "right" to me. As I learned much later, it was a photo that didn't fit into one of the typologies by which the Bechers used to organize their works, and because everybody knows everybody in Düsseldorf, Hilla Becher gave it to Ralf Hütter.

Of course I had to play this wonderful new discovery for my friends and all school mates available, and I was completely flabbergasted to learn that many of them saw this album as *funny*. With all seriousness and naiveté 14-year olds are able to display, they saw it as a sort of comedy record. KRAFTWERK – a novelty band? Really? Yes, and later we will confront this again.

Divergent from the reactions I got, the first KRAFTWERK album received good reviews in the rock music press. *Sounds*: "KRAFTWERK connects the sophistication of contemporary electronic music with the dynamic of rock music – a successful combination of intellect and emotion," including a special praise: "Here, once again, Conny Plank proves to be one of Germany's most competent sound engineers."[5] The LP sold around 60,000 copies and reached #30 in German album charts.

In 1971, when Ralf Hütter left the band for half a year with the intention of finishing his architecture studies (which he never did), Florian Schneider, Michael Rother, and Klaus Dinger worked as a trio. They made an appearance on Germany's TV show "Beat-Club", and when you watch it today, it becomes obvious that this was not really KRAFTWERK, it was NEU! with "guest musician" Florian Schneider. There was an intuitive musical connection between Rother and Dinger, while Schneider seemed to be a little bit left out, and the three of them did not know what to do with this constellation. On the afternoon of Saturday, May 22, 1971, when this "Beat-Club" episode originally aired, I was lucky to be able to watch it because, exactly on this afternoon, my grandparents (yes, the Wandervogel ones) celebrated their golden anniversary. I had a short opportunity to sneak out and watch TV for maybe half an hour with my cousin, and that was just the moment when KRAFTWERK was on screen. It was exhausting because my cousin explained to me over and over again that this was not real music. Today, this tune from the show is sometimes known under the title "Rückstoß-Gondoliere" (Repulsion Gondolier) or, on some bootleg CDs, "Vor dem Blauen Bock" (Before the Blue Buck). The latter title relates to "Zum Blauen Bock", a corny music show on German TV with folksy oompah and merry operetta melodies I've already described earlier.

The trio Rother/Dinger/Schneider at Star Studio cut what was supposed to be KRAFTWERK's second album, but it didn't work. Down to the present day this material has never seen the light of day. Quarrels came up between all three musicians, and finally Dinger and Rother left. A few weeks later, Ralf Hütter and Florian Schneider rejoined and switched on the generator again.

My schoolmates' amusement towards the band stopped when *Kraftwerk 2* was released at the end of 1971. There was nothing that could be seen as funny anymore, except maybe "Atem", but that tended to lead to headshaking, or maybe "Harmonika" which I think was just a filler to reach 40 minutes. The album's overall mood was dark, the traffic cone in day-glo green looked somehow unreal, as did the inner sleeve photos. I remember I was terribly disappointed when I gave the LP its first spin. I expected something like a continuation of the first album, but what they delivered this time was far from that. No drums this time, instead they had a rhythm machine ticking along, and on side 2 there was long strumming on guitar and bass guitar. There was no recognizable synthesizer or electronics except a wah-wah pedal and some heavy distortion. I immediately wanted to sell this album and wrote a notice for the bulletin board at school. But the next morning in school, for some reason, I didn't pin it. An inner voice probably told me to keep the album – and rightly so, because it started growing on me. It hasn't completely lost its magic up to this day (and I still stumble upon the editing flaw at 10'20" in "Kling Klang" – somebody, probably Conny, cut away one quarter note too many there.) The album reached #36 in German album charts; NDR radio even played "Kling Klang" in their daily 25-minute afternoon show "Nach der Schule – Musik für junge Leute".

My friends and I were sure the next KRAFTWERK album would take another year, be called *Kraftwerk 3*, and that the traffic cone on it would be yellow or blue. But it wasn't. It took two years, and to our surprise, it was entitled *Ralf & Florian* (lettered in a Gothic typeface, of all things!) and only had a small cone on it (half photo, half delineation, again red), like a memento. Instead, the front cover was filled with a black and white portrait photo of the two of them that looked like high school boys in anticipation of their graduation ball. The whole front cover looked unprofessional. The back cover was more interesting; it had a photo which showed a nice panorama of their studio, including Ralf's new Minimoog. The way the instruments were placed there was more or less identical with their stage set-up at that time. For some reason, friends and classmates often compared this album to Mike Oldfield's *Tubular Bells*. I could live with that, although Oldfield's recording had nothing to do with any kind of electronics.

Ralf & Florian was an important first step to more independence. This album wasn't recorded at Star Studio under usual conditions. This time, Conny Plank recorded it at Rhenus and some other studios he had the opportunity to use, and parts were recorded at their own Kling Klang Studio now. KRAFTWERK had also founded their own music publishing company. They were among the first bands to do this; record companies usually didn't accept such ideas.

Ralf Hütter made good use of his Minimoog now, still in combination with tape manipulations ("Kristallo") and some sound effects that might have been developed by Conny Plank ("Elektrisches Roulette", "Tongebirge"). The slightly flippant "Tanzmusik" and some other KRAFTWERK music was said to be used by the ballet company of the Staatsoper Stuttgart[6], which, at that time, would have been no other than world-famous choreographer John Cranko, but the theater's programs don't reveal whether this really happened. "Ananas Symphonie" was the first time KRAFTWERK used a vocoder. The words "Ananas Symphonie" were all it was used for, but it was the beginning of Florian Schneider's love for artificial voices and speech that later became one of KRAFTWERK's trademarks.

Ralf & Florian got good reviews – Hans-Joachim Krüger in *Sounds*: "… nearly a touch of nostalgia in the choice of titles (…), musically a double-jump forward by swinging electronic adaptations of such lugubrious themes"[7], but the album didn't reach any chart positions.

KRAFTWERK has never been a "band" in the word's usual meaning. Very early on, they had already started being a sort of multimedia project. The consequent design of their first two albums had shown this already, but this time there was more: The first edition of *Ralf & Florian* came with a poster-sized cartoon that illustrated the tracks; unfortunately, it was laid-out in a way that you couldn't hang it on the wall like a poster. The creator of these pages was artist Emil Schult, a Beuys student from Kunstakademie Düsseldorf. His contributions are an important part of KRAFTWERK's visual image; he also sometimes played guitar on stage and co-wrote some lyrics on later albums.

It's more than a little bit of a pity that up to this day KRAFTWERK still hasn't been willing to re-release these first three albums. Obviously, Ralf Hütter wants to see the beginning of the "real" KRAFTWERK in the *Autobahn* album from 1974, and commercially, he might be right. It's not for nostalgia reasons that I say this, it's because I seriously think that these three albums are important chapters in the story of German rock. I can't see a qualitative reason to hide them either, and there isn't any real gap between the first three and later albums. From my understanding, there is a continuous development from the first album to their fifth, *Radio-Aktivität*. *Autobahn*, especially its side 2, and *Radio-Aktivität*, are connected much deeper to *Ralf & Florian* than to, say, *Trans Europa Express* or *Die Mensch-Maschine*. The real gap in the evolution of KRAFTWERK, in my opinion, lies between *Radio-Aktivität* and *Trans Europa Express*.

Autobahn (1974) became KRAFTWERK's next strike, their last album for Philips, and a breakthrough that nobody really anticipated. Conny Plank's then assistant, Hans Lampe: "Already during the mix I thought: 'Okay, coherent concept, cool thing, hat off. Makes sense: Wir fahr'n, fahr'n, fahr'n auf der Autobahn. But there was not the feeling in the air: 'Gosh, this is a historic moment! What we are just mixing here is a milestone in music history.'"[8] I'm not so sure about this. When they heard the finished title track for the first time in its full duration of 22'30" at Conny's Studio, they may not have smelled the commercial hit, but they *must* have felt they had "something special" at hand.

"Autobahn" was and still is a unique stroke of genius, there's no other word. The track fills all of side 1; side 2 has two variations of a 45 they had made on the occasion of Comet Kohoutek that became visible in December 1973. With "Mitternacht" (Midnight) and "Morgenspaziergang" (Morning Stroll) two atmospheric tracks followed – all in all, a sort of walk through Mother Nature from dusk to sunrise. The album was not completely electronic – we also hear a violin, flutes, piano, and electric guitar, which I think gave side 2 this deep connection to its predecessors. The sound of the starting Volkswagen Beetle that opens the title track is not – as some people use to think – from Hütter's own car; it's taken from an archive record with several vehicles and other technical sounds (*Geräusche in Stereo – Stereo Sound Effects*, from the Europa label) – you can hear this same starting Volkswagen on Europa's audio play record *Die drei ???, Vol. 19: Die drei ??? und der Teufelsberg* (1980).

Autobahn received friendly reviews in Germany: "A trip on the Autobahn, by electronic devices bizarrely set to music in a way that all hell is let loose … All in all, KRAFTWERK's *Autobahn* is a varied and particularly amusing trip, especially under headphones leaving its traces",[9] said Hans-Joachim Krüger in *Sounds*, and U.S. magazine *Cash Box* assumed that "a significant role in the progressive music devolves to KRAFTWERK."[10]

In the U.S., the album had been released on Philips' affiliate label Vertigo. It had the same cover painting as the German version, on the front cover an autobahn scene, beautifully painted and collaged by Emil Schult, somehow idealizing the wirtschaftswunder era and, simultaneously, spoofing it: For Germans it was a bit like getting a pat on the back, while for U.S. and English people, it represented the image of Germany. The back sleeve showed the four musicians on the back seats of a car, still looking like a bunch of hippies. Actually, it's Emil Schult sitting on the right side, but they pasted Wolfgang Flür over his face. Only the font on the front cover was different – instead of the classic Futura (which became KRAFTWERK's corporate typeface for the next couple of years), the U.S. cover used a more art nouveau oriented one, for whatever reason, and the back cover had the "Autobahn" lyrics, including a translation (and Ralf Hütter, as often, is misspelled as "Ralph").

Since it was impossible to get any airplay on the important AM radio with a track of nearly 23 minutes in the U.S., Vertigo decided to cut "Autobahn" down to a 3'27" version. It worked; the "Autobahn" 45 got airplay, and – not least because of its unusualness – it climbed up to #23 in the *Billboard* charts. Not an earth-shaking success, but for a German band, this was respectable, and enough to get heard in the States. Young Americans who had these tiny little transistor radios that could only receive AM stations became especially curious and bought the album – just to experience a 23-minute surprise. The average John Doe listener who heard "Autobahn" in their car radio or somewhere in a supermarket took the song as a novelty record anyway. It's unlikely that many Americans realized the true potential of this tune, with the exception of some musicians.

The way Hütter and Schneider dealt with Conny Plank might be less pleasing. Ira Blacker of the U.S. record company came to Hamburg and gave them a lot of money (in cash – apparently he wasn't sure whether Germans already had bank accounts) for the right to cut the track down. Plank couldn't join this meeting, so they didn't negotiate and simply accepted the money. Back in Düsseldorf, they bought Plank out with 5000 D-Marks. He had been the producer, but now they only mentioned him as: "Engineer: Konrad Plank – Conny's Studio & mobile equipment" on the sleeve, and of course, he was disappointed. Early KRAFTWERK member, Eberhard Kranemann, sees a "bloody injustice" in this: "It's a pity that Conny took that money. He shouldn't have done that. Because from then on they didn't name him as producer anymore. From then on Florian and Ralf were the autocrats in the KRAFTWERK cosmos. ... I still hold this against them."[11] Michael Rother's view on the affair is a little bit more deliberated: "For his studio, Conny needed a lot of money he didn't have, and I think that this money was simply offered to him. For sure this was a big temptation. In return for this, he got bought out from *Autobahn* before it became a success. There are always two parties involved in a deal, as this story shows in several ways, and whether this would turn out to be a bad deal was not foreseeable at that time. 5000 D-Marks was a lot of money."[12] It might also play a role that every artist at one point in his career has to kill his mentor to find his own way – maybe this is what happened. The important point, in my view at least, is that the deal was done *before* the record hit the charts.

However, the news that a German band had reached U.S. charts gave the record a big push at home. In Germany, the 45 went up to #9 and the album reached #7. For some reason, the 45 released in Germany and the U.K. was not the same version as the U.S. one. It was shorter, only 3'05".

Meanwhile, in the United States, the DJs of several FM stations and college radios (low-power FM stations run by college and university students; they were usually only heard on and around their respective campuses) had discovered the album version of "Autobahn", and in April 1975, when Kraftwerk appeared in the U.S. for their first tour, these stations started playing it nonstop. The *Autobahn* album climbed up to #5 in the U.S. *Billboard* charts. The band was lucky. Two or three years earlier, this success would not have been possible. The main reason for this was the increasing importance of FM radio in the U.S. since the early 1970s. These stations were heard mainly in cities, but that was exactly where the main buyers for a band like Kraftwerk lived, and that's also the place to find the stores carrying the album. In small-town America, this could be a problem – the 45 was available in every mall as long as it was in the Top 40, but the album was not something to be had everywhere.

The press reactions to Kraftwerk in the U.S. were something between friendly and curious. The upcoming tour was announced in the entertainment or amusements sections of several local papers: "A blizzard unfortunately kept Kraftwerk from Philadelphia where they were slated to begin their tour. Kraftwerk ... is one of the first German groups to rise above cult status and make a heavy impact on the pop market" (*Bucks County Courier Times*, Levittown, Pennsylvania)[13]; "Many people feel that 'Autobahn', along with its electronic predecessor, Mike Oldfield's *Tubular Bells*, heralds a new era for commercial electronic rock" (*The Advocate*, Newark, New Jersey)[14]; or backstage banter like this: "Autobanned: Kraftwerk, the German group with a hit, 'Autobahn', fired opening act Greenslade from their U.S. tour after four dates [because they were] continually offending Kraftwerk and always begging for more time to play ... Greenslade told us: '... but when I tried to speak to one of them, he ran away and locked himself in his dressing room'" (*News Journal*, Mansfield, Ohio)[15] – and more highly interesting gossip like this. (It was a rather strange idea anyway to have the British prog band Greenslade as a supporting act for Kraftwerk, but nobody had a real idea about what Kraftwerk was doing.)

When Kraftwerk took American stages, they had changed their image dramatically. The hippie image from the back sleeve was passé, they had short haircuts, appeared in suits on stage, and hardly moved. They became a hot topic among college students and young people. Americans accepted Kraftwerk for doing something no American act would have done. It might also be that a slight acoustic misunderstanding had helped: The lines "Wir fahr'n, fahr'n, fahr'n auf der Autobahn" (We drive, drive, drive on the autobahn) were misheard by many as "fun, fun, fun on the autobahn" and somehow seen as a bow to the Beach Boys. This was nonsense; the Kraftwerk guys liked the Beach Boys, but that's all. There is only one vocal harmony in the piece that could be reminiscent of typical Beach Boys harmony vocals, and it's not more than one syllable: "… die Sonne scheint mit Glitzer*strahl*". However, this false Beach Boys connection goes with Kraftwerk up to present day.

More concerts were added. Nearly every evening they damaged PA speakers with extreme electronic bass, and finally, the PA rental company became furious. This was the moment when Kraftwerk decided that they needed their own PA. On their second tour, half a year later, they traveled with their own PA equipment. Seven tons of equipment now made the tour more expensive, but it had to be.

Autobahn now also entered U.K. charts; the album reached #25 and the 45 climbed up to #10. For the U.K. release, the album got a new cover. Instead of Emil Schult's painting, it showed the blue European "Autobahn" (motorway) traffic sign.

All over the years, I have felt somewhat connected to Kraftwerk: I always had a feeling that music representing the here and now of (fill in a year between 1970 and 1982) should sound like *this sound in my head* – and then, when Kraftwerk released a new album, it sounded like *this sound in my head*. I've seen Kraftwerk seven times on stage, the first time in Hamburg in 1971, the last time in Chicago in 2014. I couldn't say which concert was best. In a way, they were all special. One should never forget that when you're a teenager, or even a university student, you react much more sensitively to music because it is *new*. You have never heard it before. The older you get, the more you can compare things to earlier experiences, and this makes it less electrifying. At the first two concerts, Kraftwerk was still a completely different band, not comparable to their later performances. I'm not even sure about the line-ups anymore – had I known that half a century later I would write a book about it, I would have made some notes, but sorry, I didn't. I simply enjoyed the show without having any idea about the enormous impact they would have on the international pop music scene a decade later. I guarantee that even the band members themselves hadn't expected this.

Kraftwerk's appearance in a 1974 Easter festival in Hamburg was memorable. The *Autobahn* album wasn't out yet and Kraftwerk was the headliner of the first festival day, but because all the other bands had overrun their time schedule, Kraftwerk couldn't begin until around 10:30 pm. Their stage set-up was the same as on the back sleeve of the *Ralf & Florian* album. What was especially impressive was their custom-built bass speaker with the horn, but in addition to the cover photo, there was now an electronic drum pad played by a new guy who wasn't introduced, but turned out to be Wolfgang Flür. Half of the audience was interested in the band, the other half booed at them, catcalling and shouting for "Ruckzuck" over and over. Kraftwerk had been playing for just 25 minutes, when suddenly the hall light went on and the security started kicking the audience out – the venue had to be empty at 11 pm. It might not be connected, but after this incident, Kraftwerk stopped performing in Germany until 1981. A planned German tour in 1975 – the "Autobahn" tour, after their big success in the U.S. – was cancelled. I still have the concert poster for their cancelled Hamburg show; now framed.

Many critics and fans took Kraftwerk's U.S. tour amiss – "Now they sell out. Now they want to be big business. They can't be taken seriously anymore." This was a common way of thinking, not only among young people, but also among envious colleagues, and even more among arts & entertainment journalists who primarily saw themselves as "progressive". (This is not an especially German thing; Laurie Anderson had to go through the same experience in her circuit at home in New York when 'O Superman' unexpectedly became a hit in the U.K in 1981. She used the chance to sign with Warner Records, and many of her colleagues saw this as treason.) Besides this, there was KRAFTWERK's new image, their new look, which was now as serious as a classical string quartet. And they played synthesizers, God help us! Electronics didn't resonate well with the latent technophobia many Germans had developed during these years.

When KRAFTWERK released *Radio-Aktivität*, this phenomenon appeared even more. The album's title and most of its lyrics are a play on the meanings of "radio" and "activity" – that's why there is a hyphen in the title, but understanding this was apparently asking too much from the brains of several German journalists. I have always seen this album as a sort of homage to the airwaves produced by radio stations, especially shortwave stations. But many in Germany misunderstood the album as a homage to nuclear power, and their only possible response to that had to be refusal. Not that this is completely unjustified, but *Radio-Aktivität* simply didn't make any serious statements about this topic. However, it hit a sensitive spot (remember Roedelius' fear about the two nuclear power plants near Forst!). 1975 was the time when, all over Germany, citizen's initiative groups against nuclear power started working, and people could see the first traces of what (in 1980) began to finally manifest in the Green Party. Releasing an album named *Radio-Aktivität* in this agenda was something that couldn't be true. To make matters worse, the music on this album was not easy listening. All in all, this was a combination that made *Sounds* critic Teja Schwaner go ballistic: "The many citizen's initiatives against nuclear power plants might get the creeps when they have to listen to this voice, singing in a hushed tone: 'Für dich und mich im All entsteht / Radioaktivität' ... Gee, sometimes you don't know whether the system on the tonearm is fucked up or only a Geiger counter flips out again because the musical 'fall-out' is dangerous to life."[16] Because a critic has to be oh-so-critical, he also had to mention that "this sinus singsong is distributed now by the world's biggest record corporation EMI."[17] Still today, it's a mystery to me why *Sounds* gave this record to a critic who usually reviewed stuff like LYNYRD SKYNYRD or Bruce Springsteen; the slating review was programmed this way. But maybe this was their intention.

There were also some complaints about the record cover. The "Volksempfänger" (people's radio receiver) indeed had been a propaganda invention of the Nazi party; it was cheap, everybody could buy it, but it was intendedly insensitive. You could mainly listen to the local station, the receiver was built in a way that made it hard to catch faraway foreign stations. In the vernacular of that time, this receiver was called "Goebbelsschnauze" (snout of Goebbels). Karl Bartos had found one of these radios at a flea market and thought it might make a good record cover. In the end, they only used the rear side of the device for the back cover; the front side was replaced by a drawn volksempfänger because the real one had a swastika on its chassis.

However, the KRAFTWERKers noticed that they had unintentionally gotten themselves into a strange light. They couldn't change the record anymore, but when KRAFTWERK presented the song during their world tour in 1981, they added the little word "stop" before the word "Radio-Aktivität" and now sang about "death through radiation" and "mutation".

With the 1977 album *Trans Europa Express*, KRAFTWERK fully transitioned into a new image, and EMI treated them with their own Kling Klang Schallplatten vanity label. *Trans Europa Express* was the first KRAFTWERK album without any non-electronic instruments (except the metal plates in "Metall auf Metall"), and it divided the hearts even more. Now you were either a die-hard KRAFTWERK fan or you left the boat.

With their 1978 album *Die Mensch-Maschine* (The Man Machine), KRAFTWERK had to deal with something new, called "Neue Deutsche Welle". More about this (and further KRAFTWERK) later.

NEU!

What about NEU! in the meantime? After they had left KRAFTWERK, with Conny Plank's connections, Michael Rother and Klaus Dinger were able to use the relatively well-equipped Windrose-Dumont-Time Studio in Hamburg during the night hours for little money. The recording process didn't take more than four nights. These recordings then were mixed a couple of nights later at Star Studio, and the deal was, again, that studio owner Ralf Arnie got the publishing rights of the recorded works. The result was *NEU!*, released in 1972, and this album was unheard of in a way that we simply have to call timeless. It was another album I purchased without any prior exposure; I trusted it because there were KRAFTWERK guys involved, and the sleeve design gave the final kick.

The *NEU!* album sounds more complex than it actually is (which is not meant to be seen as negative). Listening with headphones reveals not only its simplicity, but also the richness of ideas they invested in it. *NEU!* is electronic music without a synthesizer or other electronics, but producer Conny Plank made very clever use of the possibilities the mixing desk offered to shape and modify sounds. Klaus Dinger played the drums. In parts, they were looped so he could add a second layer. He also played guitar and an instrument indicated as "japan banjo" which is not actually a banjo, but a *taishōgoto* or Nagoya harp. (An instrument of this kind can be heard more clearly in HARMONIA's "Walky-Talky" on the album *DeLuxe.*) Michael Rother played a Gibson Les Paul guitar, a modified old guitar he called "dehguitar", a bass guitar, and an upright bass. He used a fuzz box that was custom-made for him, but the guy who mounted it had built in a flaw. That's where the interesting sound comes from, and when Rother ordered a copy of this box several years later, he insisted that this flaw had to be included. Besides this, there were some delay units and wah-wah pedals, but that's mainly all they used. You rarely hear more than three sound sources at the same time on the record. The NEU! sound is mainly based on Dinger's inimitably straight drumming style (along with Dinger, I hate the often-used term "motorik") and Rother's handling of guitar feedback and the eBow. All of this combined with some snippets of field recordings Dinger had made, like the jackhammers and audience noises you can hear in "Negativland". They also used some recordings Dinger had made in Norway on a rowing boat tour with his girlfriend at the time. All of this was well balanced by Conny Plank, who also added speed variations, manually-produced tape phasing, or backing tracks running backwards. Rother: "He understood where we were going, what we had in mind, our intentions; he picked them up very early and, with his experience at the mixing desk, he organized the sounds. Klaus and I wouldn't have been able to create the organized sound. That was Conny's part. We contributed the basic ideas, the message of the music and the individual tracks, but if you listen for instance to a track like 'Hallogallo', it is still today a mystery to me how Conny could remember the good parts of my guitars and the less good parts, and that over a span of ten minutes. There was no computer aided mixing; the three of us would stand next to one another, he was the main operator and we would help out when more than two hands were needed. But to memorize these things, the tone color of my guitar, we called them 'clouds' - the short melodies, backwards and forwards - and to organize all this was such an amazing contribution. Without Conny Plank it would have been a very different and probably not as half as pleasing result, so he was a very important character in the picture. … Klaus was this kind of guy, he was very strong-headed, and to be honest, I guess he compensated his lack of technical skills on drums. If you compare him to a gifted drummer like Jaki Liebezeit, who has passed and is no longer with us, Jaki was the naturally gifted drummer. Klaus was a strong person and he invested a lot of energy and determination in his drumming, and that was Klaus and what he could do. He played the way he played and I liked it; it made it easy for me to add colors and layers on that strong basis if you had the chance to do overdubs. When we tried to play live as a duo in 1972, we failed completely because it was just the two of us, and there were not enough layers in the music - just one drum kit and one guitar, that didn't take us far. But with Conny Plank at the desk, you must always remember to point out his contribution."[18]

The original first edition of *NEU!* had an excellent sound quality and ended with the reverberated sound of water in the locked lead-out groove which made the record "never ending" if you had a record player without an automatic tone-arm lift-off; later issues (including the first official CD release in 2001) unfortunately seem to use a second generation copy of the master tape which sounds a bit muffled; these records also now end with a fade-out.

NEU! was widely ignored by the music press. *Sounds* didn't even review it. The sales numbers were modest. Klaus Dinger: "It's quite realistic when I say 30,000 within the first two years. I have no idea what it sold later."[19] Dinger's idiosyncratic cover graphics concept also cannot be ignored: The day-glo red handwritten lettering "*NEU!*" was done by a friend, but it was Dinger's decision to use it, and I guarantee it had an important influence on the way the album was received by audiences. Rother would have preferred to have a less abrasive name, but Dinger pushed it through: "It was a protest against the consumer society but also against our 'colleagues' on the Krautrock scene who had totally different taste or styling if any. I was very well informed about Warhol, Pop Art, contemporary art. I had always been very visual in my thinking. Also, during that time, I lived in a commune and in order to get the space that we lived in, I set up an advertising agency which existed mainly on paper. Most of the people that I lived with were trying to break into advertising so I was somehow surrounded by this 'new' all the time."[20]

Despite the fact that, as Dinger put it, Neu! was "pure synthetic that will probably only exist in studios and on record, because we would otherwise need to change the concept"[21], they played six test concerts with guest musicians, among them Eberhard Kranemann. The performances turned out to be a good show, especially when Dinger hurt himself with a broken cymbal he used on his drum kit and started bleeding, but in the end the events were not satisfying. (The later album *NEU! '72 Live In Düsseldorf!*, released in 1996 by Japanese label Captain Trip, is actually a rehearsal room recording, made with a cassette deck, and with all due respect, it is difficult to listen to. The fact that he felt the need to release this stuff says a lot about Dinger's monetary situation in the 1990s.)

Klaus Dinger was not easy to deal with; he was different from the cool, calm, and collected Michael Rother. One reason for this, as Rother explains, were drugs: "I was always very careful with drugs. They were around me of course. Klaus Dinger wrote on his own website once that he was proud of having taken more than a thousand LSD trips. I'm not sure whether the number is correct, but it did have quite an effect on his behavior and view of things. He had a difficult time with everyone because he was … how do you call it: alienated? Of course, smoking pot and stuff, that was no big deal. I sometimes joined in just for celebration, but never as a habit."[22]

The two of them had a musical connection, but they were never friends. Dinger: "We were incredibly contrasting from one another, and it was extremely hard to bring us into a, say, constructive situation."[23] In the studio, they were able to transform their constant conflicts into creative power – which I think is the secret behind the entire Neu! project. In any other connection it was impossible for the two of them to come to reasonable terms about nearly anything, especially potential re-releases of their records.

NEU! was released in Germany in early 1972 as the fourth release on the recently started Brain label. Some weeks later, the album was released with a different cover and extensive liner notes in the U.K. on United Artists. One year later, *NEU!* appeared in Spain on Movieplay (parallel with *NEU!2*), in the U.S. on Billingsgate, 1975 on United Artists Italy, and in 1977, a release on Brain Japan followed.

NEU! was really new. "Musik für Kopf + Hose" (music for head + pants), as stated on the inside of its hardly legible gatefold cover. The album was a shock for many – a record with some vocals, but without understandable lyrics, model, or predecessor. Even the extremely simple cover graphics were different from what most record buyers had seen before – "to somehow stand out from all the record stores' shop window crap"[24] (Dinger). Andy Warhol couldn't have done it much better.

Fans, as well as rock critics, did not really know where to put this album. Many critics felt angrily bemused, as some furious reviews may show; this was an effect that remained with Klaus Dinger's later solo albums. Radio stations rarely played parts of the record. Although some of the then existing stations had one or two hosts on a show where it would have been possible to play this record, it remained only theoretical to get tracks of the album aired; even in late night hours, the DJs shied away from playing such cross-grained material. And on the other hand, Neu! was definitely "avant-garde", but it was too much a rock project to get airplay on "serious music" broadcasts. Another problem for radio shows was the duration of the tracks. The promotion of Neu! only happened through a handful of pop magazines and, of course, through word-of-mouth.

Since they needed a 45 to promote the band and get airplay, Conny Plank managed to dredge up some hours of recording time at Giorgio Moroder's recently opened Musicland Studio in the basement of the Munich modernist Arabella House – not completely without self-interest, because this studio was known for owning one of the first Neve mixing desks, and Plank was crazy about checking it out. Rother: "The studio … was in a huge building two floors below ground level. You felt like you were in some power plant. There was no fresh air and no daylight. … Klaus was a powerful drummer. He could not survive three minutes down there because there was not enough air."[25] However, they managed to cut "Neuschnee" b/w "Super".

The 45 was released in summer 1972, and one year later it became the opener of a cheap yet well-compiled Brain sampler titled *German Rock Scene*, with Jane, Guru Guru, Lava, Thirsty Moon, Kollektiv, Embryo, Novalis, Sperrmüll, Curly Curve, Emergency, sold exclusively via Govi (its price was 5,90 D-Marks, if memory serves).

NEU! 2 followed. It started where the first album had ended. The recording took place at Windrose-Dumont-Time Studio again, but because the musicians had spent most of their advanced money from Brain on instruments and equipment, they ran out of money and studio time after they had recorded side 1 of the album. In addition, because of the modest sales figures of the first album, the label was not willing to throw in more money. Dinger: "We had a few hours on one afternoon left. … I thought it was a good idea to take this single, which we had paid a lot of money to produce with Conny … and try to clean it up, or dirty it up, or fiddle about with it and scratch it and play it at different speeds, 33, 45, 78, and Michael had this broken cassette recorder, and then this second side was finished."[26] Sometimes, emergencies lead to the best ideas – nobody had ever done it this way before, not even Faust on their first album. Günter Körber, then A&R man at Brain: "Seen from the viewpoint of a record company, to put it mildly, we were a bit irritated when for the second album simply tapes got played backwards or the tracks only differed in playing speed, just because they ran out of ideas. That came along as pretty darned sassy."[27]

Sometimes you will find descriptions like "scratching" or "remixing" about what is done on this album. I would prefer to call it "working with found objects", something the Dada and Fluxus movements had done before. When you think about the Italian Futurists and their *Intonarumori*, noise machines built between 1910 and 1930, or Nam June Paik's interactive sculpture *Record Shashlik* (1963), you might notice that Neu! was not without forerunners in this connection. Seen from this perspective, *NEU! 2* stood in a great tradition, but I don't think they thought of this. The critics, of course, grumbled. Hermann Haring in *Sounds* wrote: "Monotone rhythmic patterns constrict the scope of the melodic instruments so far that the listener gets bored nearly under compulsion. Even the interspersed sound experiments can't change this anymore. The two Neu! musicians Michael Rother and Klaus Dinger ended up in a dead end street."[28]

Klaus Dinger: "In 1974 *NEU! '75* was recorded. It was recorded when Conny left Hamburg and went close to Cologne … He started on a very low key there. This was December 1974. It was a very hard year, 1974. Michael decided in 1973 to leave Düsseldorf and went to the countryside, where he still lives today. At this time he had in mind to work with the two Cluster people, which made his group project Harmonia. … I introduced [Hans Lampe and my brother Thomas] and nobody really liked it because it wasn't necessary at that time. We could have done the third Neu! LP the same way as its predecessors. During the second Neu! LP, Hans Lampe was Conny's assistant in Hamburg. He went with Conny to the countryside to build up Conny's Studio. He seemed frustrated because he would have liked to be a musician. I thought we could try that, and the same with my brother. He had nothing – didn't finish school, didn't finish anything. At this time my experience was: everything's possible. Everybody can do what I do, which is probably not the case, by the looks of it now, because it depends a lot on your character and talent and how much time you want to involve. They played drums on the second side of the third Neu! LP."[29]

NEU! '75 is the first time that keyboards are involved, and they are played rather melodic – "Isi" is clearly an anticipation of Michael Rother's later solo recordings. But there was also a lot of aggression and rage in the record; "Hero" is a downright furious track. The record has some atmospheric tracks, sending out rays of melancholy and sehnsucht – simply great. Critic "Jogi" (= Jörg Gülden) in *Sounds* considered *NEU! '75* to be "the most mature of all three records … really pleasant for potheads, simple, and difficult at the same time …"[30]

The sales figures of the Neu! records were better than those of Harmonia, but they were not convincing. But, over the years – similar to *The Velvet Un-*

derground & Nico – NEU!, especially the first album, became a sort of insiders' tip, and today, *NEU!* is seen by fans, critics, and musicians as one of the most influential records on industrial, noise, punk, and experimental rock ever; it's a timeless masterpiece, highly appreciated all over the world.

KLAUS DINGER

When their original label, Brain, released a last small re-issue of *NEU!* in 1981, several labels (among them London's Mute Records, that also distributed CAN's own Spoon label) asked for permission to re-release the three NEU! albums. But Dinger always sensed conspiracies. He wrote about a "fake release by Teldec"[31], sensed an "industry-boycott against me"[32], he accused the German Federal President for his problems ("this is not a free country, Herr Bundespräsident"[33]), or he stipulated absurd conditions. He didn't even trust Conny Plank: "In 70-something, I had the impression that Conny betrayed us a bit. I mean he was certainly very important for KRAFTWERK, certainly for NEU!, but also he couldn't resist English intruders who came to find out what was going on. [Interposed question by the interviewer: Passed on your ideas?] Yes, something like this ..."[34] Moreover, Dinger took half-baked material from the drawer and licensed it as *NEU! 4* to the Japanese Captain Trip label – much to Rother's annoyance, to put it mildly. Klaus Dinger was the kind of artist who put all his energy into his work, regardless of the consequences. When he ran out of money once, he lived on oatmeal and milk for nearly half a year.

One thing that Rüdiger Esch clearly shows in his book is that if the Düsseldorf scene had a sub-center, it was Klaus Dinger. I'm not sure whether Dinger saw himself and his projects as part of the scene anyway, but at least "Hero", his highly emotional contribution to *NEU!'75*, made him a part of it, whether he wanted this or not, and a sort of prototype singer for the Neue Deutsche Welle. This is why it's interesting to follow his further career.

Since he wasn't completely new to the scene, Teldec offered him a contract on three albums. The first album Dinger delivered was *Düsseldorf* by his NEU! follow-up LA DÜSSELDORF, produced and recorded in 1976 by Conny Plank, released on Nova, Teldec's sublabel for German rock. To produce the second album, *Viva*, which was released on Teldec's sub-sublabel Strand in 1978, Dinger invested 200,000 borrowed D-Marks to set up his own studio. To survive during the recording, the whole band had to work in a construction site. But it paid off: *Viva* brought the band a regional hit and some airplay with "Rheinita", a 45 lifted from the album. This came as manna falling from heaven and made it possible for Dinger to sink the debt in one go.

But then things got out of hand. Dinger, for whatever reason, believed that he had gotten a "million offer" from EMI. It's not clear what gave him this idea; no written offer existed, but Dinger claimed to "have it on video"[35]. However, there was one record left to produce for Teldec, and now this company allegedly offered him 600,000 D-Marks to "prolong the contract"[36]. Even this, in view of his real sales figures, would have been an amount so enormous that it's hard to believe. Whatever the offer might have been, Dinger – in prospect of the million to come – rejected it. In 1980, he delivered the third La Düsseldorf album, *Individuellos*, which was released in 1980 on the Teldec label. Unfortunately it turned out to be a shelf warmer. Dinger himself conceded: "We loused it up."[37] – which I think was a hasty conclusion. They had simply wrecked the album with a muffled mix. The remastered and extended rerelease in 1997 on Japan's Captain Trip label proves that it's well worth a listen.

Now, EMI, whatever their actual offer might have been, suddenly wasn't interested anymore, and Teldec reduced its offer to a much more realistic 100,000 D-Marks for three albums and a 12-inch. The success of *Viva*, as well as the increasing success of music from Düsseldorf in general and the high rent he had to pay for his studio rooms, gave Dinger, who as always was deep in debt again, the idea to move his studio to Seeland in the Netherlands, not too far from Düsseldorf. The 100,000 D-Marks from Teldec were gone immediately: he had to invest 60,000 D-Marks into renovating the building, and 40,000 D-Marks went into first-class Oberheim equipment. This deal nearly broke his neck. No money for the production of the planned fourth La Düsseldorf album was left, and, into the bargain, Dinger now got into quarrels with drummer Hans Lampe. In the end, La Düsseldorf had to be buried. Dinger had lost everything and stood there empty-handed.

Instead of *La Düsseldorf IV*, with the helping hands of Conny Plank, Horst Bork (A&R head of Teldec who later left the company to become manager of Austria's rising star Falco), René Tinner from Can Studio, guest musicians Jaki Liebezeit, Bodo Staiger (of Rheingold), and bassist Raoul Walton from Anyone's Daughter, Dinger was able to finish a sort of solo album entitled *Néondian* (a contraction of "neon" and "Indian"). It was released by Teldec in 1985 and turned out to be a complete disaster. The mix was dreary, devastated lyrics filled with bitterness left even good-willed listeners at a loss. But that's not all. Dinger's biggest error in reasoning was probably his use of a drum machine: He forgot to take into account that people wanted to hear him hitting real drums. They were not interested in hearing a drum machine, even when it was him programming the patterns.

When it rains, it pours. So Dinger became entrapped in serious fights with his former bandmate Michael Rother about potential re-releases of the three NEU! albums.

This shows how much a character like Conny Plank was needed. Plank was the one who knew how to handle edgy minds like Dinger, how to deal with labels, and how to transform all this chaos into a shape that could be pressed into vinyl. Plank produced and recorded DAF, KFC, RHEINGOLD, DIE MONOPOLS, Arno Steffen and several more, and – as he often did – he did it without asking for profit. He was able to do this because he also produced and recorded several acts with more money behind them, like ULTRAVOX, DEVO, EURYTHMICS, Gianna Nannini, IDEAL and several more. Even more it makes one shake the head to hear Klaus Dinger having the nerves to hold just this against Plank: "In the end he was just a normal studio where every idiot could go and record."[38]

All of these conflicts made it impossible to officially re-release the NEU! albums for many years after 1981. The LPs were off the market and went more and more into oblivion. Ten years later, when suddenly new listeners discovered the band, Germanofon and Crown, illegal counterfeit labels both, saw their chance to supply the demand and make the profit instead of the respective rights owners. They provided fans with mediocre-sounding CDs that were rerecorded from the vinyl albums. Worse, they managed to sneak these illegal CDs into official distribution channels, so they were even available in serious record stores. Dinger's furious attacks against these products or their buyers remained empty threats.

In the end, it needed someone like Herbert Grönemeyer to make a re-release possible. Somehow, Grönemeyer (a mega-star in Germany; more about him later) had fallen in love with the NEU! records and offered a re-release on his own Grönland label. But it took him years of asking, negotiating, offering, and schmoozing, until he was finally able to reach a settlement between Dinger and Rother at the end of the 1990s. What convinced Dinger was probably the fact that Grönemeyer was a musician himself and had his own label.

In 2001, 29 years after the original release, the official rerelease of the three NEU! albums finally hit stores, released in Europe, U.K., U.S., and Japan by Grönemeyer's label and a couple of licensees. Commercially, they were still not really big hits, but for Grönemeyer, this project had been a labour of love anyway, and this time, at least the press reactions were much friendlier because the records were dealt with as "cult" now. But the promotional activities didn't work as planned – soon Dinger and Rother were at odds with each other again, and even Grönemeyer was not able to settle it. The records remained sleepers in Germany and relatively soon hit the bargain bins. At least Michael Rother could be frequently seen on stage now with a couple of guest musicians, among them Hans Lampe.

Klaus Dinger's projects after Neu! and La Düsseldorf were Die Engel des Herrn, La!Neu? and Néondian. I remember some folks who felt taken for a ride by the La Düsseldorf albums; this happened even more with Die Engel des Herrn (The Lord's Angels; 1992). Dinger released this CD without having a record company behind the project. It was an excellently produced CD he sold himself by mail order. Besides this, Dinger produced the band Lilac Angels (named after a track from *NEU! 2*), but it failed and left him 50,000 D-Marks in debt.[39]

When Klaus Dinger unexpectedly passed away at the age of 62 in March 2008, the chapter Neu! and the follow-ups had to be closed forever. The last project he had worked on was *Japandorf* (released not before 2013 and finished by his girlfriend Miki Yui), a very original record that shows what high flights he could still take if he was in the mood.

What's left is a stack of records with one of the most distinctive voices German rock music has ever had – often copied, never matched.

MORE DÜSSELDORF

Wolfgang Riechmann – "Wölfi", as his family and friends used to call him – made an electronic solo record called *Wunderbar* in 1978. Sky Records head Günter Körber: "For Sky, at the Hamburg Star Studio Wölfi recorded his solo record, his legacy. With this record he managed to do a balancing act between the Berlin and the Düsseldorf electronic scene: He unified the spherical sounds of the Berlin School around Tangerine Dream and Klaus Schulze and the minimalism of his Düsseldorf colleagues of Kraftwerk and Neu!."[40] The album has a tendency to stretch out its three or four basic ideas, but Riechmann countervailed this with a good ear for tone colors, atmospheres, and a well-thought-out use of conventional instruments (the "Röhrophon-Studio" mentioned on the cover is a vibraphone, actually). I'm sure we would have gotten some more interesting things from him – had it been granted to him to do them: On August 21, 1978, shortly before the release of *Wunderbar*, Riechmann was stabbed to death without reason by two drunks in downtown Düsseldorf. *Wunderbar* saw three rereleases yet (1985, 1991 and 2009). The wonderful blueish-decadent cover photo was shot by Michael Rother's girlfriend at the time, photographer Ann Weitz.

Wolfgang Riechmann was also part of the second album of STREETMARK, *Eileen* (1977) – prog with some hints to KRAFTWERK and NEU! rhythms which were surely induced by Riechmann and drummer Hans Schweiß (who also played on *Wunderbar*). But STREETMARK, initially produced by Conny Plank, suffered from an ongoing change of musicians. In 1979 the remaining trio line-up had a local hit with "Lovers". They split up in 1981.

STREETMARK's keyboardist Dorothea Raukes then recorded an electronic solo album under the stage name of DEUTSCHE WERTARBEIT – a bit similar to Riechmann's *Wunderbar*, clearly a "Düsseldorf" album, but with a lot of "Berlin" in it. "Intercity Rheingold" is probably its best track: "I got this idea on the train. I looked out of the window and started associating. The listener should feel like being on an air cushion"[41], as Raukes says. The compositions are quite nice to listen to once, but already in the second go it's obvious that they are not very substantial. All the tracks are played exclusively on Korg instruments; Raukes had a sponsorship contract with this company, and that's a bit how the whole album sounds like: endorsement work. Her husband at the time, Bernd Schreiber, had just finished a book about synthesizers and periphery instruments. As he writes, it shouldn't allude to being an advertising book for Korg instruments,[42] but well: Without exception, Korg instruments are mentioned throughout the whole book.

Journalist Winfried Trenkler played some tracks from *Deutsche Wertarbeit* a couple of times on WDR radio, and the album didn't sell badly. But it was anything but a hit, and since Raukes didn't want to hide herself behind a wall of keyboards, DEUTSCHE WERTARBEIT never appeared on stage. So the project died away after a while. In 1981, Raukes gave up the professional music business and went back to her original day job at the Düsseldorf district court. Today, she lives in retirement in a little village in the Westerwald area (Rhineland-Palatinate), and in her leisure time she leads a boys' choir. *Deutsche Wertarbeit* got a vinyl rerelease in the United States (!) in 2010 – the owner of a tiny independent label in Seattle had found an old copy and fell in love with it. Bureau B re-released the album on CD in 2013. Raukes, as she states, thinks about a continuation of the project,[43] but up to now, the statement is all that has happened. The term "Deutsche Wertarbeit", by the way, meaning "German high class workmanship", is not, as commonly misinterpreted, a Nazi invention (although they used it for propaganda reasons). Actually, it was coined in 1907 by the Werkbund, a group of artists, designers and architects, a bit similar to the Bauhaus.

Another link between several Düsseldorf-based projects, among them KRAFTWERK as well as NEU!, was multi-instrumentalist Eberhard Kranemann. Sadly, he only appeared on records that nobody wants to voluntarily hear anymore, and newer interviews with him sometimes show a mix of embitterment and beginning wisdom of old age: "When you get older, you see that many things are coincidence. By chance I've been at the right place at the right time. But I didn't realize it at that time. For me it was realistic, not historic, as it may sound today. It was just my life, it was what I was doing. … Afterwards you realize: 'Fuck, these four, five years, that's actually been *it*, it's really been the hammer.' In retrospect you rate things differently."[44]

An insight we all can probably relate to.

THE SEVENTIES

HAMBURG: THE HANSEATIC WAY

Hamburg's music scene was not unimportant, but compared to Berlin or Düsseldorf it was always a bit understated. It also tended to draw criticism, sometimes hate.

There was the Star-Club and there was rock music available, but it was classic British or American rock – or it was just pop. An experimental scene worth mentioning didn't come up until the 1980s, but even then it was a small one. There was high-class contemporary jazz (like Peter Herbolzheimer Rhythm Combination & Brass), but never a free jazz scene. Hamburg was home of the only authorized Moog synthesizer seller in Germany, but there was never an electronic scene like in Berlin. Hamburg became the city where rock in German language started *commercially* – with a broad impact.

There's a saying that when it starts raining in London, people in Hamburg open their umbrellas. Hamburg is, indeed, "very British". There's a sort of implicit connection between London and Hamburg at the River Elbe in North Germany; their inhabitants are tuned to similar wavelengths.

The Free and Hanseatic City of Hamburg is Germany's second-biggest city and has one of Europe's most important ports, so it has always been a place for trade and commerce. Hamburg's merchants were usually called "Pfeffersäcke" (pepper sacks), because spices, coffee, and tea were and are important parts of merchandise; the term's second meaning, of course, is something like "moneybags". They have always been a bit on the conservative side and conscious of their tradition, but nevertheless, they were and still are cosmopolitan. Hamburg has always had worldwide connections; before German Unification, it was the place with the most embassies and consulates in Europe (it's still around a hundred today). Because port and trade are important lifelines, the city has always been a liberal place populated with many foreigners of various backgrounds, and this has, of course, left its traces. (There was a dark side too: Hamburg with its port was the main connection between Germany and its overseas colonies. This is not the place to explicate this inglorious chapter, but it's part of Hamburg's history and has to be mentioned.) The University of Hamburg was founded not before 1919 (and first as a kind of trading seminar). The pepper sacks didn't see a need to have a university. They preferred following the old Hanseatic merchants' tradition: The more intelligent son had to take over the business, the other one was sent to Göttingen to study law. Daughters got married anyways, advantageously by the son of a business friend, to keep the trading connections going.

If you want to get a feel for how the people of Hamburg tick, you might be interested in knowing that native-born Hamburgers often speak a slang called "Missingsch", a mix of high and low German. They love to wear colorful clothes as long as the colors are dark blue, charcoal-gray, or black. If they are *real* born Hamburgers (being at least the third generation born in Hamburg), they don't accept medals and refuse to kneel down to anybody, except maybe to the Queen (because she's from London). If you ever go for a stroll in Hamburg: The white pigeons you see everywhere are seagulls.

In 1972, when the Hochschule für Musik und Theater decided they wanted to appoint world-famous composer György Ligeti to a professorship, they gave him an unofficial note. Ligeti agreed – and then nothing else happened. When, after a couple of months, Ligeti asked about the state of affairs, they told him: "We are still waiting for your application!" This way of thinking is also very Hamburg (however, Ligeti got his professorship). Don't forget the Star-Club; today, the City of Hamburg bursts with pride about it, but at the time when it was a highly successful venue, they did everything possible to kick its heart and soul, Manfred Weissleder, out of business.

This might give you an idea of what "Pfeffersack mentality" means.

Based on the aforesaid info, it's not hard to conclude that "being commercial" has never been seen as an offense in Hamburg. The arts and music scene has always mirrored this – Hamburg's moneybags don't have problems with any kind of experiment, but the experiment has to pay off, otherwise they'll leave it to others. This is the reason why this city was never home to any experimental scenes of relevance. This changed a bit in the 1980s, but during the 1960s and 1970s, Hamburg would have never been a good place for people like Albert Mangelsdorff or Peter Brötzmann. Hamburg proudly had James Last, Bert Kaempfert, Peter Herbolzheimer, Achim Reichel, and Les Humphries instead, and they were modern enough. Of course, there were many different excellent musicians in town. The jazz-oriented ones were usually employees of one of the ensembles or big bands of NDR radio, while the rock-oriented ones used to play in groups like the City Preachers (they started it all), Frumpy, Atlantis, Highway, Lake, Randy Pie, Novalis, Rattles, Wonderland, Les Humphries Singers, Lucifer's Friend, or later Udo Lindenberg's Panikorchester. There were connections between them all, as we will see.

In a sort of "sub scene", many of these musicians were also involved in mainstream country like Truck Stop (yes, Germany also has a country music scene), pop music, and (sometimes horrible) schlager projects; I've already mentioned schlager comedian "Willem" Wilken F. Dincklage as the business partner of Conny Plank. There was also a hullabaloo band called Torfrock (*Rata-Ta--Zong*, 1978, engineered by Conny Plank) that later melted into the enervating schlager comedy duo Klaus & Klaus ("An der Nordseeküste") – all of this was well crafted but musically trivial.

Since 1958, NDR radio at least had the "NDR Jazzworkshop", initially founded off of an idea from composer Rolf Liebermann (1910–1999) and headed by Hans Koller (1921-2003); since 1965, it's been led by Michael Naura (1934-2017). This meant public concerts at Studio 10, NDR's biggest studio (an old synagogue that had been taken out of service; today, in honor of the composer, it's named Rolf-Liebermann-Studio), with a primarily "sworn in" audience. Wes Montgomery, Kenny Wheeler, Wolfgang Dauner, Heinz Sauer, Hans Kleinschuster, or singer Karin Krog played there, as well as the Dave Pike Set with Volker Kriegel, Hans Rettenbacher, and Peter Baumeister; later, Volker Kriegel's Mild Maniac Orchestra, Albert Mangelsdorff, and Lee Konitz also made appearances. Musicians like Wolfgang Schlüter (1933-2018), Herb Geller, Jiggs Whigham, Niels-Henning Ørsted Pedersen, or Tony Inzalaco came from the NDR Big Band or NDR Tanzorchester ohne Namen. Naura frequently invited acts from the circle around the ECM label, like Jan Garbarek, Jon Christensen (1943-2020), or Palle Danielsson; Keith Jarrett came as both a soloist and with his quartet. In September 1974, Joy Fleming performed with Victor Behrens and Ralf Nowy, in October of the same year Klaus Doldinger played with Kristian Schultze, Wolfgang Schmid, Curt Cress, and Philip Catherine, joined by singer Inga Rumpf. They, and many more, were introduced to northern Germany's audience by the "Jazzworkshop". Yours Truly had his first encounter with contemporary jazz at Studio 10 in November 1975. It was from the Gary Burton Quintet (with Steve Swallow, Mick Goodrick, Bob Moses and a 19-year old guitarist nobody knew at that time: a certain Pat Metheny), joined by Albert Mangelsdorff as guest. It was an absolutely magical moment and one of the concerts I will never forget. For several artists, making an appearance at the "Jazzworkshop" was the start of a career in Germany – like the Pat Metheny Group or singer Al Jarreau, for example.

Michael Naura, jazz pianist himself, had a unique taste, was strongly opinionated, and used to follow his own ideas and ideals. His recordings with vibraphonist Wolfgang Schlüter are worth checking, like the forgotten gem *Country Children* on the ECM label (1979) that never made it onto a CD, as well as his "Jazz and Lyric" project with Hamburg poet Peter Rühmkorf. Naura had a great sense for quality, but sometimes he simply didn't like a musician or a band. He usually invited them anyway, but when he later presented a recording on air, he never hid his opinion. If one of his friends needed money, he scheduled a concert – but since most of his friends were musical heavyweights, this often led to grand events. All in all, Naura's "Jazzworkshop" was the most important source in northern Germany to get in touch with current developments in jazz. And you will never forget Naura's voice once you've heard him on the radio.

How about rock? If we were lucky and the reception conditions were well, we could listen to BBC radio on AM frequencies. Besides this, we had BFBS, the British Forces Broadcasting Service. This wasn't too bad, but I don't know how we, in the AFN-less lowlands of northern Germany, could have survived the late 1960s and 1970s without the English program of Radio Luxembourg.

Musicians from Hamburg typically don't care much about how things are done somewhere else. They have a tendency to be as perfect as possible, but they don't make much fuss about it. If you tell a musician from Hamburg how much you love his playing, his answer will probably be: "Well, I try." Bands like Randy Pie, Highway, or Lake would have hardly been possible in, say, Düsseldorf, while projects like Neu! or Tangerine Dream are hard to imagine in Hamburg. In Hamburg, musicians "do their own thing", and they rarely leave town to do it. Only a handful of musicians live and do solo projects in Hamburg while also engaging in other scenes, like Jens Fischer (who played with Tri Atma, Cyklus, Real Ax Band, Falco, and others) or Achim Gieseler (who played with Cyklus, Aera, Tri Atma, and others, and is also known as Jakino's 7th World), who also worked with the Munich scene around Eberhard Schoener. Michael Rother is originally from Hamburg, but he had to go to Düsseldorf to start his career. Violinist, multi-instrumentalist, and composer Gerd Bessler (1951-2011) lived and worked in Hamburg; he was known for theater and radio drama music, but his main jobs were commissioned by the Viennese Burgtheater or Schauspielhaus Graz. He worked with no less than Lou Reed, Tom Waits, Philip Glass, Laurie Anderson, William S. Burroughs, and was involved in Robert Wilson's stage project *The Black Rider* at Hamburg's Thalia Theater. But, if you ask somebody in Hamburg who Gerd Bessler was, they will probably reply with clueless eyes. The only artist of relevance who has worked radically on electronics and studio experiments without any commercial considerations is Asmus Tietchens, but his recording career didn't start before the 1980s. Up until then, he had worked as a copywriter for an ad agency. Michael Rother and Tietchens, by the way, are good friends; at times, and when you know the right pub, you can see them playing pool together.

Hamburg was home to a couple of pioneering Neue Deutsche Welle acts, but again, this brings us to the 1980s, so it will be part of another chapter.

As Hamburg is Germany's second-largest city and had a couple of acceptable venues and clubs, there were always big international bands and artists playing the city. Hamburg's audience is critical and not the easiest to satisfy: It's conservative, but generally open to innovation as long as it makes sense to them. I still remember the endless ovations Laurie Anderson or STEVE REICH & MUSICIANS received at their first appearances in the 1980s. When Steve Reich and his ensemble performed "Drumming" and "Music for Mallet Instruments, Voices and Organ" at the Hamburg State Opera, the next day, the 3-LP box with these tracks was sold out in every record store around noon already. Sometimes, it may take a while until the Hamburgers are convinced of something new, but once they are and take the artist to heart, these artists can return to Hamburg whenever they want for the rest of their life.

HAMBURG'S JAZZ SCENE

"Jazz" in Hamburg was not only the "NDR Jazzworkshop". For the average Hamburger, "jazz" mainly meant the preservation of traditional oldtime jazz from New Orleans or Chicago. This sort of jazz has always been cultivated in Hamburg – jazz bands that were easy-care amateurs and could be used for jazz band battles on Saturday night at the Deutsche Schauspielhaus theater, as well as the very popular "Jazzfrühschoppen" (morning jazz pints) in some clubs, the Malersaal (the experimental sub-stage of the Schauspielhaus), or at some pictorial locations at the port. You could also hire these bands for your grandpa's birthday or for the opening of a furniture store Monday morning at 10. Hamburg had a vivid club scene specializing in this kind of jazz. Some clubs were already very old and had a rich tradition, while others had the typical bulky waste charm of a 1970's student pub.

Take these traditional jazz styles seriously for a moment and let's have a closer look at this scene. You will see it was not as one-sided and boring as you might expect. Cornetist Albrecht "Abbi" Hübner for example, police emergency doctor in his day job ("Bullendoktor", as he called himself – "Bulle" was an derogatory word for police officers), formed a band called Abbi Hübner's Low Down Wizards. They specialized in the early style of King Oliver's Creole Jazz Band or Louis Armstrong's Hot Five, and compared to the Low Down Wizards' performances of classics like "Everybody Loves My Baby" or "Basin' Street Blues", most of today's New Orleans bands sound pale. Listen to the Wizards' 2-LP-set *City Jazz* (1974) if you don't believe me. In the 1980s, Abbi Hübner's Low Down Wizards became honorary citizens of New Orleans, and rightly so. Later, they tried to put German folk songs into a jazz costume. Let's forget about this as fast as possible; I think that's what they did too.

All of these guys were amateurs, yet still excellent musicians. Peter "Banjo" Meyer of Jazz Lips was one of them; Michael "Ede" Wolff played a devilish sousaphone there. Thomas Danneberg, drummer of the Low Down Wizards, masterfully handled the drums just as they were played in the early 1910s and 1920s, with snare, a giant bass drum, cymbal, several temple blocks, and of course without a hi-hat, which was yet to be invented. There was clarinetist Günther Liebetruth of the Jailhouse Jazzmen whose improvisations often reminded me of a snake charmer. Gottfried Böttger (1949-2017), an excellent ragtime pianist whom I saw a couple of times playing in some pubs, became known nationwide as the in-house pianist of the popular TV talk show "III nach 9". Later, he became a member of Udo Lindenberg's Panikorchester. Lorenz "Lonzo" Westphal (1952-2001) was as much a virtuoso on the violin as Gottfried was on the piano; later, after a serious accident that took him years to recover, he unfortunately became a severe alcoholic and passed away at the age of only 49. Singer Ingeburg Thomsen later acted in a couple of films by Horst Königstein, and I think she was also a member of the fully professional skiffle and rock'n'roll nostalgic comedy project, LEINEMANN. There was a double LP named *Hamburg Allstars*, released in 1974 on the Brunswick label, where most of these guys and girls are playing a studio session together – really a gem. There was even cornetist Günter Heide with his TRAVELIN' JAZZMEN who not only had a rock drummer and a Brazilian electric bass guitar player in his band, but seriously had the idea of performing with my lightshow group. Thankfully, the owner of the club he had in mind for this experiment waved it aside – we would have done it, but I'm sure it would have been like Viennese Schnitzel with cherry sauce.

ABBI HÜBNER'S LOW DOWN WIZARDS, the JAILHOUSE JAZZMEN, the JAZZ LIPS, HOT SHOTS, BRUNO'S SALON BAND, MOUNTAIN VILLAGE JAZZBAND (a pun on Hamburg's Bergedorf neighborhood), the BLACKBIRDS OF PARADISE, ST. JOHN'S JAZZBAND, the REVIVAL JAZZBAND, and some more, covered the spectrum between the street jazz of New Orleans and the harder Chicago style, to the swing big bands of Count Basie or Benny Goodman who played hotel lobbies, big ballrooms, and concert halls. In spite of all the flippancy these Hamburg musicians had with them, they knew very well what they were playing and which tradition they stood in. On the double LP *Hamburger Jazz-Scene*, released on the Metronome label and long out of print, you can hear some excellent recordings of these bands between 1969 and 1972. Interestingly, compared to the revival of traditional jazz in Great Britain in the late 1950s and early 1960s, these bands were more authentic to U.S. jazz and less commercially compelling than the British bands.

Why is this relevant? Because one day, someone came along and brought all these different scenes and musicians together, using their special traditions: His name was Udo Lindenberg.

UDO LINDENBERG

Udo Lindenberg of Gronau, Westphalia, played with an old time jazz band at the age of 11. After an apprenticeship as a waiter, he travelled through France and U.S. military clubs in some North African countries as a musician. For a while, he studied music in Münster, started drumming with Klaus Doldinger, and gigged as a session musician. In 1968 he hitch-hiked to Hamburg and became a member of the earlier mentioned CITY PREACHERS, a folk-oriented band where Inga Rumpf, Dagmar Krause, John O'Brien-Docker, Jean-Jacques Kravetz, or later schlager-chanson singer Alexandra, also started. After quitting this band because it ran out of steam, Lindenberg founded a band named FREE

Orbit with Peter Herbolzheimer, their only (self-titled) album appeared on the MPS label in 1970. Lindenberg wrote or co-wrote all of its ten tracks.

In 1971, Lindenberg released a solo album called *Lindenberg*. It was not a total flop. Somehow, it occurred to him to set some of its songs to German lyrics. This was an adventurous idea; the combination of rock music and German language was usually seen as impossible. Bands like Embryo, Ihre Kinder, Drosselbart, Meistersinger, and others, had done lyrics in German before, but with all due respect for their pioneering work, they sounded stiff, clumsy, and often whiny. There were singer-songwriters like Reinhard Mey, Hannes Wader, Franz-Josef Degenhardt, Dieter Süverkrüp, some of them with a more folk-oriented concept, like Knut Kiesewetter, Witthüser & Westrupp, or early Hoelderlin. Others came from the old kabarett or cabaret tradition of nonsense like Ulrich Roski, Schobert & Black, or Insterburg & Co; some had had political messages clad into more or less well-played rock music like Ton Steine Scherben, Franz K., Lokomotive Kreuzberg, Volks-Musik, Die Conrads, or Floh de Cologne. (I'm sure some friends from East Germany will say that the first bands with German lyrics came from the GDR, which is true, but the bands and music from East Germany would fill a special book, and I'm not the one to do it.)

But now Udo Lindenberg came and tried it his way. To make it completely clear, he was not the first to sing rock with German lyrics, but for some reason he was the first one to find a tolerable and authentic sounding way to do it. The result was *Daumen im Wind* (1972), produced by Lindenberg himself, and recorded and co-produced by Thomas Kukuck at Star Studio with A-list jazz musicians like Jonny Müller (harmonica), Michael Naura (e-piano), and again Peter Herbolzheimer (trombone); Kukuck added nicely made field recordings to some tracks, and also included some fine studio feats like backwards-running tapes, phased voices et cetera. In parts, Lindenberg used songs from his first solo album, but they had gotten German lyrics now. "Daumen im Wind" (Thumb in the Wind; in the meaning of hitchhiking)) and "Good Life City" were well-crafted rock ballads with a touch of melancholy, "Meer der Träume" (Ocean of Dreams), "Biochemon", "In den dunklen tiefen Gängen der Vergangenheit" (In the Dark Deep Hallways of the Past), and "Die Kinder deiner Kinder" (The Children of Your Children) were slightly floating songs with a sort of philosophical background ("your children's children won't even know your name anymore"). "Alkoholmädchen" was a depressing bouncer, using pub ambience noise until someone ends up collapsing. Lindenberg about the album: "Really a Valium record. At that time

I meditated and did strange things like yoga. I brought myself into a state of self-absorption and then started singing."[1] But there was also one real rocker on the album. This one became defining for Lindenberg's style and gave him his first minor hit: "Hoch im Norden" (Up in the North). Sung in the first person, it was a song about this craving for the faraway, this feeling that any place in the world is better than the place where you just are. A song about leaving your boring home in a North Sea village where the only choice you have is to become a sailor or a farmer, and so, around the age of 16, he's taking the next-best train south. Later, now sweating far away under the burning sun, he feels a craving to return home because the dunes at the North Sea may not have been that bad.

Udo Lindenberg (drums) with Olaf Kübler (saxophone) and Paul Vincent (guitar), performing as part of Klaus Doldinger's Passport (1971) © Manfred Rinderspacher

"Hoch im Norden" had already a lot of what would later become Udo Lindenberg's trademarks: cheeky German lyrics that nobody had believed would work, somehow a bit personal, but always with dry humor and a little wink of the eye. Lindenberg's jagged voice, guitar-oriented mainstream rock, played by first-rate musicians, were spiced up with some exotic sounds like accordion, banjo and castanets. The song was radio-compatible but not "easy listening" or schlager. The always well-informed music journalist, Werner Burkhardt (1928-2008; you can consider him Hamburg's Ralph J. Gleason), wrote the album's liner notes, starting with: "It works, after all."

Daumen im Wind had not been a big commercial hit, but it made the name Udo Lindenberg known to a wider audience. Lindenberg lived at the aforementioned "Villa Kunterbunt" with important musicians, actors, radio people, A&R guys, promoters, and journalists (remember, Conny Plank also lived there), so he knew them all, and they all knew him. He didn't need to prove he was good on drums; everybody knew he had worked with Klaus Doldinger, and Doldinger never worked with second-rate musicians.

"Hoch im Norden" included the lines "Keine Panik auf der Titanic, jetzt trinken wir erstmal einen Rum mit Tee" (Don't panic on the Titanic, first let's have a rum with tea) which became the eponym for the band Lindenberg now founded: the PANIKORCHESTER, with musicians like Karl Allaut, Gottfried Böttger, Steffi Stephan, and Carola Kretschmer. The first album under the logo UDO LINDENBERG & DAS PANIKORCHESTER was titled *Alles klar auf der Andrea Doria* (Everything's Alright on the Andrea Doria; 1973) and gave him nationwide popularity; it didn't take long for "Alles klar auf der Andrea Doria" to become a figure of speech in the vernacular.

The opening concert with this new band took place at the Musikhalle with several guest musicians and a new drummer (Peter "Backi" Backhausen). The supporting act was BRUNO'S SALON BAND who (in all probability) was the dixieland band we hear in the tune "Alles klar auf der Andrea Doria" and on some further records of Lindenberg; they were also part of the main concert. I remember this concert as pure fun. Musically, it was well balanced and ended in a sort of session; Lindenberg himself returned to a second drum kit on stage. They knew they had invented something new, and they enjoyed that it worked.

It worked because Lindenberg was clever. To get his idea of rock with German lyrics accepted and known, he had brought them all in – the rock musicians, Gottfried Böttger, Lonzo Westphal, Peter Hesslein (LUCIFER'S FRIEND, JAMES LAST ORCHESTRA), Jean-Jacques Kravetz (FRUMPY), the jazz pros from NDR BIG BAND, the oldtime jazz amateurs, and he kept this concept going for the next three albums. Inga Rumpf appeared on his next album *Ball Pompös* (1974), as well as comedian Otto Waalkes. Keith Forsey and Olaf Kübler (from Lindenberg's old Doldinger connection) came from Munich, and Michael Chevalier (Charles Bronson's German lip-synch voice in the movie *Once Upon A Time In The West*) had a short appearance in a dialogue scene with Otto Waalkes and Inga Rumpf. He got concert promoters, journalists, and a gang of real motorbike rockers ("MC Mephisto's Mob") to sing back-up vocals, and even managed to have Marlene Dietrich speak a few words on his record via phone from Paris. In short: Lindenberg included as many famous and not so famous people as possible. It didn't take long for him to become *the* voice of the Hamburg scene this way.

Once planted, it grew. In 1978, Lindenberg, to promote his new album *Dröhnland-Symphonie*, got famous theater director Peter Zadek (1926-2009) to stage a complete tour with 16 elaborate three-hour concerts. Eric Burdon was part of it, as were Inga Rumpf, Ulla Meinecke, and Freya Wippich (the latter came from ODIN and RUDOLF ROCK & DIE SCHOCKER and later had a schlager duo with her husband Bernd Wippich) who sang back-up vocals. Pantomime Samy Molcho did the choreography; about 50 actors in penguin and other costumes were part of the show. Production costs were around 70,000 D-Marks per evening, which was a very high amount for a German act at that time. It was concert promoter Fritz Rau who took the risk; Lindenberg helped him by passing a guaranteed fee and offering to carry half of a potential loss.[2] But it worked out.

A little problem for Lindenberg came up when Olaf Kübler became aware that Lindenberg had based big parts of his lyrics on phrases he had heard from him (Kübler) and filed a copyright lawsuit against Lindenberg. The judge determined an amount in dispute of 500,000 D-Marks. This affair at least didn't grow out into a personal matter; one nice evening in front of Onkel Pö's, Kübler and Lindenberg came to an agreement, and their lawyers dealt it out amicably.[3]

Udo Lindenberg is still active today. His hair seems to be glued into his now obligatory slouch hat, and he is the joint partner of Hamburg's famous Atlantic Hotel (where he lives). In 1989, he received the Cross of the Order of Merit with Ribbon of the Federal Republic of Germany (Bundesverdienstkreuz am Bande) for his efforts in keeping connections between the two German states alive.

If you can understand German, I recommend his first albums from *Daumen im Wind* to *Votan Wahnwitz* – after this, his shtick became a bit stale for my taste. In 1983, he made a cover version of Glenn Miller's "Chattanooga Choo Choo", titled "Sonderzug nach Pankow" (Special Train to Pankow). Pankow is the East Berlin neighborhood where several leading politicians of the GDR used to live, and the song was a question to Erich Honecker (then head of the Socialist Party and State Counsel of the GDR), asking why the GDR authorities didn't allow him to play for his fans in East Berlin. This resulted in an exchange between Lindenberg and Honecker – Lindenberg gave a leather jacket to Honecker, Honecker returned the favor with a shawm, a traditional wind instrument used in marching bands by the worker's movement of the 1920s. More importantly, Honecker gave Lindenberg permission to perform a televised concert at East Berlin's Palast der Republik. This took place in front of a selected audience of mainly FDJ members (Freie Deutsche Jugend, Free German Youth; the official youth organization under the whip of the Socialist Party of the GDR), but a GDR tour planned for 1984 was cancelled by the GDR authorities without giving any reasons. In 1985, Lindenberg was able to play a concert in Moscow. Lindenberg's persistent frustrations with the division of Germany are worth mentioning because he had already touched on this topic on

Alles klar auf der Andrea Doria: "Wir wollen doch einfach nur zusammen sein" (We Only Want to Be Together) was a disarmingly un-kitschy ballad about the impossible love story between a boy from West Germany and a girl he meets at East Berlin's Alexanderplatz. In 1973, when this song came out, this topic was completely against the zeitgeist: Chancellor Willy Brandt tried to approach the GDR a little bit, but there was absolutely no hope that any kind of a German unification could happen during our lifetime. Even the simple mention of such an idea sounded ridiculous, many people found it downright reactionary. But time proved Lindenberg right.

In 2011, all this and several songs became part of a musical named *Hinterm Horizont*, written by Thomas Brussig, Udo Lindenberg, and Ulrich Waller (who was also director). It premièred in Berlin and was shown there for five years. Since 2016, *Hinterm Horizont* has been shown in Hamburg.

From time to time, Lindenberg later has been able to come out with a great song – let me mention "Gegen die Strömung" (1981, a cover version of "Against the Wind" by Bob Seger & The Silver Bullet Band), "Horizont" (1987, with backup vocals by Nena), and "Ich lieb dich überhaupt nicht mehr" (1987).

TOP SZENE HAMBURG

Lindenberg's song "Alles klar auf der Andrea Doria" included the lines "Bei Onkel Pö[4] spielt 'ne Rentnerband seit 20 Jahren Dixieland / 'n Groupie haben die auch, die heißt Rosa oder so / und die tanzt auf'm Tisch wie'n Go-go-go-Girl" (At Onkel Pö's a band of retirees has been playing dixieland for 20 years / they even have a groupie, her name is Rosa or something / she's dancing on the table like a go-go-go girl). It was not Lindenberg's fault, but this song led to one of the most embarrassing ideas Hamburg's record industry has ever had: the proclaiming of the "Top Szene Hamburg".

In 1974, the lines of this above mentioned song somehow implanted an idea into the heads of Willem (Wilken F. Dincklage, you remember: business partner of Conny Plank and living in the same Villa Kunterbunt as Lindenberg) and some A&R guys to produce a "reply song" to Lindenberg's tune. So the Rentnerband (Band of Retirees) was brought to "life", as well as the "Rosa" character. This completely artificial construct had a national hit with "Hamburger Deern", a cover version of Irish singer-songwriter Dominic Behan's song "Liverpool Lou" from 1964 ("Deern" is Low German for "girl" or "young woman"). The German lyrics were written by Willem, the band behind this project consisted of schlager singer Peter Petrel, Gottfried Böttger, Lonzo Westphal, usual suspects from Leinemann, and actress Ingrid Unverdorben had to speak a few lines as "Rosa". Of course, this was not rock or jazz, this was pure schlager. The record company sold this whole thing as "the true story of how Peter Petrel met his wife". "Hamburger Deern" became a consistently played hit on popular radio waves for several weeks, including the PR story, and in December 1974, the song entered the charts. It peaked at #20 but stayed in the charts for 16 weeks. (I would still like to know why a gifted singer like Peter Petrel stooped to singing such garbage. Money, probably.)

The Rentnerband made three albums and spooked around as a live act until the early 1980s. There would be no need to deal with it at all if this project had not been the start of what became known as "Hamburger Szene". Anything that came from musicians and bands from Hamburg got a sticker now: "Top Szene Hamburg" – especially the Teldec records. Stupid samplers with collections of the now usual suspects – Lindenberg, Böttger, a young Marius Müller-Westernhagen, Truck Stop, Schulzke's Skandaltrupp, Torfrock, several Hamburg jazz bands, of course Willem under several pseudonyms – were pushed into the market. Even acts who actually had no connection to Hamburg were engrossed, like Bill Brooker's Jug Band from the Netherlands, just because the name sounded a bit like Hamburg's Billbrook neighborhood.

Teldec promotion logo (1975)

We could file this simply under schlager and ballyhoo, but the record companies even put acts like Frumpy, Atlantis, Lucifer's Friend, Les Humphries Singers, and more, under this "Hamburg Scene" label. After a while, this became so obtrusive that it began to harm serious bands and musicians. They began to hate being labeled this way, musicians from other parts of Germany started shaking their heads about this promotion fuss, and finally, even record customers and concertgoers began to react bugged out to any mention of "Hamburg". In a way, it was a sellout that is reminiscent of Rolf-Ulrich Kaiser, but with more money behind it. Luckily, it petered out about two years later, but as a phenomenon, it had to be mentioned in this book.

AGITPROP

One of the first bands in Rolf-Ulrich Kaiser's roster was Floh de Cologne, an agitprop band from Cologne. The 1970s were the prime time of political rock bands – "agitprop" is a contraction of "agitation" and "propaganda".

KABARETT

Germany has had a tradition of "kabarett" since 1900, something these bands tied up with. Kabarett means staged political or socially critical satire with theatrical approaches, sketches, songs and blackouts. It goes back to Parisian cabaret (with c and one t) but is not to be mixed up with it. Kabarett, spelled with k and two t's, is to be found mainly in Germany, Austria and Switzerland. There is no similar tradition in other countries; standup comedy or satirical TV shows like "Saturday Night Live", "Spitting Image" or "Not the Nine O'Clock News" are not really comparable. Kabarett works quite well on TV but was the original domain of cellar theaters, bars, and small venues. Kabarett uses sketches, dialogues, monologues, songs, poems, and was, for most of its time, presented by ensembles. This kind of political kabarett was popular during the Weimar Republic until the Nazis put the whammy on it. After this, the best times for political ensemble kabarett were probably the late 1950s and the 1960s, when groups like Münchner Lach- und Schiessgesellschaft (a paronomasia on "Wach- und Schließgesellschaft", a then well-known security company), Düsseldorfer Kom(m)ödchen, or the Stachelschweine of West Berlin were stars on both stage and TV screens. The Münchner Lach- und Schiessgesellschaft's annual New Year's Eve show "Schimpf vor 12" (Rant Before 12; broadcast live on TV from

1963 to 1971) was an event, seen and discussed nationwide. In the second half of the 1970s, until roughly the 1980s, these classic kabarett ensembles lost their audience more and more; connected to the upcoming commercial TV and a changing public taste, they were replaced by solo kabarett artists, and less political comedy acts and stand-up comedians.

1968 had prepared the ground to combine kabarett with rock music. Best known are Floh de Cologne and Ton Steine Scherben.

FLOH DE COLOGNE

Floh de Cologne of – as you might guess – Cologne was founded in 1966 as a student kabarett group; after a couple of changes, the line-up was Hansi Frank (drums), Dieter Klemm (percussion, vocal), Markus Schmid (guitar, bass, organ), Dick Städtler (guitar, bass, organ), Theo König (saxophone, harmonica, clarinet, vocal), and Gerd Wollschon (lyrics, usually not onstage, sometimes playing percussion). Their name, literally meaning "Flea of Cologne", is a pun on the city's most famous export hit "Eau de Cologne". The Fleas, as they were called in short, were an offspring of the student movement and its organizations, as well as of the APO (extra-parliamentary opposition); later, they joined the Moscow-devoted DKP (Deutsche Kommunistische Partei, Communist Party of Germany).

When they saw The Fugs, the Edgar Broughton Band, and Frank Zappa's Mothers of Invention at the "Essener Songtage" in 1968, they decided to add music to their shows. Markus Schmid, the Flea's keyboard and guitar player, said: "Musically, the Mothers of Invention are our role models; in view of the show, it's more The Fugs who I consider more political and show-oriented."[1] It's hard to stifle one's laughter about this statement when you listen to the Fleas' actual output. None of them was a skilled musician. They adopted some standard chords and basic rock riffs, their compositions were usually built upon short-winded building blocks and bumpy rhythms, and again and again petered out in endless repetitions and pointless escalations. Their instrumental skills were modest; the vocals were bearable but not convincing. Floh de Cologne made good use of multimedia elements like films, slide projections, or feedings of original interview snippets or quotations on stage.

In 1969, Floh de Cologne signed with Kaiser's Ohr label, being one of its first acts. *Fließbandbabys Beat-Show* (1970, meaning something like "conveyor belt baby's beat show") was already their sixth "agitation revue", as they called their programs, but the first one that could be seen as a rock show. The stale music was slightly reminiscent of the organ-affected sound of THE DOORS; the lyrics were driven by Hubert Bacia's book "Themen zur Sexualität" (Topics on Sexuality) and Karl Marx's "Lohnarbeit und Kapital" (Wagework and Capital) which were both mentioned on the record sleeve as "recommended basic lecture". The show, in a contrived "cool" language, meanders between class struggle, sexual liberation, political groaners, Marxist theories, and vulgar psychology, at times using an embarrassingly primitive vocabulary – as if a 50-year old school teacher were trying to catch up with what he believes to be the slang of his 15-year old students. Besides this, this record (as all early records) of FLOH DE COLOGNE were infused with a perception of women that can be described only as antediluvian.

Profitgeier (something like "vulture capitalist") came one year later, partially recorded live, announced as "rock opera" (rock operas, after THE WHO's *Tommy*, were a big thing then), pressed in day-glow red vinyl and packed into an expensive gimmick sleeve, showing a plucked vulture from which giblets could be pulled out.

The "opera's" main topic was the working world of apprentices, sometimes with observations to the (polemic) point, like "He, hallo Stift" ("Stift", pin, was a colloquial word for apprentice). Apprentices in the late Sixties and early Seventies, particularly in small handicraft businesses, construction firms, garages, et cetera, had often worked under bad circumstances. They were used mainly as cheap workers for errands and other jobs that had nothing to do with job training, and this needed to be changed. But again, the lyrics of *Profitgeier* were loaded with inconceivably platitudinous class struggle fantasies, stale jokes and a preposterously biased image of capitalists, used in the sense of an identity-forming concept of the enemy. The whole "opera" was covered with clumsy music. The album sold around 20,000 copies.[2]

It has always been a mystery to me why FLOH DE COLOGNE (but not only them) still portrays capitalists as cigar-smoking fat guys wearing a black suit and a bowler hat, like they were seen during the industrial revolution of the 19th century. But this was the world view the FLEAS' programs preached.

This reservation also goes for FLOH DE COLOGNE's two (most likely) best records of their Ohr years: *Lucky Streik* (recorded live in 1972) and *Geyer-Symphonie in Rock-Dur* (1973; Vulture Symphony in Rock Major), both recorded and produced by Dieter Dierks. They were slightly more intelligent than their predecessors, and in countless concerts the FLEAS had learned to use their instruments a little bit more skillfully.

The double album *Lucky Streik* (1973) was subtitled a "rock jazz rocket", but there wasn't the slightest trace of jazz in it. Again using very simple rock structures, the show depicts "one hour in the life of Karl Arsch", a 22-year old fitter, during a worker's strike at the industrial plant where he works. A couple of his co-workers involved in the strike are introduced in passing, a sort of news ticker makes the leitmotif, and the whole show is spiced up with some satirical and socially critical songs ("Schön ist ein Jugendtraum", to name one of the better ones). *Lucky Streik* again serves as the public relations department of the DKP (Communist Party), describes the GDR as the workers' paradise on earth, but is more illustrative and entertaining than its predecessors. Unfortunately, the finale grows out again into a ridiculous series of declamatory songs about a glorious socialistic future without fear and misery ("Für die Zukunft seh'n wir rot"), combined with the unconcealed request to join the SDAJ (Sozialistische Deutsche Arbeiterjugend – Socialist German Workers Youth, the youth organization of the DKP) and/or one of the trade union's youth organizations, dinged into your head.

The *Geyer-Symphonie* (1974) was a different thing. The basic idea was great: FLOH DE COLOGNE used the original recordings of the epitaphs in commemoration of Friedrich Flick (1883–1972), given at his funeral service. This collage builds up the unpleasant portrait of one of Germany's most aggravating armament industrialists, his life, and his world view. Flick belonged to the sort of fellows I talked about earlier: a coal mining and steel baron who joined the Nazi party early on and made best profits with German rearmament – and, of course, with the war itself. He also profited from Aryanizations and the work of forced laborers. In December 1947 at the Nuremberg Trials, he was sentenced to seven years of imprisonment as a war criminal. But he didn't even have to fully serve this sentence, he was pardoned in 1950. He managed to gain ground very soon and, again, became one of Germany's leading steel industrialists. He also became the biggest stockholder of Daimler-Benz and had several other major shareholdings. At the stock market he was called "the vulture" – that's where this show took its title from. The epitaphs on Friedrich Flick were held by his old accomplices, industrialists Hermann Josef Abs, Fritz Berg, Konrad Kaletsch, Hans-Günther Sohl, and former Chancellor Ludwig Erhard. The latter probably was not too happy to have to speak there, but couldn't get away.

Though these were good reasons to come up with a satiric portrait, sadly, the band partially spoiled their good ideas through inadequate workmanship. Apparently even Dieter Dierks was no help in this. As on earlier albums, too much pointless "filler music" slows down the show, and even the *Geyer-Symphonie's* culmination point, a caustic tape montage made from the mentioned funeral speeches, war sounds, military marches, Nazi songs, and real and fake newsreel snippets, falls apart into ballyhoo and stale jokes with some apt exceptions. Anyway, *Geyer-Symphonie* is worth a listen, as long as you are able to understand German.

Musically, Floh de Cologne took a step forward when skilled musician and composer Vridolin Enxing joined the band. In regard to their next show *Mumien* (Mummies, 1974) about the Chilean putsch, they also worked with composer Hans-Werner Henze, and later with Argentinian composer and musical enfant terrible Mauricio Kagel; these collaborations left their traces. With *Mumien,* the band switched to the DKP-devoted Pläne label. With their program *Tilt* (1975), now recorded by Conny Plank, they presented what is likely their musically most attractive show. Ideologically, they stuck to their line, unshakable.

I've seen Floh de Cologne a couple of times live, and I have to admit that their stage shows worked a lot better than the records. But we have to keep in mind that the audiences usually were young DKP and SDAJ members, and they would have given thunderous applause even to the Duracell Bunny, had it been made in GDR.

Besides their work on stage and record, they delivered music for a couple of radio plays and TV movies; they obviously had some friends at WDR TV: From 1978 to 1980 there was a monthly satirical 15-minute show titled "Dreizack", to which Floh de Cologne contributed music and sketches. "Dreizack" was a regional magazine, only shown in North Rhine-Westphalia. It was shut down after just three years, but these contributions are the reason why the FLEAS became one of the best-documented German bands in the media. This is the main reason why FLOH DE COLOGNE is often seen as much more important or influential today than they actually were. It had always been their biggest problem that they couldn't reach audiences outside festivals and events organized by the trade unions' youth, SDAJ and DKP.

FLOH DE COLOGNE produced a couple of further shows and records, but the political landscape in Germany changed drastically in the late 1970s and 1980s, and FLOH DE COLOGNE, who unflinchingly stuck to their orthodox GDR-adoring socialism course, continued missing the boat. In 1983, after having played 3000 concerts and selling 400,000 copies of their eleven albums, they finally called it a day.

Today, FLOH DE COLOGNE is as good as forgotten. Some stalwarts in Krautrock online forums insist on calling them a great band or a "legend" – well, there's no accounting for taste, but my conclusion is a bit different: FLOH DE COLOGNE will be remembered for their contribution to the German kabarett scene of the 1970s. But as a rock band, they left no mark simply because, for them, music had never been more than a means to an end.

TON STEINE SCHERBEN

Another political band that is still frequently mentioned and adored today is TON STEINE SCHERBEN of West Berlin. In 1966, guitarist R.P.S. Lanrue (= Ralph Peter Steitz) and singer/lyricist Rio Reiser (= Ralph Christian Möbius, 1950–1996; his pseudonym goes back to a novel character) lived in Rodgau (Hesse) and ran a band named BEAT KINGS (sometimes also spelled BEATKINKS); later, they founded DE GALAXIS. The two of them moved to Berlin in 1967 where, in a theater project, they met bass player Kai Sichtermann and drummer Wolfgang Seidel. This became the first line-up of TON STEINE SCHERBEN. In German, "Ton" can mean "sound" or "musical note", as well as "clay", but "sound" makes more sense here, so the name can probably be translated to "Sound Stones Shards". There are two possible origins for the name: One goes back to Troy discoverer Heinrich Schliemann who once said: "All I found was clay, stones, and shards." The other one is a pun, based on the name of Germany's construction workers union: "Bau, Steine, Erden".

Ton Steine Scherben, in short called "the Scherben" or simply "TSS", were mainly a product of the student movement and the squatter scene in West Berlin's Kreuzberg neighborhood. There they found a very active and in parts successful scene: The Senate of West Berlin planned to tear down lots of old tenement houses – most were in unacceptable shape. They were to be replaced by blocks of new apartment buildings. But because it was unlikely that many of the people living in Kreuzberg would be able to afford the rent for these new apartments, the houses were squatted to prevent them from being demolished – in the end, it was more than 160. The Senate finally gave in and decided to modernize big parts of the old fabric of the buildings (which then led to protests because, of course, the rent could not be kept at its former level – as always, it was impossible to please everybody).

Ton Steine Scherben, in a way, became the squatters' public relations department. Their music was simple, rough, and unpolished. Without much sense for rhythm or timing, Reiser bellowed out his lyrics – his alcohol problems were already obvious then. The band's perception of evil capitalists was as worn-out as Floh de Cologne's, but other than theirs, Reiser's and Ton Steine Scherben's songs were undogmatic and characterized by an absolute will for personal freedom – unfortunately, without caring a straw about other people's personal freedom. It was the old "them" against "us" mentality. In addition, at least on their first two albums, the Scherben were very indifferent about physical violence against persons and things, as their first underground hit shows: "Macht kaputt, was euch kaputt macht" (Destroy What Destroys You; 1970) – they meant what they said, and the slogan became a sort of street hit at many protest marches and squattings. Kreuzberg and its population was an ideal biotope for this.

In September 1970, the band played the "Love & Peace Festival" on the island of Fehmarn; for unknown reasons under the name Rote Steine. When the festival organizers decamped with the cash box without paying the bands, Reiser asked the audience to kick their asses. The audience then set the organizer's booth on fire, and later, after the band had played "Macht kaputt, was euch kaputt macht", the stage went up into flames. I'm not sure whether the band had expected to gain such a hot result, but they made it on the TV news, and this was certainly not the worst promotion they could have gotten.

Sometimes, their lyrics could cross over into the ridiculous. In "Mensch Meier" from their second album *Keine Macht für niemand* (1972; No Power For Nobody) they built up an enemy image that makes you shake your head: The band called out for mass fare dodging, and the ticket inspectors of the BVG (the Berlin transportation authority that runs buses and subway) were attacked as if they were the incarnation of the class enemy. While you can smile about this song, the unrestrained violent fantasies in "Paul Panzers Blues" were more serious. Listen to it and then think of the kidnappings and assassinations the "2 June Movement" or the "Red Army Faction" later executed – I'm quite sure this is not what the Scherben had in mind when they wrote these lyrics, but there is a parallel you'll shudder when thinking about.

It was these kinds of lyrics and the band's consistent presence at various protests that had the police visiting them every couple of weeks in search of wanted persons, and, as their manager Nikel Pallat says: "Our telephone was always bugged. In parts, this was funny because we didn't need to pay our phone bill anymore. It was more important for them [the Office for the Protection of the Constitution] to keep us wiretapped than having us pay our phone bill."[3] Certainly, the band had a lot of contacts and a lot of visitors, and some of them might have been of interest to officials. But as said in an earlier chapter: Thinking that your phone was bugged or your mail was opened and read by authorities was common at that time. It made you think of yourself as more dangerous. We shouldn't take this *too* seriously.

On the other hand, TSS did songs crammed with direct, raw, unfiltered emotion, like "Komm, schlaf bei mir" (Come Sleep With Me) or "Schritt für Schritt ins Paradies" (Step by Step Into Paradise). The combination of street fighting songs that were as tough as nails, and songs exuding pure emotion, was a bit like the graffito "Gefühl & Härte" (Emotion & Toughness) you could find on several walls in West Berlin and other cities. Just read this as "Gemütlichkeit & Brutalität" (Coziness & Brutality), and you have one of the basic principles of any totalitarian political movement. I'm sure that TSS would not accept this attribution, but both the *feeling* behind the slogan and the *feeling* behind the graffiti is something that traces back to German Romanticism. I consider Ton Steine Scherben to be a band that was deeply rooted in this early movement, despite, or precisely because of, their radicalism.

Of course "Keine Macht für niemand" estranged them from the student movement: The leaders of the student movement *wanted* political power, so the concept of living without a ruler was something they couldn't accept. You can already see the big conflict in the left-wing scene coming up that eventually exploded in the 1980s. I will come back to it then.

In 1972, Wolfgang Seidel left TSS. Under the pseudonym Sequenza, he turned to electronic music and collaborated with Conrad Schnitzler, Eruption, and Alfred 23 Harth.

The wild romanticism of Ton Steine Scherben became even more evident when, in 1975, the band waved goodbye to Berlin and relocated to a farmhouse near the tiny little village of Fresenhagen (today a district of Stadum) in the north-west of Schleswig-Holstein, not far from the North Sea. They had gotten tired of being the entertainment providers for every protest or squatting in Berlin, always expected to play for free. Nikel Pallat: "Sometimes this led to trouble when they didn't even pay for the food after a concert, not to mention a fee."[4] For about every one in five concerts, the band incurred a loss. To distribute their first 45 ("Macht kaputt, was euch kaputt macht"), the Scherben had used some bootleggers who sold the record in pubs and at protests. Soon after this, they founded their own record label named David Volksmund Produktion. The records were to be had at concerts and by mail order, and while on tour, the band visited record shops and left-wing book stores. Pallat: "They bought our records and reordered when they were sold out. This made a quite well-working distribution network. … At our performances we always sold a lot of records, and this, in the first place, made it possible for us to live on when we returned to Berlin after a tour."[5] Sales figures, as usual, are hard to obtain; but *Keine Macht für niemand* sold circa 10,000 copies within the first six months[6] – not too shabby for this way of distribution, especially since *Sounds* and most other music magazines didn't care much about them. In 1976, Ton Steine Scherben became the founding members of the self-organized and independent label April, which was later renamed to Schneeball.

With their new countryside home, political references decreased, and they put more diligence into the music; the lyrics became more poetic. Albums with the theater group Rote Rübe followed; under their own name, TSS released *Wenn die Nacht am tiefsten* (1975, When the Night Is Deepest), *IV* (1981), and *Scherben* (1983). Parts of the lyrics were now written with the help of the Tarot. (Tarot was in the air at that time, I will come back to it.) *Wenn die Nacht am tiefsten* is seen by many as their best album. "Land in Sicht" (Land Ahoy) at least is a great song, Rio sings his heart out, and I'm sure in Berlin, this song wouldn't have occurred to them.

Rio Reiser had never been cagey about his homosexuality, but he rarely made it a major topic. But now, Ton Steine Scherben started to support the growing gay movement: In 1977, they cooperated with the gay theater group Brühwarm of Hamburg which resulted in the album *Mannstoll* (Man-crazy), a second one was entitled *Entartet!* (Degenerate!), released in 1979. (Brühwarm member "Corny" Littmann, by the way, was the one who, in 1988, founded the Schmidt

Theater in Hamburg's red light district St. Pauli, which started the renaissance of the more or less down-and-out Reeperbahn.)

In 1982, Ton Steine Scherben got Claudia Roth as their new manager, but it didn't help. Although their relatively dark album *IV* could well be seen as a trailblazer of the early Neue Deutsche Welle, their time was up. In 1985, Ton Steine Scherben finally resigned, with around 200,000 D-Marks in debt.

Claudia Roth later became a member of the European Parliament and one of the heads of the Green Party. Currently, she is one of the vice presidents of the German Bundestag.

RIO REISER SOLO

Singer and songwriter Rio Reiser started a solo career in 1986 with the album *Rio I.* on the CBS label, produced by Annette Humpe and Udo Arndt. Annette came from Ideal, Udo had had a schlager band named Udo Arndt & die Safebreakers with a 45 in 1966 on the Decca label: "Patsy Girl" b/w "Hey Girl". The Safebreakers then became Orange Surprise and eventually morphed into Os Mundi. Later, Arndt became a producer for Nena, Spliff, and others. On *Rio I.*, Rio Reiser was supported by illustrious musicians like Curt Cress, FM Einheit, and Peter Weihe. With Humpe, Reiser developed a sort of pop schlager style that became a minor success; *Rio I.* reached #26 in German album charts – it was probably a bit too snotty to reach the friends of mainstream pop, but positioned high enough in charts for many of the old Scherben fans to turn their back on him. As what usually happens in Germany for such cases, they immediately saw him as a traitor who was selling off his (and their) former ideals. Some 45s extracted from this album were the sassy "König von Deutschland" (King Of Germany) and "Alles Lüge" (All Lie), the love song "Für immer und dich" (Forever And You) and the melancholic "Junimond" (Moon In June). In the two latter songs, Rio especially presents himself in the best light, but none of the 45s reached chart positions. "Junimond" still gets airplay from time to time on some oldie radio stations. In 1986, the Green Party used "Alles Lüge" as an election campaign song. Five more albums followed until Reiser's untimely death in 1996 (aged 46), but he could never repeat the commercial success of his first solo album.

Reiser's brothers Peter and Gert recently donated Rio's estate – lyrics, handwritings, letters, tapes, et cetera – to the German Literature Archive in Marbach; in 2019, the City of Berlin decided to rename the Heinrichplatz in the Kreuzberg neighborhood to Rio-Reiser-Platz.

The Ton Steine Scherben albums, as well as Rio Reiser's solo efforts might have had their time, but they've passed their expiration dates. It is still easy for me to recall feelings and thoughts connected to the albums, but they didn't age well. You might see these records as a sort of historic landmark, but don't get fooled by your own nostalgia.

OKTOBER

Oktober of Hamburg was probably one of the most musically advanced bands in the political circle. They existed from 1975 until around 1980; ideologically, they sympathized with splinter group KB (Kommunistischer Bund). The most important of their three albums was *1871 – Die Pariser Commune* (1977), a double album released on the small independent Antagon label which was run by Hamburg's lawyer and concert promoter Jens Michow. Musically, they oscillated between bands like Genesis and Grobschnitt. On stage (I saw them once), they worked with slide projections and effects like the dry ice fog we knew from most prog concerts. Some of the *1871* lyrics were taken over from their label mates Schmetterlinge of Vienna with whom they sometimes shared the stage.

To name Oktober's other two albums: *Uhrsprung*, the name is a pun on "clock" (Uhr) and "Ursprung" (origin) – essentially, it probably means something like "time warp". It was released in 1976 on the Trikont label. Their third and last one was *Himmel auf Erden* (Heaven On Earth), released in 1979 on the Cologne Eigelstein label. The band fell apart after this; their head Kalla (Karl-Heinz) Wefel founded a new wave band named Clinch nobody ever heard of; today he lives as a local kabarett artist in Osnabrück.

SCHMETTERLINGE

Schmetterlinge was a band from Vienna, Austria. But as they were a constant in the political music scene of Germany, especially in the movement against nuclear power plants, I think it's appropriate to include them here. Their name, of course, is a pun: "Schmetterling" means butterfly, but in the German language, "schmettern" can also mean "singing at the top of one's lungs". Founded in 1969, they were fully professional musicians with an unusually wide variety of styles. They gigged as session musicians and backup singers for schlager productions, made schlager themselves, as well as recordings for children. They could play rock'n'roll as well as chansons, folk songs, or vocal swing in the style of Man-

HATTAN TRANSFER or NEW YORK VOICES (okay, not really as good as these, but close), and they presented this with theatrical or kabarett elements.

Their most profound show, *Proletenpassion* (Proletarian Passion), released as a three-LP-set in 1977, was a scenic oratorio in “Geschichte von unten”, as it was called in Germany, “history seen from below”. This was the latest fad at that time; even museums and educational TV films jumped on this train. In five acts, this show analyzed the Peasant Wars, the Civic Revolution, la Commune de Paris, Fascism, the October Revolution, and the presence – always seen from the perspective of ruled classes, but unfortunately not always with the historic precision they claimed for in the liner notes. All of this was covered with adequate music which the band was absolutely proficient in. One of the most impressive songs was their adaptation of Heinrich Heine’s furious poem “Die schlesischen Weber” (The Silesian Weavers). The only flaw of the *Proletenpassion* box might be the fact that the parts were audibly mixed by different persons.

In 1977, SCHMETTERLINGE took part in representing Austria in the “Grand Prix Eurovision de la Chanson” (which today is the “European Song Contest”) with a cheeky schlager parody named “Boom Boom Boomerang”, with lyrics by kabarett artist Lukas Resetarits – and struck the right note so well that they ended up in second to last place. That was nearly a compliment. Singer and flutist Beatrix “Trixi” Neundlinger had already breathed some Grand Prix air in 1972 when she reached #5 for Austria with “Falter im Wind” (Butterfly In the Wind) with her then band MILESTONES.

With *Herbstreise* (Fall Travel), released in 1979, they presented *Lieder zur Lage*, as the subtitle said – songs on the status quo, a mildly melancholic collection of songs about several topics that were on schedule in the late 1970s (you will read about these topics later). One of the songs (“Hände über Hönnepel”, Hands Over Hönnepel) about the resident’s fight against a planned fast breeder reactor at Kalkar (a small village at the Lower Rhine) had appeared earlier among several songs by other artists on a solidarity album, released by a local action group against this power plant: *Bauer Maas – Lieder gegen Atomenergie* (1977). At that time in Germany, there was no nuclear power station that was brought on line without massive and sometimes violent protests. Usually, the protests remained unsuccessful. This fast breeder reactor was one of the few exceptions. It finished in 1983 but never started running. This was probably one of the most important successes of the movement against nuclear power in Germany.

With OKTOBER and some other artists, SCHMETTERLINGE contributed to an album entitled *Alle Türen offen* (All Doors Open), recorded at their own

Schmettersound Studio and released in 1978 on the Antagon label. The album was dedicated to author and poet Peter Paul Zahl (1944-2011) who at that time, after a contentious lawsuit, was imprisoned for attempted double murder.

The, in my opinion, most meritorious record the SCHMETTERLINGE made was released in 1981: *Verdrängte Jahre* (Suppressed Years), a collection of songs written by the then nearly forgotten Viennese kabarett/cabaret writer Jura Soyfer (1912–1939) who had died while imprisoned in the concentration camp Buchenwald. In reviving his songs, the SCHMETTERLINGE showed their whole stylistic spectrum once more.

I saw them a couple of times on stage, and they impressed me every time with their professional versatility. The SCHMETTERLINGE waved goodbye with a last double album in 1982, entitled *Die letzte Welt* (The Last World). They became a children's theater group in 1985. Their lead singer Willi Resetarits (brother of kabarett artist Lukas) successfully appeared as "Kurt Ostbahn" in a rock band named OSTBAHN-KURTI & DIE CHEFPARTIE, originally invented during a radio show by host Günter Brödl. They played blues and rock with lyrics in Viennese dialect, they also covered some songs by Bruce Springsteen. ("Ostbahn" is a railroad line in the east of Vienna and a sort of "ordinary people" neighborhood.)

AND SOME MORE

In the Stuttgart area, a blues rock oriented band named HOTZENPLOTZ was active. The most spectacular thing one could probably say about them is that they had lifted their name from the popular children's book "Der Räuber Hotzenplotz" (The Robber Hotzenplotz) by Otfried Preußler, first published in 1962. The author was not happy to see the name of his character used for a rock band without permission and threatened them with a lawsuit, so they changed the name to VOLKS-MUSIK. Which, as you might have expected already, is a pun: Written this way, you can read the name as "folklore" as well as "music for the people" or "music about the people". (Making their name ambiguous was a general fad for bands from the political scene; a tradition they took from the classic kabarett ensembles.)

VOLKS-MUSIK's singer was the later filmmaker and TV host Albrecht Metzger ("Rockpalast") who, in an interview with *Sounds,* said: "We wanted to do political rock but didn't know exactly how that should look like. And then immediately the constraints of business started. To pay for expensive production equipment, the group needed to play. We were able to develop an individual sound because we always improvised freely and never covered any other songs. During all this time we never forgot our original plan to do political work. We avoided pop events and played only low-key, until after six months our show was ready."[7] Lyric-wise, the band preferred the wooden hammer. VOLKS-MUSIK's only album, *Morgens um 7 – abends um 8* (In the Morning At 7 – In the Evening At 8), appeared on the Pläne label in 1973. It was a flop and the band later disappeared from the scene without leaving a trace.

LOKOMOTIVE KREUZBERG was another band from Berlin-Kreuzberg, ideologically near the Moscow-devoted DKP (Communist Party). They were excellent musicians and made four albums between 1972 and 1977, all released on the Pläne label, by all accounts with massive support from FLOH DE COLOGNE. The most important thing that can be said about the LOKOMOTIVE is that, in 1978, they morphed into the NINA HAGEN BAND. Nina Hagen, a phenomenal singer from East Germany, had left (or had to leave) her country because of her protest against the expulsion of her foster-father, singer-songwriter Wolf Biermann, and now lived in West Berlin. In a way, Nina had to leave the GDR anyway; she was the textbook example of a bird of paradise, and in the long run, her talent simply would have dried up in the GDR's stiff and politically organized music landscape. Their first (self-titled) album as the NINA HAGEN BAND reached #11 of German album charts and #24 in Austria. They had a hit with "TV-Glotzer", a cover version of the TUBES' hit "White Punks On Dope" (1975). As the band got into trouble with Nina, the follow-up album, *Unbehagen* (1980), was done without meeting each other – the band recorded the backings, later Nina added the vocals. The album reached #2 in Germany and #9 in Austria. After Nina Hagen had left the band, they successfully became SPLIFF. This band had a couple of hits; the best known are probably "Carbonara" and "Heut nacht" (both 1982). Nina's further career became more and more of a roller coaster tour. She came up with (probably LSD-inflicted) U.F.O. sightings and keyed-up religiousness and ended up as the buffoon of pop – which, in view of her talent, is a shame, but, things happen. With the help of Giorgio Moroder, she had a minor hit in 1983 with a well-made electronic remake of "Ich weiß, es wird einmal ein Wunder gescheh'n" (I Know One Day a Miracle Will Happen), an old morale-boosting Nazi film schlager from 1942, originally sung by Zarah Leander. In fall 2003, Nina Hagen one more time showed her old format as the guest singer on APOCALYPTICA's 45 "Seemann", a cover version of a RAMMSTEIN song, but it remained a one-off.

Spliff, after a couple of perfectly produced, successful albums, disbanded and three of their members went on to form Froon. A friend of mine simply said: "This will come to nothing. Already the name doesn't work." She was right. Froon's only album (1988) went nowhere. The song "Bobby Mugabe", taken from the album as a 45, was a chorus of praise to Zimbabwe's leader and leaves a bad taste today. To be fair, when they recorded the song, they couldn't foresee that Mugabe would become one of the worst despots the African continent has ever seen. (And Froon were not the only ones. Robert Wyatt also fell into this trap; his song "The Wind of Change", recorded 1985 with the Swapo Singers, shows that it's always dangerous to cheer revolutionary leaders on too early – after a couple of years, they usually turn into a mirror image of what they once fought.)

Franz K. of Witten (in the Ruhr area between Bochum and Dortmund) was founded in 1969 as a blues rock band. Their album *Sensemann* (local slang for the Grim Reaper) from 1972 was one of the earliest rock recordings in the German language; the title might be connected to their van, a discarded hearse. They made several albums, often about local topics like the closing of coal mines, but also about the Third World or conscientious objection. This kept them alive for a while but never turned into a bigger success, so in the 1980s, they asked schlager singer and producer Peter Orloff to work with them. He did, and it resulted in records that would have been accepted in every beer tent at every amusement park. Mick Hannes and Walter Gerke from Franz K. became songwriters for schlager singer Ibo (1961-2000). (Alex Schwers of punk band Hass, as well as Gregor Kerkmann of Kreidler, also played in Ibo's live band.)

Politically, all of these bands had the tendency to preach to the choir, and they usually never got a big audience. Alcatraz, Checkpoint Charlie, Eulenspygel, Flying Lesbians, Ihre Kinder, Komkol, Lied des Teufels, Schneewittchen, or Schroeder Roadshow can all be seen as political acts, at least in parts. Some further projects, like Die Conrads, Dadazuzu, Druckknöpfe, Interpol, Panther (founded by Klaus Schulz who produced Ton Steine Scherben's album *Keine Macht für Niemand*), Sogenanntes linksradikales Blasorchester, Teller bunte Knete, Vorschlaghammer or skiffle band Peter, Paul & Barmbek were of only local relevance (if any).

Of course, there were also several singer-songwriters (in Germany called "Liedermacher") who could sometimes be counted in – Franz-Josef Degenhardt

(1931-2011), Sonny Hennig (1946-2019), Dieter Süverkrüp, Wolf Biermann (after he was thrown out of the GDR), Hannes Wader, Klaus der Geiger, Walter Mossmann (1941-2015), Konstantin Wecker, and some more can be named here.

HÜSCH

Many jazz musicians of the Sixties and Seventies were politically thinking people and not shy about expressing their opinion on political or social topics. Nevertheless, combinations of jazz and kabarett were a rare thing. But one kabarettist took the step of working with jazz musicians: In 1970, kabarett artist, singer-songwriter, and radio host, Hanns Dieter Hüsch (1925-2005), released the album *Typisch Hüsch* on the Pläne label. With top-tier jazzers Gerd Dudek, George Gruntz, Volker Kriegel, Eberhard Weber, Günter Lenz, Peter Baumeister, and Pierre Favre, he presented an interesting mix of songs, spoken word with free musical counterpoints, poems, and improvised music. The topics changed between philosophic questions, Vietnam, conscientious objection, torture, questions to the forefathers, being a minority, people who know everything, the meaning of solidarity, church, and even pollution was already a topic – as well as why we Germans can say anything we want: because nobody listens. *Typisch Hüsch* is still a head-cleaning adventure today.

But this album gave Hüsch a lot of trouble, and not for the first time – indeed this was *typical* for him. Hüsch was never the one to run with a pack. Many of his colleagues and (student) audiences saw the album as "not left-wing enough", not radical enough, too skeptical, or blamed Hüsch for being too critical against some ideologic "truths" of the student movement. All this was nothing new to him. He had been a kabarett artist since 1946, solo as well with an ensemble named Arche Nova, so usually he knew how to deal with audience reactions. But in 1968, at the Burg Waldeck festival, he was booed off the stage after just two songs. The audience wanted to have hard-as-bone agitation instead of humor, irony, and sometimes self-skepticism. Franz-Josef Degenhardt's song lines "Zwischentöne sind bloß Krampf im Klassenkampf" (Nuances Are Just Contrived in Class Struggle) were never his cup of tea.

Hüsch left Pläne Records, as well as Germany, for three years – partly because of the hostilities against him, partly because he fell in love with a Swiss actress. In Basel (Switzerland), he wrote what is likely his most complex, surreal, disturbing, bitter, and poetic stage program, titled *Enthauptungen* (1971), released on the Intercord label. There's an untranslatable pun in this title – you can read it as "beheadings" which might be a little reference to the way he felt treated by parts of the public, but in an abstract way, it can also be seen as the opposite of "Behauptungen" ("statements" or "assertions"). Maybe there's a little bit of Zen in the title – think about it.

After his return to Germany, the Hamburg-based jazz rock band ALTONA provided him with some backing tapes for his program and resulting live album *Nachtvorstellung* (1975), recorded in dummy head stereo at Deutsches Schauspielhaus in Hamburg.

Hüsch mainly worked as a solo artist for the rest of his life, usually giving around 200 performances a year. Although he was a pretty good pianist, a little Philicorda organ became his trademark ("my stage design", as he used to say) because he could use it not only for sound accents and backing chords, he also used it as a table for his manuscript pages. In the end, he had five Philicordas, strategically placed over Germany.

In his shows, he could be funny, silly, as well as dark and philosophical. He was a strong personality on stage, satirical and political, but agitprop was never his business. He also had an open eye for the funny aspects of everyday life. He was able to bring an audience to tears and catch them up one minute later. Some of his texts, like the series of "Hagenbuch" stories, are major literature, not far from Thomas Bernhard (whom he admired as much as I do). Hüsch has never been an easy one, but this is what made him outstanding. Some of his records carried me through some dark moments. After overcoming lung cancer, he suffered a stroke in November 2001 from which he didn't recover. The "man who couched jazz into words" (*Spiegel*) passed away in 2005.

SEVENTIES IN BITS AND PIECES

There's a lot left to say about the 1970s. Be warned: This will be a jumpy chapter; please see it as a sort of slip box, picking up several aspects that haven't been mentioned yet, but are important to understand the overall atmosphere of Germany in the 1970s, as well as the way music was connected to and formed by it.

CULTURE INDUSTRY

I think it's safe to say that the era of 1968 was largely embossed by the SDS (Sozialistischer Deutscher Studentenbund, Socialistic Students Alliance of Germany). Many of these protesting students were fans of Critical Theory and opposed rock music, simply because it was popular music. They were convinced that popular music was produced and distributed by a "culture industry" to dumb people down and keep them quiet. The ambassadors of Critical Theory, Theodor W. Adorno (1903–1969), Max Horkheimer (1895–1973), and Herbert Marcuse (1898–1979), claimed the existence of such a line of industry. In his main works, "Dialektik der Aufklärung" (1947, with Horkheimer) and "Philosophie der Neuen Musik" (1949), Adorno didn't even deny that entertaining music could have a sort of quality, but because the works of artists (composers, writers, musicians) are subject to economical and industrial logic, they cannot unfold the emancipatory potential the arts originally could have had. This way, they stabilize current power dynamics. As soon as a musician follows traditional structures (like intro – verse – refrain, et cetera), he is already on the wrong path because he uses rules that are given to him by the culture industry; what he plays does not take its form from the logic of the musical material he uses. For Adorno, every single piece of music calls for its very own individual form and structure, and if the musician or composer doesn't follow this call, the piece is heteronomous.

This is, indeed, very harsh. Consequently, Adorno asked for a listener who was an expert in music theory. Only such an expert could be able to see through the way a composition is made and fully understand its meaning.[1] It's obvious that pop music is not only unable to follow these rules, it's downright the *idea* of pop music and schlagers, to follow known structures.

In 1970, Hans Magnus Enzensberger, following Adorno, Horkheimer, and also Bertolt Brecht's much older "Radio Theory" (from 1930), tightened this concept of "culture industry" into an "awareness industry" ("Bewusstseins-Industrie"), as which he saw all media. This was another idea many students immediately accepted. But not only students – in a TV portrait of CAN, also Irmin Schmidt knew exactly how to use the fitting vocabulary,[2] as did Edgar Froese[3]. There was, however, also a much simpler reason for their critical stance on rock music: The student movement's leaders, Rudi Dutschke and his pals, didn't like rock music. They preferred folk and classical music. Sometimes, they liked free jazz, but they didn't have much of an idea of what it was about; it just sounded wonderfully wild and revolutionary.

Rock music was and still is surely a part of the youth's lifestyle, but be careful whenever you hear or read about rock music being "the soundtrack of insurrection" or something like this. It probably means that somebody wants to sell you a droll story from his youth when everything was still made from wood and thus more authentic than today.

Around the years 1968 to 1970, there was no music style that was typical for a special scene.[4] This is one of the reasons why the agitprop bands, as described in the past chapter, "existed" but were not influential. In the early 1970s, however, different youth scenes developed, and with them, different music. Consequently, there were different ways for a band now to become successful – but this could also mean different ways to fail. By now you've gotten a bit of a feel for the atmosphere of the 1970s, but let me show you more of the zeitgeist and its consequences for the music scene of this decade – the decade that turned out to be *the* era of what we call "Krautrock" today.

THE DECADE OF KRAUTROCK STARTS

Culturally, it's hard to determine where the 1960s ended and the 1970s began – similar to one decade before, when the first half of the 1960s was actually more or less the closure of the 1950s. A band like AMON DÜÜL II always remained a product of 1968, although the larger part of their career happened during the 1970s. CAN, in contrast, was also founded in 1968, but was clearly a 1970s project. It's not possible to draw a clear line between the decades.

German rock still wasn't "anybody's music" in the 1970s, but it was also not quite as exotic as it had been in the 1960s. People got used to the idea that, even in Germany, it was possible to create music that was not schlager or die-hard avant-garde. This gave a bit more self-esteem to rock bands, and around 1974 their working conditions and the infrastructure they had to deal with became more professional. But in German pop magazines, most articles about German rock bands still sounded like a report on a dachshund with two heads. Somehow the writers couldn't believe that such an exotic thing like German rock was possible. There was an implicit understanding that really interesting rock music could only come from England or America, but never from German sources. Additionally – an unpleasant fact – a couple of German critics never stopped talking down successful German bands. ELOY, TANGERINE DREAM, or SCORPIONS were their preferred targets. If you look behind the scenes, you will find that several of these critics had once failed with their own bands and hadn't gotten over it – a sort of "Why them, why not me?" phenomenon. Now they were jealous of successful bands and fought tooth and nail against them. Other critics were simply too conservative, narrow-minded, or lazy to deal with other people's creativity, and of course there were also various personal tiffs between critics and musicians. Remember what I wrote about pseudonyms, fantasy band names, budget- and schlager production: In actuality, the entire German rock scene was small, and after a while, everybody knew everybody.

Sometimes, journalists from newspapers, tabloids, or illustrated magazines outside the music field were even worse. Several of these guys (usually, they were men) had no clue about music in general, but bathed in cynicism and malice regardless. When these so-called journalists had to visit a press conference on the occasion of an album release of, say, an electronic band like TANGERINE DREAM, you could bet that the most intelligent question they asked would be whether these synthesizers were equipped with coffeemakers. They were neither interested to learn about the instruments or the new sounds you could produce with them, nor why synthesizers had opened up a completely new music genre that transcended "Popcorn". Klaus Schulze once invited several journalists to visit his studio. He wanted to personally show them what a synthesizer is. Only two or three journalists accepted the offer. Average journalists were mainly interested in chart positions because this was something that didn't overstrain their intellect and was easy to integrate into the articles they had to write. The resulting articles or reviews then looked exactly like this. The only exception was when the band happened to have a record in the U.S. or U.K. charts, or just finished a successful tour in these countries. Then the journalists were proud, as if they had been personally involved in the success. All in all, serious rock journalism in Germany was a depressing chapter with very few bright spots. More open-minded rock journalists were a rare species.

In November 1973, two of these bright spots, Olaf Leitner and Walter Bachauer of radio station RIAS Berlin, organized a German rock festival with KRAAN, GURU GURU, KARTHAGO, RANDY PIE, and TANGERINE DREAM which took place at the Deutschlandhalle Berlin. This was the first time a radio station organized and aired such a festival. Later, other stations followed, like WDR radio with its "Nachtkonzert" (Night Concert) series.

This turned out to be a signal: In 1974, for the first time, concert promoters accepted German rock groups. Tours became better organized and bigger venues opened for artists – not yet the "big" big ones, but a band could now hope that playing youth center after youth center with 25 people in the audience wouldn't be their eternal fate. Record companies developed a certain interest in German bands, and at least from time to time, radio and TV programs sacrificed a couple of minutes for German rock records.

This was an important step because it meant that bands had the chance to further develop. They could refine their ideas. The originally uncut ideas from the late 1960s now became polished. It was probably a question of time, but the consequence was that the German rock scene began to split into several sub-scenes. Or, seen the other way round: The scene as a whole began to fall apart. From the fan's point of view, this meant the selection of home-grown rock had widened.

In the United States, most rock'n'roll roads lead back to the blues, and that's the way most American musicians see their business. Klaus Doldinger: "In the U.S., you get codified as soon as a sort of success becomes apparent, and you will never get away from this. In Germany I could do anything I wanted to do."[5] As we don't have a Mississippi delta, there was no authentic blues to go back to or build off of. German musicians only had the choice of continuing to copy (and maybe adapting) the music they heard from U.S. or U.K. bands, or to find other sources they could absorb. They could also try to forget all this, pave their own path, and invent something completely new, and, as there was no prototype for anything, they were then free in their decision-making. But it's hard to forget the traditions you grew up with, and that's why German rock often sounded as if somebody willfully wanted to avoid sounding like the role model he obviously follows.

Suddenly, rock music even became a subject of scientific research. The "Evangelische Akademie Tutzing" (a renowned academy and convention center at Tutzing near Munich, run by the Protestant Church) started seminars about rock music. Essays and encyclopedias tried to shed a light on the mysteries of rock music culture. In 1973, *Spiegel* writer Siegfried Schmidt-Joos published the first "Rock-Lexikon", written in German, an encyclopedia of rock musicians and bands. This book, largely written in the often snobby *Spiegel* style, was anything but objective, and had nearly no entries about German rock groups. It was very orthodox about the question of what rock music was, what its roots were, and who was allowed to call themselves a rock musician. I still have to smile when I think about this flaw in the "Rock-Lexikon"'s first edition: You remember JETHRO TULL's made-up story of 12-year old Gerald Bostock and his oh-so-dirty prize-winning poem "Thick As A Brick", "documented" in a fake newspaper named *St Cleve Chronicle*. The "Rock-Lexikon" reported this story as true. Later editions had additional co-writers, among them RIAS journalist Barry Graves (real name Hans-Jürgen Deutschmann, 1942–1994); the spectrum of entries widened and the encyclopedia was open for at least a few of the most important German acts.

In 1975, writer Günter Ehnert published the first edition of "Rock in Deutschland", an encyclopedia of German rock bands and musicians – generally useful, but should be read carefully because it is flawed with several slips. Ehnert ascribes, for example, a classical education in piano and vocals to OUGENWEIDE's singer Minne Graw (which she doesn't have); another example is his claim that the ballet company of the Württembergische Staatsoper danced to KRAFTWERK melodies, but there's no mentioning of KRAFTWERK found in the company's programs (as far back as 1970). But at that time, without having the internet, discogs, or Wikipedia, the research for such an encyclopedia was a tough challenge. Flaws happen, maybe still today, maybe even in the book you hold in your hands.

GERMAN ROCK IN FILM AND TV

The relationship between German rock musicians and the media in the late 1960s and early 1970s was a bit "at arm's length". There were some short reports about German rock or band portraits in some well-established cultural TV broadcasts like "Titel, Thesen, Temperamente" or "Aspekte", but that was it. In the mid-1970s this relationship got a little push, especially by TV stations when university graduates started their careers as editors, but connections between rock musicians and young filmmakers from film academies also formed. This was new. If we desist from a few typical music comedy movies like *Hurra, die Rattles kommen*, there had never been a close connection between film, TV, and rock music in Germany. But now, bands or musicians started writing and/or playing music for films – Wolfgang Dauner, Eberhard Schoener, CAN/Irmin Schmidt, Peter Hesslein, Klaus Doldinger, POPOL VUH/Florian Fricke, IMPROVED SOUND LIMITED, and others. But musicians were rarely cast as actors, and no band had ever been cast before to play "themselves" in a serious feature film. Here are two examples:

The first one was a TV movie, shot in 1976 and titled *Notwehr* (Self-Defense)[6]; with Günter Lamprecht the film had a top-rate actor in the lead; you may know him from Fassbinder's *Welt am Draht* or *Berlin Alexanderplatz*, several other actors from the cast were known mainly from popular TV series. A rock group lives in an old abandoned guest house in a small village and – how else could it be? – is regarded with suspicion by the villagers. Then, one day, a murder happens, and the band members are thought to be involved – wrongly, of course. The band, in the movie named DIE RATTENFÄNGER (The Pied Pipers) is played by GURU GURU, with drummer Mani Neumeier acting in a leading part. The other band members were Jürgen "Jogi" Karpenkiel, Sepp Jandrisits and Roland Schaeffer; the latter had had a connection with screenwriter Bernd Schroeder, leading to the band's hiring. Neumeier: "Unfortunately we were not allowed to use the name GURU GURU because this would have been promotion for the band"[7] – illegal covered advertising, to be precise. The movie was shot on location at Langenthal in the Odenwald region near Heidelberg where GURU GURU resided from 1974 to 1976. The film, shown in 1977 on ZDF TV, came with a sometimes painfully wagging pedagogic forefinger. Additionally, it showed that acting might be better left to actors. But of course, the band had the opportunity to play some pieces of their repertoire. No soundtrack album was made, but the film cranked up GURU GURU's record sales. Mani Neumeier: "After the broadcast, we were ten times as famous as the day before. Everybody knew us from TV. Even a policeman who stopped us said: 'Oh, I saw you on TV yesterday'. It is unbelievable that after a single appearance on TV you are more well known than after 500 regular concerts. I find this a little bit strange, but at the time it helped us very much."[8] To fully understand this phenomenon, we have to keep in mind that in the mid-1970s, Germany still only had its three public TV networks, so it was no rarity that a TV show was watched by 15 or 20 million people. This changed drastically in 1984 when the first two big commercial TV stations began broadcasting.

The second example came in 1976. A TV series called *Goldener Sonntag* (Golden Sunday), a WDR TV production, appeared on screens. Nobody was allowed to disturb me when this show was on; I even took my telephone receiver off the hook to make sure nobody would call (answering machines were not a common thing then). It was a family series, but an experimental one: It aired Sundays at 11:15 am, and that was also the time the show itself was fictitiously set – a family in their living room, kitchen or dinette on late Sunday morning between breakfast and lunch, watching TV, talking and/or bickering, sometimes about family things or relationship problems, sometimes about political or school-, university- or work-related stuff. All actors had their real first names, Hanns Dieter Hüsch played the father. The screenplays had no written dialogues, they only established topics and situations, the actors then had to improvise. Every episode opened with someone from the family entering the living room and turning on the TV set to watch a (fictitious) morning show called "Sonntagswecker" (Sunday's alarm clock), hosted by Albrecht Metzger (from Volks-Musik, later "Rockpalast" host). This fictitious "Sonntagswecker" started with jazz rock at its best, played by Wolfgang Dauner, Albert Mangelsdorff, Jiggs Whigham, Barbara Thompson, Charlie Mariano, Kenny Wheeler, Ian Carr, Ack van Rooyen, Eberhard Weber, Volker Kriegel, Jon Hiseman, and Alex Riel. This nameless bigband had been the in-house band of a real existing TV show called *11½* and now appeared in this fictitious part of *Goldener Sonntag*.

The driving forces behind the band were Wolfgang Dauner and Volker Kriegel, and they had the idea of transforming this project into the United Jazz + Rock Ensemble. It was the first time in Germany that a band that had been invented for a TV show, left its fictitious playground, and continued a real life off the screen. The United Jazz + Rock Ensemble members even founded their own record label (Mood Records, distributed by Zweitausendeins) and continued playing together until 2002; their probably best album is *Live im Schützenhaus* (1977).

Goldener Sonntag had two seasons, existed from 1976 to 1978, and had – unimaginable in today's binge watching era – not more than 18 episodes, shown once a month. The co-writer for the second season was Gerd Wollschon (1944-2012), one of the heads behind agitprop band Floh de Cologne (as said earlier: They had friends at WDR).

BUILDING SCENES

Many musicians took advantage of the now developing diversity. Several new genres, listed here in no special order, came into life this way – some innovative and some more "standard". Not all of them can be separated accurately from each other:

- A psychedelic "cosmic rock" scene came up, following the lines that Pink Floyd, Gong, Hawkwind, Amon Düül II or early Guru Guru had sketched out (like Nektar, My Solid Ground, Mythos or Grobschnitt);
- a "prog" scene developed, bands like Abacus, Embryo, Missus Beastly, Sixty-Nine, Triumvirat or Wallenstein circled around role models Yes, Genesis, King Crimson and Emerson, Lake & Palmer, other bands more or less skillfully borrowed elements from the Canterbury scene (like Satin Whale, Ramses or Eloy);
- suddenly there was a "folk" or "folk rock" scene with bands like Ougenweide, Fiedel Michel, Fraunhofer Saitenmusik, Elster Silberflug, Bröselmaschine or Wunderwald, maybe also Witthüser & Westrupp, or Achim Reichel with *Dat Shanty Alb'm*, and others. What these bands did was very different from what could be heard at the Burg Waldeck folk festivals in the 1960s, and this new movement was interesting because German folk had been frowned upon in the 1960s due to its tradition and misuse during the Third Reich;
- following the traces of project *Jazz Meets India* (1967) by Irène Schweizer Trio with Manfred Schoof, Barney Wilenand and the Dewan Motihar Trio, a highly interesting "world music" scene absorbed elements from music of non-English or non-American parts of the world, especially Embryo, Agitation Free, the Dave Pike Set with Volker Kriegel's sitar playing, Okko Bekker's *Sitar & Electronic* (1971), later Die Dissidenten, but a band like Yatha Sidhra with their Indian elements could also be counted in;
- a "hard & heavy" scene (Scorpions, Lucifer's Friend, Epitaph, Kin Ping Meh, Karthago and more);
- a "jazz rock" or "fusion" scene, a strong point in Krautrock and often interlocked with the "prog" scene (Aera, Dave Pike Set, Eiliff, Emergency, Kollektiv, Kraan, Message, Missus Beastly, Odin, Passport, Rozz, United Jazz + Rock Ensemble and several more with mostly excellent musicians);

- an "experimental" scene (like NEU!, CAN, POPOL VUH, DZYAN, ASH RA TEMPEL);
- an "electronic rock" scene (KRAFTWERK, CLUSTER, HARMONIA, TANGERINE DREAM, MYTHOS, SEESSELBERG, Klaus Schulze, also ASH RA TEMPEL and their later incarnation ASHRA and others);
- the "agitprop" scene as described in the past chapter (FLOH DE COLOGNE, LOKOMOTIVE KREUZBERG, TON STEINE SCHERBEN et cetera);
- a "rock in German language" scene (IHRE KINDER, MEISTERSINGER, EMBRYO, Sonny Hennig (1946-2019), Achim Reichel, Udo Lindenberg);
- a "romantic rock" scene (NOVALIS, in parts HOELDERLIN and JANE), not to be mixed up with the later "New Romantics" from England;
- a "soul", "funk" or "rhythm'n'blues" scene (FRUMPY, ATLANTIS, JOY & THE HIT KIDS).

This list is necessarily incomplete; there were several more styles and more bands within those styles. Not to mention all the crossbreeds that came up more and more because many musicians knew each other, listened to each other, and sometimes played sessions together. Every single sub-scene developed more and more sub-sub-branches after a while.

GOING SOLO

Many musicians now felt that it might be a good idea to go solo instead of working permanently with their usual band: Edgar Froese as well as his bandmate Peter Baumann of TANGERINE DREAM, Lutz Rahn of NOVALIS, Jean-Jacques Kravetz of FRUMPY, Manuel Göttsching of ASH RA TEMPEL, Eroc of GROBSCHNITT, Holger Czukay of CAN, Inga Rumpf of ATLANTIS (with a ridiculous album in German, titled *Second-Hand Mädchen*, 1975), to name just a few.

It was the more and more refined studio technology with its 8- or 16-track recording that made it technically easy for a musician to play all the instruments himself. It was not a new phenomenon – the American guitarist Les Paul and his wife Mary Ford first had done complex "sandwich" recordings in the 1950s; later, in the early 1960s, they started using a multitrack tape recorder, specially built for them by Ampex. In Germany, Caterina Valente, organist Klaus Wunderlich, or schlager singer-composer Hans Blum (later known as Henry Valentino) had done solo recordings using these techniques. In the U.S., Stevie Wonder had also made use of multi-tracking and overdubbing. But only a few people were aware of this, so when Mike Oldfield laid down *Tubular Bells* by playing at least ten different instruments himself, Virgin was able to promote this fact as a special highlight. The world-wide success of the *Bells* made it clear that this solo recording concept could work. Achim Reichel, Lutz Rahn, Eroc, Manuel Göttsching, and other musicians in Germany picked up this idea.

Not all solo musicians did it this way. As effective as this solo production method seems to be, there are some requirements that have to be fulfilled until you can start. First, you have to be able to play different instruments, or you must at least have the imagination for how to use them before you can write an arrangement for them. Writing a good arrangement is an art in itself; it's not without reason that arrangers receive the same amount of royalties as composers and lyricists.

Second, during the recording process, you can't communicate with other musicians, so you have to know exactly what you want, and this can be rather abstract when you work alone in the studio. This is why many solo musicians worked with hired session musicians; others preferred working with musicians they knew from befriended bands, like Carsten Bohn (of FRUMPY) and Wolfgang "Zabba" Lindner (of RELEASE MUSIC ORCHESTRA) for their joint project *Vollbedienung Of Percussion* (1974), or, like Holger Czukay who worked with members of his home base CAN for his album *Movies* (1979), as well as Hellmut Hattler who worked with his KRAAN colleagues for his solo album *Bassball* (1977).

Recording solo had another consequence: Records were no longer a simple reproduction of a session that had happened in a studio, they were a medium in their own right. On record, musicians, producers, and sound engineers could construct things that never happened in reality – Holger Czukay's *Movies* with its multiple radio snippets is an example, but also TANGERINE DREAM's "Cloudburst Flight" from their album *Force Majeure* (1979): Edgar Froese's seemingly fast guitar solo was recorded at a slowed-down tape speed.[9] It could be impossible or at least cause problems to reproduce these results live on stage without technical tricks or feeding in backing tracks from tape. Klaus Schulze did this when he performed "Ludwig II. von Bayern" from his album *X.* (1978) on stage: The orchestral strings had to be added from tape, and as it was not possible at the time to synchronize tape recordings with a live sequencer, not only the strings but also the basic sequences had to be part of the backing tape.

Well-informed people in the audience knew about this fact and understood why sometimes in electronic rock concerts there was no other way, but there were always some people perceiving it as fraud. And in some cases the suspicion that the whole concert was a playback was justified.

GET OUT TO THE COUNTRYSIDE!

Another thing that marked the early and mid-1970s was a general trend of leaving cities and relocating to the countryside. When they left West Berlin and moved to Fresenhagen, TON STEINE SCHERBEN were pioneers in this trend. CLUSTER and Michael Rother, as mentioned, moved into a 16th-century farmstead at the Weser River. GURU GURU lived in an old guest house called "Zur Krone" in the village Langenthal near Heidelberg. FAUST moved into an old school building at Wümme, a tiny little village not far from Bremen. NEKTAR lived in a farm house in Seeheim-Jugenheim near Heidelberg. Klaus Schulze moved from West Berlin to Winsen at the Aller, not far from Hanover. The KRAAN members and their loved ones relocated to a big old farm house called Wintrup, near Steinheim in the Teutoburg Forest. Usually, it's very lonesome there except once a year around summer solstice: At this time, a trail of old and young hippies, esoteric fans, druid trainees, neo-Pagans, and unfortunately also nationalists and neo-Nazis, march past there on their way to the Externsteine, a sandstone rock formation with some mythical background. KRAAN was in the lucky situation of not having to pay any rent. Count Metternich, the owner, just wanted them to play some advertising music for his mineral water. In the end, this music was not even used; it ended up as a sort of parody of a commercial on their album *Andy Nogger* (1974); "Nogger" was – and still is – the brand name of an ice cream lolly.

If living in the countryside wasn't possible, then alternatively, it became a fad to live in well-arranged flat-sharing communities, grow your own pot, and leave the big bad world at your doorstep.

ALTERNATIVE MOVEMENT

Both countryside as well as flat-sharing communities became the playground for what is known as the "alternative movement" – one of the big formative labels of the German Seventies, musically as well as sociologically.

It is not easy to determine when exactly this movement started. Political scientist Wolfgang Kraushaar sees the basic idea as already imported from Abbie Hoffman's "Woodstock Nation" (1969) in the United States: "[Hoffman] had the idea that it would be possible to take the Woodstock experience of collectivization, spread it over the whole country, and change the directness of the collective emotional state into permanence. ... This model, which had been discussed for a while in the U.S., also had its fans in Germany. ... This movement constantly assured itself of its own importance, and by the attention of the media, it mirrored how revolutionizing all this was. In the end it was about the utopia of living in the moment, feelings of delimitation, a different sexuality, and so on. 'Community' didn't mean a separate utopia, it meant the growth of a big, not abstract, but very concrete counter society that fulfills itself bit by bit."[10]

This sounds more abstract than it actually was. 1968 *had* left some traces. In Germany, the baby boomer generation started a bit later than in the U.S., because before the baby boom, destroyed Germany had the "war children" generation. It was in the Seventies when the baby boomer generation got old enough to think about the way they wanted to live. Parts of it wanted to live differently from the prissy way their parents did, and, unlike earlier generations, *they were able to do this*. This was the important impulse.

Besides living in communities and/or in the countryside, the outer signs of the "alternative scene" were brownish teapots and warmers, tea bowls without handles (you always burned your fingers, but it was very stylish), at least forty-six different sorts of aromatized tea on your kitchen shelves, piles of dirty plates in the sink, incense sticks, candles, self-rolled cigarettes, lava lamps, flokati rugs on the floor, early feminism. In every "alternative" home now you could find the German edition of J.R.R. Tolkien's "Lord Of The Rings" on the shelves (three volumes in a slipcase with green covers by Heinz Edelmann of *Yellow Submarine* fame), side by side with Michael Ende's "Momo" and "Die unendliche Geschichte" (The Never-Ending Story) – the latters often as pirated prints because, as I often heard, "we are not willing to spend our money on such bourgeois cultural crap", which everybody did want to read, but nobody wanted to pay the author for. (These prints were sold by traveling hawkers in every student pub, who were usually well accepted by the innkeepers as well as by the readers. Who cares about the fact that the "pirates" who made these typically piss-poor prints stole the authors' income and made a mint from it themselves. We've already discussed this phenomenon in a similar way in the context of fans who wanted to have bands play, but didn't want to pay any entrance fees. True artists, musicians, and writers, as we all know, live from air and love, not from profane money, and so they're expected to keep quiet when they get ripped off. Being paid for brain work has never had a big tradition in Germany, except if you are an engineer.)

Every youth center or music club now called itself a "communication center" and had a tea room with dim lighting and, of course, tea bowls without handles. On every table stood a drip candle plugged into the neck of an empty wine bottle, and music by Ravi Shankar played at low volume in the background.

Connected to these outer signs there were also some inner changes, and they were a bit more serious. One of them was that people became politicized. But while the activists of 1968 had preached, "Even the private is public", this "alternative scene" now reacted the other way round. They insisted in the conviction that changes could only happen individually and in private. The "alternative" rock audience then retreated more and more into their own private lives.

For concert promoters, this was not an easy thing to deal with: This audience didn't use the advance sale for concerts, they would just spontaneously decide in the afternoon whether they wanted to visit a concert in the evening. If so, they purchased the tickets at the door. West Berlin's audience was especially known and disliked for this. If there happened to be an important soccer game on TV that night, every band, even the biggest acts, could experience a washout. For the concert promoter, booking an artist or a band for a concert in West Berlin could be a serious risk for this reason.

An unpleasant side phenomenon was that in the mid-1970s, it became fashionable to start concerts with a heavy delay – not five or ten minutes, sometimes 45 minutes, an hour, or more, and not only in youth centers or clubs, but even in serious concert halls. Some roadie usually went up and down the stage, pretending to do something, like "testing" the mikes ("One, two, three, test, test ..."), but later, not even this happened anymore. When a concert was announced for 8 pm, you knew it would not start before quarter to nine or later. The audience accepted this as God-given, as well as – strangely – the concert promoters. Sometimes, after a while, the audience started booing, but that was taken into account as part of the game, and sadly, I have never experienced a band getting welcomed with a wave of booing that they deserved from their paying audience for the way they treated them. It was not until the mid-1980s that this nasty phenomenon finally tapered off.

MIXING SHOW ELEMENTS

Because Germany is not that big and bands closely observed what their competitors did, there were soon overlaps; different scenes influenced each other. The proggies could live with the jazz rock fans, the folk rock fans accepted some stuff from the romantic side, the psychedelic fans could also be approached with some varieties of hard rock – you get the picture. Crossbreeds were possible, a band like HOELDERLIN, for example, could be seen as romantic as well as prog and could find their audience in both camps. MY SOLID GROUND from Rüsselsheim saw their self-titled and only album from 1971 (produced by Peter Hauke and engineered by Dieter Dierks) as both hard rock and psychedelic. There was a short-lived project called Brave New World, an interesting mix of styles which could be seen as psychedelic and medieval, electronic, or jazzy, as on their only album *Impressions On Reading Aldous Huxley* (1972), developed and played by musicians from – you won't believe it – Bert Kaempfert and James Last, the NDR Studio Band and the circle around Achim Reichel. Yatha Sidhra of Freiburg, with their album *A Meditation Mass* (1974), recorded at Windrose-Dumont-Time Studio, produced by Achim Reichel and Frank Dostal, can be seen as both world music and prog or jazz rock. The band had a record deal for three albums with Brain, but *A Meditation Mass* remained their only one. It got stuck at around 4000 sold copies, so the label forfeited its option. However, the album later saw several re-releases and has a sort of secret cult status today. Mythos of West Berlin was seen as both "Berlin School electronic" and "prog". Novalis was seen as both "prog" or "romantic" and "German language" or folk rock (because sometimes they used historic German lyrics). The founding father of Guru Guru, drummer Mani Neumeier, originally came from Swiss Irène Schweizer Trio with his later band mate Uli Trepte on upright bass, playing hardcore free jazz with a heavy influence of rock (check out *Early Tapes*, recorded in 1967, released 1978 on FMP Records) – Irène Schweizer, by the way, is still a powerful pianist, and by playing with her, Mani and Uli learned the art of improvisation. Guru Guru Groove (as the band was named in the beginning) first became a raw and noisy psychedelic project, and on stage they sometimes played behind the speakers, often tripping on LSD. That might have been fun for them, but the audience was usually less convinced. Later, they deleted the "Groove" and started presenting little sketches or costumed scenes during their concerts. This had also attracted fans of Grobschnitt, whose stage show was based on slightly psychedelic prog rock combined with theatrical show elements and a sort of humor you may like, but don't have to.

The problem with this kind of theatrical material was always that if it was well made (which was the case with Grobschnitt as well as with Guru Guru), it could be nice and funny on stage, but you couldn't really put it on a record. Grobschnitt's *Solar Music Live* (1978) is an example of an album that tries to catch the spirit of their stage jokes acoustically, but it's flogging a dead horse. Guru Guru was a bit luckier with their "Elektrolurch" (Electro Amphibian): Mani with his rubber foam mask with little lightbulbs worked well on stage, but the track also worked quite well on their self-titled studio album from 1973; this is probably because they kept it compact. On the live-recorded version of this song on *Live* (1978), they dropped the ball. "Medicine Man's Overdose" from the same album also does not really work because you can "feel" that something is happening on stage, but in front of your turntable, you are left clueless. Actually, it's some nicely performed fire magic, but it doesn't help – you can't hear it. Guru Guru's eight-minute sketch "Das lebendige Radio" (The Living Radio), heard on *Tango Fango* (1976), is made only for record and spoofs a folksy radio show, hosted by "Hans Krone" (a little wink to the Haus Krone where the Gurus lived), including a real local accordion orchestra. This sketch works acoustically, but you need a pretty childlike humor to laugh about it.

Don't mistake my remarks as grumpy. I enjoy many kinds of nonsense, but all these attempts to plant humor into music, Guru Guru's as well as Grobschnitt's, or Amon Düül II's daffy "5.5.55" from *Made In Germany* (1975), share a problem that nearly all comedy records have in common: It might be fun to listen to them once, but how often can you laugh at the same joke? Holger Czukay fell into the same trap with "Bänkel Rap" from his album *Der Osten ist rot* (1984): It's funny the first time (if at all), but later you will skip the track. Besides this, most of these sketches are in German, so for an international audience, they are mostly meaningless anyway and will encumber sales in foreign countries. For this reason, it makes sense that the first international release of Czukay's record, a twofer which combines *Der Osten ist rot* and its follow-up *Rome remains Rome* (1987), omitted "Bänkel Rap", "Collage" and "Schaue vertrauensvoll in die Zukunft".

GENRE JUMPING

The 1970s of German rock were ideal for fans to catch interest in a genre they were not originally into when their favorite band switched to it: Guru Guru started with uncompromising psychedelic noise (albums *UFO* and *Hinten*), then morphed into a guitar rock trio. Sometimes they were nicknamed the "German Cream", but they didn't give up all of the psychedelia elements (*Känguru* (1972), *Don't Call Us – We Call You* (1973), *Guru Guru* (1973), *Dance Of The Flames* (1974)). Across the years, especially after the appearance of saxophonist Roland Schaeffer in the line-up, the Gurus changed into a fine jazz rock band (albums *Tango Fango* (1976), *Live* (1978) and later ones), and they took many of their old fans with them from one station to the next.

One of the most striking examples for genre-jumping is Achim Reichel. From his simple Liverpool-oriented RATTLES beat, he switched to WONDERLAND (with a little help of James Last), then to electronic and echo-laden A.R. & MACHINES psychedelia (*Die grüne Reise*, *Echo*, *Autovision*, *Erholung*). In 1973, he even presented "Meditative Improvisations" with very different musicians, such as Olaf Casalich of OUGENWEIDE, Peter Franken of DUESENBERG and TO BE, and Jochen Petersen of IKARUS and RANDY PIE, live at a "Nachtkonzert" in WDR radio. Later, he jumped to an album with rock versions of classic shanties: *Dat Shanty Alb'm* (1976) in English and Low German; maritime traditionals we all knew in North Germany because we had to learn and sing them in school. Then Reichel set classic poems to rock music: *Regenballade* (1978) – poems we also had to learn by heart in school, followed by *Heiße Scheibe* (1979) with something he called "comic rock"; an attempt he sees as "directionless" today[11]. Apparently, he was unsure where to go next. Besides these projects he became producer of NOVALIS, OUGENWEIDE, YATHA SIDHRA, and others. Not many fans followed him through all these stations, but there's no doubt that he did a good job in all these genres and never lost his overall credibility.

OUGENWEIDE

It didn't always work. OUGENWEIDE of Hamburg was a successful band that finally decided to do a style change, but fans did not follow. OUGENWEIDE took their name from a poem by Neidhart von Reuenthal, written around 1230. Today's correct spelling would be "Augenweide", meaning something like "eye candy". In a way, this band's story exemplifies the "inner" way the "alternative scene" went.

OUGENWEIDE, formed in 1970 and one of Germany's most impressive folk rock bands, did a pioneering and trendsetting job in developing what we know today as "medieval rock", although there is no real connection to today's "medieval rock groups", which are connected to Goth rock. OUGENWEIDE called it "minne rock" (Minne = Middle High German probably for "remembrance" or for "courtly love", but the exact meaning is not known anymore today). We knew bands like FAIRPORT CONVENTION or STEELEYE SPAN from England, but for Germany, this was a new concept. As a leftover from the Nazi era, German folk music was widely seen as problematic, even when it went back to much older sources. OUGENWEIDE integrated historic instruments like lute, oud, zither, flutes, hurdy-gurdy, Indian harmonium, crumhorn, and many more into a con-

Achim Reichel (on the right) with A.R. & Machines at the first British Rock Meeting (Speyer, September 1971) © Manfred Rinderspacher

temporary rock sound. Olaf Casalich and, as of the second album, Minne Graw (it's her real name!) had distinctive voices that blended beautifully together and seemed custom-made for this kind of music, just because they were not "rock" voices.

On their self-titled first album from 1973 they used original lyrics in Middle High German by minnesingers Neidhart von Reuenthal and Walther von der Vogelweide ("Nieman kan mit gerten kindes zuht beherten", a palindromic poem from around 1200, meaning "with a whip, you can't educate children"). On later albums, they discovered magic formulae like the "Merseburger Zaubersprüche" (Spells from Merseburg) or "Contra Uermes", an incantation to get your horse dewormed (maybe it also works on cats or dogs, but you better not try to sing it to your loved ones). They dedicated an album to *Eulenspiegel* (1976): Till (or Tyll) Eulenspiegel, born around 1300, was a wandering goliard (but not a court jester), known for cruel humor, holding up a mirror to everybody, to peasants as well as to nobilities or the clergy. Ougenweide used poems from the famous "Carmina Burana" ("Songs from Benediktbeuern", the manuscript of 254 poems from the 13th century is meant here; not to be mixed up with the cantata cycle of the same name by Carl Orff from 1935/36). Of course, they also used folk songs in dog Latin. Additionally, they wrote their own lyrics with a stunning feeling for the atmospheric "smell" of these long forgotten times like "Im Badehaus" (In the Bath House), "Der Schlemihl" (you know, this guy who sold his shadow to become rich) or "Bald Anders" (Soon Different), a mythic figure with a silver flute, based on a poem by shoemaker and master singer Hans Sachs around 1500. Bald Anders walks around all over the world, and he's seen with fear as well as with hope: When you happen to hear the sound of his flute, your life will change soon – turning to the good or the bad account, as the case may be. The blind might get back his eyesight, the rich might lose all his money, the lame might walk again, the lonely might find the love of his life – I'm sure you've heard his flute in your own life already. For their album *Ousflug* (Day Trip, 1979) they also used lyrics from a social-democratic songbook from the 1920s ("Denunziantenlied", Squealer Song); in 1978 they made an album entitled *Frÿheit* for a TV docu series named *Dokumente deutschen Daseins* (Documents of German Being), using lyrics by poets Georg Herwegh, Ferdinand Freiligrath or Theodor Körner from the "Sturm und Drang" (Storm and Stress) era around 1750 which induced the German Romanticism.

Ougenweide played small clubs as well as big auditoriums and open air concerts; they successfully toured England and even Russia. I saw them a couple of times on stage: They commanded a respectable amount of followers and were able to generate a Pied Piper-like power of attraction. In 1975, when Ougenweide played as the supporting act for Fairport Convention, they outacted the Brits by every trick in the book, although the Fairport's soundman did everything he could to make them sound as horrible as possible.

But then, around 1979, one half of Ougenweide got the feeling that their music had become outdated and they should make an album that included current trends. Their producer Achim Reichel: "The band thought: 'Now, as we have our own experience, we want more independence.' And this went along with: 'We bought a Moog …' This was the moment when I noticed: There's a sort of counter wave coming. … At the time I thought: The children fledge by now, they will go their own way."[12]

What was this style change based on? It was the change of the "alternative scene". Ougenweide was, again, exactly in the center of the trend. Political scientist Wolfgang Kraushaar: "Someday it had to be accepted that this model of a quasi-organic change of the society couldn't last. … I think it had been a subtle process of erosion that cannot be connected to a special date. Definitely, in the second half of the 1970s, there were already symptoms of fatigue, even if there was a certain upswing at the same time. There was a break, caused by the so-called 'Deutscher Herbst', and it interdigitated with the impulses of the Tunix meeting of 1978."[13]

TUNIX

"Tunix" was the transmogrification of "tu nichts" (do nothing); a name that was probably inspired by the popular "Asterix" comic books. Tunix, although widely forgotten today, was in fact an important impulse generator. The "Treffen in Tunix" (Meeting in Tunix) was a kind of congress, held at the Technical University of West Berlin in January 1978, organized by initiative of several independent political groups with the idea to unite the scattered groups and initiatives that had bowed out of the existing Mao-oriented or Moscow-devoted leftist groups. Around 15,000 participants came to the event.

Sometimes, Tunix is seen as the "official" starting point of the German alternative movement. I prefer to call it its culmination point; the alternative movement in the university cities of West Berlin, Münster, Konstanz, and Frankfurt had been cooking at least since 1973 or 1974, it just wasn't organized in any form.

Although its title seems to ironically point in the opposite direction, Tunix made a connection between the wishful fantasies of the "alternative scene" and the "real life". At Tunix, several projects were launched to develop alternative business concepts, set up alternative self-governing business companies, and find ways to provide them with capital. In the end, this led to the founding of the cooperatively organized "Ökobank" (Eco Bank) in Frankfurt in 1984. Considering that most Tunix participants stuck to Bertolt Brecht's old question, "What is the burgling of a bank to the founding of a bank?"[14], this might give you an idea of what a giant step this was. Several other networks and alternative institutions followed. In a way, it was what Rolf-Ulrich Kaiser had predicted in some of his books. Kraushaar: "[At Tunix] there was a certain atmosphere of departure, but at the same time, it was also a sign of wear. One had said goodbye to the claim of changing society as a whole."[15] It might be possible that somewhere behind the scenes, even Stewart Brand's "Whole Earth Catalog"[16] with its several editions between 1968 and 1972, had a little bit of influence. This project was the first try in the U.S. to organize and interconnect alternative projects of all kinds, and it had a big impact on the alternative scene there.

Finally, the Tunix' aftereffects became one of the driving forces to start citizens' initiatives against pollution and nuclear power plants, and ultimately, in the 1980s, had its part in the founding of the Green Party. But Tunix was also the starting point for many "New Age" projects to change clandestinely into for-profit businesses, as well as the starting point for the "undogmatic left", the

"Sponti" scene (a term derived from "spontaneous"), consisting of groups that teamed up occasionally and acted spontaneously (usually in a destructive way). The militant "black bloc" movement and some other not too pleasant appearances also started here.

HIPPIES

It is worth recalling in this regard that, in Germany, many people who referred to the American hippie movement had a pretty blurred perception of what the hippie movement was. They saw all hippies in the U.S. as politically left-wing, open-minded, and progressive. Of course, this was partially true, but it was by no means the case with all hippies. American hippies could be open-minded in some areas, while also extremely conservative in others. Writer T.C. Boyle made some nice novels from this. It has never been a contradiction for U.S. hippies to publicly burn their draft notices *and* be a fan of all kinds of guns, which would have been unthinkable for the German alternative scene. Many in Germany even took people in the U.S. for hippies simply because of their appearance. In Germany, JEFFERSON AIRPLANE was seen as the prototype of a hippie band, but their drummer Spencer Dryden (1938-2005) clears this up: "We weren't hippies. Hippies were the people that lived on the streets down in Haight-Ashbury. We were basically musicians and art school kids."[17] In the early 1980s, when the "alternative movement" slowly petered out, several German hippies made a last profitable hashish deal, used that money to start a bike shop or a wholefood store in the neighborhood, became gentrified, and still felt anarchic. The American hippies did basically the same, but they didn't start wholefood stores, they started *chains* of wholefood stores – and they started Silicon Valley. You see the difference.

Back to OUGENWEIDE. Their story went on. All this stuff I just described, all these movements, maybe subliminally, had left traces in the band. The result was their 1980's album *Ja-Markt* (Yes Market; a pun on the word "Jahrmarkt", which means "amusement park"). It had no lyrics from the Middle Ages anymore, its opener "Ich bin ein Folkfreak" (I'm a Folk Freak) showed the disillusioned self-portrait of a band that was obviously infected by all the great and optimistic ideas, but also the paranoia and discrepancies that had stamped the late 1970s. Other songs on the album teased some "New Age" trends or the political situation in general. *Ja-Markt* was an attempt to deal with the hiccups of a movement that the band members, in their personal life and habits, were deeply rooted in. Musically, the album was not even bad, but somehow ambiguous.

The sales figures confirmed that fans were not happy with this new concept, but they didn't give up on the band immediately. But in 1981, when the follow-up album *Noch aber ist April* (But Still It Is April) amplified this concept and became more wearily, most fans finally left the building. This was simply not the stuff one expected from Ougenweide.

The band ended up in quarrels about their next steps, got in financial trouble, and split up in 1983. Once more, they mirrored the basic discrepancies of the alternative scene: The "alternative" part only worked when it was embedded in a commercial concept – but when this worked, it wasn't alternative anymore.

For a long time, it was not possible for Ougenweide to get the rights on their recordings back from Polydor, so their eight original albums disappeared from the market, with the exception of a compilation named *Liederbuch* (Songbook, 1979). It was not until 2006 that Bear Family Records finally re-released the albums as twofers on five CDs (unfortunately without giving them a remastering). Today, some of the former members use their old rehearsal room as a professional sound recording studio (the Oton Studio in Hamburg; even Lou Reed recorded there).

Listening to the agitprop bands I introduced in the past chapter is nearly useless without having at least a basic knowledge of the German language. It is also useful when listening to Ougenweide, but you might find an alternative approach to them if you don't speak German. Their combination of mediaeval sounds and "prog rock", their profound musicianship, their feeling for atmospheres, and their high originality makes it easy to fall in love with them, even today.

DISCOTHEQUES

Every single one of the new emerging scenes in Germany had a tendency to stick to themselves and look down on the others – not so much the musicians, but the audience did this. Concert promoters especially had to keep this in mind when organizing a festival. Not that different fan groups would have fisticuffs (at least I've never seen any), but it's unpleasant enough when one half of the audience is always bored by the band that's playing.

In the 1970s, live music in general had a bit of a downfall. Singer Joy Fleming (1944-2017; Joy and the Hit Kids, Joy Unlimited): "We played old barns, crazy but live, we rocked our socks off, but suddenly, peu à peu, discotheques took over. But that is canned music! People went there more and more, they had no ears for live music anymore. So, what did I have to do after the live music era? I had to barnstorm discotheques, because live gigs decreased."[18]

This of course implied changes in the sound and style of recorded music. Not all musicians were happy with these changes because either their live business decreased, or they had to play live at discotheques, which meant short live slots, alternating with DJ sets. Under these conditions, it was impossible for a band to build up a dramaturgy for a stage show.

When records became more important, the consequence was an increasing influence from producers. Joy Fleming gnawed on this change, as her embittered statements in a TV interview still showed many years later: "This always meant: You're not allowed to sing this or to sing that. You're not allowed to wear this or that. And when the recordings were made in the studio, they had to be played to a record industry boss, one of these pinstripe guys with their tie, very distinguished, with their nice little cell phones, and they said: 'This is too modern for us', or 'We don't like it this way', or whatever – there were a thousand things they always had to criticize."[19] (Let's forget that cell phones didn't exist at that time; I think it's clear that Joy wants to characterize a certain type of businessman here.)

It was the remaining majority of "not alternative" people who now discovered the blooming discotheque scene instead of visiting concerts. *Saturday Night Fever*[20] had appeared in movie theaters in 1977, setting big parts of the agenda. People either loved it or hated it, it left nobody cold. The result, however: Record sales gained weight. But to be successful, the records of interest needed to be dance-compatible. This was not something most German rock musicians were up to. "Disco" was a cuss word for many of them. Several rock drummers had a terrible sense of rhythm, timing, or groove; many were hardly able to keep tempo or simply play a straight 4/4 rhythm without protracting it. Imagine what a hard job it was for them to play a disciplined disco rhythm! Because not all drummers were able to play their set in one go with the needed precision, it wasn't uncommon that at a recording session, the producer after two hours said something like: "This is a waste of time, let's record the drums successively. First play the bass drum only, then we record the snare drum, then the hi-hat, and so on." You might reckon this to be idiotic, but sometimes it was the only way to get the needed timing precision within a realistic studio schedule. I've seen this with my own eyes at Alster Studios. In a "making of" of Blondie's "Heart of Glass", we see the same practice: It becomes clear after a while that drummer

Chris Stein was not able to play precisely enough with the rhythm machine – which of course is a nightmare for every drummer.[21] So the looping of bass drum and snare drum became a common practice in some studios. This is one of the reasons why it may have been a relief for producers and sound engineers when, in the 1980s, drum computers appeared in the studios – as Askan Siegfried, sound engineer at Chameleon Recording in the 1980s, (the successor of Windrose-Dumont-Time) remembers: "Before these machines existed, we already tried to make machine music, this Phillysound for example. In principle, for the rhythm group, this was already 'machine music', but the machines didn't exist yet. Bass and drums were totally fettered then, and they had to play the same tune over and over for three or four hours, and of course every kind of feeling fell apart this way, and everybody in the studio got totally bugged out. I experienced this very often. And today, you fire up such a machine, and its timing is more perfect than everything a drummer could deliver. This brought back a certain relief and 'easy going' that was gone for a while."[22]

BEING TYPECAST

And now for something completely different. You all know fans who talk about a band like: "I love their first album, but what they did later is beyond me". The first Kraftwerk album is a safe candidate for such comments. There were Guru Guru fans who loved the "Elektrolurch" dearly, but were not willing to follow the band to their more jazz oriented albums. Several fans who loved Neu! didn't get the hang of Klaus Dinger's follow-up project La Düsseldorf and saw it as bogus and bullshit.

When fans reacted harshly to a band that changed from one genre to another, this indirectly meant that they didn't allow the musicians to grow, or at least that they were not willing to move along with them. They always expected something "new", but it had to remain within the box they had put the artist in.

In consideration of the small market volume available in Germany for homemade rock, changing style or genre was risky anyways, and musicians had to think twice about doing it. I remember Karlheinz Stockhausen once saying that if you want to get famous as a composer pretty soon, find something nobody else does. Write compositions exclusively for, say, snare drums. Write pieces for a single snare drum or for ensembles of hundreds of snare drums; write pieces for giant snare drums, or for tiny little snare drums, or for snare drums played underwater or on high mountain tops. If you do this, you'll be well-known within four or five years. But there's a catch: Nobody will buy anything else from you. If you write a piece now for trumpets and strings, people will say: No, this is not what we want to hear from him, he should stick to his snare drums. Then you are trapped.

This trap is not only a problem for musicians, it is one for all kinds of creative artists. In your main audience's perspective, you are connected for eternity to the one special thing they see as "yours", and they expect you to deliver variations of this thing for the rest of your life. You are typecasted, and the industry will not allow you to change your type.

The artist then can stick to his concept, like Klaus Schulze (to name one of many) who, relatively early in his career, developed a sort of formula for his recordings and varied it but rarely left this basic concept behind. You might also think of director and screenwriter Woody Allen who, for at least 30 years, has made more or less the same movie every year. If you've ever seen one of the nailed works of kinetic artist and sculptor Günther Uecker in an art museum, you might have gotten an impression like this: It looks fascinating, but this poor guy must have gone addlebrained over hammering tens of thousands of nails into wood or other material.

The other possibility would be that the artist says: "Okay, folks, your opinions are well and good, but I have no choice but to follow my own guiding star wherever it leads me, so come along with me or stay where you are." David Bowie did this a couple of times, as well as Brian Eno. In Germany, Achim Reichel, as mentioned, moved to new shores three or four times, sometimes radically, and fans and critics often reacted with total incomprehension.

This is not necessarily a question of competence or mastery. There's nothing wrong with the idea of having one big goal and the desire to reach it. Most cyclists are happy to win whichever race, but in the back of their minds, they will always know that there's the Tour de France, and that's the one that really counts. Consequently, some racing teams think: Forget all the other races, let's concentrate all our energy on Le Tour.

For musicians, this can go in a similar way. The SCORPIONS of Hanover are one of these bands. They started as THE NAMELESS without much success. They soon found out where they wanted to go. Hard rock and heavy metal are worldwide defined genres with rules you have to know and keep if you want to be successful in them. The SCORPIONS knew the specifics of the genre they aimed for, musically as well as show-wise, and they accepted and adopted them. They knew (or studied) who the competitors were and where they had their strong points.

As a test production, Dieter Dierks had asked them to do a cover version of The Sweet's "Fox On The Run" – in German: "Fuchs, geh voran" (1975, released on EMI's Colorit label) – under the fake name The Hunters. It was not even bad, but it made it clear to the band, as well as to the producer, that this couldn't be the way to go. They knew they couldn't reach their goal in their hometown Hanover or within German borders, they knew they had to go international. Result: Even (or although) being a German band, the Scorpions reached the international top league of the hard & heavy genre.

But the Scorpions were an exception. Musically, Lucifer's Friend of Hamburg operated on a similar level, and this could also be said about Epitaph of Dortmund. Lucifer's Friends' U.S. label somehow didn't do much work but cashed in, and nobody from the band knows how that worked or where the money went.[23] Even worse, Epitaph had to compensate for the U.S. record company's debt in the end. So what was the problem with them? Bad management? Inapt negotiating? Yes, but that's not all. Sometimes it simply doesn't work.

Joy Fleming, who I've previously mentioned, was an excellent singer, probably one of Germany's best. She had what it takes to be internationally known. But it didn't happen. Her problem was her (or her producer's) indecisiveness about what to do with this talent. So she played high-leveled soul rock with own bands (Joy and the Hit Kids, later Joy Unlimited); she recorded goose-bump-evoking songs in the dialect of her hometown Mannheim, like "Neckarbrücken-Blues" b/w "Mannemer Dreck" (1973 – Mannemer Dreck has nothing to do with garbage, filth, or any pollution, it's a sweet macaroon cookie). She released "Halbblut" (also 1973, a hands-on cover version of Cher's "Half Breed"); she took part in the Eurovision Song Contest in Stockholm 1975 with "Ein Lied kann eine Brücke sein" (A Song Can Be a Bridge; written by Michael Holm and Tanned Leather's Rainer Pietsch), ending up as #17. In 1978, she recorded *The Final Thing*, a disco album composed and written by Pete Bellotte and Keith Forsey, recorded at Musicland, and that's exactly what it sounds like. She made a soul pop album entitled simply *N* with a bunch of American session musicians in 1987, recorded in the States. She did jingles for "Strahler 70" toothpaste and "Tic Tac" peppermint commercials (and also sang these on stage sometimes, just for fun, because she knew the audience would recognize them). To cut to the chase, it was more and more difficult to identify a line behind all this stuff. This was a missed chance – and a textbook example of how to shipwreck a possible career. The last activity of Joy Fleming I know of was presenting the theme song of the TV game show "Glücksrad", the German version of "Wheel of Fortune".

It's on Youtube, but better don't watch it, it might bring you to tears.[24] Between 1974 and 1978, Joy Unlimited co-singer Ken Taylor also pursued a career as a schlager singer. Under the name Mike Winter, he released seven unsuccessful 45s on the Bellaphon label. Sometimes nothing works.

NEKTAR

Even when you come from one of the original rock countries, you can fail. In the late 1960s, a couple of musicians came to Hamburg with several bands from England and somehow ended up at the Star-Club. Soon, the idea of starting a new band occurred, and this band became Nektar. They moved to a farmhouse at Seeheim-Jugenheim in the Odenwald area between Darmstadt and Heidelberg (today a veterinary center is located in that house).

It has always been a bit controversial whether Nektar should be seen as a Krautrock band. They have an entry in the first edition of Günter Ehnert's "Rock in Deutschland" encyclopedia, but in the second and third edition they aren't mentioned anymore. I remember that Nektar's keyboarder Allan "Taff" Freeman once posted in a Facebook group that they neither saw Nektar as part of the German rock scene nor was their time in Germany their "big time"[25]. In reality, between 1971 and 1974, there was literally no German Rock festival without them – often enough, they were the headliner, so I think they are not misplaced in this book.

The first album they had recorded in Boston never saw the light of the day. Some of these tunes were later rerecorded for the 1973 double album *Sounds Like This* (which sounds as if Dierks recorded it with two microphones in his wine cellar). The original Boston tapes were first officially released as a bonus CD with the *Remember the Future, Anniversary Edition* (2013).

Producer Peter Hauke then signed them for his Bacillus label. Musically, the band was a bit so-so – they all knew how to play, but their style was undecided between being bombastic, psychedelic, and hard & heavy, with a tendency of repetitive idling. Roye Albrighton's technically excellent guitar playing was always in conflict with his vocals which hovered between being strident and whiny.

Nektar's lightshow was interesting (because it was unique for German means). With slides, oil wheels, colored liquid projections, and strobes, Mick Brockett and Keith Walters, Nektar's lights operators (the latter left the band in 1972), kept the tradition of psychedelic lightshows from San Francisco alive. Nektar's lightshow didn't reach the artistic quality of their American role models Joshua,

Heavy Water, or Headlights, but it went well with Nektar's sometimes trippy lyrics and their use of stage effects, like the inevitable dry ice fog.

Nektar decided to take their complete management and administration into their own hands. Many bands had similar ideas, but Nektar was one of the few bands that put this into practice. For a while it worked fine – as long as they were constantly touring and playing festivals. Additionally, their album *Remember the Future* (1973) became a veritable hit: The record went up to gold status in the States. This success led to a U.S. tour where they promoted their follow-up album *Down to Earth* with 25 concerts in front of more than 150,000 spectators.

But something messed up. Even with the gold record and 150,000 people, the tour ended with a loss in the six-digit range[26] – an amount high enough to bring their label Bellaphon/Bacillus into serious trouble.

In 1975, Nektar wasn't able anymore to recoup their fixed costs (around 30,000 D-Marks monthly for rent, office hand, roadies, travel fees, et cetera[27]) with record sales and tours through Germany and the neighboring countries. Their success in the U.S. led them to relocate to the States. But they had to learn that, in the U.S., they were by far not as successful as they had hoped. Finally, the band moved to England, their original home country. Roye Albrighton left the band to join "fusion super group" Snowball with drummer Curt Cress, keyboarder Kristian Schultze, and bass guitarist Dave King for their first album (*Defroster*, 1978), but the album went nowhere, so he returned to Nektar. They had some minor comebacks with different line-ups; in 2005, the band appeared in a "Rockpalast" show on German TV, without a lightshow now, but with background film projection, perfectly routine to the point of boredom. Nektar ended with Albrighton's passing in 2016.

If you want to listen to Nektar at their best, my recommendation is *Sunday Night at the London Roundhouse* (1974), the re-edited 2-CD version from 2002 that has the full concert. I think they have rarely been better.

TOURING U.S.

Some general annotations about the experience several bands made with touring the United States in the 1970s: It's not that German bands weren't noted here; Kraan's bassist Hellmut Hattler even thinks several American bands and artists saw German rock "more influential than one might think."[28] But there were only two realistic ways to get noticed: One was to be a perfect copy of the way a genre was seen in the States. This was the way the Scorpions did it, and they were and still are successful with it. But this is (a) hard and (b) not really original. As I see it, there will never be a German Toto, Eagles, or Steely Dan. Lake, Highway, or Randy Pie went a bit in this direction, and as the top musicians they were, they did it quite well. But not well enough. As Edgar Froese said: They didn't have "the groove", or, as Miles Davis used to call it, "this little thing".

Atlantis' album *Ooh Baby* (1974) was released on Vertigo in the States. Singer Inga Rumpf: "We were with Dieter Dierks at that time, and he had contacts with an American management. And this manager [it must have been Ira Blacker of Mr. Mouse Management] came to Germany, listened to the whole German rock scene, among them Kraftwerk, and then he brought Kraftwerk and Atlantis to America. There, we played around 40 or 50 concerts. [Interviewer: For Kraftwerk this became the start of their international career. Why didn't it work for Atlantis?] That's a good question – today, that's still something I think about. We had the opportunity to get a good amount of success, even with records, but: At our record label in New York there were three Germans working. And for some reason they didn't want to buy this from us. Or they weren't confident enough. We had reached 400,000 people with our concerts, and they loved us, but in the stores no record was to be had. Our record had not even been delivered to the radio stations. We were so wiped out that we weren't motivated anymore. And then conflicts about this stuff started within the band, and that was the end of Atlantis."[29] You know the reason why the records didn't get airplay and weren't delivered. It's the system through which the American music industry works.

BE DIFFERENT

If copying American acts doesn't work, what's left for a band to do? There's only one alternative: do something that is different from anything a U.S. band would do. This is the way Kraftwerk did it. But even for them, it only worked once: Their *Autobahn* album and tour in 1975 was a success, but already their follow-up tour in 1981 was at best "not a flop", but not something one would call a smashing success.[30]

With their album *Made In Germany* (1975) and all its edges, little gags, and electronic vignettes, Amon Düül II was another example for something Americans wouldn't do this way. But then the American label asked their producer, Jürgen Korduletsch, to cut the original double album down to one LP for the U.S. market – and he removed a lot of the stuff that made it unique. What was left was soft pop in a style that Americans had already had from a hundred local bands.

There were other attempts to get German bands to the U.S.: At the Brain Festival 1977, behind the stage, there was Herb Cohen of Frank Zappa's management to pick up some interesting acts. He had no idea who to pick. Finally, he asked Eric Burdon for advice on which bands would be able to play for an American audience, but the result was meager.[31]

Bands always had to be aware there were unwelcome things associated with Germany. RAMSES of Hanover made their first album *La Leyla* in 1976; it was produced by Klaus Hess (guitarist of JANE) and Conny Plank, recorded by the latter and released on Sky Records. It included an anti-war tune titled "War" which was spiced up with several war sounds – bomb explosions, firearm shots et cetera. When the short-lived label Annuit Coeptis (from Croydon, Pennsylvania) licensed the record for the U.S., they wanted to avoid any associations that could come up with the combination of "Germany" and "war", so the track was retitled to "Noise" and changed into a song about noise pollution, now with nasty traffic sounds. It didn't help; the album failed in the States. Even more unpleasant: The returns ended up in German stores as cut-outs for little money, much to the annoyance of Sky Records and the band.

With their unique sound and style, KRAAN was another band that should have been more successful in the States. But all of these bands were somehow spit out by their American record labels who did not know what to do with them or were too small to promote them effectively.

Another problem was the rules the American musicians' unions had set up for rock acts (not only German ones, but for all of them). One example, told by GRATEFUL DEAD's Jerry Garcia: "If you were a rock band coming into [the Shrine Auditorium in Los Angeles], the union rules said that you were usurping the job of the house band. You had to hire the house band and pay them off, because you were taking their jobs."[32] So the house band was sitting somewhere backstage, playing poker – paid in full. The rules when a band brought in a synthesizer were even crazier, which German bands tended to do: The unions had the obsessive idea that a synthesizer would replace a whole orchestra, so at least a big band had to be hired – just for not playing. For German bands, these rules essentially created an insurmountable obstacle. In his autobiography, Edgar Froese adds some more ludicrous examples for the narrow-mindedness of British and American unions – or should we say: acquisitiveness? Union officials were able to impede concerts, but for some reason, with the right amount of baksheesh, this could be solved – mostly.[33]

You see, a tour through the States was not the easiest thing. Without the help of American partner labels or their own sub-labels, German record companies preferred to keep their fingers off of U.S. tours for their acts, even when they had entered the *Billboard* charts (a rare thing anyways). An isolated hit was usually not enough to motivate these American labels to organize the needed visits of the record pluggers to radio stations all over the country. In a wide country like the U.S., a concert tour requires unbelievable finances. Hotels, transportation, local roadies, sound equipment, lights, et cetera, were very expensive, especially when the band had to deal with a lot of their own equipment (stuff that could not be rented on location). On their 1981 tour, KRAFTWERK had to transport seven tons of equipment from Germany to the U.S. and within the States from city to city. German labels usually stood in for the U.S. deficits of their acts with 20,000 dollars at maximum, and American major labels were not willing to carry any risks until a breakthrough seemed to be within reach. Independents like Passport Records who released KRAAN, NEKTAR, LUCIFER'S FRIEND or Hungarian OMEGA in the U.S. were not able to do this.

When Ingeborg Schober traveled through America with a couple of bands in 1973, she came to the conclusion that the names of some German bands were enunciated with lots of respect in some states – names like AMON DÜÜL II, CAN, or TANGERINE DREAM – but it was only a small minority of fans who saw these bands as interesting or had ever heard of them. Theoretically, the chance of success for a German band existed, but there were not the needed instruments to put it into practice.[34] German culture in America is still often seen today as either lederhosen, beer, and Bavarian veal sausage, or the oh-so-wicked Berlin of the 1920s. Edgar Froese even reports a TANGERINE DREAM concert in Sarasota, Florida, where a community of descendants of German immigrants expected them to play country rock or rock'n'roll of the Ruhr Area for dancing.[35]

How about the upcoming punk movement? Well, it was noted that something was going on in London, but it took a while until there was a reaction. In 1977, when the SEX PISTOLS' album *Never Mind The Bollocks Here's The Sex Pistols* hit the market, the shock was not as big as one might think. However, it started the countdown to the end of the 1970s.

TURN ON, TUNE IN

When we talk about the 1970s, we have to spend some words on drugs and music. Wherever it is about creativity, alcohol and other drugs aren't far away. Walt Disney's animators in the 1930s (with few exceptions) were alcoholics.[1] The heavy drinking, smoking, and consumption of pep pills in advertising agencies was and is so legendary that it ran through all seven seasons of the series *Mad Men*.[2]

Alcohol was the standard drug for most musicians as well as for the audience – it was legal, easy to obtain, and culturally accepted. Musicians apparently always had a special connection to alcohol. The reason might be stage fright and the emotional pressure to always be in a good mood at every concert and studio session. When you read Miles Davis' autobiography[3], you can easily get the impression that heavy drinking and a heroin addiction was a sort of entry requirement. It is not a secret that the James Last Orchestra always had a well-sorted mobile bar backstage, free for crew and all musicians – until finally, the whole orchestra consisted mainly of alcoholics and Mr. Last organized rehab for all of them. Since then, most of them have become hobby golfers. Classical orchestras also aren't drug-free zones; the usage of tranquilizers, valerian, and alcohol is nothing special. The hornist knows that when he cracks a note (which can easily happen, it's in the nature of his instrument) in his solo or the percussionist misses his cue, it will be noted in tomorrow's press reviews, and this, of course, will lead to stress.

The British and American rock, jazz, and blues are full of songs about drugs and booze. Some songs describe situations that might lead to drug use. Some songs, verbally or musically, and often in a coded way, describe the effect of drugs or recommend trying them. Some songs give a warning against drugs, some songs were written under the influence of drugs, and some songs were recorded under the influence of drugs, especially LSD. Some of these songs are among the finest rock tunes there are – think of The Beatles' "Tomorrow Never Knows" or "I Am The Walrus", think of Jefferson Airplane's "White Rabbit" or their "Shizoforest Love Suite", think of the drug-fueled *Live/Dead* improvisations of Grateful Dead, think of Vanilla Fudge's extremely time-expanded exuberant cover versions of popular hits. A highly original project like Gong's *Flying Teapot* trilogy would have never existed without several LSD trips, as Gong founder Daevid Allen described openly and in detail.[4]

This book is not the place to discuss the impact of LSD and other mind-altering substances on creativity or therapeutic purposes. But it is obvious that LSD was able to help create music and arts genres that would not exist otherwise. Corey Anderson Dansereau of Stanford University goes one step further: He thinks that LSD was one of the roots of Silicon Valley.[5] He might have a point.

How about the German schlager? This genre often followed the tradition of operas and operettas, many of which contain one or two drinking songs. The operetta *Ein Walzertraum* by Oscar Straus has the famous aria "Ein Schwipserl möcht' ich haben" (I Would Like to Have a Little Jag), Richard Wagner's opera *Die Meistersinger von Nürnberg* has a famous boozing scene ending with a brawl, and Heinrich Marschner's opera *Der Vampyr*, in its original first version, includes a hearty drinking song that lets us know why in all four seasons of the year there's a reason to booze.

The schlager picked up this tradition. Alcohol and cigarettes had always been a topic, usually in a played-down, positive way, especially in the 1950s and 1960s, at a time when cigarettes were seriously advertised as "salubrious"[6], smoking and drinking was seen as part of modern lifestyle – "Heute blau und morgen blau und übermorgen wieder" (Drunk Today and Drunk Tomorrow and Again the Day After Tomorrow) was a common party song, as well as the folksy "Wir versaufen unser Oma ihr klein Häuschen" (We Squander Our Granny's Little House on Booze). Even we children used to sing this. There was no music show on TV without people sitting at a bar, and being drunk was usually seen as funny and normal.

But the left-wing "alternative" scene also had its drinking songs. A Dutch band named Bots (not to mix up with the American punk band of the same name) had a song in German based on a Breton traditional ("Son Ar Chistr") that had been popularized by harpist Alan Stivell: The Bots' "Sieben Tage lang" (For Seven Days; 1980)[7], became a sort of marching song at protests against nuclear power plants, U.S. Pershing, and Soviet SS-20 missiles or festivals of the German "Rock Against Racism" branch (called "Rock gegen Rechts"), coming from sound trucks and/or PA systems – and the masses tuned in: "Was wollen wir trinken sieben Tage lang? Was wollen wir trinken? So ein Durst! / Es wird genug für alle sein / Wir trinken zusammen, roll das Fass mal rein! / Wir trinken zusammen, nicht allein!" (What do we want to drink for seven days? What do we want to drink? Such a thirst! / There will be enough for all / We drink together, roll in the barrel! / We drink together, not alone!) – The song became a real plague and always gave me the feeling to listen to left-wing Heinos.

Speed, cocaine, morphine, or other drugs, were something "one had heard of", but most people didn't really know what these were or what "addiction" meant unless they themselves were somehow involved with them. It was not until the late 1960s that the existence of stuff like hashish, LSD, and heroin finally found its way into common knowledge. The musical *Hair* made it a topic ("Walking In Space"), and Timothy Leary was a known name. The press and media were full of spooky drug stories about some c-list celebs, there were warnings as well as "reports" about wild drug orgies somewhere in the U.S., but the overall state of information about drugs was low. For us youngsters around 12 or 13, drugs, especially pot, had a certain "exotic chic of the forbidden" with them, but this image wasn't based on one's own experiences. Most adults couldn't explain this because they also had no idea what this stuff would do. However, the walls of probably thousands of teenager bedrooms were decorated with a day-glo kitsch poster entitled "Girl with Joint"[8], available for 5 D-Marks at every department store, in the trash magazines, c-list celebs like Uschi Obermaier got pictured with a joint. For young readers, drugs became sort of "theoretically stylish".

In the early 1970s, the existence of drugs finally became known enough that the schlager industry discovered the topic – interestingly, first with some stultifications (or, friendlier said: parodies). Kuno Dreysse (The Rivets, from the circle around the Rattles of the Star-Club era), under the pseudonym Kuno & The Marihuana Brass came up with a silly 45 named "Lass uns doch mal haschen" b/w "Marihuana Mantra". The record went nowhere.

Bill Ramsey, a GI who became stranded in Germany and was an excellent jazz singer and saxophonist, had become successful through the 1960s with more or less funny schlagers like “Wumba-Tumba-Schokoladeneisverkäufer” (1959), “Die Zuckerpuppe aus der Bauchtanztruppe” (1961), or “Ohne Krimi geht die Mimi nie ins Bett” (1962). These songs hit the zeitgeist – German audiences at that time expected American singers to have a funny accent and be a bit crazy, and artists like Ramsey, Gus Backus, or John Paris had no choice but to fulfil the expectations. In 1970, Ramsey continued this shtick with “Haschisch Halef Omar” b/w “High And Happy”, side A written by no other than jazz organist Ingfried Hoffmann (from the Doldinger clan) and lyricist Heinz Gietz (we've heard of him in connection to The Lords), and side B written by later schlager star Howard Carpendale.

The first real hit record in Germany about drugs followed in 1972 under the wings of – once again – producer Peter Meisel. Juliane Werding of Essen, then 16 years old, came out with “Am Tag, als Conny Kramer starb” (The Day Conny Kramer Died), a cover version of The Band's “The Night They Drove Old Dixie Down”. The song reached #1 on the German single charts and stayed for 20 weeks; in Switzerland it reached #2 and stayed for 14 weeks.

This song was not silly or funny anymore, it was deadly serious and mirrored exactly the common knowledge about drugs. The lyrics followed the concept of hashish as a “gateway drug”; one tried it out of curiosity, later ending up on the deadly syringe. They combined this with little bits of social criticism addressed to “the society”: “Doch aus den Joints, da wurden Trips / Es gab keinen Halt auf der schiefen Bahn / Die Leute fingen an zu reden / Aber keiner bot Conny Hilfe an” (The joints became trips / There was no stop on the way downhill / People started gossiping about him / But nobody offered help to Conny). Of course, the song was spiced up with a good portion of the emotional impact of teenage death drama songs as we heard them around the early 1960s, songs like Mark Dinning's “Teen Angel” (1959) or John Leyton's “Johnny Remember Me” (1961): “Beim letzten Mal sagte er / Nun kann ich den Himmel sehen / Ich schrie ihn an: Oh, komm zurück / Er konnte es nicht mehr verstehen”[9] (Last time he said / Now I can see heaven / I screamed at him: Oh come back / He couldn't hear it anymore). Marketed as “based on a true story”[10], the topic, presented by the teenaged singer with her clear, slightly dolefully voice, hit the spot in accordance with the public's opinion about drugs. As it goes for many teenage death songs, “Conny Kramer” also became a sort of cult song after a while. It is still well-known today and played on oldie radio stations every so often; Juliane Werding kept it in her live repertoire until the end of her career.

There were some more schlagers about drugs, like Udo Jürgens' "Rot blüht der Mohn" (1984) or "Amsterdam (Liebe hat total versagt)" by duo Cora (1985; Swetlana Minkow and Cornelia Freifrau von dem Bottlenberg, also known as professional backup singers The Ladygirls), perfectly produced by no less than Frank Farian (known for his projects Boney M, Milli Vanilli and others). Its moral is usually that of the old biblical saying: "Dwell in the land and you shall be fed." Those who deviate from this rule will be punished. This is the way schlagers work. But they have to do it in a way that is connected to people and personal relationships, they have to go the emotional way, otherwise they will find no interest. Schlagers are not a good medium to transport political slogans or theories about the world. No schlager, no pop song, with all their warnings and descriptions of horror and grief have ever stopped anyone from trying drugs. But they play a part in the way drugs are seen by parents, aunts, uncles, or teachers. In reality, I'm convinced, there will never be a drug-free society, with or without warnings.

Of course: When schlagers warn about drug use, it does not say anything about the way schlager singers, musicians, and producers handled drugs in reality.

The rock scene of the 1970s, especially the Krautrock bands, had a completely different way of handling the topic. Of course there were drugs involved in the German rock scene, as mentioned in earlier chapters. The culture of psychedelic drugs made its way over to Germany with the Woodstock Festival, at latest. But the public impression, as it was generated by the media, was far away from reality. There were a few bands, especially in the shipping channel of 1968, which made themselves known for excessive drug usage. In some cases, you can say they made it their business model. I've already mentioned Guru Guru. Witthüser & Westrupp and their 45 "Nimm einen Joint, mein Freund" (Take a Joint, My Friend; 1971), taken from their album *Trips + Träume* on Kaiser's Ohr label, were also well known. These two knew what they were singing about, but as with most of their songs, we should take this one with a grain of salt. But whatever pop literature tells about the wild drug (especially LSD) consumption in the German rock scene: In the long run, these bands remained the exception. Most of them lost the plot after a while, sometimes in an unfunny (psychiatric) way, and musically, it was usually not even worth it; most of the results of these explorations were meager.

Yes, there are exceptions. If you dig long enough in a waste disposal site, you may find a golden ring. But it's more realistic not to count on it. So the golden rings in music had to be edited down with the razor blade from recording sessions that sometimes consisted of hours and hours of garbage. Rarely did a band do it as systematically as GONG: On a full moon night, the whole band went into the studio, dropped a trip, and recorded whatever came into their minds. Several days later, they went carefully through all this recorded material, sorted out what was obviously garbage, thought about the usable stuff, reworked it, and finally went back into the studio to re-record the felicitous parts that had survived this procedure, but now they did the recording sober. The result was *You* (1974), one of their finest albums. While this bread was fully baked, bands like AMON DÜÜL on *Psychedelic Underground* or GURU GURU on *UFO* also tried to sell "bread", but really, they were selling something that was not much more than raw grain and required more work to be edible.

In most German bands' cases, the alleged use of hallucinogens was blatancy. When musicians told they performed most of their concerts while tripping, it was mostly hullabaloo, told to the media to look shocking and interesting. It was a sort of image some bands built up intentionally because they (or their management) thought it would amplify the impact of their music on the listeners. Think of the hogwash BRAINTICKET placed on the cover of their first album *Cottonwoodhill* from 1971: "Listen to the first recording of this LSD/Hashish/Fixy/Jointy Sound. Take a trip to your inner light. See the hallucinations of reality rise out of the groove. You've got your brainticket now! Hallelujah!"[11] This is so daffy that I'm not even sure the band members themselves believed in this rubbish. It's also possible they (or the record company) put it on the record sleeve because they thought that drug consumption was a common thing in their aimed target group. At any rate, it shows that neither the band nor the record company trusted the carrying capacity of BRAINTICKET's music.

But it's also possible the other way round: Many fans presumed the involvement of psychedelic drugs in certain music productions while the musicians actually didn't do drugs. TANGERINE DREAM might be an example for this variation: It's a common assumption that this strange music must have been a product of drugs; some of the band's blurred statements also suggested this. In the beginning, this might have been the case, but in 1974 Edgar Froese decided to become a vegetarian and stopped using any kind of drugs, including alcohol and coffee. This makes sense: You better keep a level head when you want a synthesizer to give you the results you want.

I have always thought there must have been lots of scientific studies about drug use, but I was wrong. There are not many, and sociologically, they are not too precise. For the time periods and age ranges that are important for this book, it can be said that when it comes to drug use between the late 1950s and mid-1960s, it is mainly "speed" we talk about – pep pills, amphetamine, compounds like Captagon, Dexedrine, or Preludin, at that time available as diet pills over the counter, but also easily available at or in the neighborhood of music clubs like the Star-Club.

Until 1968, only 2 percent of young people between 15 and 18 had experiences with soft drugs, which, in Germany, mainly meant hashish. This was relatively easy to obtain and affordable for young people. There was also some marijuana circulating, especially around American military bases, but other than in the U.S., it never played a real decisive role in Germany.

In 1968, an upswing started. Two years later, 22 percent of young people between ages 15 and 18 had experiences with soft drugs. In most cases, this meant having some draws once or twice, and that was that. In 1972, drug use had already gone down again; since 1975, it had leveled out constantly between 14 and 18 percent.[12] This didn't change significantly before the mid-1980s.

I remember a lot of ballyhoo in the early 1970s among parents about the stuff that was allegedly dealt on the schoolyard – which, as they had read in the tabloids, was a busy market place. In fact, the only drug dealing I've ever noticed during my education was one schoolmate trying to sell some Valium pills. In other schools, it might have been different, but that's what I saw in the early 1970s (I finished school in 1974).

LSD, as said, was known to exist, but most people had no idea what it did. They thought it was something like booze; the real effect was completely out of their world. Timothy Leary and his sermons were dragged through the press as if he would be the devil in disguise, many people had read horror stories about LSD in the tabloids or the *Reader's Digest*. LSD *existed* in Germany, but quantity-wise, it was always more a myth than a substance in wide use. Many people who actually knew the lyrics of JEFFERSON AIRPLANE's "White Rabbit" took it as a song about "Alice in Wonderland". To decipher a song like WITTHÜSER & WESTRUPP's "Karlchen", you needed to *know* what it was about, otherwise you would just take it for nonsense. In Germany, we had no "Merry Pranksters" (who, by the way, were based on an idea author Ken Kesey received from Hermann Hesse's novel "Journey to the East"), we had no "acid tests" and no books like Tom Wolfe's Kool-aid electric ones; we had no Owsley Stanley, we only had poor Rolf-Ulrich Kaiser and his Sternenmädchen, and some of their cosmic couriers – that was mainly it. I remember an article in a, at that time, still relatively serious weekly magazine called *Quick* (shut down in 1992), reporting about a scandalous "students LSD party", which, after the magazine was delivered to kiosks, turned out to be completely fake – the students had just cashed in money from the magazine and mimed to the reporters what they expected to see.

And if you really wanted? It wasn't that easy. You couldn't purchase your trip at the kiosk round the corner, and there was no online ordering (because there was no internet). In bigger cities like Hamburg, West Berlin, Frankfurt, or Munich there were some head shops where you could buy bongs, scales, extra-long cigarette paper, and this kind of stuff, but of course, if they weren't sure what to think of you, they didn't sell you any real stuff so as to avoid trouble. I can say that for Hamburg, LSD, psilocybin, and sometimes mescaline, were available at some music clubs, but you couldn't just go in there and do your shopping. Acid heads were a more or less closed circle with an esoteric aura around them. To get in touch with them, you first had to look trustworthy (cord jeans, parka, long hair, batik tee), and even then, you still got checked ideologically. These guys didn't need to sell anything, they acted on conviction. The advantage of this system was that, when they finally trusted you, you had the relative safeness that they wouldn't sell you some painkillers cut down with rat poison or other garbage as it was offered at the main station.

Unlike with hard drugs like heroin, you couldn't make much money with LSD. The market was small, and as you can't get physically addicted, the buyer is not forced to buy – a situation no professional drug dealer is interested in. In some cases, even the police knew who these LSD sellers were and let them do their little business – seen in the light of the hard drug market even in the 1970s, LSD was as good as irrelevant, and police officers knew that these dealers acted relatively responsibly (of course you will never get an official confirmation for this).

Most LSD available in Germany originated from labs in Czechoslovakia, smaller quantities came from the United States (like Rolf-Ulrich Kaiser's preferred "Orange Sunshine"), there was an obscure religious sect that actively sold LSD, psilocybin, or magic mushrooms. Only little quantities were "made in Germany" like the "Heidelberger Blitze" (flashes of Heidelberg).

Professional musicians, if they were into acid, were usually known customers, or they had their dogsbodies doing the shopping. The music scene had its own infrastructure to get supplied.

German rock musicians who were addicted to hard drugs, usually heroin, existed, but they were an exception, and if they did exist, then William S. Burroughs' old truism applies to them: he never saw a junkie who wasn't an alcoholic as well.

Most scenes, as well as most music cultures, have "their" drug. While pot was definitely a consistent part of the German rock scene of the late 1960s and 1970s – musicians as well as audiences – there was a new drug that came into circulation with the disco wave: cocaine, usually called "Koks" (charcoal) in Germany. It was not only a scene thing, it also entered studios, stages, and offices. It's hard to say whether coke changed the music, or if the upcoming new music asked for a drug that was different from the hallucinogenic stuff. Had it not always been really fun to have to deal with stoned sleepyheads on stage or in the studio, now coke also changed the way projects were planned and negotiated, and mostly not in a good way. It's not a coincidence that coke was already much in use during the 1910s and 1920s (it was not illegal then; dentists even used it as a narcotic). The techno scene coming up in the 1990s again had its own drugs, mainly designer drugs based on – again – old compounds like amphetamine or its derivatives. But this is not a topic for this book's timeframe.

Even in the United States in the 1960s and 1970s, drug use was limited. When you read about the hippie movement, Woodstock, et cetera, or watch news films about that time or talk to festival veterans, you can easily get the impression that most young Americans were into drugs and constantly high. But this is far from reality. Not unlike German youth (as described), three quarters of them never had any experiences with drugs, or they abandoned it after trying grass once or twice, and then went back to alcohol. They never touched LSD or similar substances. In the U.S., the use of grass is much more common today than it was around 1970.

Today's drug scene is much more liberal than in the 1970s. But whatever you may read about the music scene in Germany: The truth is that the main drug was and still is alcohol. Marius Müller-Westernhagen already knew this in 1978: "Johnny W." (which stands for "Johnny Walker") became one of his best-known songs.

THE SEVENTIES

LIBERATION

The overall, changing atmosphere in Germany's 1970s had left traces in the music scene. After a short breakdown in the late 1960s, the classic schlager experienced another boom phase in the 1970s. Politically and economically, times were slowly getting harder, sending out social and political shock waves; this meant that pop music had to both take up and absorb some of these shock waves. But unlike the schlagers of the 1950s and 1960s, their topics were now not quite unreachable romantic fantasy islands in the South Seas, or lovers to appear right on the day when the rain comes. Stories of this kind had no connection to the Seventies' daily life anymore. In other words: They were not needed anymore.

Many schlagers now simply and openly called on the listener to party – typical ones of this kind were "Tanze Samba mit mir" (1977; Dance Samba With Me) by Tony Holiday (1951–1990), "Sieben Fässer Wein" (1977; Seven Barrels of Wine; a cover version of a Caribbean traditional) by Roland Kaiser, or "Ein bisschen Spaß muss sein" (1972; Nothing Wrong with a Little Bit of Fun) by Roberto Blanco – simple clap-along songs without any background or deeper meaning.

In contrast to these meaningless party songs, a different (and more interesting) style of schlagers came up. It focused on social criticism and "slice of life" situations from nearby. Udo Jürgens (1934-2014) from Austria was one of the first singers to get on board. He was a pretty good composer and pianist, used to work with excellent lyricists (Michael Kunze, Wolfgang Hofer, satirist Eckart Hachfeld and others), and for a while, he became this wave's leading protagonist with songs like "Griechischer Wein" (1974; Greek Wine) about the first generation of immigrant workers in Germany and their homesickness, "Ein ehrenwertes Haus" (1975; A Respectable House) about a couple receiving a letter from all their neighbors demanding they move out because they live together unmarried, "Tante Emma" (1976) about a mom-and-pop store that has to be closed (these stores are called "Tante-Emma-Laden" in Germany), or "Gefeuert" (1977, Fired) about someone laid off from his factory job because he's not 30 anymore. With the song "Lieb Vaterland" (1971; Dear Fatherland), in which he listed several social problems Germany needed to deal with but didn't, Jürgens kicked off furious discussions in the public as well as in the media, partly about the problems, partly about whether a schlager singer was allowed to even have an opinion about them, let alone sing about them.

"Im Wagen vor mir" (1977; In the Car in Front of Me) there was another one of these "slice of life" schlagers, written and presented by Henry Valentino & Uschi alias schlager composer Hans Blum and singer Ursula Peysang (1953–1991). But in contrast to the Udo Jürgens tunes, this one was without any social criticism; it only described an everyday situation. On the autobahn, he, a gray-haired older gentleman at the wheel of his big car, follows a relatively slow-driving 2CV of a young woman, just because he enjoys being in no hurry today and she seems to look sweet. With a raspy voice, he just daydreams about whether she might be on her way to a rendezvous or just driving home, or whether she is listening to the same radio station as him or if her radio might be off. But we, the listeners, alternating to his singing, hear the situation also from *her* point of view: She becomes more and more terrified about this strange pursuer – does he want to observe her, is it the police, a kidnapper – why doesn't he simply overtake her car? Finally, she leaves the autobahn to hide somewhere, angry because now she won't get home on time, while he drives on, sending her an imaginary bye-bye, knowing his trip will end in two hours and he will never see her again. The first version of this devilish catchy tune sounded a bit too dry, so Blum then overdubbed and remixed it with a country band. In this version, the song stayed in the charts for 33 weeks, and its highest position was #8; it was probably successful not least because it was a song about driving. Cars and driving were (and still are) a German obsession, songs about them were always successful. It did not start with Kraftwerk's "Autobahn" (1974), one of the oldest songs of this kind is from around 1908: "Schorschl, ach kauf mir doch ein Automobil" (George, Oh Please Buy Me an Automobile), a cover version of "The Brooklyn Cake Walk".

Hans Blum had already been in the scene since 1959, when he had a #1 hit with a German cover version of the Coasters' hit "Charlie Brown", which he did in stereo, singing all the voices himself by overdubbing. As a member of the Hansen Quartett, also known as Hansen Boys & Girls, you can hear him singing backup on several dozens of Polydor records of the 1960s. In the 1970s, he had a couple of hits as "oldtimer" Henry Valentino, but under his real name he wrote a huge number of hits for schlager singers like Alexandra, Graham Bonney, Howard Carpendale, Katja Ebstein, Séverine, and many others.

NEW LOVE

Of course love affairs, flirts, et cetera, have always been a schlager topic. But in the 1970s, love grew into something that didn't need to be fantasized anymore, and the plots were also taken from everyday life now. "Eine neue Liebe ist wie ein neues Leben" (1972; A New Love Is Like a New Life) by Jürgen Marcus (1948-2018), with a touch of Motown rhythm, became one of the biggest hits of the era (27 weeks in the charts, peaking at #2). Another one was Marianne Rosenberg's Phillysound-fueled song "Er gehört zu mir" (1975; He Belongs to Me), memorable for the lines "Er gehört zu mir / wie mein Name an der Tür / und ich weiß, er bleibt hier" (He belongs to me / like my name on the door / and I know he will stay [While in the U.S. people usually only have apartment numbers on their door, it is usual in Germany to have a plate with your surname on the apartment door.]) Its highest chart position was only #7 (20 weeks in the charts), but this song is remarkable because it was – and still is – the secret hymn of the gay community. (Cora, the duo mentioned in the previous chapter, was singing backup here.)

HE, SHE, IT

This leads to an interesting follow-up phenomenon of the Sixty-Eights: In the 1950s and 1960s, most schlager lyrics made it completely clear whether the love interest (the "addressee" of the lyrics) was male or female by mentioning "he", "she" or a name, and of course, it had to be the opposite sex. Now this started to change more and more.

In a way, it was the rediscovery of an old game: In the 1920s, we already had cheeky schlager lyrics that intendedly left the exact kind of a relationship unclear. One of the most famous songs of this kind was the couplet "Wenn die beste Freundin mit der besten Freundin" (1928; When the Best Girlfriend With the Best Girlfriend), written by Mischa Spoliansky and Marcellus Schiffer, sung by Margo Lion and Marlene Dietrich. The lyrics leave what is going on between these two open to interpretation – are they just "best buds" on a shopping trip or are they a couple? The lyrics also mention their "husbands" – but are they male or female, or might they be a couple too? The lyrics can be read in various ways. What about the "Hausfreund" (the "lover at the gate") who's also mentioned, is he a he or a she? We aren't told; the lyrics are intentionally blurred.

With the upcoming Nazi era, lyrics of this kind of confusion were seen as "not conducive to the German nature". Mischa Spoliansky in 1920, under the pseudonym Arno Billing, had written "Das lila Lied" (The Lilac Song) and dedicated it to Magnus Hirschfeld; it became the first hymn of Berlin's gay community. Spoliansky did the right thing when he relocated to England. Marcellus Schiffer had already committed suicide in 1932 (but not for political reasons).

Sassy songs like the previously mentioned one were inconceivable in the conservative 1950s or 1960s. Schlagers at that time had to be free of direct sex (remember: "I know that such a cowboy knows how to kiss!"), only very far-fetched paraphrases were allowed. It was a bit like in today's Bollywood movies: The protagonists have no sex, they just dance – into happiness. Everybody knows what is implied, but it isn't explicit. Uptight hits like "Tanze mit mir in den Morgen" (1961; Dance With Me Into the Morning) by an oily but popular singer named Gerhard Wendland became the absolute limit for what was allowed; the film comedy titled *Wenn die Conny mit dem Peter* (When Conny With Peter) also went in this direction: indicating what was meant without saying it. In the 1960s there were also still constricted rooms; big families lived in small apartments, children were sleeping in their parent's bedroom, and having sex was a tough go under these circumstances. This might also be the reason why so many schlagers of this era were set in fantasy places and fictional worlds where "things were possible". Schlagers picked up the wishful thinking of many.

As said, in the 1970s the winds shifted. In 1971, WDR TV, after long, internal discussions, commissioned filmmaker Rosa von Praunheim with a film that got the long but accurate title *Nicht der Homosexuelle ist pervers, sondern die Situation, in der er lebt* (It's Not the Homosexual Who Is Perverse but the Situation He Lives In), a cross between documentary and feature film. The director commented: "The film was embossed by the anger and frustration that had accumulated in my gay life in Berlin up to then. I was convinced that we couldn't always passively wait for the kindness of society to change for the better for us. Our film was intended to provoke, unsettle gays and straights, and bring them into conversation with each other. Under no circumstances did we want a movie that glorifies gays or commiserate them. It was important for us to be brutally honest and disclose the god-awful situation of gays."[1] The TV broadcast became the expected scandal, BR TV skipped it completely; the movie triggered the first gay protest in Germany.

In the shipping channel of this film, but also of the sexual liberation of the late 1960s in general, schlager lyrics now became more clear – but still not *too* clear. Instead, and interestingly, they became increasingly gender-neutral. The lyrics had no names in it, and no gender pronoun was directly mentioned, only "you", so all genders could feel addressed. Most "straight" listeners probably didn't even notice this change.

Since 1969, homosexuality had not been considered a criminal offense anymore, as long as you were 21 or older, but that does not mean it immediately became widely socially accepted. The police still kept gay bars and other meeting points, even some public restrooms, under surveillance and registered gays in "pink lists", for whatever reason. It was not before 1994 that this practice finally passed – at least officially.

In schlager lyrics at this point, homosexual romance was sometimes a topic. In the beginning, it remained hidden under the surface. You had to know some code words to notice what the song was about. There was also sometimes a certain naivety on the side of the audience; listeners simply didn't understand what the lyrics were really about. A song like, say, "Y.M.C.A." (1978) by the Village People was seriously assigned to the Christian Youth Organization by many.

But as a result of 1968, it slowly became more open. The first schlager that openly dealt with queer love was "Mike und sein Freund" in 1977 (Mike and His Friend; a cover version of the Rubettes' "Under the Roof") by singer Bernd Clüver (1948-2011). The song reached #44 in the charts. Clüver was not invited to present it on TV; instead, in interviews, he had to repeatedly assure the public that the song was not about him.

Singer-songwriters whose target groups were not exactly schlager fans sometimes hinted at homosexuality – "Thorbeckeplatz" (1979) by Dutch singer Robert Long (1943-2006), for example. But this was an exception and had some radio airplay during late hours, but never found its way into one of the big TV shows or mass media.

All this is a bit strange, however, because if you would set up a list of gay or lesbian singers, musicians, and producers, it would be a long list, in schlager as well as in pop music.

In Krautrock and other German rock music, homosexuality, gay, or lesbian sex was rarely a topic (but this could also be said about sex in general). Udo Lindenberg was one of the first singers who made gay/lesbian love a topic in round terms: "Ganz egal" (No Matter; 1973). On the album *Auf freiem Fuß!* (At Large!; 1977) by Uli Hundt and Schroeder Roadshow we find a song called "Ich bin so schwul (Strichjungenwalzer)" (I am So Gay (Hustler Waltz)), but this was really underground and beyond all radio taste limits; the record appeared on the band's own label, distributed by Trikont. Rio Reiser of Ton Steine Scherben was openly gay, but he didn't make it a topic in his songs. Heiner Pudelkow (1948-1995) of Curly Curve and Interzone and Jürgen Zeltinger (of Zeltinger Band), to name two others, were also openly gay, but they remained exceptions.

The Flying Lesbians, founded in 1974 in West Berlin, saw themselves as the "voice of the autonomous women's movement". In fact, they were a sort of PR department for the lesbian community; I could have also mentioned them in the agitprop chapter. In a way, they were overdue: Male homosexuals were at least taken note of, lesbians could usually thank their stars if they were taken seriously at all. (While the aforementioned film *Not the Homosexual is perverse* … created great a stir, the TV movie *Anna und Edith*, 1975 directed by Gerrit Neuhaus, about a lesbian love story, left no serious traces.) The FLYING LESBIANS played relatively hard rock and came into existence mainly by chance when, two days before a women's festival at the Technical University of Berlin, a band from England cancelled and needed to be replaced. With the help of TON STEINE SCHERBEN and OS MUNDI the concert could be set up. The FLYING LESBIANS were, in parts, professionals; founding member, singer, and drummer was Swetlana Minkow (later she became one half of the duo CORA, who did the drug song "Amsterdam"), but she had already left the band when their first album was recorded. This album (self-titled, 1975) appeared with a double axe on the front cover (a so-called Labrys or Amazon axe), and was not released by an official label, but by feminist magazine *Frauenoffensive* and was distributed through bookstores. The *Sounds* critic, nameless, but probably male, poured out buckets of malice: "Really the worst bullshit I've heard in a long time. … All the commendable intentions these seven women surely had and have, go downhill. And then there is this overdrawn pretension. On the cover it says: This (the record) is an important part of 'women's culture'. The cultureless heterosexual females in our staff laughed loud and resounding, and the men were simply at a loss for words …"[2] Okay, the album is not really a cabinet piece, but it fits in with the time it was made. In its aggression, it might have been a healthy shock for *Sounds*- and other machos. It sold around 17,000 copies – not too bad for its distribution. It remained their only album; the FLYING LESBIANS fell apart in 1977.

It might be worth mentioning that even in the agitprop department of German rock, women were only a topic that crossed the line of being sex objects at random; even FLOH DE COLOGNE who were so proud of their realistic approach, used to mention women only as girlfriends or wifes in their lyrics.

The way the relationships between men and women were depicted in rock music and schlagers changed drastically in the 1990s. The record industry discovered gays and lesbians as a market; Atlantic Records even has a "Gay Marketing Department". The ongoing and now established women's movement was one reason. Another reason was the upcoming Techno music culture and its side-effects, like the annual Berlin Love Parade, which, on the one hand, was much more directly sex-oriented than the music scenes of former decades, but also much more gender-neutral on the other.

Blixa Bargeld, Lead singer of Einstürzende Neubauten (London, UK – August 19th, 1983)

THE EIGHTIES

"Over the city lies a haze of gray
that my mother has yet to wash away"

FEHLFARBEN

THE EIGHTIES

NEW TECHNOLOGY

In 1983, Germany went through a highly emotional election battle for the Bundestag – keywords: NATO's double-track decision, unemployment exceeded 2 million people, ongoing conflicts about controversial methods against terrorism. The liberal FDP had ended the social-democratic SPD coalition, and now, after a tricky parliamentary procedure, a new election followed. A new coalition with the conservative CDU and the FDP got the majority of votes and Helmut Kohl became Chancellor. Comedians made lots of fun of him; nobody at that time would have dared to predict that Kohl would stay in office for 16 years. This election was also the first time the Green Party moved into the Bundestag with 5.6 percent of the votes. Immediately, several augurs saw the downfall of the Occident coming. Of course, no downfall happened, but the social-democratic atmosphere of departure that had been a defining part of the 1970s vanished into thin air. Germany preferred to dance the safety dance again and became conservative, but while the conservatism of the 1960s was based on the desire to keep the formula of success working – prosperity and general optimism – the 1980s started as an era of depression, economic uncertainty, and the desire to get the good old times of economic growth back.

During the 1950s and 1960s, it was normal to view average life as the standard one had to strive for. When you reached this goal of having a job, a family, and a car, you had navigated life correctly. Being mainstream was the way to be. Even the student movement was a collective idea; individualism did not belong to its goals. This changed in the 1970s, pushed slightly by the Sixty-Eight movement, but mainly as a countercyclical reaction to it: Now average life became more and more like something you had to differ from. Individual fulfillment came to the fore and swimming in the mainstream was no longer en vogue. Now you had to show that you were different from the masses – the clothing you wore, the books you read, the music you listened to, the movies you watched, and ideally the job you did: All of this became the public sign of your individuality. And you had to show it.

In the 1980s, the AIDS virus became a topic. Living the concept of free love that had defined wide parts of the late 1960s and 1970s could become life-threatening now. This changed not only behavior on a personal level, but also the overall atmosphere. As always, the arts adjusted accordingly.

Propelled by the economic situation, increasing pollution problems, nuclear power plants, AIDS, and the arms race between East and West, a touch of self-pity and fatalism became a fad that intermixed with the open atmosphere of the 1970s. Questions of social solidarity, which had been very important in the 1970s, were seen as dowdy now, as something from yesterday. Being an individual was the important thing. "No Future" became the label of the decade, and of course arts, music, films, et cetera, mirrored and empowered this. Even schlager singer Peter Maffay wallowed in a dystopic kitsch scenario: "Eiszeit" (Ice Age); the song entered the charts in 1982.

For Yours Truly, the 1980s were just the opposite: a time to start over. WAVES, my lightshow group, had been buried. We had the same experience as most rock groups: We were three people who had grown in different directions. The chemistry didn't work anymore. One guy was a gifted projection tinkerer, but his creative input to the show became smaller and smaller, and the other guy viewed being stoned as his main mission during the shows. Not that I had never engaged in such activities, but being under the influence too often results in this sort of "don't care" approach – something I've always seen as professionally inept, and this led to increasingly grumpy, unnecessary quarrels about peanuts. Furthermore, we grew to feel that a lightshow, as we did it, was a relic of a finished era. So WAVES eventually fell apart. In a way, I wasn't too unhappy about it – for me, there were new goals approaching on the horizon.

NEW SYNTHESIZER GENERATION

I've never systematically learned to play a musical instrument, which I continue to regret. It was never even considered in my family. I played drums in a band of two schoolmates for a couple of months, but that was it.

As you may have noticed, I was interested in electronic music in general and synthesizers in detail. Now, around 1980, synthesizers became affordable, especially the ones from Japanese manufacturers. They were not cheap, but I had some money saved up, and one fine summer day, I went to Steinway's music store, played along with the synthesizers they had there, and in the end, I spontaneously balanced my checkbook for a Yamaha CS-15. It was a good one, following the concept of the Minimoog, but I soon noticed that there's not much you can do with just one monophonic synthesizer, besides "playing around" and getting familiar with the instrument. So, two or three weeks later, I added a string keyboard and, to give its sound a bit more color, a flanging pedal. I played them through a Fender Vibro Champ, a nice little tube amp that I still have today, and it was also great for guitar and an Ibanez bass (the latter was eventually stolen from my attic, I hope it fell on the thief's big toe). These devices formed the starting point for me to jump off of. I became addicted to keyboards for the next fifteen years. In addition to my growing synth and home recording equipment collection, I made myself a bit more familiar with guitar, bass guitar, drums, percussion, and – still one of my favorites – vibraphone.

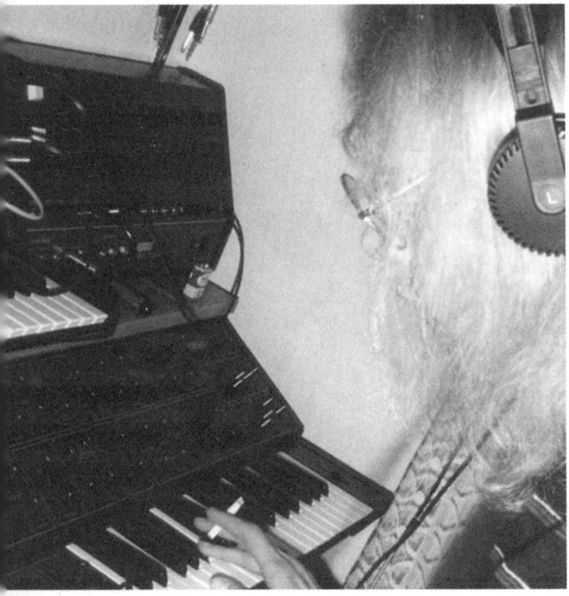

Yours Truly (circa 1981)

I was not the only one who jumped. The decreasing prices of synthesizers and music electronics opened a whole new world to amateur musicians. But they discovered synthesizers in a different way and with different intentions than their predecessors had done in the early 1970s, like Schoener, Schulze, TANGERINE DREAM, and others.

The early 1980s turned out to be the golden years for the manufacturers of electronic instruments. New synthesizer models hit stores nearly every month. The important steps were the development of polyphonic synthesizers, touch-sensitive keyboards, and the possibility of storing self-developed sounds. Besides this, the innovations were usually not too impressive; the new models had one or two new features, or could provide sound effects a bit better than the "old" ones, but the main difference was often just the design. Obviously, there were also many bands and musicians who could easily be talked into consistently being up to date. The now blooming special interest magazines (*Keys* and *Keyboards, Homerecording und Computer*, to name the two leading German ones) had a major part in this game. They had interviews with professional musicians and monthly new test reports. This way, they tried to convince us readers that we definitely needed the latest devices to be on top of musical advancement. It's not that these magazines didn't try to be serious, but like all special-interest magazines, they had to deal with one big conflict: They had to write critical reviews on instruments they got from the same manufacturers whose advertising budgets they needed to tap to save their own existence.

SAMPLING

Another new development that came up was *sound sampling*: putting short samples of sounds on a chip and reproducing them in an organized way. First this idea was used to replace the artificial drum sounds of rhythm machines with the sound of real drums. This had first been done with a unique device called "Wendel" on STEELY DAN's album *Gaucho* (1980), as well as on Donald Fagen's *The Nightfly* (1982). It was developed by sound engineer Roger Nichols (1944-2011) and had an endless amount of memory capacity which made it extremely expensive, but the stored drum and cymbal sounds had a quality that made it nearly impossible to sense that it was a machine drumming. (Interestingly, the drummers whose sounds were used to feed into this machine were paid as if they had taken part in the recording session.) But for the commercial market, this drum machine was not usable.

The Linn Drum then became the first machine available on the market; the price was around 5000 Dollars. The first time I noticed the Linn was in Falco's "Der Kommissar" (1982). It didn't take long until the sound of this machine dominated commercial pop productions; the hand clapping sound in particular became a plague after a while.

If you can sample drum sounds, you can also sample other sounds, and the more memory space you have, the better. The development of chips made it possible. This meant the possibility to feed samples of every imaginable sound into a computer, edit them on a screen, and play the results on a keyboard – it could be the sound of a church organ or even a creaking door or trumpeting elephant.

The first sound sampler came from Australia, was developed by Peter Vogel and Kim Ryrie, and named Fairlight CMI (= Computer Musical Instrument); besides being a sampler, this instrument was also a highly complex synthesizer. The basic version was available for around 25,000 dollars, but to be able to really work with the instrument, you needed to get some additional units and devices, which rose costs to between 40,000 and 100,000 dollars. Kate Bush, Peter Gabriel, YELLO, ART OF NOISE, and others became the first adopters of this new tool with its characteristic "breathy" sound (because of the eight-bit storage). One special sound, the so-called "orchestra hit", was overused immediately and became a sort of plague on hundreds of records. The success of the Fairlight was followed by the Synclavier from U.S. company New England Digital. Originally a synthesizer, it was expanded to a sampler around 1982. It was even more expensive than the Fairlight. Users became Laurie Anderson, Lyle Mays (1953-2020), KRAFTWERK, DEPECHE MODE, Benny Andersson of ABBA, Harold Faltermeyer, and some others used it, and NDW band TRIO or schlager producer, sound engineer and singer Hanne Haller (1950-2005) integrated a Synclavier into their productions. Even the stars of the folksy schlager scene, the ORIGINAL NAABTAL DUO (superhit: "Patrona Bavariae", 1988), recorded their stuff with drum machines and Synclavier, while on TV they always appeared in knee-length lederhosen and mimed playing drums and accordion.

The first record that was completely produced with a Fairlight and exclusively used natural sounds was the "computer-acoustic sound symphony" *Erdenklang* by Austrians Hubert Bognermayr and Harald Zuschrader of EELA CRAIG fame, produced by Ulrich Rützel and premiered in September 1982 during the Ars Electronica Arts and Media Festival at the Brucknerhaus in Linz (Austria). A record version was released on the Teldec label. Its impact on musicians can be compared to Wendy Carlos' *Switched-On Bach.* It was a success – not as big as Carlos' success, but every keyboardist knew it, and it became the basis for Rützel's Erdenklang label for computer-acoustic music.

The expensive Fairlight CMI and Synclavier weren't the last word, cheaper devices followed. Of course, they didn't have all of the features their big brothers had, but they were a practical alternative. One of the first devices was the "Ensoniq" sampler, a stuffy sounding device for around 6000 D-Marks. But there was also the "Emulator" (in short "Emu") by E-mu Systems, followed by Emu II in 1984. The latter was a big success. Musician Gerd Bessler: "For me, all my imaginations about how a music instrument had to be, came true with the Emu. I'd always looked for something like this, but it didn't exist. And then, one day,

I spotted it at the Frankfurt Music Fair, and I knew: That's the one! The price, if memory serves, was 25,000 D-Marks or so, for me an absolutely unaffordable amount at that time, but one month later I owned this thing!"[1]

Since the prices were also extremely high when the early Moog synthesizers came out, one would think it should have been similar now with samplers. But there was a difference. The Big Moog was highly interesting, but if you didn't have one, you didn't have one. At that time there was no existential need for it. With sampling, it was different: It had an immediate influence on the sound of contemporary pop music. Sampled sounds became a "must"; they were expected. This meant that keyboardists had to get a sampler to stay on trend. Ulrich Rützel explained the consequence: "Due to the high initial costs I would recommend musicians to go back to the good old conventional recording contracts with record companies instead of licensing deals."[2] Michael Haentjes, co-founder of Klaus Schulze's IC label, then head of marketing at Teldec, later founder and still CEO of Edel Music: "The risk lay not so much with the musicians but with the producers. They had to carry the risk to a great extent. Of course they compensated this by selling their productions at a higher price than the actual production costs made. This way they minimized the risk in case a production didn't find a label."[3] This is put into perspective a bit when the musicians – as Gerd Bessler, nearly all solo musicians and more and more bands – were their own producers, even more when they created not only pop music but also advertising jingles, film music, or executed other similar commissioned jobs. The musician had to be a good business man himself, or he needed a good agent or manager.

LOW-TECH

If you cannot win this high-priced rat race, then what can you do as a musician? The best idea is probably to forget about reaching for the stars and simply work systematically with the equipment you already own, even if it's not top-notch. There are recordings proving that this can lead to good results. Even Cluster, who were always under financial pressure and had never been able to own even a Minimoog or another device from the middle price range, worked on their album *Curiosum* (1981) with a simple Korg MS-20 (which cost around 1300 D-Mark at that time), and the results were anything but trivial. The duo Tyndall did at least two albums with relatively inexpensive Roland equipment: *Sonnenlicht* (1980) and *Traumland* (1981). But to come to acceptable results with this kind of equipment you need imagination, patience, and a studio for the mix

– something not everybody has access to, and you have to accept that TANGERINE DREAM or Klaus Schulze cannot be your benchmark.

But you can go the other way. You can use the cheap sound for exactly what it is: cheap sound, and you make it your trademark. A band like GRAUZONE of Zürich produced a whole album with not much more than a Korg MS-20 synthesizer, the matching analog sequencer SQ-10, a KR-55 rhythm machine, a guitar, and a saxophone – and this worked, their 45 "Eisbär" (Polar Bear; 1981) became a Neue Deutsche Welle hit and is still known today. It was the cheap sound of the MS-20 and the artificial drum sounds of the KR-55 that made the perfect match for their tracks.

For the technically more proficient readers: The MS-20 was a well thought-out and flexible device. The problem was its cheap sound. It could have been a really great instrument, had only Korg provided it with better filters. The KR-55 rhythm machine was not programmable and thus was relatively rarely used, but when it was used, the sound is immediately recognizable: Listen to "Steppin' Out" by Joe Jackson, the *Deutsche Wertarbeit* album by Dorothea Raukes, "I Can't Take It Anymore" by Vangelis, and some early recordings of DEPECHE MODE: "Dreaming Of Me", "Just Can't Get Enough", or some tracks from Jean-Michel Jarre's *Magnetic Fields*.

We shouldn't stick too long in technical aspects, but we also cannot ignore them: Technology had consequences for the way music was produced, as well as for the way we listened to music. This, in turn, had consequences for the way music was thought up by musicians and producers. Both influenced each other. Technology progressed, and as always, the arts were the first to reflect, ignite or even invent new concepts.

ICE AGE

Like it had been at the end of the 1960s, the transition from the 1970s to the 1980s was not an abrupt jump. On the one hand, the prog rock bands of the 1970s didn't dissolve on New Years' Eve 1979. Their sound had caught a bit of dust and some already considered them dinosaurs, but they still went on playing, and with them the 1970s lived on. But on the other hand, in 1977, the Sex Pistols' album *Never Mind The Bollocks Here's The Sex Pistols* had hit the market in Germany. The punk revolution (and with it the 1980s) had its liftoff.

A revolution? It was a bit more complex. Most of the media (but only few music fans) were familiar with the guy who had put the Sex Pistols project on tracks: Malcolm McLaren (1946-2010) had always been someone with a sixth sense for latent changes. In the 1970s, he ran a boutique with Vivienne Westwood in London's King's Road; later in New York, he managed the New York Dolls and designed their costumes. Back in London, he took over the management of a band called The Strand, re-named them Sex Pistols and organized their career. This was a fully commercial and well-planned project, based mainly on the good old method of setting up a calculated scandal to spread the name. A provocative appearance on ITV with their first 45, "Anarchy In The U.K.", did the job. EMI, their label, gave them the sack after this, which turned out to be first-class publicity for the band. Assistance came from another side: When the *New Musical Express* in 1976 conducted a reader's poll, asking for "the biggest hope for 1977", the chief editor doctored the result into the Sex Pistols – in fact the majority of readers had voted for Brand X.[1] McLaren licensed the next Sex Pistols 45, "God Save The Queen", to A&M Records, but when the police stormed the release party, this label gave the SEX PISTOLS the boot and (allegedly) trashed the already pressed records. This was even more first-class publicity and made the band attractive enough for, of all things, the hippie label Virgin. The record went up to #2 in charts, the album followed.

In Germany, music producer Axel Klopprogge and TV director Eckehard "Ecki" Ziedrich of Frankfurt thought that what had worked in the U.K. should work in Germany just as well. They used experienced musicians from the band TIGER B. SMITH that had split up in 1975, renamed them with pseudonyms, called them STRASSENJUNGS (Guttersnipes), and released their debut album *Dauerlutscher* (Lollipop, 1977) on the well-established CBS label. STRASSENJUNGS was not far from what we would call a casting project today; obviously the production team's idea was to simulate a punk band to get a foot in the door of a potential new youth scene. In this case, however, it didn't work; the STRASSENJUNGS remained without much success. Critic Hans Keller in *Sounds* conceded they had some inventive lyrics, but eventually came to the conclusion: "Harmless average rock without character."[2]

Hans Keller is not really important, but is nevertheless an interesting name in this connection. In the late 1970s, he was a layout man on the board of *Sounds*. When he decided to become a punk, most of the magazine's "classic" rock editors smiled at him, but also gave him space to review some punk albums. His early writing style was full of phrases he had learned under the assumption punks used them.

The old-established *Sounds* writers found it ridiculous, but after a while they realized that they couldn't stop this new wave that was coming up. Some more new writers found their way to *Sounds* – writers who were well informed about this new wave because they were involved in homegrown material. The most important of them turned out to be the earlier mentioned Diedrich Diederichsen. He played in a band with the arty name NACHDENKLICHE WEHRPFLICHTIGE (Reflexive Draftees – they had probably spent more time in finding this name than in thinking about their music). It was not an important band itself, but with West Berlin's FM Einheit, Frieder Butzmann, Timo Blunck, and Bettina Köster playing in the band, it became a sort of germ cell. They released an EP named *Politik für junge Leute* (Politics For Young People – you have to know the German radio programs of that time to get the irony behind this title) on the Hamburg-based Zickzack label in 1980. Some dashes of "no wave" (SWANS, SONIC YOUTH, MATERIAL, SUICIDE, Lydia Lunch and some more) mixed into a few of these band projects now. Timo Blunck later founded PALAIS SCHAUM-

BURG (named after the then Federal Chancellery in Bonn), a counterpart to Düsseldorf's DER PLAN and probably one of Hamburg's two groups that formed the foundation for what was to become Neue Deutsche Welle (the other band was ABWÄRTS).

Hans Keller was also in a band, GEISTERFAHRER (literally "ghost drivers", meaning wrong-way drivers) of Hamburg; Keller played violin, synthesizer, and bass. After their first EP had been released on Zickzack, they signed with Konkurrenz, a sublabel of Philips. Their first album was *Schatten voraus* (Shadow Ahead, 1980). Their sound, dominated by dry drums, the Korg MS-20 synthesizer and shaky, effect-laden vocals, was a little bit like what later would become known as Goth or Dark Wave. Keller later relocated to New York to work as a music journalist; his (taped) voice can be heard in Laurie Anderson's *United States I-IV* performance (1983).

It didn't take long until all of this was categorized under "Neue Deutsche Welle" or, in short, NDW. This term originated from an advertisement for the first album of Düsseldorf's DEUTSCH-AMERIKANISCHE FREUNDSCHAFT, which their distributor Burkhard Seiler (a.k.a. Der Zensor), a local record dealer in West Berlin, had taken out in *Sounds*. Later, music journalist Alfred Hilsberg of Hamburg picked this phrase up in an article titled "Neue Deutsche Welle – aus grauer Städte Mauern" (New German Wave – Out of Gray Cities' Walls). In 1980, Hilsberg had founded the mentioned independent label Zickzack and piled up a bunch of bands and projects that became important: ABWÄRTS, ANDREAS DORAU & DIE MARINAS, EINSTÜRZENDE NEUBAUTEN, FREIWILLIGE SELBSTKONTROLLE, Andy Giorbino, KOSMONAUTENTRAUM, DIE KRUPPS, PALAIS SCHAUMBURG, DIE RADIERER, SPRUNG AUS DEN WOLKEN, DIE TÖDLICHE DORIS, THE WIRTSCHAFTSWUNDER, XMAL DEUTSCHLAND, DIE ZIMMERMÄNNER, and several more, even Jello Biafra (DEAD KENNEDYS) or the No Wave keyboardist and sax player Peter Gordon of New York (LOVE OF LIFE ORCHESTRA with David Van Tieghem, he also worked with Laurie Anderson) had releases on this label. You can hear several of these acts on a sampler called *Lieber zuviel als zuwenig* (Better Too Much Than Too Little), somewhat ironically subtitled "Zickzack Sommerhits 81".

The most important and original NDW bands came from West Berlin and Düsseldorf. From West Berlin there were EINSTÜRZENDE NEUBAUTEN (Collapsing New Buildings – in Germany, "Neubauten" doesn't simply mean "new buildings", it's a sort of architectural term, usually relating to apartment buildings erected after 1945, during the 1950s and early 1960s. Earlier buildings are called "Altbauten", old buildings. The difference between Altbauten and Neubauten is very distinct). Then there were PVC, MANIA D, DIE TÖDLICHE DORIS (The Deadly Doris, more an art project than a band), IDEAL, NEONBABIES, NINA HAGEN BAND, ERSTER FUTUROLOGISCHER KONGRESS (named after a novel by Stanisław Lem), or MALARIA. These plants couldn't have grown anywhere else besides the chaotic "alternative" narrowness of West Berlin's Kreuzberg neighborhood, where ten years earlier, TON STEINE SCHERBEN had already flourished.[3]

Hanover chipped in with some bands that had their very own flavor: BÄRCHEN UND DIE MILCHBUBIS, HANS-A-PLAST, MYTHEN IN TÜTEN, and DER MODERNE MAN were released on No Fun Records, a local label founded by music writer Holger Poscich (a.k.a. Hollow Skai).

Also Hagen at the southeastern edge of the Ruhr area, known as the city ruled by GROBSCHNITT, had a couple of NDW bands: EXTRABREIT, ERSTE WEIBLICHE FLEISCHERGESELLIN NACH 1945, KEIN MENSCH, X-QUADRAT, and of course, NENA (which initially was the name of the band, not of its singer).

From Switzerland the previously mentioned GRAUZONE came in when their 45 "Eisbär" in 1981 became something like an underground hit in Germany – it never reached charts, but the tune became relatively popular and is still known today. Their guitarist, Stephan Eicher, later became a remarkable solo songwriter.

Besides Berlin, Hamburg, and Hanover, it was Düsseldorf that had the most distinctive acts, like DER PLAN (The Plan). Their member Moritz Rrr (sometimes Moritz R®, real name Moritz Reichelt) ran the influential local label Ata Tak (to be read as "art attack"). There were DEUTSCH-AMERIKANISCHE FREUNDSCHAFT (or in short DAF), MITTAGSPAUSE (Lunch Break), ROTZKOTZ (something like Snortpuke), DIE KRUPPS, S.Y.P.H. (who appeared as guests on Holger Czukay's very fine album *On the Way to the Peak of Normal* in 1981), and, probably still the best-known of them, FEHLFARBEN (Off-Colors). Their 45 "Ein Jahr (Es geht voran)" (One Year (Moving On), 1981) reached #22 of German single charts in April 1982; their album *Monarchie und Alltag* (Monarchy and Everyday Life, 1980) became a gem that finally made it to a golden record – 20 years later! (And rightly so, it's still an impressive, high-energy record.) FEHLFARBEN's keyboard player was Kurt Dahlke, he played on DAF's debut album *Ein Produkt der Deutsch-Amerikanischen Freundschaft* (1979), became known for a couple of solo records under the project name DER PYROLATOR, and is still active as a producer today. Guitarist Thomas Schwebel also played with MITTAGSPAUSE and S.Y.P.H.; sax player Frank Fenstermacher (with Dahlke also known as A CERTAIN FRANK) came from DER PLAN and was co-runner of Ata Tak. "Militürk", one of Fehlfarben's album tracks, was co-written by singer Gabriel "Gabi" Delgado-López (1958-2020) who took the song along with him to DAF when he left Mittagspause.

Düsseldorf, as you can see, was a playground where everybody knew everybody. The scene mainly centered at a pub called Ratinger Hof. It's not overblown to call this former juke joint one of the most important places for the Düsseldorf music scene at that time, and one of the germ cells of the NDW, memorialized in at least one book[4] and a TV docu[5]. Every NDW band had to play at this place and deal with the (sometimes violent) audience reactions. In a way, the Ratinger Hof was for NDW bands what the Star-Club had been for beat bands in the 1960s: Having been accepted there meant a sort of approval for everywhere else. Of course, all these bands listened to each other and learned (or stole) from each other.

Let's not forget there was also the artistic scene around the Kunstakademie. The Düsseldorf music landscape was deeply influenced by the students and some professors from this art school. In 1982, even Joseph Beuys became part of the NDW scene when he participated in a 45 titled "Sonne statt Reagan". This could be heard as "Sun instead of rain" or as "Sun instead of Reagan" – an untranslatable pun, based on the acoustic similarity of the word "Reagan" (U.S. President from 1981 to 1989) and the German word for rain, "Regen". It was, with all due respect for Beuys, a slightly crackbrained campaigning song for the Green Party of which Beuys had been a founding member. The lyrics had been written by a copywriter at a local ad agency. Beuys was not accompanied by musicians from Düsseldorf but by members of BAP, a band based in neighboring city Cologne, certainly without their head, heart, singer, and songwriter, Wolfgang Niedecken, who wasn't informed about this project. Which is a bit juicy because from time immemorial the citizens of Düsseldorf and Cologne used to pick on each other, but that shouldn't be taken too seriously.

Rüdiger Esch, member of Die Krupps (a precursor of what would later become Electronic Body Music, EBM) and well-informed chronologist of the Düsseldorf scene[6], makes it clear that, interestingly, Kraftwerk had always remained the benchmark. Most of the other Düsseldorf projects either circled around Kraftwerk, felt annoyed by Kraftwerk, tried to match Kraftwerk, tried to do something comparable to Kraftwerk, or tried to do something *contrastable* to Kraftwerk. Today, it's still stunning to see the amount of hate and malice shown toward Kraftwerk after they had become internationally known and played in a completely different league: The scene wanted and still wants to see them as their "very own". This shows the mechanisms of such a "scene" quite well: Everyone is best friends as long as they are in the same boat, but as soon as one of them becomes successful, all friendship is perdu.

Most tunes produced by NDW bands were short, simple, and noisy; the musicians, to put it nicely, didn't have golden voices and weren't virtuosos on their instruments. West Berlin's Einstürzende Neubauten didn't even use musical instruments as a basis, but rather all sorts of tools, scraps, and building-site finds. A TV report showing them in their then "rehearsal room" is unforgettable – a claustrophobically low-ceilinged hollow space inside of an autobahn bridge. But this might have been faked for the camera; who knows. However (or maybe because of it), they were able to later establish themselves as an art project, but they had to survive their quantum of hunger years. Blixa Bargeld had a remarkable voice that stuck in your mind. He wasn't even the worst guitarist I've ever heard, as his work with Nick Cave & The Bad Seeds shows.

Although Düsseldorf is somehow characterised by the mechanism through which NDW worked, this wave was not a specific Düsseldorf phenomenon, not even a German one. However, most NDW bands remained local acts. There were no more than five or maybe six bands that reached a sort of importance outside their respective cities. When you watch a documentary like filmmaker Stephanie Beroes' *Debt Begins at 20* (1980) on the local punk and new wave scene of Pittsburgh, Pennsylvania, you will see many parallels with the German NDW bands, their situation and their way of thinking.[7]

This movie, by the way, also makes it clear that "punk" in the U.S. did not carry the same meaning as in England or Germany. Why artists and bands like Patti Smith, Blondie, Talking Heads, Television, or even Mink DeVille/Willy DeVille (1950-2009) went under "punk" in the States would be inexplicable for Europeans. In England, these bands would have been "new wave" or "pub rock". In Germany, the term "pub rock" didn't exist, so Blondie was seen first as "new wave", later as "disco", and the other three bands always went under "new wave". But what was seen as "new wave" in Germany was not the same as in England: The stars of new wave in Germany were what went under "new romantic" in the U.K., bands like Duran Duran, Haircut 100, Japan, Spandau Ballet, Ultravox, Visage. Yes, it's complicated.

In Germany, part of this new wave was the "popper" movement, meaning young folks wearing asymmetric bangs, tapered jeans (called "carrot jeans"), expensive clothes from brands like Burberry, Diesel, Fiorucci, Benetton, Lacoste et al, preferably cashmere. They smoked "international sounding" cigarette brands like Dunhill, Kent, or JPS, and acted demonstratively conservative, apolitical, and spend-happy. This made a very welcomed enemy image for the punks that sometimes led to brawls in front of clubs. This popper movement started in Hamburg (are you surprised?) and spread over Germany's metropolises as a subset of what was called the "Generation Golf", people who spent their youth in the later 1970s and 1980s, the German equivalent of "Generation X" in the United States. The term "Generation Golf" became part of the vernacular in Germany; originally, it was the title of a book by journalist Florian Illies, a humorous portrait of the generation born between 1965 and 1975. This generation grew up with the Volkswagen Golf (in the U.S. its name was "Rabbit"), a car that was said to be so economically and ecologically reasonable that it had to become a giant success – and it did. Everybody either had a Golf or at least knew somebody who had one. Musically, this generation contributed to bands like PROPAGANDA, ALPHAVILLE and some others – something between "new wave" and "electronic". It was a short-lived trend. But the NDW went on.

Similar to the punk movement, the NDW derived from certain weariness. It was a reaction to the increasingly bombastic stadium acts and prog bands. The drug-fueled excursions through faraway galaxies had also gone stale. Being a virtuoso was not a priority; music simply had to be short, loud, full of energy, sometimes full of pathos, and often came with a sort of "there is no point in doing anything" attitude. The language had to be German and the instrumental in-your-face aggressiveness of many songs is still striking, especially the barrack yard attitude of many of their vocalists. A lot of this reflected a depressed personal and/or political situation, but always without propagating any methods on how to change it. Not even CARAMBOLAGE, a band founded in Fresenhagen by people from the TON STEINE SCHERBEN circle, called for a better world or rioted against class enemies as their parents had done.

What many musicians (and critics) didn't seem to notice was how close all these bands were to the concepts of their early forefathers AMON DÜÜL, FAUST, KLUSTER, and companions. They built up their own infrastructures and said goodbye to the past, not realizing that they acted, in fact, quite similar.[8] But there's one aspect that Moritz Rrr of DER PLAN and Ata Tak brings in: "Even the punks of the second generation didn't get all these ironic elements of punk. They took that seriously. Even this 'No Future' thing. We then explicitly distanced ourselves from this and intentionally spread opposite paroles. Like: 'The world is bad, but life is good!' … We simply didn't want the wit and the irony of punk to open out into such a new, deadly seriousness."[9] I'm not sure whether Moritz Rrr took all the components of the punk movement into account. Of course, there were "Sunday punks" who saw punk as a sort of fashion trend they followed from Friday night to Sunday morning, while during the week they wore business attire. There were also punks who saw the irony that was included in the movement. But there were also punks hanging out on some streets and public open spaces, who seriously had this "no future" idea in their heads. It was of course a sort of self-fulfilling prophecy, but *these* punks behaved and looked in a way that destroyed nearly any chance of a personal future, and they meant it.

NEUE DEUTSCHE WELLE SELLOUT

It was the "not too serious" view that led to a direction which was not intended by the founding bands of NDW. The NDW went into a much more commercial direction when "Fred vom Jupiter" accidentally became a hit. This 45 was made in 1981 as a slightly crackbrained (but indeed funny) schlager parody, published under the project name Die Doraus und die Marinas, invented and produced by Andreas Dorau of Hamburg and a handful of female schoolmates of his. The production consisted of a synthie, a sequencer, and a cheap rhythm machine, recorded at the studio of their pals Geisterfahrer, more or less under home recording conditions. When the song was released on Ata Tak, nobody could have foreseen what would happen: In spring 1982, the tune climbed up to #21 of German charts and remained in charts for 18 weeks. In Austria, it reached #13, and Ata Tak licensed "Fred vom Jupiter" to major label Teldec.

This production (and its success) could happen not only because prog rock had become an old hat that needed an answer, but also because synthesizers and home recording equipment had become affordable for nearly everybody. The sound aesthetic resulting from this cheap equipment had become accepted by a broad audience because it was new and fresh.

This, however, had consequences. The record industry suddenly sensed there was potential in this seemingly strange NDW. The majors tried to jump on the bandwagon. The result was the biggest hype campaign Germany had probably seen since "Top Szene Hamburg".

In 1982, the aforementioned Axel Klopprogge (producer of Strassenjungs) became deeply involved in setting up a commercial leg of the NDW with the songs "Ich will Spaß" (I Want Fun) and "Kleine Taschenlampe brenn'" (Little

Flashlight Shine) with singers Markus (full name: Markus Mörl) and Nena. The singers as well as the songs were part of the film *Gib Gas, ich will Spaß*[10] (Hit the Gas, I Want Fun; U.K. title: *Hangin' Out*) from 1983. It became a moderate success, and director Wolfgang Büld claimed: "The wide breakthrough of German pop music made a combination of feature film and music possible, a situation we had to wait a long time for in Germany."[11] The movie was a direct continuation of the infantile schlager comedies of the 1950s and 1960s, and I'm not sure that anyone really waited for those.

However, since her first hit "Nur geträumt" (1982), Nena had become a household name, and the naiveté, the sentimentality, and the easygoing humor of this film opened the gate for her. Now all hell began to let loose. Dozens of bands, singers and projects were catapulted into the orbit, all under the label "NDW": Hubert Kah ("Sternenhimmel", "Engel 07"), UKW ("Sommersprossen"), Combo Colossale ("Puppen weinen nicht"), Peter Schilling ("Major Tom [Völlig losgelöst]", of course a hint to Bowie's "Space Oddity"), Lilli Berlin ("Ostberlin-Wahnsinn", with Harald Großkopf on drums and lyrics by Jürgen Barz, former member of musical comedy group Insterburg & Co), ZaZa ("Zauberstab"), Clit ("Keine Probleme Marlene"), Steinwolke ("Katherine Katherine"), Vera Kaa ("Bye Bye Baby, das war's schon"), Fräulein Menke ("Hohe Berge"; Franziska Menke is the daughter of producer and Studio Maschen owner Joe Menke), and of course Nena ("99 Luftballons"; under the title "99 Red Balloons" the tune charted on #1 in the U.K., on #2 in the U.S., and sold more than 2 million copies).

There were many more – most of these acts became one hit wonders. Some of them were even incorporated in the NDW without really being NDW, like the slightly ironic schlager "Bruttosozialprodukt" (Gross National Product) by Geier Sturzflug (Vulture Nosedive; 1983, #1 in Germany, Austria and Switzerland) or the pseudo-ecological tearjerker "Karl der Käfer" (Karl The Beetle) by Gänsehaut (Goosebumps), a project formed by members of the editorial staff of *Keyboards, Homerecording und Computer* including chief editor Gerald Dellmann, former keyboardist of Satin Whale; the song reached #17.

The Neue Deutsche Welle finally ended where this book started: being schlager.

Only a few projects were more substantial; one worth mentioning is Ideal. They played in West Berlin as the supporting act for Barclay James Harvest in front of 150,000 people and were shown for a couple of seconds in Germany's leading newscast "Tagesschau". Their self-titled debut album from 1980 was produced a bit clumsily by Klaus Schulze's music publisher Klaus D. Müller (a.k.a. kdm) and released on Schulze's IC label. (Klaus Schulze's track "Weird Caravan" on his album *Dig It* (1980) is based on a loop taken from IDEAL's song "Telephon".) The record reached #3 in album charts and stayed in charts for exactly one year. The record went gold for 250,000 sold copies, which made it the first golden record for a release from an independent label. IDEAL consisted of fully professional musicians; their instrumental skills were criminally underestimated by many. Bass player Ernst Deuker and guitarist/singer Frank Jürgen "Eff Jott" Krüger (1948-2007) from the X-PECTORS played as tough as nails, drummer Hans-Joachim Behrendt had played with VOLKER KRIEGEL'S MILD MANIAC ORCHESTRA and the RELEASE MUSIC ORCHESTRA, and the patterns he played were often much more complicated than they sounded. IDEAL's main person of interest was singer and organist Annette Humpe. Her lyrics were original, clever, and on point, with sometimes surreally radical themes: "Erschießen" (Shoot Dead), "Eiszeit" (Ice Age; luckily not the same song as Peter Maffay's), "Wir zerstören unser Glück" (We Destroy Our Happiness), "Spannung" (Suspense), "Sex in der Wüste" (Sex in the Desert), "Spion" (Spy). Sometimes the songs were not far from being schlager, but they came with a little wink and could be seen as subversive: "Blaue Augen" (Blue Eyes), "Monotonie" (Monotony). Annette Humpe's singing was vigorous. Sometimes rolling the "r" a bit too dramatically, on stage her playing the Yamaha Electone organ was always slightly reminiscent of typewriting (but she had studied piano and composition). Usually, she appeared with a captain's hat, but even without, it was obvious that this was not just "another band with a female singer". IDEAL was *her* band. I'm sure it was her idea to ignite the band's career with a hymn to their city: "Berlin", a song still well-known today, evoking the atmosphere of Kreuzberg in the early Eighties and mentioning all of West Berlin's then hip places.

Conny Plank produced their second album, *Der Ernst des Lebens* (1981; The Serious Side Of Life) which is probably their best album except for its slightly muffled sound, followed by *Bi Nuu* (a nonsense title), produced by Gareth Jones in 1982 and mixed at Hansa Studio.

IDEAL represents the substance of NDW and is still one of the strongest acts of 1980's Germany. They were clever enough to disband in March 1983, in the zenith of their success, announcing they had planned it this way from the beginning.

After the end of Ideal, Annette Humpe had a mega NDW hit with "Codo – Düse im Sauseschritt" by DÖF in 1983. DÖF, clearly a parody of DAF, stands for "Deutsch-Österreichisches Feingefühl" (German-Austrian Sensitiveness) and was a project with her sister Inga Humpe (former Neonbabies) and the Austrian comedy duo Tauchen & Prokopetz. The 45 is a textbook example of a catchy tune, reached #1 in German and Austrian charts and #4 in Switzerland, and the non-existent verb "düsen" (meant in the sense of "to run" or "to hurry") became a common phrase in German vernacular. A production company Annette Humpe co-founded with Siggi Loch didn't fly; the two of them had too different ideas about what this company should be about. (Loch finally in 1988 founded Act, now one of Germany's most important independent jazz labels next to ECM and Enja.) I remember seeing Annette Humpe in a TV interview a couple of years ago where she stated that she hadn't become really successful until she found out what she was *not* able to do and simply stopped trying it. Not the worst way to see things. She had several ups and downs in her further career but can be seen still today as one of Germany's most original producers and lyricists.

Annette Humpe was also involved as a backup singer for another NDW smash hit with the full title: "Da Da Da Ich lieb dich nicht Du liebst mich nicht Aha Aha Aha" (1981), usually simply known as "Da Da Da", by Trio of East Frisia village Großenkneten (no, you don't have to memorize this). In its ironic simplicity it can't be called anything other than a stroke of genius; its producer was no other than Klaus Voormann. The guitarist was Gert "Kralle" Krawinkel (1947-2014), who formerly played in country-folk bands Cravinkel and Emsland Hillbillies; later he worked with Marius Müller-Westernhagen. Drummer Peter Behrens (1947-2016) had worked as a clown, played with Silberbart, and finally died from alcoholism. Trio's singer Stephan Remmler had been a schlager singer before joining Trio: "I Know It's Over" b/w "Now I'm Leaving Home" under the pseudonym Rex Carter, released in 1971 on the Philips label, had Frumpy as a backing band; the follow-up "Ich liebe die Sonne" b/w "Melanie" was written by Manfred Oberdörffer – we remember him being schlager singer Tony, his band was the Tonics. After the end of Trio, Remmler went back to the schlager scene. His biggest solo success was probably "Alles hat ein Ende, nur die Wurst hat zwei" (1986; Everything Has an End, Only the Sausage Has Two; a common German proverb). In the U.S., "Da Da Da" achieved a certain level of fame as the song was used in a Volkswagen commercial. As always, as a German artist, you have to do something special to receive recognition in the U.S., and Trio did it.

This also goes for Klaus Nomi (1944–1983, real name Klaus Sperber). The pseudonym "Nomi" resulted from switching the letters of "omni", which is a data transfer modus for synthesizers. As a skilled countertenor, Nomi relocated to New York in 1973 because no German opera house wanted to hire him. There, he started his career with a little help from David Bowie, who hired him as back-up singer for a TV gig on "Saturday Night Live". Nomi made black and white kabuki makeup his trademark, wore a Cubist costume, and moved on stage in a way he had picked up from German expressionism.

He wrote some songs ("Keys of Life", "Nomi Song") using Dada elements and an intentionally overdone German accent. His best-known song was probably the aria "Oh What Power Art Thou (Cold Song)" from Henry Purcell's opera *King Arthur*. Around 1981, Klaus Nomi was discovered to be HIV positive, something that was still relatively unexplored at that time. An appearance on German TV at "Klassik Rock Night" in 1982, with a full symphony orchestra conducted by Eberhard Schoener, shows him already visibly weak. This touching "Cold Song" turned out to be one of his last stage appearances ever, and he knew it. Klaus Nomi passed away in 1983.

Joachim Witt of Hamburg, a former singer of Duesenberg, is also significant. He landed a smash hit with "Goldener Reiter" (Golden Rider) from his album *Silberblick* (Squint), a slightly unpleasant song about a loony bin. The song was not new, it had already been recorded in 1980 by René Tinner at Inner Space Studio (later Witt became the co-owner of it). Nobody wanted the song until Witt's exalted vocal style, Harald Gutowski's straight bass, and Jaki Liebezeit's on-the-point drumming fit perfectly into the NDW, and WEA decided to release it. The 45 went up to #2 of German charts in December 1981 and stayed in the charts for more than half a year. *Silberblick* reached #10 of album charts in the following January. Part of the album was "Der Weg in die Ferne", a charming cover version of Talking Head's "Heaven". A second hit followed in September 1982, "Tri Tra Trullala (Herbergsvater)", a wonderful hypnotic nonsensical number, reaching #39 of charts ("Tri Tra Trullala" is the song Kasper sings, who is the Punch from the Punch and Judy show in Germany; a Herbergsvater is a youth hostel warden, I'm sure you know these kinds of guys). Several attempts followed, but no further success was to be had for Joachim Witt, so he relocated to Portugal for a while. In 1998 he had a stunning comeback with "Die Flut" (The Flood; a duet with Peter Heppner of Wolfsheim) which established him as a star in Germany's then quite vivid Goth scene. "Die Flut" was another "calculated scandal song". Some radio hosts and newspapers thought they had heard a right-wing undertone in the lyrics because the word "Flut" was often used by right-wing folks and politicians as a synonym for the "unwanted mass immigration" of Muslim asylum seekers to Germany. In reality, the lyrics had no connection to this topic. The problem was the video showing miserable people in the rain trying to get on board an ark and sent away. What the video showed had no direct connection to the lyrics, but it played with refugees connected to the keyword "Flut". This was enough for several radio stations to ban the song. As always, this helped make it cult.

As we talk about calculated scandal songs (again), here's another one: DAF (Deutsch-Amerikanische Freundschaft) precisely used this method to get media attention, and once more, it worked. Gabi Delgado-López and drummer Robert Görl, now as a duo, stripped the band's sound down to a skeleton made of not more than short sequencer patterns and drums, and used these as backing tracks for Gabi's sweaty vocals. Their album *Alles ist gut* (Everything Is Good; 1981), not released on Ata Tak anymore but on Virgin, was produced and recorded by Conny Plank. He contributed the idea to cut off the decaying sound of the cymbals with a noise gate after a second – a striking effect which is missed on later remastered rereleases. Probably only few people outside of Düsseldorf would have noticed the album, had DAF not taken the song "Der Mussolini" from the LP and released it as a 45. The tune asked listeners to clap their hands, move their ass and dance the Mussolini, the Adolf Hitler, the Jesus Christ, and the Communism – utter nonsense, but it served its purpose: Radio stations, newspapers, magazines, the church, and some politicians went overboard about the question of whether it was acceptable to banalize Mussolini and Hitler this way and mention Jesus Christ in the same breath. What was planned, happened: The discussion carried *Alles ist gut* up to #15 of German album charts and #16 of Austrian album charts. DAF used their window of opportunity and went on tour with this success. Since they didn't want to deal with synthesizers and sequencers on stage, they simply piled up around 20 or so cassette decks for the backing tracks, one cassette with one track in every deck, accompanied by live drumming from Robert Görl. *Alles ist gut* is still a sort of NDW solitaire and an early example of what would later become Industrial or EBM. "Als wär's das letzte Mal", "Der Räuber und der Prinz", and "Alles ist gut" are still charming, but the concept only worked for this one album and one summer. Further DAF albums offered the same stuff but without much variation, and the basic idea fizzled out.

Even KRAFTWERK, without much ado, was now assigned to the NDW. In 1981, just after the release of the *Computerwelt* album, they were at the peak of their creativity and enthusiasm. When their 1981 world tour made a stop at Hamburg's time-honored Musikhalle, they were simply fantastic. It was crowded, the sound was great, and their retro-futuristic stage setting was similar to the bridge of a spaceship. Like the earlier mentioned "fast space cruiser Orion" of TV series *Raumpatrouille*, their usage of the curtain, lights, neon, and video projections clearly targeted producing a sort of overwhelming aesthetic. It worked; they left an ecstatic and happy audience. When I think of Ralf Hütter's dance movements (which looked as if he scythed a lawn), the attribution to the NDW didn't seem to be too far out. (The stage scenes in KRAFTWERK's "The Model" video, by the way, were shot at this concert.)

Several 1970s bands gave up in the 1980s. Some musicians tried to integrate NDW elements into their sound to stay up to date. The CHRIS BRAUN BAND was one of those. In the 1970s, they were already a second-rate band with two albums, *Both Sides* (1972) and *Foreign Lady* (1974), and tried to make a comeback as an NDW band in 1983 with *Ultrabraun.* It was too late for them.

The opposite also happened: to start as an NDW act and then change to something different. But as mentioned earlier, genre-change is a hard business. Miko (Petra Mikolajczak, sometimes also known as Miko Lay Czak or Mico Layczak) started as a singer with NEONBABIES, then later joined the NDW project 1. FUTUROLOGISCHER CONGRESS on the album *Schützt die Verliebten* (Protect the People in Love; 1982). After, she tried to start a solo career as Miko with the album *The Voice and the Beat* (1983). This was obviously intended to bring in a good portion of funk, it even contains a cover version of Billie Holiday's "Lady Sings the Blues", but it turned out a half-baked record. At least it brought her a contract with Polydor. The outcome was *Visionen von Schönheit* (Visions of Beauty; 1986). This LP is the soundtrack for the half-biographical film *Miko – Aus der Gosse zu den Sternen* (From the Gutter to the Stars) by Frank Ripploh (1949-2002). In the same year, she played in Hans-Christoph Blumenberg's film *Der Sommer des Samurai* and sometimes worked as a TV host. Her career as a singer never really took off.

Other established musicians ignored the trend and kept on doing their shtick.

CLUSTER fell apart in 1981 for personal reasons after the release of the *Curiosum* album. They didn't reappear until the mid-1990s.

Klaus Schulze went digital and integrated a Crumar GDS (General Development System) in his equipment, which was probably the first synthesizer combined with a computer. This device was not a big success. Aside from Klaus Schulze, only Chris Franke and Wendy Carlos used one. To my knowledge, all in all, not more than ten units were built. On his album *Dig It*, released in 1980, Schulze features the GDS, and this brought audible changes to his basic sound. Musically, Schulze just went on doing what he had always done.

Tangerine Dream turned more and more to film music productions and churned out album after album for, unfortunately, mainly second- and third-rate movies. This generated a good income, but musically, most of their soundtrack albums were stale – I would name *Sorcerer* (1977), *Thief* (1981) and *Wavelength* (1983) as exceptions. In 1982, they managed to land a hit in Germany: "Das Mädchen auf der Treppe" (The Girl on the Stairs) was the end title track of an episode of the popular TV series *Tatort* (Crime Scene) and went up to #13 in the charts. It was a remixed variation of the title track of their album *White Eagle*. In my opinion, Tangerine Dream's last interesting album was *Hyperborea* (1983). *Poland (The Warsaw Concert)* (1984) and *Underwater Sunlight* (1986), both highly rated by many fans, didn't do much for me, and for several years I gave up following the band.

Eberhard Schoener was pioneering once more, this time in the use of samples. His album *Spurensicherung* (Securing Of Evidence, 1983) had an interesting concept: Songs with vocals were followed by instrumental tracks based on sound samples that were related to the topic of the song they followed. As sound sources, Schoener used different sounding stones, a Mexican market, the singing of monks from the Sama monastery in Tibet, and others. Although singers Hazel O'Connor and George Kochbek (who sounds nearly like Sting here), and actor Rolf Zacher were part of the line-up, the whole album was a bit clueless. It never got a CD rerelease and seems to be more or less forgotten today.

This was different with Schoener's follow-up, *Sky Music/Mountain Music* (1984), a solo recording. The album was based on a multi-media live event at Lake Tegernsee near Schoener's home. Musicians played on a stage in the middle of the lake, loudspeakers were placed on the mountains around the lake, and there was a laser show and hang-gliders with specially-painted lit gliders. Hundreds of carrier pigeons were set free over the lake, with each of them carrying a tiny little flute, and the flight wind produced a swirling sound. Schoener had found these flutes in Bali. Later, this event was partly recreated in the studio. Because there was no way to record the pigeons in the air, the flutes were attached to sticks and put into the wind tunnel of BMW. The resulting sound cloud was fed into the Fairlight and mixed with several Oberheim and Moog sounds to become the "Sky Music". "Mountain Music", the album's second track, is based on modified samples of birds singing, combined with electronic sounds. *Sky Music/Mountain Music* can be considered Schoener's most beautiful ambient work.

The late 1970s and 1980s were also Michael Rother's most successful time. After his first three solo albums (*Flammende Herzen*, 1977; *Sterntaler*, 1978; *Katzenmusik*, 1979), he had left Sky Records; *Fernwärme* (1982) and the following three albums (*Lust*, 1983; *Süßherz und Tiefenschärfe*, 1985; *Traumreisen*, 1987) appeared on Germany's still biggest label, Polydor. Rother had always avoided taking on debt, so it was this Polydor deal that now made it possible for him to acquire a Fairlight CMI. For the first time, the instrument appeared on his album *Lust* (1983), the opening track "Palmengarten" (Palm Garden) was released as a 45. Polydor tried to establish Rother as "Germany's answer to Jean-Michel Jarre"; they managed to place a portrait in the TV gossip magazine "Bitte umblättern", and they sent him on a tour through the daytime programs of German radio stations. Usually, the hosts didn't know what to ask him and he didn't know what to tell them. Rother is a friendly and intelligent guy, but he's not an extroverted show person like Jarre. His music, as "easy" as it seems to be sometimes, was not "music for the masses", there were no concerts to announce, and the chosen TV and radio shows weren't the right places to catch an audience that would have been seriously interested in his music. Rother's albums were slow burners, and nobody seemed to have a clear idea about who his target audience was. The 45 "Glitzerglanz" (something like "Glittergloss") from his album *Süßherz und Tiefenschärfe* (Sweetheart and Depth of Field; 1985) was used by NDR radio for several years as a sort of interlude, but it never entered the charts.

Outside of Germany, Rother was nearly unknown. Having been in NEU! or HARMONIA was no help, and in the U.S., you could only get his records as imports. So, inevitably, after *Traumreisen* (Dream Journeys; 1987), Polydor abandoned the option. On the other hand, Rother was too well known in Germany to be easily affordable for small independents, so he fell silent for roughly the next ten years, aside from doing a few film music tracks.

JAPAN

In the early and mid-1980s, Germany had an interesting phenomenon of exchange: Parts of the German pop culture had popularized in Japan. The YELLOW MAGIC ORCHESTRA would have been a different band without KRAFTWERK anyway, but now YMO even used German track titles – in the German language! "Neue Tanz", grammatically wrong, but definitely German, opened their album *Technodelic* (1981); YMO's Ryuichi Sakamoto titled one of his solo tracks "Das Neue Japanische Elektronische Volkslied" (The New Japanese Electronic Folk Song), and singer Miharu Koshi came up with pop versions of "Ave Maria" and Goethe's "Heideröslein" on her album *Boy Soprano* (1985), both composed by Franz Schubert. Electronic ambient duo INOYAMA LAND presented "Shüffer" (which probably meant "Schiffe", ships), "Wässer" (Waters) and "Meine Reflexion" (My Reflection) on their album *Danzindan-Pojidon* (1983). At the same time, German innerspring mattresses also became a fad in Tokyo's hipster apartments.

Germany's late hippies and followers of the alternative scene, as well as hipsters and people who considered themselves avant-garde, in exchange, discovered Japan. Every flat-sharing community now had futons on the floor. Besides this, far-eastern things like Japanese design (especially electronics, like telephones or TV sets – Sony TV sets were a must-have for a while because of their design), tea ceremonies, meditation, Japanese movies, and Zen Buddhism became a topic – not that people always understood everything, but it was something exotic and interesting, like the expensive kimonos you could now buy.

This fad went on for three or four years before falling into oblivion – but today, Japan is still an important market for German music.

PATHWAYS BETWEEN SCHLAGER AND ROCK

There were also still "standard" rock groups. One of them was the earlier mentioned BAP from Cologne, founded in 1976. The name means "Papa" (Dad) in Kölsch, the region's dialect. BAP played mainstream rock, loosely based on the ROLLING STONES, the KINKS, Bob Dylan, or Bruce Springsteen – the kind of rock that is usually seen as "honest". Their relatively substantial lyrics, written and performed by Wolfgang Niedecken, were consequently sung in Kölsch. Sometimes, the lyrics had a local connection ("Stollwerck-Leed", about a squatted factory building), sometimes they came with clearly political undertones, like "Kristallnaach", "Südstadt verzäll nix", or "Stellt üch vüür" (a cover version of John Lennon's "Imagine"). Other songs spoofed the "alternative scene" ("Wellenreiter", "Müsli Män"), discussed personal things (like the problematic relationship between Niedecken and his father in "Verdamp lang her", probably their best-known song), or simply told love stories ("Do kanns zaubere"). After being a local act for a while, with their records released on the Cologne independent label Eigelstein, they switched over to EMI's Musikant label in 1981 with the album *Für usszeschnigge* (For Cutting-Out). BAP's career got its biggest push in 1982 when they performed at an open air festival on the Loreley Stage with a beautiful view of the River Rhine; "Rockpalast" aired the concert nationwide on TV. Although their dialect was hard to understand outside the Cologne area, BAP became extremely successful: During the next 22 years they reached the #1 spot of German album charts with no less than eleven albums.

BAP was a pioneer for the development of a strange crossbreed of bands. BAP was clearly a rock band and had a special place because of their dialect, but they opened the door for something that had been unheard of: Songs in the German language with mostly ambitious lyrics that were not schlagers anymore. But you wouldn't call them real rock songs, and they also were not singer-songwriter music. They were not what Udo Lindenberg did, they were something between all three worlds.

This trend had already started in the mid-1970s with Austrian musicians Wolfgang Ambros, Georg Danzer (1946-2007), Ludwig Hirsch (1946-2011), or Rainhard Fendrich, but their breakthrough hadn't come until the 1980s when the time was apparently right for them. Obviously, after the crazy and overtorqued Neue Deutsche Welle, people were waiting for something more serious.

Heinz Rudolf Kunze started in the singer-songwriter area with excellent, sometimes melancholic or satirical lyrics. In the mid-1980s, he became a hopper between the worlds. With his album *Dein ist mein ganzes Herz* (With All My Heart I'm Yours; 1985), the title picking up an old operetta song, he discovered the stage and became popular among a wide audience. Besides this, he translated the lyrics for some musicals.

In parts (and, as far as I'm concerned, with raised eyebrows), Peter Maffay can also be named here. He started out as a pure schlager singer in the early 1970s. With his tearjerker "Du" (You) from 1970 he stormed the charts. With "Und es war Sommer" (And It Was Summer; 1976) he crooned an unintendedly funny song about his defloration at a beach ("… and as a man I saw the sun arise"). Maffay's lyrics were and always are free of any kind of humor. I'm sure this is a big part of his success; as every advertising copywriter knows, humor, even more so irony, is always dangerous because most people either don't understand it or misunderstand it. In the 1980s, Maffay changed his style into something that, musically, came nearer to rock music, and his sincereness made it credible. Concert promoter Fritz Rau loved him, and in 1982, Maffay even became a supporting act for the Rolling Stones. He is still a superstar in Germany, even more so with his children's record series *Tabaluga*. But he could never get rid of his pathetic schlager voice, and his records never did much for me.

Marius Müller-Westernhagen of Düsseldorf, actor as well as singer, was one of the earliest protagonists in this genre. In the 1960s, he was in a band called Harakiri Whoom with later Rheingold founder Bodo Staiger (1949-2019). The first time I noted his name was in 1974 in Roland Klick's film *Supermarkt*[12], where, under the pseudonym Marius West, he sang the title track. The music was written by Peter Hesslein of Lucifer's Friend, and Udo Lindenberg was also somehow involved in the music. Klick had worked with rock musicians before: He was the one who commissioned Can with the *Deadlock* soundtrack in 1970. Müller-Westernhagen's first album, *Das erste Mal* (1975; The First Time), was produced and composed again mainly by Peter Hesslein; most of the involved musicians were rock musicians, but something inside me jibs against the idea to mark songs like "Marion aus Pinneberg" or "Wir waren noch Kinder" (We Were Still Children) as rock songs. But they were not schlagers like Peter Maffay did them, and they were not singer-songwriter stuff. On later albums, this didn't change much. MMW, as he was called, kept the concept, but scarfed his lyrics, often to a point of polemics or deliberate provocation, and in the 1980s and 1990, Marius Müller-Westernhagen became extremely successful. From the beginning, I have had the impression of seeing an actor playing a rock singer, and his recordings never did anything for me. But polarizing was always part of his business model.

Another one of these "halfbreeds" was the Klaus Lage Band who had a smash hit with "1001 Nacht" (1984), along with two or three further hits. One of them was the title track for a *Tatort* TV crime movie ("Faust auf Faust", 1985). But then, the Klaus Lage Band somehow disappeared into thin air (although the band made a nice little instrumental album featuring trombonist Albert Mangelsdorff: *Listen and Lay Back*, 1988, without singer Klaus Lage).

The most successful of all of these musicians, Herbert Grönemeyer, mentioned already as the runner of the Grönland label, started his singing career in the 1980s. Grönemeyer was and still is a superstar in Germany. First he was an actor, best known internationally since 1981 when he appeared as "war correspondent Leutnant Werner" in Wolfgang Petersen's movie *Das Boot*.[13] But he was also a musician: Already in the 1970s, he had worked as a musical director at Schauspielhaus Bochum and Württembergisches Staatstheater Stuttgart. He had even worked with choreographer Pina Bausch (1940-2009). In 1983, his enervating song "Currywurst" became a sort of Kohlenpott (Ruhr Area) classic that, for the first time, showed Grönemeyer's characteristic vocal style; it was something between nervous singing and bellowing. In contrast to the others, his lyrics can be humorous. A rare experience in German rock.

His real big career started one year later with his album *4630 Bochum* (the city he then lived in; 4630 was its postal code). It stayed in German album charts for 79 weeks. Several records and tours followed; *Mensch* (2002) became the (then) best-selling album of all time in the German language, and stayed in the charts for 96 weeks, selling more than 3 million copies.

It was not before 2013 that somebody outnumbered this success: Schlager singer Helene Fischer's album *Farbenspiel* stayed in the charts for 241 weeks. Don't ask me why.

Like a bridge between the schlager area and the Kunzes, Grönemeyers, et cetera, Ulla Meinecke of Frankfurt invented a sort of rock chanson style. She was originally employed as a secretary at Udo Lindenberg's office, and after a while she became his protégé. Her first album, *Von toten Tigern und nassen Katzen* (About Dead Tigers and Wet Cats; 1977) was produced and partly written by Lindenberg, and you could hear this, word by word and line by line. But Ulla is an excellent lyricist on her own. She found her voice and individual style very soon. Her best albums are probably *Nächtelang* (Nightlong; 1981), *Wenn schon nicht für immer, dann wenigstens für ewig* (If Not Forever, Then at Least Eternally; 1983), and *Der Stolz italienischer Frauen* (The Pride of Italian Women; 1985).

THE EIGHTIES

WOMEN'S POWER

We have already heard about Annette Humpe, but she doesn't represent what this chapter will be about. In connection with the alternative movement, an important social movement that came up in the 1970s found its way into rock and popular music of the 1980s. But as popular music tends to work, this movement soon got hijacked by commerce and esotericism.

Since the late 1970s, Germany has had a growing feminism movement. It resulted from the 1968 movement; as this had primarily been a male movement, the female image hadn't changed in a significant way. A lot of activities circled around the German §218 (prohibition of abortion), but there were a lot of other topics that also had to be dusted off. Up to the late 1960s, a married woman was not allowed to open up a bank account, get a driver's license, or take up a job without her husband's written approval. Not to mention the disparity of salaries, inequality of educational opportunities, and several more old hats. There was a lot to do.

In the 1980s, this feminism movement was still growing, but it was established enough to already have some side effects.

One of them was a load full of novels coming into book stores under the label "Neue Frau" (New Woman); some of the significant writers of that time were Hera Lind, Gaby Hauptmann, Eva Heller (1948-2008). This kind of literature didn't have much in common with real feminist ideas or goals, it were old stories in new clothes: old-fashioned, pseudo-emancipatory, platitudinous love stories, dime novels, told in a modern tone. These books flooded the market and sold by the millions.

It didn't take long for the schlager scene to take on the same topics, but it sometimes conveyed them in a different color. A time of highly emotional lyrics about "adult" topics began. Interestingly, there were three female singers, each one representing a unique aspect. But at one point, they were united: What they did was highly commercial.

Gitte Haenning (the one who wanted a cowboy as her husband when she was 17) started this trend with a new image in a sort of second wind career. She came up with songs about failing relationships, starting over, women's power, and living a self-determined life as she wants it, implying that life isn't over after crossing the 40.

The first sign of this new start in 1981 was a cover version of Gene Pitney's high-drama song "Something's Gotten Hold of My Heart" (1967) titled "Etwas ist geschehen (Es ist nie zu spät)" (Something Happened (It's Never Too Late)), German lyrics by Michael Kunze. This "nie" (never) in the song was stretched out like a siren over four bars, making window panes vibrate. Its peak chart position was #28, but Gitte reached her targeted audience: Follow-ups tunes like "Ich bin stark" (I Am Strong), "Ich will alles" (I Want it All) or "Gib mich frei" (Set Me Free), presented again with dramatic background music, solemn arrangements, and insistent singing, became chart hits as well as airplay successes.

The release of all of this was covered very effectively with press reports about Gitte's career obstacles as a woman, being forced to be especially strong, her failing relationships, and other drama. The album was called *Ungeschminkt* (Unvarnished) – of course, it was intended to make it look like a confession without reserve.

It worked. Every middle-aged female social studies highschool teacher eventually copied Gitte's fringe haircut and took her songs seriously, believing she was working on her real life relationship problems. In actuality, Gitte has never written a song herself, but her material fit perfectly into the zeitgeist, made to measure for a growing women's movement that was seen as a promising market.

Ina Deter of Cologne hit this line as well, but her way to popularity was different; something between rock and NDW, and her concept was less personal but more aggressive. She was originally from Berlin but relocated when her employer, an advertising agency, moved to Cologne. Starting there as a singer-songwriter, she had a minor hit with "Wenn du so bist wie dein Lachen" (If You Are Like Your Laughing), released in 1976 on the CBS label, presented with a bell-like head voice and an enormously gurgling throat-"R". The song failed in the preliminaries of the Eurovision Song Contest.

In the following years, Ina Deter discovered more and more the circle around magazine *Emma*, one of the leading voices of Germany's feminist movement, and radicalized not only her world view but also her lyrics, her singing style, and her music. With the help of producer and bass guitarist Micki Meuser, and guitarist Manni Holländer (both from the NDW band NERVOUS GERMANS), she set up a band and came out with the album *Neue Männer braucht das Land* (The Country Needs New Men) in 1983. A friend of mine bought the album to give it to his girlfriend, and when we listened to it, we both felt like we were listening to the same song eight times. Sung in a dashy tone, the lyrics fulminated against men, but it was the kind of pseudo-radicalism the "Neue Frau" novel readers could accept.

1983 was the big time of lilac dungarees and scarfs; the feminist movement was in a phase of delimitation and in search of clear goals. *Neue Männer braucht das Land* mirrored this. It became Ina Deter's biggest success, the 45 reached #22 in charts and the album peaked at #13. A tour with no less than 180 concerts followed; Ina's trademark on stage became her pink electric guitar (which is an exhibit at the Rock'n'Pop Museum in Gronau today).

Ina Deter was portrayed for a TV documentary titled "Frauen unter Strom" (Switched-on Women) in 1984, and the line "Neue Männer braucht das Land" went into the vernacular, at least among university students. It might have been coincidence or cleverness of Ina, who came from the advertising business, that the song had the line: "Ich sprüh's auf jede Wand: Neue Männer braucht das Land" (I spray it on every wall: …). Graffiti were beginning to be a growing everyday annoyance all over Germany; kids had discovered the New Yorker graffiti scene (which was a constant topic in all zeitgeist magazines), and even NDW electro project RHEINGOLD had a song about graffiti on their debut album in 1980, so this line hit the spot.

But as it happens sometimes after a hit, Ina Deter couldn't repeat it. Whatever she did, it was measured in comparison to this first big hit. Two follow-up albums still worked relatively well, but the trend went down, and in 1993 she decided to call it a day as a rock singer.

ESOTERICS, U.F.O.'S AND OTHER STRONG FEELINGS

Here is the third aspect: In the 1970s, the "classic" German schlager hit its prime time. When it had to compete with NDW hits in the 1980s, it lost a lot of its market shares and had to search for new fans. But the schlager genre is very flexible, so the makers gained new ground following a part of the "alternative" scene. It was a child of the 1970s that had become established in the 1980s, so now there was a search for new sensations for a personal way of life, but also simply for commercial reasons: Whole food stores became a thing of the past, biodynamic food now was offered even by supermarket chains. Something new had to be found. This led to several fads, most of them short-lived.

One of these fads came in the shipping channel of Dark Wave and Independent music (Joy Division, The Cure, Bauhaus et cetera). A Goth scene had been established. In Germany, it was called the "Schwarze Szene" (black scene), because bands as well as fans of this scene used to wear black with symbolic meaning. Consequently, this scene's music was called "Schwarze Musik" (black music; not to be mixed up with the meaning of "black music" in America). It was not a big, but rather an optically striking scene that soon became a topic in the media – seen as exotic and strange, often misunderstood as right-wing, satanic, or BDSM-oriented. Connected to this scene, medieval markets became popular in the second half of the 1980s.

Some elements of this Gothic movement became everyday fashion, especially when they came in combination with some "New Age" aspects: Astrology, the Bhagwan movement, homeopathy, mental healing, "alternative" healing methods, the supernatural in general, telepathy, extra-terrestrial visitors, and mystery TV series like *Twin Peaks* or *The X-Files*. Hair salons, at horrendous prices, offered midnight haircuts under the light of the full moon (usually the fringy kind Gitte Haenning had), and in flower shops you could buy wire pyramids that assisted in the growth of your home plants. Topics like guardian angels, Tarot, Kabbalah, moon calendars, Celtic symbols, and stuff like this, became small talk topics at every party. Extremely simplified variations of far-eastern religions were presented in expensive lectures, usually by ranters who, in their former lives, must have sold snake oil or magic all-purpose slicers at farmer's markets. It became more and more of a fad to wear enormous layers of kohl, in combination with black clothes – on some people, this looked fascinating, but in most cases one was tempted to ask whether their dog happened to pass away last night.

The schlager scene, always in search of new fads and always one of its promoters, discovered this mystery fad very soon – and one of its protagonists, intentionally or not, hit the bull's eye: our friend Juliane Werding of Essen.

After her "Conny Kramer" hit, Juliane Werding had had some success with a gruesome cover version of the Rolling Stones' "Angie", a couple of harmless pseudo-feminist songs like "Wenn du denkst, du denkst, dann denkst du nur, du denkst" (1975; When You Think You Think, You Only Think You Think) or truisms like "Man muss das Leben eben nehmen wie das Leben eben ist" (1976; You Have to Take Life Just as Life Is), written mainly by Gunter Gabriel (1942-2017), Germany's Johnny Cash for beginners. Besides this, Werding had worked in the Public Relations sector. Then she stopped this, became a nonmedical practitioner for a while (perfect background info for her new target group), then she changed her musical team.

Now, lyricist Michael Kunze, whom we know in connection with Udo Jürgens and Gitte Haenning, composer and arranger Harald Steinhauer, an old hand in the schlager business, and guitarist and producer Mats Björklund (who worked with the Spotnicks, Boney M, Amanda Lear, Demis Roussos, Mandrake, Silver Convention, Joe Dassin and many more), now became the staff behind her recordings. Proven helmsmen like Drafi Deutscher or Michael Cretu were also involved in some tracks. The backing musicians used were the finest studio cracks from Munich and Hamburg, like Curt Cress, Hermann Weindorf, Frank Loef, as well as ex-members of the Rattles.

In 1984, Juliane Werding, perfectly timed, ignited her new style with "Nacht voll Schatten" (Night Full of Shadows), a cover version of Mike Oldfield's "Moonlight Shadow" which had been a smash hit in Germany, Austria, and Switzerland. This dark song about a nightly duel defined the atmosphere of Juliane's following four albums: *Ohne Angst* (Without Fear; 1984), *Sehnsucht ist unheilbar* (Desire Is Incurable; 1986), *Tarot* (1988) and *Zeit für Engel* (Time for Angels; 1990) – descriptive titles of all four. These albums were deeply dark: Presentiments of death, prophecies of accidents, scary guests in black, soothsayers, a lonely woman living in rooms painted all black, a pendulum over a red cloth, sadness, unhappy love, fateful games of dice, being bound to the secret Tarot, blows of fate, a sighting of an alien spaceship: The complete collection of esoteric keywords is present in these albums. Artificially blurred wondrous rescues happen because "there are no coincidences", everything has a predestined meaning. Listening to these records is like watching these cheap 1950s horror movies by Jack Arnold: a full moon covered by clouds, thunderstorms, rain on the windshield, a cross on the asphalt. Invisible, deadly powers descend on the car and kill the co-driver during the ride home ("Nebelmond"; Hazy Moon, a modernized version of Goethe's "Erlkönig" poem). A woman murders her boyfriend who wants to leave her – because "Herzen, die brennen, erschreckt kein Verbot / Starke Gefühle besiegt nur der Tod" (No forbiddance can startle burning hearts

/ Only death can defeat strong feelings). A man she walks with under the moonlight doesn't cast a shadow. Every evening a woman on the beach talks to invisible people from a sunken ship – but she might calm down: "Was ruht in tiefen Meeren / wird einmal wiederkehren / Deine schwere Zeit ist bald vorbei" (What rests in deep seas / Will return one day / Your hard time will soon be done).

Another type of song on these records belongs to the aforementioned category depicting everyday situations, but here they are sometimes carbonated with a dash of social criticism: "Drei Jahre lang" (For Three Years) describes a love relationship in which one of the two is in prison; "Geh nicht in die Stadt heut' nacht" (Don't Go to Town Tonight) is about a woman who suspects that her jobless partner has gotten himself a gun and is going to do something criminal. Many of these songs come with an intentionally open end; you are left without a solution, some are ambiguous on purpose or just lack a bit of logic (a really nice flaw is the stranger in "Das Würfelspiel" who throws 19 pips with three dice).

All of this was presented through simple, melodic songs, made to measure Juliane's mournful schlager voice, perfectly arranged mainly in the plastic pop sound of the 1980s, but sometimes also embellished with well-done instrumental parts and solos. All songs are free of humor, lightness, or any trace of irony (which in her Gunter Gabriel era was sometimes a factor), perfect pop, delivered on point to a mainly female clientele ready to consume this kind of zeitgeist food. Interestingly, even people who say they would never listen to schlagers know at least some of these songs.

Juliane Werding became one of the most successful schlager acts of the 1980s, was a consistent guest on radio stations, appeared in the "ZDF-Hitparade" and other music shows on TV, received lots of awards, golden records, and made several tours.

In the 1990s, Udo Arndt and keyboardist Reinhold Heil (ex-Nina Hagen Band and Spliff) took over the production for several more albums, but they were not as interesting anymore. In 2009, Juliane Werding finished her career.

When, in 30 years, somebody happens to listen to the records this chapter describes, he or she will learn a lot about what people did and thought in the 1980s, in the same way we learn a lot about the 1950s and early 1960s when we listen to the schlagers of that time.

SILVER & SCREEN

Two things of far-ranging importance for the media infrastructure happened in the 1980s. The first was that the recording and reproducing of music on a wide scale went digital – the Compact Disc (CD) was developed. My first two CDs were Brian Eno's *Thursday Afternoon* (1985), a recording made especially for this new medium and probably still his definitive ambient opus. The other one was David Van Tieghem's *Safety In Numbers*, another record I still love, released on Private Music, a label started by ex-TANGERINE DREAM member Peter Baumann who had moved to New York. I had purchased both CDs without having a player yet – not only the CDs itself, but also the CD players were expensive. Two or three weeks later, I found a demonstration device that was reduced in price. I bought it together with the CD box set of Philip Glass's opera *Einstein On The Beach*, hoping it might sound better than the vinyl pressing I had loved to death – and it did.

First, we all thought the CD would mean the end of most of the German rock recordings that existed on vinyl. Only new productions, we thought, would be released on CD, the old LPs would be sold off and not be available for much longer.

But we underestimated the record industry. In fact, the opposite happened. Some record companies re-released some highlights of their back catalogue on CD for test purposes, and it turned out, many music fans began replacing their vinyl albums with these. Besides this, the CD was also playable in the car. This gave the record industry and dealers a giant push, leading to a drop in prices for CDs as well as for CD players. The CD turned out to be a giant success.

But there was a flaw: The CD, as well as the whole digital process of recording, mixing, re-mixing, mastering, and remastering, was uncharted land for everyone involved. This is why a lot of re-releases on CD were free of scratches, sizzling, and distortions, but also sounded flat, came with weak bass, and revealed tape hissing and other flaws that came from the analogue recording process. On vinyl records, this was inaudible or camouflaged by surface noise. It took a couple of years until sound engineers got the hang of how to deal with digital recording. It was around this time that the never-ending debate on whether digital recordings were better than analogue recordings started. This debate goes on and can't be settled here.

Interestingly, the schlager and folksy music scene largely ignored these changes. Of course, new recordings were released on CD now, but the majority of fan communities had always bought Compact Cassette tapes and now stayed with them. The same went for the audio play recordings for children. It took more than a decade until the CD outran vinyl and cassettes.

The CD was not just a new sound carrier. It came with its own aesthetic. Its existence had already changed the way we listened to music. Most German rock bands had been album bands. Their music was conceived for being presented on two sides of an LP; you couldn't skip or repeat a track without getting on your feet for a walk to your turntable. The duration of an LP was also limited to about 2 × 20 minutes. Longer recordings were possible, but this affected the sound quality: The overall volume, but especially the bass volume, needed to be reduced, and this made surface noise more audible.

The CD did not have these limitations, and, per definition, it offered 74 minutes of playing time in one go. As the saga goes, it was Herbert von Karajan who demanded that the playing time had to be long enough for Beethoven's Ninth Symphony, but in all likelihood, this is an urban legend. Actually, two manufacturers were working on digital systems: Philips wanted a 14-bit system with one hour of playing time, Sony wanted a 16-bit system which would need half a centimeter more in diameter of the disc, but would offer 15 minutes more. The Sony system turned out to have better error correction, which is why Sony won the race. (As it showed, five minutes more of playing time was possible. In fact, even more than 80 would be possible, but the limit became a standard because several early CD players simply stopped when 79'59" was reached.)

HOW TO FILL A WHOLE CD?

Most bands and singers had been happy when they managed to fill the 40 minutes of an album. But now producers and record companies felt the need to use all the running time available. As a result, a lot of music was stretched out, and many tunes found their way on an album that wouldn't have been good enough to be a filler on a standard LP. In addition, because many (not all) CD players were programmable, the bands and producers had to now keep in mind that the listener could skip tracks or arrange their own track sequence. This was a problem for concept albums. Only a few artists were powerful enough to push through their original concept – sometimes with questionable methods, like Prince on his album *Lovesexy* (1988): He forced the listener to listen to the tracks in the given sequence by simply turning them into one long track. I'm not sure whether every listener was happy with this. Some musicians, however, embraced this new concept: *Erdenklang* composer Hubert Bognermayr of the Blue Chip Orchestra, used the CD booklet to give three different recommendations on how to program the track sequence on their first self-titled album (1988) – a "Blue Line", a "Philharmonic Line", and a "Walking Line". This would have been impossible on a vinyl album.

While this could make sense, many CDs came with several more or less funny, but useless, gimmicks. One of the most annoying ones was the "hidden track": When the seemingly last tune had ended, the track silently ran on and on for several minutes, and then suddenly, another tune or an acoustic gag followed. You couldn't even skip the silent minutes. The strangest CD gimmick I've ever seen was probably on *Repetitive Movement* (1998) by Asmus Tietchens & Achim Wollscheid: The CD has a hidden track at the *beginning* of the album – you have to put the disc into the player and scroll *backwards* from track 1 to reach the hidden track. This might be funny for a moment (it's the kind of humor Tietchens loves), but it is only funny once. When you play the record a third or fourth time, the joke gets tiring. I'm sure that several people who bought the CD never even found out there was one more track (a really "hidden" one then).

COPYING AND FILE SHARING

Another aspect of the CD was that, since it presented the music in a digital form, it allowed lossless copying. This way, the record industry itself gave the starting shot for music piracy. Illegal file sharing services like Napster or blogs run by fans now offered free (illegal) downloads of all kinds of music. Fans, but also journalists and experts, soon predicted "the end of the music industry". The industry developed several copy protection systems, but in the digital world, anything that is coded can be decoded. These systems became a peeve but didn't work for very long.

Many bands and musicians now saw the internet as their big chance to become famous without the industry's help. Suddenly we heard stories about bands who had put their self-produced material on their website, Youtube, or Myspace, soon had tens of thousands of clicks and fans, and immediately, all majors had beaten a path to the band's door to give them a record deal. In 99.9 per cent of all these cases, however, these stories had been made up in the PR departments of just these majors. All the bands that really attempted this path to fame had to learn very soon that the internet marketing idea was not much more than a nice theory.

MUSIC TELEVISION

Another important thing happened in the 1980s, and it had consequences that turned the music business upside down: In August 1981, on the cable network of New York City, media group Viacom started MTV (Music Television). Their first video was "Video Killed the Radio Star" by The Buggles; a project under producer Trevor Horn and an unremarkable little pop schlager, the most interesting thing in the video is probably seeing a very young Hans Zimmer.

Not that there hadn't been music promotion films before. Actually, under the name "soundies" or the brand "Scopitones" they go back to the 1920s. Most of you have probably seen one of the tiny little music films the Beatles or Pink Floyd made for their tunes, but all this stuff had been a sort of addition to the tune. But now, MTV started a 24/7 TV program with this, and that changed the music world completely. MTV didn't simply "present music videos", MTV created a new environment for all acts that sailed under the pop music flag. The old promotion methods didn't work anymore. Immediately, MTV was needed to keep established acts alive, and by far not all of them (as well as their labels and producers) were able to keep up with this new challenge. MTV also played a key role suddenly in launching new bands and projects.

After MTV had started, it was no longer possible to carry a record into the hit zone without a video. This needed acts who were able to perform well in front of a camera and were willing to present themselves in a visually attractive way.

Some musicians liked this idea. Others didn't. But in the end, both had no choice – they weren't asked. MTV was unavoidable.

As it's mostly the case when a new medium or a new arts genre comes into existence, many of the productions during MTV's early years were highly interesting because there were no rules and ruts yet. Once the labels and record producers had accepted that there was no way to escape from presenting their acts on video, they had to ask themselves: Who can shoot these videos? There were two obvious possibilities: commercial and artistic film producers. This way, some first-class film and video artists and directors got involved in the pop video business. To name a couple of outstanding results:

- Rebecca Allen – Kraftwerk: "Musique Non Stop", 1986, not the first computer-animated pop video, but the first one that included the band members *as* computer animations, created at the Computer Graphics Lab of New York Institute of Technology. Nam June Paik later used the video for one of his sculptures made from TV sets.
- Steve Barron – Dire Straits: "Money For Nothing", 1985, the first computer-animated pop video. (Actually, it was no real computer animation. It was done like a classic animation film, frame by frame, with Quantel's Paint Box; it must have been an enormous amount of work. But what wouldn't you do to be "the first"?)
- Dancer and choreographer Philippe Decouflé – New Order: "True Faith", 1987.
- Jonathan Demme (1944-2017) – New Order: "The Perfect Kiss", 1985. Demme was also the director of Talking Heads' film *Stop Making Sense* in 1984 – still one of the best concert films ever made.
- Kevin Godley & Lol Creme of 10cc – Visage: "Fade To Grey", 1980, Herbie Hancock: "Rockit", 1982).
- Annabell Jankel & Rocky Morton – Donald Fagen: "New Frontier", 1982.
- Stephen R. Johnson (1952-2015) – Talking Heads: "Road to Nowhere", 1985; Peter Gabriel: "Sledgehammer", 1986.
- Bill Mather – Dire Straits: "Brothers in Arms", 1985, a video that combines pictures like animated pencil drawings with optically manipulated documentary war films.
- Dieter Meier – Yello: "Oh Yeah", 198). A classic back projection, probably made on classic film.
- Video artist Zbigniew Rybczynsky – Art of Noise: "Close to the Edit", 1984.

- Video artist John Sanborn – David Van Tieghem: "Galaxy", 1987; John Sanborn and Dean Winkler – "Luminare", 1985, (music by Daniel Lentz); both in collaboration with Mary Perillo.

These are only a handful of artists who have pushed this new genre forward; all these videos can be found on Youtube today. Many of them were very experimental and would have been a thing for art galleries, but MTV put them into a framing that challenged and changed audiences' viewing habits. This went so far that even the newscasts of serious TV stations felt the need to change their optical outfit, sometimes up to a ridiculous degree.

This was driven not only by MTV, there was a second source: Brazil's Rede Globo TV network which, with its head designer Hans Donner, was also pioneering in all kinds of electronic and computer-generated design elements on TV. As this happened in parallel, it's hard to say who followed whom.

Music videos were expensive; their production costs could be 200,000 dollars or more – this was often more than the production costs of the record they were made for. Record companies threw in the money because otherwise their acts wouldn't be shown on MTV, and that meant they wouldn't have the ghost of a chance to enter the charts anymore. This became a big problem for independent labels and sadly killed several of them.

MUSIC TV IN GERMANY

At the beginning of the video era, these music videos (or "videoclips", as they were called in Germany) were a rare thing to see on German TV screens. Remember: There had not yet been commercial TV in Germany, and the stations under public law normally expected bands and singers to appear in the studio to present their song, usually lip-synching. But now, a music video was sometimes shown in the "Musikladen", the follow-up TV show of the shut-down "Beat-Club", and they were presented as "something very new and very special". The first one I saw there, if memory serves, was Blondie's "The Tide Is High" from 1982.

These videos soon became popular, and the public ARD TV was the first to start a weekly one-hour music video show called "Formel Eins" in 1983. The show was chart-oriented, became very popular and, with different hosts, ran until 1990.

In 1981, the German Bundestag, after hot tempered discussions, finally came to the conclusion of allowing commercial radio and TV. Very soon, commercial radio stations were on air. Their transmission area was local, nearly none of them was of interest for German rock music; most of them were simple Top 40 radio.

Private TV took a bit longer to start, but finally in 1984, in Ludwigshafen (near Mannheim), the first cable TV pilot project was established, soon followed by other cities. One year later (and usually against the fierce resistance of the Green Party), cable TV was available almost all over Germany. The monopoly of radio and TV under public law was officially broken, Germany had commercial TV now, and this became visible.

MTV, which had only been receivable with satellite receivers in Germany, was now available on cable. It became the model for Musicbox, a music TV channel that started in 1984 in Munich without the help of big companies (not to mix up with the English channel Music Box that later became Super Channel). Musicbox was soon available nationwide on cable. Some young journalists saw their chance here, and Musicbox was soon presented by relatively competent hosts with primarily journalistic backgrounds. Not only did they show the videos provided by international record companies, the Musicbox crew also produced videos with German acts themselves. These videos were relatively simple; they were not allowed to cost much money. But they were a signal, and finally even the German record companies accepted that they needed to start some video activities of their own. From then on, German labels also produced videos with their acts.

It didn't take long for Musicbox to get more and more in financial trouble. After only four years, they had to deal with a joint partner: Silvio Berlusconi from Italy. Soon, he changed Musicbox into Tele 5, and the music shows became an increasingly small part of the program.

In 1988, RTLplus (= Radio Télé Luxembourg; the TV branch of Radio Luxembourg and one of the two big commercial stations that had been established since 1984, later they deleted the "plus") started a short-lived rock music show titled "RockTL", but even live concerts and the popular host Alan Bangs of "Rockpalast" fame couldn't prevent the show from soon going downhill. "Heimatmelodie", a weekly show with folksy music (1984 to 1994), which was a reaction to the giant success of the folksy "Musikantenstadl" (something like "minstrel barn") in the ARD, was more successful. This kind of music experienced a boom around these years in Germany. Germany's second big commercial TV channel, Sat.1, never made an attempt to start a rock music show, as well as the smaller third one, Pro7.

The public ZDF TV started a sub-channel called ZDF-Musikkanal in 1984, available on cable and via satellite. It was a kind of reaction to Musicbox, but it was different because the ZDF-Musikkanal mainly showed reruns of music shows from the ZDF archives (like several episodes of "RockPop in Concert"). The ZDF-Musikkanal remained on air for nine years, in 1993 it merged into what was to become 3sat, a channel with cultural focus, made by public stations from Germany, Austria, and Switzerland.

In August 1987, MTV started a European branch: MTV-Europe. It was first based in Amsterdam, later moving to one-and-a-half floors in a factory building in London's hip Camden neighborhood. MTV-Europe operated as professionally as its mother in New York; the VJs came from several European countries, the program language was English, and the shows were U.K.-centered. I enjoyed these early years of MTV-Europe, especially in the 1990s when, from time to time, they aired experimental electronic stuff late at night. Even a video with Klaus Schulze could be seen there.

It took six years for a direct reaction to MTV-Europe to come up in Germany. It was called Viva and started in 1993, based in Cologne, and the station's founding was a sort of tour de force by Sony, Polygram, EMI, and a couple of private media persons and TV production companies, among them Me Myself & Eye, a company that had been founded by some leftover Musicbox editors and the Austrian video and TV producers Rudi Dolezal and Hannes Rossacher (DoRo).

With the end of the 1980s, the time of interesting videos petered out. Of course, videos still had to be produced, but as the novelty factor was gone, they became more and more routine. MTV-Europe finally dug its own grave in June 1995 when it decided to become a pay-TV channel. Viva became a launch pad for a couple of talented hosts, but the program itself was more or less a copy of MTV-Europe, just in German. Viva floundered when they installed a second channel named Viva 2 and became an excessive and exhausting hub for ringtone commercials.

Kraftwerk 3D Concert "The Mix" (Tokyo, Japan – May 15th, 2013)

THE FUTURE

"TV is great because when you close your eyes, it sounds like radio."

DOUGLAS DAVIS

RETROPIA

The U.S. *Rolling Stone* listed four German albums under the "50 best Prog Rock Albums of All Time" in 2015: *Illusions on a Double Dimple* by Triumvirat (1974), *Yeti* by Amon Düül II (1970), *Phaedra* by Tangerine Dream (1974; it's open to dispute whether "prog" is the right label for this album), and *Future Days* by Can (1973).[1] *Future Days* is the only German record that has made it under the Top Ten, flanked by *Thick as a Brick* by Jethro Tull and *The Lamb Lies Down on Broadway* by Genesis.

Four out of fifty – in view of the competitors, it could be worse. Triumvirat, to be honest, would not have been on my shortlist, but the other three albums can, indeed, be seen as classics of German rock.

All the still, or again, active German bands and musicians share a problem: They are expected to continue with the material they had done in the 1960s or 1970s because this is what they are known for. But if they really do continue, most listeners would say: "Oh no, you can't do this anymore." These long-living or reunited bands are expected to have inhaled all the new trends and musical aspects we have seen since the 1970s. But if they integrate these trends into their new music, they will be told: "No, this is not what we want from you". Their fans want them to play what they had played in the olden days. They should sound "modern", but without changing anything of significance.

A band only has two ways to handle this dilemma: First, the musicians can give up creativity and try to be a perfect copy of what they were in the past. This can work for a while (Nektar exemplifies this), but for creative musicians, even for those already over retirement age, this is an imposition. Could you seriously imagine Kraftwerk, still playing "Ruckzuck" on stage, ideally with the original instruments of 1970? It would be ridiculous and, in the end, boring. You have to change to remain yourself.

I can hear some of you saying: "But aren't there several bands using this old equipment, and it works?" Yes, there were and are some, like ADD N TO (X), PORTISHEAD or STEREOLAB, but don't get it wrong: They used old equipment as a sort of quotation. Of course they *refer* to the music of the 1970s, but they *are* not of the 1970s, and that's an important difference.

In America, the "classic rock" of "Stairway to Heaven" fame still has its fans and its place on the radio. Still today, the EAGLES' "Hotel California" is aired every eleven minutes on one of the 5000 U.S. stations. But let's face it: This kind of music is on the downswing. The soundtrack of neo-capitalism is hip-hop (and there are good reasons for it). When you hear a powerful distorted rock guitar today, you can bet it's a sample.

And in this moment, German rock, with all its 1970's bells and whistles, has a sort of renaissance? How can this be – especially when you see that there are only a handful of German bands that have retained a certain international significance? AMON DÜÜL II, CAN, CLUSTER, Holger Czukay, EMBRYO, HARMONIA, KRAAN, KRAFTWERK, LA DÜSSELDORF, NEU!, PASSPORT, POPOL VUH (mainly for film music), Michael Rother, Klaus Schulze, TANGERINE DREAM, maybe (in their musical department) the SCORPIONS: When push comes to shove, these would be the names I'd list as *the important German rock acts*. In the U.K. they are still known by a not even small circle of fans. But in the U.S.? CAN, KRAFTWERK, TANGERINE DREAM. Out of the newer ones, you might add RAMMSTEIN, but that's it, I think. Okay, sometimes there's also some pop music from Germany's trio infernal – Dieter Bohlen, Michael Cretu and Frank Farian – but it's usually not even common knowledge that their protégés are German acts. Which, in some way, is alright, because pop music is meant to be international. Most people have heard of Harold Faltermeyer of Munich and his *Axel F.* theme, but who knew that the drummer in the main title track of TV soap *Dallas* was Curt Cress? German vocal schlagers might have an international level, but because they are always in German, they don't have a chance in England or America – Nena might have been the exception. But I'm sure most of you know the instrumental "Be My Boogie Woogie Baby" (1976) by a certain Mr. Walkie Talkie – you might not know the title or the performer, you probably don't know it from any charts, but I'm sure you've heard it in an amusement park at the bumper cars. Who knew that this "Mr. Walkie Talkie" was one of the more than 40 pseudonyms of Drafi Deutscher?

Let's look inside this "Krautrock" circle. What kind of truth or authenticity is it that makes these bands and musicians still interesting today, even for listeners who weren't born when this music first came out?

If you follow one of the several "Krautrock" forums on Facebook, you might notice that some people are still very active in making discoveries. At record fairs, in attics, and on eBay or Discogs, they try to find the last hidden private pressing with a print run of 300 copies by bands that, even in the 1970s, were at best only locally known. Nice work, folks, and I mean it – but it doesn't help, I have to stick to what I said earlier: There were hundreds of bands playing, and many of them made their privately pressed record, so it is still possible to dig out forgotten stuff somewhere. But we should not wait for buried treasures.

How about the leftover tracks we find today as a "bonus" on re-released albums? Where do they come from? Usually, when there are ten tracks on an album, the musicians recorded at least 15, maybe more, and all of them were recorded in at least four takes. After the recording process, musicians and producers decided which tunes and which versions should finally find their way onto the album. The rest went into a drawer and stayed there for decades. But this means that there were good reasons for why these tracks remained unused, as well as the outtakes. The musicians and/or producers decided not to release them, and they usually had a good feeling about which takes or tunes are the best ones to release. The unused ones might be of interest for music historians or die-hard fans of a band, but hardly for anybody else.

Sometimes, "sensational findings" are announced in a Facebook group. They usually turn out to be soap bubbles, if not ridiculous – they might be "alternate versions" of known tunes, throwouts, stuff that has been long forgotten or never been released by a real label, or chance recordings from when musicians met somewhere in a studio while working on other projects. The (beautiful) *Liliental* album is one of those, or the (pointless) stuff Timothy Leary added to some Tangerine Dream recordings in 1973, connected to the Cosmic Jokers sessions. Some "sensations" might be even fake.

In the 1970s, when a band had a little bit of potential, it was not difficult to find a label. When German bands got rejected by labels specializing in German rock, it was mostly for good reasons. But all these tapes, test recordings, demos, and whatever else there is, are lying around somewhere, and somebody might pick them up.

When I say this, I'm usually replied with: "But there are dozens of examples showing that great talents were ignored by the sleepyheads doing a nine-to-five job at record companies!" My answer: Of course, misjudgments were and are a daily occurrence in every record company or publishing house. Neither producers nor A&R people have standards other than their own subjective feeling. There is no recipe to cook success. Rejecting bands that later turn out to be top acts is a thing that happens every day, but usually not to all of them at the same time. If artists have true potential and regularly come out with works of good quality, then it is hardly imaginable that they will *always* be rejected by *everybody*. In all probability, *someone will* notice, even if it might take a while and cost the artist lots of effort. Finally: Getting published does not mean immediate success (if any). Nobody can tell why one record takes off and a similar one fails. But both are released, and that's the point here.

OH, NOSTALGIA ...

In 2015, for the first time in the U.S., albums from the years 1960 to 1980 were sold in bigger numbers than current releases.[2] Of course, this has something to do with the situation of today's record industry, but that's not the whole reason. It's the customers who grew up with rock music and are now old enough to want to dive back into their youth, to try to get back the sense of wellbeing they remember from the olden days.

Krautrock has now reached an age that gives you a bit of a funny feeling when you look at the old pictures or watch videos of the bands – a similar thing will happen when, in 40 years, today's young generation looks at their photos or videos from today – when *they* were young. But while the 1950s, 1960s, 1970s and 1980s had clearly identifiable designs and fashions, nothing like this has proven to exist in the last three decades. We have to bemoan the stagnancy of new ideas and styles; everything that seems to be new is, in reality, the merger of older ideas into one big remix.

If this is the case, then one question suggests itself: What do we see when we look at these musicians from the past now, and what do we hear today when we listen to their 40- or 50-year old music? It's obvious that what they wanted to share was produced within a different frame of conditions. Today's listeners, if they aren't the same age as the musicians, might have no idea about this. So what do they hear? It's not a question of equipment. Older listeners will experience a flashback of their own youth (even if they notice that the music sounds better in their memory than in today's reality). Younger listeners will hear a part of the older generation's youth, but without having this older background. One thing goes for all generations: Even if we sit stoned on a flokati on the floor in front of a Dual turntable, a tube amplifier, and big speakers, listening to an original LP or the finest reissues on 180-gram vinyl while looking at its big album sleeve in the light of a dripping candle with the scent of incense sticks in the background: We will never be able to listen to the music of the 1960s and 1970s the same way the people in the 1960s and 1970s did. We can simulate time travel, but we cannot go back in time. We cannot exclude our experiences or our socialization, and we cannot listen against the way we have learned to listen. It might be the same record, but we will not receive the same message it sent on the day of its original release. It will always be an act of nostalgia or an act of guessing of what it might have been.

Something in some of these old records must have kept its meaning over time. It's possible that it's not the original meaning anymore, but even then, it's still a valid meaning. If this wasn't possible, we wouldn't be listening to classical music anymore. But we do, and Mr. Brahms still speaks to us.

Most of yesterday's rock musicians are forgotten. What they had to say – like most pop and rock music – was made for the moment. Many of these musicians never really lifted off. Some did, they had their time, and they stepped back when they felt their time was done. Many passed away, some of them are dearly missed. Others are either still active or have become active again. Some of the better ones have reached a sort of "late work". Yes, even in rock music we have this now. But who of these artists still reaches an audience? Who still has something to say today, and what is their message?

Mani Neumeier never stopped. His way of thinking is that of a "Sixty-Eight" veteran, but of one who adapted. He's just celebrating his 50th stage anniversary and still has his project Guru Guru going, its musical style changing with line-ups over the years, a bit old-fashioned, a bit classic, but a band still at its best. Aside from this, Mani discovered his love for Japanese culture and people, which led to some interesting results. *Moshi Moshi* (1997), to name an example, shows Mani Neumeier on the Koto. The collaboration album *Acid Guru Pond* (2016) by Bardo Pond, Acid Mothers Temple, and Guru Guru, however, is a trip back into the deep past, reminiscent of Guru Guru's firstling *UFO*; I'm sure they had a lot of fun. In 2018, Neumeier released *Rotate*, a powerful celebration of Guru Guru's 50th anniversary.

Hans-Joachim Roedelius, still one of the big names of Krautrock, now finally receives the appreciation he's deserved after many years of being underestimated as a solo artist – at least in Europe and Japan. He consequently follows his nose. Since CLUSTER cannot continue after the passing of Dieter Moebius, Roedelius started QLUSTER as a sort of side project with different musicians. The man is 86 now. In Germany, he has recently received an invitation to play at Hamburg's prestigious new Elbphilharmonie (as well as his colleagues TANGERINE DREAM and Manuel Göttsching). This might have resulted from his recording for the also prestigious Deutsche Grammophon label, but regardless of the reason: This is the place where he belongs. In the U.S., much too often, he's still expected to play back rooms at third-rate clubs with ridiculously low entrance fees, accompanied by the noise of a pool table and shouting drunks.

Michael Rother, having been silent for nearly ten years after *Traumreisen*, decided to set up his own label, Random Records, but he only released two further albums: *Esperanza* in 1996 and, again eight years later, *Remember (The Great Adventure)*. Even Herbert Grönemeyer contributed some vocals to the latter, but it's a faceless album that went nowhere. Besides this, Rother wrote some film and theater music. In a backstage interview in 2014, he stated that he was "not too interested in releasing new stuff" but was thinking about releasing some of his film soundtracks online for download[3] (which still has not happened). Putting it this way is as cautious as it is typical for him. Rother has always been a person who thinks at least twice before he answers a question, and when he says "not too interested", we are allowed to assume that he considers new album releases on CD or vinyl not worth the effort anymore. He wouldn't be the only one; Karl Bartos mentioned something similar around 2010 already.[4] In 2019, Grönemeyer's Grönland label released a box set titled *Solo* with Rother's first four albums (the ones with Jaki Liebezeit); the vinyl version of this set also has some soundtrack and live material (the CD version doesn't). Instead of making new records, Rother is active on stage today, presenting tracks of NEU!, HARMONIA, and his solo works, mostly with drummer Hans Lampe and guitarist Franz Bargmann. Recently, they even toured Mexico. It's stunning how modern this old stuff still sounds today.

Klaus Doldinger, after releasing an uncountable number of records, unflinchingly goes on and on. At home and abroad he is still on the road with PASSPORT; several times his international tours have been supported by Germany's Goethe Institute. He still writes film and TV music and still knows what's going on in the world. His latest sign of life was a self-titled album in 2016 with PASSPORT and several prominent guest musicians honoring his 80th birthday, presenting powerful new recordings of older compositions. His last film music was from 2018 for a *Tatort* episode.

Since 1970, EMBRYO has made more than 40 albums. Not all of them are "official", many of them have guest musicians like Charlie Mariano, Mal Waldron, or the KARNATAKA COLLEGE OF PERCUSSION contributing, but most of them are adventurous – still today. Like Mr. Doldinger, EMBRYO had done several tours organized by the Goethe Institute. Filmmaker Werner Penzel's documentary film *Vagabundenkarawane*, showing EMBRYO's 1978 Goethe tour through Greece, Turkey, Iran, Afghanistan, Pakistan, and India, is now on Youtube[5], and it's still fascinating, despite its cutback of nearly half an hour. EMBRYO even outlived their split-off DIE DISSIDENTEN (recommendable album: *Sahara Electric*, 1984). When Christian Burchard, EMBRYO's founder, passed away in 2018, his daughter Marja took over the wheel. The caravan of vagabonds continues on as a generation project – and it works.

After the passing of Edgar Froese in 2015, the current line-up of TANGERINE DREAM – Thorsten Quaeschning, Ulrich Schnauss, and Hoshiko Yamane, all three chosen by Froese himself – decided to continue the project under its original name. Some of the older fans are not happy with the decision; they feel a band comes to its natural end with the death of a key member, so the name shouldn't be used anymore. But the majority of fans seem to accept this line-up as legitimate successors. For a while, this trio may follow the tracks Edgar Froese had prepared and left unfinished, but in the long run they will have to develop their own tracks and their own style. They even revitalize the old TANGERINE DREAM practice to improvise on stage. All three of them are musically skilled enough to be more than just an Edgar Froese memorial band.

Klaus Schulze is also still active. After some not-very-convincing attempts to catch up with "modern" stuff, like his dance album *Are You Sequenced?* from 1996 (one of the tracks even brought him onto an MTV show), the partially unbalanced albums with digital sounds and computerized synthesizers like *Miditerranian Pads* (1990) or *Beyond Recall* (1991), the failed *Klaus Schulze Goes Classic* (1994), or the undecided recordings with Lisa Gerrard from 2008 and 2009, he came out with the surprisingly late work *Silhouettes*, which is simply Schulze at his best again in 2018.

Manuel Göttsching, another heavyweight of the "pioneering Krautrock generation", has been active throughout the years, both on stage as well as on record. The kaleidoscopic sounds of his ASHRA productions *Blackouts* (1978) and *Cor-*

relations (1979) with Harald Grosskopf and Lutz "Lüül" Ulbrich, even more his successful solo album *E2-E4* (1984, named after a chess opening), had pumped more than a few impulses into what was to become techno and trance music in the 1990s.

After the passing of three core members – Michael Karoli, Jaki Liebezeit, Holger Czukay – CAN found themselves in the strange situation of merely being a label today. This "label" is more successful now than the band was during their active time, but today, this still does not mean we can call CAN a well-known band. In fact, CAN has always mainly been an insiders' tip and, similar to TANGERINE DREAM or AMON DÜÜL II, is better known in the U.K. than in Germany – and this might have been their lucky star. They can't produce new music, but the better part of their records is still timeless and flawless.

When it comes to wringing out repertoire to its last drop, KRAFTWERK is not less busy than CAN, probably even more busy. KRAFTWERK hasn't released any new music since 2003, but the band has been more active than ever on stage. They developed a show which is mainly based on 3-D projections and (sometimes) a very high-tech multi-channel sound system, called "wave field synthesis", and they seem to be on a sort of never-ending tour.

Florian Schneider passed away from cancer in April 2020. He had left the band already in 2008. Since then, although the band usually still plays in front of sold-out venues, it's mainly Ralf Hütter's nostalgia project today – a sort of mobile museum that presents its own story. "Museum" can be perceived literally: KRAFTWERK defines itself as a multimedia art project and prefers playing at venues like museums, galleries, opera houses, and other cultural institutions. If possible, they play their album catalogue ("1-2-3-4-5-6-7-8", as the headline goes) in eight concerts en suite, which include the albums from *Autobahn* to *Tour de France Soundtracks*. This 3-D *Catalogue* idea was tested in 2011 at Lenbachhaus in Munich and received its successful world première at the Museum of Modern Art in New York City in 2012, after having grown into a ticketing chaos, probably because many fans feared this event might be a goodbye concert.

Over the years, KRAFTWERK has grown its own core audience, consisting of people "in the know". Some of these die-hard, longtime fans have never missed a single show. This is an interesting phenomenon, at least in the U.S., because the average audience of younger pop music fans and concertgoers hardly has an idea about who this band is. And if you ask the older generation about "Autobahn", you might have to play it to them, otherwise not many people will remember. Most of them, *if* they remember, had seen "Autobahn" as a novelty song; in 1975, nobody thought that KRAFTWERK would turn out to be the beginning of a new branch of pop music. "Trans Europe Express" is also hardly remembered in the U.S. – if it is remembered, it's usually ascribed to Afrika Bambaataa (if anyone of the young generation remembers who *that* was).

In Germany, it's still seen as relatively sensational if a German act makes it into American charts because it doesn't happen very often. But when it does happen, Germans immediately tend to think this band or this song must be "influential". It looks like this: Every rapper, every hip-hop artist, every DJ, when asked today to name their main influences, knows what he is expected to reply – without fail, he will drop the name KRAFTWERK, usually acknowledged by an approving nod from the interviewer. But does anybody seriously think that, without KRAFTWERK there would be no hip-hop? No rap? No House? This is not the way music works. KRAFTWERK did a good job in providing electronic rhythm patterns that could be used as a model, and they are one of the most-sampled bands ever, but let's not overestimate it. Herbie Hancock or Quincy Jones didn't need KRAFTWERK to invent straight rhythm patterns on their own. Miles Davis' album *On The Corner* (1972) was at least as important for hip-hop as KRAFTWERK, even though many of today's hip-hop artists and fans have never heard it. Even if there was an influence made by KRAFTWERK, how long ago was it in effect? Mentioning KRAFTWERK's influence on whatever scene has become an act of nostalgia itself, and the fact that they *are* sampled, proves it. KRAFTWERK has lost its unique feature while electronic pop music in general has become established and professional in countless implementations, especially in the shape of duos – PET SHOP BOYS, YAZOO, EURYTHMICS, SOFT CELL, ERASURE, LFO, to name a couple. KRAFTWERK, on the other hand, couldn't ignore what these other artists and producers did – on the contrary, KRAFTWERK began using them as a reference.[6] The fathers began to copy their children, while in reality, the grandchildren had already taken over the shift levers of pop.

Today, mainstream pop audiences think KRAFTWERK has lifted the hookline of "Computer Love" from COLDPLAY's "Talk". In Facebook forums centered on KRAFTWERK, the band has increasingly become an object of parodies, caricatures, and other kinds of more or less funny humor. It's especially striking that more than anything else, KRAFTWERK is still associated with the mechanical "robots" and their red shirts and black ties. The band members gave up these accessories many years ago, but *this* is the image that sticks. Apparently people only want to have *one* point that makes their image, and in the case of this band, there are these red shirts and black ties, like the black and white made-up faces of Kiss. This won't change anymore. The last time I saw Kraftwerk on stage was in Chicago in 2014, and the appearance of the "robots" with their sleepy moving arms and slow turning heads was still greatly acclaimed by the audience, although the band has always done this exact routine since their 1990s tour. (The precursors of these robots were already on stage in 1981, but they were classic "showroom dummies" that couldn't move yet.) The appearance of these devices is a gimmick free of surprise that begins to be a bit tedious.

It is obvious to me that Ralf Hütter sees the eight albums from *Autobahn* (1974) to *Tour de France Soundtracks* (2003) as the definite ones. All of them are made by the same masterminds, but they are different; each of these albums is its own universe. The band's whole image is now built on the numbers one through eight. This is the reason why I think there will be no new album anymore – the concept leaves no space for a number nine. Admittedly, the concerts still have everything you expect from Kraftwerk – the crystal-clear visuals, the retro-futurism, the undercooled presentation. A Kraftwerk show is more performance art than a concert. For a while, the 3-D effect grabs you. Sometimes it's amazing, like when "Numbers" are flying through the venue or the "Spacelab" seems to pull into the room. But after 30 minutes or so, the effect wears off. The 3-D fad in general has also jumped the shark. In movie theaters, people have noticed that 3-D effects don't make the movies better. 3-D did not become the "next big thing". The manufacturers of TV sets gave up on developing 3-D devices. The demand was not sufficient enough. It is no longer possible to astound an audience for two hours just with 3-D effects. To boot, some of the newer Kraftwerk videos are somehow loveless; "Trans Europe Express" and "Neon Lights" are especially unimaginative now – yet, at one point in time, these were two of Kraftwerk's most magical tunes and videos.

MYTH MAKERS

You know this phenomenon: Something in your apartment hasn't been used for years, but you think it's too good to be thrown away and might come in handy one day. So you store it somewhere out of sight. But yonce this old stuff is stashed in the basement or the attic, it is as good as thrown away. Somewhere in the back of your brain, you know you will never touch it again.

Same here. When a musician (writer, painter …) is called "cult", "iconic", or "a legend", a similar thing happens: Their talents are generally acknowledged, they are an institution that doesn't need to prove anything anymore. But it also means that we don't expect surprises from them anymore; they are a friendly memorial of passed times. We all know that the graveyards are full of forgotten artists who were once considered "too important to be forgotten". From time to time, at notable anniversaries, these artists are upheaved into shining lights, only to fall even deeper into oblivion immediately after. The artists who are still with us usually don't complain about the nonsense published about them on significant birthdays.

Today, as the death messages from Germany's rock and pop scene become a more and more regular occurrence and there are not many findings left to discover, how is it possible to keep the cult, especially around Krautrock, alive and sometimes even commercially still profitable? Why is second- and third-rate stuff consistently a topic in respective forums, sometimes over and over?

To answer this, we have to enter the fields of *fandom* and *collectors*. They are the folks searching for hidden treasures, but what they do is a business not so much for music lovers anymore, it's becoming more and more a thing for collectors who are mainly interested in *completeness* or in *obscurities*, without taking a look at the musical quality.

Surely you know these kinds of collectors. Their world consists of limited editions, runout numbers, inscriptions scratched into the deadwax, or hardly visible differences in the label print of different LP editions. Other fans of this kind hunt for all the foreign pressings of a certain record; they are over the moon when they manage to find an ultra-rare Peruvian pressing of KRAFTWERK's "Kohoutek Comet Melody" at a record fair, or they put lots of energy and money into getting a copy of TANGERINE DREAM's *Ricochet* in clear vinyl, even when they know it's a counterfeit. These collectors have the tendency of considering their expensive findings as something very special – the longer they had to search for it, the more special the finding is. They lose all their interest in a record when it's been remastered and re-released as a CD they could buy in the store next door or order it online.

This is the mechanism that makes third-rate stuff look "cult".[7] These people mistake what they do as connoisseurship. Often, their joy in hunting overrides their critical abilities. They could also collect Steiff teddy bears from the Fifties or Swatch watches from the Eighties. There's nothing wrong with that, but it is a way of thinking nobody who's really into the *music* would fall for.

These collectors are very important for record labels, so the labels care for them. Not all labels of course, only the ones that are interested in keeping the demand for these old records alive because they either own the rights or they do their business without having the rights. Labels including Spalax, Zyx, Bureau B, Garden Of Delights, and in parts, Grönland, officially specialize in the ministration of Krautrock records. Since we are not talking about a big market here, it's not always an easy job for them to find the right balance between engaging in business and the labor of love. It's a little bit like throwing spaghetti at the wall – in the age of online second-hand shops, Youtube, bootleggers, counterfeiters, streaming services, and all kinds of illegal download portals, you can hardly calculate which re-releases might sell. Regardless of whatever nonsense Rolf-Ulrich Kaiser might have talked about, at one point he was right: A label can't be a benevolent society. But even if there's not too much money in it anymore, it can be enough to keep a one-person business afloat (with the help maybe of one or two unpaid interns who take care of routine office tasks).

The work of these labels can be a meritorious thing. Many German rock or jazz records would have wound up lost without these treasure seekers. Even some major labels went down to their archives, re-released their Krautrock stuff, and revived their old sublabels (like Brain or MPS) with the purpose of making it look more authentic. Several artists bought back the rights over their old recordings for little money when nobody else wanted them and distribute them single-handedly now. As Holger Czukay once said to his CAN colleagues: This stuff will be our pension one day.

But what can be done if the reservoir of quality is running out? This is the moment when record companies have to perform some marketing feats to sell second- and third-rate material as attractive or important. This is the point at which the previously mentioned collector groups come into play. You have to systematically search for special target groups and serve them well-directed. Building up myths and legends around bands and artists is the most important way to wring some money out of long forgotten German beat bands or Krautrock recordings that only few people were interested in when they were originally released.

How does this mythmaking, this creation of a "legend" or a "cult figure", work? Here are some ways that are in practice:

A myth about a band can arise when only few people (ideally one person) in a circle of record-collecting friends own a certain record that is known to be rare – bands like EJWUUSL WESSAHQQAN, GÄA, GEBÄRVÄTERLI, KALACAKRA, MORGENSCHEIN, come to mind. It then goes without saying that the owner will attribute an especially important role in the history of German rock to his treasure. (And yes: "his", because this is mainly a male game.)

A myth centered on a band can also arise the other way round: When the entire group of friends *owns* a certain obscure record, this can lead to the desire to share this "tacit knowledge" with a bigger, yet still select, circle of people.

In both cases, social media like Facebook, online discussion forums, et cetera, come in handy to spread the feeling of having "something really special" and, in case the reaction is lukewarm, may even build up a sort of "us against them" attitude. It's often not even the music that is important, it is what Adorno called the "stage value" ("Inszenierungswert"): What the music does or is about doesn't really play a role, the important thing is how your cultural environment looks at you when you present yourself as a connoisseur of it.

A myth can also come into existence after a span of many years, when the public's view of a band changes. Example: When CLUSTER's or HARMONIA's records were first released, nearly no one had taken note of them. Today, they are seen as outstanding blueprints of the Krautrock substance. This makes the records interesting, even for collectors who are not especially interested in CLUSTER's or HARMONIA's music. I would even go as far to say: The fact that these records were without commercial success makes up a big part of their credibility today.

A myth can be created by making up facts about a band – the more absurd, the better. This can be done by a record label as well as by the musicians themselves or their management. For German rock, it works especially fine in the U.S. and the U.K., simply because as a German, you can tell journalists from these countries any kind of bullshit – they will buy it because they think: "He's a German, he must be serious." In regard to KRAFTWERK, today, you can still hear the story that they had a telephone without a bell in their studio, because the ringing might have disturbed them. When you wanted to call Ralf Hütter, according to the myth, you had to arrange a time to meet down to the second, and he would pick up his receiver at exactly that moment. CAN, as described earlier, was clever in spreading news about "supernatural phenomena" that allegedly happened in the presence of the band. Other artists never miss a chance to tell the press (and fans) that, during many of their concerts, they tripped on acid. In old press articles, you find breathtaking stories about the stars' sex adventures on tour or the hotel rooms they left in chaos and destruction. In reality, no ghost ever stopped the clocks during these concerts, the musicians probably smoked some pot, in their hotel rooms they had the TV set too loud, and stole the ashtrays like every other tourist, and that was it. Most of the rest was and is made up – the longer ago, the better, because the less likely it is that anyone can verify. There are always fans who love gossip of this kind. You don't need a Rolf-Ulrich Kaiser for stuff like this. In the offices of teenage pop gazettes, the chief editor sometimes gave funny or strange photos of a band to his editorial staff with the instruction: "Invent a nice story about them." And they did. The tabloids also love this game. When there is no story, they invent one, still today, often with the (unspoken) consent from the artists. This can be risky – journalists working for the tabloid *Bild* have a saying: If you use *Bild* as your elevator to the top, you have to accept that *Bild* will also be with you on your way back down.

The death of an artist is often a good thing for the record business. It's usually an opportunity to release a box set, or maybe even a tribute album by some label mates. The audience is always part of this calculation: As macabre as this may sound, the tragic homicide of Wolfgang Riechmann has its part in the recognition of his promising, but in no way earthshaking, solo firstling *Wunderbar* as "cult" today. Holger Czukay was barely under the sod when a box set with five records was released (*Cinema*), including a "vinyl video", a gimmick that only some technology museums can play. Only a few weeks later, a "remixed" re-release of Holger's albums *Plight & Premonition* (1988) and *Flux + Mutability* (1989) with David Sylvian, now as a double CD, was announced. There's no doubt that both records are worth it, but nobody will convince me that that point in time was not "jumping on the chance". Record labels can act very fast when they see the chance to cash in some fast bucks.

It doesn't even always have to be the death of an artist. If he is successful and decides to leave the label, that's also an opportunity a label usually won't miss out on. For the label, both reasons amount more or less to the same thing.

Releasing a luxurious box set has always been an effective way to artificially reactivate interest in acts that have left the sphere of popularity a while ago; that's one reason why we see this method more and more often today. The forgetfulness of the audience is part of the calculation. TANGERINE DREAM, for example, saw a luxury box set entitled *In Search of Hades – The Virgin Recordings 1973–1979* with 16 CDs, two Blu-ray discs, and an 80-page booklet in 2019 – of course the recordings were *remastered*. But wasn't there already a remastered reissue of their Virgin albums titled "definitive edition" in the mid-1990s that most fans probably own? So when the industry starts remastering the remasters, then the "definitive" edition was not too "definitive" – or the industry tries to rely on fans' short memory. Of course, one reason for this is the general breakdown of record sales, so the record companies have to find alternatives. Luxury editions, remastered recordings, remixes of the original recordings, anniversary editions with new liner notes, unpublished photos, repeated announcements, and some little video appetizers several months before the release date, highlighted presentation in record stores, bonus tracks that mostly aren't worth it – all this stuff can be used to wring money out of the back catalogue (usual rule: 15 months to three years old = "recent catalogue"; older than three years = "deep catalogue").

I don't know how you feel about them, but as carefully as box sets might be arranged and edited, for me they often have the aftertaste of being a sort of coffin – a box set finalizes the work of an artist. You'll probably listen to the content of such a set once or maybe twice and you'll skim through the booklet, but then you'll put the box onto a shelf. You can rarely listen to five or six albums (or even 16) of an artist in one go. Often, the track sequence is different from the original albums, or tracks are missing. So, in most cases, you will listen to the original albums (if ever), and the box set will remain untouched for the rest of your life.

Re-releases on vinyl have been especially popular for a while. The eternal debate between the purist fans of "analogue" and "digital" will not be taken up here, but the big LP sleeve can definitely be more aesthetic than a CD booklet. But there are some things one should know about vinyl re-releases: When you listen to the old original LPs from the 1960s or 1970s, you'll find that they often sound muffled and don't match today's standard of sound quality. So, for the re-release, the recordings have to be remastered, and since the old master tapes are usually in a bad shape and shouldn't be played very often anymore, they are copied onto a digital medium. This copy is then the basis for further treatments. A specialized sound engineer can do an excellent job of this, but to keep the process cheap, the recordings often simply get pumped up with emphasized bass and treble, and to reach a higher overall volume, they are often audibly compressed (keyword: loudness war). To reach an even higher volume, what originally was on one LP is now spread out onto two LPs. Of course, in most cases, it is "180 grams" vinyl. The latter especially doesn't make sense. The record is thick and heavy and gives you a solid feeling, but it is actually a waste of mineral oil. A record that weighs 100 or 120 grams is as good as the thicker one; the thickness has no effect on the sound quality. What makes the quality is this: The record needs to be pressed for around 25 seconds at a temperature of at least 140°C (284°F). To beat down the costs, some pressing plants shorten this process to 15 or 18 seconds and/or use a lower, often uneven, temperature, with the result that the record has inner tensions and might warp after a while. Besides this, sometimes the vinyl they use is cut with re-melted material – the labels of old returns are punched out and the vinyl is reused. This is of course cheaper, but it almost inevitably leads to crackling and sizzling surface noise after a while.

Let's just wait a while: My prediction is that one day, in the not-so-far future, many of the fans who now dump their CD collection for nearly no money will kick themselves for doing this.

It may sound petty-minded, but it's worth thinking about this: Our generations are the first in history to have comprehensive knowledge about ecological correlations. Vinyl is made from the same mineral oil that we need as raw material for lots of important things, from the paint on our walls to textiles to several pharmaceutical products. One day, we will have to stop blowing oil through the tailpipes of our cars – and all the old records? They will end up at the junkyard – maybe in fifty years, maybe in a hundred and fifty years. There, they will live the same fate as old auto tires: They will corrode into the oil they were made of, but this oil cannot be reused. It will sink into the ground and the groundwater.

Back to the reissues: Another nice game is a "limited edition" of an album on colored vinyl, as a shape disc, a picture disc, or packaged into something gimmicky. The "limited" number of copies often correlates with the number of copies that would be expected to be sold anyways, and in many cases it is too high to really become a rarity. But a numbered copy gives the collector the feeling of owning something rare and special. Not to mention the sometimes ridiculous number of remixes – DEPECHE MODE or the PET SHOP BOYS specialized in this business. For record companies, this is a sort of "extra income", aimed mainly at collectors. The fans who are interested in a band because of its *music* will rarely buy this sort of stuff.

How about myth building? One way to artificially create a myth can be assigning run-of-the-mill recordings to a producer who is seen as "legendary". Conny Plank is one of these names. He did a lot of important productions, that's where his reputation comes from. But he also did stuff that was just commercial – he didn't make much ado about them, but he needed to do these jobs because this was his way to fund risky productions. It has become a common practice now to connect these (otherwise usually long-forgotten) "standard" productions with his name, and suddenly they look interesting even though there's nothing special about the acts or the productions.

Another effective way to create an artificial myth can be collecting statements from currently successful musicians claiming a certain band (like CAN or KRAFTWERK) as "influential" for their own work. Often, they "document" their worship by weaving in some samples taken from tracks of their heroes into their own tunes. As producer Moses Pelham had to learn, this is not always welcome, but in the end it might go under the old marketing lore that "any publicity is good publicity" – sometimes, this can be the little brother of the calculated scandal.

Portrait films, TV documentaries, or biopics about bands, musicians, or personalities, especially about deceased ones, are always helpful in creating a myth. Wolfgang Kraesze's 1976 TV documentary *Signale aus der Schwäbischen Straße* (the then home address of Edgar Froese in Berlin-Wilmersdorf), about TANGERINE DREAM, was well received, can still be found on Youtube, and gets posted on Facebook forums from time to time; it's also part of the mentioned box set *In Search of Hades*. A portrait film about TANGERINE DREAM by Margarete Kreuzer was shown on German-French TV channel Arte in 2016, a crowdfunded longer version appeared on DVD in 2017. The TV movie *Notwehr* (1977) boosted the popularity of GURU GURU and even found its way on DVD, combined with some TV pearls of Krautrock bands. The TV screening of Werner Penzel's film *Vagabundenkarawane* in 1980 helped make EMBRYO more popular and promoted their album *Embryo's Reise*. Michael Meert's little TV movie *Krieg der Töne* (1987) lifted the popularity of Holger Czukay – in fact, it was more or less a film about him, just wrapped into a thin slapstick plot. (I have the feeling that today, this film would fall prey to the suspicion of belittlement of pedophilia. I'm sure it was never meant this way, but maybe that's the reason why it has never been shown again on TV. However, that makes it even more an appetizer for the mentioned *Cinema* box set.) A portrait film on Conny Plank by Reto Caduff and Conny's son Stephan Plank is available on DVD now, after having been sent through selected German and international movie theaters (*The Potential of Noise*, 2017). An unbelievably daffy Swedish documentary film on Klaus Dinger was shown on Arte TV in 2019 (*The Heart is A Drum* by Jacob Frössén). A "making of" movie about the *Seven Up* album by ASH RA TEMPEL and Timothy Leary is still in its planning stage, and a crowdfunded documentary about Damo Suzuki is under discussion.

Books can also be helpful in keeping names alive or reviving them. A well-researched biography on Manuel Göttsching[8] was published in 2015. Wolfgang Flür was not as lucky: His autobiography[9], first published in 1999, became known mainly because he got sued for it. Karl Bartos recently wrote his autobiography[10] and toured through TV, radio stations, and newspapers for several weeks, which helped not only him, but also revived the interest in KRAFTWERK. A sort of biography on Klaus Dinger[11], combined with an exhibition of his art, was published in 2012 by a Düsseldorf art gallery. Irmin Schmidt, as well as Damo Suzuki and Hans-Joachim Roedelius, have autobiographies out, and CAN and Kraftwerk have already been topic of several books – Kraftwerk has recently become subject of more or less useful scientific papers; even a congress about the band and their work was held. Edgar Froese's heirs released parts of his unfinished autobiography[12]; I'm not sure whether he would be very happy with the result. Even Olaf Kübler's originally self-published autobiography[13] made it through the media and found its readers at least in some inner circles.

GOING WITH THE STREAM

Listening to an album via one of today's streaming services is a completely different experience compared to having a physical carrier. This means two things: There is no time limit anymore like the LP once had with its 2 x 20 minutes, or the CD with its 79 minutes. Money also doesn't create a limit anymore; for roughly 10 dollars a month, you can listen to whatever you want, as long as you want and as often as you want. The success of a music release cannot be measured by sales figures anymore.

Many people never listen to the full length of the x-thousands tracks on their smartphone anymore. Guaranteed, several tracks will remain unheard forever. How many people still have the patience to listen to a 20-minute piece of music without checking Whatsapp? How many people can still listen to a whole Bruckner or Mahler symphony today and note that it's not just a sequence of four pieces, but understand that the 4th movement *refers* to the 1st?

How about Artificial Intelligence? No, I don't fear artificially computer-composed music, computer-written novels, or screenplays. They will not reach the quality of work that real artists can create. But will you ever hear about the works real artists did? *This* is the question to be concerned about. Every time you give your automatically generated personal playlist a run, the algorithm will decide more deeply about the kind of music it chooses for you next time. No, this is not nostalgic groaning. It's just the diagnosis of a cultural change of values. This goes not only for listeners; today's musicians also have to think in a different way in order to reach an audience.

The usual streaming services today offer 50 million tracks. Every day, around 40,000 new tracks are added. It's obvious that nobody is able to listen to even a tiny little fraction of all. Musicians and record companies already react to these trends. Still, in the 1990s, it was the standard production rhythm for a band or an artist to produce an album every two years, alternating with tours. Today, presenting a new album after two years, is seen as a "comeback" already. To keep the act in public view, today, labels and artists prefer to publish two EPs a year instead of one album every two years, additionally supported by remixes, re-releases of the current album with extra tracks, and re-releases of old material in the shape of box sets, live versions, dub versions, "lost" versions, alternate versions, and whatever you can imagine. The only goal is to keep the act known. As Anne Haffmanns of indie label Domino Records says: "We have to fill the time to generate attention for your own brand as an artist. Otherwise you'll simply drown."[14] It's not the music or the personality of the artist anymore, it's the *brand* that has to be kept alive.

Never again will we listen to music as we did when the music this book deals with was new. This, of course, has consequences for the way yesterday's rock music is located in today's canon of music.

The social media, Facebook groups, et cetera, sometimes act like newsgroups that document their own disappearance. The music talked about there is historic and will never come back as a living thing. But the group doesn't notice because of its self-imposed limits. This way, the stuff that is talked about, becomes more and more insignificant and gets lost in the ever same loop of the same topics, until finally it ends up in the absurd. You can see what I mean when you look at some of the Krautrock or KRAFTWERK fan groups on Facebook. As I said before, they take their topic out of context. As there is no new stuff to discuss, they have no real function anymore, but they go on and on like a regulars' table because they are so gemütlich. In German, the word for this phenomenon is *Dekontextualisierung* – fans take their topic (Krautrock) out of the initial context in which it originated. They are busy following a topic without knowing its roots. Is it possible to *understand* a topic without knowing where it came from?

SOMETHING WE WOULDN'T KNOW WITHOUT

The Polish sociologist and philosopher Zygmunt Bauman (1925-2017) described a phenomenon he called a "retropia". He meant it politically, but it also fits here: KRAFTWERK, as well as most Krautrock acts, provide (and their fans discuss) visions that feel like future, but the visions can never become true because they are built on a long lost past.

We could go on naming bands and artists and try to make up the balance. There would be AERA, AGITATION FREE, ALTONA, ATLANTIS, BIRTH CONTROL, BRÖSELMASCHINE, CITY PREACHERS, DZYAN, EELA CRAIG, FRUMPY, GROBSCHNITT, HIGHWAY, HOELDERLIN, JADE WARRIOR, JANE, KOLLEKTIV, LAVA,

Novalis, Odin, Randy Pie, Rattles and more … Their records are still available, but all these names are "past", even if some of them still exist or recently reunited. The latter can especially be a double-edged sword: Aside from just commercial reasons, it can be a bit ridiculous to have to watch a club of veterans who still consider themselves as avant-garde. On the other hand: If an artist had something substantial to say in his twenties, then why shouldn't he have something substantial to say in his sixties or seventies – unless he has maybe injected his brain into an eternal orbit around Jupiter. Jazz musicians have always known this, and some of them got better every year.

German rock – as all music in the world – is a continuing process. It didn't start with Amon Düül and it didn't end after the Krautrock era. In parts, it's still going on. In other parts, it has become a blueprint for later developments. Techno, Eurodance, et cetera, can be traced back to Kraftwerk, Giorgio Moroder, or the Munich sound. Other electronic music of the 1980s and 1990s, like industrial, trance, noise, and more – all this ambient and drone music that is produced today by laptop musicians, can, in the end, be traced back to Tangerine Dream's *Zeit*, Edgar Froese's *Epsilon In Malaysian Pale,* or Eberhard Schoener's *Meditation*.

If streaming is the way we listen to music in the future, it is quite clear that curated playlists and algorithms will choose what we listen to more and more, and then, to a decreasingly less degree, *what* we are listening to won't matter anymore. But if sound carpets of this kind become the standard, then German rock of the 1970s and 1980s in particular, with its high recognition value, will stand out as a beacon of individualism. As it has always been with music: If it is *good* music, it will have a secret to it. Something we wouldn't know without it.

NOTES

WHAT'S IT ALL ABOUT?

1 Brand 2009, p. 21
2 Cp. Sailer 2016
3 Lundberg 1977
4 *New Musical Express*, September 6, 1975
5 Qtd. in Morawietz 2006

RUBBLE YEARS

1 Qtd. in Stubbs 2014
2 Qtd. in *Spiegel* 50/2009
3 Qtd. in Pertou 2015
4 Cp. Prieberg 2000, p. 242ff
5 Cp. Storjohann 1993, p. 108
6 Cp. Storjohann 1993, p. 119ff
7 NSDAP = Nationalsozialistische Deutsche Arbeiterpartei (National Socialist German Worker's Party); the Nazi party.
8 Cp. Sloterdijk 2014, p. 182

TEENAGER MELODY

1 Cp. Whalley 2009
2 Qtd. in Dallach 2015
3 Advertisement in *Metzinger Volksblatt*, September 24, 1966, facsimile in Matheja 2007, p. 23
4 In English texts, by the way, these umlauts often are transformed into a, o and u. But ä, ö and ü are vowels in their own right and have a different pronunciation than a, o and u, so this is not just a laxness, it's wrong.
5 Cp. Matheja 2007. In addition to his book Bear Family Records released a series of (currently) 12 CDs under the same title.
6 Cp. Klatt 2013
7 "Der richt'ge Fahrstuhl für Sie fährt unter Umständen nie." (Lyrics by Hans Feltz.)
8 "Weiße Rosen aus Athen / sagen dir: Komm recht bald wieder"; lyrics by Hans Bradtke.
9 "Rastlos zieh' ich um die Erde / in die weite Welt hinaus / ohne Freund und ohne Liebe / denn ich hab ja kein Zuhaus"; German lyrics by Ernst Bader. The song was a cover version of „The Carnival is Over" (which was a cover version itself; the original was the Russian traditional "Stenka Rasin").
10 „Jimmy wollt' ein Mädchen lieben / doch ein anderer kam daher / und als Trost sind ihm geblieben: / die Gitarre und das Meer" (From the movie *Die Gitarre und das Meer*, lyrics by Aldo Pinelli.)
11 „Er hörte den Schuss / aber nie mehr das Echo / und nie mehr sah er / Jenny Lees gold'nes Haar". (Lyrics by Dolf Bokler; a cover version of „Only the Heartaches", a tune from Joe Meek's kitchen.)
12 „Heißer Sand und ein verlorenes Land / und ein Leben in Gefahr / Heißer Sand und die Erinn'rung daran / dass es einmal schöner war" (Lyrics by Kurt Feltz).
13 „Ich mach mir Sorgen, Sorgen um dich / Denk auch an morgen, denk auch an mich!" (Lyrics by Walter Rothenburg).
14 Völker 2010, p. 206
15 „Am Tag als der Regen kam / lang ersehnt, heiß erfleht / auf die glühenden Felder / auf die durstigen Wälder / Da kamst du." (Original written by Gilbert Bécaud, German lyrics by Ernst Bader – a guy who always had a great sense for drama).
16 "Da rief ich no, no, no, no, no / mit dem werd' ich des Lebens nicht mehr froh / Ich will 'nen Cowboy als Mann / Dabei kommt's mir gar nicht auf das Schießen an / denn ich weiß, dass so ein Cowboy küssen kann!" (Lyrics by Peter Ström).
17 Napier-Bell 2002, p. 12
18 Cp. Miller 2015 – far from being rock'n'roll, but at least a nice dancing tune, it has to be admitted.
19 Cp. Grotum 1994
20 Cp. Werthmann 1958. Eberhard Werthmann was an insider: As "Donald Wolf" ("Gold in der Sierra") he worked as a schlager singer for a couple of years; with this dissertation he received his Ph.D. in political science from Karl-Franzens-Universität in Graz, Austria, and became an entrepreneur later.
21 Qtd. in Bremer 2009
22 Cp. Weber 2015, p. 94
23 Qtd. in Fuchs-Gamböck n.d.

SOME QUESTIONS OF INFRASTRUCTURE

1 These were Nordwestdeutscher Rundfunk (NWDR) in Hamburg and Cologne, Sender Freies Berlin (SFB), Radio Bremen (RB), Hessischer Rundfunk (HR) in Frankfurt, Südwestfunk (SWF) in Baden-Baden, Süddeutscher Rundfunk (SDR) in Stuttgart and Bayrischer Rundfunk (BR) in Munich. In the mid-1950s the NWDR was split up into Norddeutscher Rundfunk (NDR) in Hamburg and Westdeutscher Rundfunk (WDR) in Cologne. After the German reunification two GDR stations were added and renamed: Rundfunk Berlin-Brandenburg (RBB) in Potsdam and Mitteldeutscher Rundfunk (MDR) in Leipzig. In 1998, SDR and SWF merged into SWR. A country-wide radio station is Deutschlandfunk in Cologne and Berlin. All these are stations under public law. Different from this is the Deutsche Welle (DW), broadcasting around the world in several languages. The DW is run by the German government.
2 Cp. Bailey 2006

3 CDU = Christlich-demokratische Union (Christian-democratic Union); Germany's conservative party. "Union" in this case has nothing to do with trade unions.
4 Cp. Haus Mödrath 2020
5 Cp. Werthmann 1958, p. 19
6 Cp. Simon Frith 2004, p. 120.
7 Cp. Rudorf 1979, p. 199.
8 Cp. Matheja 2007, p. 11.
9 Cp. Loch 2010, p. 32.
10 Cp. Rudorf 1979, p. 199
11 Cp. SDW n.d. (retrieved May 2, 2015)
12 Cp. Murphy 2014, p. 230
13 Cp. *Musikmarkt* 2013
14 Cp. Statista 2015
15 Cp. *Frankfurter Rundschau,* September 20, 1968
16 Cp. Czarnecky/Siebert 2009; cp. also Loichinger 2010
17 Cp. Kübler/Augustin 1996, chapter 1

CHOO-CHOO TRAINS AND TELSTAR

1 Mr. Meek is a completely different, but highly interesting beast, and if you want to know more about him, feel free to go to www.joemeekpage.info
2 *Heimat, eine deutsche Chronik* (11 films, 1984); *Die zweite Heimat, Chronik einer Jugend* (13 films, 1992); *Heimat 3, Chronik einer Zeitenwende* (6 films, 2004) – all in all 52 hours of film, written and directed by Edgar Reitz. If you have to choose only one German film production to see in your life, choose the first season.
3 CDU = Christlich-demokratische Union (Christian-democratic Union); Germany's conservative party. "Union" in this case has nothing to do with trade unions.
4 Gesellschaft für Konsumforschung (GfK), today number four in the world.
5 "Solang' noch die Zigarre glüht, so lange geht's uns gut." Die Schaumburger Hofsänger, lyrics by Ronny Hein.
6 Cp. Stenke 2018
7 "Und sie werden nicht mehr frei ihr ganzes Leben." https://www.youtube.com/watch?v=-JbtgQM0uP8s
8 A rather harsh example is Prabel 2015.
9 Höppener, n.d.
10 Cp. Giordano 1987
11 Cp. Mitscherlich 1967
12 Cp. Ziok 2010
13 *Cabaret*, USA 1972, directed by Bob Fosse, with Liza Minnelli, Michael York, Helmut Griem, Joel Grey, Fritz Wepper and several others. The film is based on the Broadway musical of the same title with music by John Kander and Fred Ebb, which is based on the stage play *I am a Camera* by John Van Druten, which is based on the novel "Goodbye to Berlin" by Christopher Isherwood – and still one of my all-time favorite films.
14 "Hundert Mann und ein Befehl / und ein Weg, den keiner will / tagein, tagaus, wer weiß wohin / Verbranntes Land, und was ist der Sinn?" German lyrics again by Ernst Bader, the guy who already had written the German lyrics of "Am Tag, als der Regen kam".
15 Adenauer: „Nach meiner festen Überzeugung, nach der Überzeugung eines jeden Deutschen, der die Dinge unvoreingenommen betrachtet, gibt es vor dieser konsequent fortgeführten Politik des totalitären Sowjetrusslands nur eine Rettung für uns alle: uns so stark zu machen, dass Sowjetrussland erkennt, ein Angriff darauf ist ein großes Risiko für Sowjetrussland selbst!" – Qtd. in Baag 2006

THE STAR-CLUB: WHERE IT ALL STARTED

1 Günter Zint by email.
2 Qtd. in Rockarchiv, n.d.
3 Cp. Fascher/Flesch 2007, p. 191f
4 Cp. Flür 1999, photo section "Beathovens im Ostseebad Dahme, 1965"
5 Cp. Loch 2010, p. 36ff
6 Krüger 2010, p. 293
7 Qtd. in Lange 2012
8 Cp. Wikipedia (Salambo)
9 Cp. Zint 1987, p. 115ff

BEAT OF THE WIRTSCHAFTSWUNDER

1 Written by the very productive schlager lyricist Rudolf-Günter Loose (1927-2013).
2 Qtd. in Spittler 2015
3 Cp. Spittler 2015
4 Qtd. in Graves/Schmidt-Joos/Halbscheffel 1998, p. 755
5 Cp. Last/Macho 2006, p. 261
6 Cp. Last/Macho 2006, p. 67f
7 Qtd. in Last/Macho 2006, p. 261

MUSICIAN'S DAILY ROUTINES

1 Cp. Temme 2014
2 Hesslein and Horns, qtd. in Morawietz 2006

BEAT-CLUB & CO.: MUSIC ON GERMAN TV

1 Cp. Augustin 2008

THE MISLEADING MAGIC OF SIXTY-EIGHT

1 Mann 1942, p. 100
2 Cp. Jobs 1917
3 Cp. Gabler 2006, p. 517
4 Cp. Reetze 1992, p. 256ff
5 Cp. Mann 1932, p. 221ff
6 Qtd. in Legath 1979, p. 35

7 Cp. Shapiro 2018
8 Cp. Mansnerus 1996
9 Cp. Didion 2008, p. 84-128
10 Qtd. in Iliffe 2003, p. 23
11 Ensslin, qtd. in Aust 1985, p. 69
12 Qtd. in *Spiegel* 19/1968
13 Qtd. in *Spiegel* 19/1968
14 Reinders and Fritzsch 1995

MUNICH RIOTS AND THE START OF KRAUTROCK

1 Cp. Stefanie Schoener 2010, p. 66ff
2 Cp. Stefanie Schoener 2010, p. 69
3 Qtd. in Schober 1979, p. 25
4 Qtd. in Stefanie Schoener 2010, p. 70
5 Qtd. in Stefanie Schoener 2010, p. 70
6 Qtd. in Schober 1979, p. 25
7 Qtd. in Schober 1979, p. 25
8 Qtd. in Stefanie Schoener 2010, p. 70
9 Qtd. in Mervis 2016
10 Qtd. in Legath 1979, p. 72
11 Qtd. in Schober 1979, p. 28
12 Stockhausen 1971, p. 110
13 Joseph Beuys, qtd. in Reinartz
14 Joseph Beuys, qtd. in Staub
15 Joseph Beuys, qtd. in Reinartz
16 Joseph Beuys, qtd. in Reinartz

ANGELS OF CHAOS

1 Schober 1979, p. 43
2 Kübler, qtd. in Schober 1979, p. 57
3 Loch 2010, p. 78f
4 Cp. Kübler/Augustin 1996, p. 72
5 Kübler/Augustin 1996, p. 72f
6 Kübler/Augustin 1996, p. 73
7 Qtd. in Schober 1979, p. 57f
8 Loch 2010, p. 78f
9 In: Mießgang 1997
10 Kübler/Augustin 1996, p. 73
11 Schober 1979, p. 52
12 Qtd. in Schober 1979, p. 61
13 Qtd. in Schober 1979, p. 59
14 Qtd. in Mineur 2003, p. 4
15 Qtd. in Mineur 2003, p. 4
16 Qtd. in Schober 1979, p. 63
17 Qtd. in Schober 1979, p. 64
18 In: *Kölner Stadt-Anzeiger*, July 1, 1972; qtd. in Schober 1979, p. 157f
19 Kübler, qtd. in Schober 1979, p. 152
20 Karrer, qtd. in Schober 1979, p. 152
21 Qtd. in Schober 1979, p. 159
22 Qtd. in Schober 1979, p. 161
23 Cp. Schober 1979, p. 56
24 Qtd. in Schober 1979, p. 213

CONFOUNDING THE GHOSTS

1 Qtd. in Granini 1977, p. 4
2 Cp. Warner 2015, p. 91ff
3 Qtd. in Ehnert/Kinsler 1984, p. 55
4 Qtd. in Zahn 2006, p. 37f
5 Stockhausen Vol. 3, 1971, p. 200
6 Qtd. in Morawietz 2006
7 See Mießgang 1997
8 Qtd. in Kumpf n.d.
9 Qtd. in Schmidt/Kampmann 1998, p. 384-387
10 Qtd. in Schmidt/Kampmann 1998, p. 382
11 Cp. Ehnert/Kinsler 1984, p. 56
12 Qtd. in Ehnert/Kinsler 1984, p. 56
13 Qtd. in Ehnert/Kinsler 1984, p. 56
14 Holger Czukay and Irmin Schmidt in a live interview, WDR TV 1977
15 Cp. Balzer 2017
16 Qtd. in Schmidt/Kampmann 1998, p. 388-390
17 In case you want more: Cp. Zahn 2006, p. 34
18 Qtd. in Schmidt/Kampmann 1998, p. 388
19 Qtd. in Grissemann 2013
20 Qtd. in Ehnert/Kinsler 1984, p. 373
21 Loch 2010, p. 81
22 Loch 2010, p. 81
23 Qtd. in Schmidt/Kampmann 1998, p. 380
24 Cp. Lippegaus 2017
25 Qtd. in Schmidt/Kampmann 1998, p. 388
26 Qtd. in Zahn 2006, p. 35
27 In: Corso, Deutschlandfunk, May 29, 2012
28 *Das Messer*, directed by Rolf von Sydow, written by Francis Durbridge
29 Qtd. in Dallach 2016
30 Granini 1977, p. 8
31 Granini 1977, p. 8
32 Cp. Luhmann 1987, p. 60ff
33 Qtd. in Ehnert/Kinsler 1984, p. 56
34 Cp. Legath 1979, p. 227
35 Qtd. in Kitching 2015
36 Cp. Lippegaus 1984
37 Qtd. in Schneider 1986, p. 161
38 Qtd. in Wagner 2019

FUTURE'S CALLING

1 Qtd. in Kraushaar 2017, taz
2 Meinhof 1970
3 Cp. Kraushaar 2017, NZZ
4 Cp. Kraushaar 2017, NZZ
5 Cp. *Spiegel* 3/1972
6 *Die verlorene Ehre der Katharina Blum* (The Lost Honor of Katharina Blum), Germany 1975, directed by Volker Schlöndorff, with a select ensemble of excellent actors, especially Angela Winkler, Mario Adorf, Dieter Laser, Jürgen Prochnow and Hannelore Hoger.
7 Böll 1974, p. 5
8 *Deutschland im Herbst* (Germany in Autumn), Germany 1978, episode movie by 11 directors, among them Edgar Reitz, Volker Schlöndorff, Rainer Werner Fassbinder and Alexander Kluge. Partly fictional, partly documental.
9 *Der Baader Meinhof Komplex*, Germany 2008, directed by Uli Edel, screenplay by Bernd Eichinger after the book of the same title by Stefan Aust (1985).
10 Qtd. in Kraushaar 2017, taz
11 Qtd. in *Spiegel* 35/2017, p. 1
12 Cp. Schwabe 2016
13 Lachenmann 2002, p. 39
14 Lachenmann 2002, p. 39

AMATEURS AND PROFESSIONALS

1 Cp. Rau 2005, p. 27f
2 Qtd. in Simmeth 2016, p. 166
3 Qtd. in Kraushaar 2016, p. 50
4 Cp. Olivier 1976, p. 11
5 Qtd. in Haring 1984, p. 55
6 Cp. Koers 1994, p. 47
7 Cp. Jerry Garcia, qtd. in Jackson/Gans 2016, p. 185
8 Cp. Lesh 2006, p. 295f
9 From a Nazi songbook: "Heil Hitler Dir", written by Bruno Schestak, 1937. "Deutschland erwache aus deinem bösen Traum / Gib fremden Juden in deinem Reich nicht Raum" (Germany, awaken from your bad dream / don't give space to foreign Jews in your empire).
10 DiCesare 2010

BEING PROFESSIONAL

1 Cp. Diederichsen 2014, p. 40ff
2 Qtd. in Morawietz 2006
3 Cp. Olivier 1976, p. 11
4 Cp. Rudorf 1979, p. 199
5 Cp. *Musikspiegel* 1972
6 Cp. *Pop Aktuell*, n.d.
7 This is a conservative rough estimate, based on the acts listed in Ehnert 1979 and some additional research. It is not possible today anymore to find out the exact number of German rock acts that were signed by a record label, but 250 should give you an idea.
8 Cp. chartsurfer.de
9 Cp. *Rock & Folk*, n.d.
10 Qtd. in Haring 1984, p. 246
11 Qtd. in Murphy 2014, p. 315
12 Cp. Schmidt 2017
13 Cp. Murphy 2014, p. 279
14 Qtd. in Haring 1984, p. 252f
15 Qtd. in Schneider 1986, p. 52f
16 Cp. Enwezor 2012, p. 81-91
17 Cp. Kahlefendt 2016
18 Cp. Morawietz 2006

STUDIOS AND PRODUCERS

1 Qtd. in Boettcher 2002, p. 104
2 Qtd. in Hentschel 2004
3 Cp. Napier-Bell 2002, p. 35ff
4 Qtd. in Murphy 2014, p. 137
5 Cp. Lake/Griffiths 2007, p. 1
6 Eicher, qtd. in Linke 2019
7 Eicher, qtd. in Linke 2019
8 Jennings 2012

CONNY PLANK, DIETER DIERKS

1 Qtd. in Haring 1984, p. 227
2 Wikipedia (Conny Plank)
3 By email
4 Correspondingly qtd. in Haring 1984, p. 227
5 Qtd. in Morawietz 2006
6 Qtd. in Morawietz 2006
7 Qtd. in Haring 1984, p. 223
8 Qtd. in Haring 1984, p. 228f
9 Qtd. in Haring 1984, p. 229
10 Roedelius 2016, p. 218/220
11 Qtd. in Stichtag 23. Januar 1986

KAISER'S REICH

1 Qtd. in *Spiegel* 41/1968
2 Qtd. in Morawietz 2006
3 Qtd. in Schober 1979, p. 39
4 Qtd. in *Spiegel* 41/1968
5 Kaiser 1972, p. 367
6 Kaiser 1972, p. 367
7 Cp. Hub 1997
8 Qtd. in Hub 1997
9 Qtd. in Legath 1979, p. 408
10 Cp. Morawietz 2006
11 Cp. *Spiegel* 43/1971
12 Qtd. in Hub 1997
13 By email
14 Cp. Higgs 2006, p. 145f
15 Greenfield 2006, p. 437
16 Qtd. in Higgs 2006, p. 162
17 Higgs 2006, p. 162
18 Qtd. in Hub 1997
19 Cp. Westrupp n.d.
20 Cp. *Spiegel* 40/1973
21 Qtd. in *Spiegel* 40/1973
22 Hub 1997
23 *Spiegel* 40/1973
24 Press release, n.d.
25 From a press release, n.d.
26 Qtd. in *Spiegel* 40/1973
27 Cp. *Spiegel* 40/1973
28 Cp. Pieper 2007, p. 54
29 Patterson 2011
30 Qtd. in Hub 1997.
31 Qtd. in Hub 1997
32 Cp. Hub 1997
33 Qtd. in *Spiegel* 40/1973
34 Qtd. in Hub 1997
35 Qtd. in Hub 1997
36 Press release, n.d.
37 Press release, n.d.
38 Qtd. in Hub 1997
39 Qtd. in *Spiegel* 40/1973
40 Pieper 2007, p. 54
41 Cp. Hub 1997
42 Hub 1997
43 Westrupp n.d.
44 By email
45 Cp. Pieper 2007
46 Hub 1997

STOCKHAUSEN, CARLOS, SALA & CO.: ELECTRONIC REVOLUTION

1 Edgar Froese, facsimile of a magazine interview from 1997, original source unknown
2 Cp. Ehnert/Kinsler 1984, p. 197
3 Davis 1990, p. 329
4 Qtd. in Stockhausen 1978, p. 504
5 Qtd. in Stockhausen 1978, p. 504
6 Qtd. in Ehnert/Kinsler 1984, p. 197
7 Cp. Jackson/Gans 2015, p. 14
8 Qtd. in Stockhausen 1978, p. 505
9 Mießgang 1997
10 Qtd. in Stockhausen 1978, p. 505
11 Qtd. in Stockhausen 1978, p. 505
12 Qtd. in Stockhausen 1978, p. 505
13 Cp. Betschon 2015
14 Cp. Wikipedia (Giorgio Moroder)
15 Qtd. in Maconie 2000, p. 133

SCHOENER, FRICKE, MORODER: THE MUNICH MOOG PIONEERS

1 By email (as several parts of this chapter), also cp. Schoener 2010, p. 74ff
2 Qtd. in Haring 1984, p. 235
3 Qtd. in Haring 1984, p. 235
4 Cp. Schoener 2010, p. 131
5 Qtd. in Ehnert/Kinsler 1984, p. 300
6 Qtd. in Miersch 1/2007
7 Qtd. in Florian Secundus Fricke 2010
8 In: Mießgang 1997
9 *Pop* magazine, n.d., qtd. in Ehnert/Kinsler 1984, p. 300
10 Qtd. in Legath 1979, p. 183
11 Fricke, qtd. in Ehnert/Kinsler 1984, p. 300
12 Qtd. in Legath 1979, p. 294
13 Qtd. in Miersch 1/2007
14 Qtd. in Ehnert/Kinsler 1984, p. 300
15 Qtd. in Florian Secundus Fricke 2010
16 Qtd. in Florian Secundus Fricke 2010
17 Qtd. in Florian Secundus Fricke 2010
18 Qtd. in Florian Secundus Fricke 2010
19 Qtd. in Florian Secundus Fricke 2010
20 Qtd. in Florian Secundus Fricke 2010
21 Qtd. in Florian Secundus Fricke 2010
22 Qtd. in Florian Secundus Fricke 2010
23 Qtd. in Florian Secundus Fricke 2010
24 Qtd. in Geisenhanslüke 2014

BERLIN SCHOOL

1 Eberhard Schoener by email
2 Qtd. in Kestrel n.d.
3 Cp. Miersch 1/2007
4 Qtd. in Miersch 1/2007
5 Qtd. in Kestrel n.d.
6 Qtd. in Miersch 1/2007
7 Qtd. in Miersch 1/2007
8 Miersch by email
9 Cp. Behrendsen/Rüsenberg 1978
10 Qtd. in Frank 1976, p. 16
11 Qtd. in Miersch 1/2007
12 In: Quotefancy.com
13 Cp. Fechner 1988, p. 167ff
14 Qtd. in Frank 1976, p. 16

MUSIC FROM THE ROAD OF FAIRY TALES

1 Qtd. in Iliffe 2003, p. 24
2 Cp. Iliffe 2003, p. 24f
3 Qtd. in Legath 1979, p. 205
4 Iliffe 2003, p. 93
5 Qtd. in Legath 1979, p. 336
6 Cp. Morawietz 2006
7 Cp. Ehnert/Kinsler 1984, p. 109
8 Qtd. in Iliffe 2003, p. 40
9 Today: www.alter-weserhof.de
10 Qtd. in Esch 2014, p. 108
11 Qtd. in Crane 2015
12 Qtd. in Legath 1979, p. 737
13 Haring 1984, p. 122
14 Qtd. in Ehnert/Kinsler 1984, p. 70
15 Qtd. in Crane 2015
16 Qtd. in Crane 2015
17 *Live 1974* was released in 2007.
18 Reetze 2015
19 Roedelius 2016, p. 162
20 Qtd. in Engelbrecht 2017
21 Cp. Dotzauer 2015
22 Qtd. in Legath 1979, p. 1533
23 Cp. Roedelius 2016, p. 220-222
24 Cp. Roedelius 2018
25 Qtd. in Jürgens 2006, p. 125
26 Qtd. in Esch 2014, p. 105
27 Qtd. in Legath 1979, p. 1498
28 Qtd. in Ehnert/Kinsler 1984, p. 322
29 Cp. Ingenhoff 2015
30 Cp. Ehnert/Kinsler 1984, p. 323

DÜSSELDORF SCHOOL

1 Cp. Esch 2014, passim
2 Qtd. in Amend 2017
3 Qtd. in Amend 2017
4 Qtd. in Amend 2017
5 Nameless review, qtd. in Legath 1979, p. 184
6 Cp. Ehnert/Kinsler 1984, p. 196
7 Qtd. in Legath 1979, p. 684
8 Qtd. in Esch 2014, p. 98
9 Qtd. in Legath 1979, p. 864
10 Qtd. in Ehnert/Kinsler 1984, p. 196
11 Qtd. in Esch 2014, p. 99f
12 Qtd. in Esch 2014, p. 100
13 *Bucks County Courier Times* 1975
14 *The Advocate* 1975
15 *News Journal* 1975
16 Qtd. in Legath 1979, p. 1144
17 Qtd. in Legath 1979, p. 1144
18 Qtd. in Klotschkow 2017
19 Cp. Dinger 2012
20 Qtd. in Dinger (Wikipedia)
21 Qtd. in Ehnert/Kinsler 1984, p. 272
22 Qtd. in Holden/Rother 2015
23 Qtd. in Esch 2014, p. 84
24 Qtd. in Ehnert/Kinsler 1984, p. 272
25 Qtd. in Crane 2015, p. 30
26 Dinger 2012
27 Qtd. in Esch 2014, p. 83
28 Qtd. in Legath 1979, p. 594
29 Dinger 2012
30 Qtd. in Legath 1979, p. 963
31 Dinger 1999
32 Dinger 1999
33 Dinger 1999
34 Dinger 2012
35 Cp. Dinger 2012
36 Cp. Dinger 2012
37 Qtd. in Ehnert/Kinsler 1979, p. 208
38 Dinger 2012
39 Cp. Dinger 2012
40 Qtd. in Esch 2014, p. 199
41 Qtd. in Holstein 2014
42 Cp. Schreiber 1980, p. 98
43 Cp. Holstein 2014
44 Qtd. in Esch 2014, p. 411f

HAMBURG: THE HANSEATIC WAY

1 Qtd. in Ehnert 1975, p. 131
2 Cp. Rau 2005, p. 174f
3 Cp. Kübler/Augustin 1996, p. 168ff and 178f

4 Probably Hamburg's most famous jazz club.

AGITPROP

1 Qtd. in Haring 1984, p. 68
2 Cp. Wagner 2013, p. 52
3 Qtd. in Wagner 2013, p. 49
4 Qtd. in Wagner 2013, p. 50f
5 Qtd. in Wagner 2013, p. 51
6 Cp. Wagner 2013, p. 51
7 Qtd. in Haring 1984, p. 69

SEVENTIES IN BITS AND PIECES

1 Cp. Adorno 1962, p. 14-34
2 Cp. Schmidt, in WDR 1971
3 Cp. Froese's remarks in Kraesze 1976
4 Cp. Kraushaar 2016, p. 54f
5 Source unknown (radio interview, probably NDR)
6 *Notwehr*, TV movie, Germany 1977, directed by Hartmut Griesmayr, screenplay written by Bernd Schroeder.
7 Neumeier 2007
8 Neumeier 2007
9 Cp. Froese 2017, p. 213
10 Kraushaar 2016, p. 64f
11 Cp. Reichel n.d.
12 Qtd. in Jahn n.d.
13 Kraushaar 2016, p. 66
14 Macheath, in *The Threepenny Opera*, Act 3, scene 3.
15 Kraushaar 2016, p. 66f
16 Cp. Brand 1968-1972
17 Qtd. in Tamarkin 2003, p. 154
18 Qtd. in Morawietz 2006
19 Qtd. in Morawietz 2006
20 *Saturday Night Fever (Nur Samstag Nacht)*, USA 1977, directed by John Badham, written by Norman Wexler.
21 Cp. Blondie n.d.
22 Qtd. in Reetze 1987, p. 87
23 Cp. Peter Hesslein, in: Morawietz 2006
24 Cp. Fleming n.d.
25 On Facebook, exact source unknown
26 Cp. Haring 1984, p. 116
27 Cp. Ehnert 1975, p. 147
28 Cp. Morawietz 2006
29 Qtd. in Morawietz 2006
30 Cp. Bartos 2017, p. 369-371
31 Cp. *Musik Express* 4/1977: Brain Festival
32 Qtd. in Jackson and Gans, p. 247
33 Cp. Froese 2017, p. 69f and 330
34 Cp. Schober 1979, p. 194
35 Cp. Froese 2017, p. 331

TURN ON, TUNE IN

1 Cp. Gabler 2006, p. 239f
2 *Mad Men*, USA 2007-2015, 92 episodes
3 Cp. Davis 1990
4 Cp. Allen 2009, several chapters
5 Cp. Anderson Dansereau 2020
6 Cp. Overstolz vom Rhein
7 German lyrics written by writer Günter Wallraff and the not undisputed singer-songwriter Diether Dehm a.k.a. Lerryn.
8 Cp. Psychedelic Pictures
9 Lyrics by Hans-Ulrich Weigel, a well-known schlager lyricist.
10 Cp. Werding 2018
11 On the album back cover.
12 Cp. Reuband 1994, p. 71f

LIBERATION

1 Praunheim
2 In: Legath 1979, p. 1223

NEW TECHNOLOGY

1 Qtd. in Reetze 1987, p. 100
2 Qtd. in Reetze 1987, p. 100
3 Qtd. in Reetze 1987, p. 100

ICE AGE

1 Cp. Jekal 2018
2 Qtd. in Legath 1979, p. 1533
3 Cp. Müller 2013. Author Wolfgang Müller was the driving force behind Die Tödliche Doris. Although his book mainly centers the story of this project, it has a lot of detailed information about the West Berlin NDW scene.
4 Cp. Zeigermann 2010
5 Cp. Schwabe 2016
6 Cp. Esch 2014, no special chapter
7 *Debt Begins at 20*, USA 1980, docu with intermixed acted footage, directed by Stephanie Beroes. For more info, cp. Ahwesh 2017.
8 A pretty good overview of the whole NDW scene and its way of thinking can be found in Teipel 2001, no special chapter.
9 Qtd. in Teipel 2001, p. 175
10 *Gib Gas, ich will Spaß*, Germany 1983, director: Wolfgang Büld. In the U.K. the movie appeared as *Hangin' Out*.
11 Qtd. in Hobsch 1998, p. 208
12 *Supermarkt*, Germany 1974, directed by Roland Klick
13 *Das Boot*, Germany 1981, directed by Wolfgang Petersen, after the novel by Lothar-Günther Buchheim, music by Klaus Doldinger. Original duration 145 minutes, Director's Cut (1997) 208 minutes. Since 2014 there's also a version made for TV available on Bluray, six episodes with an overall duration of 308 minutes.

RETROPIA

1 Cp. *Rolling Stone* 06/2015
2 Cp. Schwesig 2016
3 Cp. Rother 2014
4 By email.
5 Cp. Penzel 1979
6 Cp. Bartos 2017, p. 479
7 Cp. Reynolds 2011, p. 102f
8 Wheeldon 2015
9 Flür 1999
10 Bartos 2017
11 Dinger 2012
12 Froese 2017
13 Kübler/Augustin 1996
14 Qtd. in Plodroch 2019

SOURCES

Translations from German by Yours Truly except when marked otherwise. Some books listed here are Kindle versions. In these cases, the page numbers may not always be precise.

Adorno, Theodor W.: Einleitung in die Musiksoziologie. Frankfurt 1962, edition 1975

The Advocate, Newark, June 16, 1975, p. 21

Ahwesh, Peggy: Bored in Pittsburgh – The Obscure Film That Immortalized 1980s Punk. In: Carnegie Museum of Art, https://blog.cmoa.org/2017/01/bored-in-pittsburgh-the-obscure-film-that-immortalized-1980s-punk/

Allen, Daevid: Gong Dreaming 2 – The Histories & Mysteries of Gong from 1969-1975. London 2009

Amend, Christoph: Wenn Roboter reisen. In: *Zeit Magazin* 21/2017, p. 15-23

Anderson Dansereau, Corey: Wie Millionen untereinander kommunizierende Menschen sich in ein millionenäugiges Monster verwandeln. In: Neue Zürcher Zeitung, March 11, 2020. https://www.nzz.ch/feuilleton/silicon-valley-seine-anfaenge-haben-auch-mit-lsd-zu-tun-ld.1543857

Augustin, Gerd: Als das Fernsehen rocken lernte. In: *Der Spiegel*, January 23, 2008, http://www.spiegel.de/einestages/beat-club-a-950035.html (retrieved June 14, 2015)

Aust, Stefan: Der Baader-Meinhof-Komplex. Hamburg 1985

Baag, Robert: Das Erbe von „Fremde Heere Ost". Deutschlandfunk, Cologne, April 4, 2006

Bailey, Alan: Radio Luxembourg. 208 – It Was Great! An Affectionate Anecdotal Journey Between 1958 and 1975. UK 2006

Balzer, Jens: Zum Tod von Holger Czukay – Unser unermüdlichster musikalischer Erneuerer. In: *Rolling Stone* (German edition), September 6, 2017. https://www.rollingstone.de/zum-tod-von-holger-czukay-unser-unermuedlichster-musikalischer-erneuerer-1341641/

Bartos, Karl: Der Klang der Maschine – Autobiografie. Cologne 2017

Behrendsen, Peter and Rüsenberg, Michael: Der Synthesizer – Je größer der Apparat ... In: Rock Session 2, p. 136-154. Reinbek 1978

Betschon, Stefan: Think small – Wie der Käfer nach Amerika kam. In: *Neue Zürcher Zeitung*, November 22, 2015

Blondie: The Making of "Heart of Glass". https://www.youtube.com/watch?v=2K4zdG0QfOA

Boettcher, Marc: Stranger in the Night – Die Bert Kaempfert Story. Hamburg 2002

Böll, Heinrich: Die verlorene Ehre der Katharina Blum, oder: Wie Gewalt entstehen und wohin sie führen kann. Cologne 1974

Brand, Stewart: Whole Earth Catalog. Menlo Park, CA, 1968

Brand, Stewart: Whole Earth Discipline - An Ecopragmatist Manifesto. New York 2009

Bremer, Ulrike: Legenden – Rex Gildo. Documentary film. Hessischer Rundfunk, Frankfurt 2009

Bucks County Courier Times, May 25, 1975, p. C14

Cailloux, Bernd: Das Geschäftsjahr 1968/69. Frankfurt 2005

Chartsurfer.de: http://www.chartsurfer.de/musik/album-charts-deutschland/jahrescharts/alben-1977-2x1.html; http://www.chartsurfer.de/musik/single-charts-deutschland/jahrescharts/hits-1977-2x3.html

Corso. Deutschlandfunk, Cologne, May 29, 2012

Crane, Alan: Interview with Michael Rother. In: *Tape Op*, Nov./Dec. 2015, p. 28-31

Czarnecky, Axel and Siebert, Daniel: Roll Over Hanau – Eine Stadt, die Amerikaner und ihre Musik. Documentary film. Germany 2009

Czukay, Holger and Schmidt, Irmin in interview. WDR TV, Cologne 1977. https://www.youtube.com/watch?v=c2kzNcw-9Eg

Dallach, Christoph: Dada dada dada. Interview with Giorgio Moroder. In: *Die Zeit* 14/2015

Dallach, Christoph: Solowerk von Irmin Schmidt – Blaupausen für Bowie. In: *Der Spiegel*, February 6, 2016, http://www.spiegel.de/kultur/musik/irmin-schmidt-can-electro-violet-rezension-a-1075646.html (retrieved February 7, 2016)

Davis, Miles (with Quincy Troupe): Miles – The Autobiography. New York 1990

Der Spiegel: see *Spiegel*

Deutsche Welle: PopXport, August 28, 2015. http://www.dw.com/en/popxport-ranking-the-top-10-music-acts-from-germany-2015-08-28/e-18627089-9798

DiCesare, Pat: Janis Joplin's '69 show at the Civic Arena was a raucous affair from start to finish. In: *Pittsburgh Post-Gazette*, Oct 3, 2010

Didion, Joan: Slouching Towards Bethlehem. New York 2008 (first released 1968)

Diederichsen, Diedrich: Über Pop-Musik. Cologne 2014

Dinger, Klaus: *Blue* by La!Neu? – Liner notes, Captain Trip Records 1999

Dinger, Klaus: Ihr könnt mich mal am Arsch lecken. Düsseldorf 2012 (no page numbers)

Dinger, Klaus: Wikipedia https://en.wikipedia.org/wiki/Klaus_Dinger (retrieved May 24, 2017)

Dotzauer, Gregor: Lasst 1000 Klangschleifen kreisen. In: *Tagesspiegel*, July 21, 2015

DW: see Deutsche Welle

Ehnert, Günter: Rock in Deutschland. Hamburg 1975

Ehnert, Günter: Rock in Deutschland. 2nd edition, Hamburg 1979

Ehnert, Günter and Kinsler, Detlev: Rock in Deutschland. 3rd edition, Hamburg 1984

Eidam, Klaus and Schröder, Rudolf: Die Hit-Fabrik –

Chronik eines Berliner Musikverlages. Edition Intro Meisel GmbH. Berlin 2001

Engelbrecht, Michael: An invitation for summer (last call), comment #2. In: http://manafonistas.de/2017/05/19/four-decades-ago-cluster-harmonia-eno-in-der-deutschen-provinz-ein-road-movie-fuer-freigeister/#comments

Enwezor, Okwui (ed.): ECM – Eine kulturelle Archäologie. Catalog of Exhibitions. Munich 2012

Esch, Rüdiger: Electri_City – Elektronische Musik aus Düsseldorf. Berlin 2014

Fascher, Horst with Flesch, Oliver: Let The Good Times Roll! – Der Star-Club-Gründer erzählt. Munich 2007

Fechner, Eberhard: Die Comedian Harmonists – Sechs Lebensläufe. Weinheim 1988

Fleming, Joy: „Glücksrad" theme. https://www.youtube.com/watch?v=BTESDpLGlxQ_

Flür, Wolfgang: Ich war ein Roboter. St. Andrä-Wördern 1999

Frank, Merlin W.: Interview with Klaus Schulze. In: *Fachblatt* 44, November 1976, p. 16-18

Frankfurter Rundschau, September 20, 1968: Razzia im „Heidi Loves You"-Shop

Fricke, Florian Secundus: Miesbach, der Moog und die Mayas. Radio feature, Bayrischer Rundfunk, Munich 2010 (Music journalist, not related to musician Florian Fricke, but indeed named after him.)

Frith, Simon: Popular Music – Music And Society. London 2004

Froese, Edgar: Tangerine Dream – Force Majeur. Die Autobiografie. Berlin 2017

Fuchs-Gamböck, Michael: Weg mit dem Staub vom ollen Adolf H. – Drei Fragen an Mani Neumeier. Facsimile; source and date unknown

Gabler, Neal: Walt Disney – The Triumph of the American Imagination. New York 2006

Geisenhanslüke, Ralph: Giorgio Moroder – „Damals habe ich begriffen, dass man in der Musik alles darf". In: *ZeitMagazin* 33/2014

Giordano, Ralph: Die zweite Schuld oder Von der Last, Deutscher zu sein. Hamburg 1987

Glass, Philip: Words Without Music – A Memoir. New York 2015

Granini, Pierre: Es ist gefährlich, die Geister zu verwirren – Das magische Weltbild der Can. In: Rock Session 1, p. 3-9. Reinbek 1977

Graves, Barry and Schmidt-Joos, Siegfried and Halbscheffel, Bernward: Das neue Rock-Lexikon. Reinbek 1998

Greenfield, Robert: Timothy Leary – A Biography. Orlando, FL, 2006

Greve, Bettina: Sternenhimmel – Die Chronik einer deutschen Schallplattenmarke (Polydor). Höfen 2001

Grissemann, Stefan: Can-Mastermind Irmin Schmidt – Es gab nur Streit, die ganze Zeit. In: *Profil*, December 11, 2013. http://www.profil.at/gesellschaft/can-mastermind-irmin-schmidt-es-streit-zeit-370553 (retrieved February 13, 2016)

Grotum, Thomas: Die Halbstarken – Zur Geschichte einer Jugendkultur der 50er Jahre. Frankfurt 1994

Haring, Hermann: Rock aus Deutschland/West – Von den Rattles bis Nena: Zwei Jahrzehnte Heimatklang. Reinbek 1984

Haus Mödrath: WDR nimmt das Angebot von Haus Mödrath nicht an. Press release, January 10, 2020. http://www.haus-moedrath.de/de/studio.html

Hentschel, Joachim: The Beatles feat. Tony Sheridan; CD booklet, Polydor 06024982132-3; Hamburg 2004

Higgs, John: I Have My Life Surrounded – The Life of Timothy Leary. Fort Lee, NJ, 2006

Hobsch, Manfred: Liebe, Tanz und 1000 Schlagerfilme. Berlin 1998

Holden, James and Rother, Michael: Encounters. In: Red Bull Music Academy Daily; July 15, 2015. http://daily.redbullmusicacademy.com/2015/07/encounters-james-holden-michael-rother (retrieved July 6, 2017)

Holstein, Philipp: Neue deutsche Wertarbeit. In: *RP-Online*, November 12, 2014. http://www.rp-online.de/nrw/staedte/duesseldorf/kultur/neue-deutsche-wertarbeit-aid-1.4663323 (retrieved June 16, 2017)

Höppener, Hugo: Lichtgebet (painting)

http://www.damals.de/img/damals_news/0827_Fidus_Lichtgebet.jpg (retrieved July 18, 2015)

Hub, Andreas: Das Kraut der frühen Jahre. In: *Rolling Stone* (German Edition), April 1997, p. 42-46

Iliffe, Stephen: Painting With Sound – The Life and Music of Hans-Joachim Roedelius. London 2003

Ingenhoff, Sebastian: Die anlassfreie Rezension #2. In: *Spex*, July 7, 2015

Jackson, Blair and Gans, David: This Is All A Dream We Dreamed – An Oral History Of The Grateful Dead. New York 2015

Jahn, Lothar: Eine fruchtbare, freudvolle Zusammenarbeit – Achim Reichel über seine Zusammenarbeit mit Ougenweide. In: http://www.minnesang.com/Interviews/Interview-Achim-Reichel-und-Ougenweide.html (retrieved December 12, 2017)

Jekal, Jan: Keine bleichen Männer mehr. In: *Die Tageszeitung*, March 9, 2018. http://www.taz.de/!5490564/

Jennings, Dana: CDs know that Ears have Eyes. In: Art & Design, *New York Times*, December 26, 2012

Jobs, Richard Ivan: Backpack Ambassadors – How Youth Travel Integrated Europe. Chicago and London 2017

Jürgens, Kai U. (ed.): Monographie Asmus Tietchens. Erweiterte Neuausgabe, Kiel 2006

Kahlefendt, Nils: Totgesagte leben länger – Linker Buchhandel in der Bundesrepublik. Deutschlandradio Kultur, Berlin 2016

Kaiser, Rolf-Ulrich: Rock-Zeit – Stars, Geschäft und Geschichte der neuen Popmusik. Düsseldorf 1972

Kestrel, Elana: Christopher Franke – Impressions of a So-

nic Painter. In: http://christopherfranke.com/interview.html (retrieved April 3, 2017)
Kirby, Jack: Panel from "The Mighty Thor" #134, November 1966. https://www.facebook.com/groups/2210740370/permalink/10160419717310371/
Kitching, Sean: The Spirit Is The Thing – Irmin Schmidt's Favorite Records. In: *The Quietus*, December 4th, 2015. http://thequietus.com/articles/19386-irmin-schmidt-can-favourite-records-interview?page=3 (retrieved February 15, 2016)
Klatt, Oliver: Hitlers Disney. In: *Der Spiegel*, April 25, 2013
Klotschkow, Paul: Michael Rother Interview. In: *Left-Lion*, April 12, 2017. https://www.leftlion.co.uk/read/2017/april/michael-rother-interview
Koers, Peter: Creedence Clearwater Revival – Rocking All Over The World. Augsburg 1994
Kraesze, Wolfgang: Signale aus der Schwäbischen Straße. Docu, Sender Freies Berlin, Berlin 1976
Kraushaar, Wolfgang: Good Vibrations – Ein Gespräch mit Wolfgang Kraushaar. In: *Mittelweg 36, Zeitschrift des Hamburger Instituts für Sozialforschung*, 4-5/2016, p. 50-80
Kraushaar, Wolfgang: Mythos und Wahrheit. In: *Die Tageszeitung*, September 2, 2017. https://www.taz.de/!5442455/
Kraushaar, Wolfgang: Deutscher Herbst – Eine Republik im Ausnahmezustand. In: *Neue Zürcher Zeitung*, September 5, 2017. https://www.nzz.ch/feuilleton/deutscher-herbst-eine-republik-im-ausnahmezustand-ld.1314349
Krüger, Ulf: Star-Club – The Most Famous Beat-Club In The World. Höfen 2010
Kübler, Olaf and Augustin, Gert: Klartext/Voll daneben. Pfaffenhofen 1996
Kumpf, Hans: Neugierig ein ganzes Leben lang – Irmin Schmidt. In: *JazzPages*, n.d. http://jazzpages.com/jazz-interviews/Irmin-Schmidt-interview-Hans-Kumpf.htm (retrieved February 13, 2016)
Lachenmann, Helmut: Sounds are Natural Phenomena – Excerpt from an interview with Klaus Zehelein and Hans Thomalla. In: *Das Mädchen mit den Schwefelhölzern*, CD booklet. Kairos Production 2002
Lake, Steve and Griffiths, Paul (ed.): Horizons Touched – The Music of ECM. London 2007
Lange, Tino: Rock & Roll – Der Star war der Club. *Hamburger Abendblatt*, April 4, 2012, http://www.abendblatt.de/hamburg/article107774167/Rock-n-Roll-Der-Star-war-der-Club.html (retrieved July 18, 2015)
Last, James with Macho, Thomas: Mein Leben – Die Autobiografie. Munich 2006
Leary, Timothy: Flashbacks – A Personal and Cultural History of an Era. New York, NY, 1997
Legath, Jürgen (ed.): *Sounds*: Platten 66-77 – 1827 Kritiken. Hamburg/Frankfurt 1979
Lesh, Phil: Searching for the Sound – My Life with the Grateful Dead. New York and Boston 2006
Linke, Hans-Jürgen: Label ECM – Dimensionen der Freiheit. In: *Frankfurter Rundschau*, November 14, 2019. https://www.fr.de/kultur/musik/label-ecm-dimensionen-freiheit-13220678.html
Lippegaus, Karl: Holger Czukay – Der liebe Onkel von Boy George. In: *Spex*, Cologne 1984 (exact edition unknown)
Lippegaus, Karl: Radionacht Can. Deutschlandfunk, May 1, 2017
Loch, Siggi: Plattenboss aus Leidenschaft. Hamburg 2010
Loichinger, Stephan: Avantgarde in Altenhaßlau. In: *Frankfurter Rundschau*, January 11, 2010
Luhmann, Niklas: Soziale Systeme – Grundriss einer allgemeinen Theorie. Frankfurt 1987
Lundberg, Camilla: Taktfast stöveltramp. In: *Expressen*, Stockholm, March 23, 1977. Translation: Andréas Hagström
Maconie, Robin: Stockhausen on Music – Lectures and Interviews, compiled by Robin Maconie. London 2000 (Reprint from 1989)
Mann, Klaus: Treffpunkt im Unendlichen. First release 1932. Reinbek 1981
Mann, Klaus: Der Wendepunkt – Ein Lebensbericht. First release as "The Turning Point", 1942. Reinbek 1981
Mansnerus, Laura: Timothy Leary, Pied Piper of Psychedelic 60's, Dies at 75. In: *New York Times*, June 1, 1996
Matheja, Bernd: 1000 Nadelstiche – Amerikaner und Briten singen deutsch, 1955 – 1975. 3rd edition, Hambergen 2007
Meinhof, Ulrike: Natürlich kann geschossen werden. In: *Der Spiegel* 25/1970. http://www.spiegel.de/spiegel/print/d-44931157.html
Menand, Louis: Out of Bethlehem. In: *The New Yorker*, Aug 24, 2015, p. 66-73
Mervis, Scott: Kraut Legends. In: *Pittsburgh Post-Gazette*, March 24, 2016, p. WE 10
Miersch, Manfred: Elektronische Instrumente im Film, Folge 1. In: *Synthesizer-Magazin* 1/2007, p. 48-51
Mießgang, Thomas: Schlagsahne, Irrengesang, Kirmesgeister – Karlheinz Stockhausen testet Krautrock. In: *Die Zeit*, April 18, 1997, p. 72
Miller, Gerd: Ray Conniff – ein Sound erobert die Welt. In: Rock & Roll-Schallplattenforum, http://www.rocknroll-schallplatten-forum.de/viewtopic.php?t=4815&start=0 (retrieved May 10, 2015)
Mineur, Matthias: Liner notes, DVD Booklet *Amon Düül II Play Phallus Dei*. Repertoire Records 2003
Mitscherlich, Alexander and Margarete: Die Unfähigkeit zu trauern – Grundlagen kollektiven Verhaltens. Munich 1967
Morawietz, Stefan: Kraut und Rüben. Docu film in 6 parts. WDR TV, Cologne 2006
Müller, Wolfgang: Subkultur Westberlin 1979-1989. Hamburg 2013

Murphy, Gareth: Cowboys and Indies – The Epic History of the Record Industry. New York 2014
Musik Express: Brain Festival – Fete für frisch gebackene Millionäre. *Musik Express* 4/1977
Musikmarkt September 4, 2013. http://www.musikmarkt.de/Aktuell/News/Universal-Music-Vertriebstagung-Wir-sind-heute-besser-aufgestellt-denn-je
Musikspiegel (a music trade magazine, founded in 1972 as a counterpoint to the established *Musikmarkt*, shut down only two years later). Quoted from memory.
Napier-Bell, Simon: Black Vinyl, White Powder. London 2002
Neumeier, Mani: DVD liner notes for *Notwehr*, ZDF/Novafilm 2007
News Journal, Mansfield, Ohio, May 13, 1975, p. 10
Olivier, Thomas: Kraan – Sie sind Klasse, aber machen wenig Kasse. In: *Musik Joker* 10/1976, p. 11
Overstolz vom Rhein. Cigarettes ad, mid-1950s. https://www.youtube.com/watch?v=ieuJLnZE8sk
Patterson, Archie: The Mythos of Rolf-Ulrich Kaiser. http://www.rocksbackpagesblogs.com/2011/05/the-mythos-of-rolf-ulrich-kaiser/ (retrieved May 23, 2011)
Penzel, Werner: Vagabundenkarawane. Documentary film, Germany 1979. https://www.youtube.com/watch?v=lN6xMtDvJCQ&t=8s
Pertou, Jacob: Manuel Goettsching – Rebuilding Culture, re-envisioning the guitar, http://passiveaggressive.dk/manuel-gottsching-interview/, April 12, 2015 (retrieved July 18, 2015)
Pieper, Werner: Kaiser Schmarrn süß/sauer. In: Pieper (ed.) 2007, p. 50-55
Pieper, Werner (ed.): Alles schien möglich – 60 Sechziger über die 60er Jahre und was aus ihnen wurde. Löhrbach 2007
Plodroch, Ina: Festival-Schlacht ums beste Line-Up. In: Corso, Deutschlandfunk, July 29, 2017
Plodroch, Ina: Masse statt Klasse – Wie Streaming den Output von Musikern bestimmt. Deutschlandfunk, July 24, 2019. https://www.deutschlandfunkkultur.de/wie-streaming-den-output-von-musikern-bestimmt-masse-statt.2177.de.html?dram:article_id=454682
Pop aktuell: n.d., probably 1978
Prabel, Wolfgang: Der Bausatz des Dritten Reiches – Die deutsche Kulturrevolution 1890 bis 1933. Kindle e-book 2015
Praunheim, Rosa von: Qtd. in https://de.wikipedia.org/wiki/Nicht_der_Homosexuelle_ist_pervers,_sondern_die_Situation,_in_der_er_lebt (retrieved May 31, 2019)
Prieberg, Fred K.: Musik im NS-Staat. Cologne 2000
Psychedelic Pictures. https://twitter.com/psychdelicpics/status/1022089968833843200
Quotefancy.com: https://quotefancy.com/quote/1726429/Nam-June-Paik-The-only-way-to-win-a-race-is-to-run-alone
Rau, Fritz: 50 Jahre Backstage – Erinnerungen eines Konzertveranstalters. Heidelberg 2005
Reetze, Jan: Musikcomputer – Computermusik. Gegenwart und Zukunft eines neuen Mediums. Stuttgart 1987
Reetze, Jan: Harmonia live. In: Klanghorizonte, Deutschlandfunk December 19, 2015
Reichel, Achim: Heiße Scheibe – mein missratenes Werk? In: http://www.achimreichel.de/heisse-scheibe.html (retrieved October 3, 2017)
Reinartz, Burkhard: Auferstehen muss der Mensch schon selbst – Joseph Beuys und die Religion. Deutschlandfunk, December 25, 2019.
Reinders, Ralf and Fritzsch, Ronald: Quotation from 1995 in Wikipedia, https://de.wikipedia.org/wiki/Bewegung_2._Juni
Reuband, Karl-Heinz: Soziale Determinanten des Drogengebrauchs – Eine sozialwissenschaftliche Analyse des Gebrauchs weicher Drogen in der Bunderepublik Deutschland. Opladen 1994
Reynolds, Simon: Retromania – Pop Culture's Addiction to Its Own Past. New York 2011
Rock & Folk. French music magazine, facsimile n.d.
Rockarchiv: Statt Striptease Beat-Musik. Manfred Weißleder und sein Star-Club-Imperium. http://www.rockarchiv.infopartisan.net/starclub/sc08.html (retrieved July 18, 2015)
Roedelius, Hans-Joachim: Roedelius – Das Buch. Bad Vöslau 2016
Roedelius, Hans-Joachim: Heilende Hände spielen heilende Töne. In: *Kurier*, November 4, 2018. https://kurier.at/kultur/interview-mit-roedelius-heilende-haende-spielen-heilende-toene/400314423
Rolling Stone 06/2015: 50 Greatest Prog Rock Albums of All Time. https://www.rollingstone.com/music/lists/50-greatest-prog-rock-albums-of-all-time-20150617/happy-the-man-happy-the-man-1977-20150617
Rother, Michael: Michael Rother spielt einziges Konzert in Deutschland. *Weser-Ith-News*, July 31, 2014. http://archiv.meine-onlinezeitung.de/gesellschaft/54-gesellschaft/7270 (retrieved March 7, 2018)
Rudorf, Reginald: Das Geheimnis der schwarzen Rille. Quoted after Haas, Walter: Das Jahrhundert der Schallplatte – Eine Geschichte der Phonographie. Bielefeld 1979
Sailer, Niklas: Oh-oh oh Amadeus. In: *Spiegel*, March 31, 2016. http://www.spiegel.de/einestages/rock-me-amadeus-von-falco-die-geschichte-des-deutschen-us-nr-1-hit-a-1084647.html
Schmidt, Hildegard and Kampmann, Wolf: Can Box Book. Münster 1998
Schmidt, Irmin: Interview in „Aspekte", ZDF TV 1971. https://www.youtube.com/watch?v=d4Jz_c4cAQM
Schmidt, Thorsten: Knut Kiesewetter war Jazzer durch und durch. In: http://www.rocknroll-schallplatten-forum.de/viewtopic.php?t=15545, April 2017
Schneider, Nobert Jürgen („Enjott"): Handbuch Filmmusik – Musikdramaturgie im Neuen Deutschen Film. Munich 1986
Schober, Ingeborg: Poesie und Abenteuer heutiger Musik.

In: Rock Session 1, p. 295-309. Reinbek 1977
Schober, Ingeborg: Tanz der Lemminge – Amon Düül II. Eine Musikkommune in der Protestbewegung der 60er Jahre. Reinbek 1979
Schöler, Franz: High-Fidelity-Technik für Aufsteiger – Vom Klangerlebnis über Tonstudiopraktiken bis zur digitalen Revolution. Reinbek 1981
Schoener, Stefanie: Eberhard Schoener – Grenzen gibt es nicht. Munich 2010
Schreiber, Bernd: Das Synthesizer-Handbuch – Synthesizer transparent gemacht. Germany 1980
Schwabe, Oliver: Keine Atempause – Düsseldorf, der Ratinger Hof und die neue Musik. Docu film, WDR, Cologne 2016
Schwesig, Oliver: Flucht in die Musik von früher – Oliver Schwesig im Gespräch mit Albert Koch. Deutschlandfunk Kultur, February 3, 2016
SDW (Stiftung deutscher Wald) n.d. http://www.sdw.de/waldwissen/weihnachtsbaum/ (retrieved May 2, 2015)
Shapiro, Ari: Nixon's Manhunt For The High Priest Of LSD. In: NPR, January 5, 2018. https://www.npr.org/2018/01/05/575392333/nixons-manhunt-for-the-high-priest-of-lsd-in-the-most-dangerous-man-in-america
Simmeth, Alexander: Krautrock – „Heimatmusik aus dem Rhein-Ruhr-Gebiet". In: *Mittelweg 36, Zeitschrift des Hamburger Instituts für Sozialforschung*, 4-5/2016, p. 157-178
Sloterdijk, Peter: Die schrecklichen Kinder der Neuzeit – Über das anti-genealogische Experiment der Moderne. Frankfurt 2014
Spiegel 19/1968: Eine ‚Bild'-Schlagzeile ist mehr Gewalt als ein Stein am Polizisten-Kopf. *Der Spiegel*, Mai 6, 1968. http://www.spiegel.de/spiegel/print/d-46039870.html (retrieved September 9, 2015)
Spiegel 41/1968: Größtes Ding. In: *Der Spiegel*, October 7, 1968, p. 213-214. http://www.spiegel.de/spiegel/print/d-45922258.html (retrieved July 18, 2015)
Spiegel 43/1971: Szene - Popmusik. In: *Der Spiegel*, October 18, 1971, p. 177. http://www.spiegel.de/spiegel/print/d-44916493.html (retrieved July 18, 2015)
Spiegel 3/1972: Will Ulrike Gnade oder freies Geleit? Essay by Heinrich Böll. In: *Der Spiegel*, January 10, 1972. http://www.spiegel.de/spiegel/print/d-43019376.html
Spiegel 40/1973: Prinzip der Freude. In: *Der Spiegel*, October 1, 1973, p. 186-188. http://www.spiegel.de/spiegel/print/d-41911372.html (retrieved July 18, 2015)
Spiegel 50/2009: Maschinen sind einfach lockerer. Interview mit Ralf Hütter. http://www.spiegel.de/spiegel/print/d-68074001.html (retrieved July 18, 2015)
Spiegel 35/2017: Es ist scheiße, ein Mörder zu sein. http://www.spiegel.de/spiegel/print/index-2017-35.html
Spittler, Christoph: Deutschland hatte Angst vor dieser Band. In: Kalenderblatt, Deutschlandradio Kultur, September 11, 2015. http://www.deutschlandradiokultur.de/erster-stones-auftritt-vor-50-jahren-deutschland-hatte.932.de.html?dram:article_id=330753
Statista: Durchschnittlicher Brutto-Jahresarbeitslohn je Arbeitnehmer in Deutschland von 1960 bis 2014. http://de.statista.com/statistik/daten/studie/164047/umfrage/jahresarbeitslohn-in-deutschland-seit-1960/ (retrieved August 16, 2015)
Staub, Samantha: Joseph Beuys – Jeder Mensch ist ein Künstler. In: modernperformanceart, n.d. https://modernperformanceart.wordpress.com/joseph-beuys-jeder-mensch-ist-ein-kuenstler/
Stenke, Wolfgang: Beate Klarsfeld – die Frau, die Kanzler Kiesinger ohrfeigte. Deutschlandfunk, November 7, 2018. https://www.deutschlandfunk.de/vor-50-jahren-beate-klarsfeld-die-frau-die-kanzler.871.de.html?dram:article_id=432491
Stichtag 23. Januar 1986. WDR 2 radio, January 26, 2011. http://www1.wdr.de/stichtag/stichtag5372.html
Stockhausen, Karlheinz: Texte zur elektronischen und instrumentalen Musik, Band 1 (1952-1962). Cologne 1963
Stockhausen, Karlheinz: Texte zur Musik, Band 3 (1963-1970). Cologne 1971
Stockhausen, Karlheinz: Texte zur Musik, Band 4 (1970-1977). Cologne 1978
Storjohann, Uwe: Hauptsache Überleben – Eine Jugend im Krieg 1936-1945. Hamburg 1993
Stubbs, David: Too Much The Darkness – The Werner Herzog Soundtracks of Popol Vuh. In: *The Quietus*, August 29, 2014
Tagesschau: Deutscher Musikmarkt – Streaming schlägt erstmals CD. Tagesschau, ARD TV July 18, 2018. http://www.tagesschau.de/wirtschaft/streaming-cd-103.html
Tamarkin, Jeff: Got A Revolution! – The Turbulent Flight of Jefferson Airplane. New York 2003
Teipel, Jürgen: Verschwende Deine Jugend – Ein Doku-Roman über den deutschen Punk und New Wave. Frankfurt 2001. Accompanying to the book a 2-CD set is available.
Temme, Anna Lena: Heikedine Körting – Die Hörspielkönigin. Docu film, NDR, Hamburg 2014
Völker, Klaus: Kabarett der Komiker – Berlin 1924 bis 1950. München 2010
Wagner, Christoph: Der Klang der Revolte – Die magischen Jahre des westdeutschen Musik-Underground. Mainz 2013
Wagner, Christoph: Irmin Schmidt – Klang-Kalligraphie. Interview in: Jazzthetik 05/06, 2019, p. 64
Warner, Alan: 33 1/3 – Tago Mago. New York and London 2015
Weber, Eberhard: Résumé – Eine deutsche Jazz-Geschichte. Stuttgart 2015
Weber, Julian: Los Angeles ist keine einfache Stadt – Giorgio Moroder über seine Karriere. In: *die Tageszeitung*, December 20, 2014. http://www.taz.de/!5025680/
Wenske, Helmut: Scheiss drauf! Eine Rock'n'Roll Bio in

Bildern, ein Leben gegen den Strich. Berlin 2003
Werding, Juliane: Wer war Conny Kramer? http://www.juliane-werding.de/service/faqs.htm#9 (2018)
Werthmann, Eberhard: Die Entwicklung der deutschen Schallplattenindustrie, ihre gegenwärtige Situation und ihre Marktformen. Doctoral thesis, Karl-Franzens-Universität Graz, 1958
Westrupp, Walter: 68er nach Noten. http://www.computopia.de/westrupps/w+w/seiten/buch/frame_buch.htm (retrieved July 18, 2015)
Whalley, Ben: Krautrock – The Rebirth of Germany. Documentary film. BBC 2009
Wheeldon, Christian: Deep Distance – The Musical Life of Manuel Göttsching. UK 2015
Wikipedia (Conny Plank): https://en.wikipedia.org/wiki/Conny_Plank (retrieved June 3, 2018)
Wikipedia (Giorgio Moroder): https://de.wikipedia.org/wiki/Giorgio_Moroder (retrieved July 28, 2018)
Wikipedia (Salambo): https://de.wikipedia.org/wiki/Salambo_%28Nachtlokal%29 (retrieved August 18, 2015)
Zahn, Robert von: Can. Kunststiftung NRW series Energien/Synergien 6. Cologne 2006
Zeigermann, Ralf: Ratinger Hof – Fotos und Geschichten. Königswinter 2010
Zint, Günter: Große Freiheit 39 – Vom Beat zum Bums, vom Star-Club zum Salambo. Munich 1987
Ziok, Ilona: *Fritz Bauer – Tod auf Raten*; documentary film, Germany 2010, directed by Ilona Ziok; English version: *Fritz Bauer – Death by Instalments.*

PHOTOS

Page 18: The ruins of the Reichstag, destroyed in World War II, are removed (March 18th, 1948). © Bundesarchiv, Image 183-M1203-303/Otto Donath.

Page 58: Franz-Josef Degenhardt at the "German Song Night" (opening of the "Internationale Essener Songtage" – September 25th, 1968). © Manfred Scholz/Fotoarchiv Ruhr Museum (Detail). The image has been cropped in favour of the page format.

Page 82: Entrance of the Star-Club, Hamburg. © ThomasFHH via Wikimedia Commons, licensed under the Creative Commons Attribution-ShareAlike 4.0 International License. To view a copy of this license, visit http://creativecommons.org/licenses/by-sa/4.0/ or send a letter to Creative Commons, PO Box 1866, Mountain View, CA 94042, USA.

Page 141: "Under the gowns – bad smell of 1000 years!" is written on a banner that students hold on September 11th, 1967, when both the new and old president of the University of Hamburg enter the Auditorium Maximum. On the left, behind the banner, is the former president, Prof. Dr. med. Schöfer; on the right is the new president, Prof. Dr. rer. pol. Ehrlicher. During the president's inauguration, students protested and chanted loudly in unison to demand the acceleration of university reform. © picture alliance/dpa, Image 2607897.

Page 153: Klaus Doldinger, live at Heidelberg City Hall (1971). © Manfred Rinderspacher

Page 159: Amon Düül II at the second British Rock Meeting (Germersheim, May 22nd, 1972). © Manfred Rinderspacher

Page 192: Mani Neumeier of Guru Guru, live at Heidelberg Thingstätte (1970). © Manfred Rinderspacher

Page 209: © Frank Thiele (Author's private collection).

Page 221: Audience at the second British Rock Meeting on the island Grün near Germersheim (1972). © Manfred Rinderspacher

Page 303: Eberhard Schoener and his Moog (photographer unknown). © Produktionsbüro Eberhard Schoener.

Page 375: Udo Lindenberg (drums) with Olaf Kübler (saxophone) and Paul Vincent (guitar), performing as part of Klaus Doldinger's Passport (1971). © Manfred Rinderspacher

Page 413: Achim Reichel (on the right) with A.R. & Machines at the first British Rock Meeting (Speyer, September 1971). © Manfred Rinderspacher

Page 442: Blixa Bargeld, Lead singer of Einstürzende Neubauten (London, UK – August 19th, 1983). © Jeremy Bannister. Comment from the photographer: *"Once inside, the punters were locked in and the heaters were turned on to full power. This factor, combined with the fires onstage, made it the most uncomfortable gig I've ever been to. Added to this were angle grinders covering the audience in sparks, and Blixa Bargeld smashing bottles into huge iron plates, with shards of glass showering the audience."*

Page 446: © Maria Müller (Author's private collection).

Page 486: Kraftwerk 3D Concert "The Mix" (Tokyo, Japan – May 15th, 2013). © Takahiro Kyono via Flickr, licensed under the Creative Commons Attribution 2.0 Generic License. To view a copy of this license, visit http://creativecommons.org/licenses/by/2.0/ or send a letter to Creative Commons, PO Box 1866, Mountain View, CA 94042, USA. The image has been cropped in favour of the page format.

INDEX

C

D

E

H

I

Q

R

S

THANKYOUS

Thanks for this and that, now and then: Karl Bartos, Gerd Bessler (†), Thorsten Breyer, Holger Czukay (†), Michael Engelbrecht, Sapana Gupta, Michael Haentjes, Hellmut Hattler, Andreas Hub (†), Harold Faltermeyer, Günter Körber (†), Adorján F. Kovács, Christoph Kowollik, Hubert Maessen, Uwe Meilchen, Manfred Miersch, Dieter Moll, Stefan Morawietz, Lajla Nizinski, Kathinka Pasveer, Werner Pieper, Philippe Ressing, Hans-Joachim Roedelius, Michael Rother, Ulrich Rützel, Oskar Sala (†), Günter Schlienz, Thorsten Schmidt, Ingeborg Schober (†), Eberhard Schoener, Frank Thiele, Walter Westrupp, Klaus Zäpke, Günter Zint, members of Rock'n'Roll-Schallplattenforum, members of Memoryradio-Forum, my fellow Manafonistas.

YOU WANT MORE?

LEGEND

This map shows a selection of active bands and solo artists with at least one record release in the heyday of Krautrock between 1969 and 1974 (with few exceptions). Due to space restrictions, and the fact that the term Krautrock is not clearly defined, this presentation cannot in any way show all of the genre's corresponding artists (insert your favourite underground band here).

The color markings for each musical style serve to represent the main style of the respective artists and should give a simplified overview of the musical diversity of Krautrock. Many of the artists mentioned here were much broader in terms of sound during the course of their career and certainly did not strictly follow the styles listed here.

The places listed here refer primarily o each artist's main place of creation hroughout their career. In cases of loubt, place of birth was used. If no oncrete place could be identified at ll (e.g. in the case of supergroups and rojects), the artists were spread out ver undefined areas within the map vithout connection.

KRAUTROCK LABELS

- ❄ April/Schneeball*
- Bacillus
- Brain
- ★ Kosmische Kuriere/Kosmische Musik
- Kuckuck
- Ohr
- Pilz
- Spiegelei
- Zebra

*Catalogue starts after 1974

COUNTRIES AND PLACES

- ● ABC City/Place
- //// German Democratic Republic (GDR)
- ⋰⋰ Austria/Switzerland

FEDERAL STATES (BUNDESLÄNDER)

1. Schleswig-Holstein
2. Hamburg*
3. Lower Saxony
4. Bremen*
5. North Rhine-Westphalia
6. Hesse
7. Rhineland-Palatinate
8. Saarland
9. Baden-Württemberg
10. Bavaria
11. (West-)Berlin*

*City-State

ARTISTS

- ● Band (Variation/Previous Name)
- ⊕ Supergroup/Project
- ○ Solo-Artist
- ¦ Band/Artist has worked with this Producer
- * Discography starts after 1974

MAIN STYLES

- ● Rock (Psychedelic-, Prog-, Blues-, Space-)
- ● Jazz (-Rock), Fusion
- ● Folk (-Rock)
- ● Electronic, Ambient, Drone, Avantgarde (-Rock), Experimental

ROLF-ULRICH KAISER (*1943)
Controversial music critic, author, producer, and label director of the key Krautrock labels, who later disappeared into oblivion.

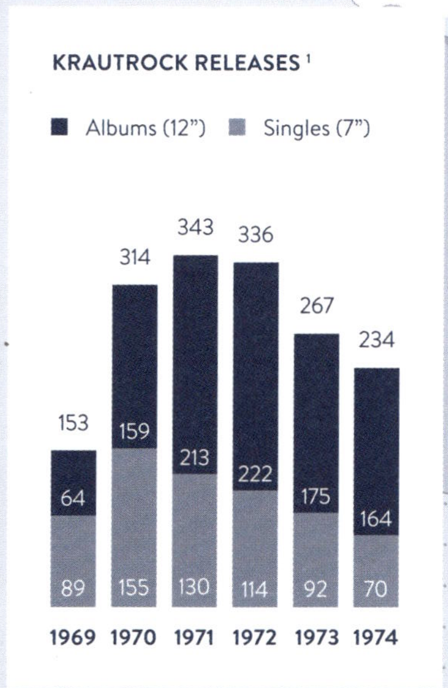

Sources:
[1] Klatte, Ulrich – Cosmic Price Guide. CPG Books, Hamburg (Germany) 2018
Discogs, discogs.com
Krautrock-Musikzirkus, krautrock-musikzirkus.de
Babyblaue Seiten, babyblaue-seiten.de